SolidWorks 2012
Part I - Basic Tools

Introductory Level Tutorials
Parts, Assemblies and Drawings

Written by: Sr. Certified SolidWorks Instructor
Paul Tran, CSWP, CSWE, CSWI

Schroff Development Corporation
P.O. Box 1334
Mission KS 66222
(913) 262-2664
www.SDCPublications.com

Publisher: Stephen Schroff

Disclaimer

The author makes a sincere effort to ensure the accuracy of the material described herein, however the author makes no warranty, expressed or implied, with respect to the quality, correctness, reliability, currency, accuracy, or freedom from error of this document or the products it describes.

The author disclaims all liability for any direct, indirect, incidental or consequential, special or exemplary damages resulting from the use of the information in this document or from the use of any products described in this document. Data used in examples and sample data files are intended to be fictional.

Trademarks

SolidWorks is a registered trademark of Dassault Systems.
Microsoft Excel / Word are registered trademarks of Microsoft Corporation.
All other brand names or trademarks belong to their respective companies.

Acknowledgments

Thanks as always to my wife Vivian and daughter Lani for always being there and providing support and honest feedback on all the chapters in the textbook.

I would like to give a special thanks to Dave Worcester for his technical editing, advice, and corrections. Additionally thanks to Peter Douglas for writing the foreword.

I also have to thank SDC Corp. and the staff for its continuing encouragement and support for this edition of SolidWorks 2012 Part 1 Basic Tools. Thanks also to Zach Werner for putting together such a beautiful cover design.

Finally, I would like to thank you, our readers, for your continued support. It is with your consistent feedback that we were able to create the lessons and exercises in this book with more detailed and useful information.

ISBN: 978-1-58503-696-7

Foreword

I first met Paul Tran when I was busy creating another challenge in my life. I needed to take a vision from one man's mind, understand what the vision looked like, how it was going to work and comprehend the scale of his idea. My challenge was I was missing one very important ingredient, a tool that would create a picture with all the moving parts.

A vision born in the mind of man only becomes a reality when seen through that man's eyes, and that man was blind. Over time and many conversations, mostly with him talking and me asking endless questions, I came to understand his idea and adopt his vision. The challenge now became, how do I make it real, *how to help a blind man build his dream?*

Research led me to discover a great tool, SolidWorks. It claimed to allow one to make 3D components, in picture quality, on a computer, add in all moving parts, assemble it and make it run, all before money was spent on bending steel and buying parts that may not fit together. I needed to design and build a product with thousands of parts, make them all fit and work in harmony with millimeters tolerance. The possible cost implications of failed experimentation were daunting.

To my good fortune, one company's marketing strategy of selling a product without an instruction manual and requiring one to attend an instructional class to get it, led me to meet a communicator who made it all seem so simple.

Paul Tran has worked with and taught SolidWorks as his profession for more than 25 years. Paul knows the SolidWorks product and manipulates it like a fine musical instrument. I watched Paul explain the unexplainable to baffled students with great skill and clarity. He taught me how to navigate the intricacies of the product so that I could use it as a communication tool with skilled engineers. **He teaches the teachers**.

I employed Paul as a design engineering consultant to create the thousands of parts for my company's product. Paul Tran's knowledge and teaching skill has added immeasurable value to my company. When I read through the pages of these manuals, I now have an "instant replay" of his communication skill with the clarity of having him looking over my shoulder - *continuously*. We can now design, prove and build our product and know it will always work and not fail. Most important of all, Paul Tran helped me turn a blind man's vision into reality and a monument to his dream.

Thanks Paul.

These books will make dreams come true and help visionaries change the world.

Peter J. Douglas – CEO, Cake Energy, LLC

Images courtesy of C.A.K.E. Energy Corp.

Preface

The modern world of engineering design and analysis requires an intense knowledge of Computer Aided Design (CAD) tools. To gain this deep understanding of unique CAD requirements one must commit the time, energy, and use of study guides. Paul Tran has invested countless hours and the wealth of his career to provide a path of easy to understand and follow instructional books. Each chapter is designed to build on the next and supplies users with the building blocks required to easily navigate SolidWorks 2012. I challenge you to find a finer educational tool whether you are new to this industry or a seasoned SolidWorks veteran.

I have been a part of the CAD industry for over twenty five years and read my share of instructional manuals. I can tell you Paul Tran's SolidWorks books do what most promise; however what others don't deliver. This book surpasses any CAD instructional tool I have used during my career. Paul's education and vast experience provides a finely tuned combination, producing instructional material that supports industry standards and most importantly, industry requirements.

Anyone interested in gaining the basics of SolidWorks to an in-depth approach should continue to engage the following chapters. All users at every level of SolidWorks knowledge will gain tremendous benefit from within these pages.

Dave Worcester
System Administer
Advanced Sterilization Products - A Johnson & Johnson Company

Author's Note

SolidWorks 2012 Basic Tools and Advanced Techniques are comprised of lessons and exercises based on the author's extensive knowledge on this software. Paul has over 25 years of experience in the fields of mechanical and manufacturing engineering; 16 years were in teaching and supporting the SolidWorks software and its add-ins. As an active Sr. SolidWorks instructor and design engineer, Paul has worked and consulted with hundreds of reputable companies including; IBM, Intel, NASA, US- Navy, Boeing, Disneyland, Medtronic, Guidant, Terumo, Kingston and many more. Today, he has trained more than 6000 engineering professionals, and given guidance to nearly ½ of the number of Certified SolidWorks Professionals and Certified SolidWorks Expert (CSWP & CSWE) in the state of California.

Every lesson and exercise in this book was created based on real world projects. Each of these projects have been broken down and developed into easy and comprehendible steps for the reader. Learn the fundamentals of SolidWorks at your own pace, as you progress form simple to more complex design challenges. Furthermore, at the end of every chapter, there are self test questionnaires to ensure that the reader has gained sufficient knowledge from each section before moving on to more advanced lessons.

Paul believes that the most effective way to learn the "world's most sophisticated software" is to learn it inside and out, create everything from the beginning, and take it step by step. This is what the **SolidWorks 2012 Basic Tools & Advanced Techniques** manuals are all about.

About the CD

This text includes a CD containing copies of the various files that are used throughout this book. They are organized by the file names that are normally mentioned at the beginning of each chapter or exercise.

In the Built Parts folder you will also find copies of the parts, assemblies and drawings that were created for cross references or reviewing purposes.

It would be best to make a copy of the content to your local hard drive and work from these documents, and then safely store the original CD.

Who this book is for

This book is for the beginner, who is unfamiliar with the SolidWorks program and its add-ins. It is also a great resource for the more CAD literate individuals who want to expand their knowledge of the different features that SolidWorks 2012 has to offer.

The organization of the book

The chapters in this book are organized in the logical order in which you would learn the SolidWorks 2012 program. Each chapter will guide you through some different tasks, from navigating through the user interface, to exploring the toolbars, from some simple 3D modeling and move on to more complex tasks that are common to all SolidWorks releases. There is also a self-test questionnaire at the end of each chapter to ensure that you have gained sufficient knowledge before moving on to the next chapter.

The conventions in this book

This book uses the following conventions to describe the actions you perform when using the keyboard and mouse to work in SolidWorks 2012:

Click: means to press and release the mouse button. A click of a mouse button is used to select a command or an item on the screen.

Double Click: means to quickly press and release the left mouse button twice. A double mouse click is used to open a program, or showing the dimensions of a feature.

Right Click: means to press and release the right mouse button. A right mouse click is used to display a list of commands, a list of shortcuts that is related to the selected item.

Click and Drag: means to position the mouse cursor over an item on the screen and then press and hold down the left mouse button; still holding down the left button, move the mouse to the new destination and release the mouse button. Drag and drop makes it easy to move things around within a SolidWorks document.

Bolded words: indicated the action items that you need to perform.

Italic words: Side notes and tips that give you additional information, or to explain special conditions that may occur during the course of the task.

Numbered Steps: indicates that you should follow these steps in order to successfully perform the task.

Icons: indicates the buttons or commands that you need to press.

SolidWorks 2012

SolidWorks 2012 is program suite, or a collection of engineering programs that can help you design better products faster. SolidWorks 2012 contains different combinations of programs; some of the programs used in this book may not be available in your suites.

Start and exit SolidWorks

SolidWorks allows you to start its program in several ways. You can either double click on its shortcut icon on the desktop, or go to the Start menu and select the following: All Program / SolidWorks 2012 / SolidWorks, or drag a SolidWorks document and drop it on the SolidWorks shortcut icon.

Before exiting SolidWorks, be sure to save any open documents, and then click File / Exit; you can also click the X button on the top right of your screen to exit the program.

Using the Toolbars

You can use toolbars to select commands in SolidWorks rather than using the drop down menus. Using the toolbars is normally faster. The toolbars come with commonly used commands in SolidWorks, but they can be customized to help you work more efficiently.

To access the toolbars, either right click in an empty spot on the top right of your screen or select View / Toolbars.

To customize the toolbars, select Tools / Customize. When the dialog pops up, click on the Commands tab, select a Category, and then drag an icon out of the dialog box and drop it on a toolbar that you want to customize. To remove an icon from a toolbar, drag an icon out of the toolbar and drop it into the dialog box.

Using the task pane

The task pane is normally kept on the right side of your screen. It display various options like SolidWorks resources, Design library, File explorer, Search, View palette, Appearances and Scenes, Custom properties, Built-in libraries, Technical alerts and news, etc,.

The task pane provides quick access to any of the mentioned items by offering the drag and drop function to all of its contents. You can see a large preview of a SolidWorks document before opening it. New documents can be saved in the task pane at anytime, and existing documents can also be edited and re-saved. The task pane can be resized, close or move to different location on your screen if needed.

Table of Contents

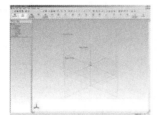

Setting the System Parameters

Table of Contents

Table of Contents

Basic Modeling Topics

Table of Contents

Table of Contents

Table of Contents

Table of Contents

Table of Contents

Table of Contents

Drawing Topics

Table of Contents

Table of Contents

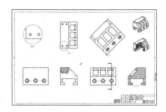

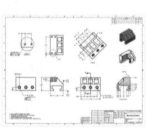

Table of Contents

Table of Contents

Table of Contents

CSWP Core Preparation Practice

Student Testimonials:

Some of the actual student testimonials after completing the training courses from the Author. All documents are filed at local SolidWorks resellers.

SolidWorks 2012 Quick-Guides:

Quick Reference Guide to SolidWorks 2012 Command Icons and Toolbars.

Introduction

SolidWorks User Interface

The SolidWorks 2012 User Interface

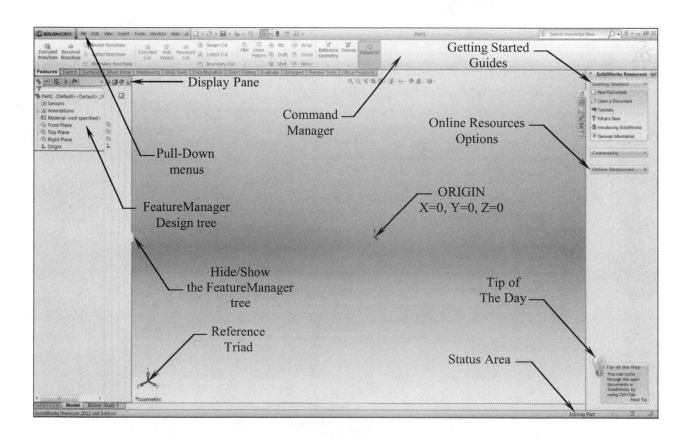

Introduction

The 3 reference planes:

- The Front, Top and the Right plane are 90°apart. They shared the same center point called the Origin.

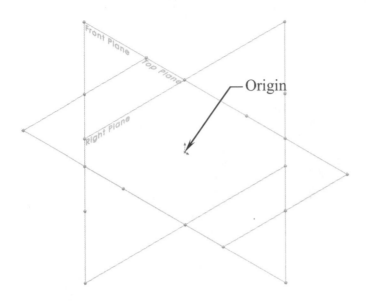

Origin

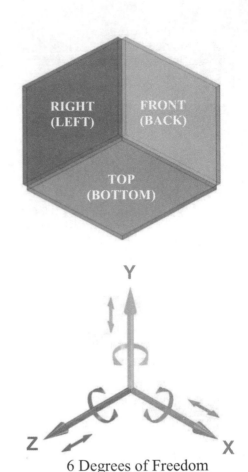

6 Degrees of Freedom

The Toolbars:

- Toolbars can be moved, docked or left floating in the graphics area.

- They can also be "shaped" from horizontal to vertical, or from a single to double rows when dragging on their corners.

- The CommandManager is recommended for the newer releases of SolidWorks.

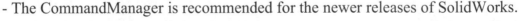

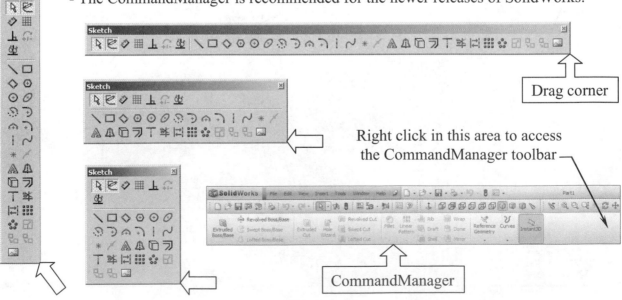

Drag corner

Right click in this area to access the CommandManager toolbar

CommandManager

Introduction

- If the CommandManager is not used, toolbars can be docked or leave floating.

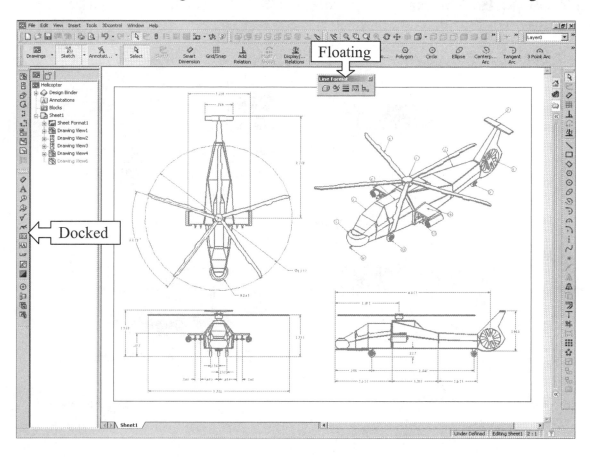

- Toolbars can be toggled off or on by activating or de-activating their check boxes:

- Select **Tools / Customize / Toolbars** tab.

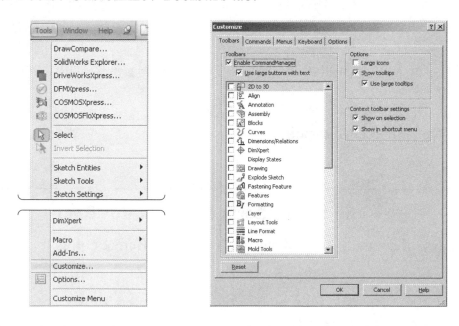

- The icons in the toolbars can be enlarged when its check box is selected [ ] Large icons

Introduction

The View ports: You can view or work with SolidWorks model or an assembly using one, two or four view ports.

View Orientation

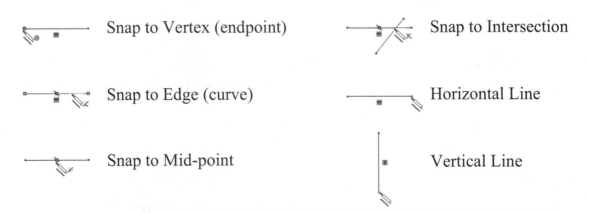

- Some of the **System Feedback symbols** (Inference pointers):

Snap to Vertex (endpoint)	Snap to Intersection
Snap to Edge (curve)	Horizontal Line
Snap to Mid-point	Vertical Line

The Status Bar: (View / Status Bar)

Displays the status of the sketch entity using different colors to indicate:

Green = Selected	**Blue** = Under defined
Black = Fully defined	**Red** = Over defined

2D Sketch examples:

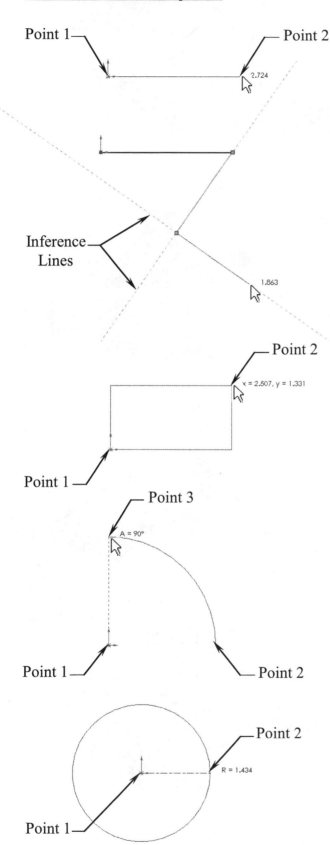

Click-Drag-Release: Single entity.

(Click Point 1, hold the mouse button, drag to point 2 and release).

Click-Release: Continuous multiple entities.

(The Inference Lines appear when the sketch entities are Parallel, Perpendicular or Tangent with each other).

Click-Drag-Release: Single Rectangle

(Click point 1, hold the mouse button, drag to Point 2 and release).

Click-Drag-Release: Single Centerpoint Arc

(Click point 1, hold the mouse button and drag to Point 2, release; then drag to Point 3 and release).

Click-Drag-Release: Single Circle

(Click point 1 [center of circle], hold the mouse button, drag to Point 2 [Radius] and release).

<u>3D Feature examples:</u>

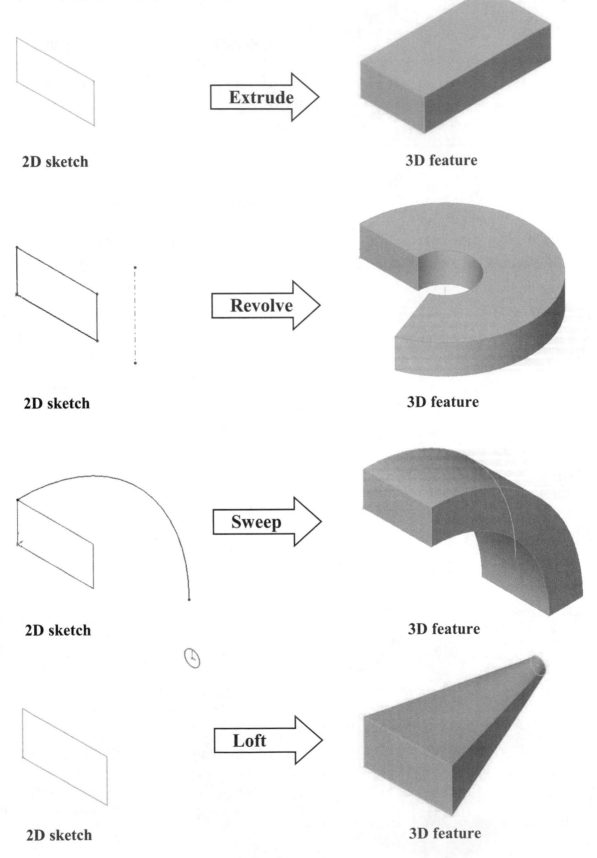

2D sketch → **Extrude** → 3D feature

2D sketch → **Revolve** → 3D feature

2D sketch → **Sweep** → 3D feature

2D sketch → **Loft** → 3D feature

Box-Select: Use the Select Pointer 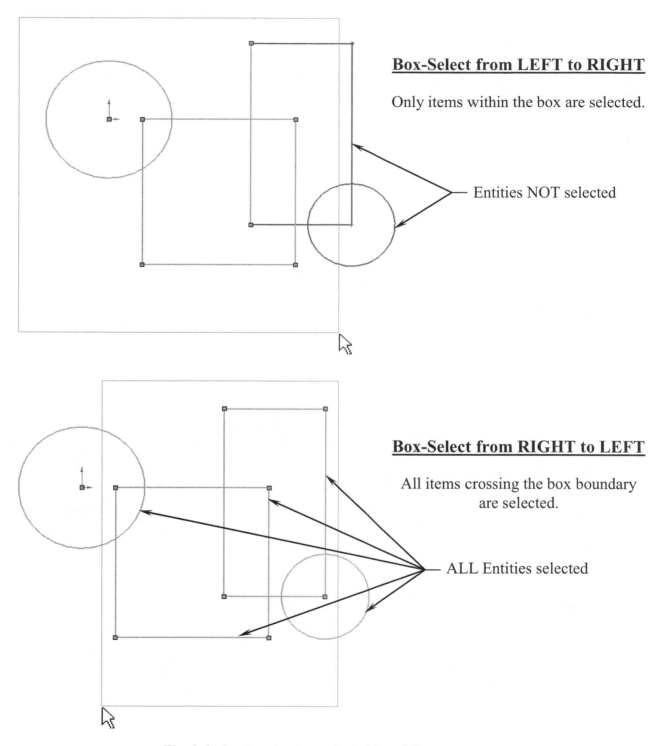 to drag a selection box around items.

Box-Select from LEFT to RIGHT

Only items within the box are selected.

Entities NOT selected

Box-Select from RIGHT to LEFT

All items crossing the box boundary are selected.

ALL Entities selected

The default geometry type selected is as follows:

* Part documents – edges * Assembly documents – components * Drawing documents - sketch entities, dims & annotations. * To select multiple entities, hold down **Ctrl** while selecting after the first selection.

Introduction

The <u>Mouse Gestures</u> for Sketches, Drawings and Parts

- Similar to a keyboard shortcut, you can use a Mouse Gesture to execute a command. A total of 8 keyboard shortcuts can be independently mapped and stored in the Mouse Gesture Guides.

- To activate the Mouse Gesture Guide, **right-click-and-drag** to see the current eight-gestures, then simply select the command that you want to use.

Mouse Gestures for Sketches

Mouse Gestures for Parts & Assemblies

Mouse Gestures for Drawings

- To customize the Mouse Gestures and include your favorite shortcuts, go to:

Tools / Customize.

- From the **Mouse Gestures** tab, select **All Commands** and enable the **Show only commands with Mouse Gestures assigned** checkbox.

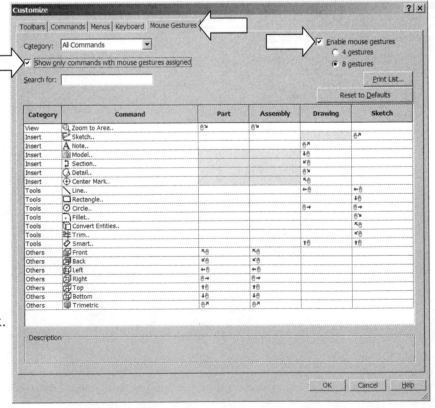

Introduction

Fit to Left display ———   ——— Fit to Right display

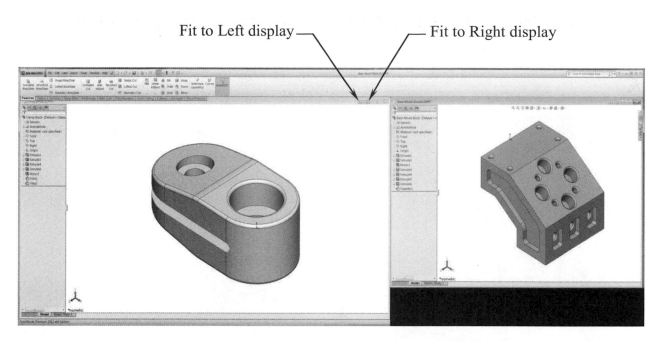

Dual monitors display

Image courtesy of ABCO Automation, Inc.

Text and images created using Windows 7 SP1 and SolidWorks 2012 64bit SP0

CHAPTER 1

System Options

The System Options

One of the first things to do after installing the SolidWorks software is to setup the system options to use as the default settings for all documents.

System Options such as:

- Input dimension value, Face highlighting...

- Drawing views controls, edge and hatch display.

- System colors, errors, sketch, text, grid, etc.

- Sketch display, Automatic relation.

- Edges display and selection controls.

- Performance and Large assembly mode.

- Area hatch/fill and hatch patterns.

- Feature Manager and Spin Box increment controls.

- View rotation and animation.

- Backup files and locations.

... are all set and saved in the **system registry**. While not part of the document itself, these settings affect all documents, including current and future documents.

This chapter will guide you through some of the options settings for use with this textbook; you may need to modify them to ensure full compatibility with your applications or company's standards.

System Options

The **General** Options

- To start setting up the system options, go to: **Tools / Options.**

- Select the **General** options.

- Select only the check boxes as shown in the General Options dialog box.

- Go down the list and select the **Drawings** Options.

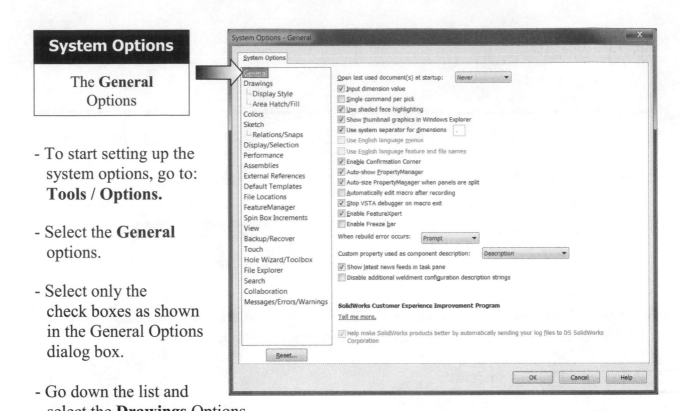

System Options

The **Drawings** Options

- Enable only the check boxes as indicated in this dialog box.

(These settings are intended for use with this training manual only, you may need to adjust them to meet your company's requirements).

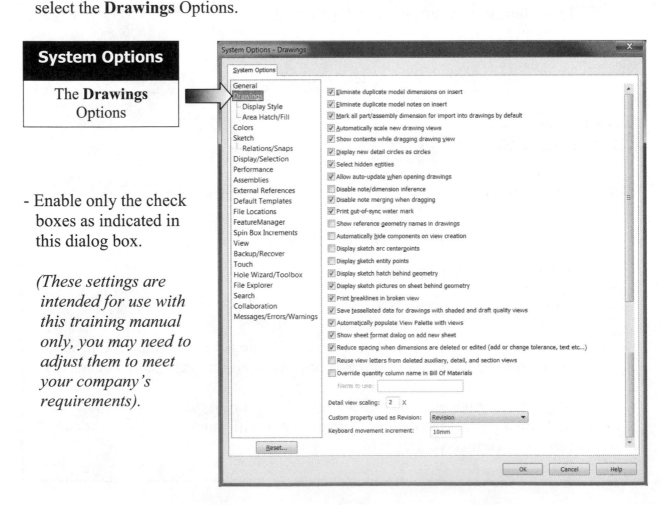

System Options

The **Display Style** Options

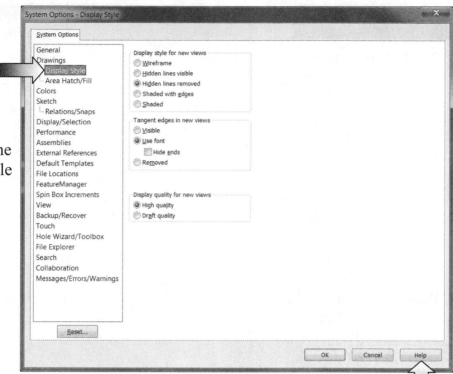

- Continue going down the list and follow the sample settings shown in the dialog boxes to setup your System Options.

- For detail explanation on these settings click the Help button at the lower right corner of the dialog box (arrow).

System Options

The **Area Hatch/Fill** Options

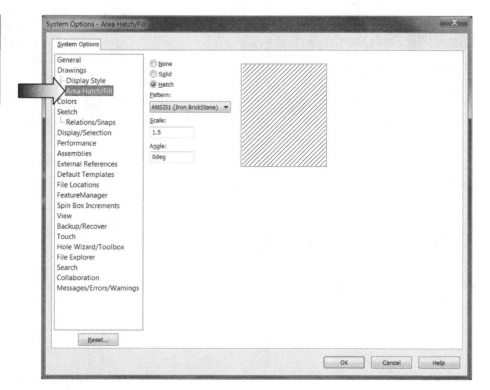

- The Area Hatch/Fills option sets the hatch pattern and Spacing (Scale).

System Options

The **Colors** Options

- The Colors options set the colors of the background and the Feature-Manager Design tree.

- For Background-Appearance select the PLAIN option, and for Viewport Background color click Edit and select the White color.

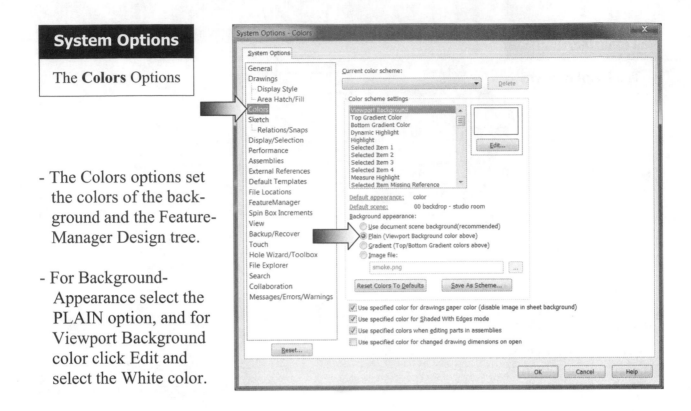

System Options

The **Sketch** Options

- These options control the displays of the sketch entities and orientation.

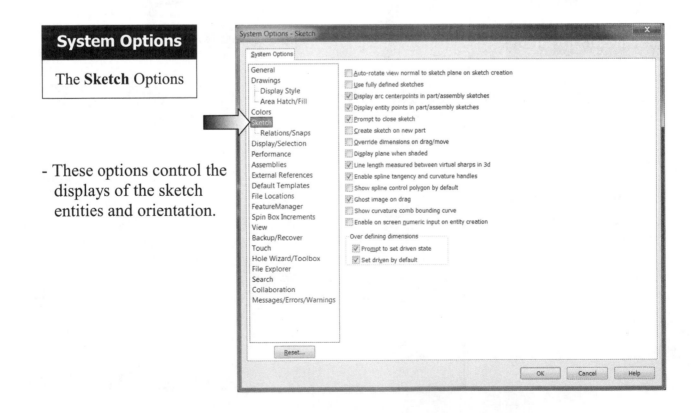

System Options

The **Relations / Snaps** Options

- Enable all Automatic-Relation options, except the Grid and Angle options.

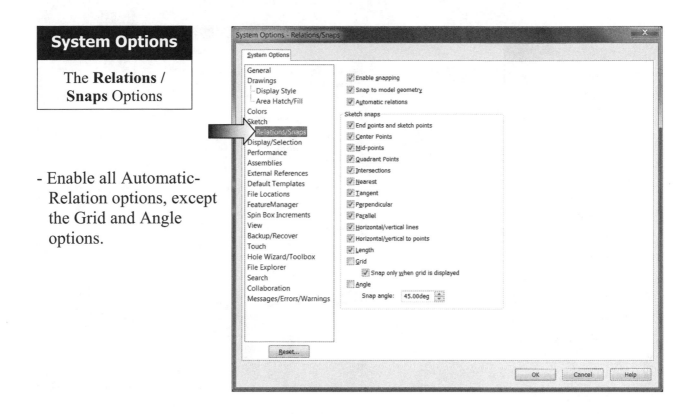

System Options

The **Display / Selection** Options

- The controls for Displays and Selection options in the Part, Assembly, and Drawings modes.

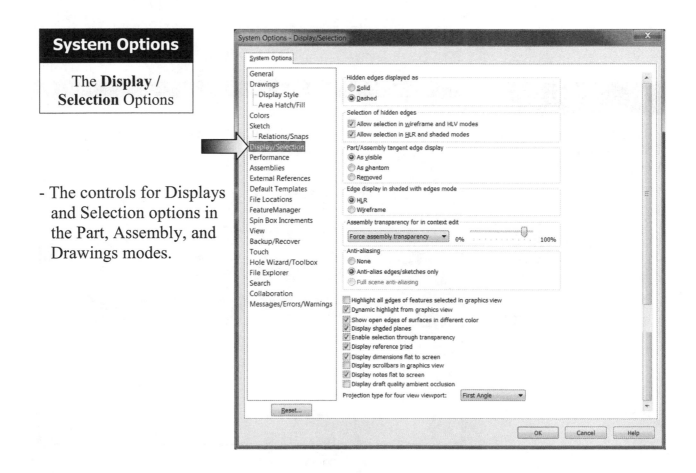

System Options

The **Performance** Options

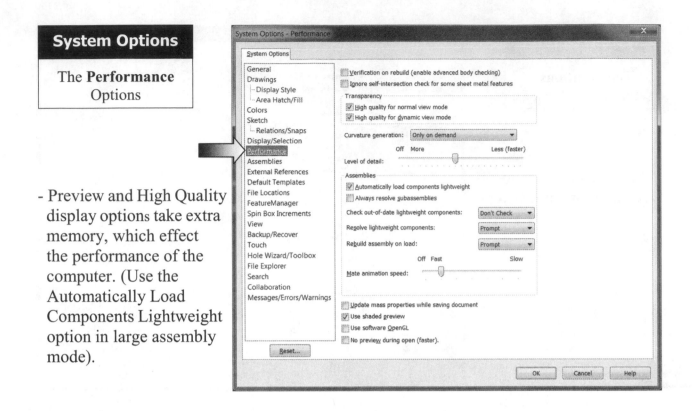

- Preview and High Quality display options take extra memory, which effect the performance of the computer. (Use the Automatically Load Components Lightweight option in large assembly mode).

System Options

The **Assemblies** Options

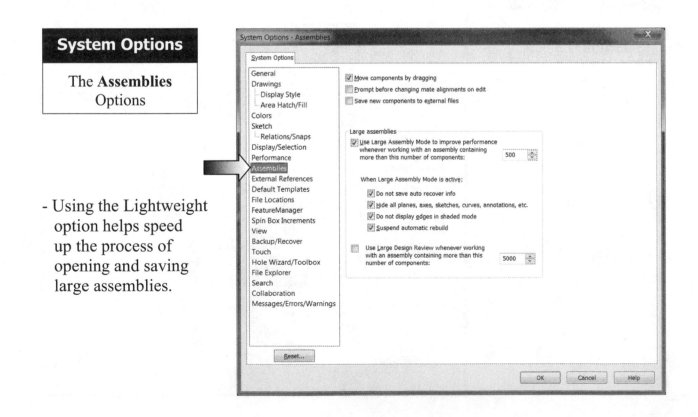

- Using the Lightweight option helps speed up the process of opening and saving large assemblies.

System Options

The **External References** Options

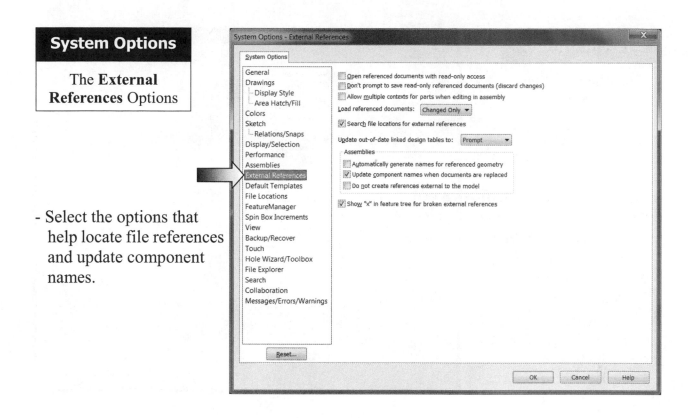

- Select the options that help locate file references and update component names.

System Options

The **Default Templates** Options

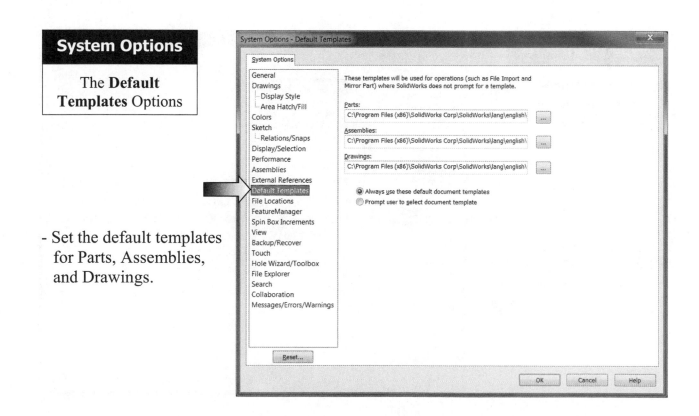

- Set the default templates for Parts, Assemblies, and Drawings.

System Options

The **File Locations**
Options

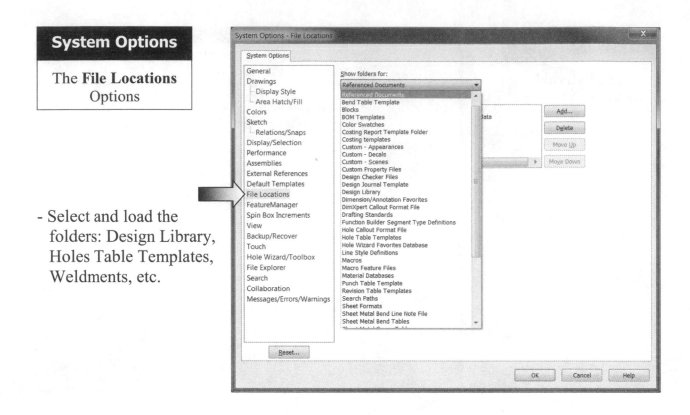

- Select and load the
folders: Design Library,
Holes Table Templates,
Weldments, etc.

System Options

The **Feature-
Manager** Options

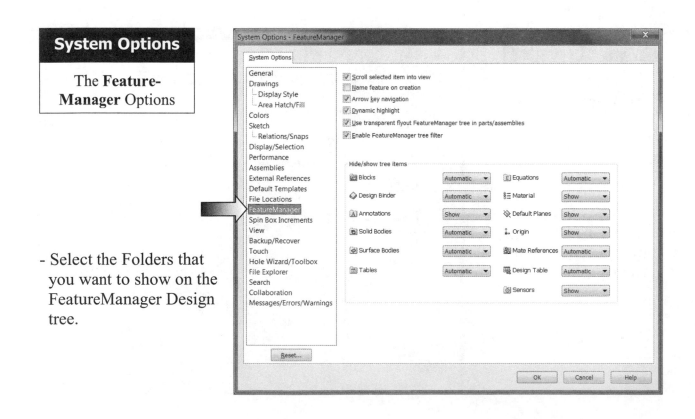

- Select the Folders that
you want to show on the
FeatureManager Design
tree.

System Options
The **Spin Box Increments** Options

- Set the default increments for the Modify Spin Box (when creating or editing dimensions).

System Options
The **View** Options

- Set the Rotation, Mouse Speed, and Transitions of the view.

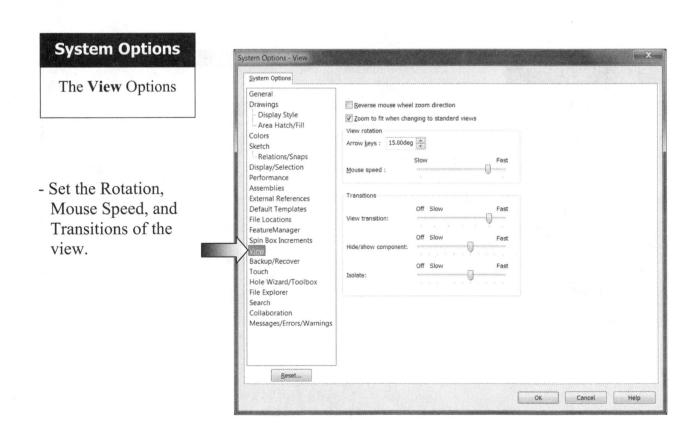

System Options

The **Backups / Recover** Options

- Set the Auto-Recover-Time and the Number of Backup Copies.

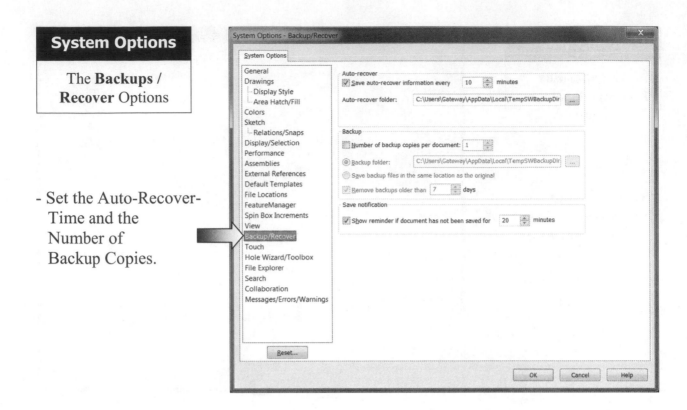

System Options

The **Touch** Options

- With a Touch-enabled computer, you can use flick touch and multi-touch gestures in SolidWorks 2012.

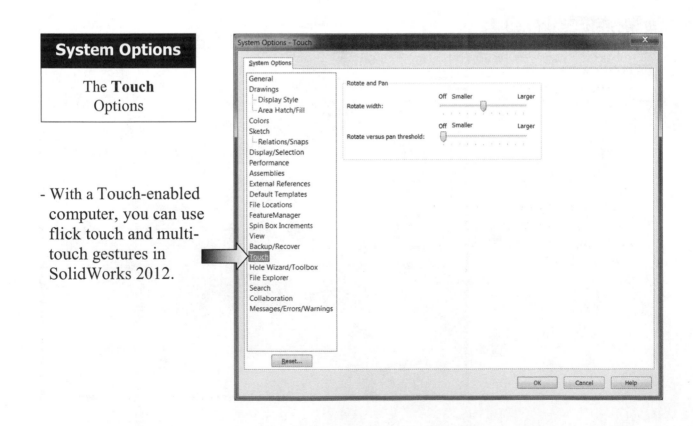

System Options

The **Hole-Wizard/Toolbox**
Options

- Locate the Hole Wizard
and Toolbox folder.

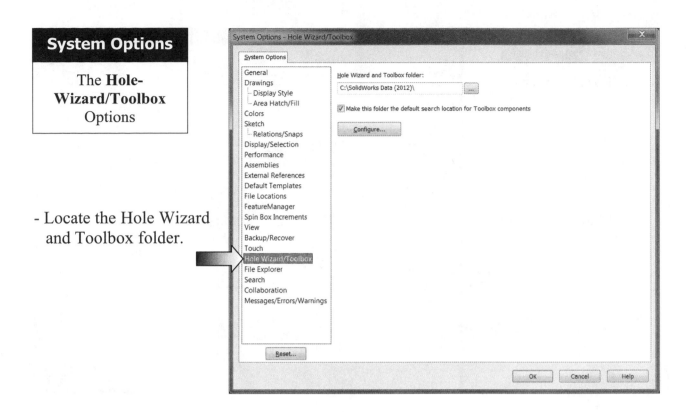

System Options

The **File Explorer**
Options

- Enable the File Locations
for accessing the SW
documents.

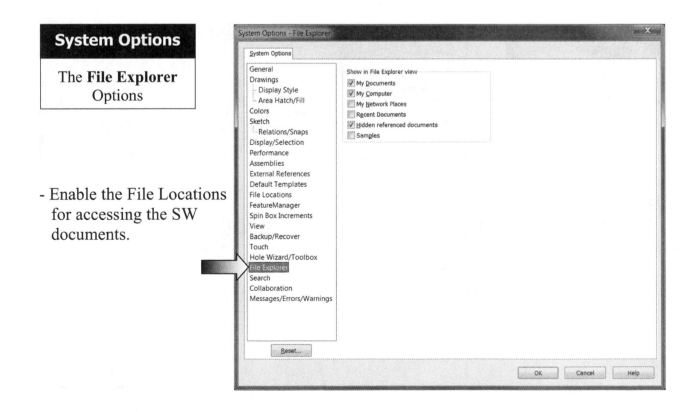

System Options

The **Search** Options

- Set the Search options.

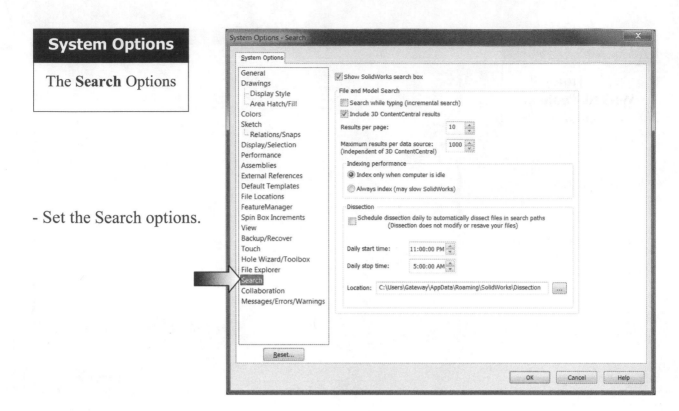

System Options

The **Collaboration** Options

- Enable / Disable the Multi-User Environment.

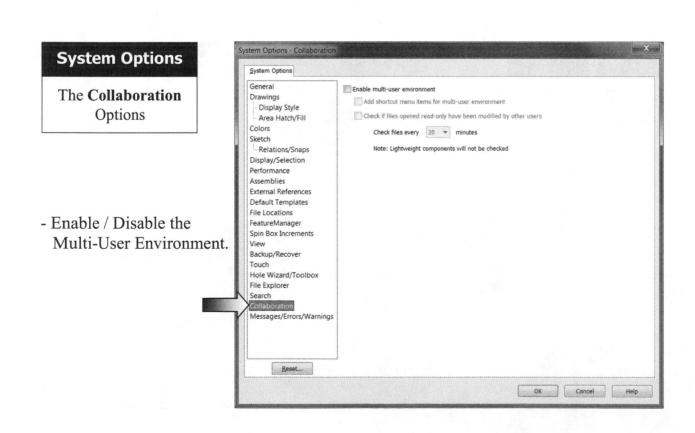

System Options

The **Advanced**
Options

- Set the Error and
  Warning messages.

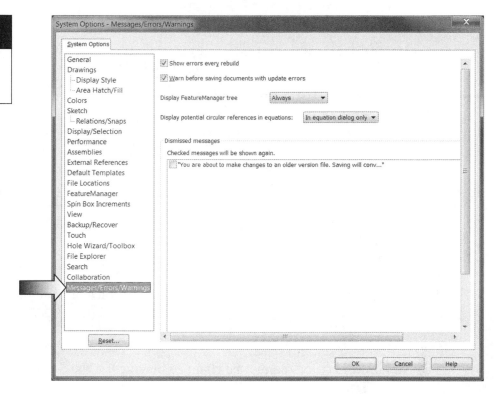

- Continue to setup the Document Properties in Chapter 2...

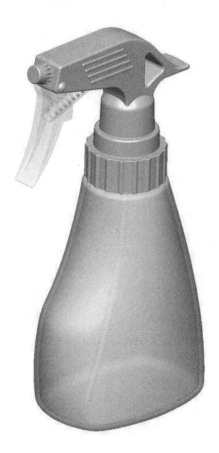

Questions for Review

System Options

1. The settings in the System Options affect all documents including the current and the future documents.
   - a. True
   - b. False

2. The sketch display and automatic relations are samples of System Options.
   - a. True
   - b. False

3. The background colors cannot be changed or saved in the System Options.
   - a. True
   - b. False

4. The mouse wheel zoom direction can be reverse and saved.
   - a. True
   - b. False

5. Default document templates can be selected and saved in the System Options.
   - a. True
   - b. False

6. The spin box increment is fixed in the System Options; its value cannot be changed.
   - a. True
   - b. False

7. The number of backup copies for a document can be specified and saved in the System Options.
   - a. True
   - b. False

8. The System Options can be copied using the SolidWorks Utility / Copy Settings Wizard.
   - a. True
   - b. False

1. TRUE
2. TRUE
3. FALSE
4. TRUE
5. FALSE
6. FALSE
7. TRUE
8. TRUE

CHAPTER 2

Document Templates

The Document Properties

After setting up the System Options, the next task is to setup a document template, where drafting standards and other settings can be set, saved and used over and over again as a template. The Document Properties such as:

- Drafting Standard (ANSI, ISO, DIN, JIS, etc.).

- Dimension, Note, Balloon, and Fonts Sizes.

- Arrowhead sizes.

- Annotation display.

- Grid spacing and grid display.

- Units (Inches, Millimeters, etc.) and Decimal places.

- Feature Colors, Wireframe, and Shading colors.

- Material Properties.

- Image quality controls.

- Plane display controls.

… are all set and saved in the templates, all settings affect only the **current document** (C:\Program Files\SolidWorks Corp\SolidWorks Data\Templates) OR (C:\Program Files\SolidWorks Corp\SolidWorks\Lang\English\Tutorial).

The following are examples of various document settings which are intended for use with this textbook only; you may need to modify them to ensure full compatibility with your applications.

Document Properties
The **Drafting Standard** options

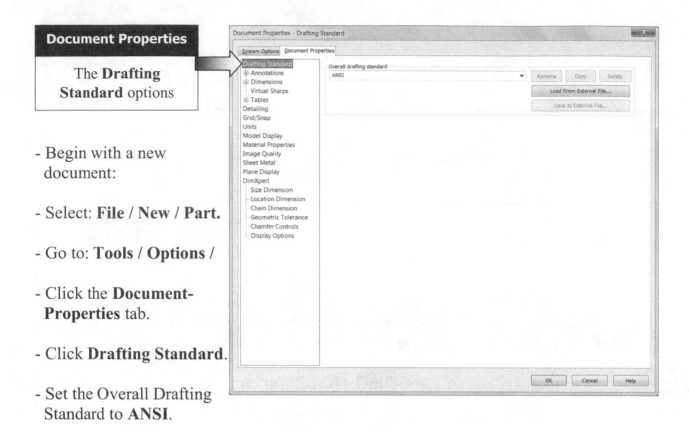

- Begin with a new document:

- Select: **File / New / Part.**

- Go to: **Tools / Options /**

- Click the **Document-Properties** tab.

- Click **Drafting Standard**.

- Set the Overall Drafting Standard to **ANSI**.

Note: If your Units is in Millimeter, skip to the Units options on page 2-13 and set your units to IPS, then return to where you left off and continue with your template settings.

Document Properties
The **Annotations** options

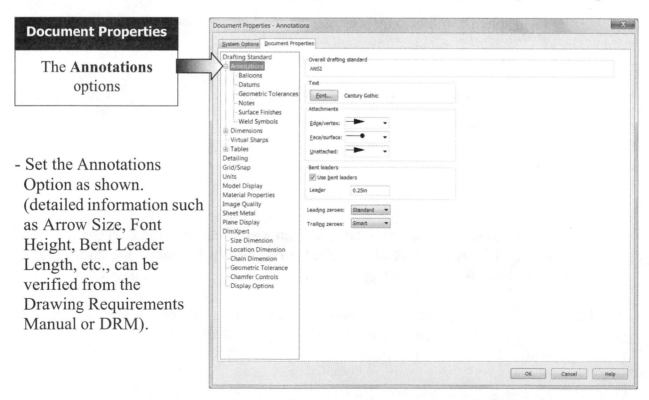

- Set the Annotations Option as shown. (detailed information such as Arrow Size, Font Height, Bent Leader Length, etc., can be verified from the Drawing Requirements Manual or DRM).

Document Properties

The **Annotations /
Balloons** options

- Set the Balloons standard
to ANSI and the other
options as shown.

- Click on the Help button at
any time to access the detail
information on these topics.

Document Properties

The **Annotations /
Datums** options

- Set the Datums standard
to ANSI and other options
as shown.

Note:

1982 Datum symbol $-A-$

1994 Datum symbol $\boxed{A}$

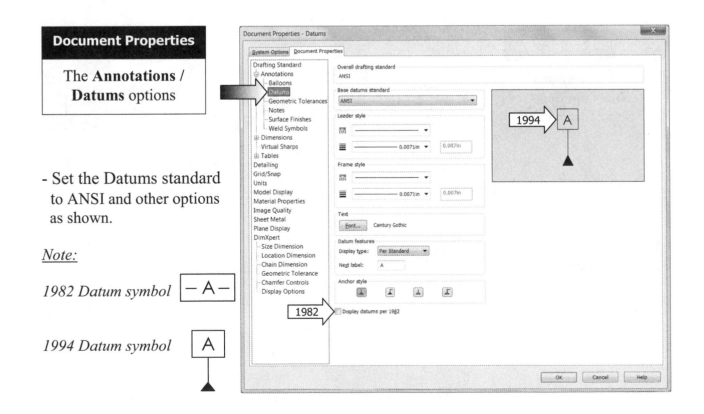

Document Properties

The **Annotations /
Geo. Tol.** options

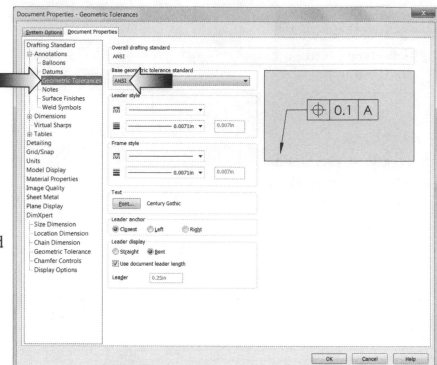

- Set the Geometric-
Tolerance standard to
ANSI.

- The Font selection should
match the other options
for all annotations.

Document Properties

The **Annotations /
Notes** options

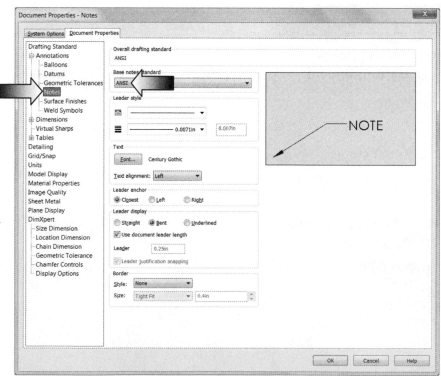

- Set the Notes standard to
ANSI.

- Use the same settings for
Font and Leader display.

Document Properties

The **Surface Finishes** options

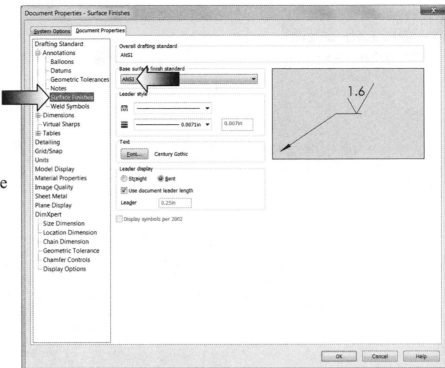

- Set the Surfaces Finish standard to ANSI and the same Leader Display as in the previous options.

The **Annotations / Weld Symbols** options

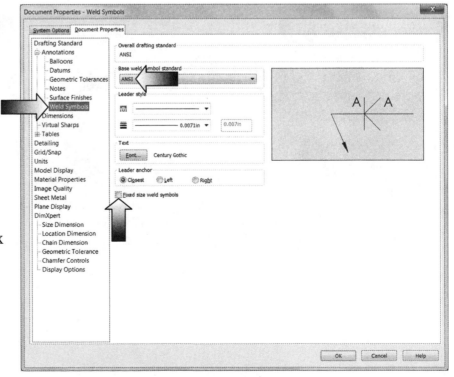

- Set the Weld Symbols standard to ANSI.

- Clear the Fixed Size Weld Symbols checkbox to scale the size of the symbol to the symbol font size.

Document Properties

The **Dimensions**
options

- Continue with setting the
options as shown in the
next dialog boxes.

- Document-level drafting
settings for all dimensions
are set here.

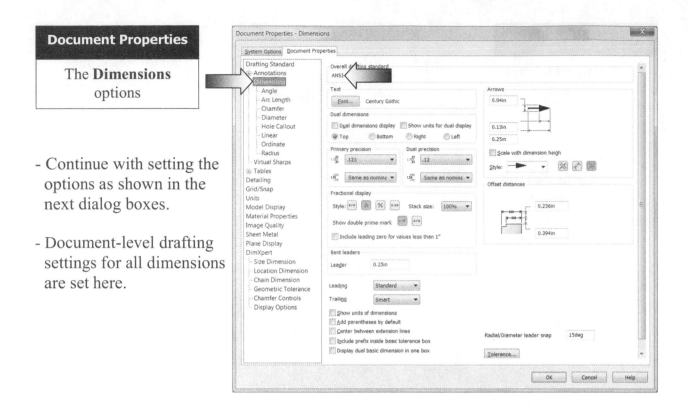

Document Properties

The **Dimensions** /
Angle options

- Set the Angle Dimension
standard to ANSI and set
the other options shown.

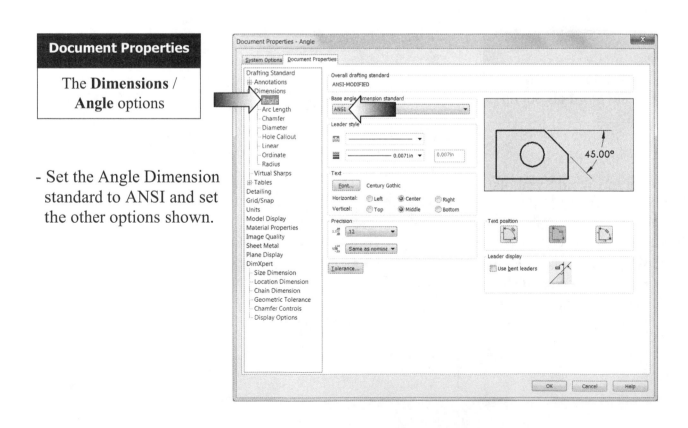

Document Properties

The **Dimensions /
Arc Length** options

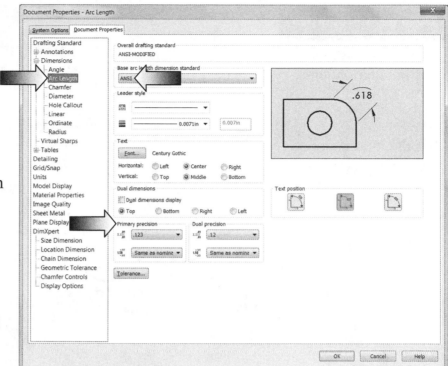

- Set the Arc Length
Dimension standard to
ANSI, Primary Precision
to 3 decimals, and Dual
Precision to 2 decimals.

- The Arc Length
dimension is created by
holding the Control key
and clicking the arc and
both of its endpoints.

Document Properties

The **Dimensions /
Chamfer** options

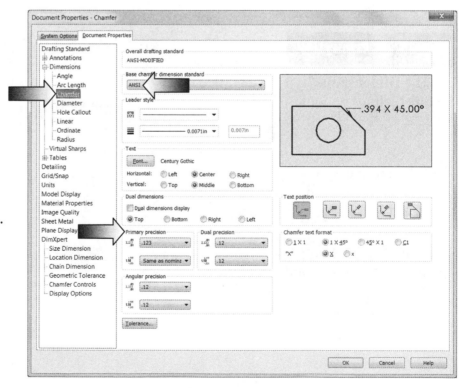

- Set the Chamfer-
Dimension standard to
ANSI and the Primary-
Precision to 3 decimals.

Document Properties

The **Dimensions /
Diameter** options

- Set the Diameter-
Dimension standard to
ANSI.

- Set the Leader Style and
thickness here.

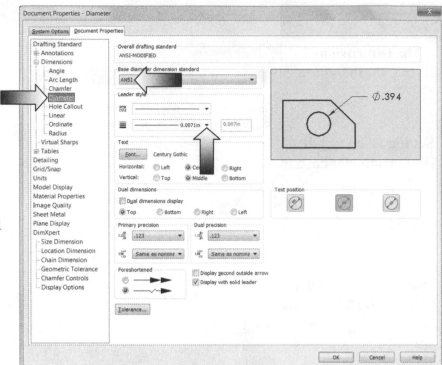

Document Properties

The **Dimensions /
Hole Callout** options

- Set the Hole Callout
Dimension standard
to ANSI.

- Set the Text justification
positions to Center and
Middle.

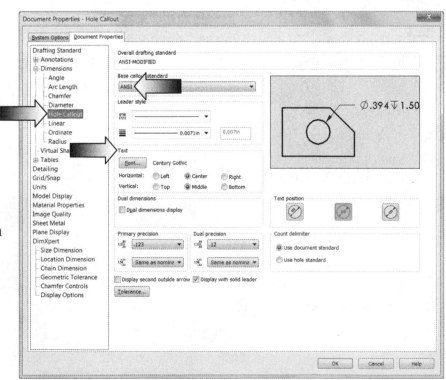

Document Properties

The **Dimensions /
Linear** options

- Set the Linear Dimension standard to ANSI.

- Enable (or disable) the Use Bent Leader checkbox.

Document Properties

The **Dimensions /
Ordinate** options

- Set the Ordinate-Dimension standard to ANSI.

- Enable the Automatically Jog Ordinates, when dimensions overlaping or too close to one another.

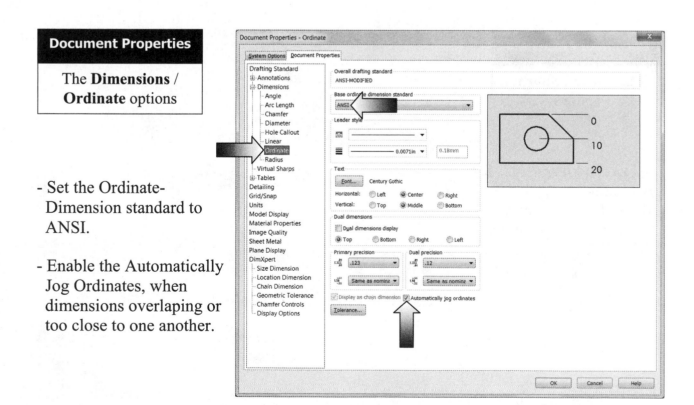

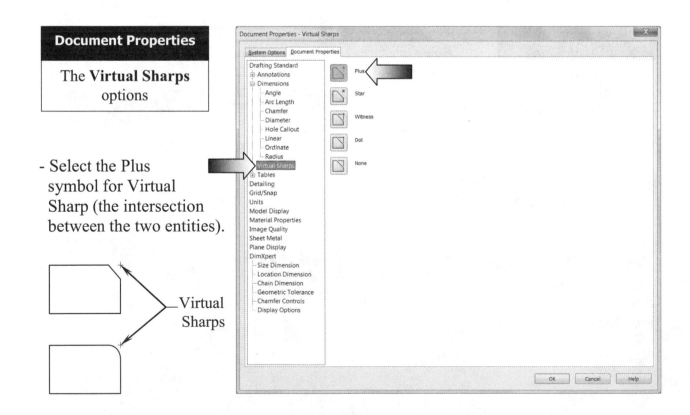

Document Properties

The **Dimensions** / **Radius** options

- Set the Radius-Dimension standard to ANSI.

- Enable (or disable) the Display With Solid Leader Checkbox.

Document Properties

The **Virtual Sharps** options

- Select the Plus symbol for Virtual Sharp (the intersection between the two entities).

Virtual Sharps

Document Properties

The **Tables** options

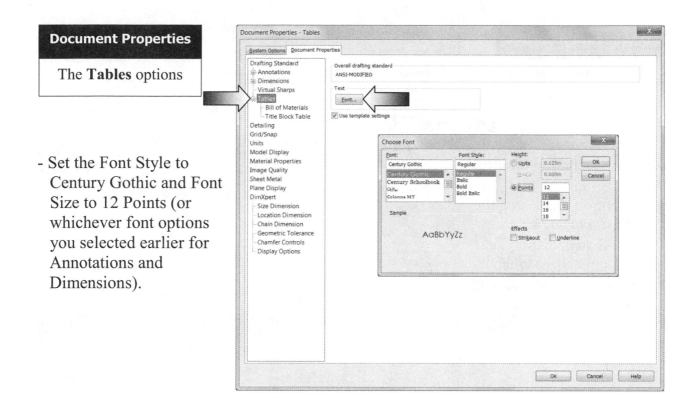

- Set the Font Style to
  Century Gothic and Font
  Size to 12 Points (or
  whichever font options
  you selected earlier for
  Annotations and
  Dimensions).

Document Properties

The **Bill of Materials**
options

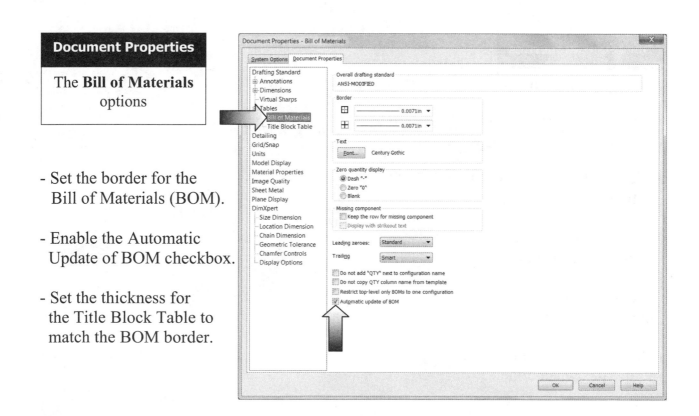

- Set the border for the
  Bill of Materials (BOM).

- Enable the Automatic
  Update of BOM checkbox.

- Set the thickness for
  the Title Block Table to
  match the BOM border.

Document Properties

The **Detailing** options

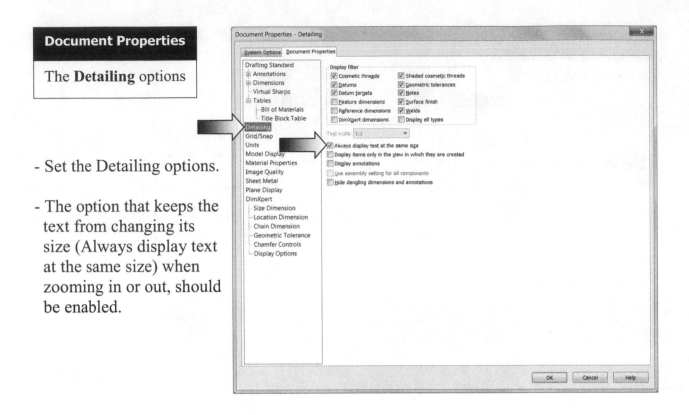

- Set the Detailing options.

- The option that keeps the text from changing its size (Always display text at the same size) when zooming in or out, should be enabled.

Document Properties

The **Grid/Snap** options

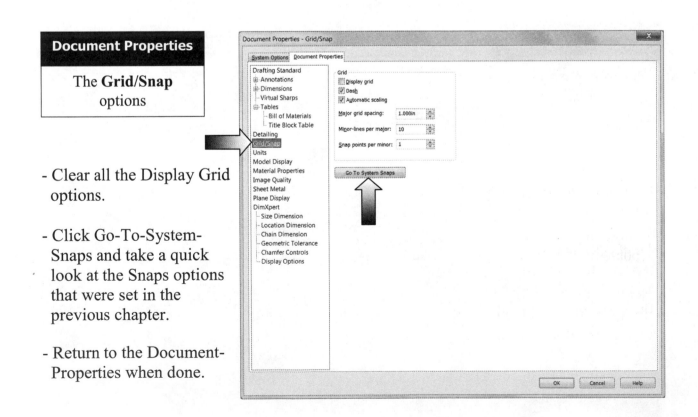

- Clear all the Display Grid options.

- Click Go-To-System-Snaps and take a quick look at the Snaps options that were set in the previous chapter.

- Return to the Document-Properties when done.

Document Properties

The **Units** options

- Set the Unit options to IPS, and number of decimals as indicated.

(The Dual Dimension options are set in the Dimension section).

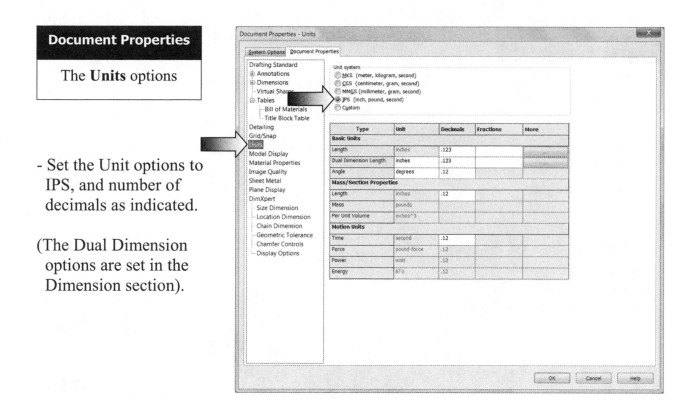

Document Properties

The **Model Display** options

- Keep all default Colors as they are, do not change.

- Uncheck the Store Appearance, Decal, and Scene… to help reduce the file size.

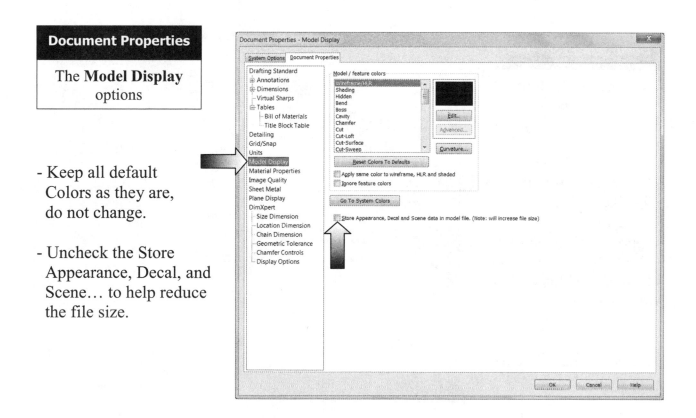

Document Properties

The **Material Properties** options

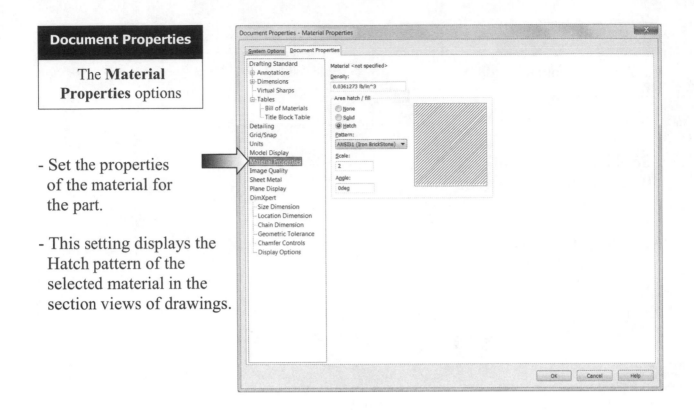

- Set the properties of the material for the part.

- This setting displays the Hatch pattern of the selected material in the section views of drawings.

Document Properties

The **Image Quality** options

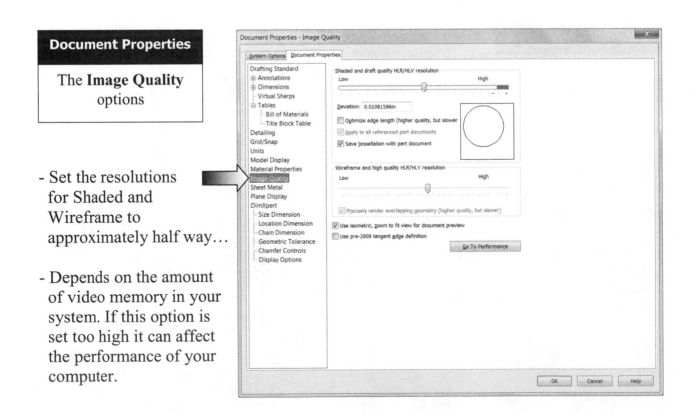

- Set the resolutions for Shaded and Wireframe to approximately half way...

- Depends on the amount of video memory in your system. If this option is set too high it can affect the performance of your computer.

Document Properties

The **Sheet Metal**
options

- Set the Sheet Metal
options as shown.

- These options vary
depending on whether
you are working with a
part, assembly, or drawing.
Click the Help button for
more information about
these settings.

Document Properties

The **Plane Display**
options

- Change the Plane
colors and its
transparency only
as needed.

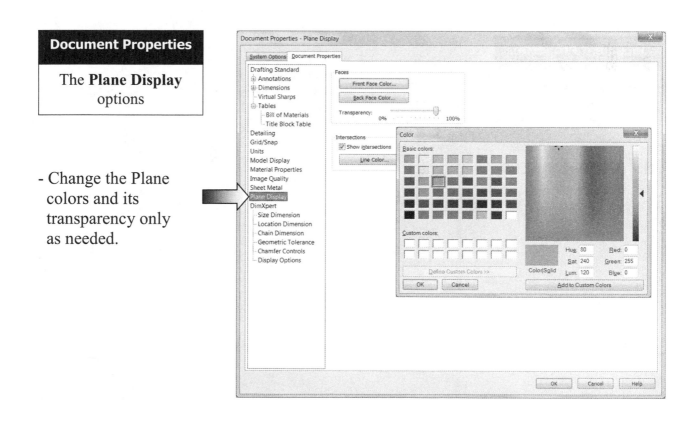

Document Properties

The **DimXpert** options

- Set the DimXpert to your company's specifications.

- Block Tolerance: is a common form of tolerancing used with inch units.

- General Tolerance: is a common form of tolerancing used with metric units in conjunction with the ISO drawing standard.

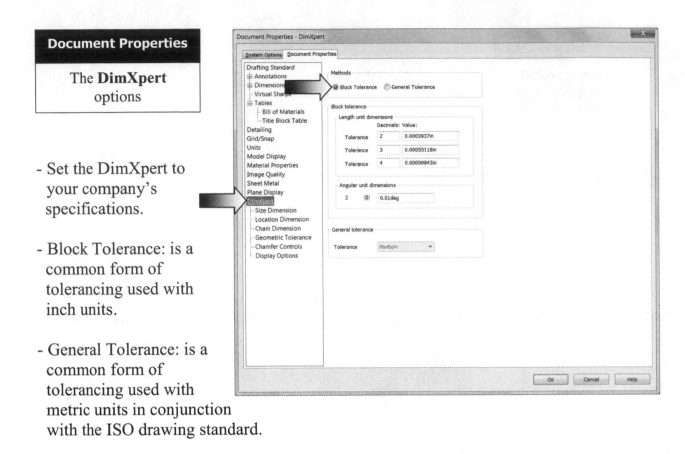

Document Properties

The **Size Dimension** options

- Set per company Std.

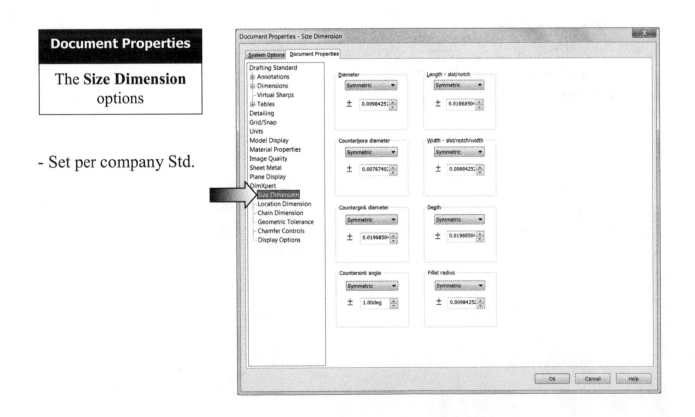

Document Properties

The **Location-Dimension** options

- Set per company Std.

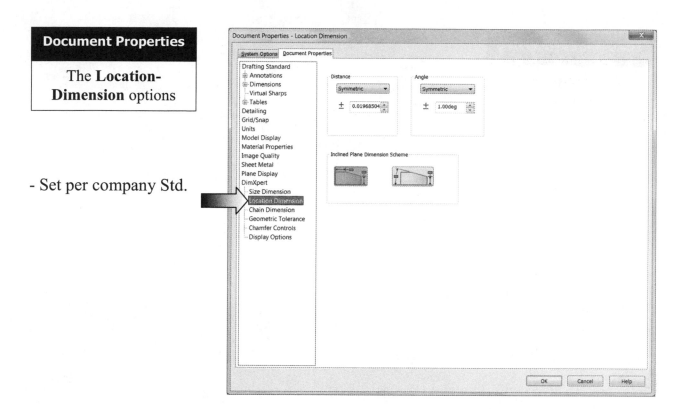

Document Properties

The **Chain Dimension** options

- Set per company Std.

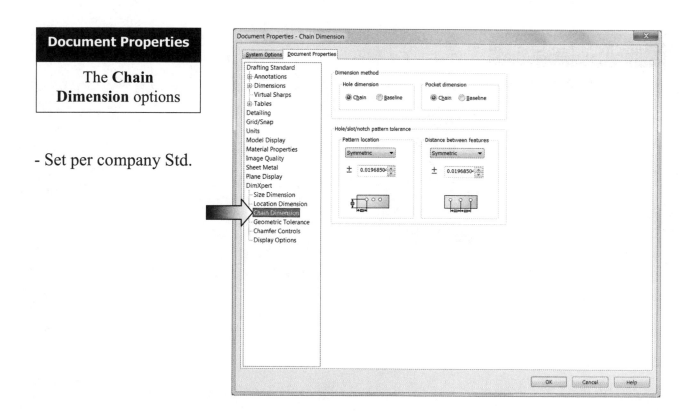

Document Properties

The **Geometric-Tolerance** options

- Set per company Std.

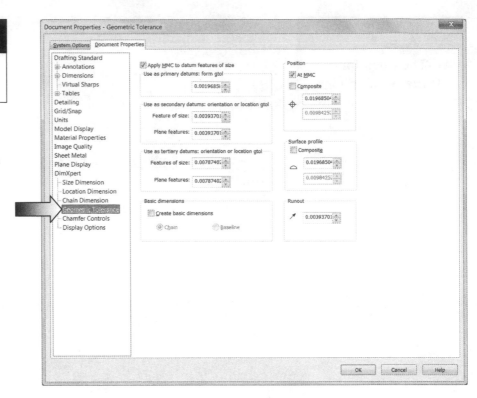

Document Properties

The **Chamfer-Controls** options

- Set per company Std.

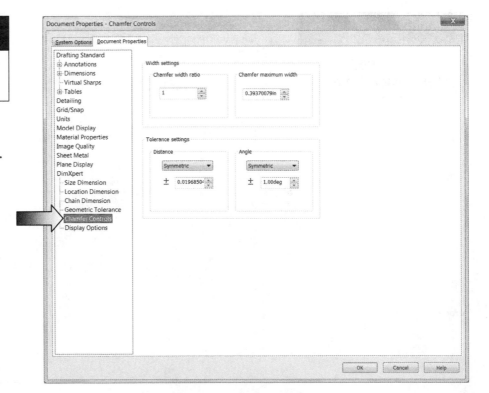

Document Properties
The **Display** options

- Set per company Std.

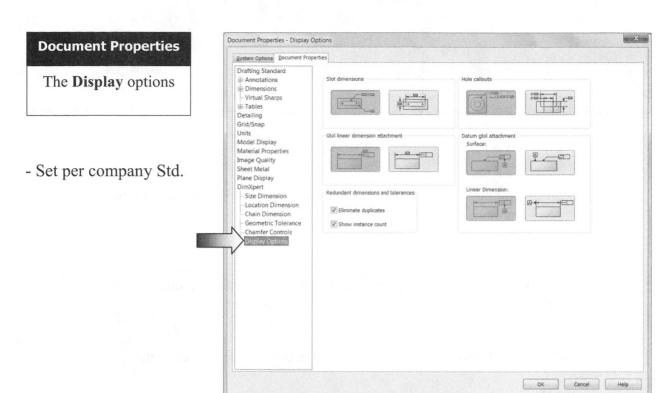

Saving the settings as a Part Template:

- These settings should be saved within the Document Template for use in future documents.

- Go to **File / Save As.**

- Change the Save-As-Type to: **Part Templates** (*.prtdot - part document template).

- Enter **Part-Inch.prtdot** for the file name.

- Save either in the Templates folder *(C:\Program Files\Solidworks Corp\ SolidWorks\Data\Templates).* – or – in the Tutorial folder *(C:\Program Files\SolidWorks Corp\Solidworks\ Lang\English\Tutorial).*

- Click **Save**.

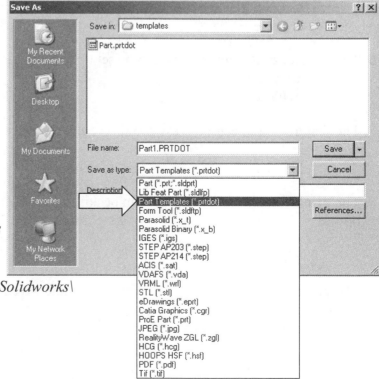

Questions for Review

Document Templates

1. The ANSI dimensioning standard (American National Standards Institute) can be set and saved in the System Options.
   - a. True
   - b. False

2. The size of dimension arrows can be controlled globally from the Document Templates.
   - a. True
   - b. False

3. The balloon's size and shape can be set and saved in the Document Templates.
   - a. True
   - b. False

4. Dimension and note fonts can be changed and edited both locally and globally.
   - a. True
   - b. False

5. The Grid option is only available in the drawing environment, not in the part or assembly.
   - a. True
   - b. False

6. The number of decimal places can be set up to 10 digits.
   - a. True
   - b. False

7. The feature colors can be pre-set and saved in the Document Templates.
   - a. True
   - b. False

8. The display quality of the model can be adjusted using the settings in the Image Quality option.
   - a. True
   - b. False

9. The plane colors and transparency can be set and saved in the Document Templates.
   - a. True
   - b. False

9. TRUE
7. TRUE   8. TRUE
5. FALSE   6. FALSE
3. TRUE   4. TRUE
1. FALSE   2. TRUE

CHAPTER 3

Basic Solid Modeling

Basic Solid Modeling
Extrude Options

- Upon successful completion of this lesson, you will be able to:

  * Sketch on planes and/or planar surfaces.

  * Use the sketch tools to construct geometry.

  * Add the geometric relations or constraints.

  * Add/modify dimensions.

  * Explore the different extrude options.

- The following 5 basic steps will be demonstrated throughout this exercise:

  * Select the sketch plane.

  * Activate Sketch pencil .

  * Sketch the profile using the sketch tools .

  * Define the profile with dimensions or relations .

  * Extrude the profile .

- Be sure to review self-test questionnaires at the end of the lesson, prior to going to the next chapter.

Basic Solid Modeling
Extrude Options

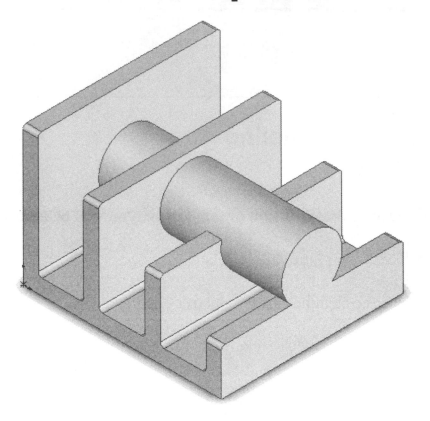

| Dimensioning Standards: **ANSI** |
| Units: **INCHES** – 3 Decimals |

Tools Needed:

	Insert Sketch		Line		Circle
Add Geometric Relations		Dimension		Sketch Fillet
	Boss / Base Extrude			

1. Starting a new Part:

- From the **File** menu, select **New / Part**, or click the **New** icon.

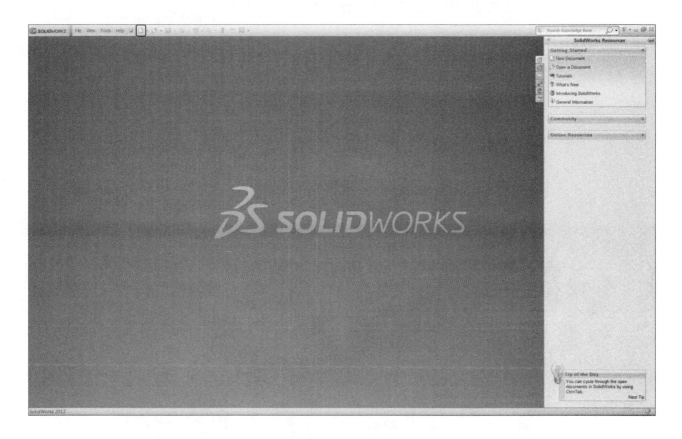

- Select the **Part** template from either the Templates or Tutorial folders.

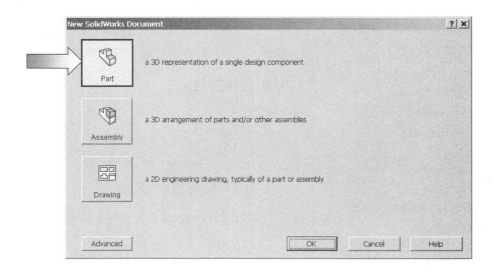

- Click **OK** [OK]; a new part template is opened.

2. Changing the background color:

- From the View (Heads-up) toolbar, click the Apply Scene button (arrow) and select the Plain White option (arrow).

- By changing the background color to Plain White we can better view the colors of the sketch entities and sketch dimensions.

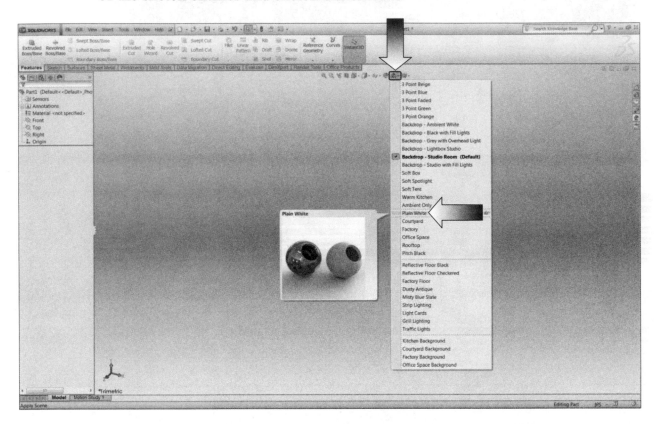

- To show the Origin, click the View dropdown menu and select Origin.

- The Blue Origin is the Zero position of the part and the Red Origin is the Zero position of a sketch.

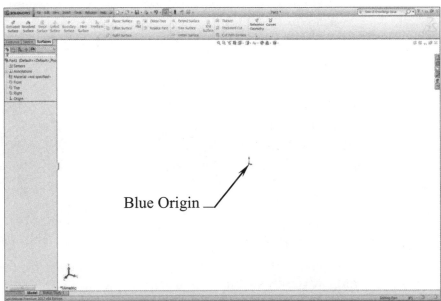

3. Starting a new Sketch:

- Select the Front plane from the Feature-Manager tree and click the Pencil icon  to start a new sketch.

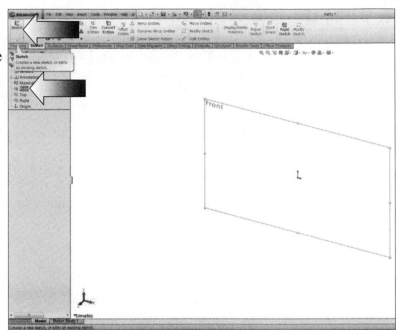

- A sketch is normally created first, relations and dimensions are added after, then it gets extruded into a 3D feature.

- From the Command-Manager toolbar, select the Line  command.

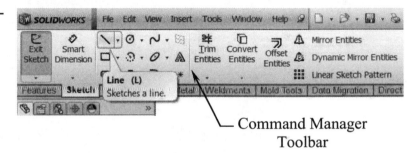

Command Manager
Toolbar

Mouse Gesture

OPTION:
Right-Drag to display the Mouse Gesture guide and select the Line command from it. (See the Introduction section, page XVIII for details on customizing the Mouse Gesture).

- Position the mouse cursor at the Red Origin point, a yellow feedback symbol pops up to indicate that a relation (Coincident) is going to be added automatically to the 1st endpoint of the line. This endpoint will be locked at the zero position.

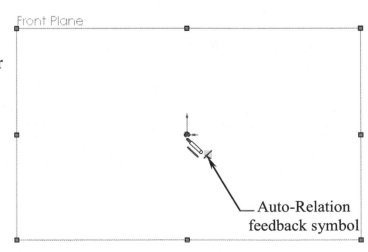

Auto-Relation
feedback symbol

4. Using the line command:

- Click on the Origin point and **hold** the mouse button to start the line at point 1, **drag upwards** to point 2, then release the mouse button.

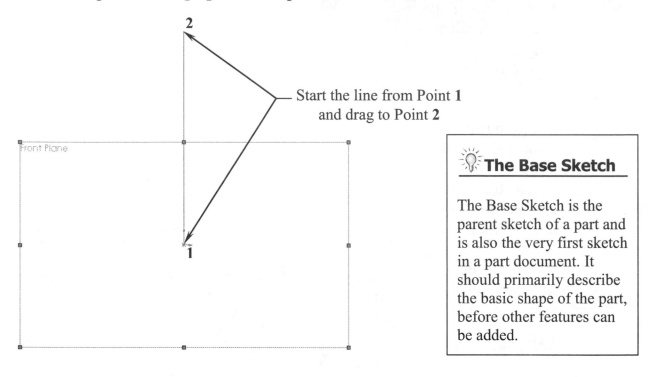

Start the line from Point **1**
and drag to Point **2**

> ### The Base Sketch
>
> The Base Sketch is the parent sketch of a part and is also the very first sketch in a part document. It should primarily describe the basic shape of the part, before other features can be added.

- Continue adding other lines using the **Click-Hold-Drag** technique.

- The relations like Horizontal and Vertical are added automatically to each sketch line. Other relations like Collinear and Equal are added manually.

- The size and shape of the profile will be corrected in the next few steps.

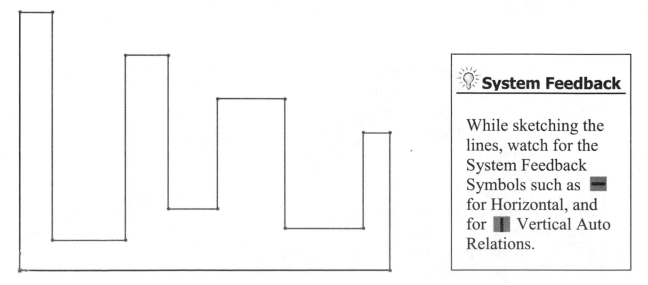

> ### System Feedback
>
> While sketching the lines, watch for the System Feedback Symbols such as ▬ for Horizontal, and for ▮ Vertical Auto Relations.

5. Adding Geometric Relations*:

- Click **Add Relation** 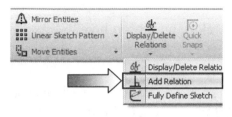 under Display/Delete Relations - OR - select **Tools / Relations / Add**.

- Select the 4 lines shown below.

- Click **EQUAL** from the Add Geometric Relation dialog box. This relation makes the length of the two selected lines equal.

* Geometric relations are one of the most powerful features in SolidWorks. They're used in the sketch level to control the behaviors of the sketch entities when they are moved or rotated and to keep the associations between one another.

When applying geometric relations between entities, one of them should be a 2D entity and the other can either be a 2D sketch entity or a model edge, a plane, an axis, or a curve, etc.

Equal Relations

Adding the EQUAL relations to these lines eliminates the need to dimension each line.

Geometric relations can be created manually or automatically. The next few steps in this chapter will demonstrate how geometric relations are added manually.

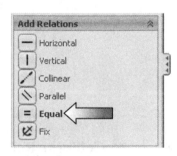

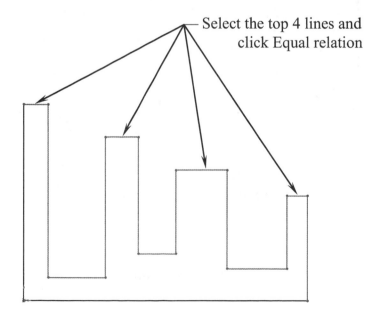

Select the top 4 lines and click Equal relation

The top 4 lines are now Equal in size.

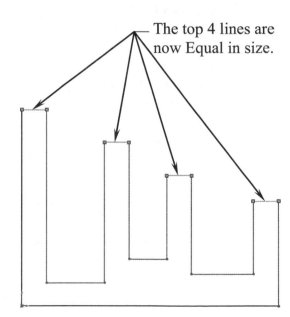

6. Adding a Collinear relation**:

- Select the **Add Relation** 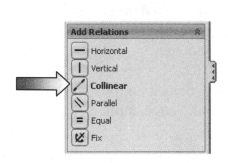 command again.

- Select the 3 lines as shown below.

- Click **COLLINEAR** from the Add Geometric Relations dialog box.

- Click **OK** ✅.

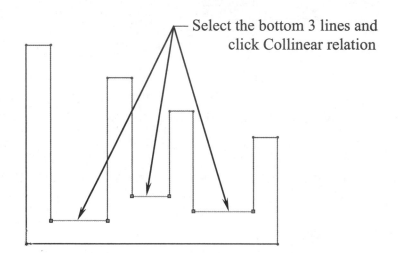

Select the bottom 3 lines and click Collinear relation

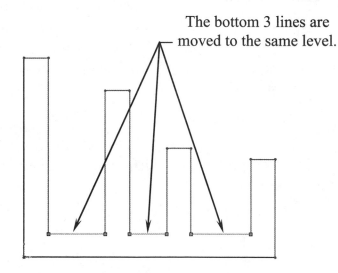

The bottom 3 lines are moved to the same level.

💡 **Collinear Relations**

Adding a Collinear relation to these lines puts them on the same height level; only one dimension is needed to drive the height of all 3 lines.

** Collinear relations can be used to constrain the geometry as follow:

- Collinear between a line and another line(s) (2D and 2D).

- Collinear between a line(s) to an edge of a model (2D and 3D).

Geometric Relations Examples

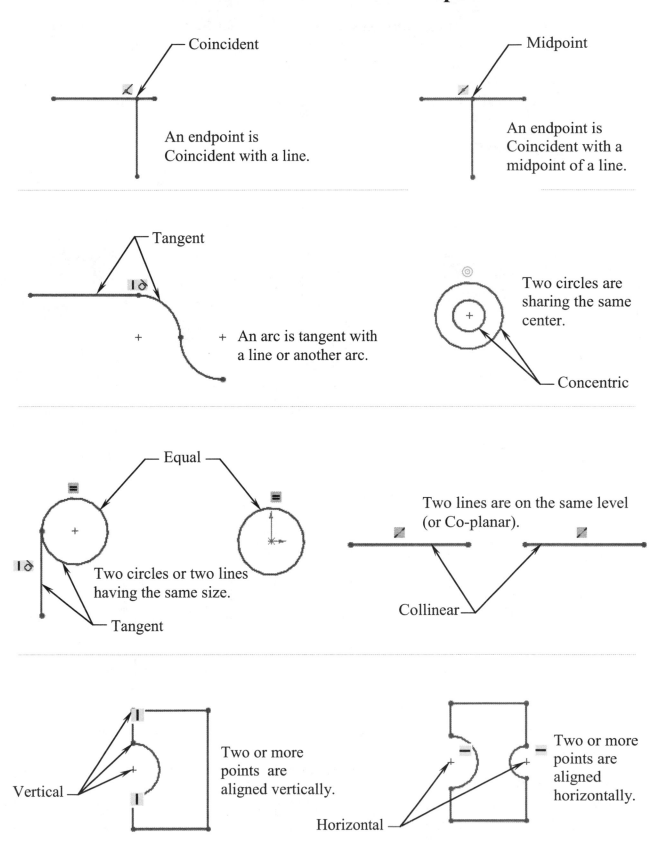

Coincident

An endpoint is
Coincident with a line.

Midpoint

An endpoint is
Coincident with a
midpoint of a line.

Tangent

An arc is tangent with
a line or another arc.

Two circles are
sharing the same
center.

Concentric

Equal

Two circles or two lines
having the same size.

Tangent

Two lines are on the same level
(or Co-planar).

Collinear

Vertical

Two or more
points are
aligned vertically.

Horizontal

Two or more
points are
aligned
horizontally.

7. Adding the horizontal dimensions:

- Select 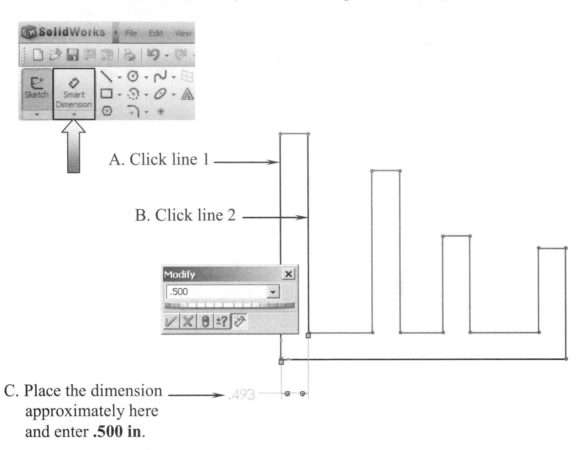 from the Sketch toolbar - OR - select **Insert / Dimension**, and add the dimensions shown below (follow the 3 steps A, B and C).

A. Click line 1

B. Click line 2

C. Place the dimension approximately here and enter **.500 in**.

- Continue adding the horizontal dimensions as shown here.

NOTE:
The color of the sketch lines changes from Blue to Black, to indicate that they have been constrained with a dimension.

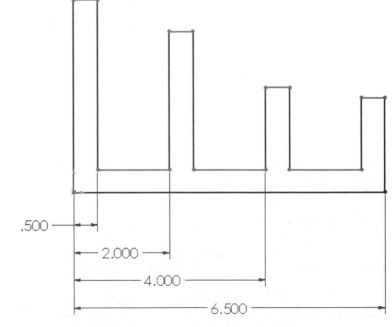

8. Adding the Vertical dimensions:

- With the Smart-Dimension tool still selected, click on line 1 and line 2; place the dimension approximately as shown, and change the value to **.500 in**.

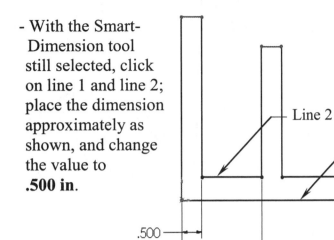

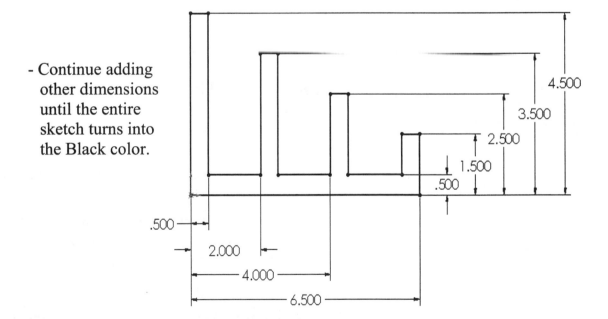

- Continue adding other dimensions until the entire sketch turns into the Black color.

The Status of a Sketch:

The current status of a sketch is displayed in the lower right corner of the screen.

Fully Defined	=	**Black**	Fully Defined
Under Defined	=	**Blue**	Under Defined
Over Defined	=	**Red**	Over Defined

Sketch Relation Symbols

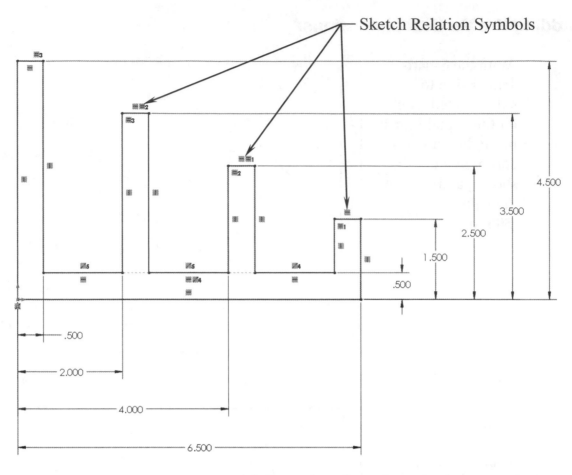

4.500

3.500

2.500

1.500

.500

.500

2.000

4.000

6.500

9. Hiding the Sketch Relation Symbols:

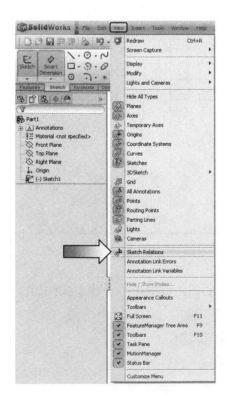

- The Sketch Relation Symbols indicates which geometric relation a sketch entity has, but they get quite busy as shown.

- To hide or show the Sketch Relation Symbols, go to the **View** menu and Click off the **Sketch Relations** option.

Sketch Relation Symbols at a Glance

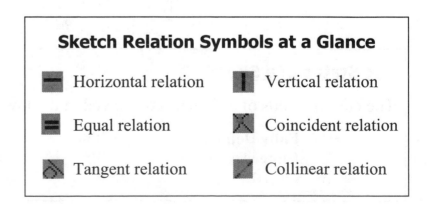

Horizontal relation   Vertical relation

Equal relation   Coincident relation

Tangent relation   Collinear relation

10. Extruding the Base:

- The **Extrude Boss/Base** command is used to define the characteristic of a 3D linear feature.

- Click  from the Features toolbar - OR- select **Insert / Boss Base / Extrude**.

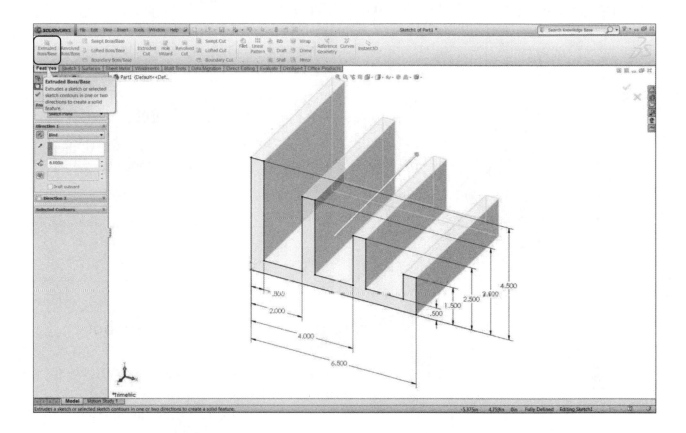

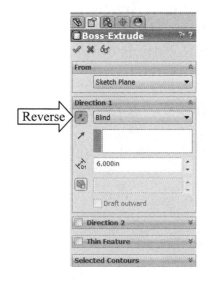

- Set the following:

- Direction: **Blind**.

- Depth: **6.00 in**.

- Enabled **Reverse** direction.

- Click **OK** ✓.

11. Sketching on a Planar Face:

- Select the face as indicated.

- Click ✎ or select **Insert/Sketch**.

- Click ⊕ from the Sketch Tools toolbar
  Or select **Tools / Sketch Entity / Circle**.

(From the View toolbar above the CommandManager, click the Isometric icon
or press the shortcut keys **Ctrl+7**).

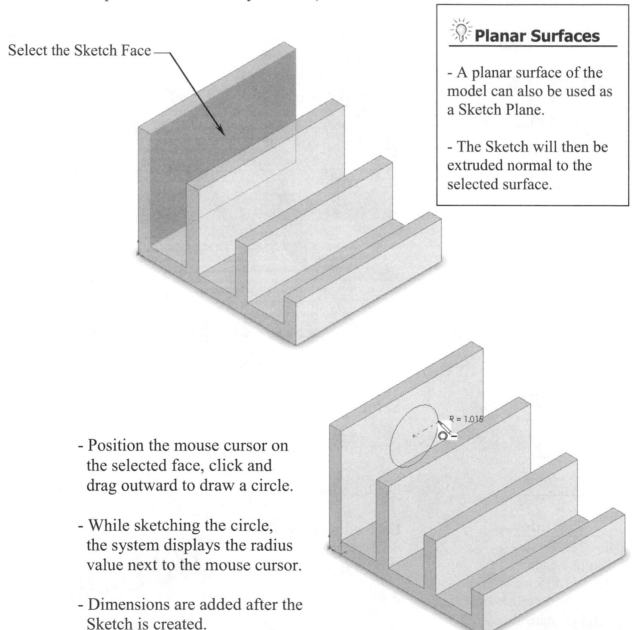

Select the Sketch Face

> ### 💡 Planar Surfaces
>
> - A planar surface of the model can also be used as a Sketch Plane.
>
> - The Sketch will then be extruded normal to the selected surface.

- Position the mouse cursor on the selected face, click and drag outward to draw a circle.

- While sketching the circle, the system displays the radius value next to the mouse cursor.

- Dimensions are added after the Sketch is created.

- Select the **Smart Dimension**

    command  and add a
    diameter dimension to the
    circle.

    (Click on the circle and move
    the mouse cursor outward, at
    approximately 45 degrees,
    and place it).

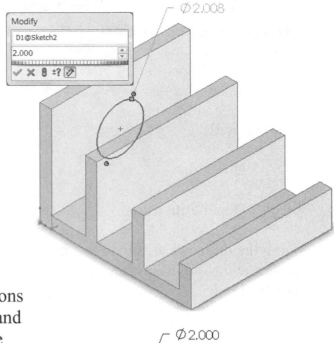

- To add the location dimensions
    click the edge of the circle and
    the edge of the model, place
    the dimension, then correct
    the value.

- Continue adding the
    location dimensions
    as shown, to fully
    define the sketch.

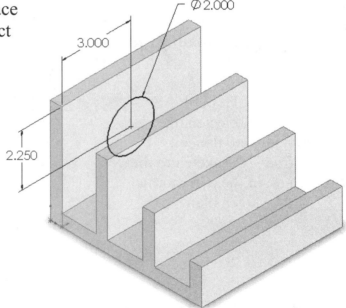

12. Extruding a Boss:

- Click 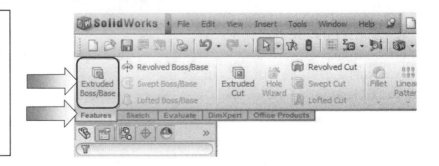 or select **Insert / Boss-Base / Extrude**.

🔆 Extrude Options...

Explore each extrude option to
see the different results.
Press Undo to go back to the
original state after each one.

(A) Using the Blind option:

- When extruding with the Blind option, the following conditions are required:

* Direction

* Depth dimension

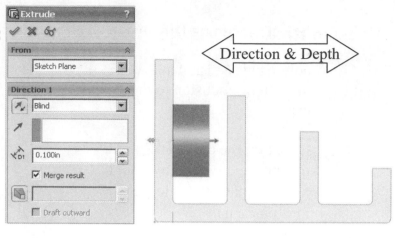

Direction & Depth

Blind
Condition

- Drag the direction arrow on the preview graphics to define the direction, then enter a dimension for the depth.

(B) Using the Through All option:

- When the Through All option is selected, the system automatically extrudes the sketch to the length of the part, normal to the sketch plane.

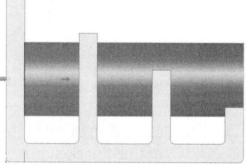

Through All
Condition

(C) Using the Up To Next option:

- With the Up To Next option selected, the system extrudes the sketch to the very next set of surface(s), and blends it to match.

Up To Next
Condition

D **Using the Up To Vertex option:**

- This option extrudes the sketch from its plane to a vertex, specified by the user, to define its depth.

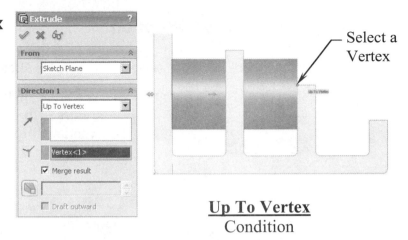

Select a Vertex

<u>Up To Vertex</u>
Condition

E **Using the Up To Surface option:**

- This option extrudes the sketch from its plane to a single surface, to define its depth.

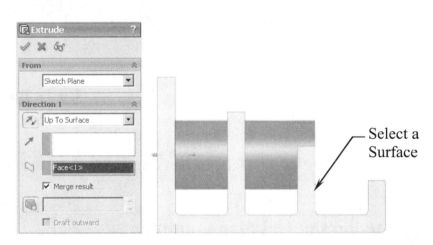

Select a Surface

<u>Up To Surface</u>
Condition

F **Using the Offset From Surface option:**

- This option extrudes the sketch from its plane to a selected face, then offsets at a specified distance.

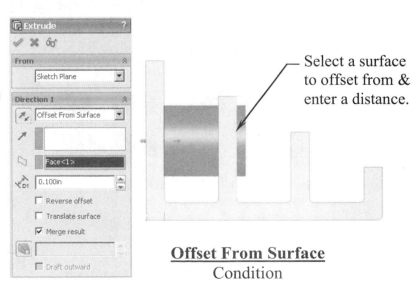

Select a surface to offset from & enter a distance.

<u>Offset From Surface</u>
Condition

G Using the Up To Body option:

- This option extrudes the sketch from its sketch plane to a specified body.

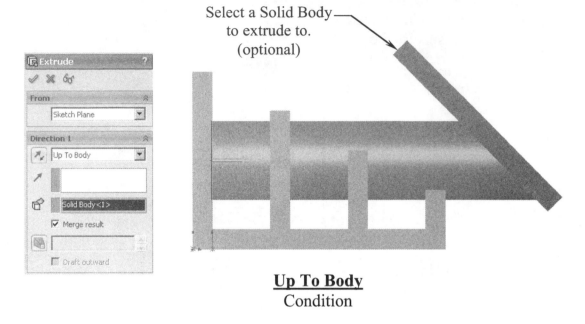

Select a Solid Body
to extrude to.
(optional)

Up To Body
Condition

- The Up To Body option can also be used in assemblies or multi-body parts.

H Using the Mid Plane option:

- This option extrudes the sketch from its plane equally in both directions.

- Enter the Total Depth dimension when using the Mid-Plane option.

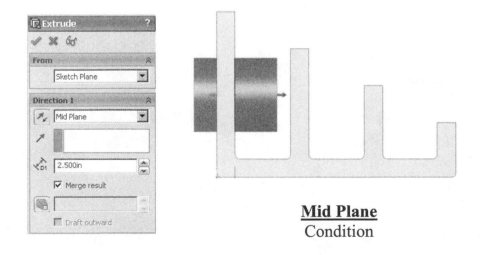

Mid Plane
Condition

- After you are done exploring all the extrude options, change the final condition to: **Through All**

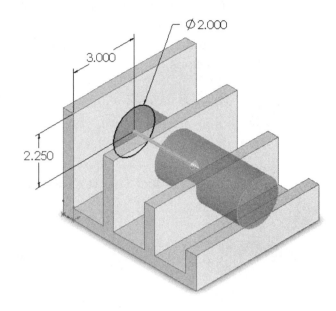

- Click OK ✅.

- The system extrudes the circle to the outer most surface as the result of the Through All end condition.

- The extra material between the first and the second extruded features are removed automatically.

- Unless the Merge Result checkbox is cleared, all interferences will be detected and removed.

Extrude summary:

* The Extrude Boss/Base command is used to add thickness to a sketch and to define the characteristic of a 3D feature.

* A sketch can be extruded in both directions at the same time, from its sketch plane.

* A sketch can also be extruded as a solid or a thin feature.

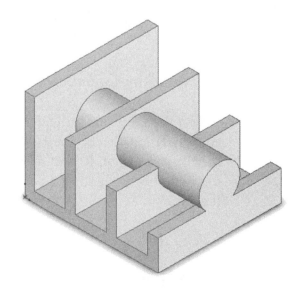

13. Adding the model fillets*:

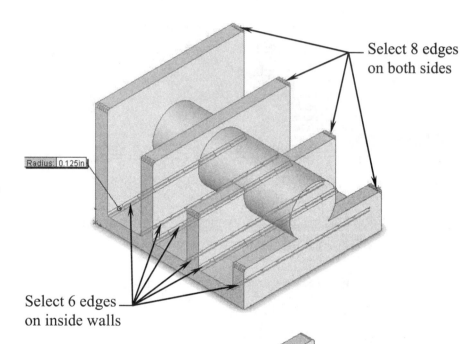

- Fillet/Round creates a rounded internal or external face on the part. You can fillet all edges of a face, select sets of faces, edges, or edge loops.

- The **radius** value stays in effect until you change it. Therefore, you can select any number of edges or faces in the same operation.

- Click 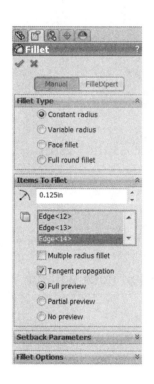 or select **Insert / Features / Fillet/Round**.

Select 8 edges on both sides

Radius: 0.125in

Select 6 edges on inside walls

- Enter **.125 in**. for radius value.

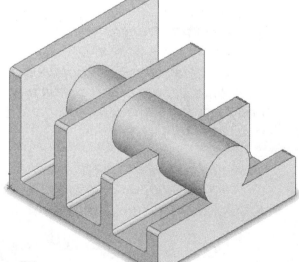

- Select the edges as indicated to add the fillets. Since the fillets are the same size, it is quicker to create them together as one feature.

- Click **OK** ⊘.

- Zoom or rotate to view the complete fillets.

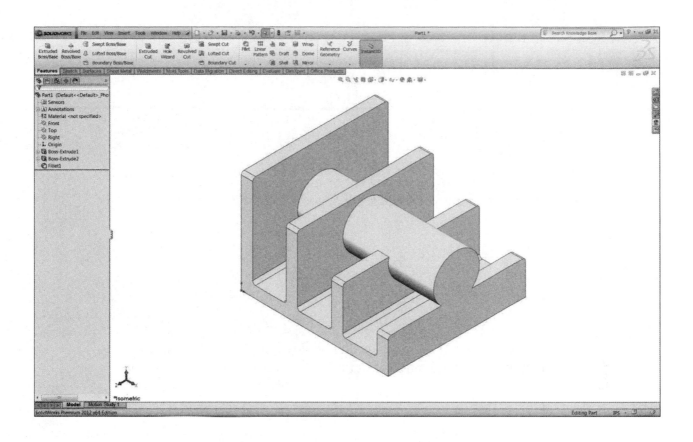

* In the attached CD, in the <u>Built Parts folder</u> you will also find copies of the parts, assemblies, and drawings that were created for cross references or reviewing purposes.

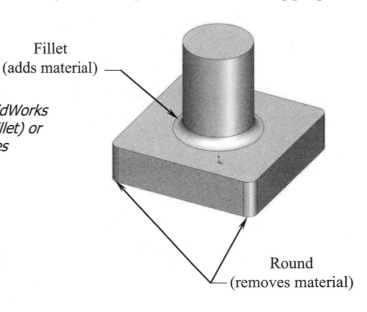

Fillet
(adds material)

Round
(removes material)

* Fillets and Rounds:

Using the same Fillet command, SolidWorks "knows" whether to add material (Fillet) or remove material (Round) to the faces adjacent to the selected edge.

14. Saving your work:

- Select **File / Save As**.

- Enter **Extrude Options** for the name of the file.

- Click **Save**.

Questions for Review

Basic Solid Modeling

1. To open a new sketch, first you must select a plane from the FeatureManager tree.
    a. True
    b. False

2. Geometric relations can be used only in the assembly environments.
    a. True
    b. False

3. The current status of a sketch is displayed in the lower right area of the screen as: Under defined, Fully defined, or Over defined.
    a. True
    b. False

4. Once a feature is extruded, its extrude direction cannot be changed.
    a. True
    b. False

5. A planar face can also be used as a sketch plane.
    a. True
    b. False

6. The Equal relation only works for Lines, not Circles or Arcs.
    a. True
    b. False

7. After a dimension is created, its value cannot be changed.
    a. True
    b. False

8. When the UP TO SURFACE option is selected, you have to choose a surface as an end-condition to extrude up to.
    a. True
    b. False

9. UP TO VERTEX is not a valid Extrude option.
    a. True
    b. False

1. TRUE   2. FALSE
3. TRUE   4. FALSE
5. TRUE   6. FALSE
7. FALSE   8. TRUE
9. FALSE

Exercise: Extrude Boss & Extrude Cut.

1. Dimensions are in inches, 3 decimal places.
2. Use Mid-Plane end condition for the Base feature.
3. The part is symmetrical about the Front plane.
4. Use the instructions on the following pages if needed.

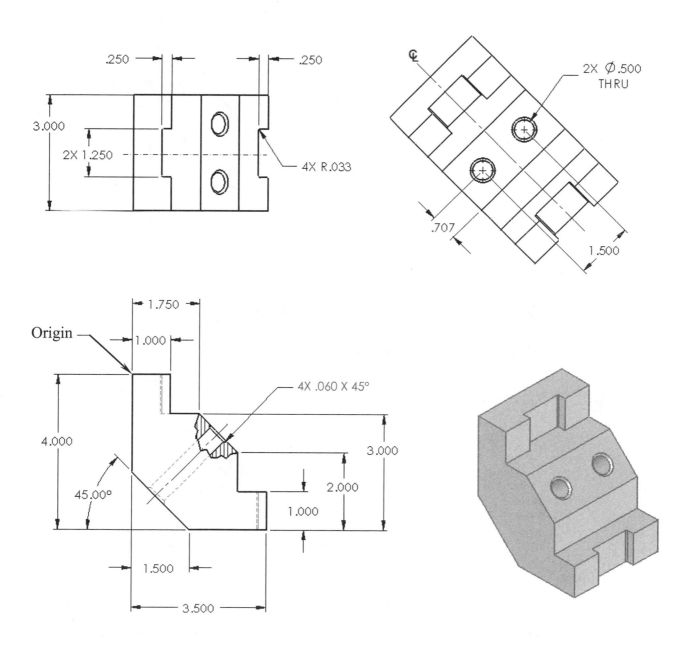

1. Starting with the base sketch:

- Select the **Front** plane and open a new sketch.

- Starting at the top left corner, using the line command, sketch the profile below.

Origin

Parallel

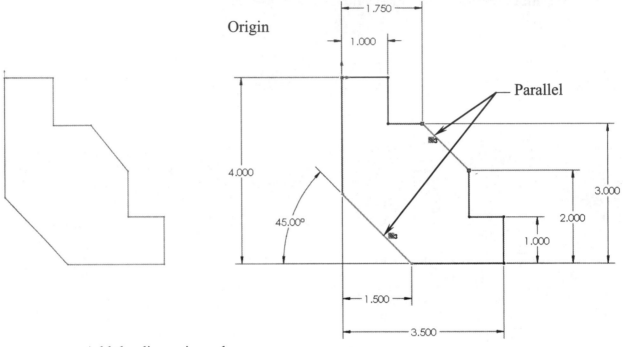

- Add the dimensions shown.

- Add the Parallel relation to fully define the sketch.

- Extrude Boss/Base with **Mid Plane** at **3.000"** deep.

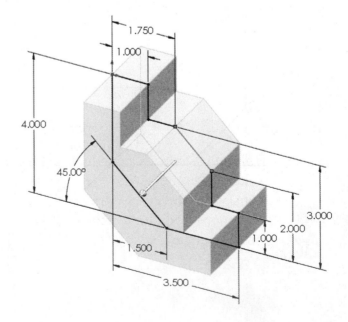

2. Adding the through holes:

- Select the face as indicated and click the Normal-To button.

- This command rotates the part normal to the screen.

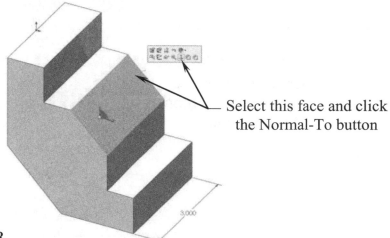

Select this face and click the Normal-To button

- The hot-key for this command is **Cntrl + 8**.

- Sketch a centerline that starts from the origin point.

- Sketch 2 circles on either side of the centerline.

- Add the diameter and location dimensions shown.

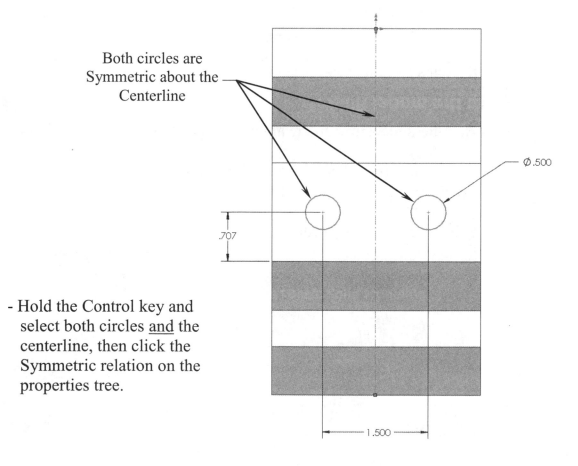

Both circles are Symmetric about the Centerline

Ø.500

.707

- Hold the Control key and select both circles <u>and</u> the centerline, then click the Symmetric relation on the properties tree.

1.500

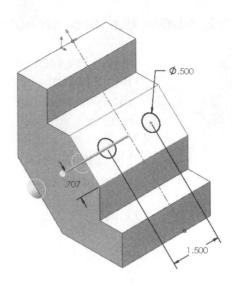

- Create an extruded
  cut using the Through-
  All condition.

3. Adding the upper cut:

- Select the upper face and click the
  Sketch pencil to open a new sketch.

- Sketch a centerline
  that starts at the
  Origin.

Both lines are
Symmetric about the
Centerline

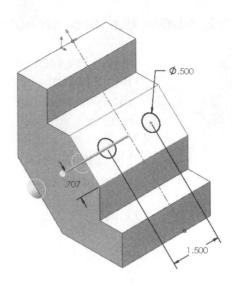

- Sketch a rectangle as
  shown.

- Add the dimensions and relations as indicated.

- Create an extruded cut using the **Up-To-Vertex**
  condition (up-to-surface also works).

- Select the Vertex indicated.

Select Vertex

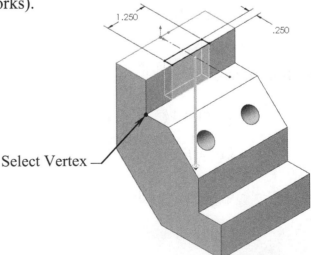

- Click **OK**.

4. Adding the lower cut:

- Select the lower face of the part and open a new sketch.

- Sketch a rectangle on this face.

- Add a Collinear <u>and</u> an Equal relations to the lines and the edges as noted.

The line is Collinear <u>and</u> Equal with the edge on both sides.

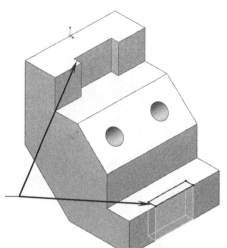

- Extrude a cut using the Through All condition.

5. Adding a chamfer:

- Click Chamfer under the Fillet button.

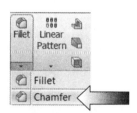

- Enter **.060** for depth.

- Select the 4 circular edges of the 2 holes.

- Click **OK**.

Select 4 edges

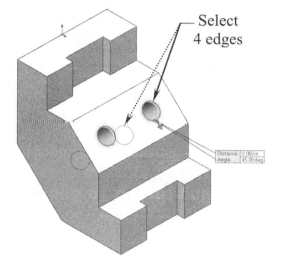

6. Saving your work:

- Click **File / Save As**.

- Enter **Extrudes_Exe1** for the file name.

- Select a location to save the file.

- Click **Save**.

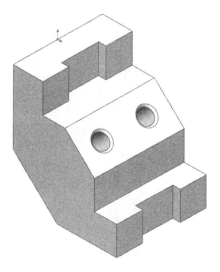

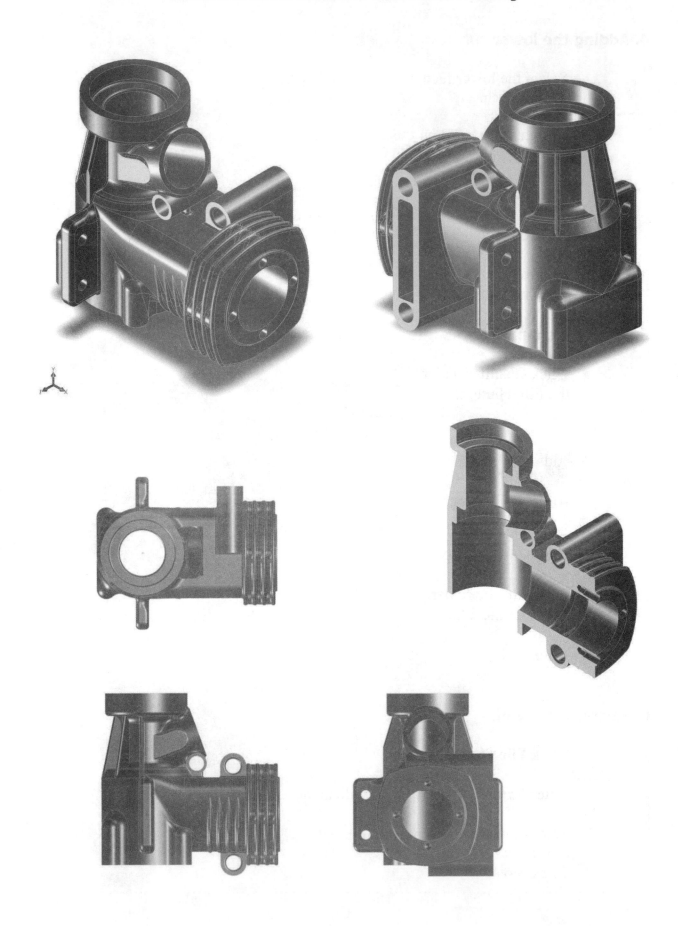

CHAPTER 4

Basic Solid Modeling

Basic Solid Modeling
Extrude & Revolve

- Upon successful completion of this lesson, you will be able to:

  * Perform basic modeling techniques.

  * Sketch on planar surfaces ✏️.

  * Add dimensions ◇.

  * Add geometric relations or constraints ⊥.

  * Use extrude with Boss / Base 🔲.

  * Use Extruded Cut ▣.

  * Create revolved features ⊕.

  * Create Fillets ◉ and Chamfers ◈.

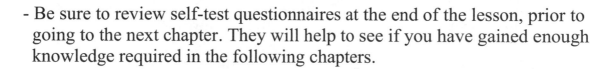

- The components created in this lesson will be used again later in an assembly chapter to demonstrate how they can be copied several times and constrained to form a new assembly, check for interferences, and dynamic motion of an assembly.

- Be sure to review self-test questionnaires at the end of the lesson, prior to going to the next chapter. They will help to see if you have gained enough knowledge required in the following chapters.

Link Components
Basic Solid Modeling

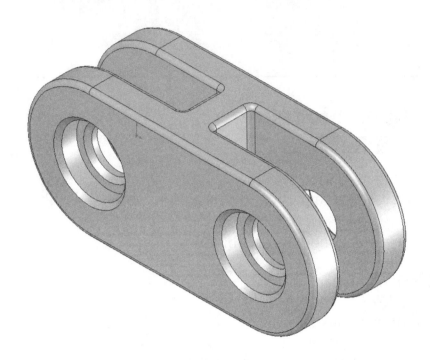

Dimensioning Standards: **ANSI**	
Units: **INCHES** – 3 Decimals	

Tools Needed:

✎	Insert Sketch	╲	Line	┋	Centerline
⊕	Circle	⚠	Mirror	◈	Dimension
⊥	Add Geometric Relations	◳	Fillet	◈	Chamfer
⬓	Extruded Boss/Base	▣	Extruded Cut	⊕	Boss/Base Revolve

1. Sketching the first profile:

- Select the FRONT plane from the FeatureManager tree.

- Click 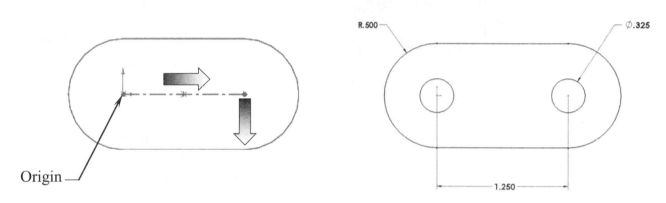 (Insert Sketch) and select the **Straight Slot** command .

- First start at the origin, sketch a straight line and then move downward (or upward) to complete the slot (arrows).

- Add 2 circles on the same centers of the arcs.

- Add Dimensions and Relations as shown.

Origin

2. Extruding the first solid:

- Click on the Features toolbar or select **Insert / Boss-Base / Extrude**.

- End condition: **Mid Plane**

- Extrude depth: **.750 in**.

- Click **OK**.

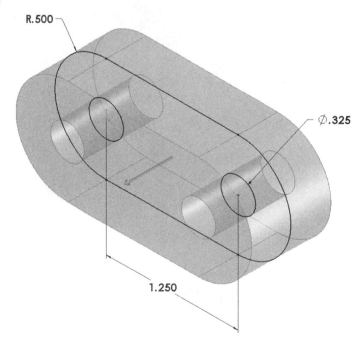

3. Creating the Bore holes:

- Select the front face as indicated and click 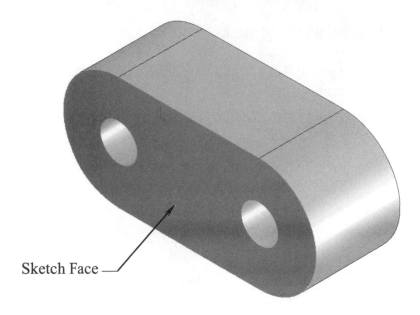 (Insert / Sketch).

Planar Surfaces

The planar surfaces of the model can also be used as sketch planes; sketch geometry can be drawn directly on these surfaces.

Sketch Face —

(The Blue origin is the Part origin and the Red origin is the Sketch origin).

- Sketch a circle ⊕ starting at the center of the existing hole.

- Add **Ø.500** dimension 🗇 as shown.

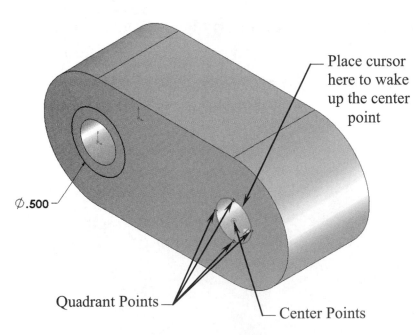

Place cursor here to wake up the center point

Ø.500 —

Quadrant Points —

Center Points

Wake-Up Entities*

To find the center (or the quadrant points) of a hole or a circle:

* In the Sketch mode, select one of the sketch tools (Circle, in this case), then hover the mouse cursor over the circular edge to "wake-up" the center point & its quadrant points.

- Sketch a 2nd Circle ⊕ and add an EQUAL relation between the 2 circles.

- Click off the Circle command. Hold the Control key, select the 2 Circles and click the **Equal** relation (arrow).

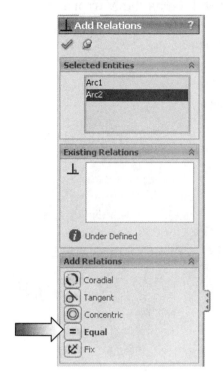

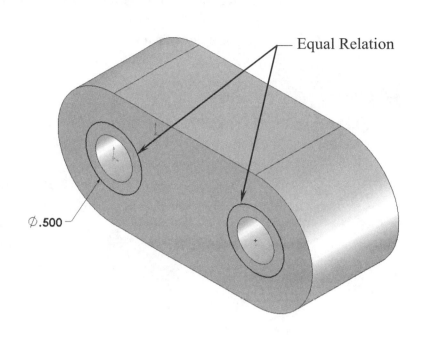

Equal Relation

∅.500

4. Cutting the Bore holes:

- Click  Extruded Cut or select **Insert / Cut / Extrude**.

- End Condition: **Blind**

- Extrude Depth: **.150 in**.

- Click **OK** ✅.

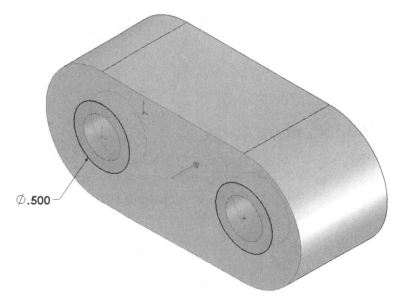

∅.500

5. Mirroring the Bore holes:

- Select the FRONT plane from the FeatureManager Tree as the Mirror Plane.

- Click 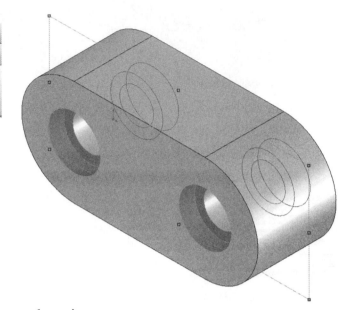 or select **Insert / Patent Mirror / Mirror**.

- The Mirror command copies one or more features about a plane or a planar face.

- Select the **Cut-Extrude1** from the FeatureManager Tree, or click one of the Bore holes from the graphics area.

- Click **OK** ✅.

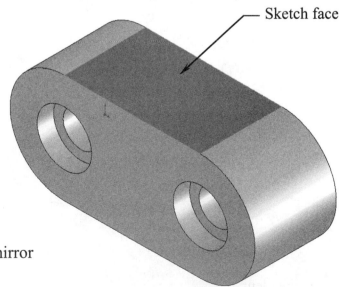

— Sketch face

6. Adding more Cuts:

- Select the face as indicated and open a new sketch ✏️ .

- We will learn to use sketch mirror in this next step.

- Sketch 2 Centerlines 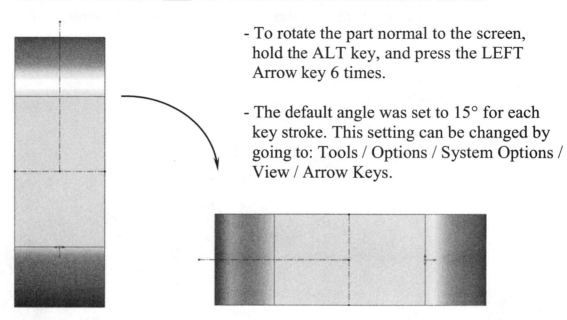 one vertical and one horizontal as shown.

- To rotate the part normal to the screen, hold the ALT key, and press the LEFT Arrow key 6 times.

- The default angle was set to 15° for each key stroke. This setting can be changed by going to: Tools / Options / System Options / View / Arrow Keys.

- Select the vertical centerline and click the **Dynamic Mirror** command or click: **Tools, Sketch Tools, Dynamic Mirror**.

- Sketch a Rectangle on one side of the centerline; it will get mirrored to the other side automatically.

- Click off the Dynamic mirror button. Add a Symmetric relation to the 3 lines as noted .

- Add Dimensions to fully define the sketch.

- Click **OK** .

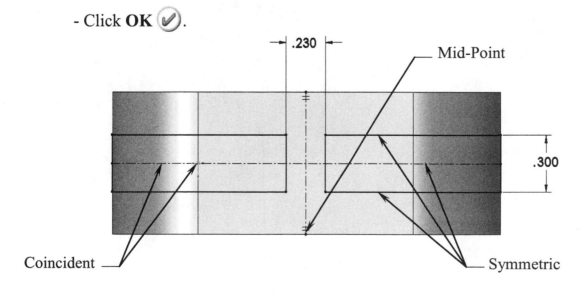

.230

Mid-Point

.300

Coincident

Symmetric

7. Extruding a Through All cut:

- Click  (Extruded Cut) or select **Insert / Cut / Extrude**.

- Direction 1: **Through All**

- Click **OK** ✓.

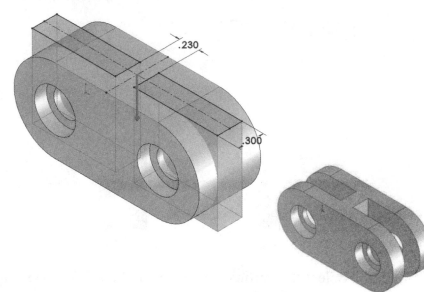

8. Adding the .032". fillets:

- Click 🔲 Fillet or select **Insert / Features / Fillet/Round**.

- Enter **.032 in.** for Radius ⟋ .

- Select the edges as indicated below 🔲 .

- Click **OK** ✓.

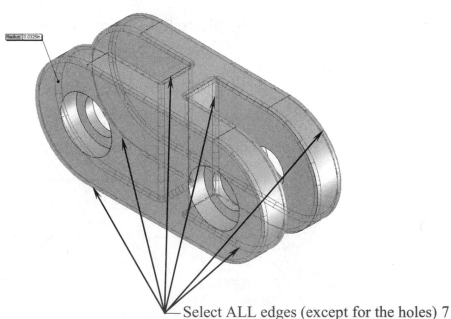

Select ALL edges (except for the holes) 7

9. Adding the .032 in. chamfers:

- Click 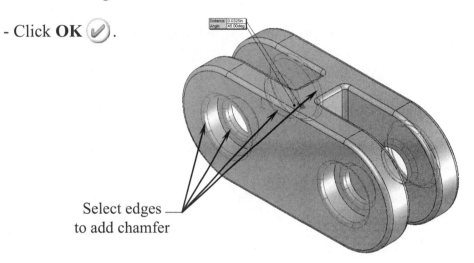 or select **Insert / Features / Chamfer.**

- Enter **.032 in.** for Depth .

- Select the edges of the 4 holes.

- Click **OK** .

Select edges
to add chamfer

10. Saving your work:

- Select **File / Save As / Double Link / Save**.

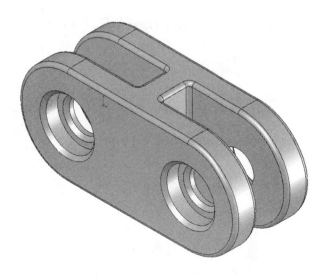

11. Creating the Sub-Components:

- The 1st sub-component is the **Alignment Pin**.

- Select the RIGHT plane from the FeatureManager Tree.

- Click 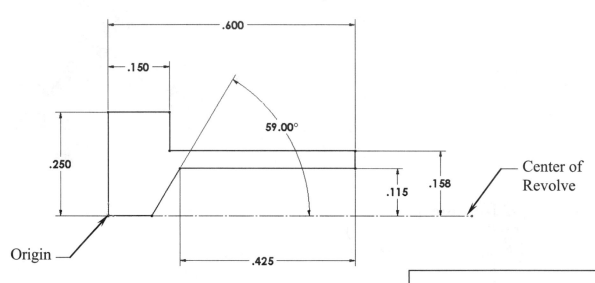 or select **Insert / Sketch**.

- Sketch the profile below using the Line tool.

- Add dimensions as shown to fully define the sketch.

.600

.150

59.00°

.250

.115   .158

Center of
Revolve

Origin

.425

12. Revolving the base feature:

- Click or select **Insert / Boss-Base / Revolve**.

- Revolve Type: **Blind**.

- Revolve Angle: **360 deg**. (default).

- Click **OK**.

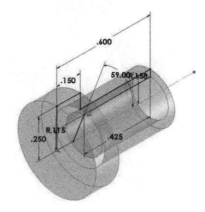

> ### Center of Revolve
>
> A centerline is used when revolving a sketch profile.
>
> A model edge, an axis, or a sketch line can also be used as the center of the revolve.

13. Adding chamfers:

- Click  or select **Insert / Features / Chamfer**.

- Enter **.032** for Distance.

- Enter **45 deg**. for Angle.

- Select the 2 Edges as indicated.

- Click **OK**.

Select 2 edges

14. Saving your work:

- Select **File / Save As / Alignment Pin / Save**.

15. The 2nd Sub-Components:

- The 2nd sub-component is the **Pin Head**:

- Select the FRONT plane from the FeatureManager Tree.

- Click 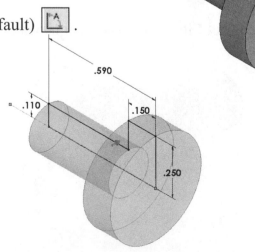 or select **Insert / Sketch**.

- Sketch the profile below using the Line tool .

- Add dimensions as shown to fully define the sketch.

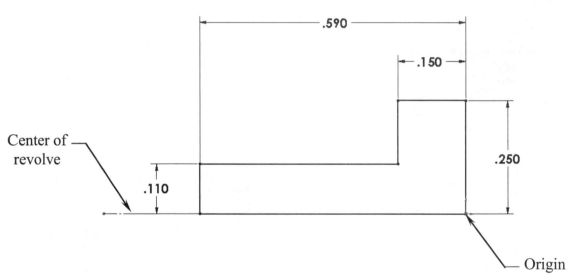

Center of revolve

.590

.150

.250

.110

Origin

16. Revolving the base feature:

- Click or select **Insert / Boss-Base / Revolve**.

- Revolve Type: **Blind** .

- Revolve Angle: **360 deg**. (default) .

- Click **OK** .

17. Adding chamfer:

- Click  or select **Insert / Features / Chamfer**.

- Enter **.025** for Distance 🔲 .

- Enter **45 deg**. for Angle 🔲 .

- Select the Edge as indicated.

- Click **OK** ✅ .

Select 2 Edges

18. Saving your work:

- Select **File / Save As / Pin Head / Save**.

19. Creating the 3rd Sub-Components:

- The 3rd sub-component is the **Single Link**:

- Select FRONT plane from FeatureManager Tree.

- Click  Insert Sketch and select the **Straight Slot** command.

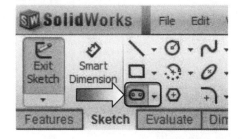

- Enable the Add Dimensions checkbox.

- Start at the origin, sketch a horizontal line as shown, then move the cursor downward to make a straight slot.

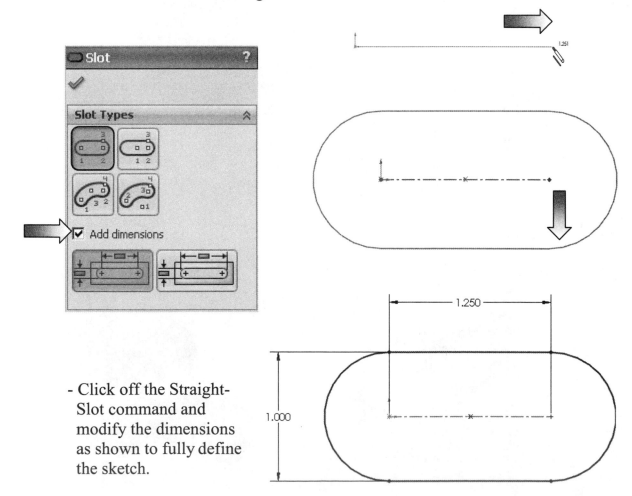

- Click off the Straight-Slot command and modify the dimensions as shown to fully define the sketch.

20. Extruding the base:

- Click  Extruded Boss-Base or select **Insert / Boss-Base / Extrude**.

- End condition: **Mid Plane**

- Extrude depth: **.750 in**.

- Click **OK** ⊘ .

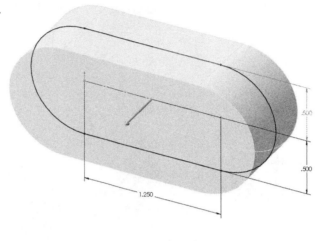

21. Sketching the Recess Profiles:

- Select the face indicated and open a new sketch .

- Sketch 2 Circles ⊕ at the centers of the circular edges.

- Add a **Ø1.020 in.** dimension ⟨⟩ to one of the circles. (The circles are slightly larger than the part).

- Add an Equal relation ⊥ between the 2 circles.

Sketch Face

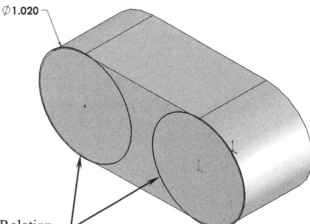

Ø1.020

Equal Relation

22. Extruding a blind cut:

- Click  Extruded Cut or select **Insert / Cut / Extrude**.

- End condition: **Blind**

- Extrude Depth: **.235 in.**

- Click **OK** ✓.

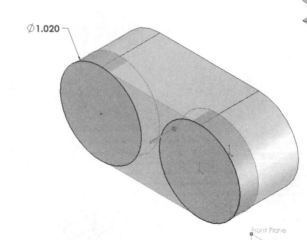

Ø1.020

23. Mirroring the cut:

- Click 🔲 or select **Insert /
Pattern- Mirror / Mirror**.

- Select the **FRONT** plane
from the FeatureManager
tree for Mirror Plane.

- Select the **Cut-Extrude1**
for Features-to-Pattern.

- Click **OK** ✓.

- Rotate the part to verify
the mirrored feature on
the far side.

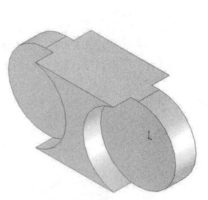

24. Adding the Holes:

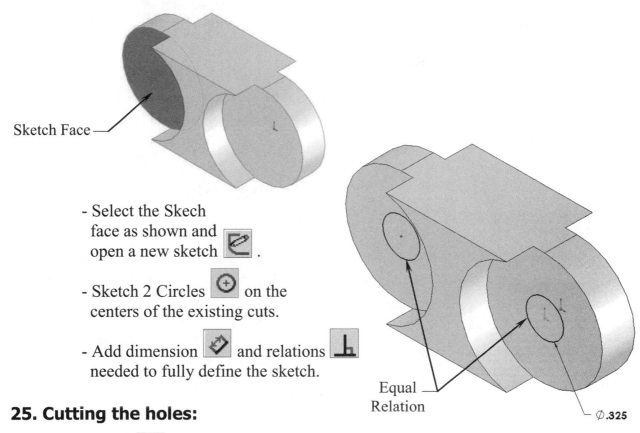

Sketch Face

- Select the Skech face as shown and open a new sketch 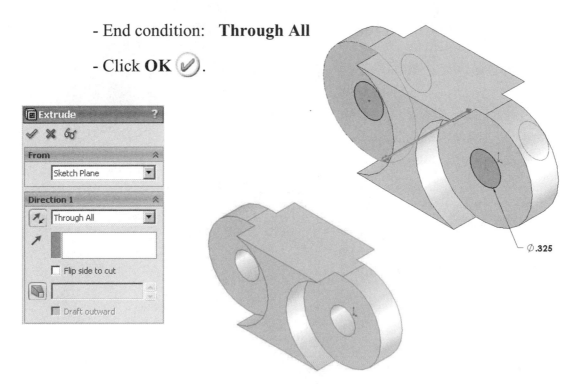.

- Sketch 2 Circles on the centers of the existing cuts.

- Add dimension and relations needed to fully define the sketch.

Equal Relation

⌀.325

25. Cutting the holes:

- Click Extruded Cut or select **Insert / Cut / Extrude**.

- End condition: **Through All**

- Click **OK**.

⌀.325

Extrude

From

Sketch Plane

Direction 1

Through All

☐ Flip side to cut

☐ Draft outward

26. Adding the .100" fillets:

- Click Fillet or select **Insert / Features / Fillet/Round**.

- Enter **.100 in.** for Radius .

- Select the **8 edges** as indicated below .

- Click **OK** .

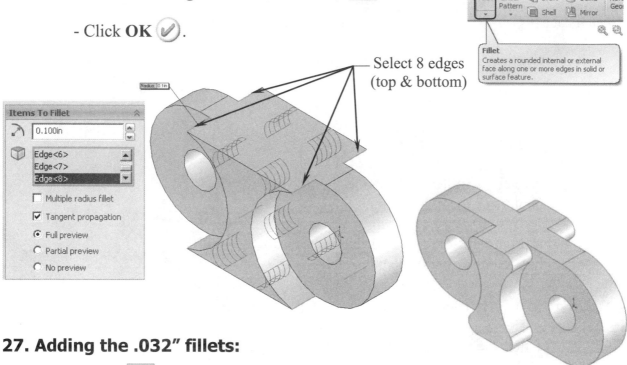

Select 8 edges
(top & bottom)

27. Adding the .032" fillets:

- Click Fillet or select **Insert / Features / Fillet/Round**.

- Enter **.032 in.** for Radius .

- Select the edges as shown .

- Click **OK** .

NOTE:

There are no fillets on the 4 edges as indicated.

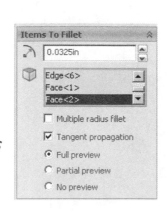

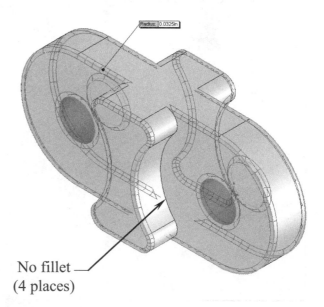

No fillet
(4 places)

28. Saving your work:

- Click **File / Save As / Single Link / Save.**

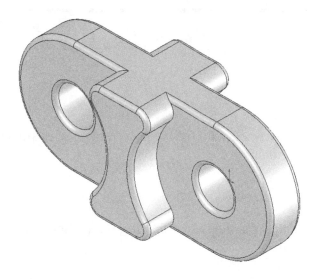

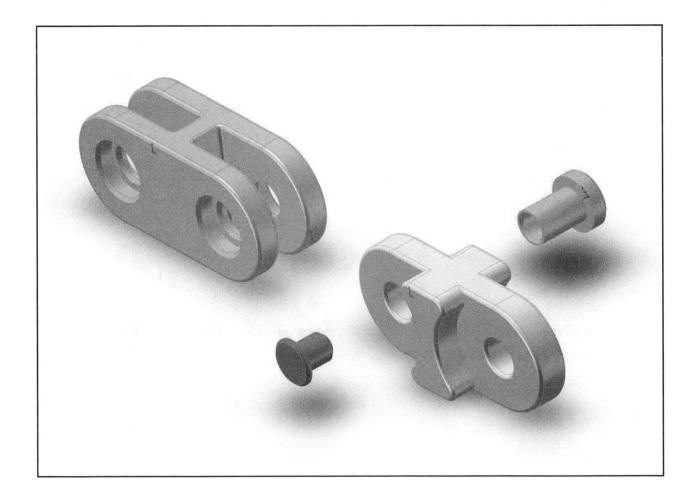

Questions for Review

Basic Solid Modeling

1. Tangent relations only work with the same type of entities such as an arc to another arc, not between a line and an arc.
   a. True
   b. False

2. The first feature in a part is the parent feature, not a child.
   a. True
   b. False

3. The dimension arrows can be toggled to flip inwards or outwards when clicking on its handle points.

   a. True
   b. False

4. The Shaded with edges option cannot be used in the part mode, only in the drawing mode.
   a. True
   b. False

5. The Concentric relations make the diameter of the circles equal.
   a. True
   b. False

6. More than one model edges can be selected and filleted at the same time.
   a. True
   b. False

7. To revolve a sketch profile, a centerline should be selected as the center of the revolve.
   a. True
   b. False

8. After a sketch is revolved, its revolved angle cannot be changed.
   a. True
   b. False

7. TRUE   8. FALSE
5. FALSE   6. TRUE
3. TRUE   4. FALSE
1. FALSE   2. TRUE

Exercise: EXTRUDE BOSS & EXTRUDE CUT

1. Create the solid model using the drawing provided below.
2. Dimensions are in Inches, 3 decimal places.
3. Tangent relations between the transitions of the Arcs should be used.
4. The Ø.472 holes are Concentric with R.710 Arcs.
5. Use the instructions on the following pages,
   if needed.

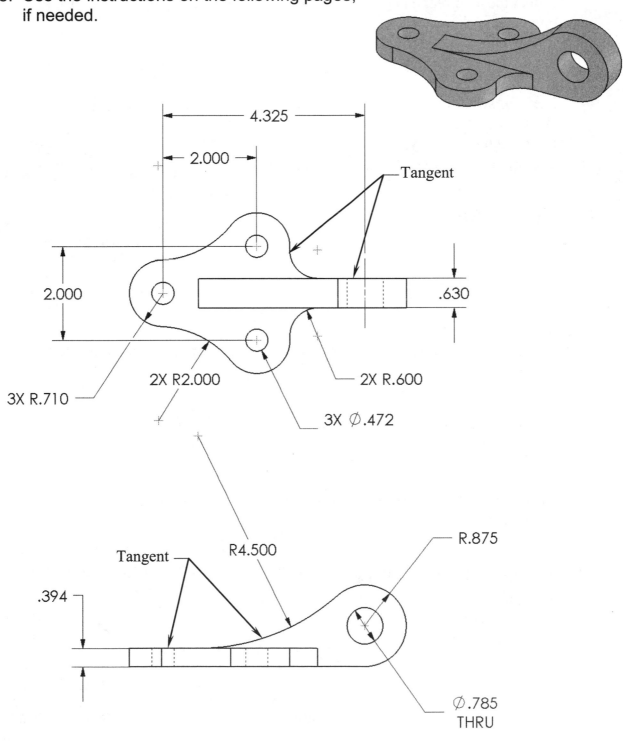

1. Creating the Base sketch:

- There are many ways to create this part but let try this basic method first.

- Select the Top plane and open a new sketch.

- Create the construction circles (toggle the **For Construction** checkbox), then create the Sketch Geometry over them.

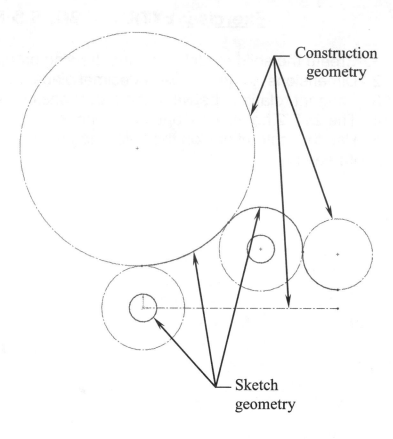

Construction geometry

Sketch geometry

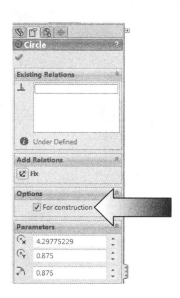

- Either re-create the rest of the geometry or mirror them as noted.

- To mirror the sketch geometry, hold the Control key and select the entities that you want to mirror AND the centerline as noted, then click the Mirror-Entities command.

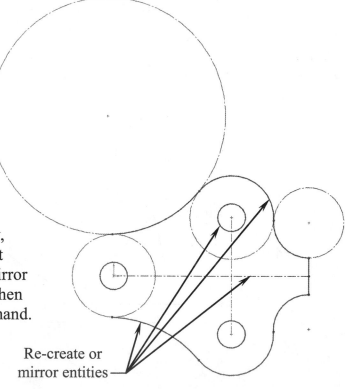

Re-create or mirror entities

- Add the geometric relations as indicated. Remember to add the Equal relations for the circles and the arcs.

- Add the Smart-Dimensions to fully define the sketch.

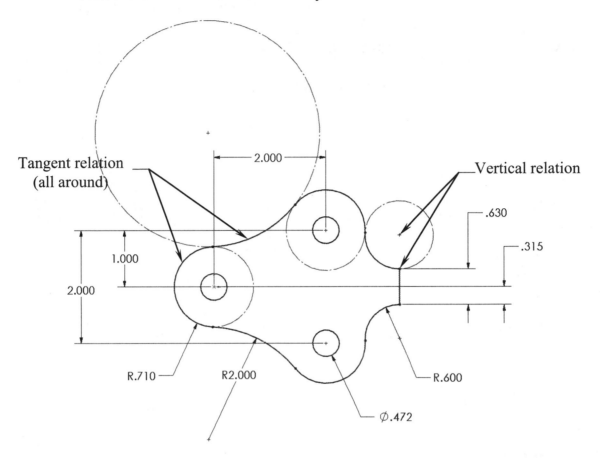

Tangent relation (all around)

Vertical relation

2.000

.630

.315

1.000

2.000

R.710

R2.000

R.600

Ø.472

2. Extruding the Base:

- Click **Extruded Boss-Base**.

- Use the **Blind** type for Diretion1.

- Enter **.394"** for extrude Depth.

- Click **OK**.

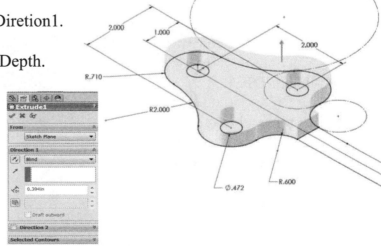

3. Creating the Tail-End sketch:

- Select the Front reference plane from the Feature tree and open another sketch.

- Sketch the construction circles and add the sketch geometry right over them.

- Add the Tangent relation as noted.

- Add the Smart Dimensions to fully define the sketch.

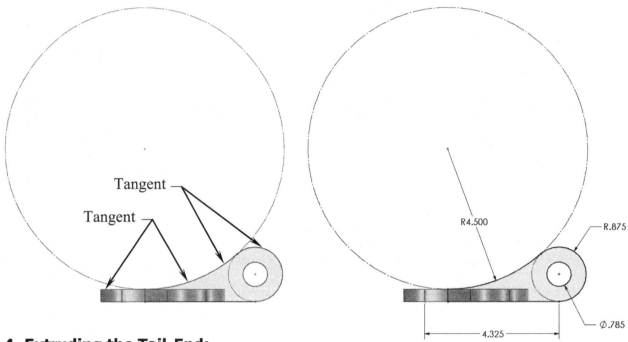

4. Extruding the Tail-End:

- Click **Extruded Boss-Base**.

- Use the **Mid Plane** type for Diretion1.

- Enter **.630"** for extrude Depth.

- Click **OK**.

5. Saving your work:

- Click **File / Save As**.

- Enter **Extrudes_Exe2**.

- Click **Save**.

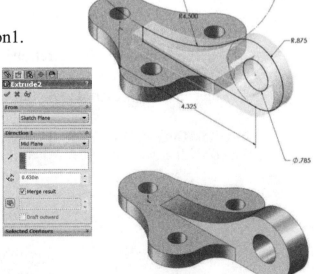

CHAPTER 5

Revolved Parts

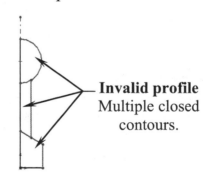

Revolved Parts
Ball Joint Arm

- The Revolve command rotates one or more sketch profiles around a centerline, up to 360° to create a <u>thin</u> or a <u>solid</u> feature.

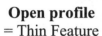

Open profile
= Thin Feature

Closed profile
= Solid Feature

- The revolved sketch should have a continuous closed contour and it can either be a polygon, a circle, an ellipse, or a closed spline.

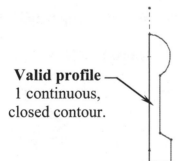

Valid profile
1 continuous,
closed contour.

Invalid profile
Multiple closed
contours.

- If there is more than one centerline in the same sketch, the center of rotation must be specified when creating the revolve.

- In the newer releases of SolidWorks, the center of the revolve (centerline) can be replaced with a line, an axis, or a linear model edge.

- The revolve feature can be a cut feature 🔟 (which removes material) or a revolve boss feature ⚙ (which adds material).

- This chapter will guide you through the basics of creating the revolved parts.

Ball Joint Arm
Revolved Parts

Dimensioning Standards: **ANSI**	
Units: **INCHES** – 3 Decimals	

Tools Needed:

	Insert Sketch		Line		Circle
	Rectangle		Sketch Fillet		Trim
	Add Geometric Relations		Dimension		Centerline
	Base/Boss Revolve		Fillet/Round		Mirror Features

1. Creating the Base Profile:

- Select the FRONT plane from the FeatureManager tree.

- Click  or select **Insert / Sketch**.

- Sketch the profile using the Lines and Circles commands.

- Trim the circles as shown.

- Add Dimensions and Relations needed to fully define the sketch. (It is easier to add the R.050" fillets after the sketch is fully defined).

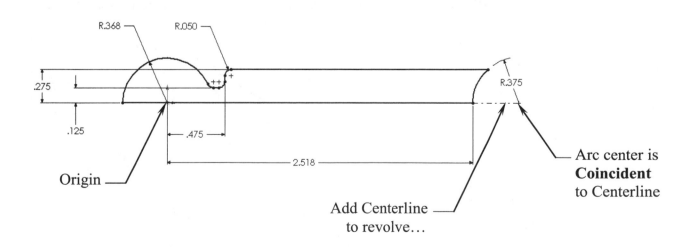

R.368   R.050

R.375

.275

.125

.475

2.518

Origin

Arc center is **Coincident** to Centerline

Add Centerline to revolve…

2. Revolving the Base Feature:

- Click  Revolve, or select **Insert / Boss-Base / Revolve**.

- Revolve Type: **Blind** .

- Revolve Angle: **360 deg.** .

- Click **OK** .

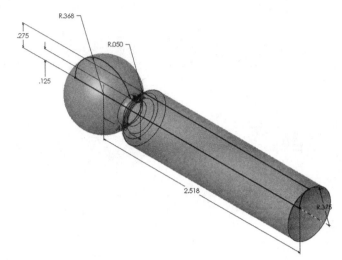

3. Sketching the Opened-End Profile:

- Select the TOP plane from the FeatureManager tree.

- Click or select **Insert / Sketch**.

- Switch to Hidden Lines Visible mode: click on the VIEW toolbar.

- Sketch 2 circles as shown.

- Add a **Coradial** relation between the small circle and the hidden edge.

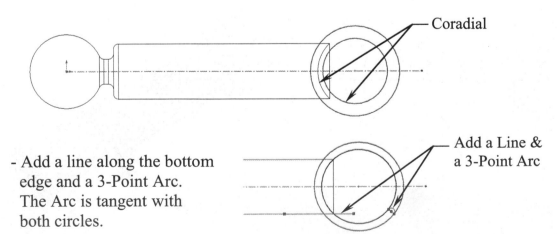

Coradial

- Add a line along the bottom
edge and a 3-Point Arc.
The Arc is tangent with
both circles.

Add a Line &
a 3-Point Arc

- Trim 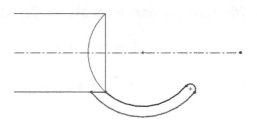 the line and the 2 circles.

- Add a Collinear relation  between the line and the bottom edge of the part.

Collinear relation

.250

R.425

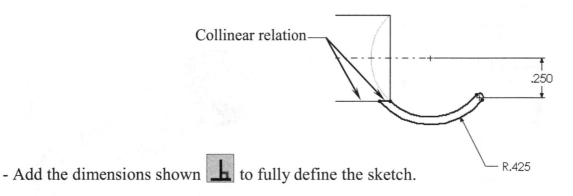

- Add the dimensions shown  to fully define the sketch.

4. Revolving the Opened-End Feature:

- Click Revolve  , or select **Insert / Boss-Base / Revolve**.

- Revolve Type: **Mid Plane**  .

- Revolve Angle: **75 deg.**  .

- Click **OK**  .

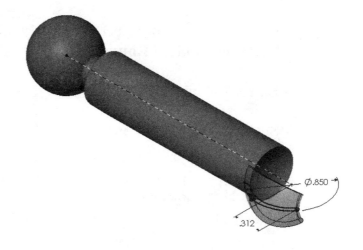

Ø.850

.312

5. Mirroring the Revolved feature:

- Click 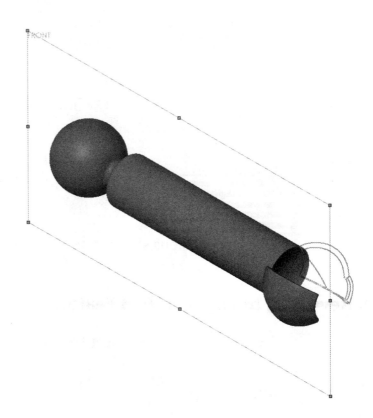 or select **Insert / Pattern Mirror / Mirror**.

- Select the FRONT plane from the FeatureManager tree as mirror plane ⬜ .

- Select the Revolve2 feature either from the graphics area or from the Feature-Manager tree, as Features to Mirror ⬛ .

- Click **OK** ✅ .

6. Adding the .080" Fillets:

- Click Fillet 🔘 or select **Insert / Features / Fillet / Round**.

- Enter **.080** in. as the Radius ⬛ .

- Select the two edges as shown for Items to Fillet ⬜ .

- Click **OK** ✅ .

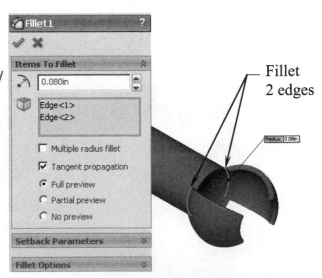

Fillet 2 edges

7. Adding the .015" Fillets:

- Click Fillet  or select **Insert / Features / Fillet / Round**.

- Enter **.015** in. as the Radius .

- Select the edges of the 2 revolved features as shown.

- Click **OK** .

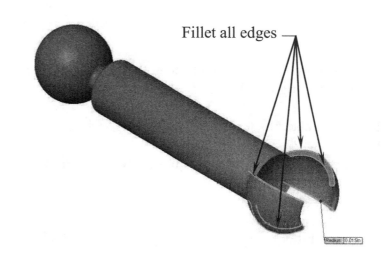

Fillet all edges

8. Saving Your Work:

- Select **File / Save As / Ball-Joint-Arm / Save**.

Questions for Review

Revolved Parts

1. A proper profile for use in a revolved feature is a single closed contour, created on one side of the revolved centerline.
   a. True
   b. False

2. If there is more than one centerline in the same sketch, one centerline should be selected prior to revolving the sketch.
   a. True
   b. False

3. A revolve feature should *always* be revolved a complete 360°.
   a. True
   b. False

4. The Sketch Fillet command can also be used on solid features.
   a. True
   b. False

5. To mirror a 3D feature, a plane, or a planar surface should be used as a mirror plane.
   a. True
   b. False

6. To mirror a series of features, a centerline can be used as a mirror plane.
   a. True
   b. False

7. After a fillet feature is created, its parameters (selected faces, edges, fillet values, etc.) cannot be modified.
   a. True
   b. False

8. Either an axis, a model edge, or a sketch line can be used as the center of the revolve. (Newer releases of SolidWorks only).
   a. True
   b. False

7. FALSE   8. TRUE
5. TRUE   6. FALSE
3. FALSE   4. FALSE
1. TRUE   2. TRUE

Exercise: Flat Head Screw Driver

1. Create the part using the drawing provided below.
2. Dimensions are in Inches, 3 decimal places.
3. The part is symmetrical about the Top plane.
4. Unspecified radii to be R.050 max.
5. Use the instructions on the following pages, if needed.

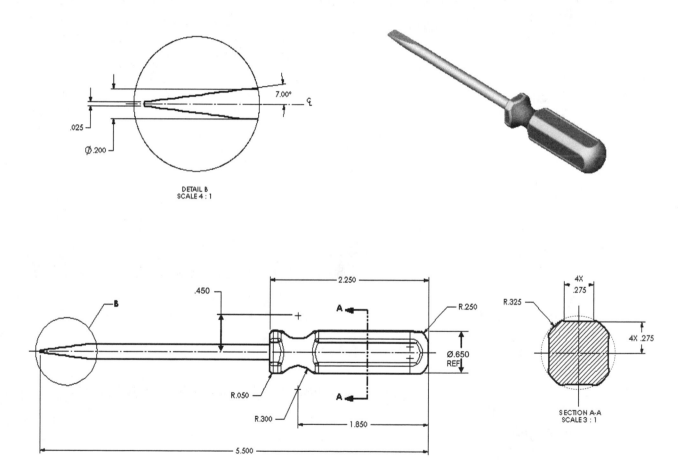

6. Save your work as: **Flat Head Screw Driver**.

1. Creating the base sketch:

- Select the Front
  plane and open
  a new sketch.

- Sketch the profile
  shown and add the
  dimensions noted.

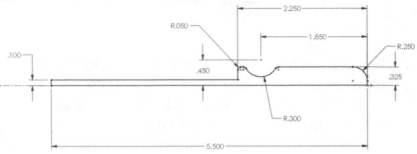

2. Revolving the base:

- Click **Revolve /
  Boss-Base**.

- For Direction 1:
  Use **Blind**.

- Angle = **360°**

- Click **OK**.

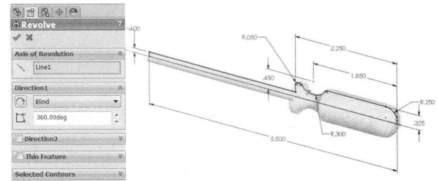

3. Creating the flat head:

- Select the Front
  plane and open
  another sketch.

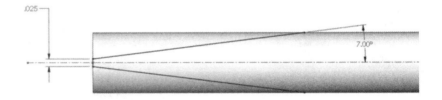

- Sketch the lines as
  shown and add the
  dimensions to fully
  define the sketch.

- Create an **extruded
  cut** using **Through-
  All** for both
  directions.

- Since the sketch was
  open, Through All
  was the only extrude
  option in this case.

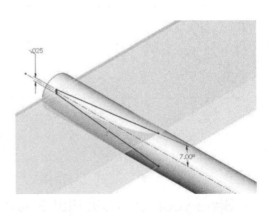

4. Creating the flat handle:

- Select the flat surface on the right end of the handle and open a new sketch.

- Sketch a rectangle and mirror it using the vertical and horizontal centerline.

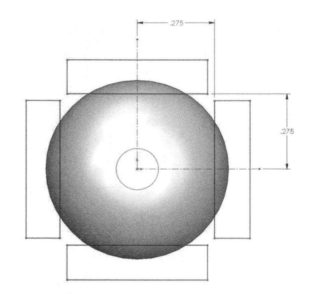

- Create an extruded cut using the opposite end of the handle as the end condition for the Up-To-Surface option.

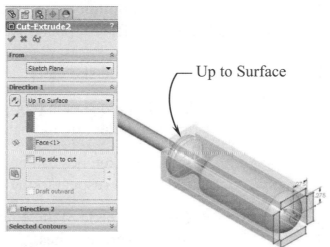

Up to Surface

5. Adding the .050" fillets:

- Apply a **.050"** fillet to the 4 flat surfaces and the curved surface of the neck.

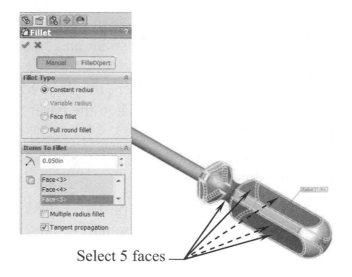

Select 5 faces

6. Saving your work:

- Save your work as **Flat Head Screw Driver**.

Revolved Parts cont.

Derived Sketches

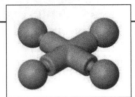

Derived Sketches
Center Ball Joint

- The derived sketch option creates a copy of the original sketch and places it on the same or different plane, within the same part document.

    * The derived sketch is the child feature of the original.

    * The derived sketch (copy) cannot be edited. Its size and shape are dependent on the parent sketch.

    * Derived sketches can be moved and related to different planes or faces with respect to the same model.

    * Changes made to the parent sketch are automatically reflected in the derived sketches.

- To break the link between the parent sketch and the derived copies, right click on the derived sketch and select **Underived**.

- After the link is broken, the derived sketches can be modified independently and will not update when the parent sketch is changed.

- One major difference between the traditional copy / paste option and the derived sketch is:

    * The copy/ paste creates an Independent copy. There is no link between the parent sketch and the derived sketch.

    * The derived sketch creates a dependent copy. The parent sketch and the derived sketch are fully linked.

Center Ball Joint
Derived Sketches

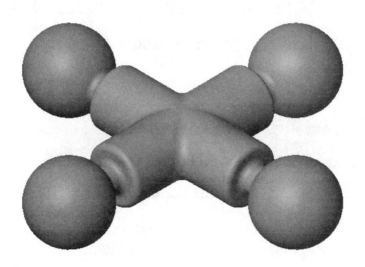

Dimensioning Standards: **ANSI**

Units: **INCHES** – 3 Decimals

Tools Needed:

Insert Sketch	Line	Center Line
Circle	Sketch Fillet	Trim
Add Geometric Relations	Dimension	Plane
Derived Sketch	Fillet/Round	Base/Boss Revolve

1. Creating the Base Profile:

- Select the FRONT plane from the Feature Manager tree.

- Click 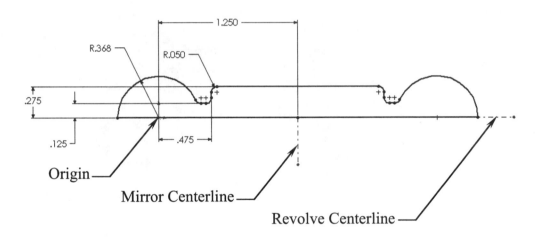 or select **Insert / Sketch**.

- Sketch the profile using Lines , Circles , Sketch Fillets and

the Trim tools (Follow step 1 on page 5-3 to create this sketch).

- Add the Dimensions and Relations needed to fully define the sketch.

R.368   R.050   1.250

.275

.125   .475

Origin

Mirror Centerline

Revolve Centerline

2. Revolving the Base Feature:

- Click Revolve , or select **Insert / Boss-Base / Revolve**.

- Revolve Type: **Blind** .

- Revolve Angle: **360 deg**. .

- Click **OK** .

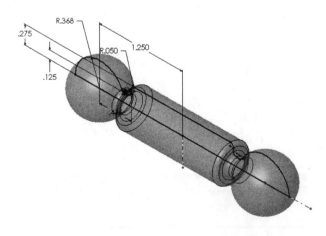

R.368

.275

R.050   1.250

.125

3. Creating a new work plane*:

- Click 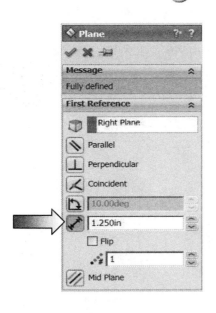 or select **Insert / Reference Geometry / Plane**.

- Select the RIGHT plane from the FeatureManager tree 🔲 .

- Choose the **Offset Distance** option 🔲 .

- Enter **1.250** in. (place the new plane on the right side).

- Click **OK** ✓.

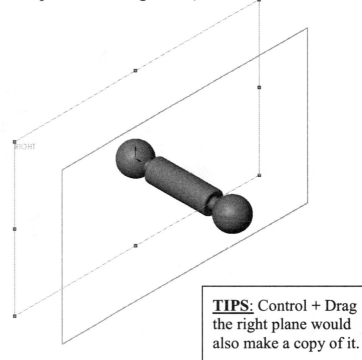

> **TIPS**: Control + Drag the right plane would also make a copy of it.

4. Creating a Derived Sketch:

- Hold the CONTROL key, select the new plane (**Plane1**) and the **Sketch1** (under Base-Revolved1) from the FeatureManager tree.

- Select **Derived Sketch** under the **Insert** menu.

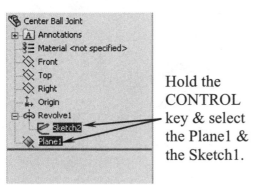

Hold the CONTROL key & select the Plane1 & the Sketch1.

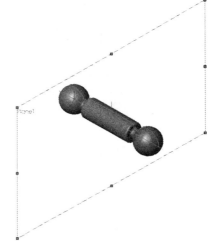

- A copy of Sketch1 is created and placed on Plane1, and is automatically activated for positioning.

5. Positioning the Derived Sketch:

- Add a **Collinear** relation between the TOP plane and the Line as indicated.

- Add a **Collinear** relation between the FRONT plane and the Centerline as shown.

- Click **OK** ✅.

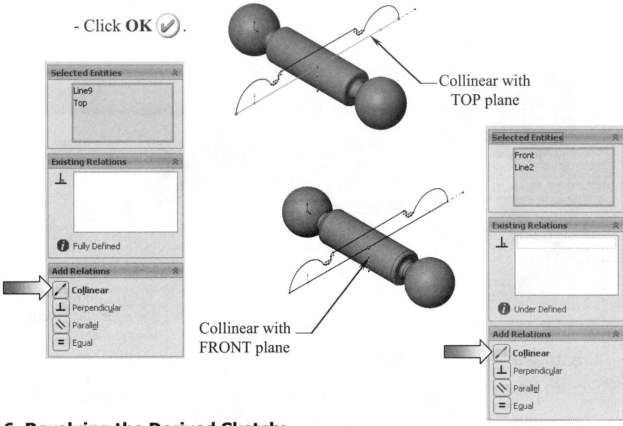

Collinear with
TOP plane

Collinear with
FRONT plane

6. Revolving the Derived Sketch:

- Click 🔄 or select **Insert / Boss-Base / Revolve**.

- Revolve Type: **Blind** 🔲.

- Revolve Angle: **360 deg**. 🔲.

- Click **OK** ✅.

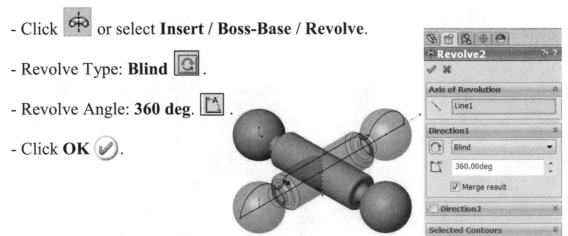

7. Adding Fillets:

- Click Fillet  or select **Insert / Features / Fillet / Round**.

- Enter **.100 in.** as the Radius ⟋ .

- Select the Edges shown as the Edges-To-Fillet ⬜ .

- Click **OK** ✓ .

Fillet
2 edges

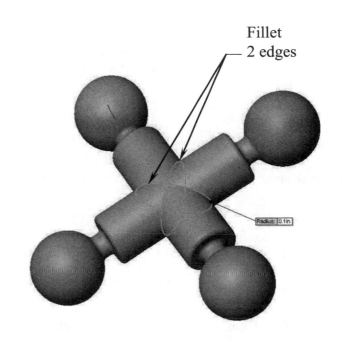

Fillet1

Items To Fillet

0.100in

Edge<1>
Edge<2>

☐ Multiple radius fillet
☑ Tangent propagation
◉ Full preview
○ Partial preview
○ No preview

Setback Parameters

Fillet Options

Radius: 0.1in

8. Saving Your Work:

- Select **File / Save As / Center Ball Joint / Save**.

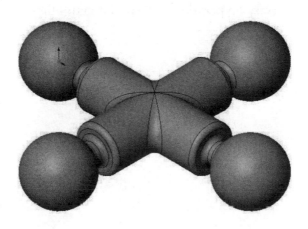

Questions for Review

Derived Sketches

1. The first feature in a part is the parent feature.
   - a. True
   - b. False

2. More than one centerline can be selected at the same time to revolve a sketch profile.
   - a. True
   - b. False

3. A parallel plane can be created from another plane or a planar surface.
   - a. True
   - b. False

4. A derived sketch can be copied and placed on a different plane / surface.
   - a. True
   - b. False

5. A derived sketch can be edited just like any other sketch.
   - a. True
   - b. False

6. A derived sketch is an independent sketch. There is no link between the derived sketch and the parent sketch.
   - a. True
   - b. False

7. A derived sketch can only be positioned and related to other sketches / features.
   - a. True
   - b. False

8. When the parent sketch is changed, the derived sketches will be updated automatically.
   - a. True
   - b. False

7. TRUE   8. TRUE
5. FALSE   6. FALSE
3. TRUE   4. TRUE
1. TRUE   2. FALSE

<u>Exercise</u>: Revolved Parts

1. Create the 3D model using the drawing provided below.
2. Dimensions are in inches, 3 decimal places.
3. The part is Symmetrical about the horizontal axis.
4. The 5 mounting holes should be created as a Circular Pattern.
5. Use the instructions on the following page if needed.

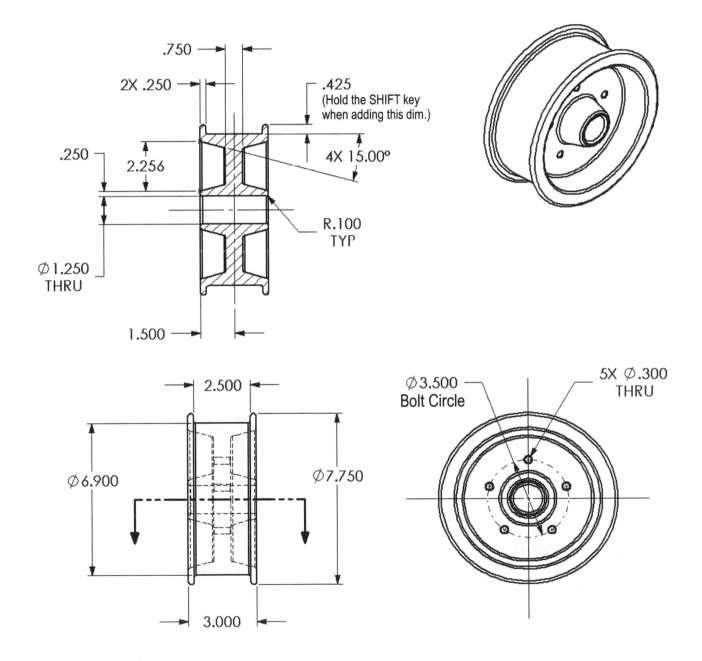

6. Save your work as: **Wheel_Exe**.

1. Start with the Front plane.

- Sketch 2 centerlines and use the vertical centerline for Dynamic Mirror.

- Sketch the profile as shown.

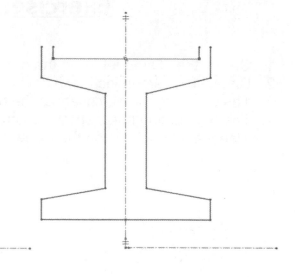

- Add a tangent arc to close off the upper portion of the sketch.

- Add the dimensions and relations as indicated.

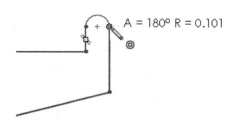

A = 180° R = 0.101

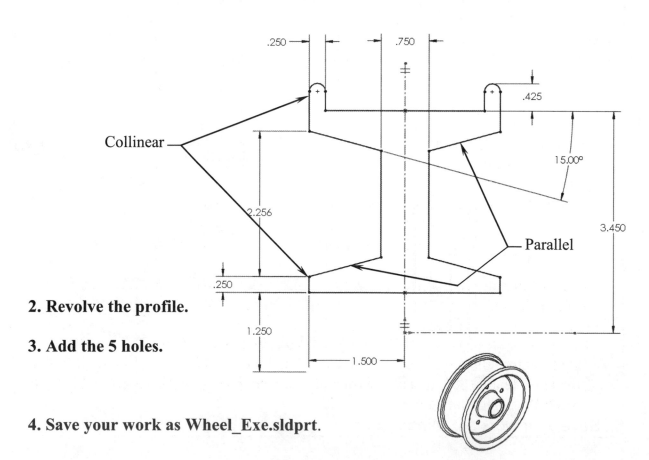

Collinear

15.00°

Parallel

.250

.750

.425

2.256

3.450

.250

1.250

1.500

2. Revolve the profile.

3. Add the 5 holes.

4. Save your work as Wheel_Exe.sldprt.

CHAPTER 6

Rib & Shell Features

The Rib and Shell Features
Formed Tray

- A **Rib** is a special type of extruded feature created from open or closed sketched contours. It adds material of a specified thickness in a specified direction between the contour and an existing part. A rib can be created using single or multiple sketches.

- Rib features can have draft angles, inward, or outward.

- The **Detailed Preview** Property Manager can be used with multi-body parts to enhance detail and select entities to display.

- The **Shell** tool hollows out a part, leaves selected faces open, and creates thin walled features on the remaining faces. If nothing (no face) is selected on the model, a solid part can be shelled, creating a closed hollow model.

- Multiple thicknesses are also supported when shelling a solid model.

- In most cases, the model fillets should be applied before shelling a part.

- One of the most common problems when the shell fails is when the wall thickness of the shell is smaller than one of the fillets in the model.

- If errors appear when shelling a model, you can run the **Error Diagnostics**. The shell feature displays error messages and includes tools to help you identify why the shell feature failed. The diagnostic tool **Error Diagnostics** is available in the **Shell** Property Manager.

Formed Tray
Rib & Shell Features

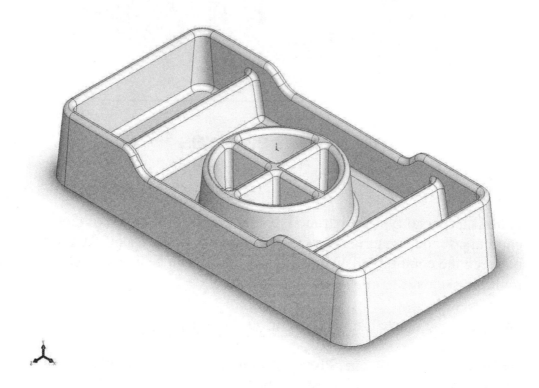

| Dimensioning Standards: **ANSI** |
| Units: **INCHES** – 3 Decimals |

Tools Needed:

Insert Sketch	Line	Circle
Add Geometric Relations	Dimension	Fillet
Boss/Base Extrude	Rib	Shell

1. Sketching the Base Profile:

- Select the TOP plane from the FeatureManager tree.

- Click Sketch 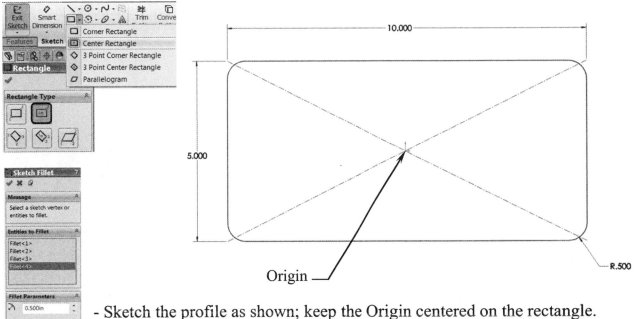 or select **Insert / Sketch**.

- Sketch the profile as shown; keep the Origin centered on the rectangle.

- Add Sketch Fillets and Dimensions as shown to fully define the sketch.

2. Extruding the Base feature:

- Click Extruded Boss-Base or select **Insert / Boss-Base / Extrude**.

- End condition: **Blind**

- Extrude depth: **2.00 in.**

- Draft angle: **5.00 deg.**

- Click OK

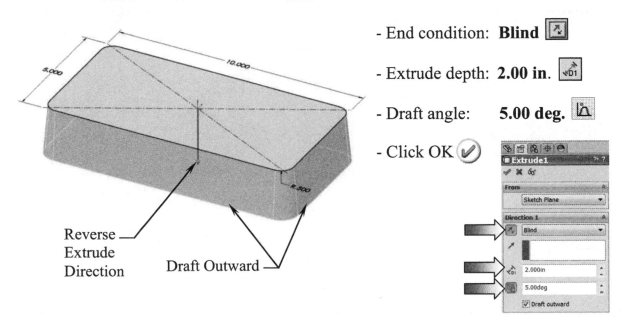

Reverse Extrude Direction

Draft Outward

3. Adding the Side Cutouts:

- Select the FRONT plane from the FeatureManager tree.

- Click Sketch 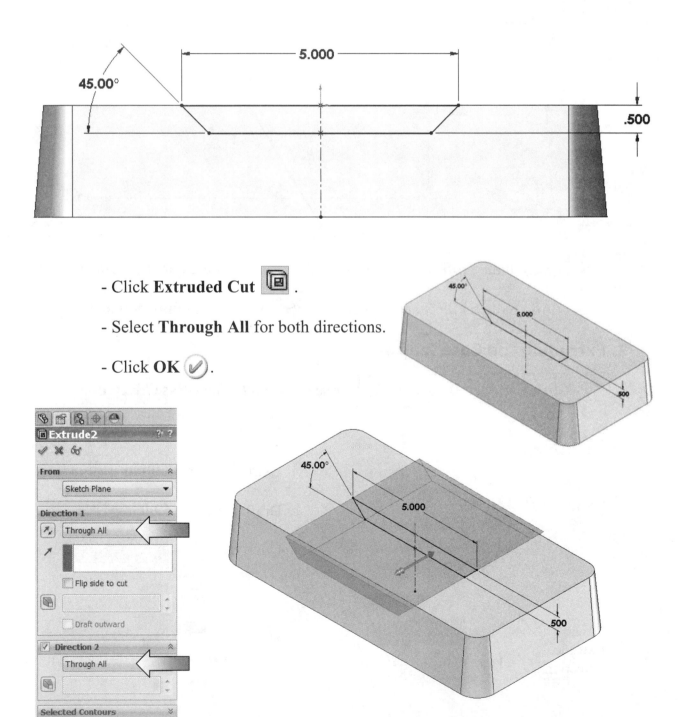 or select **Insert / Sketch.**

- Sketch the profile as shown and add Dimensions / Relations necessary to fully define the sketch.

- Click **Extruded Cut** .

- Select **Through All** for both directions.

- Click **OK** .

4. Removing more material:

- Select the Top surface and open a new sketch.

- Select the outer edges and create an **offset** of **.250"** as indicated.

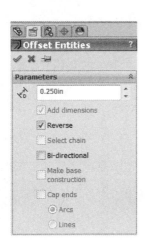 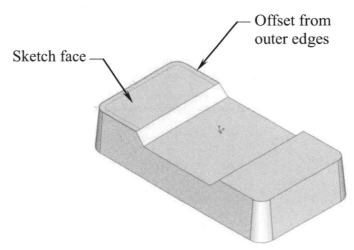

Sketch face

Offset from outer edges

- Offset the opposite edges using the same offset value.

- Drag the endpoint of the lines to merge the 2 ends into one continuous profile.

- Extrude a **cut** with **5°** draft using the bottom surface to offset the cut.

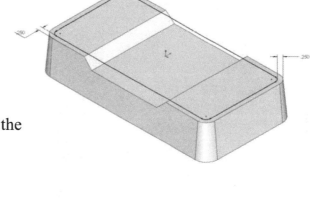

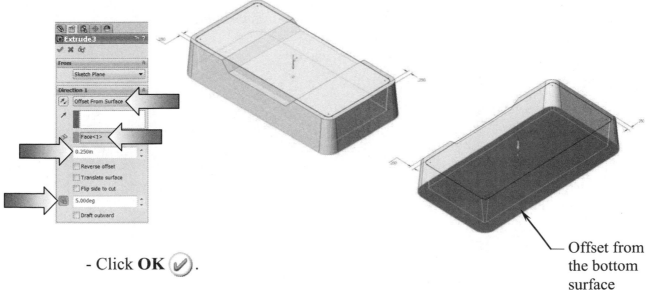

Offset from the bottom surface

- Click **OK** ✔.

5. Creating the Rib Profiles:

- Select the Face as indicated and open a new sketch .

- Sketch the profile and add Dimensions / Relations needed to fully define the sketch.

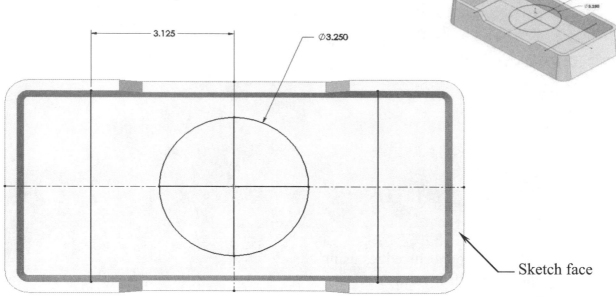

Sketch face

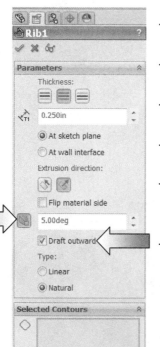

- Click Rib 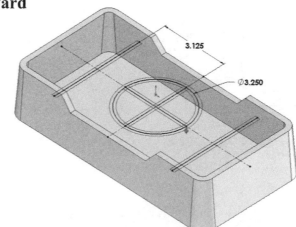 or select **Insert / Features / Rib**.

- Enter **.250 in.** for Thickness.

- Select the **Normal To Sketch** option.

- Click the **Draft** option and enter **5.00** deg.

- Enable **Draft Outward** check box.

- Click **OK**.

6. Adding the .500" Fillets:

- Click Fillet 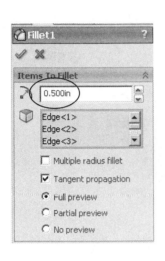 or select **Insert / Features / Fillet-Round**.

- Enter **.500 in.** as the Radius and select the **8 Edges** as shown.

- Click **OK** ✅.

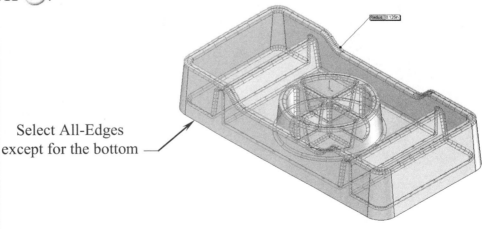

Select 8 Edges
(Both Sides)

7. Adding the .125" Fillets:

- Click Fillet  or select **Insert / Features / Fillet-Round**.

- Enter **.125 in.** as the Radius and select All-Edges **except** for the bottom edges.

- Click **OK** ✅.

Box select

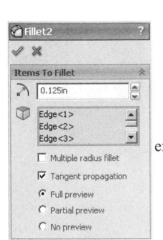

Select All-Edges
except for the bottom

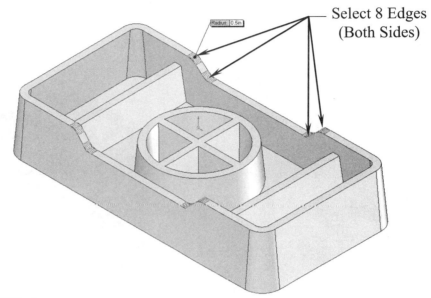

8. Shelling the lower portion:

- Click Shell  or select **Insert / Features / Shell**.

- Select the Bottom-Face and enter **.080** in. for Thickness.

- Click **OK** ✓.

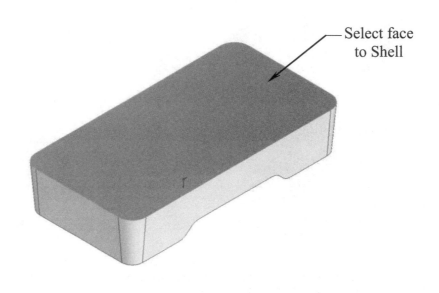

Select face
to Shell

9. Saving Your Work:

- Click **File / Save As / Rib and Shell / Save**.

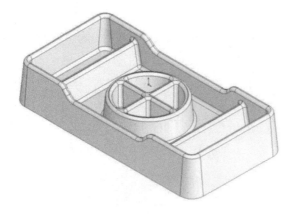
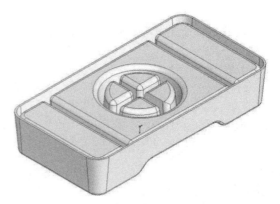

Questions for Review

Ribs & Shell

1. A fully defined sketch can be re-positioned after its relations/dimensions to the origin have been removed.
    a. True
    b. False

2. The Mid-Plane extrude option extrudes the profile in both directions and at equal depths.
    a. True
    b. False

3. Draft Outward is the only option available; the Draft Inward option is not available.
    a. True
    b. False

4. The Shell feature hollows out the part starting with the selected face.
    a. True
    b. False

5. If nothing (no face) is selected, a solid model cannot be shelled.
    a. True
    b. False

6. A Rib is a special type of extruded feature; no drafts may be added to it.
    a. True
    b. False

7. A Rib can only be created with a closed-sketch profile; opened-sketch profiles may not be used.
    a. True
    b. False

8. The Rib features can be fully edited, just like any other feature in SolidWorks.
    a. True
    b. False

7. FALSE   8. TRUE
5. FALSE   6. FALSE
3. FALSE   4. TRUE
1. TRUE   2. TRUE

Exercise: Basic Solid Modeling
Extrude / Revolve / Sweep and Circular Pattern

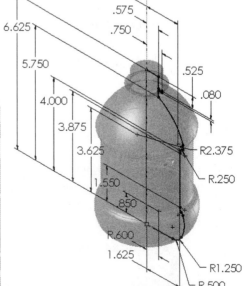

1. Copying the document:

Go to:
Training CD
Basic Solid Modeling_Bottle

Make a Copy of this file and **Open the copy**.

(To review how this part was made, open the sample part from the provided CD, in the Built-Parts folder).

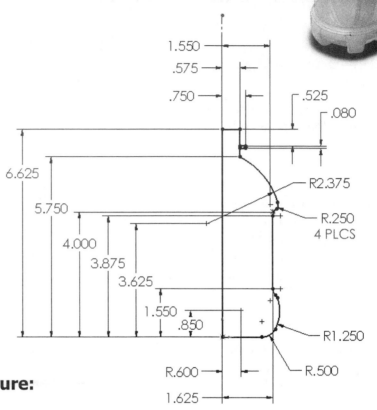

2. Revolving the Base feature:

- Click Revolve or select **Insert / Boss-Base / Revolve**

- Select the **Vertical Centerline** as Center of the rotation.

- Direction: **Blind** (Default).

- Revolve Angle: **360 deg**.

- Click **OK**.

3. Creating the Upper Sketch:

- Select the FRONT Plane and open a new sketch.

- Sketch the profile as shown and add dimensions and/or relations needed to fully define the sketch.

4. Revolving the Upper Cut:

- Click Revolved Cut 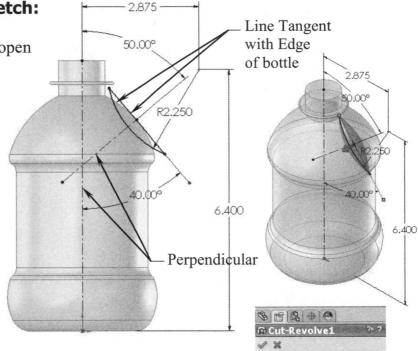 or select **Insert / Cut / Revolve**.

- Select the **Angular Centerline (40°)** as Center of the rotation.

- Revolve **One-Direction** (Default).

- Revolve Angle: **360 deg**.

- Click **OK** ✅.

5. Creating the Bottom Cut:

- Select the FRONT Plane and open a new sketch.

- Sketch the profile as shown, use **Convert-Entities** where needed.

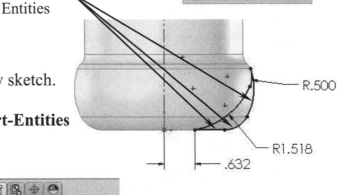

- Add Dimensions and Relations to fully define the sketch.

- Click **Revolve Cut** .

- Revolve Direction: **Mid-Plane**

- Revolve Angle: **45 Deg**.

- Click **OK** ✅.

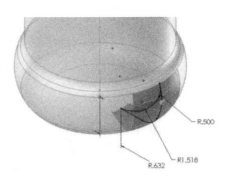

6. Adding .075" Fillets:

- Click Fillet 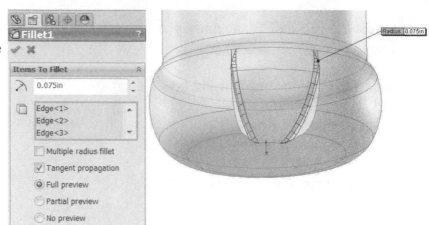 or select: **Insert / Feature / Fillet-Round**

- Enter **.075 in**. for Radius.

- Select the **2 inner edges**.

- Click **OK** .

7. Adding .125" Fillets:

- Click Fillet or select: **Insert / Feature / Fillet-Round**

- Enter **.125 in**. for Radius.

- Select the **2 outer edges**.

- Click **OK** .

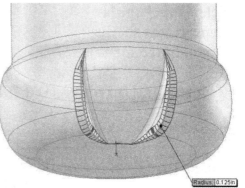

8. Circular Pattern the Cutouts:

- Click Circular Pattern or select **Insert / Pattern-Mirror /Circular Pattern**.

- Select the **Center Axis** for use as the Pattern-Axis.

- Pattern Angle: **360deg**.

- **Equal Spacing** enabled.

- Number of Copies: **5**

- Select the **Upper Cut,** the **Lower Cut,** the **Fillet 1,** and **Fillet 2**.

- Click **OK** .

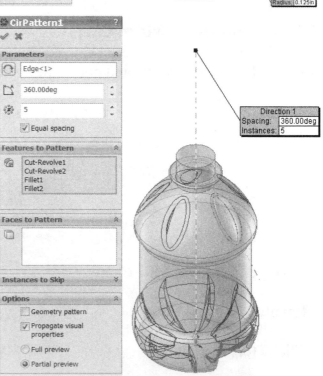

9. Shelling with Multi-Wall:

- Click Shell  or select: **Insert / Feature / Shell.**

- Select the **uppermost face** and enter **.025 in**. for default thickness.

- Select the **side face** as indicated and enter **.050 in**. for multi-thickness.

- Click **OK** ✅.

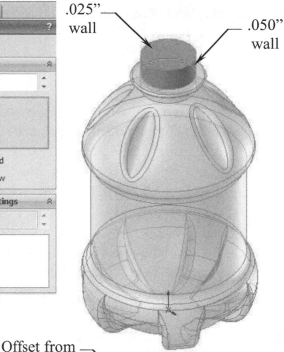

.025" wall

.050" wall

10. Creating an Offset Plane:

- Click Plane or select **Insert / Reference Geometry / Plane.**

- Select the **upper face** as noted.

- Enter **.450 in**. for offset Distance.

- Click **OK** ✅.

Offset from top surface

11. Creating the Helix (Sweep Path):

- Select the New Plane and open a new sketch.

- **Convert** the uppermost circular edge into a circle.

- Select: **Insert / Curve / Helix-Spiral.**

- Pitch: **.115 in**.

- Revolution: **3.5**

- Start Angle: **0.00deg**.

- Enable Counterclockwise.

- Click **OK** ✅.

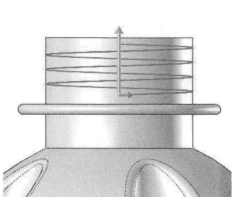

12. Sketching the Thread Profile:

- Select the RIGHT Plane and open a new sketch.

- Sketch the profile (Triangle), add the dimensions and relations needed to fully define the sketch.

- Use Dynamic Mirror 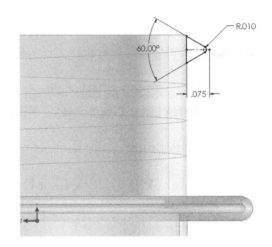 to keep all sketch entities symmetrical.

- Add a **PIERCE** relation (between the the endpoint of the centerline and the helix) to properly snap the sweep profile on the Helix.

- **Exit the Sketch** .

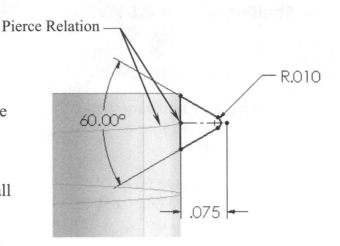

Pierce Relation

13. Adding the Threads:

- Click Swept Boss Base or select: **Insert / Boss-Base / Sweep**.

- Select the Sketch Profile (the triangle) for use as the Sweep Profile.

- Select the Helix for use as the Sweep Path.

- Click **OK** .

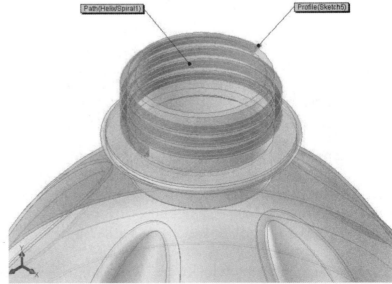

14. Rounding the ends:

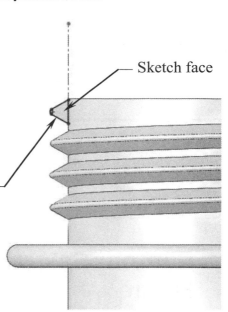

Sketch face

Convert Entities

- Select the End-Face of the Swept feature and open a new sketch.

- Click **Convert-Entities** to covert the selected face into a new sketch profile.

- Add a **Vertical Centerline** as shown.

- Click Revolve 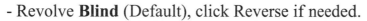 or select: **Insert / Boss-Base / Revolve**.

- Revolve **Blind** (Default), click Reverse if needed.

- Revolve Angle: **100 deg**.

- Click **OK** ✅.

- *Repeat Step 14 to round off the other end of the threads.*

15. Saving your work:

- Click **File / Save As / Basic Solid Modeling_Bottle**.

- Click **Save.**

CHAPTER 6 (cont.)

Contour Selection

Contour Selection
Fixture

- The **Contour Selection** tool allows the SolidWorks user to select one or more closed contours in a sketch for use in a feature.

- Any sketches created in SolidWorks or imported from another CAD program, can be <u>reused</u> by using the Contour Select tool. This useful command allows the user to use a partial sketch to create features.

- The examples below show many possible contours available for extruding solid features within a single sketch.

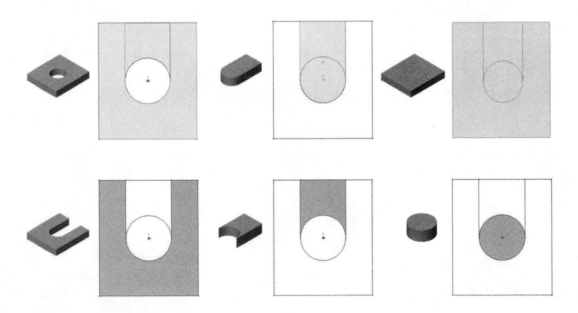

- This chapter and its exercise will guide you through the use of the Contour-Selection tool to convert 2D sketches into 3D models.

Fixture
Using Contour Selection

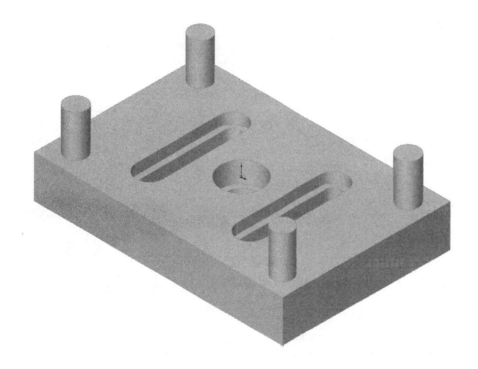

Dimensioning Standards: **ANSI**
Units: **INCHES** – 3 Decimals

Tools Needed:

Insert Sketch	Line	Centerline
Circle	Mirror	Dimension
Add Geometric Relations	Fillet	Chamfer
Extruded Boss/Base	Extruded Cut	Contour Select Tool

1. Opening the main sketch:

- From the Training CD, open a SolidWorks document named:
  Contour Selection.sldprt

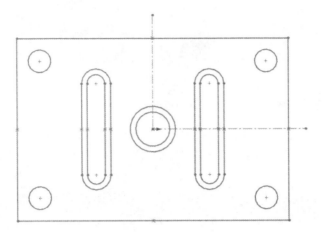

- **Edit** the sketch. Verify that the sketch is fully defined.

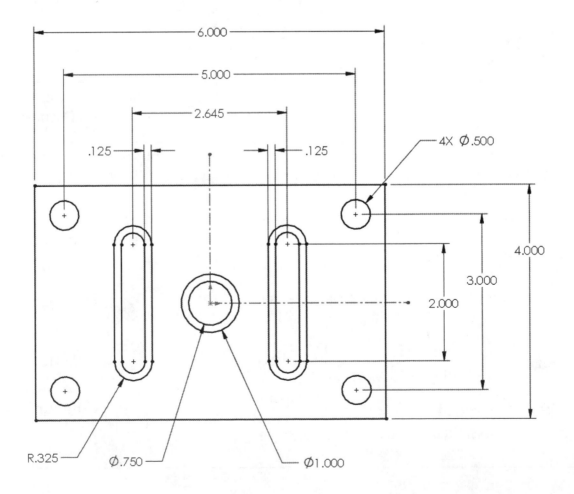

2. Extruding the Base:

- Click 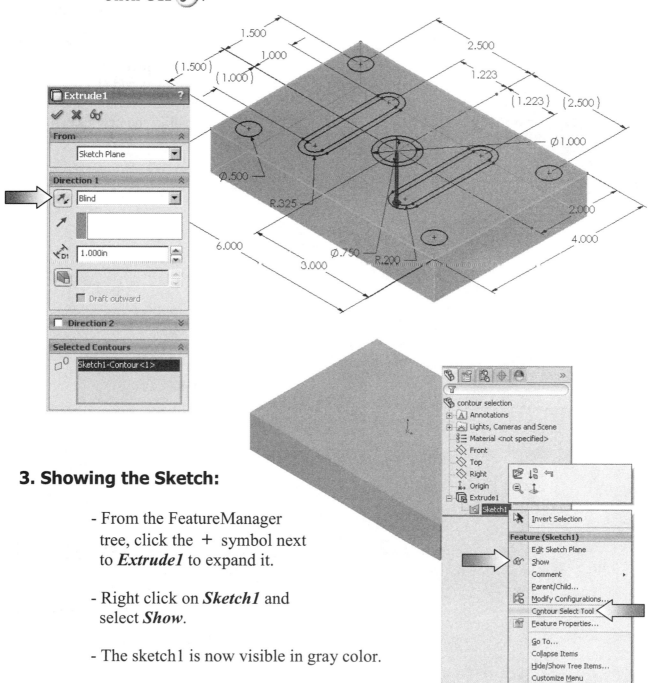 or select **Insert / Boss-Base / Extrude**.

- End Condition: **Blind**.

- Extrude Depth: **1.00 in**.   - Reverse Direction **Enabled**

- Click **OK**.

3. Showing the Sketch:

- From the FeatureManager tree, click the **+** symbol next to **Extrude1** to expand it.

- Right click on **Sketch1** and select **Show**.

- The sketch1 is now visible in gray color.

4. Using the Contour Selection Tool:

- Right click on the line as indicated and select *Contour Selection Tool* .

Right click on
one of the lines...

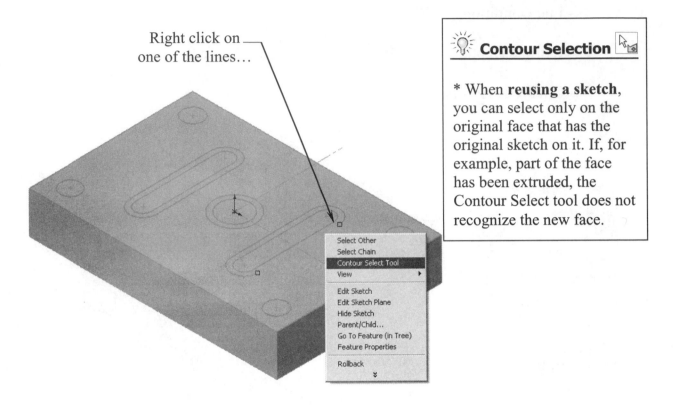

💡 **Contour Selection**

* When **reusing a sketch**, you can select only on the original face that has the original sketch on it. If, for example, part of the face has been extruded, the Contour Select tool does not recognize the new face.

- Hold down the CONTROL key and select the areas as indicated.

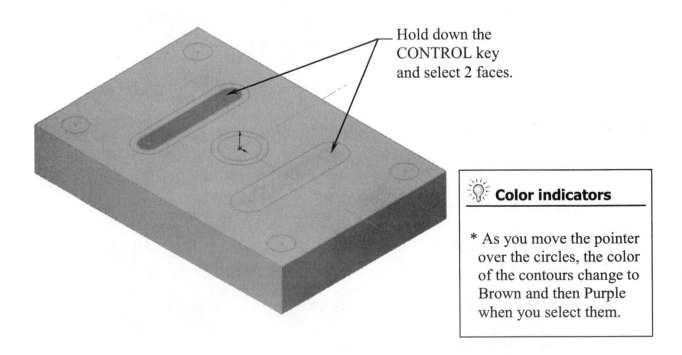

Hold down the
CONTROL key
and select 2 faces.

💡 **Color indicators**

* As you move the pointer over the circles, the color of the contours change to Brown and then Purple when you select them.

5. Extruding the selected contours as cut features:

- Click 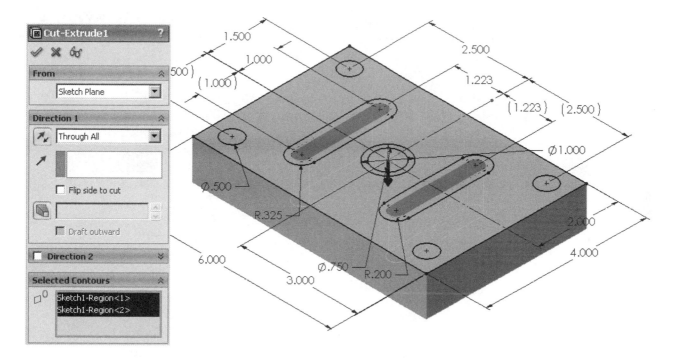 or select **Insert / Cut / Extrude**.

- End Condition: **Though All**

- Click **OK** .

- The slots are created from a sketch containing multiple contours.

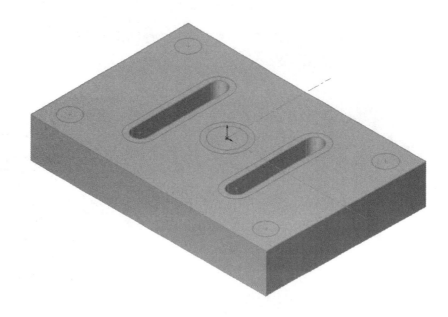

6. Re-using the same sketch:

- Right click on the line indicated and select **Contour Selection Tool** .

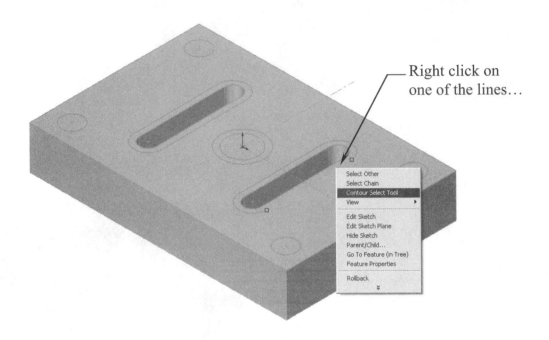

Right click on
one of the lines…

- Hold down the *CONTROL* key and select the faces as indicated.

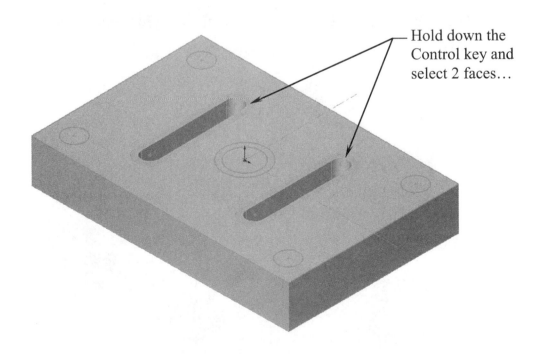

Hold down the
Control key and
select 2 faces…

7. Cutting the selected contours:

- Click 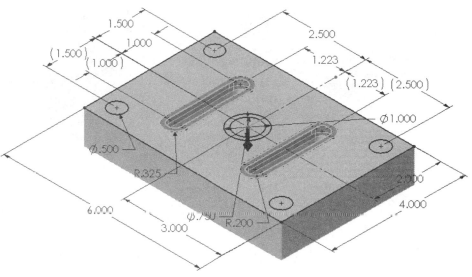 or select **Insert / Cut / Extrude**.

- End Condition: **Blind.**

- Extrude Depth: **.250 in**.

- Click **OK** ✓.

- The Recesses are
created from
the same sketch.

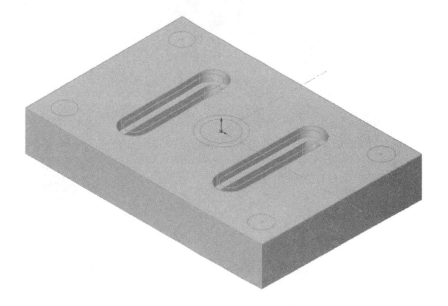

8. Continuing with other contours:

- Right click on the circle indicated and select: **Contour Selection Tool** .

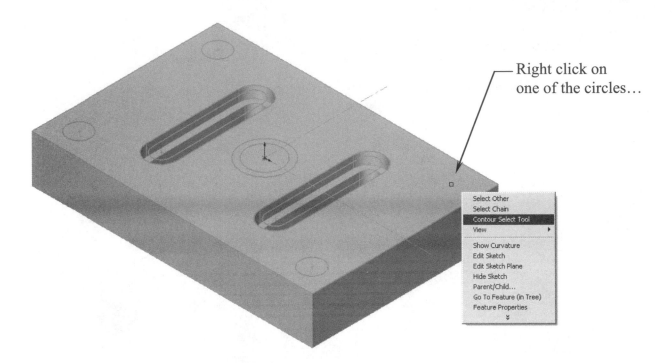

Right click on
one of the circles…

- Hold down the CONTROL key and select the faces as shown below.

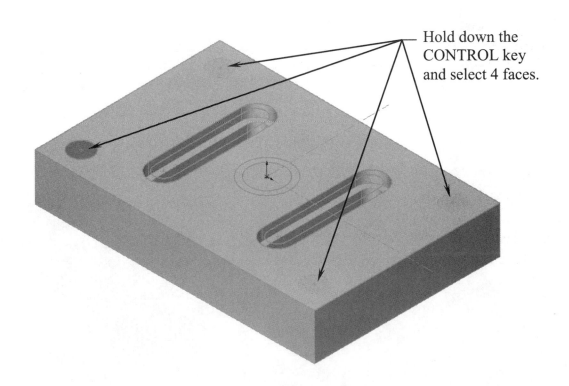

Hold down the
CONTROL key
and select 4 faces.

9. Extruding the selected contours:

- Click 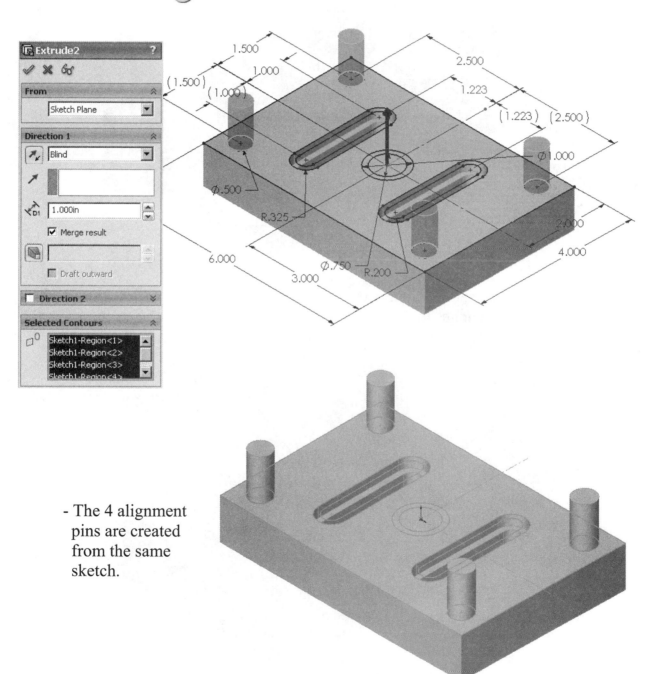 or select **Insert / Boss-Base / Extrude**.

- End Condition: **Blind.**

- Extrude Depth: **1.00 in**.

- Click **OK**.

- The 4 alignment pins are created from the same sketch.

10. Selecting the center contours:

- Right click on the circle indicated and select: **Contour Selection Tool** .

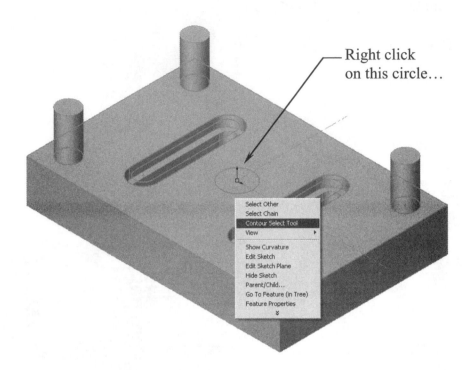

Right click
on this circle...

- Hover the mouse cursor over the circle in the center, select the contour when the color changes to Brown.

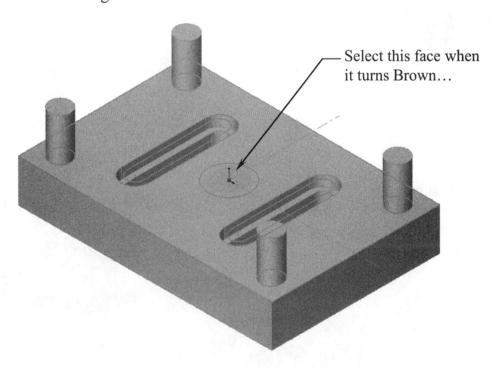

Select this face when
it turns Brown...

11. Extruding the selected contours as cut features:

- Click 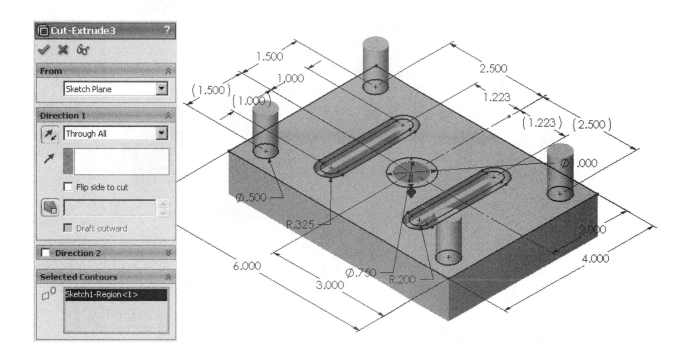 or select **Insert / Cut / Extrude**.

- End Condition: **Though All.**

- Click **OK** .

- The center hole
  is created from
  the main sketch.

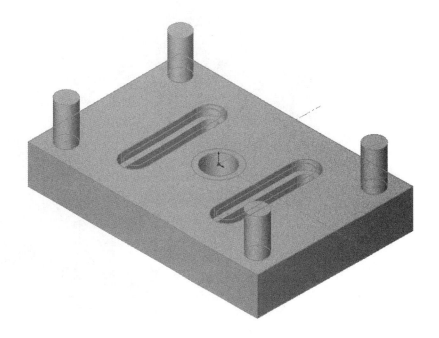

12. Selecting the next contour:

- Right click on the circle indicated and select: **Contour Selection Tool** .

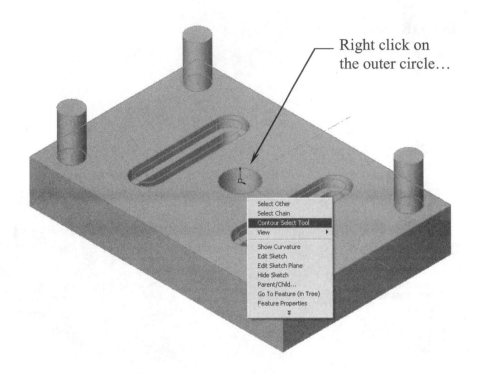

Right click on
the outer circle...

- Select the face as indicated when its color changes to Brown.

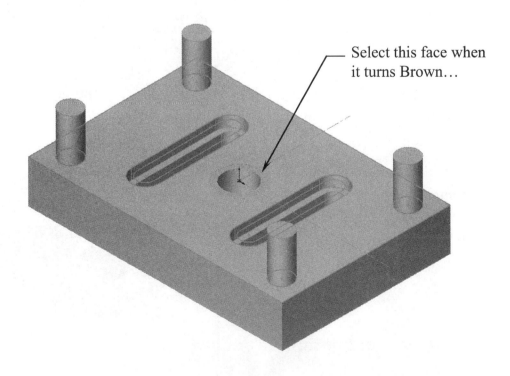

Select this face when
it turns Brown...

13. Cutting the center hole:

- Click or select **Insert / Cut / Extrude**.

- End Condition: **Blind.**

- Extrude Depth: **.500 in**.

- Click **OK** ✅.

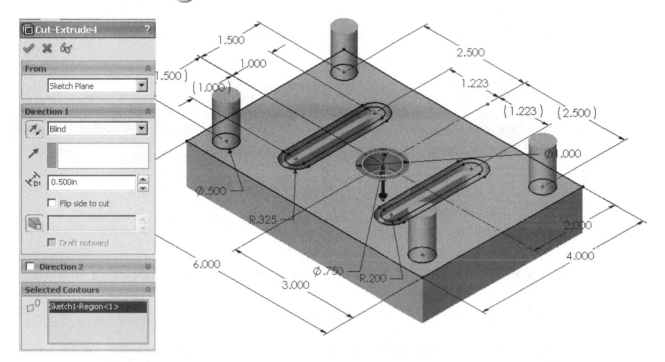

- The center hole is created from the main sketch.

💡 Hide Sketch

* When the Contour Select Tool is being used, the sketch remains visible (Yellow Icon) so that it can be reused in other features.

* When finished, right-click on the sketch and select **Hide**.

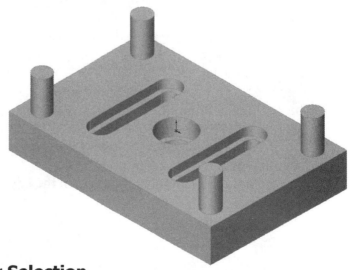

14. Save your work as: Contour Selection.

Questions for Review

Contour Selection

1. The Contour Select Tool allows you to select one or more closed contours in a sketch to convert into a feature.
    a. True
    b. False

2. When extruding several contours at the same time, they can have different depths.
    a. True
    b. False

3. Opened contours can be selected and extruded.
    a. True
    b. False

4. If several contours are selected, they will have to be extruded to the same depth.
    a. True
    b. False

5. As you drag the pointer over the contours, their colors change from Brown to Purple when selected.
    a. True
    b. False

6. The sketches cannot be reused; a new sketch has to be made each time.
    a. True
    b. False

7. The selected contours can be edited at anytime.
    a. True
    b. False

8. To select multiple contours, hold down the key:
    a. Shift
    b. Control
    c. Alt

1. True   2. False
3. False   4. True
5. True   6. False
7. True   8. B

Exercise: Contour Selection

1. From the Training CD, open a
   document named:
   Contour Selection_Exe.
2. Use the Contour Selection tool to
   extrude all features.
3. The 4 holes are thru holes.
4. The upper boss is centered of the thickness.
5. Use the instructions on the next page, if needed.

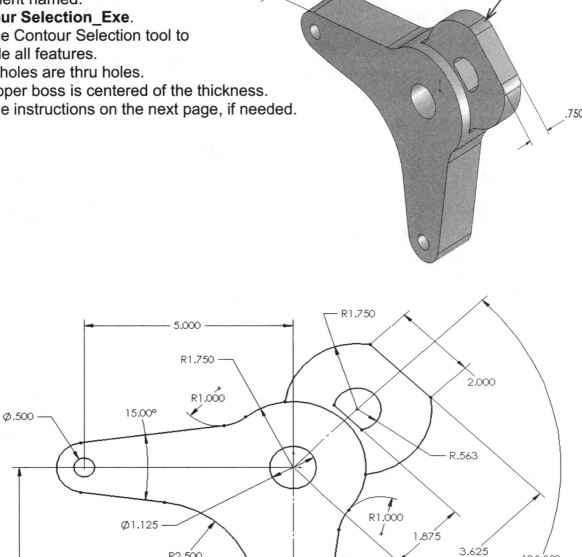

6. Save a copy of your work as: **Contour Selection_Exe**.

1. Activating the Contour Select tool:

- Right click on one of the lines and pick: **Contour-Select Tool**.

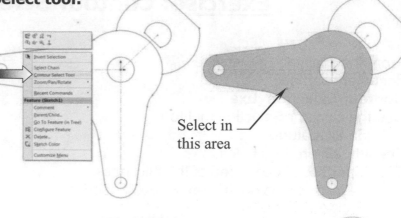

Select in this area

- Hove the mouse in the area as noted and select it when the color changes to magenta.

2. Extruding the base:

- Create an **Extruded Boss-Base** using **Mid Plane** at **1.500"** thick.

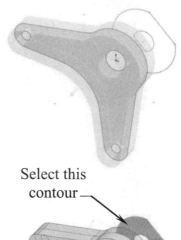

3. Selecting another contour:

Select this contour

- Expand the Boss-Extrude1 feature and **show** the **Sketch1**.

- Right click on one of the lines and pick: **Contour Select Tool**.

- Select the upper contour when the color changes to magenta.

4. Extruding the upper boss:

- Extrude the selected contour using **Mid Plane** at **.750"** thick.

5. Adding fillets:

- Add a **.500"** fillet to the 4 Edges as indicated.

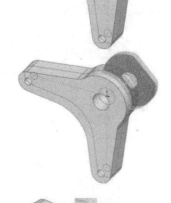

6. Saving your work:

Fillet 4 edges

- Save a copy of your work as: **Contour_Selection_Exe**.

CHAPTER 7

Linear Patterns

Linear Patterns
Test Tray

- The Linear Pattern is used to arrange multiple instances of selected features along one or two linear paths.

- The following 4 elements are needed to create a linear pattern:

  * Direction of the pattern (linear edge of the model or an axis) .

  * Distance between the pattern instances .

  * Number of pattern instances in each direction .

  * Feature(s) to the pattern .

- When the features used to create the pattern are changed, all instances within the pattern will be updated automatically.

- The options available in Linear Patterns:

  * Pattern instances to skip. This option is used to hide / skip some instances in a pattern.

  * Pattern only the seed feature. This option is used when only the original feature gets repeated, not its instances.

- This chapter will guide you through the use of the pattern commands such as: Linear, Circular, and Curve Driven Patterns.

Test Tray
Linear Patterns

| Dimensioning Standards: **ANSI** |
| Units: **INCHES** – 3 Decimals |

Tools Needed:

Insert Sketch	Rectangle	Circle
Dimension	Add Geometric Relations	Base/Boss Extrude
Shell	Linear Pattern	Fillet/Round

1. Sketching the Base Profile:

- Select the TOP plane from the FeatureManager tree.

- Click 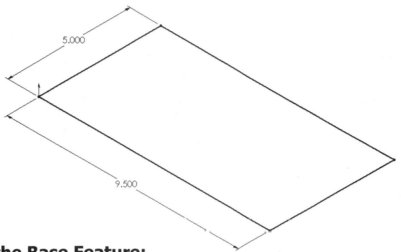 or select **Insert /Sketch**.

- Sketch a rectangle ☐ starting at the Origin.

- Add dimensions ⬧ as shown.

5.000

9.500

2. Extruding the Base Feature:

- Click 🔲 or select **Insert / Boss-Base / Extrude**.

- End Condition: **Blind.**

- Extrude Depth: **.500 in**.

- Click **OK** ✅.

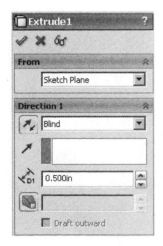

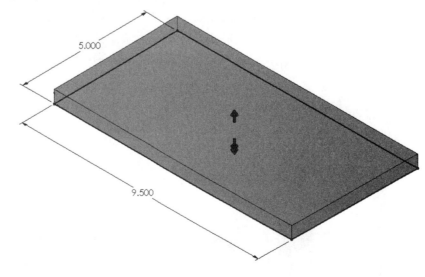

3. Sketching the seed feature:

- Select the face indicated as the sketch plane.

- Click  or select **Insert / Sketch**.

- Sketch a circle and add dimensions as shown.

Sketch Face

Ø1.000

1.000

1.000

4. Extruding a seed feature:

- Click or select **Insert / Boss-Base / Extrude**.

- End Condition: **Blind.**

- Extrude Depth: **2.00 in**.

- Draft On/Off: **Enabled.**

- Draft Angle: **7 deg**.

- Click **OK** .

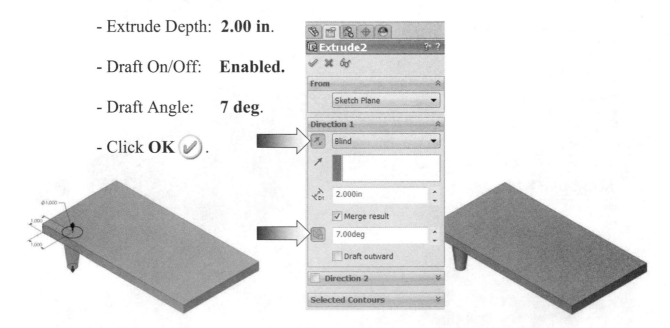

Extrude2

From
Sketch Plane

Direction 1
Blind

2.000in

✓ Merge result

7.00deg

Draft outward

Direction 2

Selected Contours

5. Creating a Linear Pattern of the Boss Feature:

- Click ⊞ or select **Insert / Pattern Mirror / Linear Pattern**.

For **Direction 1**:

- Select the bottom **horizontal edge** as Pattern Direction1 ↗.

- Enter **1.500** in. as the Spacing.

- Enter **6** as the Number Of Instances.

For **Direction 2**:

- Select the **vertical edge** as Pattern Direction2 ↗.

- Enter **1.500** in. as the Spacing.

- Enter **3** as the Number of Instances.

- Click Extrude2 as the Features to Pattern.

- Click **OK** ✓.

> 💡 **Linear Patterns**
>
> The Linear Pattern option creates multiple instances of one or more features uniformly along one or two directions.

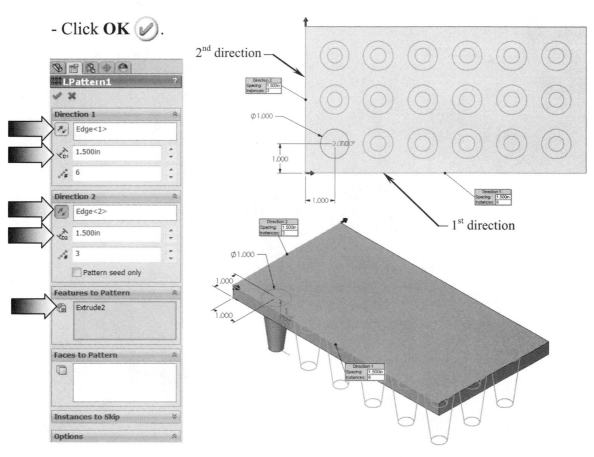

6. Shelling the Base feature:

- Select the upper face as shown.

- Click or select **Insert / Features / Shell**.

- Type **.100** in. for the Thickness.

- Click **OK** ✓ .

> ### Shell
>
> The Shell option hollows out the part, starting with the selected face. Constant or multi-wall thickness can be done in the same operation.

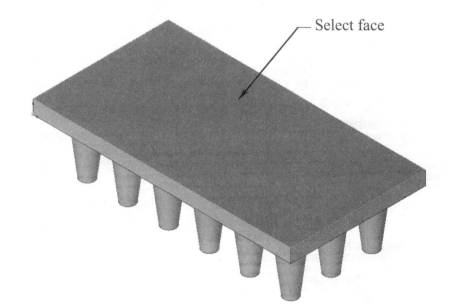

Select face

- The shelled part.

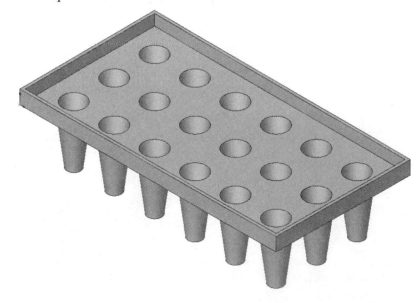

7. Adding Fillets:

- Click Fillet  or select **Insert / Features / Fillet / Round.**

- Enter **.050** in. as the Radius .

- Select the edges as shown .

- Click **OK** .

> ### 💡 Fillets
>
> A combination of faces and edges can be selected within the same fillet operation.
> (Box-select the entire part to select all edges).

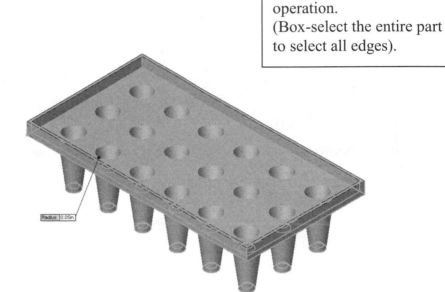

8. Saving your work:

- Select **File / Save As / Test Tray / Save.**

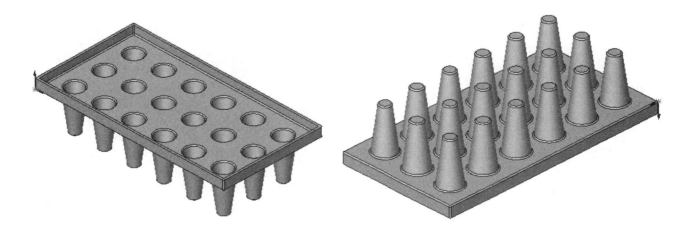

Questions for Review

Linear Patterns

1. SolidWorks only allows you to pattern one feature at a time. Patterning multiple features is not supported.
   a. True
   b. False

2. Only the spacing and number of copies are required to create a linear pattern.
   a. True
   b. False

3. SolidWorks does not require you to specify the 2nd direction when using both directions option.
   a. True
   b. False

4. The Shell feature hollows out the part using a wall thickness specified by the user.
   a. True
   b. False

5. After the Shell feature is created, its wall thickness cannot be changed.
   a. True
   b. False

6. A combination of faces and edges of a model can be selected in the same fillet operation.
   a. True
   b. False

7. The value of the fillet can be changed at anytime.
   a. True
   b. False

8. "Pattern a pattern" is not supported in SolidWorks.
   a. True
   b. False

7. TRUE   8. FALSE
5. FALSE   6. TRUE
3. FALSE   4. TRUE
1. FALSE   2. FALSE

Circular Patterns

Spur Gear

Circular Patterns
Spur Gear

- One or more instances can be copied in a circular fashion or around an Axis.

- The center of the pattern can be defined by a circular edge, an axis, a temporary axis, or an angular dimension.

- In the newer releases of SolidWorks, a circular edge can be used as the center of the pattern, instead of an axis.

- The information required to create a circular pattern are:

> * Center of rotation.
>
> * Spacing between the instances.
>
> * Number of copies.
>
> * Feature(s) to copy.

- Only the original feature can be edited; changes made to the original are automatically updated within the pattern.

- The features to the pattern can be selected directly from the graphics area or from the Feature Manager tree.

- The instances in a pattern can be skipped. The skipped instances can be edited during or after the pattern is made.

Spur-Gear
Circular Patterns

Dimensioning Standards: **ANSI**

Units: **INCHES** – 3 Decimals

Tools Needed:

Insert Sketch	╲ Line	┊ Center Line
Dynamic Mirror	┴ Add Geometric Relations	Dimension
Convert Entities	Trim Entities	Base/Boss Revolve
Circular Pattern	Base/Boss Extrude	Extruded Cut

1. Sketching the Body profile:

- Select the FRONT plane from the FeatureManager Tree.

- Click or select **Insert / Sketch**.

- Sketch a Centerline starting at the Origin.

- Select the Mirror tool and click the centerline to active the Dynamic Mirror mode.

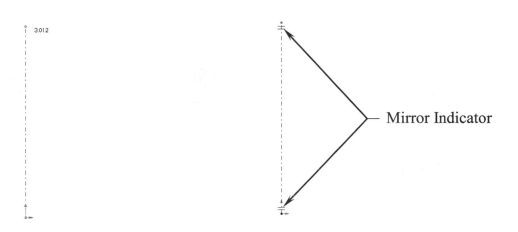

Mirror Indicator

- Sketch the profile below using the Line tool .

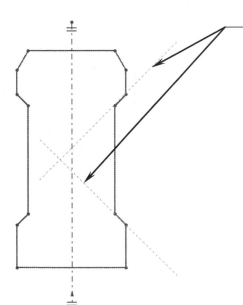

To avoid Auto-Relations (dotted inference lines), either hold down the Control key while sketching the lines – OR – just simply avoid sketching over the dotted lines.

Using the Dynamic Mirror:

- Sketch on one side of the centerline only.

- The sketch should not cross the centerline.

- The system creates **Symmetric** relations between all mirrored sketch entities.

- Add the following Geometric Relations 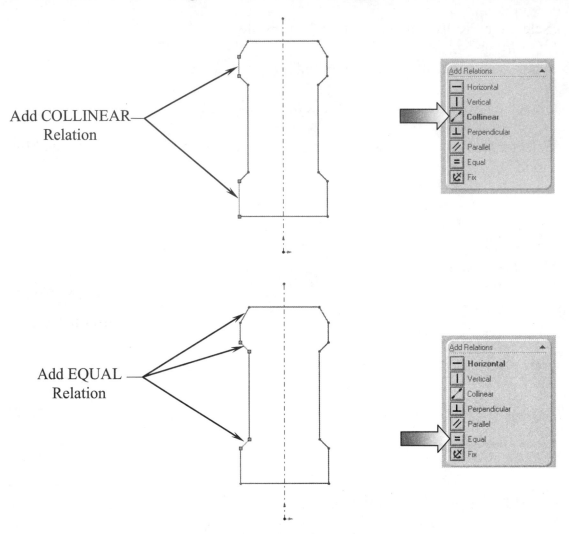 to the entities indicated below:

Add COLLINEAR Relation

Add EQUAL Relation

- Sketch a horizontal Centerline starting at the Origin.

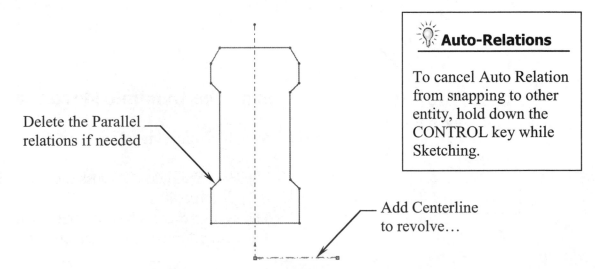

Delete the Parallel relations if needed

Add Centerline to revolve…

Auto-Relations

To cancel Auto Relation from snapping to other entity, hold down the CONTROL key while Sketching.

- Add the dimensions as shown below:

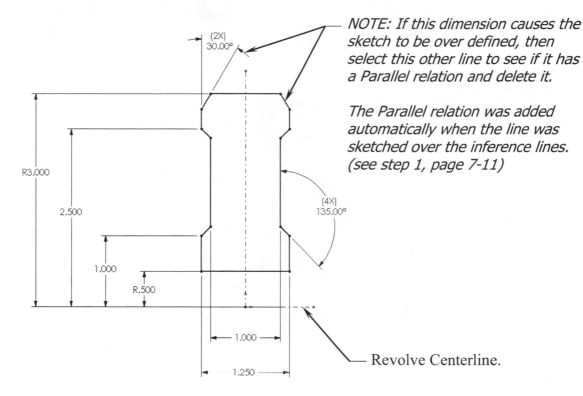

NOTE: If this dimension causes the sketch to be over defined, then select this other line to see if it has a Parallel relation and delete it.

The Parallel relation was added automatically when the line was sketched over the inference lines. (see step 1, page 7-11)

(2X) 30.00°

R3.000

2.500

(4X) 135.00°

1.000

R.500

1.000

1.250

Revolve Centerline.

2. Revolving the Base Body:

- Select the Horizontal Centerline as indicated above.

- Click 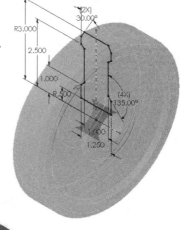 or select **Insert / Boss-Base / Revolve**.

- Revolve direction: **One Direction**

- Revolve Angle: **360°**

- Click **OK** ✓.

Revolve1

Axis of Revolution

Line1

Direction1

Blind

360.00deg

3. Sketching the Thread Profile:

- Select the face as indicated and click 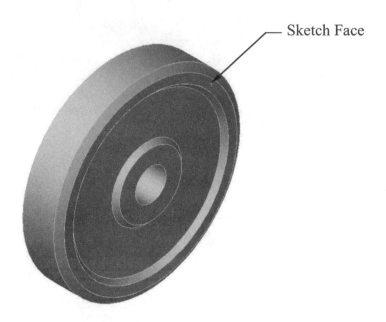 or select **Insert / Sketch**.

Sketch Face

- Click Normal To ⬆ from the Standard View Toolbar.

- Sketch a vertical Centerline ⫶ starting at the origin.

- Select the Mirror tool 🔁 and click the centerline to active the Dynamic-Mirror mode.

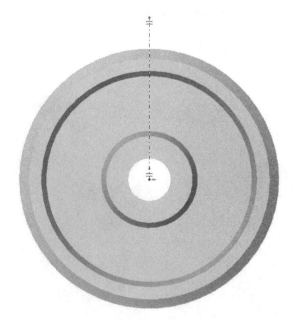

- Sketch the profile using the Line 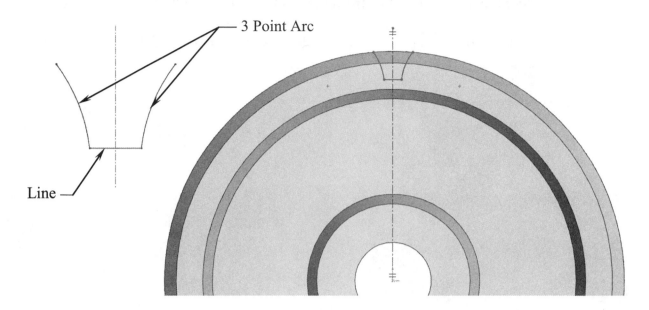 and the 3-Point-Arc tools.

3 Point Arc

Line

4. Converting the entities:

- Select the outer edge of the part and click **Convert Entities** from the Sketch-Tools toolbar.

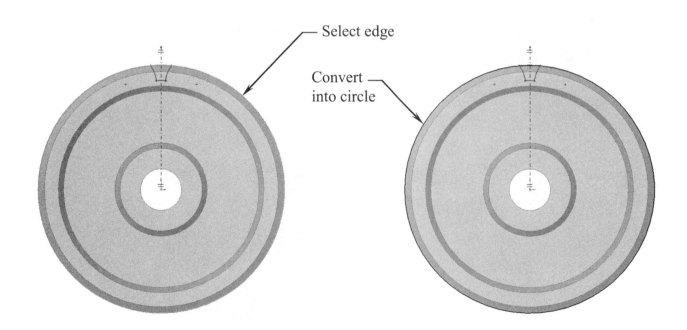

Select edge

Convert into circle

- The selected edge is converted into a circle.

5. Trimming the Sketch Entities:

- Select the Trim tool 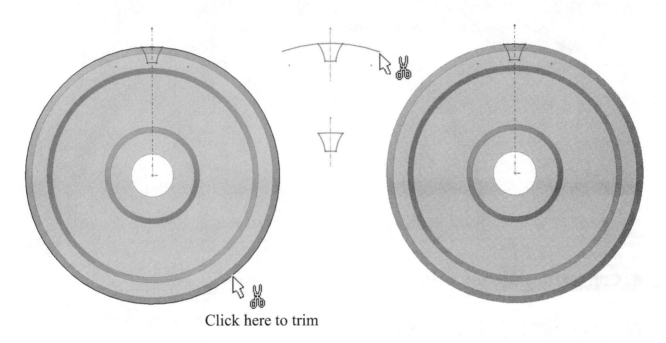 from the Sketch-Tools toolbar; select the **Trim-to-Closest** option , and click on the lower right edge of the circle to trim.

Click here to trim

6. Adding Dimensions:

- Select the Dimension Tool from the Sketch-Tools toolbar and add the dimensions as shown.

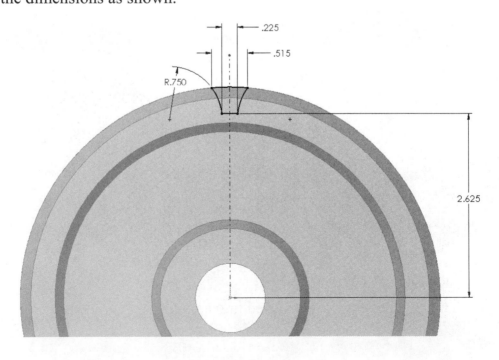

- Switch to the Isometric View  or press Ctrl + 7.

7. Cutting the First Tooth:

- Click Extruded Cut ⬛ from the Features toolbar.

- End Condition: **Through All**.

- Click **OK** ✓.

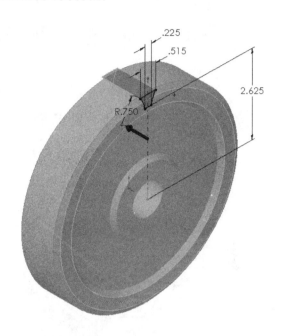

8. Circular Patterning the Tooth:

- Select **Temporary Axis** from the **View** pull-down menu. An axis in the center of the hole is created automatically; this axis will be used as the center of the pattern.

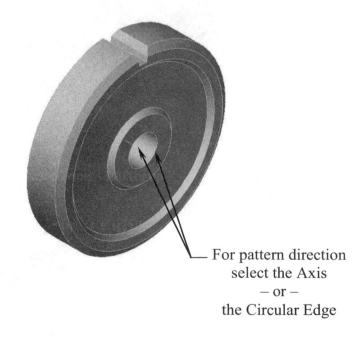

For pattern direction
select the Axis
– or –
the Circular Edge

- Click Circular Pattern 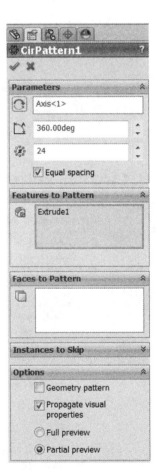 from the Features toolbar.

- Click on the center axis as Direction 1 .

- Click the **Equal Spacing** check box.

- Set the Total Angle to **360°** .

- Set the Number of Instances to **24** .

- Click inside the Features to Pattern box and select one of the faces of the cut feature (or select the previous Extruded Cut feature from the tree).

- Click **OK** .

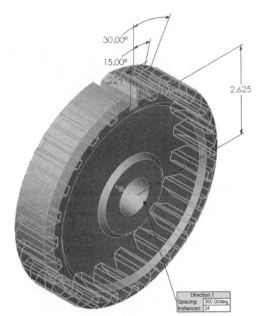

- The resulting circular Pattern.

9. Adding the Keyway:

- Select the face as indicated and click 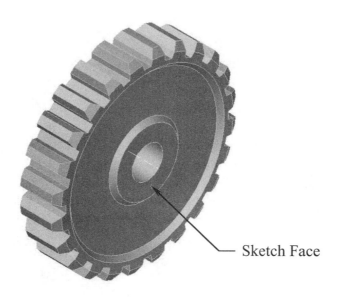 or select **Insert / Sketch**.

Sketch Face

- Click Normal To ⚓ from the Standard Views toolbar (Cntrl + 8).

- Sketch a vertical Centerline ⦙ starting at the Origin.

- Select the Mirror tool ⌗ and click the centerline to activate the Dynamic-Mirror mode.

💡 Sketch Mirror

Use the Mirror option in a sketch to make a symmetrical profile.

When a sketch entity is changed, the mirrored image will also change.

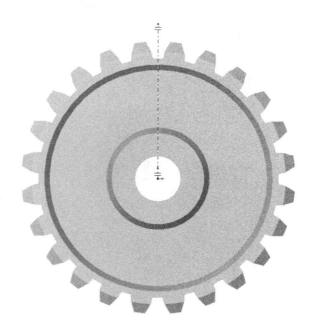

- Sketch the profile of the keyway and add dimension 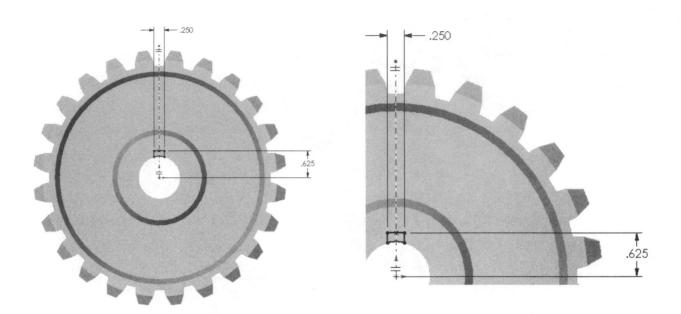 as shown:

10. Extruding a Cut:

- Click on Extruded Cut 🔳 from the Features toolbar.

- End Condition: **Through All**

- Click **OK** ✓.

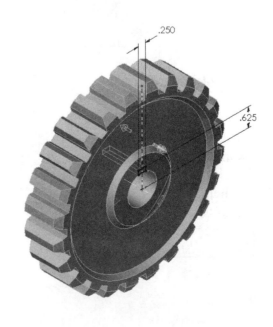

11. Saving Your Work:

- Select **File / Save As**.

- Enter **Spur Gear** for the file name.

- Click **Save**.

Questions for Review

Circular Patterns

1. The Revolve sketch entities should not cross the Revolve centerline.
    a. True
    b. False

2. The system creates **symmetric** relations to all mirrored sketch entities.
    a. True
    b. False

3. An Equal relation makes the entities equal in size.
    a. True
    b. False

4. The system creates an On-Edge relation to all converted entities.
    a. True
    b. False

5. The Trim tool is used to trim 2D sketch entities.
    a. True
    b. False

6. The center of the circular pattern can be defined by an axis, a linear edge, or an angular dimension.
    a. True
    b. False

7. The center of rotation, spacing, number of copies, and features to copy are required when creating a circular pattern.
    a. True
    b. False

8. When the original feature is changed, all instances in the pattern will also change.
    a. True
    b. False

7. TRUE   8. TRUE
5. TRUE   6. TRUE
3. TRUE   4. TRUE
1. TRUE   2. TRUE

Circular Patterns (cont.)

Circular Base Mount

Circular Patterns
Circular Base Mount

- As mentioned in the 1st half of this chapter, the Circular Pattern command creates an array of feature(s) around an axis.

- The elements required to create circular patterns are:

    * Center axis (Temporary Axis, Axis, an Edge, etc.)

    * Spacing between each instance

    * Number of instances in the pattern

    * Feature(s) to the pattern

- Only the original feature may be edited and changes made to the original feature will automatically be passed onto the instances within the pattern.

- The features to the pattern can be selected directly from the graphics area or from the Feature Manager tree.

- Instances in a pattern can be skipped. The skipped instances can be edited during or after the pattern is complete.

- The Temporary axis can be toggled on or off (View/Temporary Axis).

- This 2nd half of the chapter will guide you through the use of the Circular Pattern command, as well as the Curve Driven Pattern command.

Circular Base Mount
Circular Patterns

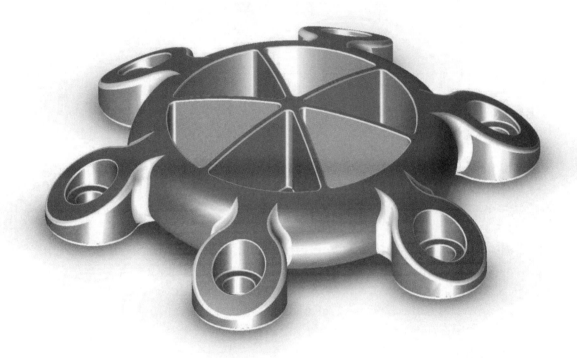

Dimensioning Standards: **ANSI**
Units: **INCHES** – 3 Decimals

Tools Needed:

Insert Sketch	Line	Mirror Dynamic
Add Geometric Relations	Dimension	Base/Boss Revolve
Revolve Cut	Circular Pattern	Fillet/Round

1. Creating the Base Sketch:

- From the FRONT plane, start a new Sketch .

- Sketch the profile on the right side of the revolve centerline as shown.

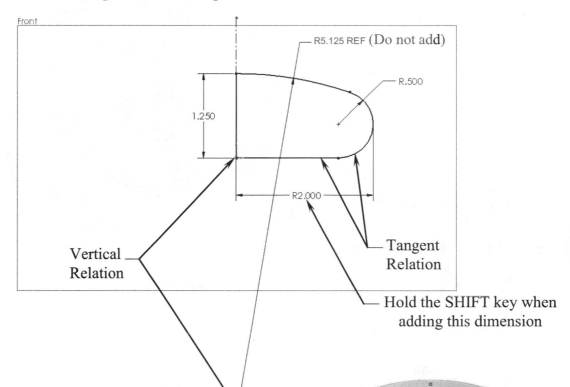

Front

R5.125 REF (Do not add)

R.500

1.250

R2.000

Vertical Relation

Tangent Relation

Hold the SHIFT key when adding this dimension

2. Revolving the Base Feature:

- Click  or select: **Insert / Boss Base / Revolve**.

- Revolve Direction: **Blind**.

- Revolve Angle: **360 deg**.

- Click **OK** ✓ .

3. Creating the first Side-Tab sketch:

- Select the TOP plane and open a new Sketch

- Sketch the profile as shown; add the dimensions and relations needed to fully define the sketch.

- Add the R.250 after the sketch is fully defined.

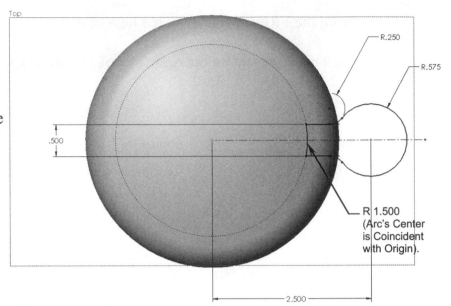

4. Extruding the Side-Tab:

- Click 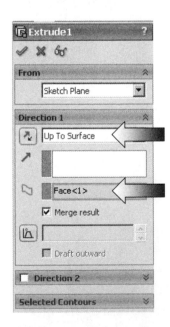 or select **Insert / Boss-Base / Extrude**.

- Direction 1: **Up To Surface**.

- Select the upper surface for End Condition.

— Select face

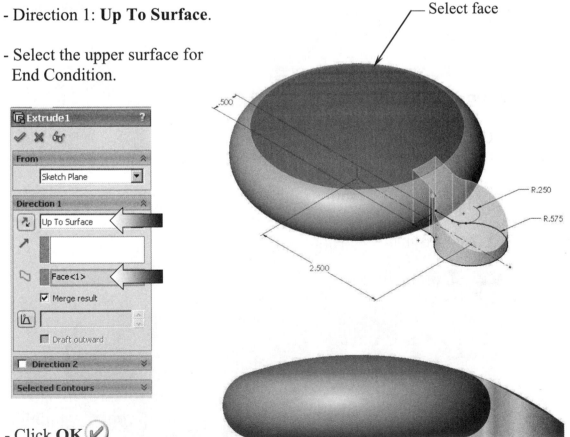

- Click **OK** ✅.

5. Adding a CounterBore Hole:

- Using the "traditional method" sketch the profile of the Counter-Bore on the FRONT plane.

(To create the "Virtual Diameter" dimensions click the centerline 1st then any entity thereafter).

Virtual Diameter: Add dimension from the centerline to the end point of the line on the left of the profile.

- Add the 2 Diameters and the 2 Depth dimensions.

- Add the relations needed to fully define the sketch.

Mid-Point Relation

6. Cutting the C'Bore:

- Click or select: **Insert / Cut / Revolve**.

- Revolve Direction: **Blind**.

- Revolve Angle **360 deg**.

- Click **OK**.

7. Creating the circular pattern:

- Click 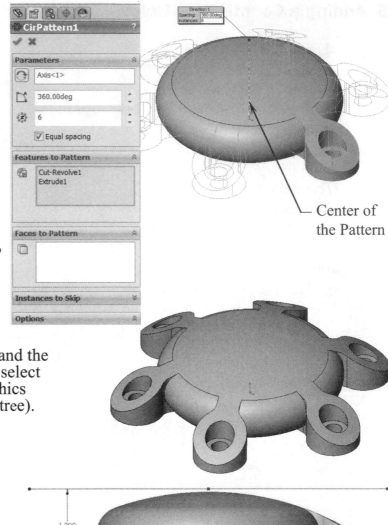 Circular Pattern (below Linear).

- From the **View** menu, select the **Temporary-Axis** option.

- Select the **Axis** in the middle of the part as noted.

- Set Pattern Angle to **360°**

- Enter **6** for the Number of Instances.

- For Features to Pattern, select both the **Side Tab** and the CounterBore hole (either select the C'Bore from the graphics area or from the Feature tree).

- Click **OK** ✅.

Center of the Pattern

8. Creating a new Plane:

- Click ◇ or select: **Insert / Reference Geometry / Plane**.

- Select **Offset Distance** option.

- Enter **1.300** in. as the distance.

- Select the **TOP** reference plane from the Feature Manger tree to offset from.

- Click **OK** ✅.

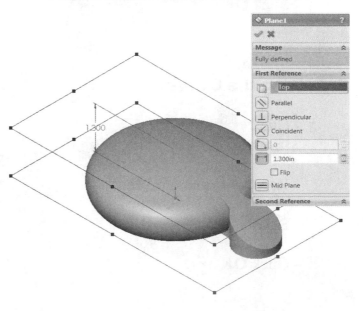

9. Creating the Pockets Sketch:

- Select the new plane (Plane1) and open a new sketch.

- Use the **Dynamic Mirror** 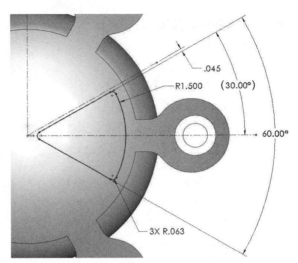 and sketch the profile as shown.

- Add the dimensions and relations as needed to fully define the sketch.

- Use **Circular Sketch Pattern** to make a total of 6 instances of the pocket.

10. Cutting the Pockets:

- Click or select: **Insert / Cut / Extrude**.

- For direction 1: use **Offset From Surface**.

- Select the **bottom surface** to offset from.

- Enter **.125** in. for Depth.

- Click **OK**.

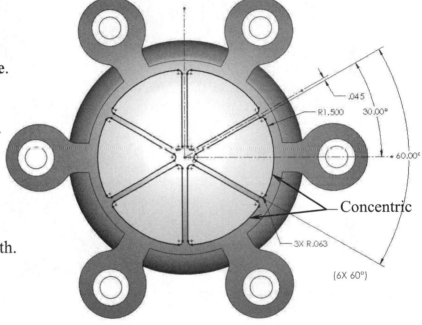

Concentric

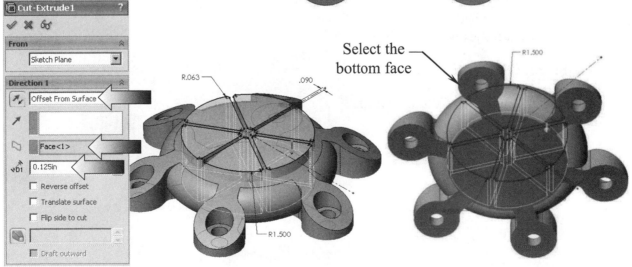

Select the bottom face

11. Adding the .0625" Fillets:

- Click Fillet
  or select: **Insert /
  Features / Fillet-
  Round**.

- Enter **.0625** in.
  for Radius size.

- Select all upper
  and lower edges
  of the 6 tabs.

Top & bottom
12 edges

- Click **OK** ✓.

12. Adding the .125" Fillets:

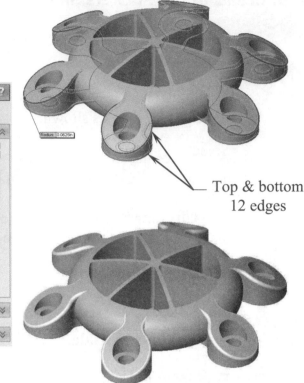

- Click Fillet 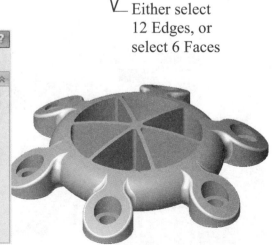 or select:
  Insert / Features / Fillet-Round.

- Enter **.125** in. for Radius size.

Either select
12 Edges, or
select 6 Faces

- Select all edges on
  the side of the 6 tabs
  or select the 6 faces
  as noted.

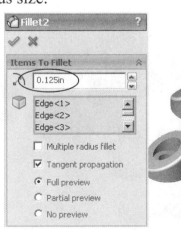

- Click **OK** ✓.

13. Adding the .015" Fillets:

- Click Fillet 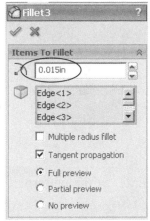 or select
  Insert / Features / Fillet-Round.

- Enter **.015** in. for
  radius size.

- Select all edges
  of the 6 Pockets
  and the 6 Counter-
  bores.

- Click **OK** .

14. Saving your work:

- Click **File / Save As**.

- Enter **Circular Base Mount** for file name.

- Click **Save**.

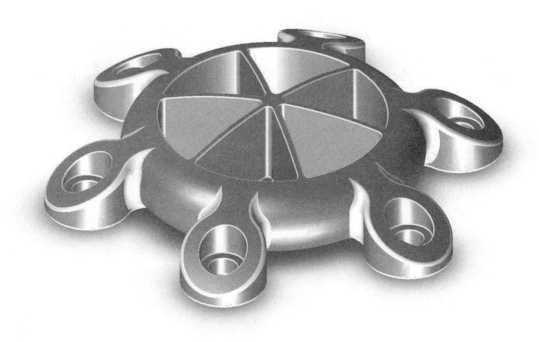

Questions for Review

Circular Patterns

1. The Circular Patterns command can also be selected from Insert / Pattern Mirror / Circular Pattern.
   a. True
   b. False

2. A Temporary Axis can be used as the center of the pattern.
   a. True
   b. False

3. A linear edge can also be used as the center of the circular pattern.
   a. True
   b. False

4. The Temporary Axis can be toggled ON / OFF under View / Temporary Axis.
   a. True
   b. False

5. The instances in the circular pattern can be skipped during and after the pattern is created.

   a. True
   b. False

6. If an *instance* of the patterned feature is deleted, the whole pattern will also be deleted.
   a. True
   b. False

7. If the *original* patterned feature is deleted, the whole pattern will also be deleted.
   a. True
   b. False

8. When the Equal spacing check box is enabled, the total angle (360°) must be used.
   a. True
   b. False

7. TRUE	8. FALSE
5. TRUE	6. FALSE
3. TRUE	4. TRUE
1. TRUE	2. TRUE

Curve Driven Patterns

Universal Bracket

Curve Driven Patterns
Universal Bracket

- The **Curve Drive Pattern** PropertyManager appears when you create
  a new curve driven pattern feature or when you edit an existing curve driven pattern feature.

- The PropertyManager controls the following properties:

> **Pattern Direction**: Select a curve, edge, sketch entity, or select a sketch from the
> FeatureManager to use as the path for the pattern. If necessary, click Reverse Direction to
> change the direction of the pattern.

> **Number of Instances**: Set a value for the number of instances of the seed feature in the
> pattern.

> **Equal spacing**: Sets equal spacing between each pattern instance. The separation between
> instances depends on the curve selected for Pattern Direction and on the Curve method.

> **Spacing:** (Available if you do not select Equal spacing) Set a value for the distance between
> pattern instances along the curve. The distance between the curve and the Features to Pattern
> is measured normal to the curve.

Curve method: Defines the direction of the pattern by transforming how you use the curve selected
for Pattern Direction. Select one of the following:

> * **Transform curve**. The delta X and delta Y distances from the origin of the
> selected curve to the seed feature are maintained for each instance.

> * **Offset curve**: The normal distance from the origin of the selected curve to the seed feature
> is maintained for each instance.

Alignment method: Select one of the following:

> * **Tangent to curve**: Aligns each instance tangent to the curve selected for Pattern direction

> * **Align to seed**: Aligns each instance to match the original alignment of the seed feature of
> **Curve method** and **Alignment method** selections.

> * **Face normal:** (For 3D curves only) Select the face on which the 3D curve lies to create the
> curve driven pattern.

Curve Driven Pattern and Hole Wizard
Universal Bracket

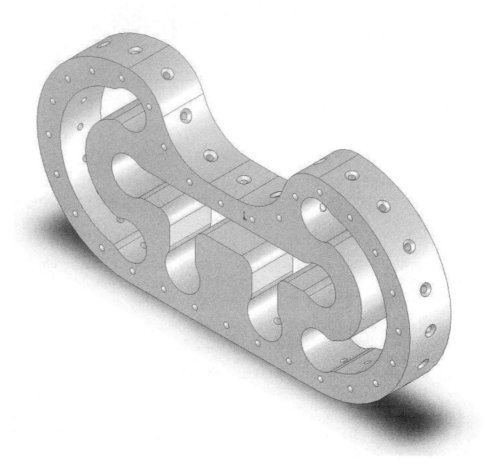

Dimensioning Standards: **ANSI**	
Units: **INCHES** – 3 Decimals	

Tools Needed:

 Insert Sketch   Convert Entities   Offset Entities

 Boss Base Extrude   Hole Wizard   Curve Driven Pattern

1. Opening the existing file:

- Go to: The Training CD
              Open a copy of the file named:
              Curve Driven Pattern.sldprt

- **Edit** the **Sketch1.**

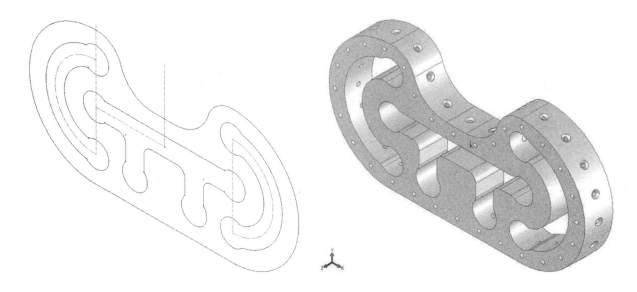

- Make sure the sketch1 is fully define before extruding.

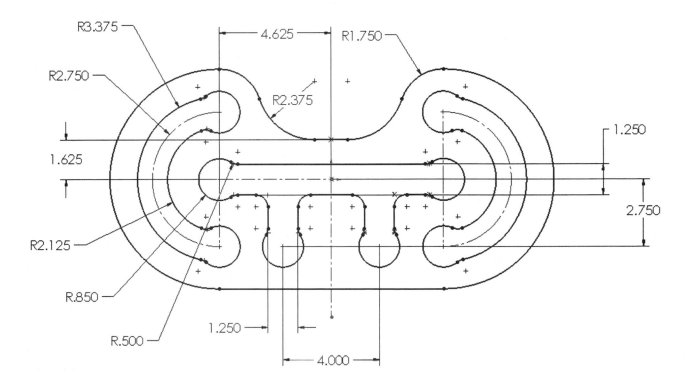

2. Extruding the Base:

- Click 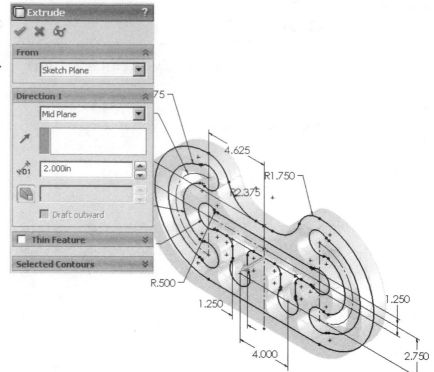 or select:
**Insert / Features /
Boss Base Extrude**.

- Use **Mid Plane**
for Direction1.

- Enter **2.00 in**. for
Depth.

- Click **OK** ✅.

3. Creating the sketch of the 1ˢᵗ hole:

- Select the face as indicated and open a new sketch 🖉 .

- Sketch a Centerline at the
Mid-Point of the two arcs.

- Add a Circle on the Mid-
Point of the centerline.

- Add a **Ø.250 in**. dimension .

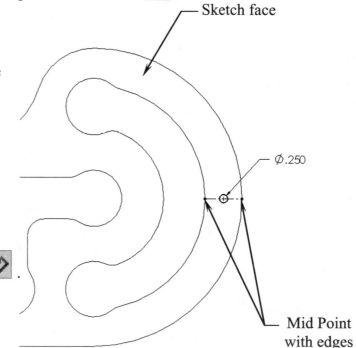

Sketch face

Ø.250

Mid Point
with edges

4. Cutting the hole:

- Click 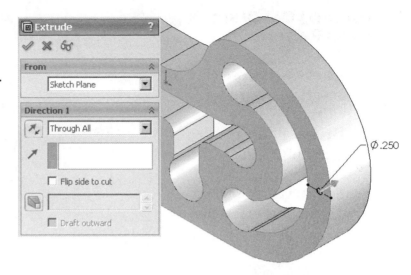 or select: **Insert / Cut / Extrude**.

- Select **Through All** for Direction1.

- Click **OK** ✓.

Ø.250

5. Constructing the Curve-Sketch to drive the Pattern:

- Select the face as noted* and open a new sketch 📝 .

- Select all Outer-Edges of the part (Right mouse click on an edge & Select-Tangency).

- Click ⟭ or select **Tools / Sketch Entities / Offset Entities**.

- Enter **.563 in**. for Offset Distance.

- Click Reverse if necessary to place the new profile on the **INSIDE**.

- **Exit** the sketch mode and change the name of the sketch to **CURVE1**.

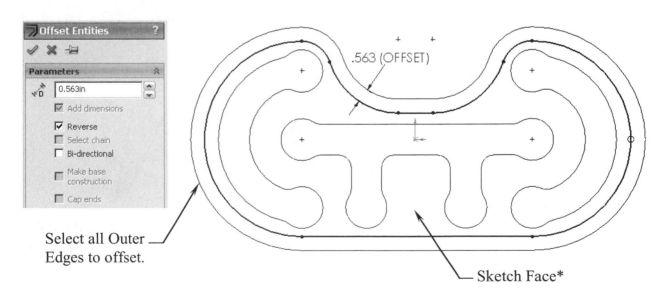

.563 (OFFSET)

Select all Outer Edges to offset.

Sketch Face*

6. Creating the Curve-Driven Pattern:

- Click 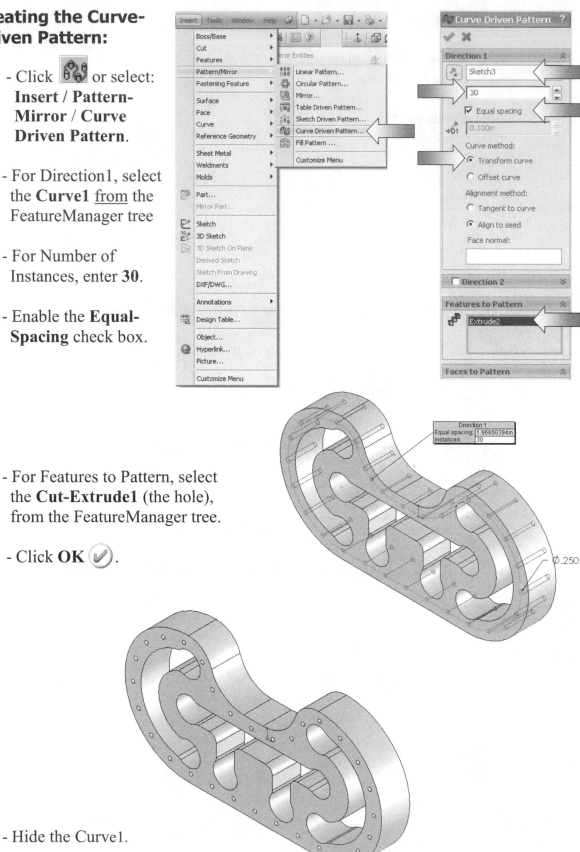 or select: **Insert / Pattern-Mirror / Curve Driven Pattern**.

- For Direction1, select the **Curve1** from the FeatureManager tree

- For Number of Instances, enter **30**.

- Enable the **Equal-Spacing** check box.

- For Features to Pattern, select the **Cut-Extrude1** (the hole), from the FeatureManager tree.

- Click **OK**.

- Hide the Curve1.

7. Constructing the 2ⁿᵈ Curve:

- Select the FRONT plane and open a new sketch.

- Select all Outer-Edges of the

part and click 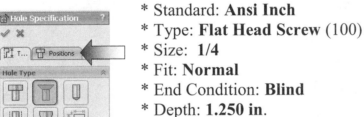 or select: **Tools / Sketch Entities / Convert Entities**.

- **Exit the Sketch** and change the sketch name to: **CURVE2**.

Front Plane

Right click & pick Select Tangency

8. Adding the Hole Wizard:

- Click or select **Insert / Features / Hole Wizard**.

- Select the Counter-Sink button and set the following:

* Standard: **Ansi Inch**
* Type: **Flat Head Screw** (100)
* Size: **1/4**
* Fit: **Normal**
* End Condition: **Blind**
* Depth: **1.250 in**.

- Select the **Position** tab (arrow) and click the **3D Sketch** button [3D Sketch]
  This option allows the holes to be placed on non-planar surfaces as well.

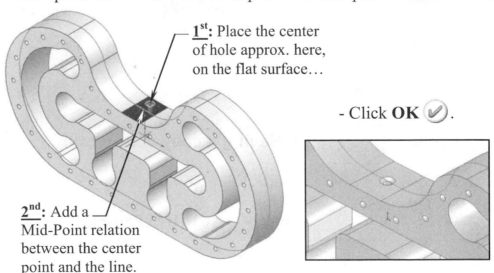

1ˢᵗ: Place the center of hole approx. here, on the flat surface...

- Click **OK** ✓.

2ⁿᵈ: Add a Mid-Point relation between the center point and the line.

9. Creating the Curve Driven Pattern:

- Click 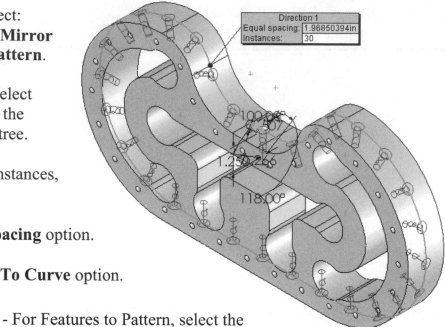 or select:
**Insert / Pattern-Mirror
Curve Driven Pattern**.

- For Direction1, select
the **Curve2** from the
FeatureManager tree.

- For Number of Instances,
enter **30**.

- Enable **Equal Spacing** option.

- Enable **Tangent To Curve** option.

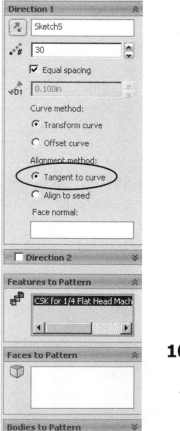

- For Features to Pattern, select the
CSK-Hole from the FeatureManager tree.

- Click **OK** ✅.

10. Saving a copy your work:

- Click **File / Save As**.

- Enter **Curve Driven Pattern** for file name.

- Click **Save**.

CHAPTER 8

Part Configurations

Part Configurations
Machined Block

- This chapter reviews most of the commands that were covered in the previous chapters. Upon successful completion of this lesson, you'll have a better understanding of how and when to:

    * Sketch on planes and planar surfaces.

    * Sketch fillets and model fillets.

    * Dimensions and Geometric Relations.

    * Extruded Cuts and Bosses.

    * Linear Patterns.

    * Using the Hole-Wizard option.

    * Create new Planes.

    * Mirror features.

    * Create new Part Configurations; an option that allows the user to develop and manage families of parts and assemblies.

- Configuration options are available in Part and Assembly environments.

- After the model is completed, it will be used again in a drawing chapter to further discuss the details of creating an Engineering drawing.

Machined Block
Part Configurations

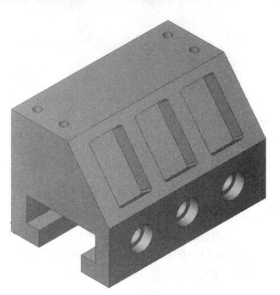

Dimensioning Standards: **ANSI**
Units: **INCHES** – 3 Decimals

Tools Needed:

Insert Sketch	Line	Rectangle
Circle	Sketch Fillet	Dimension
Add Geometric Relations	Extruded Boss/Base	Extruded Cut
Hole Wizard	Fillet	Linear Pattern

1. Sketching the base profile:

- Select the FRONT plane from the FeatureManager tree.

- Click 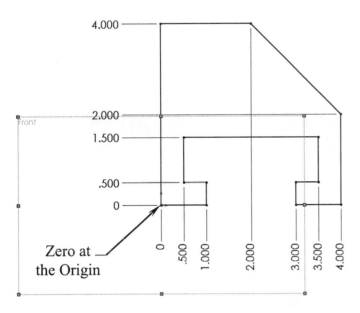 or select **Insert / Sketch**.

- Sketch the profile below using the Line tool .

- Add dimensions as shown.

Zero at the Origin

Ordinate Dimensions

To create Ordinate dimensions:

1. Click the small drop down arrow below the Smart-Dimension command and select either Vertical or Horizontal Ordinate option.

2. First click at a vertex to specify the Zero dimension, then click the next entity to create the next dimension.

3. Repeat step 2 for the other entities / dimensions.

---

2. Extruding the base feature:

- Click or select **Insert / Boss-Base / Extrude**.

- End Condition: **Blind** .

- Extrude Depth: **6.00 in**. .

- Click **OK** .

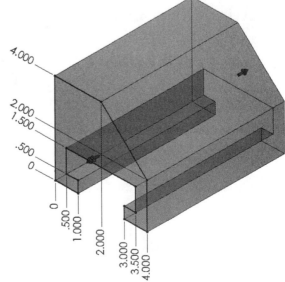

Reverse Direction

3. Creating the pocket profiles:

- Select the face* as indicated below for sketch plane.

- Click 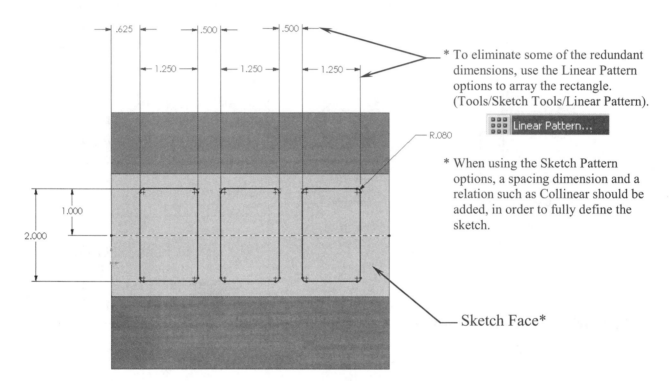 or select **Insert / Sketch**.

- Sketch the profile below using Rectangle and Sketch Fillet tools.

- Add dimensions* or Relations needed to fully define the sketch.

* To eliminate some of the redundant dimensions, use the Linear Pattern options to array the rectangle. (Tools/Sketch Tools/Linear Pattern).

Linear Pattern...

* When using the Sketch Pattern options, a spacing dimension and a relation such as Collinear should be added, in order to fully define the sketch.

R.080

Sketch Face*

.625   .500   .500

1.250   1.250   1.250

1.000

2.000

4. Cutting the pockets:

- Click  or select **Insert / Cut / Extrude**.

- End Condition: **Blind**.

- Extrude Depth: **.500 in**.

- Click **OK** .

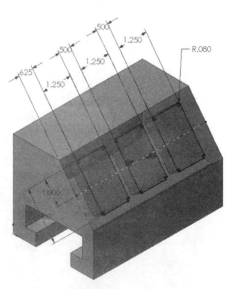

Cut-Extrude1

From
Sketch Plane

Direction 1
Blind

0.500in

Flip side to cut

Draft outward

.500   1.250
.500   1.250
.625   1.250
R.080
1.000

5. Adding a CounterBore from the Hole Wizard:

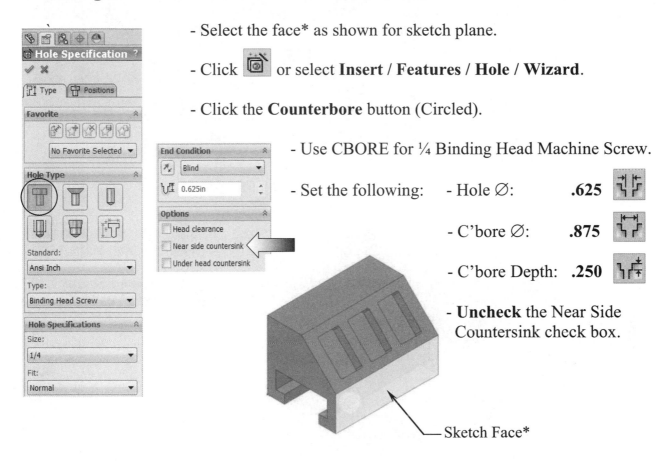

- Select the face* as shown for sketch plane.

- Click [icon] or select **Insert / Features / Hole / Wizard**.

- Click the **Counterbore** button (Circled).

- Use CBORE for ¼ Binding Head Machine Screw.

- Set the following:
  - Hole ∅:   **.625**
  - C'bore ∅:   **.875**
  - C'bore Depth: **.250**

- **Uncheck** the Near Side Countersink check box.

———— Sketch Face*

- Select the **Positions Tab** (arrow). (Note: the 3D Sketch button is only available if none of the faces were selected prior to clicking the HoleWizard).

- Add Dimensions [icon] as shown to position the C'bore.

- Click **OK** [icon].

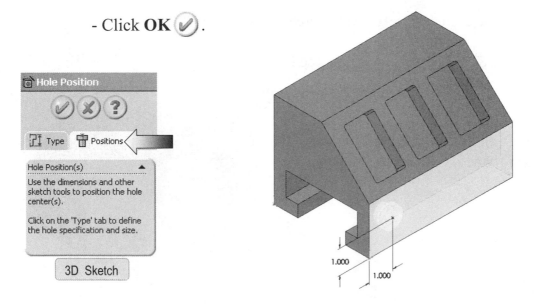

1.000

1.000

6. Patterning the Counterforce:

- Click 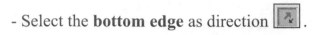 or select **Insert / Pattern Mirror / Linear Pattern**.

- Select the **bottom edge** as direction .

- Enter **2.00 in**. for Spacing .

- Type **3** for Number of Instances .

- Select the C'bore feature as Features to Pattern .

- Click **OK** .

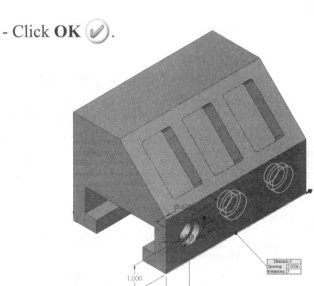

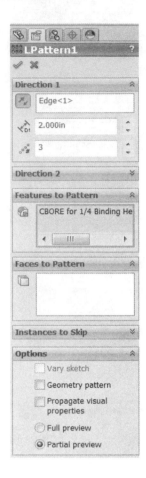

7. Creating the Mirror-Plane:

- Click 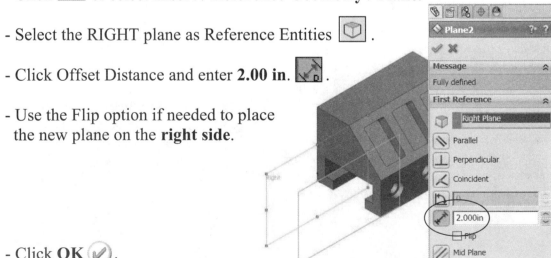 or select **Insert / Reference Geometry / Plane.**

- Select the RIGHT plane as Reference Entities .

- Click Offset Distance and enter **2.00 in**. .

- Use the Flip option if needed to place the new plane on the **right side.**

- Click **OK** .

8. Mirroring the C'bores:

- Click  or select **Mirror** under **Insert / Pattern Mirror menu**.

- Select the new plane (Plane1) as Mirror Face/Plane .

- Choose the C'bore and its Pattern as Features to Pattern .

- Click **OK** .

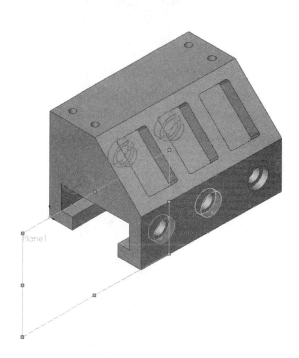

- Rotate the model around to verify the results of the mirror.

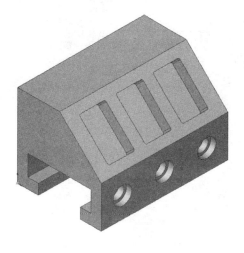

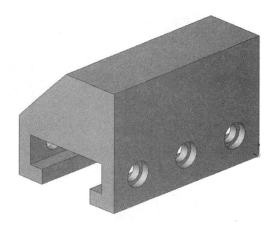

9. Creating the blind holes on the top surface:

- Select the top face* as the new sketch plane.

- Click 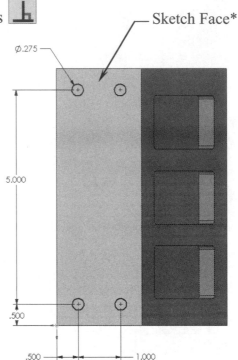 or select **Insert / Sketch**.

- Sketch 4 Circles ⊕ as shown.

- Add Dimensions ⟨⟩ and Relations ⊥ needed to fully define the sketch.

— Sketch Face*

⌀.275

5.000

.500

.500   1.000

10. Cutting the 4 holes:

- Click 🔲 or select **Insert / Cut / Extrude**.

- End Condition: **Blind.**

- Extrude Depth: **1.00 in**.

- Click **OK** ✓.

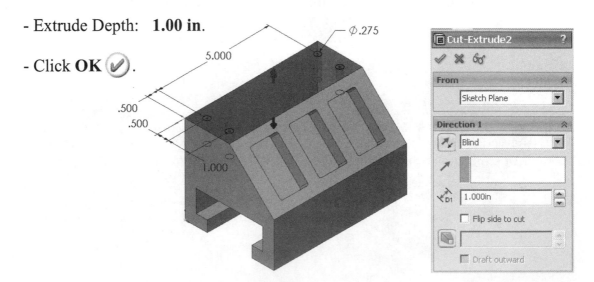

11. Creating a Cutaway section: (in a separate configuration).

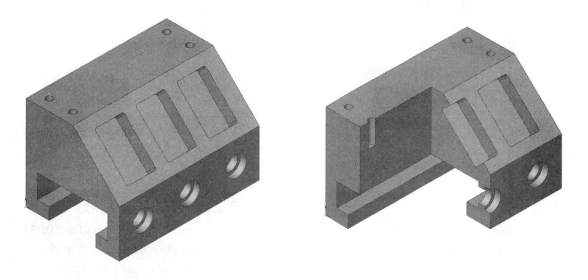

Default Configuration   **New Cutaway Configuration**

- At the top of the FeatureManager tree, select the Configuration tab.

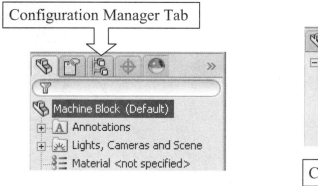

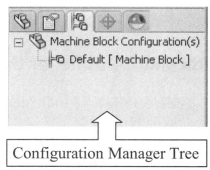

- Right click on the name of the part and select **Add Configuration**.

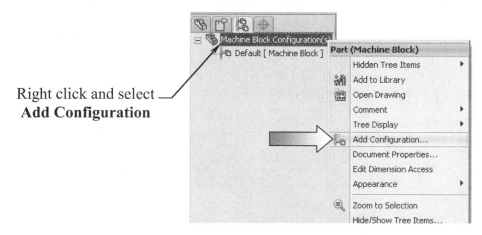

Right click and select ——
Add Configuration

- Under Configuration Name, enter: **Cutaway View.**

- Click **OK** OK

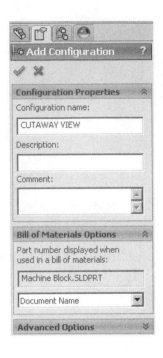

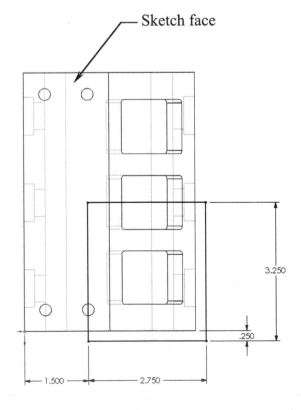

> ### Configurations
>
> The Configuration options allow the SolidWorks user to create multiple variations of a part or assembly and save all changes within the same document.

12. Sketching a profile for the cut:

- Select the face indicated as the new sketch plane.

- Click ✏️ or select **Insert / Sketch**.

- Sketch the profile as shown using the Rectangle ▭ tool.

- Add the dimensions or relations needed to fully define the sketch.

Sketch face

13. Making the section cut:

- Click  or select **Insert / Cut / Extrude**.

- End Condition: **Through All.**

- Click **OK** ✓.

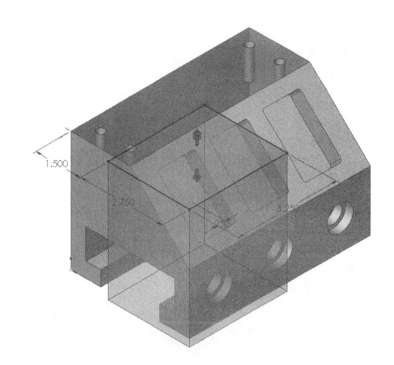

- The Cutaway section view.

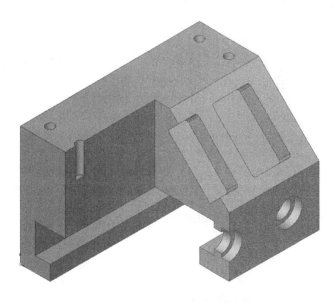

14. Switching between the Configurations:

- Double-click on Default configuration to see the original part.

- Double-click on Cutaway View configuration to see the cut feature.

Double-click to toggle
between Configurations*

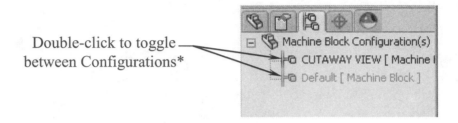

* The Yellow icon next to the name of the configuration means it is active.

* The Grey icon next to the name of the configuration means it is inactive.

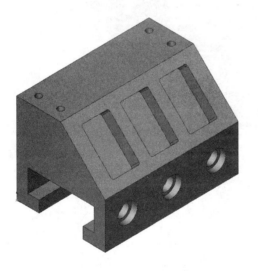

Default Configuration

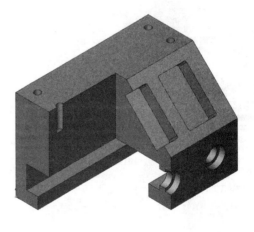
Cutaway Configuration

- The Cutaway configuration will be used again in one of the drawing chapters.

- There is no limit on how many configurations can be created and saved in a part document. If a part has many configurations, it is might be better to use a design table to help manage them.

15. Saving your work as:

- Select **File / Save As / Machined Block / Save**.

Questions for Review

Machined Block

1. The five basic steps to create an extruded feature are:
   - Select a sketch Plane OR a planar surface
   - Activate Sketch Pencil (Insert / Sketch)
   - Sketch the profile
   - Define the profile (Dimensions / Relations)
   - Extrude the profile
     a. True
     b. False

2. When the extrude type is set to Blind, a depth dimension has to be specified as the End-Condition.
     a. True
     b. False

3. More than one closed sketch profiles on the same surface can be extruded at the same time to the same depth.
     a. True
     b. False

4. In the Hole Wizard definition, the Counter bore's parameters such as bore diameter, hole depth, etc. cannot be changed.
     a. True
     b. False

5. Holes created using the Hole Wizard cannot be patterned.
     a. True
     b. False

6. Configurations in a part can be toggled ON / OFF by double clicking on their icons.
     a. True
     b. False

7. Every part document can only have *one* configuration in it.
     a. True
     b. False

7. FALSE
5. FALSE   6. TRUE
3. TRUE   4. FALSE
2. TRUE   1. TRUE

Exercise: Using Vary-Sketch.

1. The Vary Sketch allows the pattern instances to change dimensions as they repeat.
2. Create the part as shown, focusing on the Linear Pattern & Vary-Sketch option.

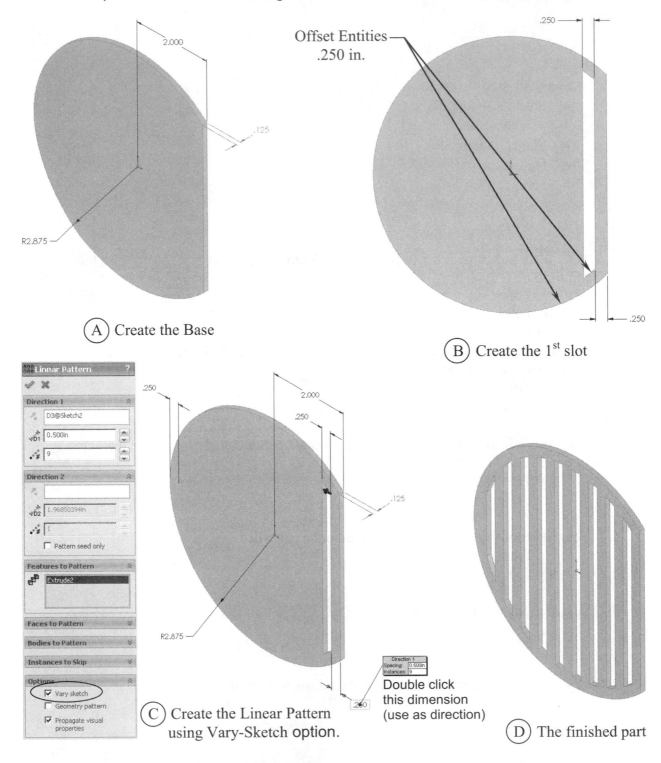

(A) Create the Base

Offset Entities
.250 in.

(B) Create the 1st slot

(C) Create the Linear Pattern using Vary-Sketch option.

Double click
this dimension
(use as direction)

(D) The finished part

3. Save your work as: **Vary Sketch_Exe**.

Using the Wrap feature

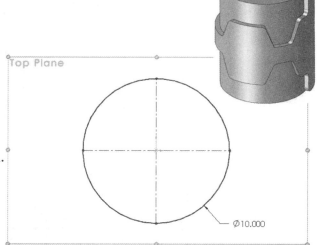

1. Creating the Base Cylinder:

- Select the TOP plane and open a new sketch.

- Sketch a circle starting at the Origin and add a **10.000"** diameter dimension.

- Add vertical and horizontal centerlines as shown.

2. Extruding the Base:

- Extrude the circle using the **Blind** option and a depth of **6.000** in.

- Click **OK**.

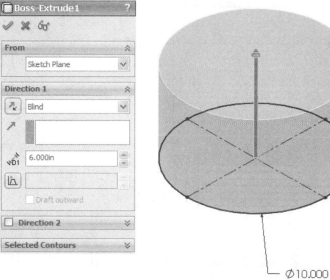

3. Creating a Plane on Surface:

- Show the Sketch1 under the Extrude1 feature.

- Create a plane on the cylindrical face using the references as noted.

- **Click OK.**

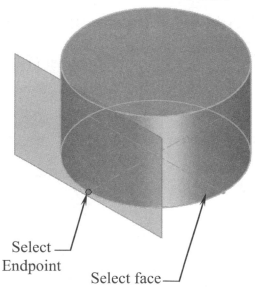

Select Endpoint

Select face

4. Sketching the Wrap sketch:

- Select the new PLANE1 and open a new sketch.

- Sketch the profile shown below and add the ordinate dimensions and the relations as indicated.

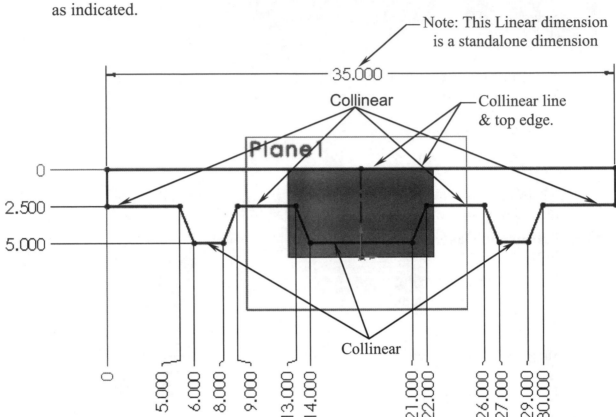

Note: This Linear dimension is a standalone dimension

- **EXIT** the sketch and Show the Feature Dimensions (under Annotations).

5. Adding an Equation: Click **Tools / Equations** and create an Equation as follows:

- The cylinder diameter (10.000") is equals to **pi** times the overall length of the sketch2 (35.000").

- The equation should reads:
  "D1@Sketch2" = pi * "D2@Sketch1".

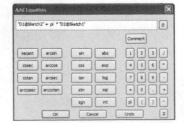

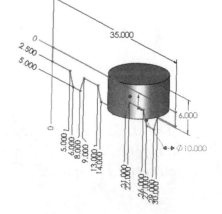

- This equation should correct the overall length of the sketch so that it can wrap perfectly around the cylinder.

- The overall length of the sketch2 is updated to: **31.416"**.

- The equation symbol is placed next to the overall length dimension. This dimension is now driven by the cylinder diameter.

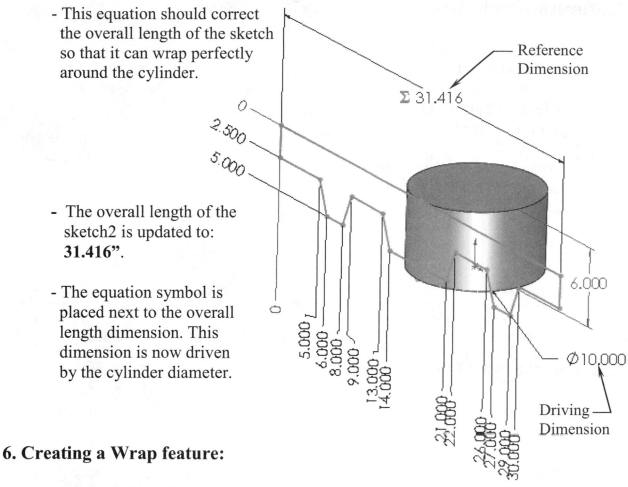

Reference Dimension

Σ 31.416

6.000

Ø10.000

Driving Dimension

6. Creating a Wrap feature:

- Select **Insert / Features / Wrap**.

- Select the Sketch2 or click on one of its lines.

- Select the **Deboss** option to remove material.

- Click the **outer face** of the cylinder.

- Enter **.500** for depth.

- Click **OK**.

- *The sketch2 is wrapped around the cylinder and .500 worth of material is removed.*

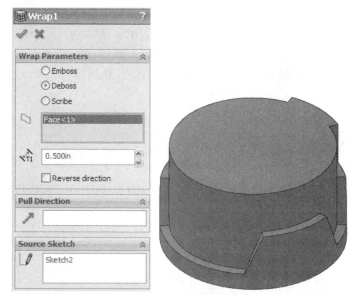

7. Mirroring the body:

- From the Features toolbar, click the **Mirror** button.

- Select the **bottom face** of the part for Mirror Face/Plane.

- Expand the Bodies to Mirror section and click anywhere on the part.

- Click **OK**.

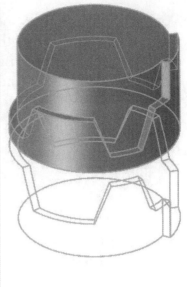

8. Adding the .500" fillets:

- Click the **Fillet** command from the Features toolbar.

- Enter **.500in** for radius value.

- Select the Edges that were created by the wrap feature.

- Click **OK**.

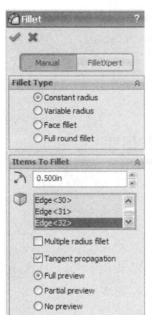

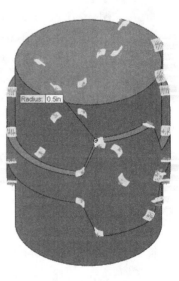

9. Saving your work:

- Save the part as **Wrap Feature** in your folder.

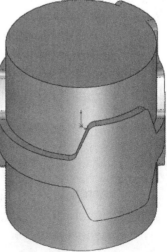

CHAPTER 8 cont.

Repair Part Errors

Understanding and Repairing Part Errors

When an error occurs, SolidWorks will try and solve it based on the settings below:

To pre-set the rebuild action:

A. Click **Options** (Standard toolbar) or **Tools**, **Options**.

B. Select **Stop**, **Continue**, or **Prompt** for **When rebuild error occurs**, then click **OK**. With **Stop** or **Prompt**, the rebuild action stops for each error so you can fix feature failures one at a time.

Error Symbols and Description

Indicates an error with the model. This icon appears on the document name at the top of the FeatureManager design tree, and on the feature that contains the error. The text of the part or feature is in red.

Indicates an error with a feature. This icon appears on the feature name in the FeatureManager design tree. The text of the feature is in red.

Indicates a warning underneath the node indicated. This icon appears on the document name at the top of the Feature-Manager design tree and on the parent feature in the FeatureManager design tree whose child feature issued the error. The text of the feature is in Olive Green.

Indicates a warning with a **feature** or **sketch**. This icon appears on the specific feature in the FeatureManager design tree that issued the warning. The text of the feature or sketch is in Olive Green.

1. Opening a part document:

- Insert the Training CD, browse to the Repair Errors folder, and open the part named: **Repair Errors**.

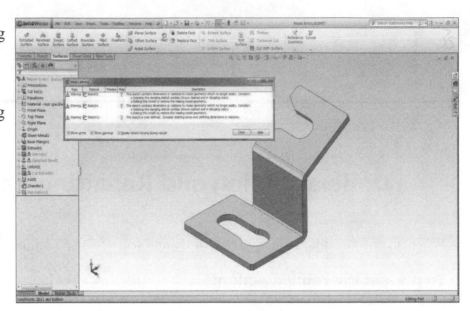

- When opening a document that contains errors, the What's Wrong dialog box will appear and display where the errors are located and suggest some solutions in solving them.

- **Expand** each feature on the FeatureManager tree and hover the pointer over the **Sketch3**.

- An explanation about the error or the warning is displayed in the tooltip. This is the same as right clicking on the error and selecting What's Wrong.

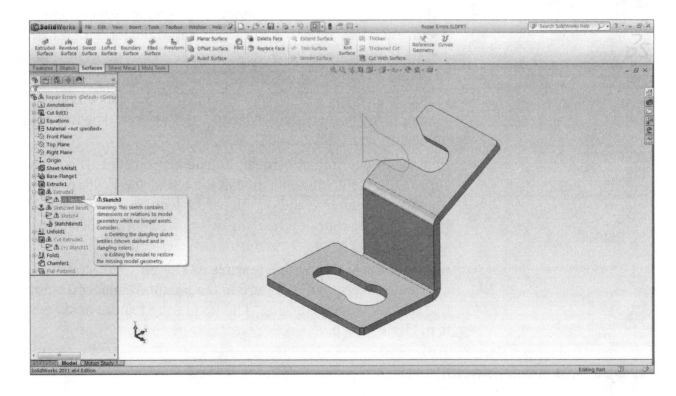

- Another way to see the explanation about the error is to right click on the error and select: What's Wrong.

- The What's Wrong dialog box pops up displaying the same explanation about the selected error. Enable the **Show Warnings** checkbox (arrow) to see the warnings after each rebuild.

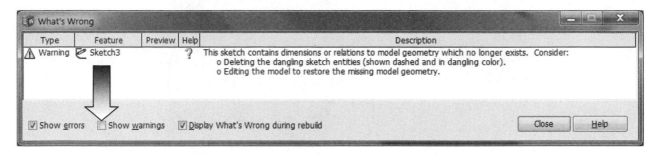

- From the Sketch toolbar click the **Display / Delete-Relations** button.

- The relations or dimensions that contain errors will appeared in different colors, Olive Green in this case.

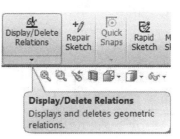

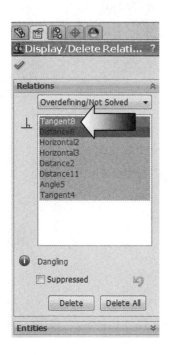

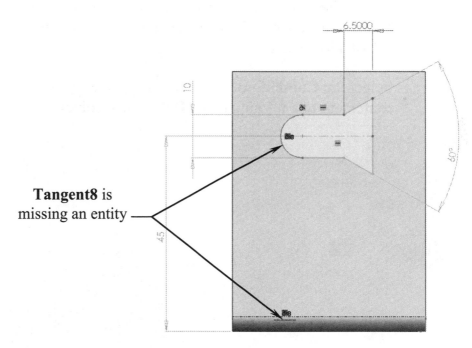

Tangent8 is missing an entity

- **Select** the relation **Tangent8** from the relation dialog box. An arc and the missing entity are highlighted. The missing entity appears in **Red** along with an **Olive Green** tangent symbol above.

- **Delete** the **Tangent8** relation.

- A message on the bottom right of the screen appears, indicating that: **The sketch can now find a valid solution**.

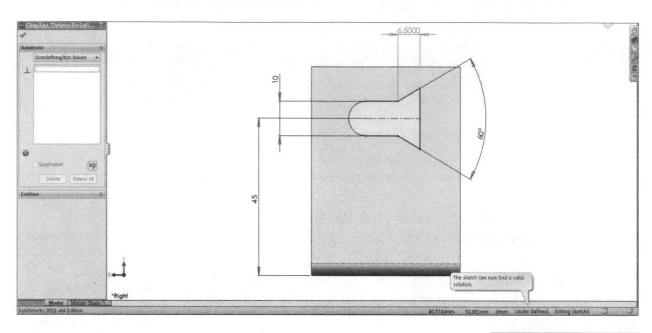

- To see the status for the rest of the relations and dimensions, change from **Over Defining / Not Solved** to **All In This Sketch**.

- Select the **Coincident3**. An endpoint of the line is coincident to a missing edge. **Delete** this Coincident3.

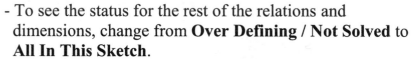

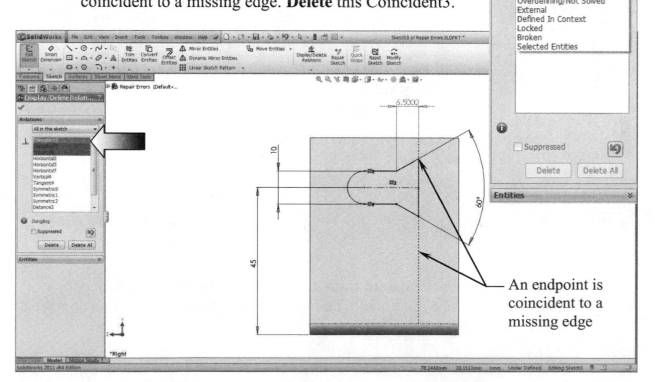

An endpoint is coincident to a missing edge

- **Delete** also the **Coincident5**. It's missing the same edge as the previous relation.

- The dimension **6.500** is dangling. It was also measured to a missing entity, **delete it**.

- **Add** 3 new dimensions as indicated to fully define this sketch. **Exit** the sketch when completed.

Delete this
Dangling dimension —

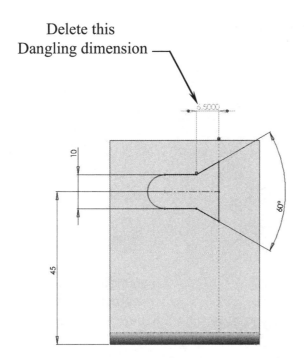

Add 3 new —
dimensions

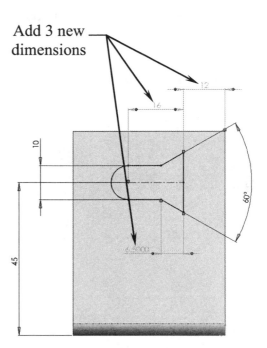

- After exiting the sketch, SolidWorks continues to report other errors still remained in the part. The **Sketch4** and **Sketch11** still need to be repaired.

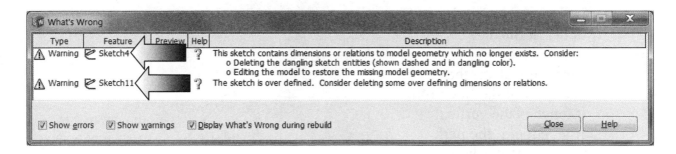

- **Close** the What's Wrong dialog box.

2. Repairing the 2nd error:

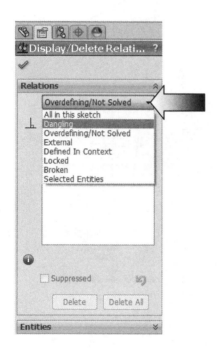

- Right click the **Sketch4** (under the Sketched Bend1 feature) and select **Edit Sketch**.

- Click the **Display / Delete Relations** button once again.

- Change the display relations option to **Dangling** (arrow).

- The **Coincident1** is dangled and has the Olive Green color. **Delete it**.

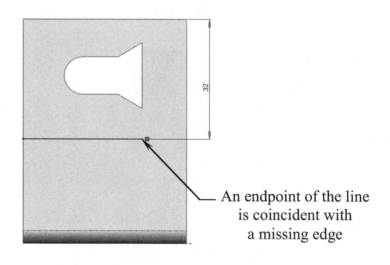

An endpoint of the line is coincident with a missing edge

- The endpoint of the line turns to Blue color. This indicates the sketch is under defined.

- **Drag and drop** the endpoint of the line until it touches the vertical right edge of the part. A coincident relation should be created automatically.

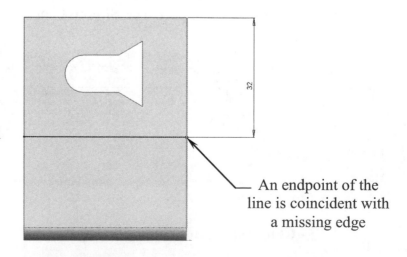

An endpoint of the line is coincident with a missing edge

- **Exit** the sketch or press **Control + Q**.

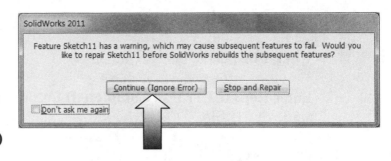

- SolidWorks continues to report the last error in the model. Click the **Continue (Ignore Error)** button to continue.

3. Repairing the 3rd error:

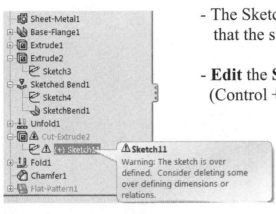

- The Sketch11 has a plus sign next to its name, this indicates that the sketch is Over Defined.

- **Edit** the **Sketch11**. Change to the Top orientation (Control + 5).

     - Click the **Display / Delete Relations** button.

- Set the display relations option to: **Over Defining / Not Solved**.

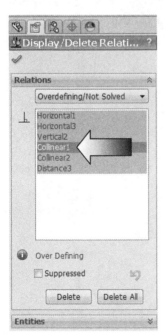

- Select the **Collinear1** from the list. This relation shows a **Magenta** color next to its Collinear symbol.

     - Delete the **Collinear1** from the list.

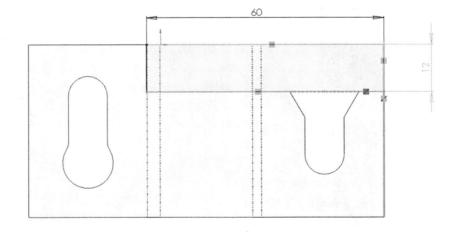

- This last step should bring the sketch back to its Fully Define status.

- **Exit** the Sketch or press **Control + Q**.

4. Saving your work:

- Click **File / Save As**.

- Enter **Repair Errors (Completed)** for the name of the file.

- Click **Save**.

- All errors have been repaired. The Feature-Manager tree is now free of errors.

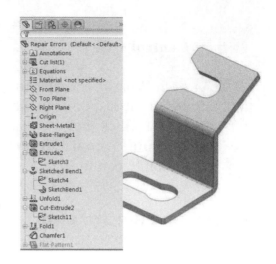

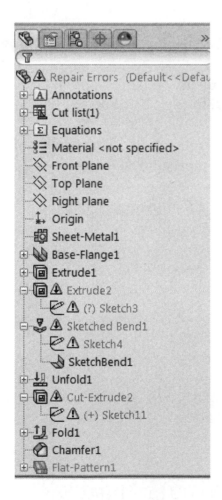

CHAPTER 9

Modeling Threads

Modeling Threads (external)
Threaded Insert

- Most of the time threads are not modeled in the part, instead they are represented with dashed lines and callouts in the drawings. But for non-standard threads they should be modeled in the part for use in some applications such as Stereo Lithography, Finite Element Analysis, etc.

- Two sketches are involved in making the threads:

    * A sweep path (a helix that controls the pitch, revolutions, starting angle, and left or right hand threads).

    * A sweep profile (shape and size of the threads).

- The sweep profile should be related to the sweep path with a **pierce** relation, which will move the sketch profile to the end of the path.

- The profile is swept along the path with the command swept cut and the interfered material is removed as the result of the cut.

- In some cases, the sweep boss command is used to add material to the sweep path when making the external threads.

- This chapter and its exercises will guide you through some special techniques on how internal and external threads can be modeled in SolidWorks.

Modeling Threads – External
Threaded Insert

| Dimensioning Standards: **ANSI** |
| Units: **INCHES** – 3 Decimals |

Tools Needed:

	Insert Sketch		Line		Convert Entities
	Dimension		Add Geometric Relations		Helix/Spiral
	Extruded Base / Revolve		Cut Sweep		Chamfer

1. Sketching the base profile:

- Select the FRONT plane from the FeatureManager Tree.

- Click Sketch 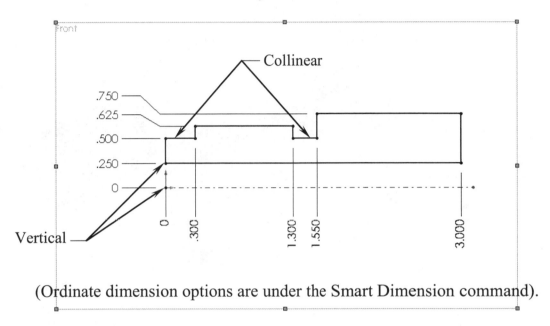 or select: **Insert / Sketch**.

- Sketch the profile as shown below using the Line tool .

- Add dimensions to fully define the sketch.

(Ordinate dimension options are under the Smart Dimension command).

2. Revolving the base feature:

- Click Revolve or select **Insert / Base / Revolve**.

- Revolve Direction: **Blind**.

- Revolve Angle: **360°**

- Click **OK** .

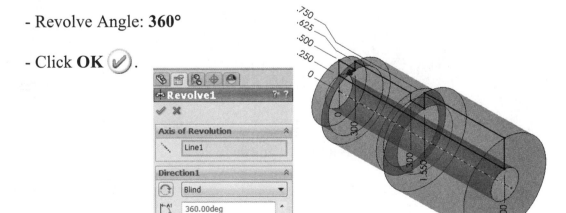

3. Creating the Sweep path:

- Select the face indicated as sketch face.

- Click Sketch 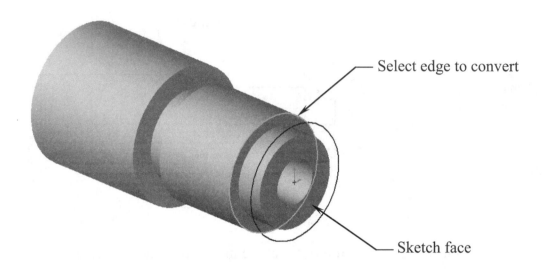 or select: **Insert / Sketch**.

- Select the circular edge as indicated.

- Click **Convert Entities** , the select edge is converted into a circle and brought onto the front face at the same time.

Select edge to convert

Sketch face

4. Creating the Helix:

- Click or select **Insert / Curve / Helix Spiral**.

- Defined by: **Pitch and Revolution.**

      * Pitch: **.125 in**.

      * Revolution: **11.00**

      * Start Angle: **0.00°**

      * Reverse direction: **Enabled.**

- Click **OK** .

- The resulting Helix (sweep path).

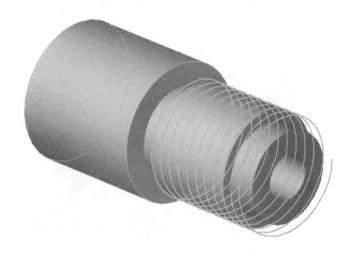

5. Sketching the Sweep profile:

- Select the TOP plane from the FeatureManager Tree.

- Click 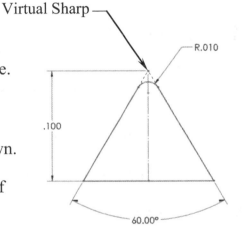 or **Insert / Sketch**.

- Sketch a Triangle and dimension as shown.

- Add a Pierce relation between the upper endpoint of the centerline and the Helix.

Virtual Sharp

R.010

.100

60.00°

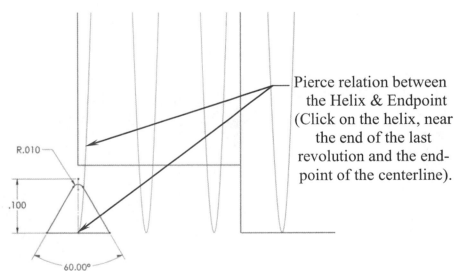

Pierce relation between the Helix & Endpoint (Click on the helix, near the end of the last revolution and the endpoint of the centerline).

R.010

.100

60.00°

- The sketch should be fully defined at this point.

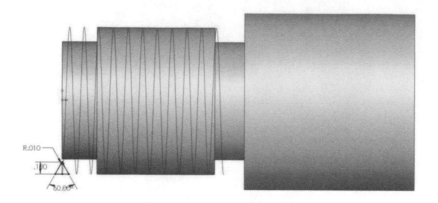

- **Exit** the Sketch or click  .

6. Sweeping the profile along the path.

- Click 🗐 or Select **Insert / Cut / Sweep.**

- Select the triangular profile as sweep profile 🗀 .

- Select the helix as sweep path 🗀 .

- Click **OK** ✅.

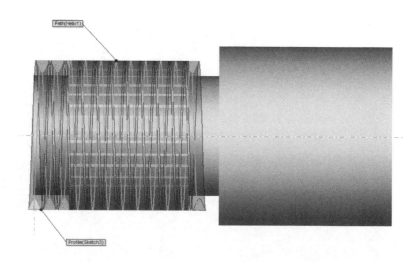

- The 1st half of the threads, clockwise direction (right hand).

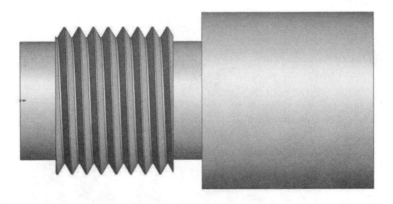

7. Using the Mirror Bodies option:

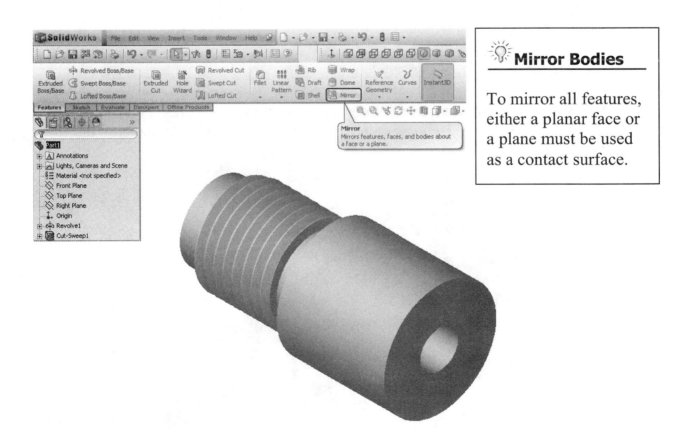

Mirror Bodies

To mirror all features, either a planar face or a plane must be used as a contact surface.

- Select Mirror from **Insert / Pattern Mirror**.

- Select the mirror face as indicated.

- Expand the Bodies To Mirror Option and in the graphics area, click on the body of the part as shown.

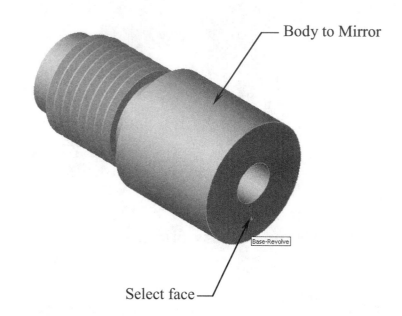

Body to Mirror

Select face

Base-Revolve

- Click **OK** ⊘.

- The "2 halves" are jointed as one solid. Additional features can be added to either half, but changes to the mirrored half cannot be passed onto the original.

- The 2nd half of the threads, counterclockwise direction (left hand).

8. Adding chamfers:

- Click Chamfer 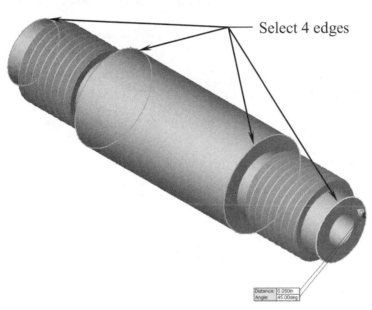 or **Insert / Features / Chamfers**.

- Select the **4 edges** as indicated.

- Enter **.050 in**. for Depth 🔲.

- Enter **45°** for Angle 🔲 .

- Click **OK** ✅.

Select 4 edges

9. Saving the finished part.

- Save your work as Threaded Insert.

- Select **File / Save as / Threaded Insert / Save**.

Questions for Review

Modeling Threads

1. It is proper to select the sketch plane first before activating the sketch pencil.
   a. True
   b. False

2. To create a sweep feature, the sweep path should be created first and the sweep profile created later.
   a. True
   b. False

3. The Helix / Spiral command can be selected from Insert / Curve / Helix-Spiral menus.
   a. True
   b. False

4. Taper Helix option is not supported in SolidWorks.
   a. True
   b. False

5. A Helix can be defined by pitch and revolution.
   a. True
   b. False

6. The Sweep profile should not have any relations with the sweep path.
   a. True
   b. False

7. Either a planar surface or a plane can be used to perform a Mirror-Bodies (All) feature.
   a. True
   b. False

8. Several model edges can be chamfered at the same time if their values are the same.
   a. True
   b. False

9. The mirrored half is a dependent feature; it cannot be used to change the original half.
   a. True
   b. False

9. TRUE
7. TRUE   8. TRUE
5. TRUE   6. FALSE
3. TRUE   4. FALSE
1. TRUE   2. TRUE

Exercise: Modeling Threads (Internal)

1. Dimensions provided are for solid modeling practice purposes.
2. Dimensions are in Inches, 3 decimal places.
3. Use the instructions on the following pages, if needed.

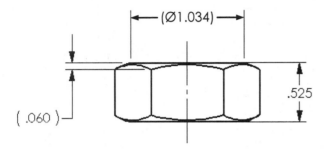

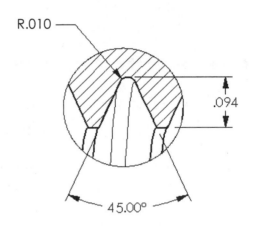

DETAIL B

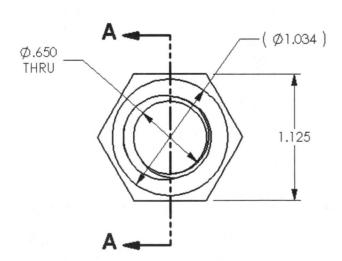

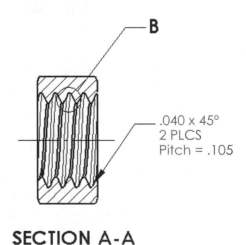

SECTION A-A

1. Starting with the base sketch:

- Select the **Front** plane and open a new sketch.

- Sketch a 6 sided Polygon and add the dimensions and relation shown.

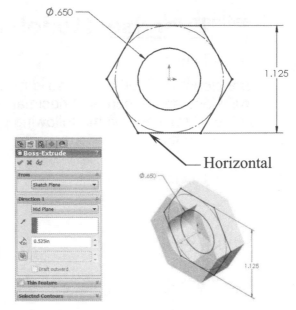

Horizontal

2. Extruding the base:

- Extrude the sketch using **Mid Plane** and **.525"** thick.

3. Removing the Sharp edges:

- Select the **Top** plane and open another sketch.

- Sketch the profile shown.

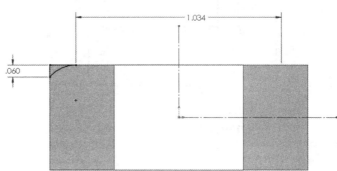

Tangent

- Add the dimensions and the Tangent relation as noted.

- Mirror the profile using the horizontal centerline.

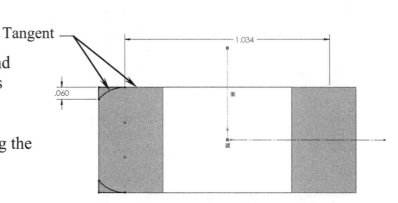

- Revolve Cut with **Blind** and **360°** angle.

- Click **OK**.

4. Creating a new plane:

- Select the front face of the part and click **Insert / Reference Geometry / Plane**.

- The **Offset Distance** should be selected automatically; enter **.105"** for distance.

- Click **OK**.

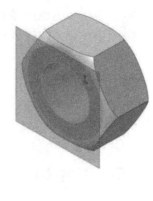

5. Creating the sweep path:

Convert this edge

- Select the new plane and open a new sketch.

- Select the circular edge as indicated and click: **Convert Entities**.

- The selected edge turns into a sketch circle.

- Click the **Helix** command or select: **Insert / Curve / Helix-Spiral**.

- Enter the following:
  * Pitch = **.105"**
  * Reverse Direction: **Enabled**.
  * Revolutions: **7**
  * Start Angle: **0.00 deg**.
  * **Clockwise**

- Click **OK**.

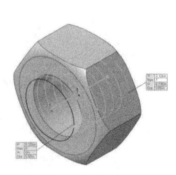

6. Creating the sweep profile:

- Select the Top plane and open a new sketch.

- Sketch the profile using Dynamic Mirror.

- Add the dimensions as shown to fully define the sketch.

- Add a **.010"** sketch fillet to the tip.

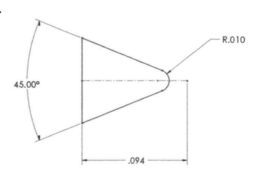

- Add a **Pierce** relation between the midpoint of the vertical line and the 1st revolution of the helix.

- **Exit** the sketch.

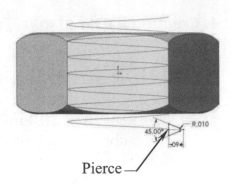

Pierce ⎯

7. Creating the swept cut:

- Change to the **Features** toolbar.

- Click **Swept Cut**.

- Select the triangular sketch for Profile.

- Select the Helix for Path.

- The Profile is Swept along the Path.

- Click **OK**.

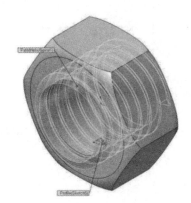

8. Verifying the cut:

- Select the **Right** plane and click **Section View**.

- Verify the cut. Look at the section view from different orientations.

- Change the dimension **.094"** in the profile sketch to **.100"**. Click Rebuild to execute the change.

9. Saving your work:

- Save your work as **Nut – Internal Threads**.

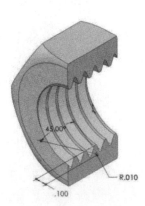

<u>Exercise:</u> Internal & External Thread

A. Internal Threads:

1. Creating the Revolve Sketch:

- Select the FRONT plane and open a new sketch plane as shown.

- Sketch the profile and add relations & dimensions as shown.

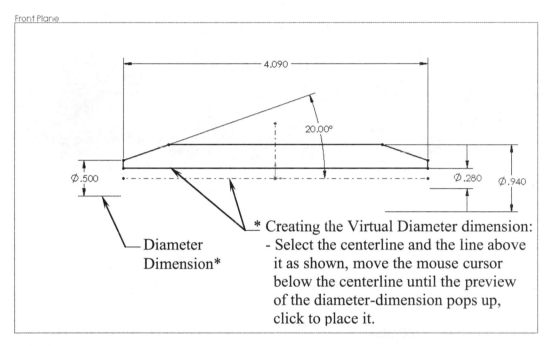

Diameter Dimension*

* Creating the Virtual Diameter dimension:
- Select the centerline and the line above it as shown, move the mouse cursor below the centerline until the preview of the diameter-dimension pops up, click to place it.

2. Revolving the Body:

- Revolve the sketch a full 360 deg. and click **OK**.

3. Creating the cutout features:

- From the FRONT plane, sketch the profiles of the cutouts.

- Use MIRROR where applicable. Add Relations & Dimensions to fully define the sketch.

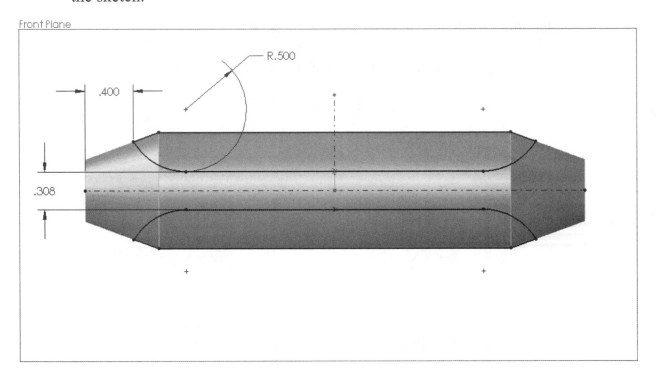

4. Extruding the Cutouts:

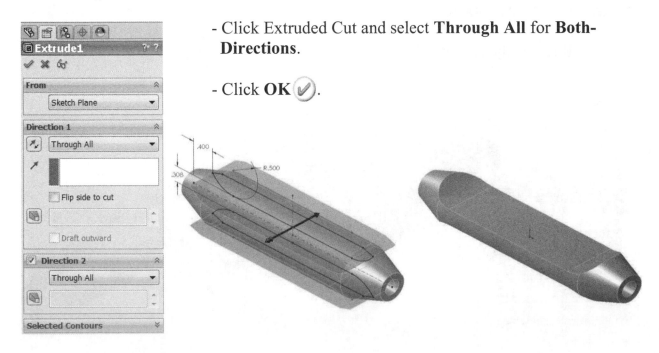

- Click Extruded Cut and select **Through All** for **Both-Directions**.

- Click **OK** ✓.

5. Sketching the Slot Profile:

- From the TOP plane, sketch the profile of the slot (use the Straight Slot options).

- Add Relations & Dimensions to fully define the sketch.

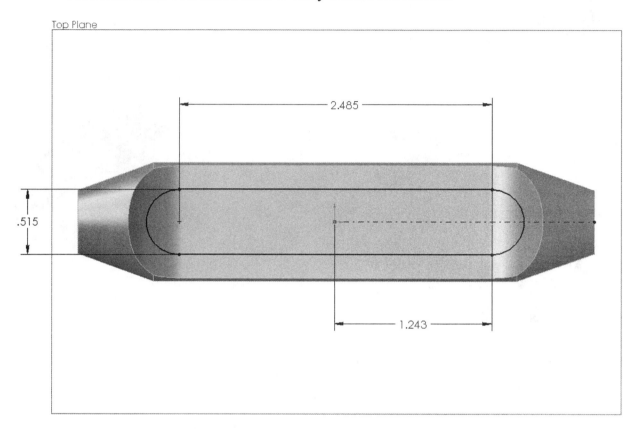

6. Cutting the Slot:

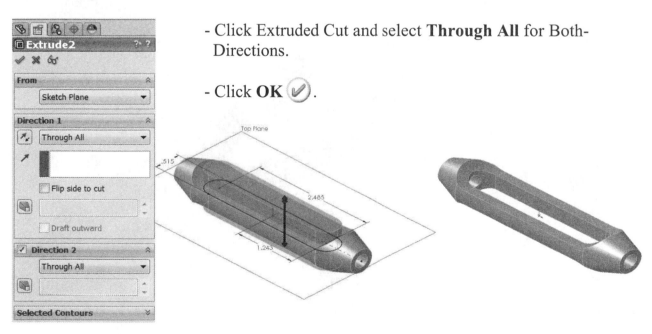

- Click Extruded Cut and select **Through All** for Both-Directions.

- Click **OK**.

7. Adding Chamfers:

- Add a chamfer to both ends of the holes.

- Chamfer Depth = **.050 in**.   - Chamfer Angle = **45 deg**.

- Click **OK** .

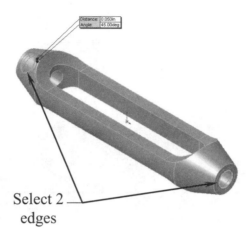

Select 2 edges

8. Adding Fillets:

- Add fillets to the 4 edges as shown.

- Radius = **.250 in**.

- Click **OK** .

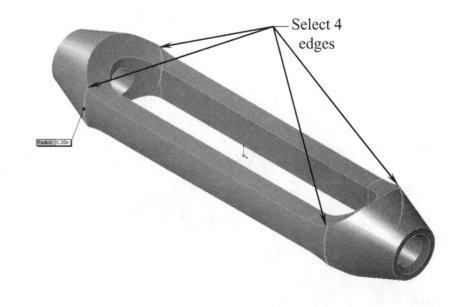

Select 4 edges

9. Filleting all edges:

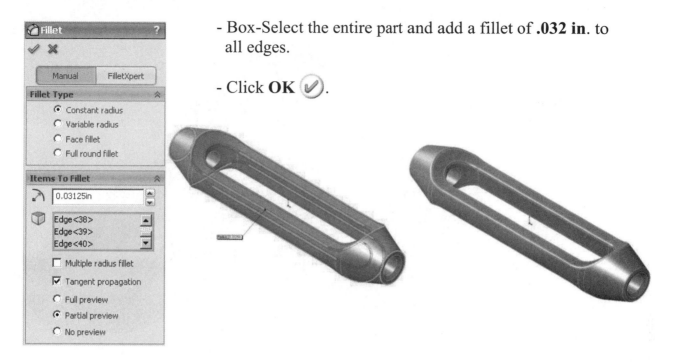

- Box-Select the entire part and add a fillet of **.032 in**. to all edges.

- Click **OK** ✅.

10. Creating an Offset-Distance Plane:

- Click Plane or select **Insert / Reference Geometry / Plane**.

- Click **Offset-Distance** option and enter **2.062 in**.

- Select the RIGHT plane to copy from; place the new plane on the right hand side.

- Click **OK** ✅.

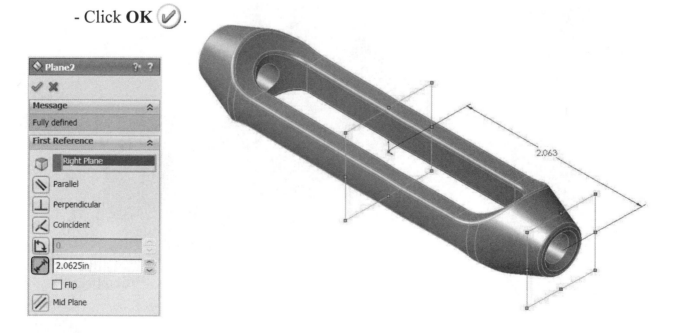

11. Creating the Helix (the sweep path):

- Select the new plane and open a new sketch.

- Convert the Inner Circular Edge into a Circle.

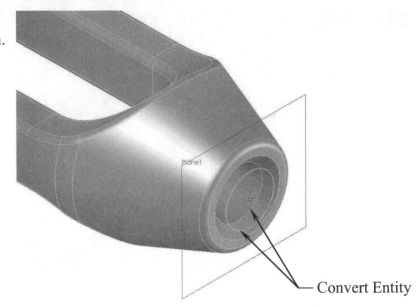

Convert Entity

- Click Helix or select **Insert / Curve / Helix-Spiral**.

- Pitch: **.055 in**.

- Revolutions: **11**

- Start Angle: **0 deg**.

- Clockwise   - Click **OK** .

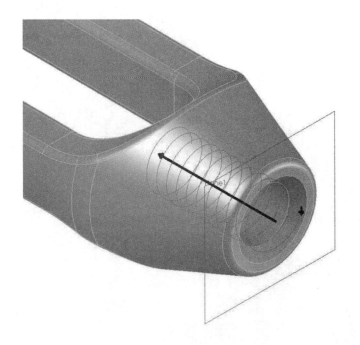

12. Sketching the Thread Profile:

- Select the TOP reference plane and open a new sketch.

- Sketch the thread profile as shown. Add the relation and dimensions needed to define the profile.

- **Exit** the Sketch.

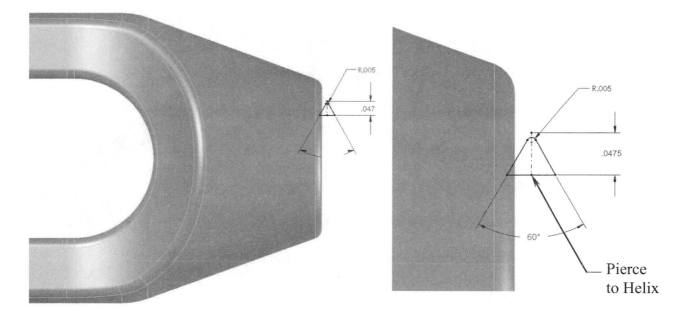

13. Sweeping the Cut:

- Click Cut-Sweep or select **Insert / Cut / Sweep**.

- Select the triangular sketch as Profile and select the helix as Sweep Path.

- Click **OK** ✓.

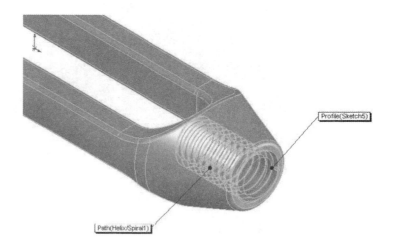

14. Mirroring the Threads:

- Click **Mirror** or select **Insert / Pattern Mirror / Mirror**.

- Select the **RIGHT** plane as the Mirror Plane.

- For Features to Mirror select the **Cut-Sweep1** feature.

- Click **OK** ✓.

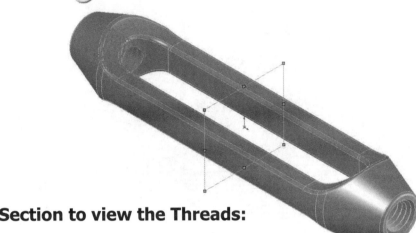

15. Creating the Cross-Section to view the Threads:

- Select the FRONT plane from the FeatureManager tree.

- Click Section View or select **View / Display / Section**.

- Zoom in on the threaded areas and examine the thread details.

- Click Cancel when you are done viewing.

- Save the part as **Internal Threads**.

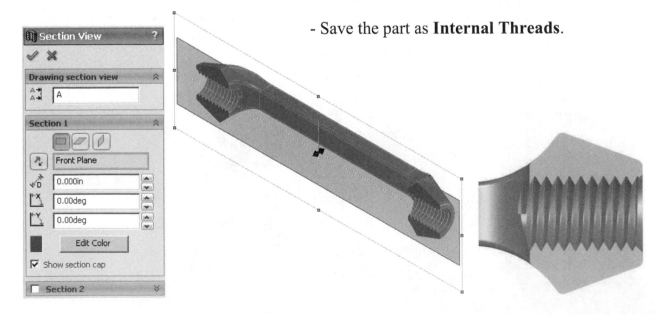

B. External Threads

1. Sketching the Sweep Path:

- Select the FRONT plane and open a new sketch.

- Sketch the profile as shown, add Relations & Dimensions needed to fully define.

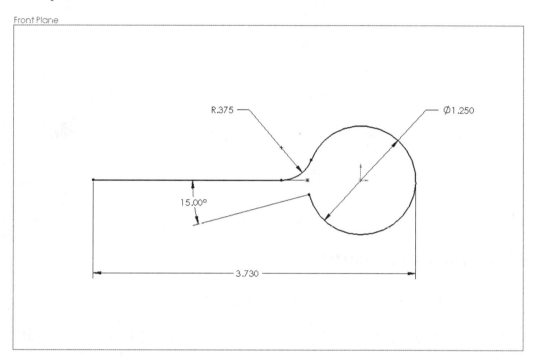

2. Creating a plane Normal-To-Curve:

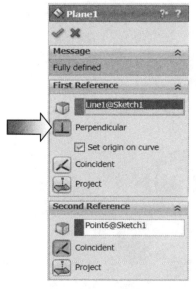

- Click Plane or select **Insert / Reference Geometry/ Plane**.

- Select the Horizontal line and the Endpoint on the left side.

- A new plane is created normal to the line

- Click **OK**.

Select this Line and its Endpoint

3. Sketching the Sweep Profile:

- Select the New plane and open a new sketch.

- Sketch a Circle as shown and add
  a diameter dimension.

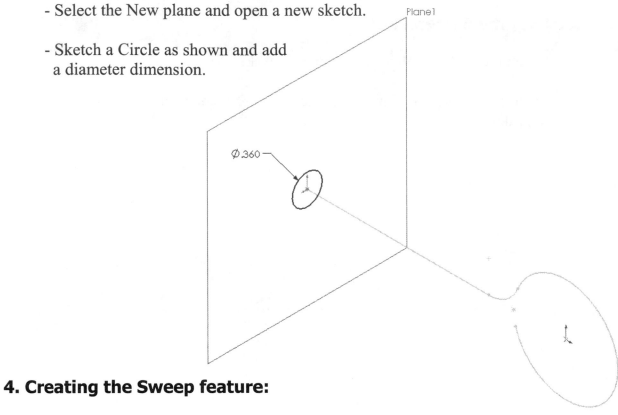

4. Creating the Sweep feature:

- Click Sweep or select **Insert / Features / Sweep**.

- Select the Circle as Sweep Profile and select the Sketch1 as Sweep Path.

- Click **OK** .

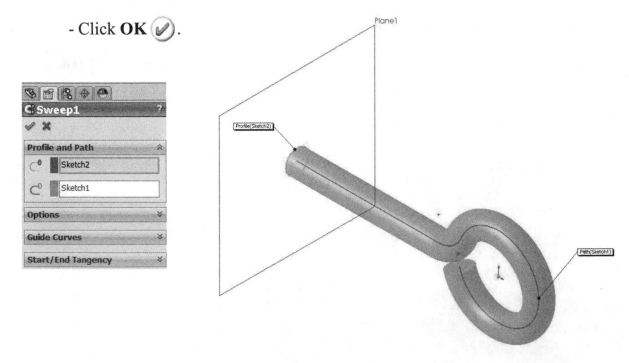

5. Adding Chamfers:

- Click Chamfer or select
  Insert / Features / Chamfer.

- Select the 2 Circular Edges
  at the ends.

- Enter **.050 in**. for Depth.

- Enter **45 deg**. for Angle.

- Click **OK** .

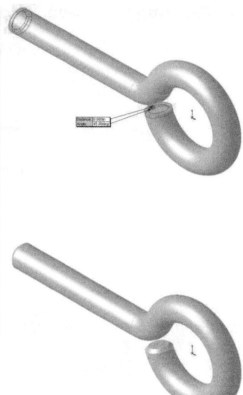

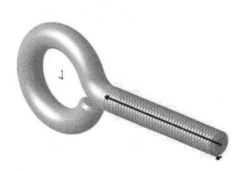

— Sketch face

6. Creating the Helix:

- Select the Face as indicated
  and open a new sketch.

- Select the Circular Edge on
  the end and click Convert or
  select **Tools/Sketch Tools/
  Convert Entities**.

- Click Helix or select **Insert/
  Curve/Helix-Spiral**.

- Enter **.055** in. for Pitch.

- Enter **39** for Revolutions.

- Enter **0 deg**. for Start Angle.

- Click **OK** .

Convert
Entity

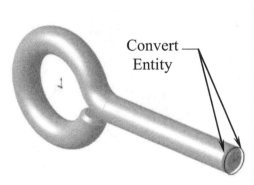

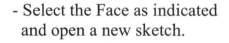

7. Creating the Thread Profile:

- Either copy the previous thread profile or recreate.

- Add a Pierce relation to position the thread profile at the end of the helix.

- Click **OK** ✅.

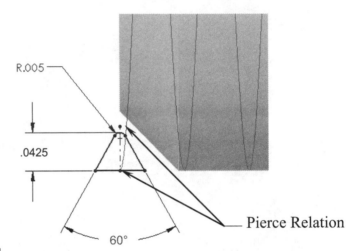

<u>NOTE:</u>
There should be a clearance between the 2 threaded parts so that they can be moved back and forth easily.

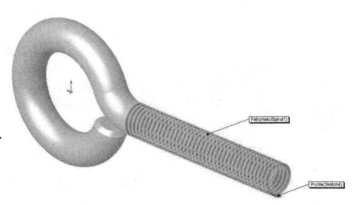

Pierce Relation

8. Sweeping Cut the Threads:

- Click Sweep Cut or select **Insert / Cut / Sweep.**

- Select the triangular sketch as the Sweep Profile.

- Select the Helix as the Sweep path.

- Click **OK** ✅.

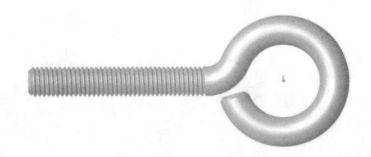

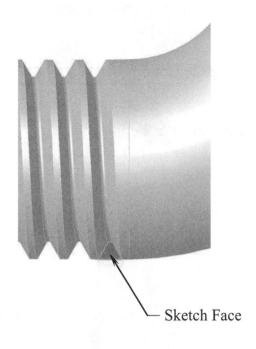

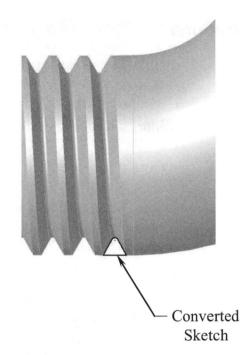

Sketch Face

Converted
Sketch

9. Removing the Undercut:

- Select the Face as noted and open a new sketch.

- **Convert** the selected face into a new triangular sketch.

- Click Extruded-Cut or select **Insert / Cut / Extrude**.

- Select **Through All** for End Condition.

- Click **OK** ✅.

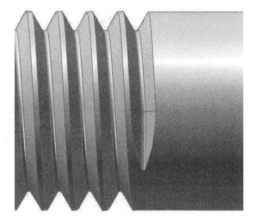

10. Saving your work:

- Save a copy of your work as **External Threads**.

11. Optional:

(This step can also be done after completing the Bottom Up Assembly chapter).

- Start a New Assembly document and assemble the 2 components.

- Create an Assembly Exploded View as shown below.

- Save the assembly as: **TurnBuckle.sldasm**

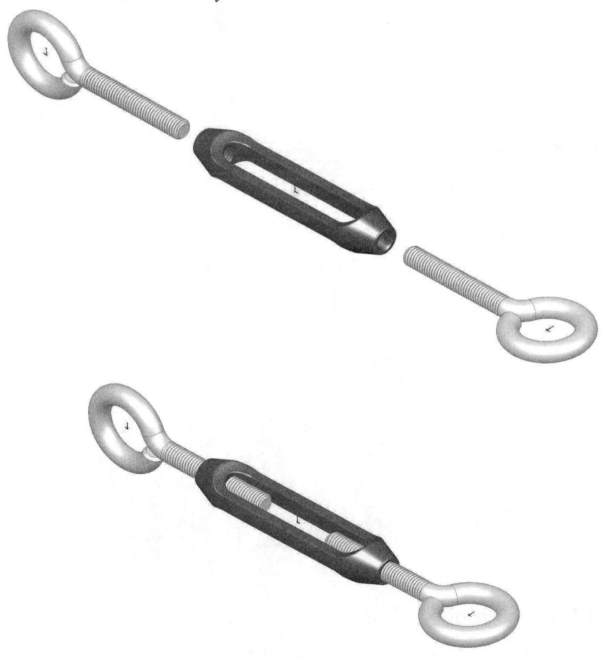

CHAPTER 10

Bottom Up Assembly

Bottom Up Assembly
Ball Joint Assembly

- When your design involves multiple parts, SolidWorks offers 3 different assembly methods to help you work faster and more efficient. The first method is called Bottom-Up-Assembly, the second method is called Layout-Assembly, and the third Top-Down-Assembly.

- We will explore the first two methods in this Part-1 book and the last method is covered in the Part-2, Advanced textbook.

- Individual components inserted into an assembly document that get re-oriented, and mated (constrained) together, is called Bottom Up Assembly.

- The first component inserted into the assembly will be fixed by the system automatically. If it is placed on the Origin, then the Front, Top, and the Right planes of the first component will automatically be aligned with the assembly's planes.

- Only the first part will be fixed by default, all other components are free to move or be re-oriented.

- Each component has a total of 6 degrees of freedom; depending on the mate type, once a mate is assigned to a component one or more of its degrees of freedom are removed, causing the component to move or rotate only in the desired directions.

- All Mates (constraints) are stored in the FeatureManager tree under Mates group. They can be edited, suppressed, or deleted.

Ball Joint Assembly
Bottom-Up Assembly

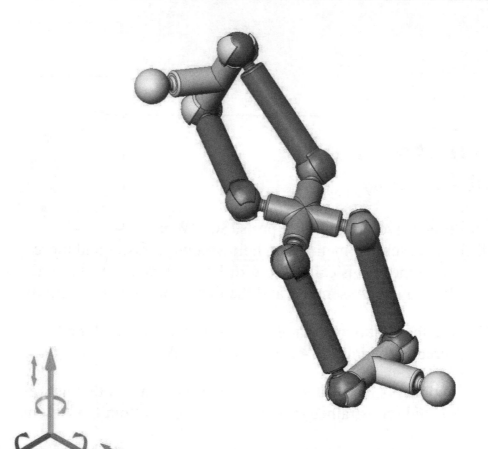

6 Degrees of Freedom

Dimensioning Standards: **ANSI**

Units: **INCHES** – 3 Decimals

Tools Needed:

 Mates

 Move Component

 Rotate Component

 Concentric Mate

 Inference Origins

 Placing New Component

1. Starting a new Assembly template:

- Select **File / New / Assembly / OK**.

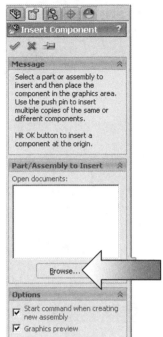

- In the Insert Component dialog, click Browse [Browse...] .

- Select the **Center Ball Joint** document and click **Open**.

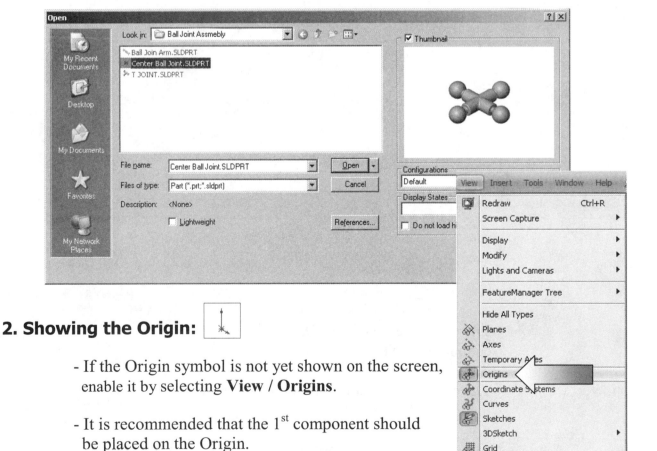

2. Showing the Origin:

- If the Origin symbol is not yet shown on the screen, enable it by selecting **View / Origins**.

- It is recommended that the 1st component should be placed on the Origin.

3. Inserting the 1ˢᵗ component (the Parent) on the Origin:

- Position the mouse cursor on the origin, an Origin-Inference symbol appears to confirm the location of the 1ˢᵗ component.

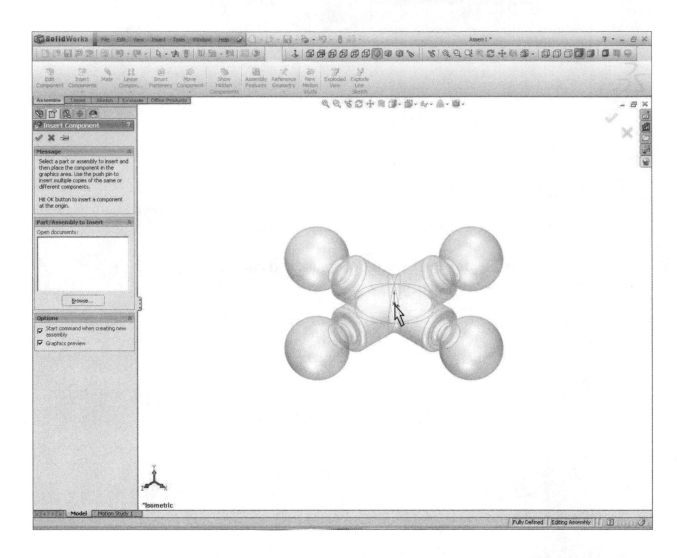

- The symbol 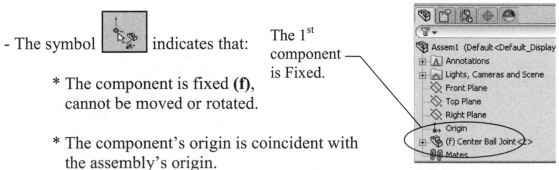 indicates that:

The 1ˢᵗ component is Fixed.

* The component is fixed **(f)**, cannot be moved or rotated.

* The component's origin is coincident with the assembly's origin.

* The planes of the component and the assembly are aligned.

4. Inserting the second component (a child) into the assembly:

- Click 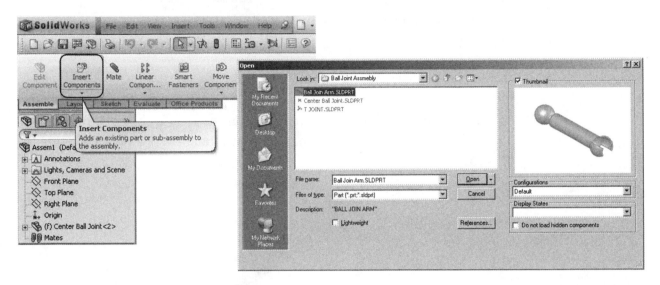 or Select **Insert / Component / Existing Part/Assembly**.

- Click Browse Browse... .

- Select **Ball Joint Arm.sldprt** from the pop-up dialog box and click **Open**.

- The preview graphic of the component is attached to the mouse cursor.

- Click any where to place the part, approximately as shown below.

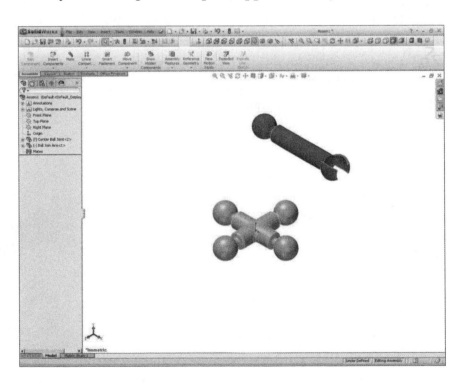

5. Mating the components:

- Click 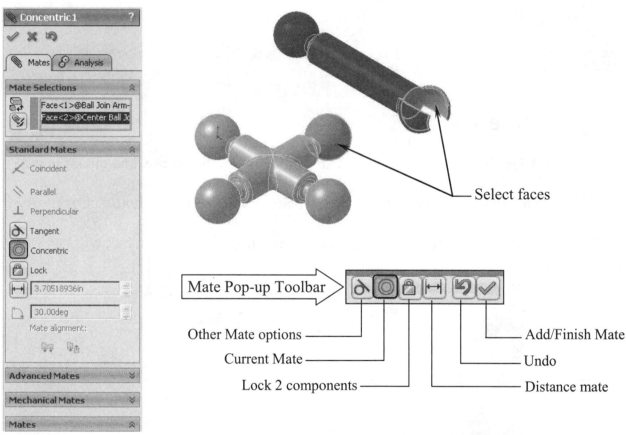 or select **Insert / Mate**.

- Assembly mate options appear on the FeatureManager tree.

- Select the two **(2) faces** as indicated below.

- The **Concentric** mate option is selected automatically and the system displays the preview graphics of the two (2) mated components.

Select faces

Mate Pop-up Toolbar

Other Mate options ——

Current Mate ——

Lock 2 components ——

Add/Finish Mate

Undo

Distance mate

- Review the options on the Mate Pop-up toolbar.

- Click **OK**.

- The two faces are constrained.

- The second component is still free to rotate around the cylindrical surface.

6. Moving the component:

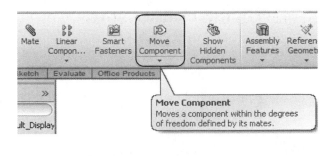

- Click  **Move Component**.

- Click and drag the face as noted.

- Move the component to the approximate shown position.

- Click **OK** ✅.

Drag here ⟶

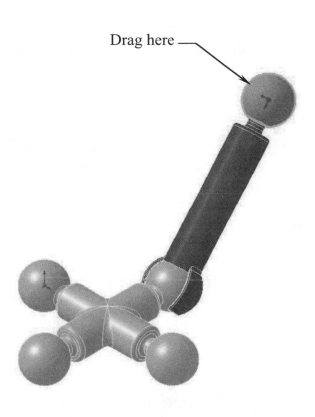

7. Inserting another instance into the assembly:

- Click [Insert Compon...] Select **Insert / Component / Existing Part/ Assembly**.

- Click [Browse...].

(NOTE: Not all assemblies are fully constrained. In an assembly with moving parts, leave at least one degree of freedom open so that the component can still be moved or rotated.

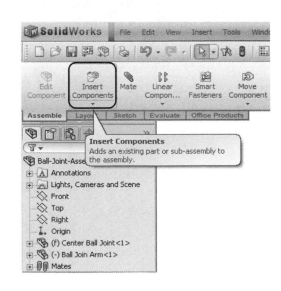

- Select **Ball Joint Arm.sldprt** (same part) and click **Open**.

- Place the part next to the first one as shown.

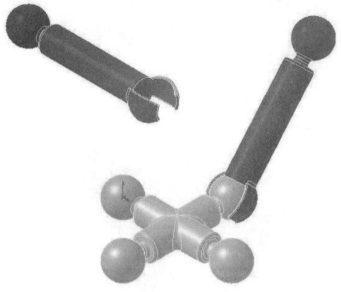

8. Constraining the components:

- Click  or select **Insert / Mate**.

- Select the two **faces** as shown.

- The **Concentric** mate option is selected automatically and the system displays the preview graphics of the two mated components.

- Click **OK** ✓.

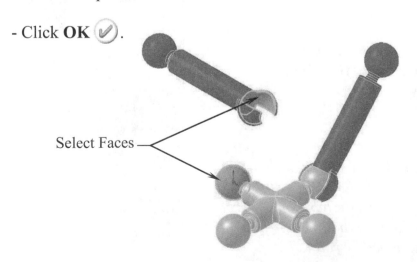

Select Faces

- The two selected faces are mated together with a Concentric mate.

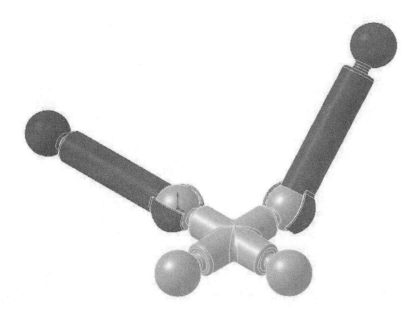

9. Repeating the step 5:

- Insert (or copy) two more instances of the **Ball Joint Arm** and add the mates to assemble them as shown.

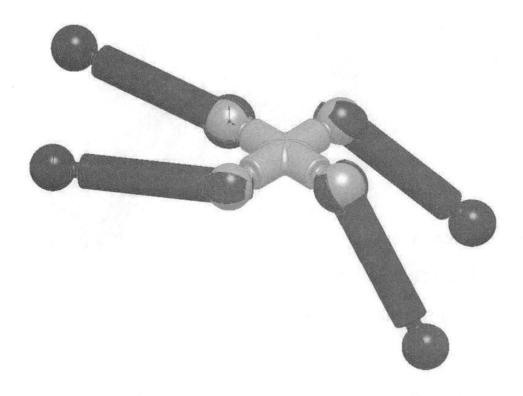

<u>**Optional**</u>:

- Insert the T-Join part (either from the Training CD or from the web link) as pictured below and mate it to the assembly.

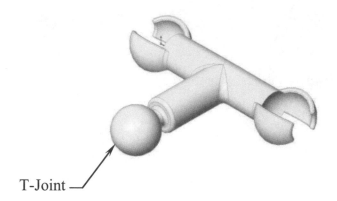

T-Joint

- Check the assembly motion by dragging one of the T-Joints back and forth.

- Each component has only one mate applied, they are still free to move or rotate around their constrained entities.

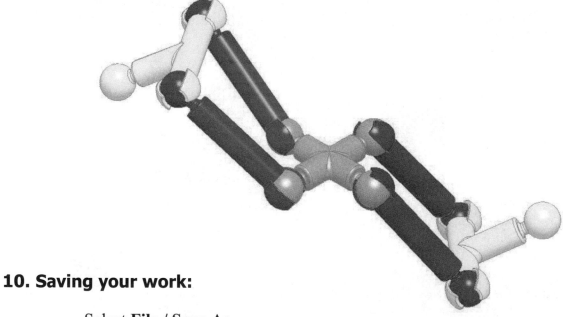

10. Saving your work:

- Select **File / Save As**.

- Enter **Ball-Joint-Assembly** for the name of the file.

- Click **Save**.

(On the CD, in the Built-Parts folder, open the pre-built assembly to compare your work).

Questions for Review

Bottom Up Assembly

1. The 1ˢᵗ component should be fixed on the Origin.
   a. True
   b. False

2. The symbol (f) next to a file name means:
   a. Fully defined
   b. Failed
   c. Fixed

3. After the first component is inserted into an assembly, it is still free to be moved or re-oriented.
   a. True
   b. False

4. Beside the first component, if other components are not yet constrained they cannot be moved or rotated.
   a. True
   b. False

5. You cannot copy multiple components in an assembly document.
   a. True
   b. False

6. To make a copy of a component, click and drag that component while holding the key:
   a. Shift
   b. Control
   c. Alt
   d. Tab

7. Once a mate is created, its definitions (mate alignment, mate type, etc.) cannot be edited.
   a. True
   b. False

8. Mates can be suppressed, deleted, or changed.
   a. True
   b. False

7. FALSE	8. TRUE
5. FALSE	6. B
3. FALSE	4. FALSE
1. TRUE	2. C

CHAPTER 10 (cont.)

Bottom Up Assembly

Bottom Up Assembly
Links Assembly

- After the parts are inserted into an assembly document, they are called components. These components will get re-positioned and mated together. This method is referred as Bottom Up Assembly.

- The first component inserted into the assembly will be fixed by the system automatically. If it is placed on the Origin, then the Front, Top, and Right planes of the first component will also be aligned with the assembly's planes.

- Only the first part will be fixed by default, all other components are free to be moved or re-oriented. Depending on the mate type, once a mate is assigned to a component, one or more of its degrees of freedom are removed, causing the component to move or rotate only in the desired directions.

- Standard mates [icon] are created one by one to constraint components.

- Multi-Mates [icon] can be used to constrain more than one component, where a common entity is used to mate with several other entities.

- This second half of the chapter will guide you through the use of the Bottom Up assembly method once again. Some of the components are exactly identical. We will learn how to create several copies of them and then add 2 mates to each one, leaving one degree of freedom open, so that they can be moved or rotated when dragged. There will be an instance number <1> <2> <3> etc., placed next to the name of each copy, to indicate how many times the components are used in an assembly.

Links Assembly
Bottom-Up Assembly

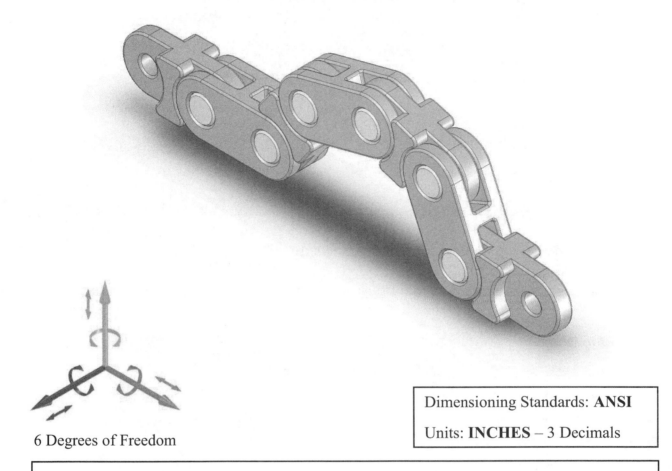

6 Degrees of Freedom

| Dimensioning Standards: **ANSI** |
| Units: **INCHES** – 3 Decimals |

Tools Needed:

 Mates

 Insert New Component

 Rotate Component

 Move Component

 Inference Origins

 Place/Position Component

 Align & Anti-Align

 Concentric Mate

 Coincident Mate

1. Starting a new Assembly Template:

- Select **File / New / Assembly / OK**.

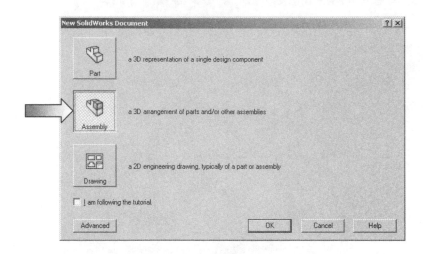

- The new assembly document is opened.

- Select **Insert Component** command from the CommandManager.

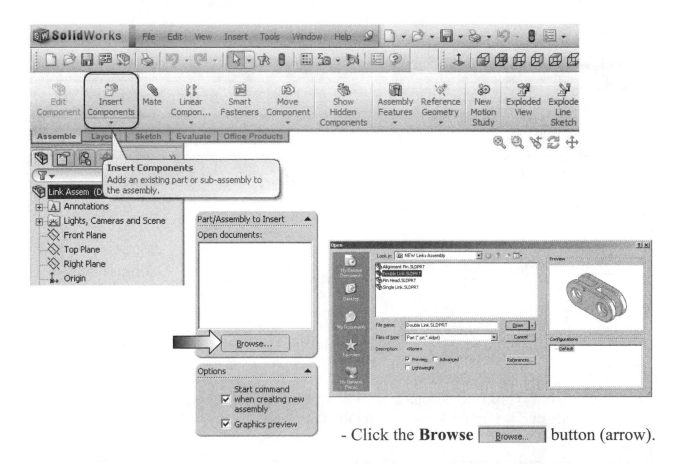

- Click the **Browse** button (arrow).

2. Inserting the 1ˢᵗ Component:

- Go to: The Training CD and open the part **Double Link.sldprt**.

- Place the part Double Link on the assembly Origin.

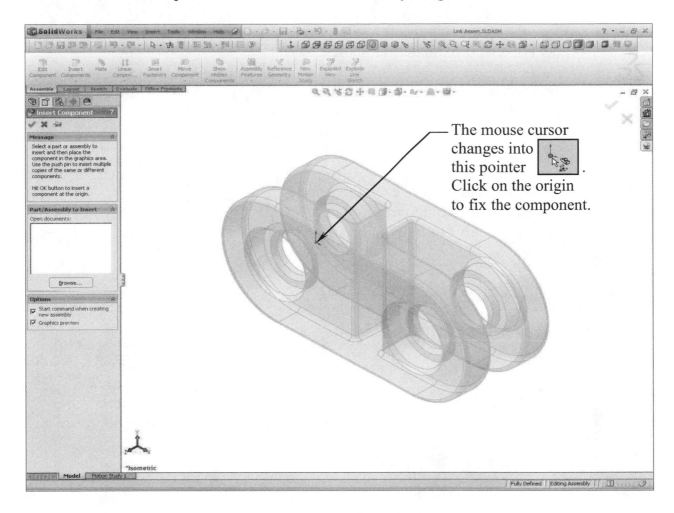

The mouse cursor changes into this pointer. Click on the origin to fix the component.

☼ "Fixing" the 1ˢᵗ component

- The first component inserted into the assembly will be fixed automatically by the system, the symbol (f) next to the document's name means the part cannot be moved or rotated.

- Other components can be added and mated to the first one using one of the three options:

    1. Drag & Drop from an opened window
    2. Use the Windows Explorer to drag the component into the assembly.
    3. Use the Insert Component command.

3. Adding other components:

- Select **Insert / Component / Existing Part/Assembly** (or click 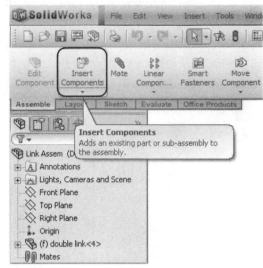) and add five (**5**) more copies of the first component into the Assembly document.

- Place the new components around the Fixed one, approximately as shown.

- The Feature Manager tree shows the same name for each component with an indicator of how many times used **<2>**, **<3>**, **<4>**, etc...

- The **(-)** signs in front of each file name indicate that the components are under defined, still able to move or rotate freely.

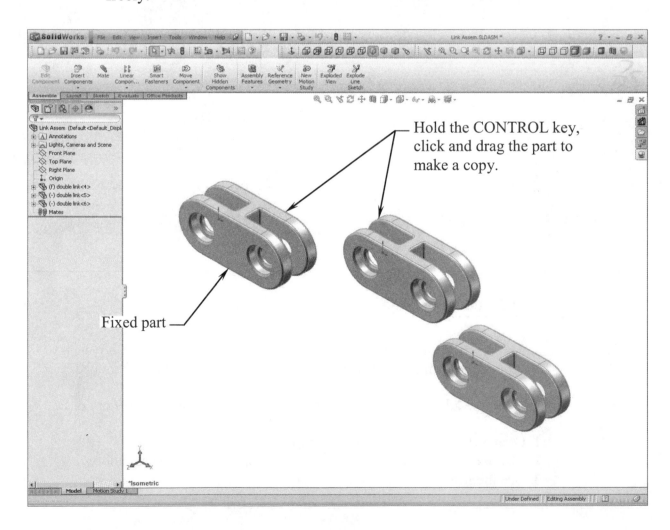

Hold the CONTROL key, click and drag the part to make a copy.

Fixed part

4. Changing colors:

- For Clarity, change the color of the 1st part to a different color, this way we can differentiate the parent part from the copies.

- Click the 1st part and select the **Appearances** button (the beach ball) and click the Edit Part color (arrow).

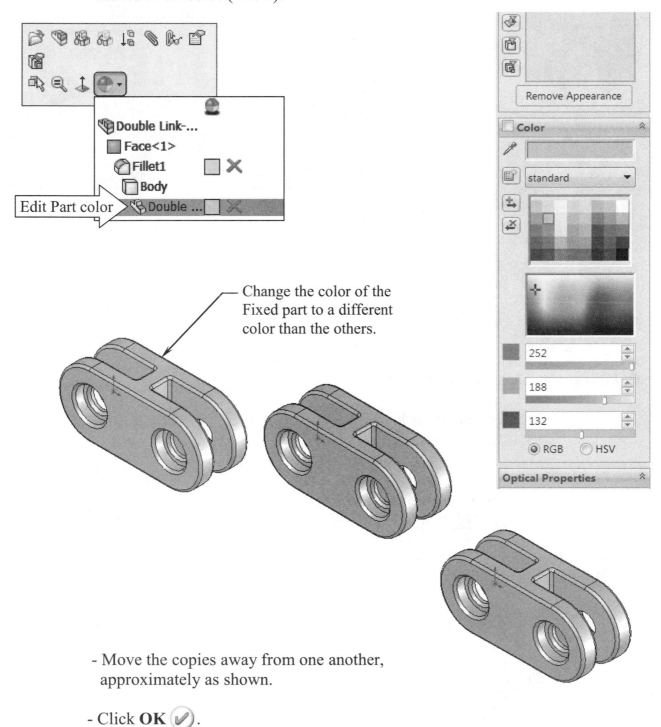

Change the color of the Fixed part to a different color than the others.

- Move the copies away from one another, approximately as shown.

- Click **OK** ✓.

5. Inserting the Single Link into the assembly:

- Click **Insert Component** on the Assembly toolbar and select the part **Single Link**, from the previous folder.

- Place the Single Link approximately as shown.

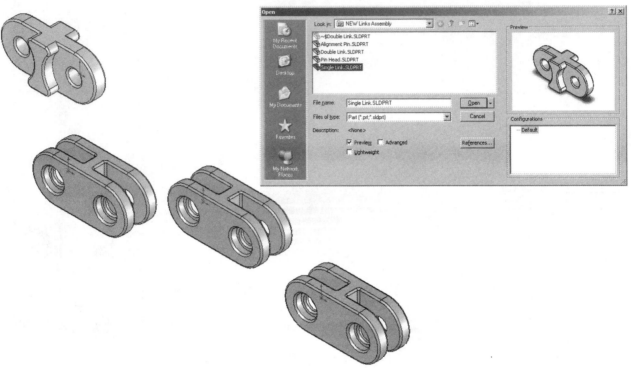

6. Using the Selection Filters:

- The Selection Filters help select the right type of geometry to add mates such as filter Faces, Edges, Axis or Vertices, etc...

- Click **Selection Filter** icon, or press the **F5** function key.

- Select **Filter Faces** option .

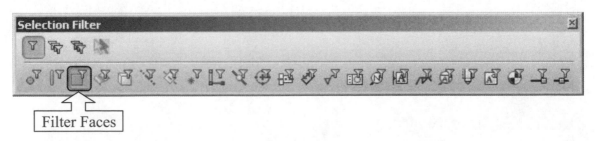

Filter Faces

7. Adding Mates:

- Click **Mate** on the Assembly toolbar or select **Insert / Mate**.

- Select the faces of the two (2) holes as indicated.

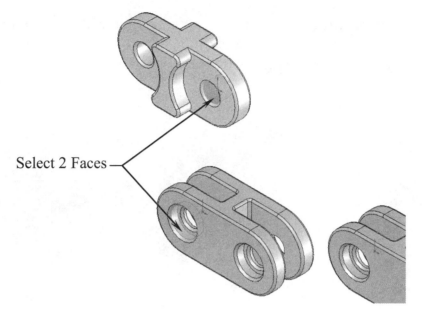

Select 2 Faces

- The **Concentric** mate option is selected automatically and the system displays the preview graphics for the two mated components.

- Click **OK** to accept the concentric mate.

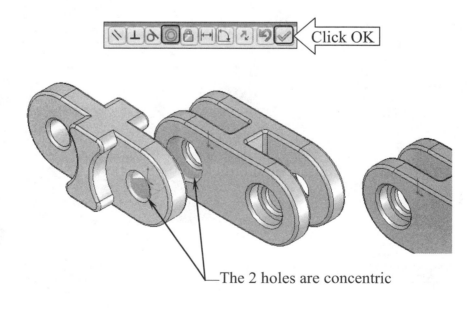

Click OK

The 2 holes are concentric

8. Adding a Width mate:

- The Width mate centered the 2 parts (width of part 1 and groove/tab of part 2).

- Click **Mate** on the Assembly toolbar or select **Insert / Mate**.

- Expand the **Advanced Mates** section and click the **Width** option.

- Select **2 faces** for **each part** as indicated. A total of 4 faces must be selected.

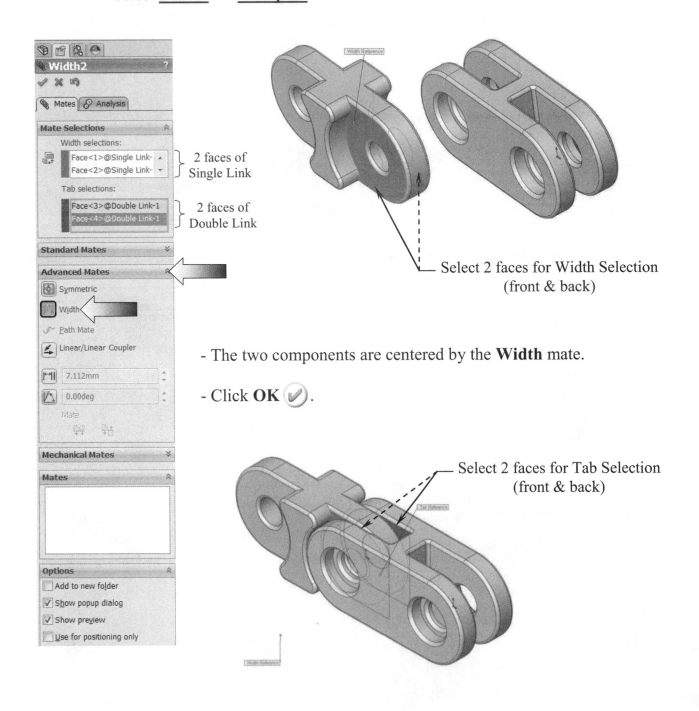

2 faces of
Single Link

2 faces of
Double Link

Select 2 faces for Width Selection
(front & back)

- The two components are centered by the **Width** mate.

- Click **OK**.

Select 2 faces for Tab Selection
(front & back)

9. Making copies of the component:

- Select the part Single-Link and click **Edit / Copy**, click anywhere in the graphics area and select **Edit / Paste**
– OR – Hold down the CONTROL key, click/hold and drag the part Single-Link to make a copy.

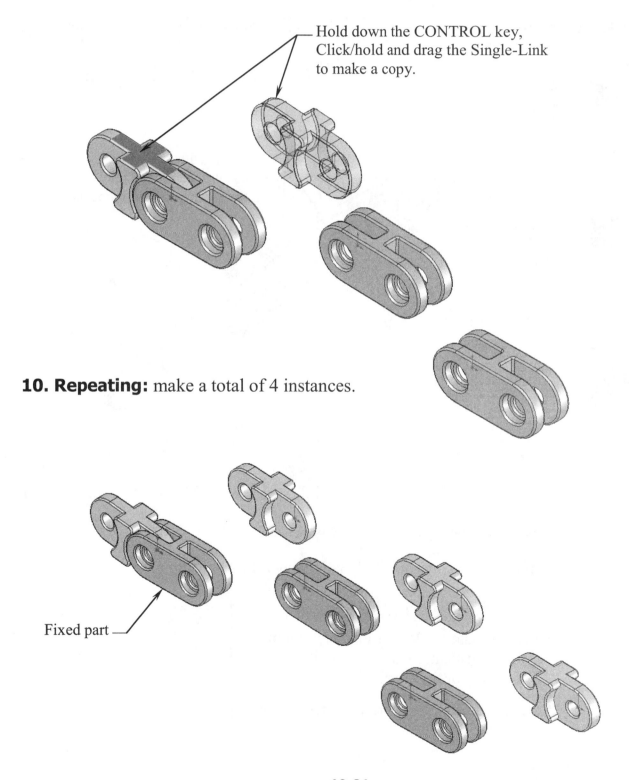

Hold down the CONTROL key,
Click/hold and drag the Single-Link
to make a copy.

10. Repeating: make a total of 4 instances.

Fixed part

Notes:

- *The correct mates are displayed in Black color* 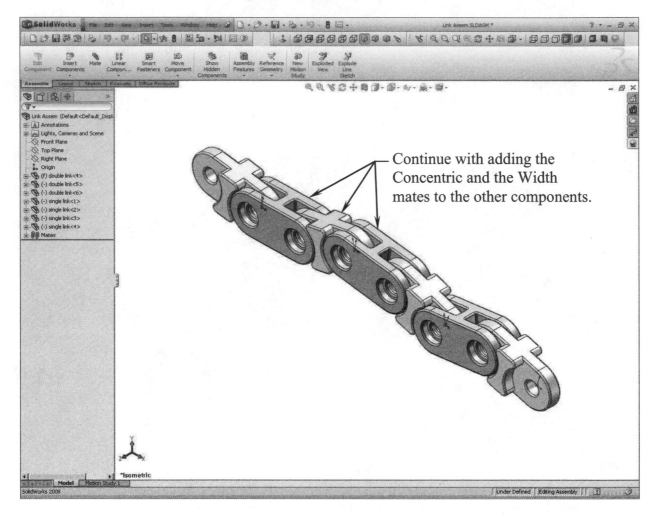 *on the FeatureManager tree.*

- *The Incorrect mates are displayed with a red X* ✎ ⊗ (+) *or a yellow*

exclamation mark ✎ ⚠ (+) *next to them.*

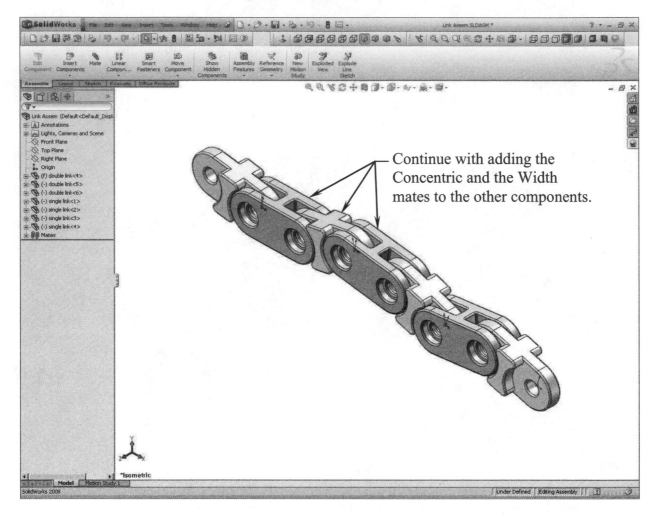

Continue with adding the Concentric and the Width mates to the other components.

- Expand the Mate group ⊟ 🔗 Mates (Click on the **+** sign).

- Verify that there are no "Red Flags" under the Mate Group.

- If a mate error occurs, do the following:

** Right-mouse click over the incorrect mate, select Edit-Feature, and correct the selections for that particular mate - **OR** -

** Simply delete the incorrect mates and re-create the new ones.

11. Inserting other components into the Assembly:

- Click 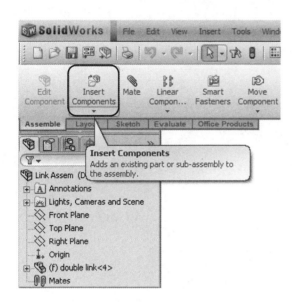 or select **Insert / Component / Existing Part/Assembly.**

- Click **Browse**, select **Alignment Pin** and click **Open**.

- Place the component on the left side of the assembly as shown.

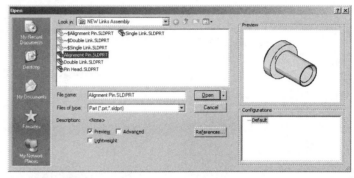

- Insert the **Pin Head** and place it on the right side.

12. Rotating the Pin Head:

- Select the Rotate 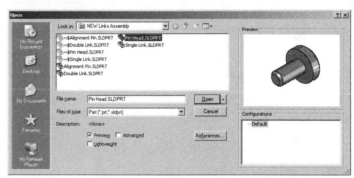 Component command and rotate the Pin-Head to the correct orientation

Make 5 more copies of both, the Pin-Head and the Alignment Pin.

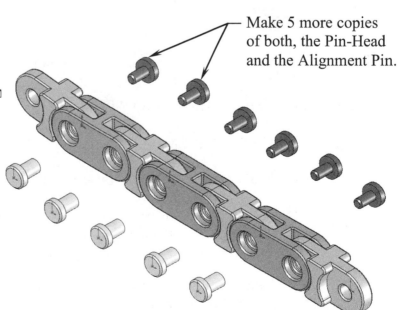
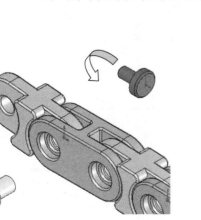

13. Constraining the Alignment Pin:

- Click 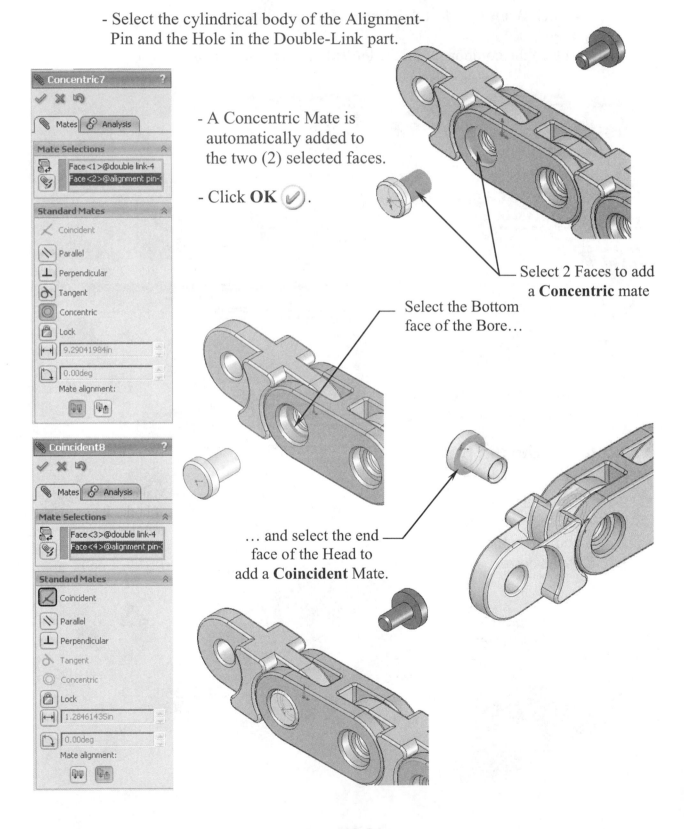 **Mate** on the Assembly toolbar.

- Select the cylindrical body of the Alignment-Pin and the Hole in the Double-Link part.

- A Concentric Mate is automatically added to the two (2) selected faces.

- Click **OK**.

Select 2 Faces to add a **Concentric** mate

Select the Bottom face of the Bore…

… and select the end face of the Head to add a **Coincident** Mate.

Concentric7

Mates | Analysis

Mate Selections

Face<1>@double link-4
Face<2>@alignment pin-

Standard Mates

Coincident
Parallel
Perpendicular
Tangent
Concentric
Lock
9.29041984in
0.00deg

Mate alignment:

Coincident8

Mates | Analysis

Mate Selections

Face<3>@double link-4
Face<4>@alignment pin-

Standard Mates

Coincident
Parallel
Perpendicular
Tangent
Concentric
Lock
1.28461435in
0.00deg

Mate alignment:

14. Constraining the Pin-Head:

- Align the Pin-Head with its mating hole, using a Concentric Mate.

Select the cylindrical
body of the Pin-Head…

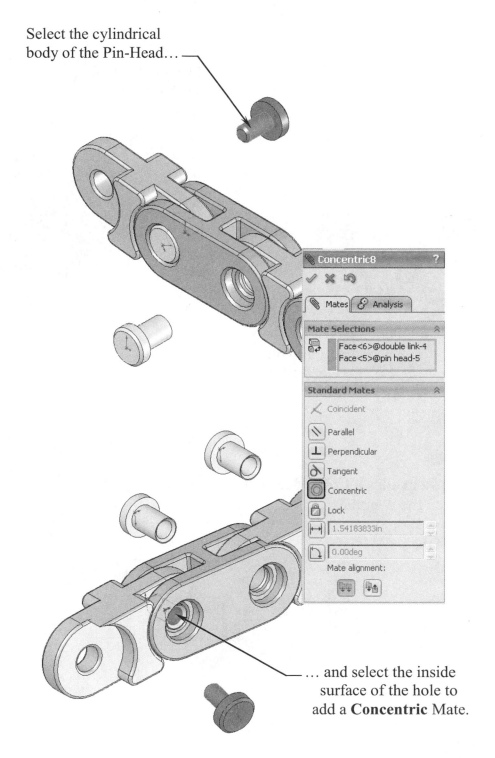

… and select the inside
surface of the hole to
add a **Concentric** Mate.

- Click **OK** ✅.

- Click  **Mate** again, if you have already closed out of it from the last step.

- Select the two (2) faces as indicated to add a Coincident Mate.

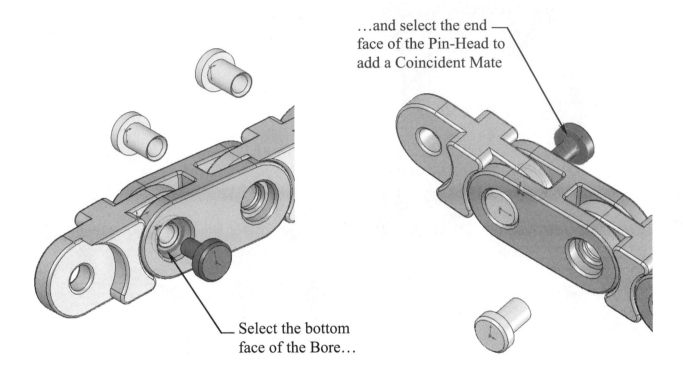

…and select the end
face of the Pin-Head to
add a Coincident Mate

Select the bottom
face of the Bore…

- The system adds a **Coincident** mate
between the 2 entities.

- Click **OK** .

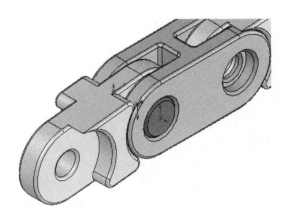

Coincident9

Mates | Analysis

Mate Selections

Face<7>@double link-4
Face<8>@pin head-5

Standard Mates

Coincident

Parallel

Perpendicular

Tangent

Concentric

Lock

1.54183833in

0.00deg

Mate alignment:

15. Using the Align & Anti-Align Options:

- When the Mate command is active, the options **Align** and **Anti-Align** are also available in the Mate dialog box.

- Use the alignment options to flip the mating component 180° .

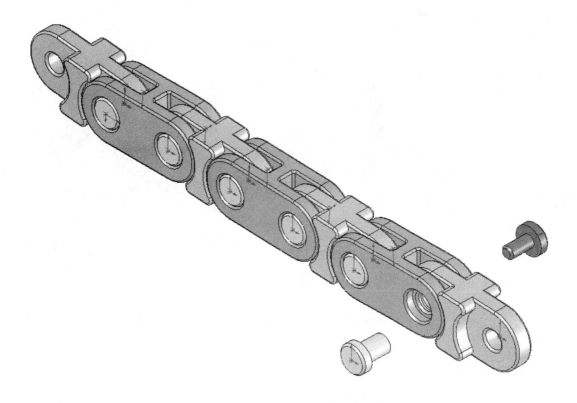

- The last two (2) pins will be used to demonstrate the use of Align and Anti-Align (see step 16).

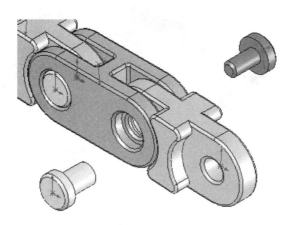

16. Using Align and Anti-Align:

- When mating the components using the **Concentric** option, the **TAB** key can be used to flip the component 180° or from Align into Anti-Align.

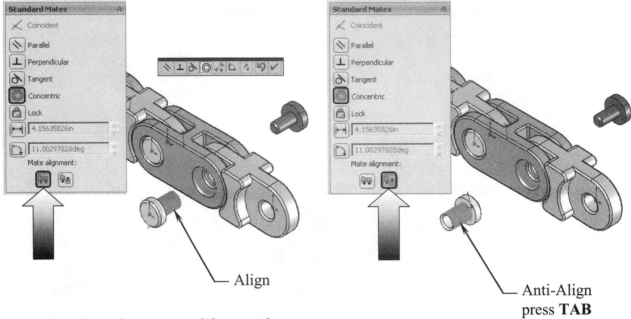

Align

Anti-Align
press **TAB**

17. Viewing the assembly motion:

- Drag one of the links to see how the components move relative to each other.

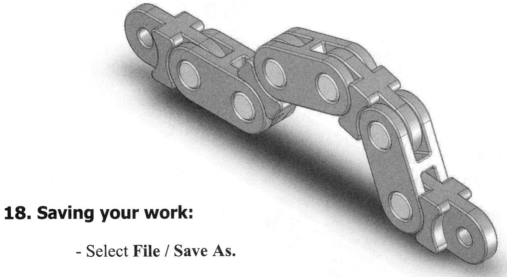

18. Saving your work:

- Select **File / Save As.**

- Enter **Links Assembly** for the name of the file**.**

- Click **Save**.

(On the CD, in the Built-Parts folder, open the pre-built assembly to compare your work).

Questions for Review

Bottom Up Assembly

1. Parts inserted into an assembly document are called documents.
   - a. True
   - b. False

2. Each component in an assembly document has six degrees of freedom.
   - a. True
   - b. False

3. Once a mate is applied to a component, depends on the mate type, one or more of its degrees of freedom is removed.
   - a. True
   - b. False

4. Standard mates are created one by one to constraint the components.
   - a. True
   - b. False

5. A combination of a Face and an Edge can be used to constraint with a Coincident mate.
   - a. True
   - b. False

6. Align and Anti-Align while in the Mating mode can toggle by pressing:
   - a. Control
   - b. Back space
   - c. Tab
   - d. Esc.

7. Mates can be deferred so that several mates can be done and solved at the same time.
   - a. True
   - b. False

8. Mates can be:
   - a. Suppressed
   - b. Deleted
   - c. Edited
   - d. All of the above

7. TRUE   8. D
5. TRUE   6. C
3. TRUE   4. TRUE
1. FALSE   2. TRUE

Exercise: Gate Assembly

Go to: The Training CD
Gate Assembly Folder.

1. Create an Assembly document from the components provided.
2. Create a Mirror plane at **26.125 in.** offset from the RIGHT plane.

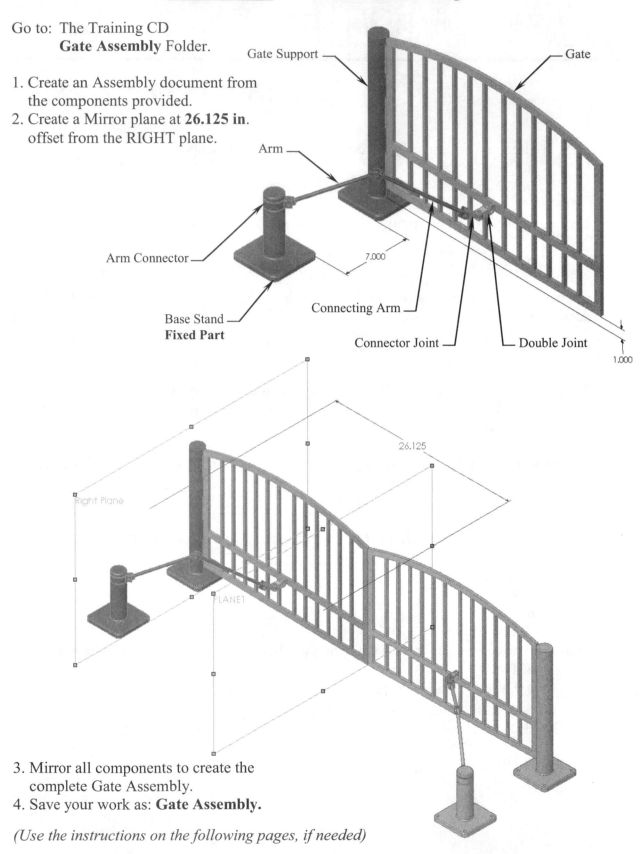

Gate Support

Gate

Arm

Arm Connector

7.000

Base Stand
Fixed Part

Connecting Arm

Connector Joint

Double Joint

1.000

26.125

Right Plane

PLANE1

3. Mirror all components to create the complete Gate Assembly.
4. Save your work as: **Gate Assembly.**

(Use the instructions on the following pages, if needed)

1. Starting a new assembly:

- Click **File / New / Assembly**.

- From the Assembly tool-bar, select **Insert / Components**.

- Brows to the part **Base Stand** and place it on the assembly's origin.

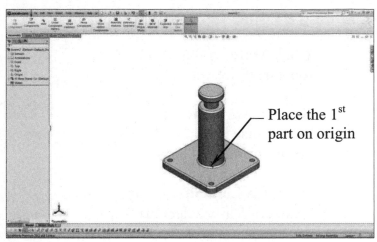

Place the 1st part on origin

2. Inserting other components:

- Insert all components (total of 8) into the assembly.

- **Rotate** the **Gate** <u>and</u> the **Gate-Support** approximately **180 degrees**.

- Move the Gate and the Gate-Support to the positions shown.

- By rotating and positioning the components before mating them, it helps seeing the mating entities a little easier.

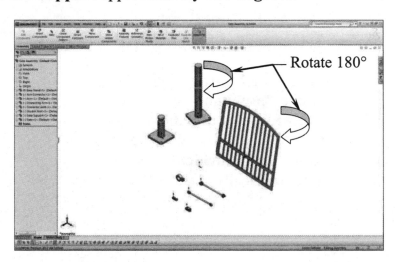

Rotate 180°

3. Adding a Distance mate:

- Click **Mate** on the Assembly toolbar.

- Select the **2 side faces** of the **Base Stand** and the **Gate-Support** as indicated.

- Click the **Distance** button and enter **7.00"**.

- Click **OK**.

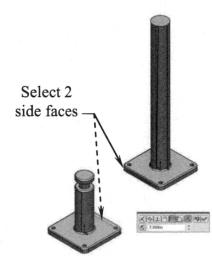

Select 2 side faces

4. Adding a Coincident mates:

- Click **Mate** on the Assembly toolbar, if not yet selected.

- Select the **2 front faces** of the **Base Stand** and the **Gate Support** as indicated.

- Click the **Coincident** button (Automatically selected).

- Click **OK**.

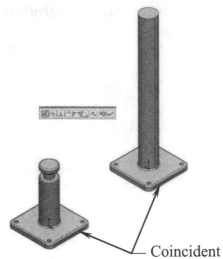

Coincident

5. Adding other mates:

- The **Mate** command should still be active, if not, select it.

- Select the **2 bottom faces** of the **Base Stand** and the **Gate Support** as indicated.

- Click the **Coincident** button (Automatically selected).

- Click **OK**.

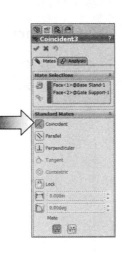

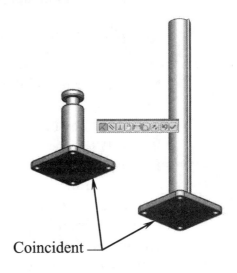

Coincident

Concentric

- Click the Circular Bosses on the sides of the **Gate** and the **Gate Support**; a **concentric** mate is automatically added.

- Click **OK**.

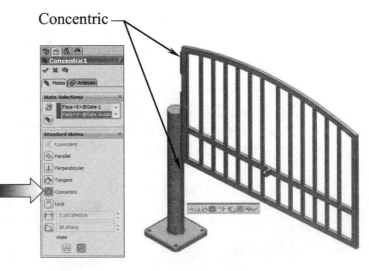

- Add a **Distance** mate of **1.000"** between the **upper face** of the Gate Support and the **bottom face** of the Gate, as noted.

1.00"distance

- Add a **Concentric** mate between the **circular face** of the Base-Stand and the **center hole** of the Arm-Connector.

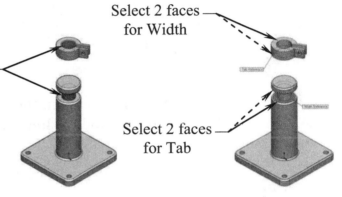

Concentric

Select 2 faces for Width

Select 2 faces for Tab

- Add a **Width** mate between the **4 faces** of the same components.

- Add a **Concentric** mate between the side Hole of the Arm Connector and **the hole** in the Arm.

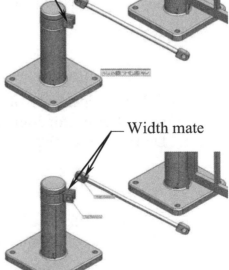

Concentric mate

Width mate

- Add another **Width** mate between the **4 faces** of these two components.

- Add a **Concentric** mate between
the hole in the Arm and **the hole**
in the Connecting Arm.

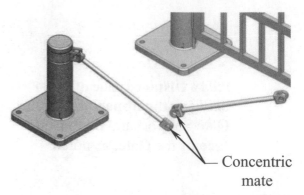

Concentric
mate

- Add a **Width** mate between the
4 faces of the same components.

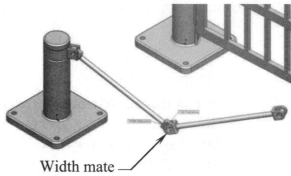

Width mate

- Add a **Concentric** mate between **the hole**
of the Connecting Arm and **the hole** in the
Connector Joint.

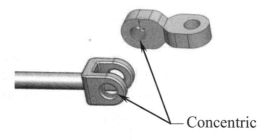

Concentric

- Add another **Width** mate between the **4 faces**
of these two components.

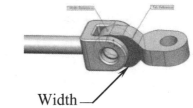

Width

- Add a Concentric mate between **the hole**
in the Connector Joint and **the hole** in the
Double Joint.

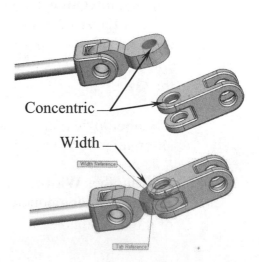

Concentric

Width

- Add a **Width** mate between the **4 faces**
of these two components.

- Click **OK**.

- Move the components to the position shown.

- Since the Double Joint has several components connected to its left side, this time it might be a bit easier if we created the Width mate before the Concentric mate.

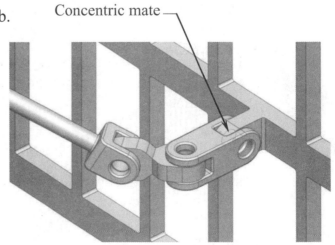

6. Adding more mates:

- Click the **Mate** command again, if not yet selected.

Move the components to approx. here

- Select the **Advanced** tab.

- Click the **Width** option.

- Select the **2 faces** of the **Double Joint** for Width selection.

- Select the other **2 faces** of the tab on the **Gate** for Tab selection.

- Click **OK**.

Select 2 faces for each part

- Change to the **Standard Mates** tab.

Concentric mate

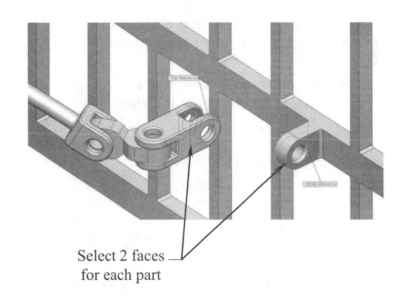

- Select **the hole** in the Double-Joint and **the hole** on the tab of the Gate.

- A **Concentric** mate is added automatically to the selected holes.

- Click **OK** twice to close out of the mate mode.

7. Creating an Offset Distance plane:

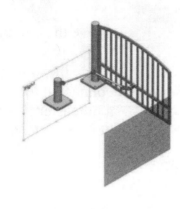

- Select the **Right** plane of the assembly and click the **Plane** command, or **select Insert / Reference Geometry / Plane**.

- The **Offset Distance** button is selected by default.

- Enter **26.125"** for distance.

- Click **OK**.

8. Mirroring the components:

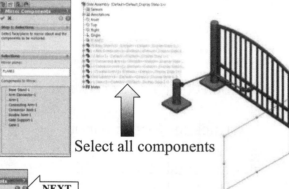

- Select the **new plane** and click: **Insert / Mirror Components**.

Select all components

- Expand the Feature tree and **select all components** from there.

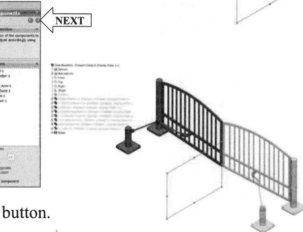

NEXT

- Click the **NEXT** arrow on the upper corner of the Feature tree.

- Select the part **Gate** from the list and click the **Create Opposite Hand Version** button.

- Click **OK** and drag one of the gates to test your assembly.

- **Save** and **Close**.

Gate Closed

Gate Open

CHAPTER 11

Using Advanced Mates

Rack & Pinion Mates

The Rack and Pinion mate option allows linear translation of the Rack to cause circular rotation in the Pinion, and vice versa.

For each full rotation of the Pinion, the Rack translates a distance equal to π multiplied by the Pinion diameter. You can specify either the diameter or the distance by selecting either the Pinion Pitch Diameter or the Rack Travel / Revolution options.

1. Open an assembly document:

- From the Training CD, browse to the Rack & Pinion folder and open the assembly namcd **Rack & Pinion mates**.

- The assembly has two components, the Rack and Gear1. Some of the mates have been created to define the distances between the centers of the two components.

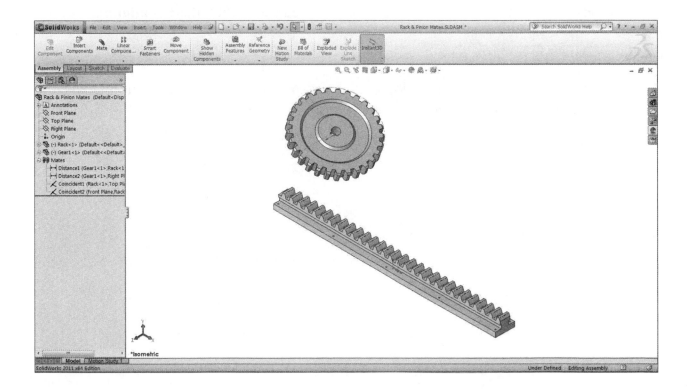

2. Adding standard mates:

- Click the **Mate** command 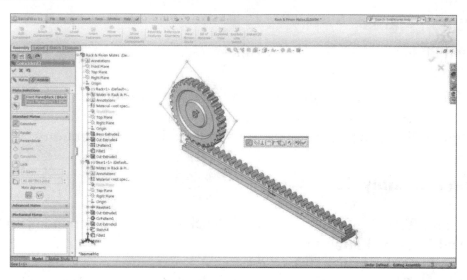 from the assembly toolbar, or select **Insert / Mate**.

- Expand the FeatureManager tree and select the **Front planes** for both components. The software automatically creates a coincident mate for the two selected plane.

- Click **OK**

- Click the **Mate** command if not already selected.

- Select the **Right planes** for both components and click the **Parallel** mate option.

- Click **OK**

- This mate is used to position the starting position of the Gear1, but it needs to be suppressed prior to adding the Rack & Pinion mate.

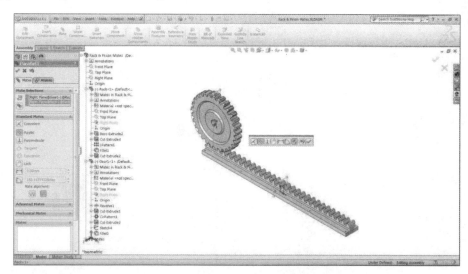

3. Suppressing a mate:

- Expand the **Mate Group** (click the + sign) at the bottom of the FeatureManager tree.

- Right click the Parallel mate and select the **Suppress** button from the pop-up window.

- The Parallel icon should turn grey to indicate that it is suppressed.

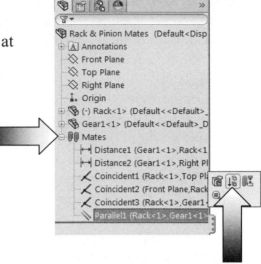

4. Adding a Mechanical mate:

- Move down the Mate properties and expand the Mechanical section (arrow).

- Click the **Rack Pinion** button. The option Pinion Pitch Diameter should be selected already. For each full rotation of the pinion, the rack translates a distance equal to π multiplied by the pinion diameter, and the Pinion's diameter appears in the window.

- In the Mate Selections, highlight the Rack section and select the **Bottom-Edge** of one of the teeth on the Rack.

- Click in the Pinion section and select the **Construction-Circle** on the gear.

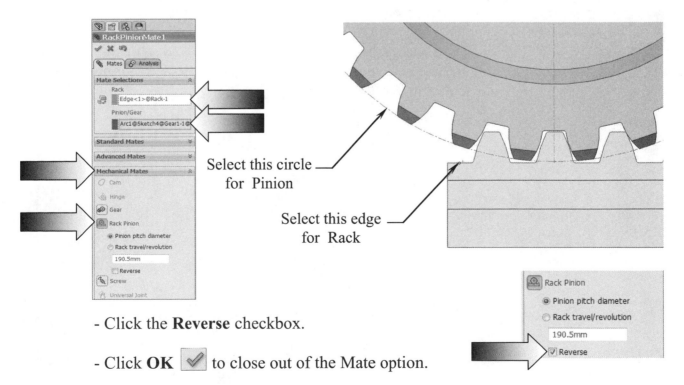

Select this circle for Pinion

Select this edge for Rack

- Click the **Reverse** checkbox.

- Click **OK** to close out of the Mate option.

5. Testing the mates:

- Change to the Isometric orientation (Control + 7).

- Drag either the Rack or the Gear1 back and forth and see how the two components will moved relative to each other.

- Hide the construction circle. Next we'll create an animation using a linear motor to drive the motions.

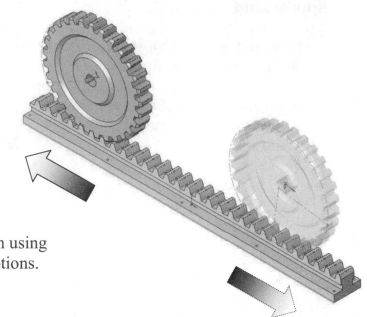

6. Creating a Linear Motion:

- Remain in the Isometric view, click the **Motion Study1** tab on the lower left corner of the screen.

- The screen is split into 2 viewports showing the Animation program on the bottom.

- Click the **Motor** button 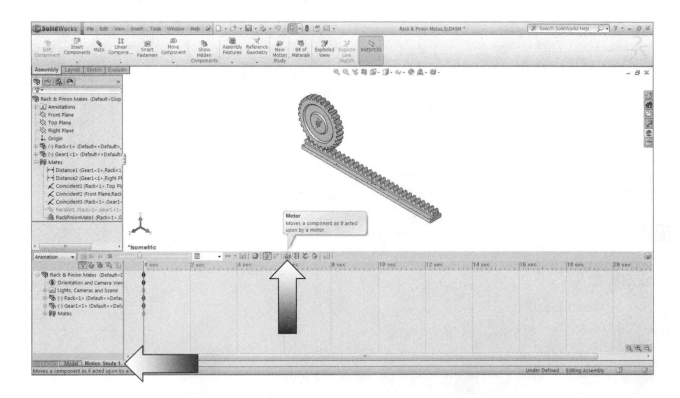 (arrow) on the Motion Study toolbar.

- Under the **Motor Type**, select the **Linear Motor (Actuator)** option.

- Under the **Motion** section, use the default **Constant Speed** and set the speed to **50mm/s** (50 millimeters per second).

- Click **OK**

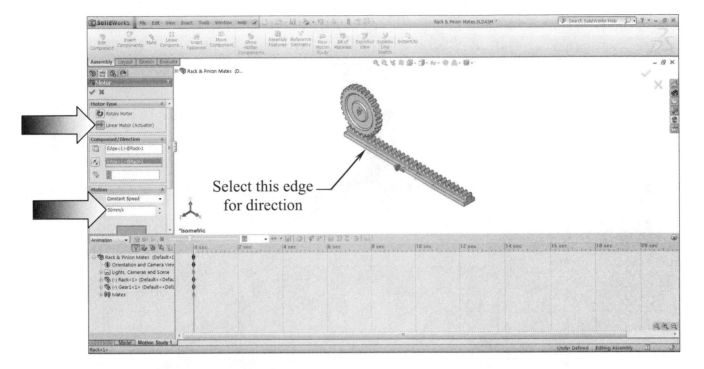

Select this edge for direction

7. Creating a Linear Motion:

- Click the Playback Mode arrow and select: **Playback Mode Reciprocate**.

- Click the **Play** button to view the animation.

- By default the Solid-Works-Animator sets the play time to 5 seconds.

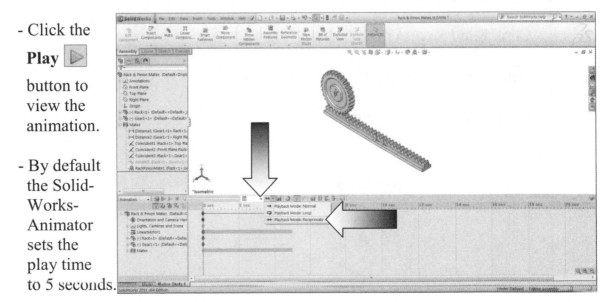

- To change the **Playback Time**, drag the diamond key to **10 second** spot (arrow).

- To change the **Playback Speed**, click the small arrow and select **5X** (arrow).

- Click the Play ▷ button again to re-run the animation.

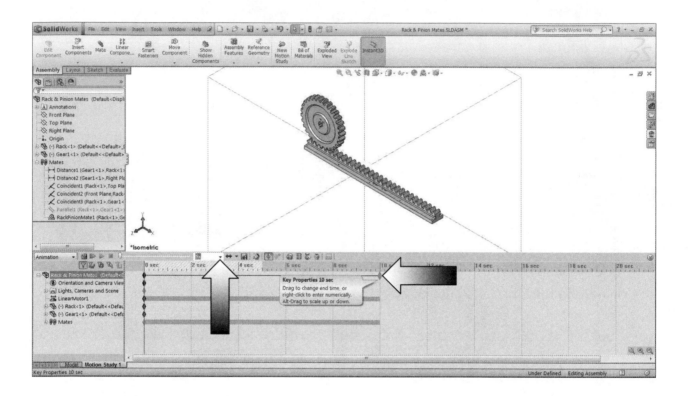

8. Saving your work:

- Click **File / Save As**.

- Enter **Rack & Pinion Mates** for the name of the file.

- Overwrite the old file with the new.

- Click **Save**.

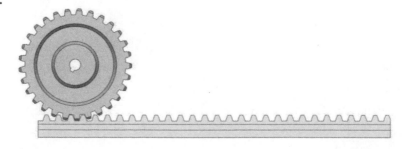

CHAPTER 11 cont.

Limit & Cam Mates

1. Opening a part file:

- Browse to the attached CD and open the part file named: **Limit & Cam Mates**.

Limit mates: Allow components to move within a specified distance or angle. The user specifies a starting distance or angle as well as a maximum and minimum value.

Cam Mate: is a type of coincident or tangent mate. Where a cylinder, plane, or point can be mated to a series of tangent extruded faces.

- This assembly document has 2 components. The Part1 has been fixed by the Inplace1 and the Part2 still has 6 degrees of freedom.

- We will explore the use of Limit and Cam mates when positioning the Part2.

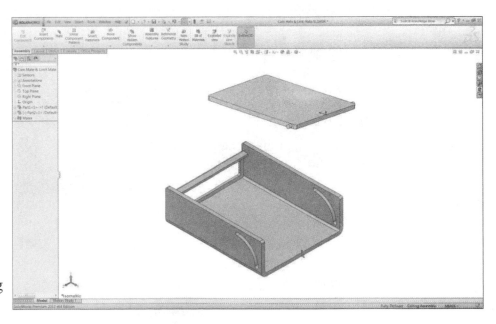

2. Adding a Width mate:

- Click the **Mate** command from the Assembly tab.
- Click the **Advanced Mates** tab and select the **Width** option.

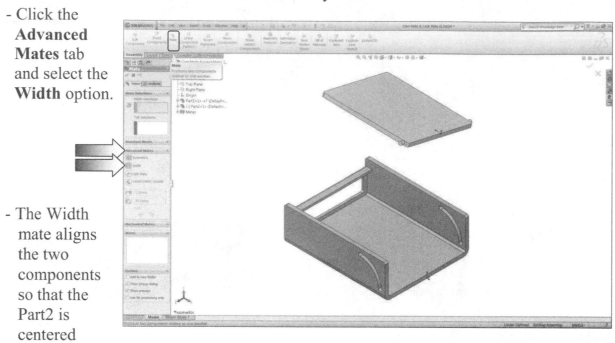

- The Width mate aligns the two components so that the Part2 is centered between the faces of the Part1 (Housing). The Part2 can translate along the center plane of the Housing and rotate about an axis normal to the center plane. The width mate prevents the Part2 from translating or rotating side to side.

- For the **Width Selection**, select the **2 side faces** of the **Part2** (arrow).

- For the **Tab Selection**, select the **2 side faces** of the **Part1** (Housing).

- It doesn't matter which component you select first or second, just be sure to select both faces of the same part before selecting the next set.

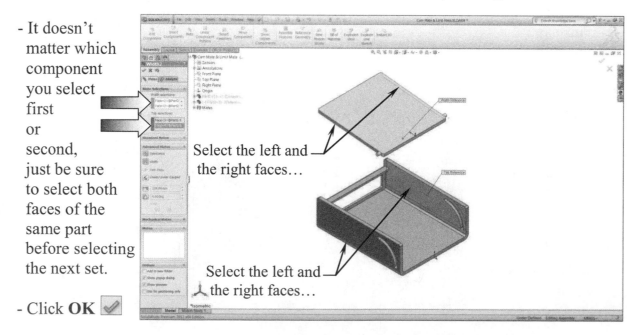

Select the left and the right faces...

Select the left and the right faces...

- Click **OK**

3. Adding a Cam mate:

- Click the **Mechanical Mate** tab below the Standard and Advanced tabs (Arrow).

- Select the **Cam** mate button from the list.

- A Cam mate forces a cylinder, a plane, or a point to be coincident or tangent to a series of tangent extruded faces.

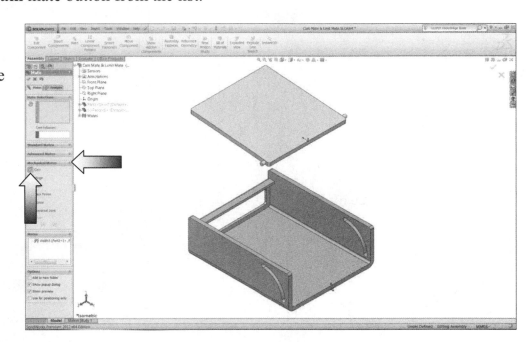

- For the **Cam Selection**, <u>right click</u> a face of the slot and pick: **Select Tangency**.

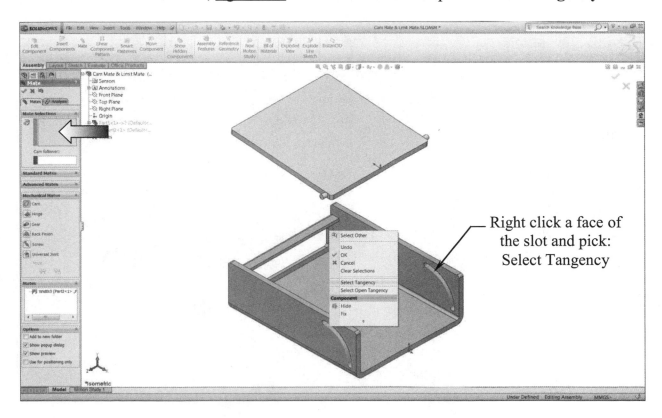

Right click a face of the slot and pick: Select Tangency

- For the **Cam Follower**, select the <u>cylindrical face</u> of one of the 2 pins.

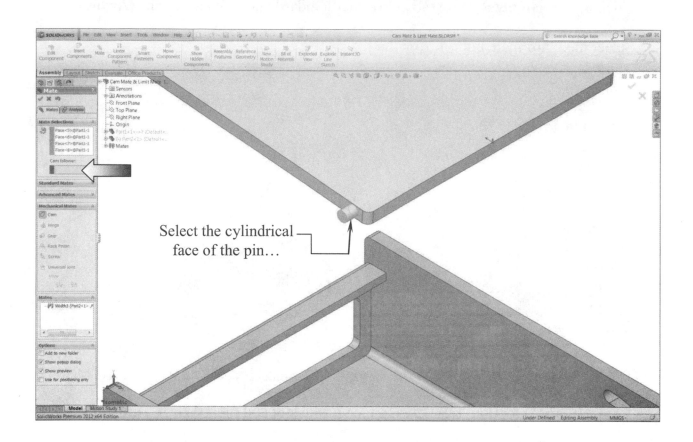

Select the cylindrical — face of the pin…

- Toggle between the 2 mate alignment buttons (arrow) to make sure the two components are properly mated.

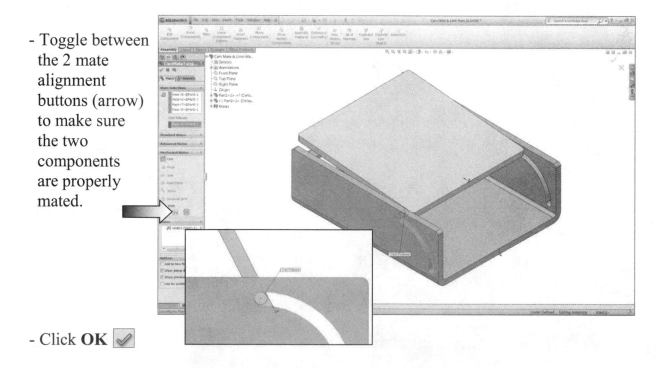

- Click **OK**

4. Adding a Parallel mate:

- Click the **Standard Mates** tab (arrow) and select **Parallel** from the list.

- Select the **2 faces** as indicated to make parallel.

- Click **OK** ✅

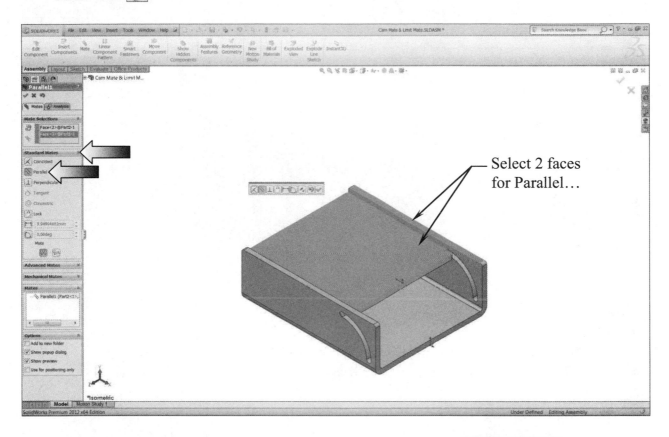

Select 2 faces
for Parallel...

- The Parallel mate was use to precisely rotate the Part2 to its vertical position. We will need to suppress it so that other mates can be added without over defining the assembly.

- Expand the Mate group by clicking the plus sign (+) next to the Mates folder.

- Right (or left) click the Parallel mate and select the **Suppress** button (arrow).

- Do not move the component, a Limit mate is going to be added next.

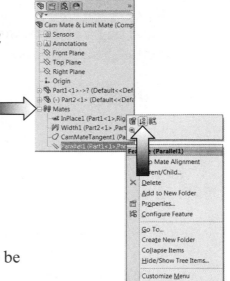

5. Adding a Limit mate:

- Click the **Advanced Mates** tab (arrow) and select **Angle** from the list.

- Select the 2 faces of the 2 components as indicated.

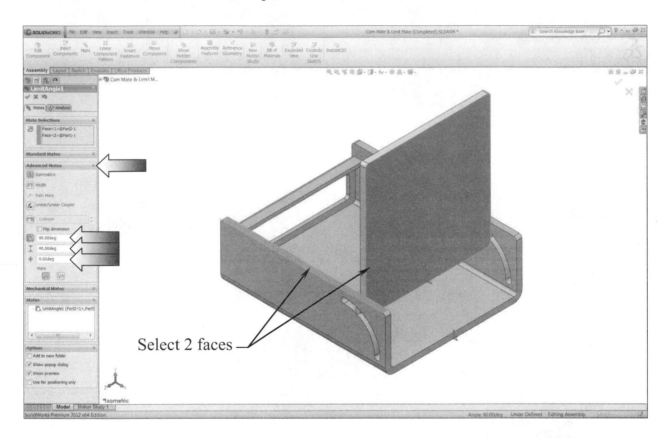

Select 2 faces

- Enter the following:

> **0.00 deg** for "starting" Angle.
> **90.00 deg** for **Maximum** value.
> **0.00 deg** for **Minimum** value.

- Click **OK** ✅

- Test the mates by dragging the Part2 up and down.

- It may take a little getting used to when moving a cam part. (Changing to other orientations may make it easier).

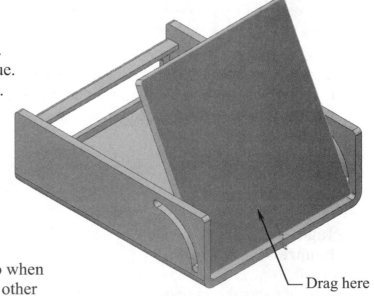

Drag here

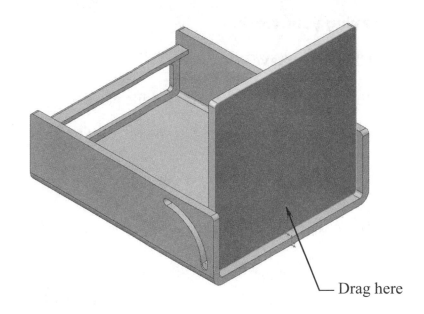

- Try pulling the right end of
 the Part2 downward.
 It should stop when reaching
 the 90 degrees angle.

Drag here

- Let us explore some other options of
 dragging a cam part.

- Change to the Front orientation
 (Control + 1).

- Drag the **circular face** of the Pin
 upward. Start out slowly at first,
 then move a bit faster when the
 part starts to follow your cursor.

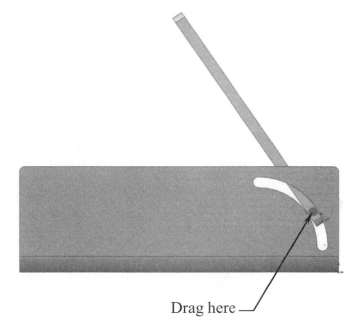

Drag here

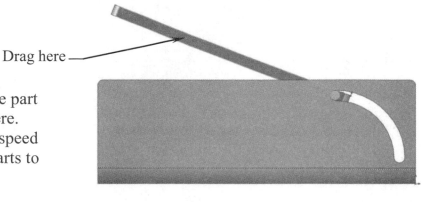

Drag here

- Now try dragging the same part
 from the side as shown here.
 Also start out slowly then speed
 up a little when the part starts to
 catch on.

6. Saving your work:

- Click **File / Save As**.

- Enter **Limit & Cam Mates** for file name.

- Click **Save**.

- Overwrite the document if prompted.

(In the CD, locate the Built-Parts folder; open the pre-built assembly to compare your work).

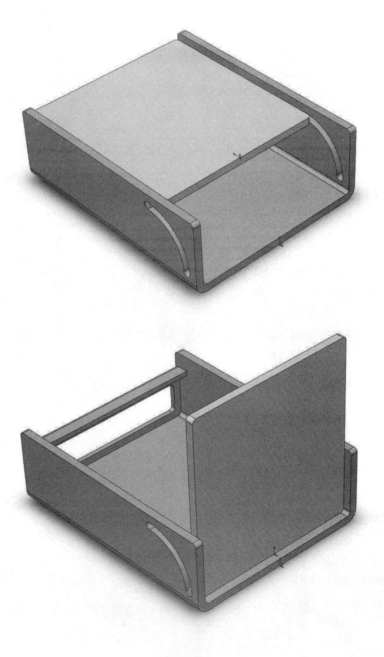

Exercise: Using Cam Followers*

1. Copying the Cam Followers Assembly folder:

- Go to: The Training CD
- Copy the entire folder named **Cam Followers** to your desktop.

A Cam-Follower mate is a type of tangent or coincident mate. It allows you to mate a cylinder, plane, or point to a series of tangent extruded faces, such as you would find on a cam. You can make the profile of the cam from lines, arcs, and splines, as long as they are tangent and form a closed loop.

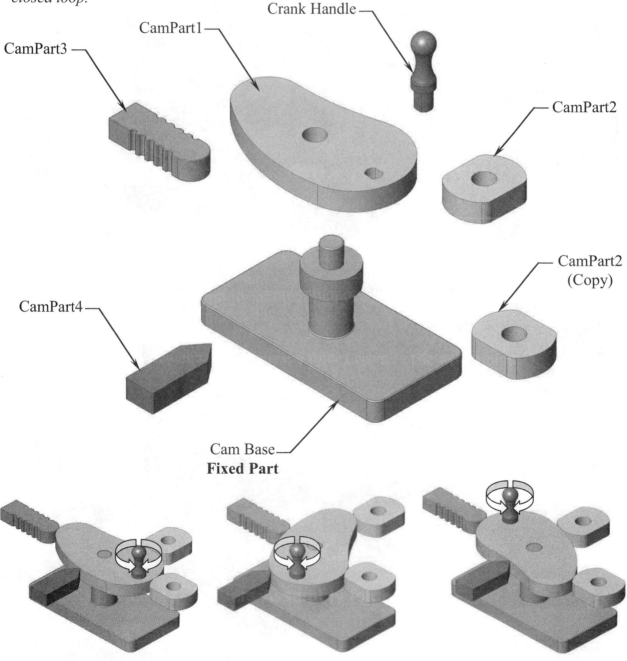

CamPart3

CamPart1

Crank Handle

CamPart2

CamPart4

CamPart2 (Copy)

Cam Base
Fixed Part

2. Assembling the components using the Standard Mates:

- Create a **Concentric mate** between the shaft and the hole as shown below.

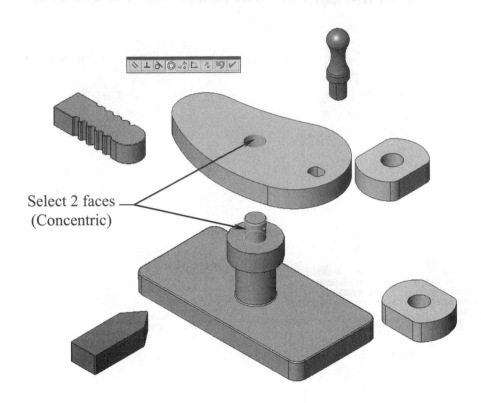

Select 2 faces
(Concentric)

- Create a **Coincident mate** between the two faces as shown below.

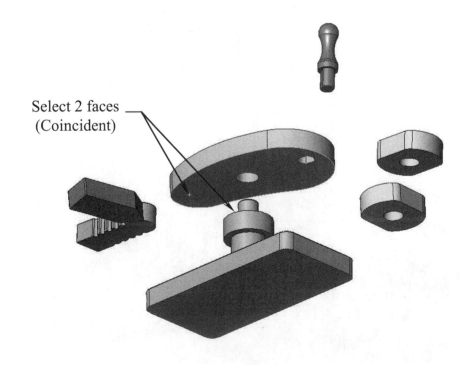

Select 2 faces
(Coincident)

- Create a **Coincident Mate** between the **2 upper surfaces** of the 2 parts as shown.

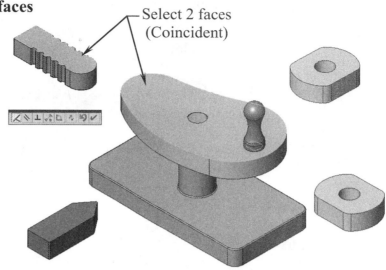

Select 2 faces (Coincident)

- Repeat the Coincident Mates for all other parts (except for the Crank-Handle) to bring them up to the same height.

3. Using Mechanical Mates:

All Upper Faces are Coincident with the Campart1.

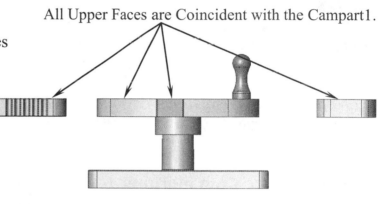

- Below the Advanced mates expand the **Mechanical Mate** section.

- Select the **CAM** option (arrow).

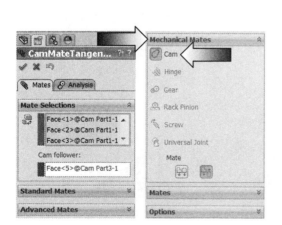

- **Right click** on the side of the CamPart1 and pick **Select-Tangency** from the menu.

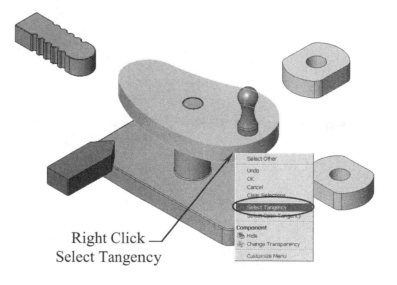

Right Click
Select Tangency

- Click in the **Cam-Follower** section (circled) and select the **left face** of the part CamPart2,

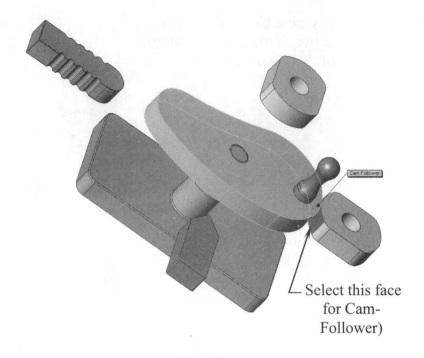

Select this face for Cam-Follower)

NOTES:

- *In order for the components to "behave" properly when they're being rotated, their center-planes should also be constrained.*

- *Create a Coincident Mate between the FRONT plane of the CamPart1 and the FRONT plane of the CamPart3, then repeat the same step for the others.*

4. Viewing the Cam Motions

- Drag the Crank Handle clockwise or counter-clockwise to view the Cam Motion of your assembly.

Move the Crank Handle to test the Cam Motions

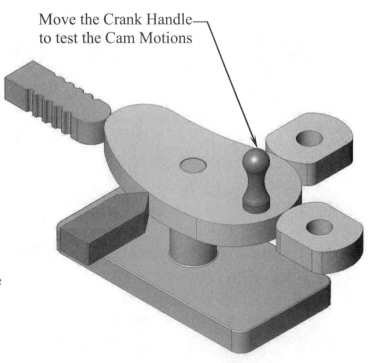

5. Saving your Work:

- Click **File / Save As**.

- Enter **Cam Follower** for the name of the file.

- Click **Save**.

Level 1 Final Exam

Files location: Training CD.

Bottom Up Assembly Folder.
Copy the entire folder to your
Desktop.

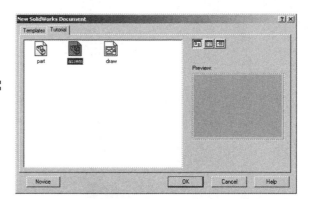

1. Starting a new Assembly document:

- Select **File / New / Assem**. (Assembly)
from either the Template or the
Tutorial folder.

2. Inserting the Fixed component:

- Click the **Insert Component** command from the Assembly toolbar.

- Locate the **Molded Housing** and place it on the assembly's origin.

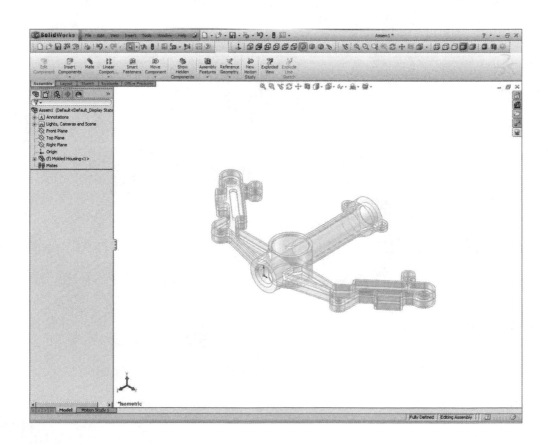

Note: _To show the Origin symbol, go to **View / Origins.**_

3. Inserting the other components:

- Insert the rest of the components as labeled, from the Bottom Up Assembly folder into the assembly.

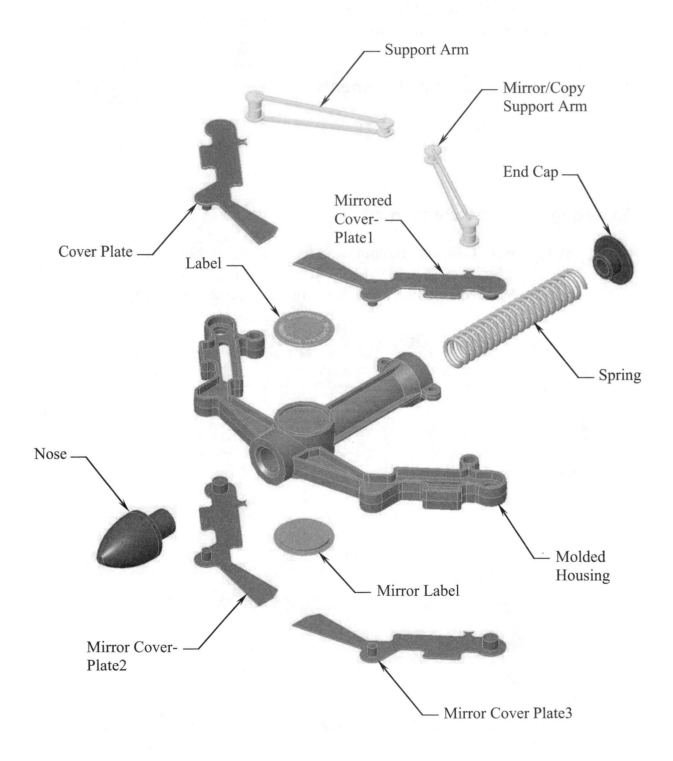

4. Mating the components:

- Assign Mate conditions such as Concentric, Coincident, etc., to assemble the components.

- The finished assembly should look like the one pictured below.

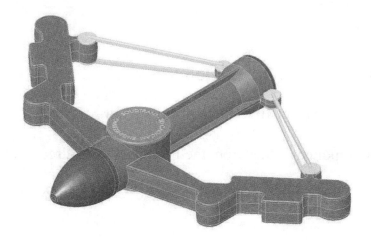

5. Verifying the position of the Spring:

- Select the Right Plane and click Section View.

- Position the Spring approximately as shown to avoid assembly's interferences.

- Click-off the section view option when finished.

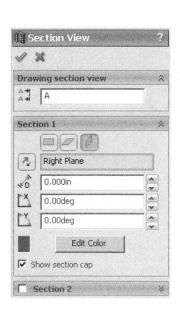

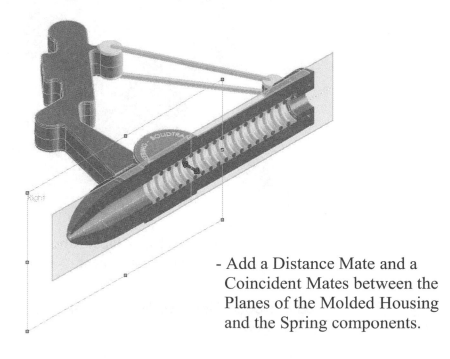

- Add a Distance Mate and a Coincident Mates between the Planes of the Molded Housing and the Spring components.

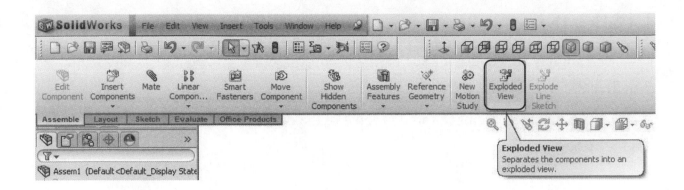

6. Creating the Assembly Exploded View:

- Click 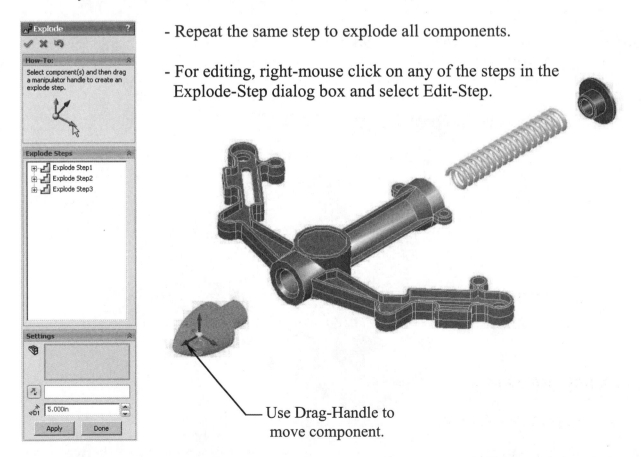 or Select **Insert / Exploded View**.

- Select a component either from the Feature tree or directly from the Graphics area.

- Drag one of the three Drag-Handles to move the component along the direction you wish to move.

- Repeat the same step to explode all components.

- For editing, right-mouse click on any of the steps in the Explode-Step dialog box and select Edit-Step.

Use Drag-Handle to move component.

Note: _The Finished Exploded View can be edited by accessing the ConfigurationManager under the Default Configuration._

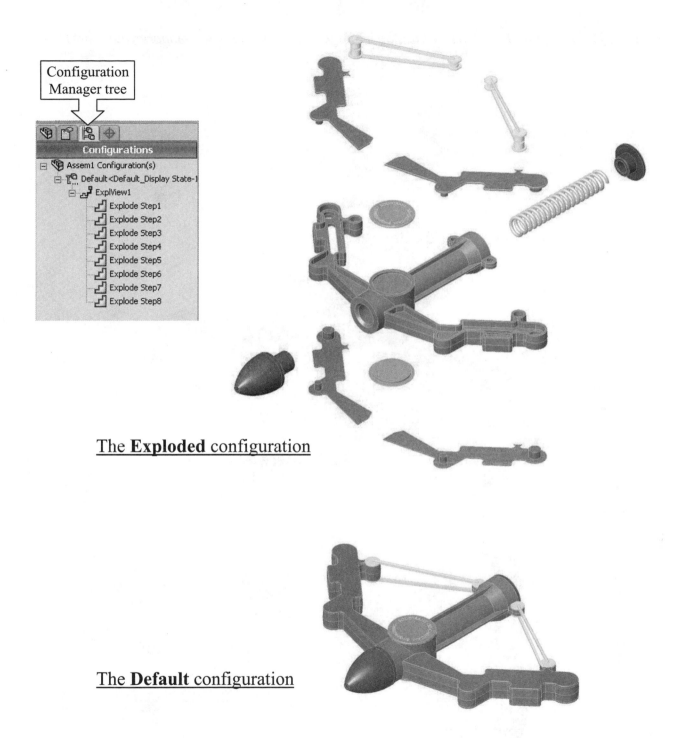

Configuration
Manager tree

The **Exploded** configuration

The **Default** configuration

7. Saving your work:

- Select **File / Save As**.

- Enter **L1 Final Exam** for the name of the file.

- Click **Save**.

(In the CD, locate the Built-Parts folder; open the pre-built assembly to compare your work).

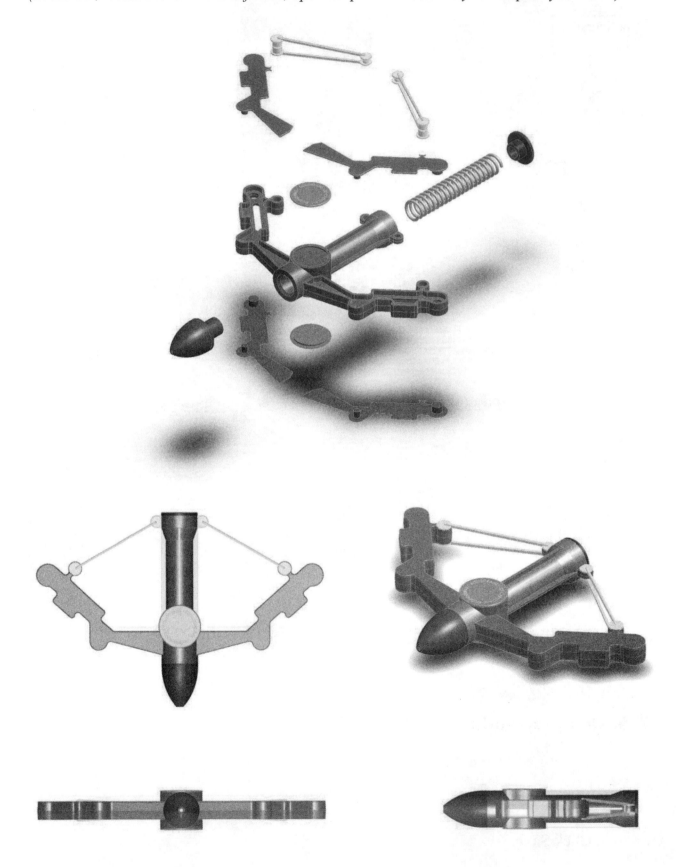

CHAPTER 11 cont.

Using PhotoView 360

PhotoView 360 enables the user to create photo-realistic renderings of the SolidWorks models. The rendered image incorporates the appearances, lighting, scene, and decals included with the model. PhotoView 360 is available with SolidWorks Pro or SolidWorks Premium only.

1. Activating the PhotoView 360 Add-In:

- Click **Tools / Add-Ins**…

- Select the PhotoView 360 checkbox.

- Click **OK**.

- *NOTE:*

Enable the checkbox on the right of the PhotoView 360 add-in if you wish to have it available at startup. Otherwise only activate it for each use.

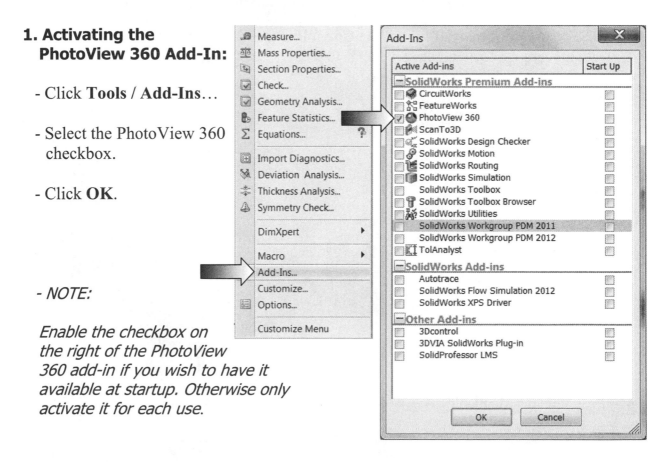

2. Setting the Appearance:

- Click **Edit Appearance** from the PhotoView 360 pull down menu (arrow).

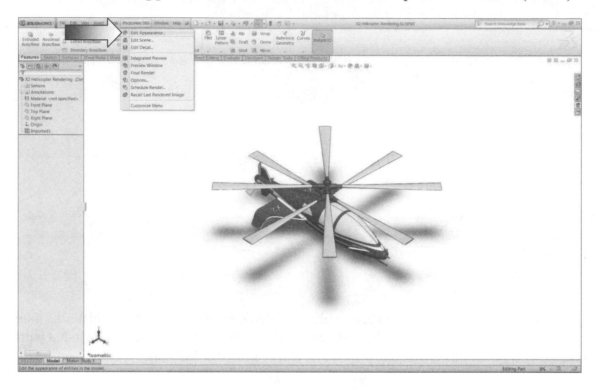

- Expand the **Painted** folder, the **Car** folder (arrows) and <u>double click</u> the **Siena** appearance to select it. Click **OK** to close.

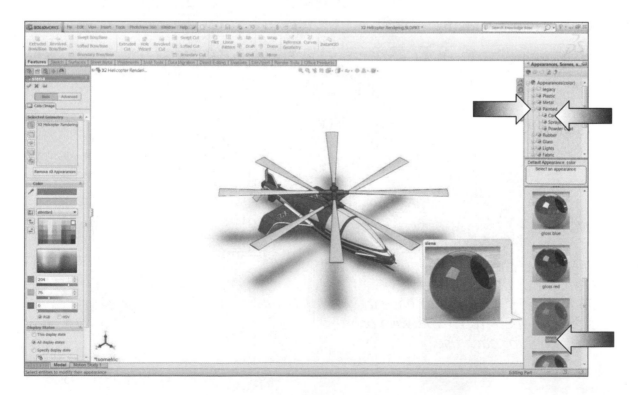

3. Setting the Scene:

- Click **Edit Scene** from the PhotoView 360 pull down menu (arrow).

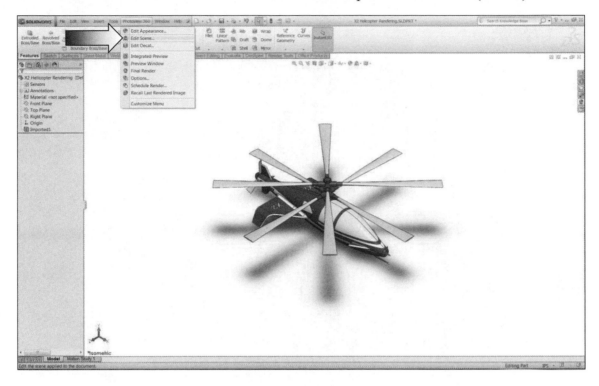

- Expand the **Scenes** folder, the **Studio Scenes** folder (arrows) and <u>double click</u> the **Reflective Floor Black** scene to select it. Click **OK** to close.

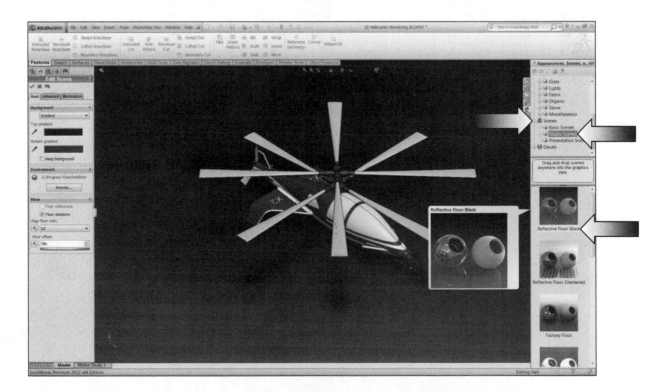

4. Setting the Image Quality options:

- Click **Options** from the PhotoView 360 pull down menu (arrow).

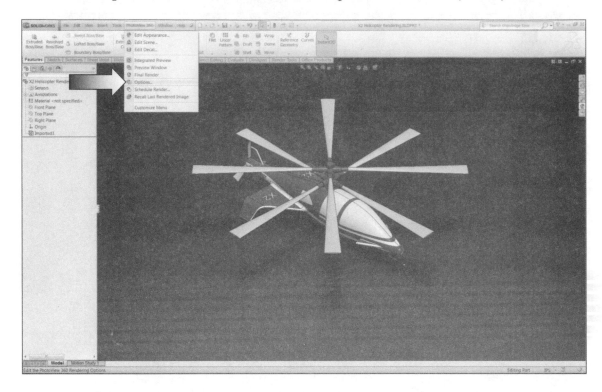

- Set the **Output Image Width** to **1600**, the Image Height is set automatically.
- Under Render Quality, set the **Final Render** to **Best** (arrow). Click **OK** to close.

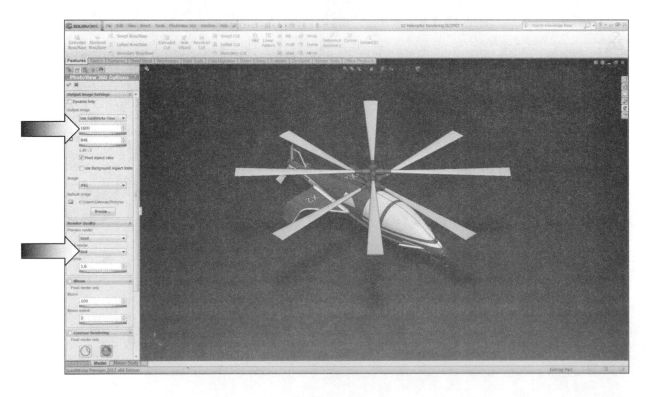

5. Rendering the image:

- Click **Rende**r. After the rendering is completed, click **Save Image** (arrow).

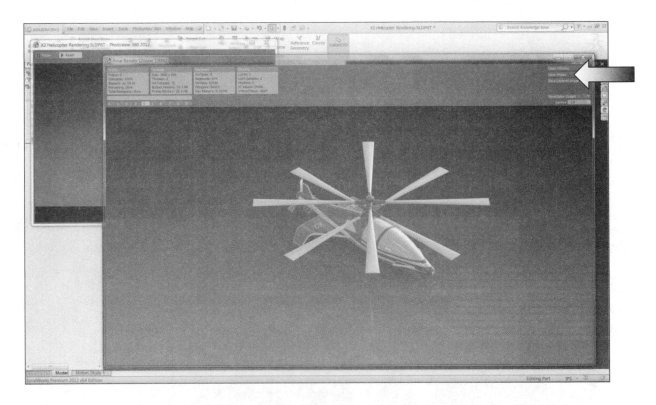

- Select the **JPEG** format from the Save-as-Type drop down list.

- Enter a file name and click **OK**.

NOTE:

- Different file formats may reduce the quality of the image and at the same time, it may increase or decrease the size of the file.

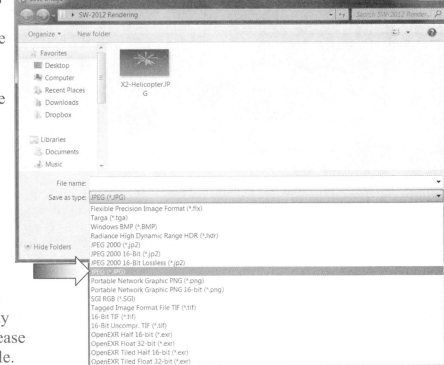

CHAPTER 12

Layout Assembly

Layout Assembly

- You can design an assembly from the top-down using layout sketches. You can construct one or more sketches showing where each assembly component belongs. Then, you can create and modify the design before you create any parts. In addition, you can see the assembly motions ahead of time and how the components are going to behave when they are being moved around.

- The major advantage of designing an assembly using a layout sketch is that if you change the layout sketch, the assembly and its parts are automatically updated. You can make changes quickly, and in just one place.

- In a Layout Assembly, blocks are created from each sketch to help handle them more efficiently. A block is created by grouping the sketch entities, dimensions, callouts, etc., into one unit and then saving them as a Block. A block can easily be moved, positioned, or re-used in other assembly documents.

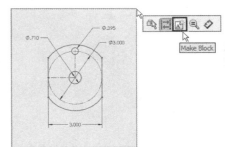

- In layout-based assembly design, you can switch back and forth between top-down and bottom-up design methods. You can create, edit, and delete parts and blocks at any point in the design cycle without any history-based restrictions. This is particularly useful during the conceptual design process, when you frequently experiment with and make changes to the assembly structure and components.

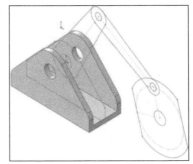

- This chapter will guide you through the use of Layout Assembly, as well as making new blocks and converting them to 3D models.

Assembly Motions
Layout Assembly

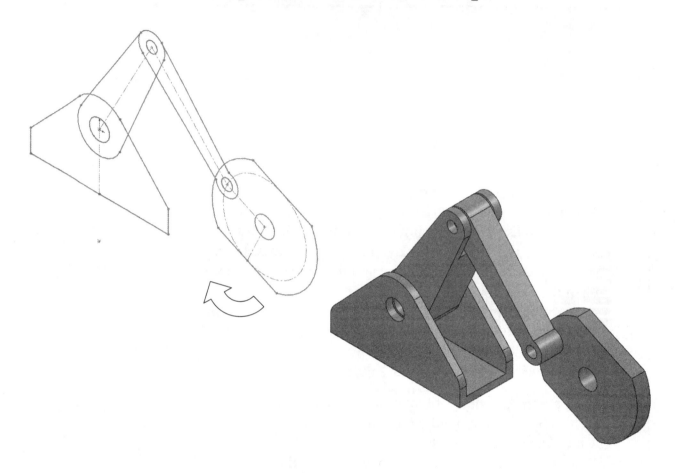

| Dimensioning Standards: **ANSI** |
| Units: **INCHES** – 3 Decimals |

Tools Needed:

 Layout

 Make Block

 Make Part From Block

 Animation Wizard

 Motors

 Add New Key

1. Opening an assembly document:

- Open the **Layout Assembly.sldasm** document from the Training CD, in the Class Files folder.

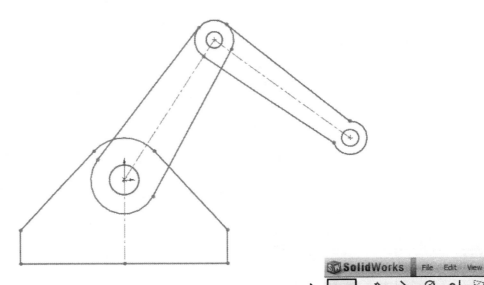

2. Activating the layout mode:

- In order to see the motions in the Layout mode, each sketch must be converted into a Block.

- In a block, a set of sketch entities and Dimensions are grouped into one unit or one block so that they can be moved, positioned easily, or re-used in other assembly documents.

Block 2

Block 1

- Click the **Layout** button on the Layout tab, next to the Assembly toolbar (arrow).

Block 3

NOTE: Recreate the mates if needed.

3. Creating a new sketch:

- Sketch the profile below and add the dimensions as shown.

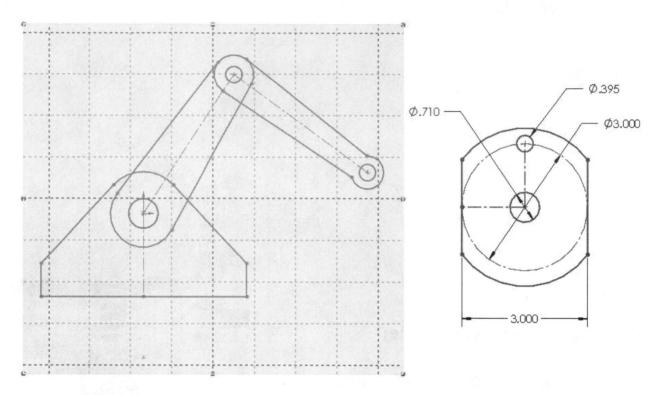

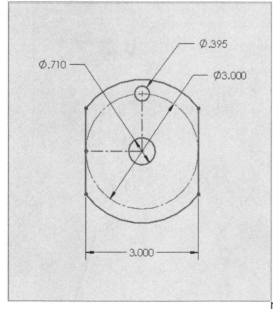

4. Making a Block:

- A block is created by grouping the Sketch entities, dimensions, callouts, etc., into one unit and then saving them as a Block.

- Box-select the entire profile, click the **Make Block** button from the pop up toolbar – OR – select **Tools / Block / Make** from the pull down menus.

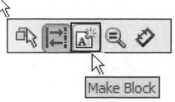

5. Setting the Insertion Point:

- Each block should have an Insertion Point (or Handle Point), which will allow the block to move and position more easily.

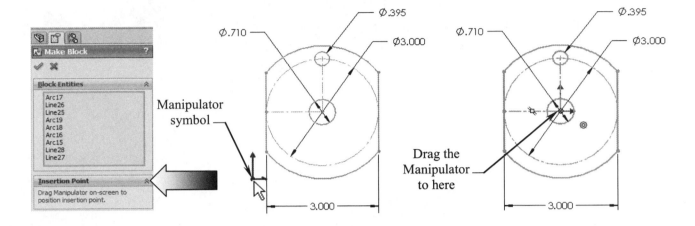

Manipulator symbol

Drag the Manipulator to here

- Expand the **Insertion Point** option (arrow) and drag the Blue Manipulator symbol and place it on the center of the middle circle.

- Click **OK** ✓ .

6. Adding relations:

- Add a **Horizontal** relation between the centers of the 2 circles as shown below.

Note: *The center of the circle on the left side is Coincident with the Origin.*

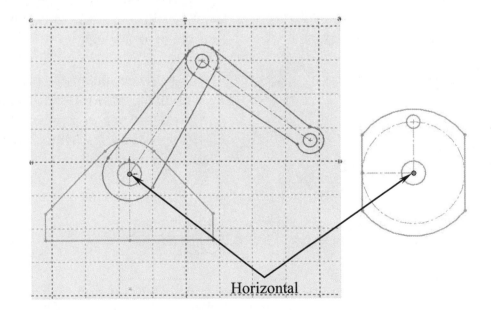

Horizontal

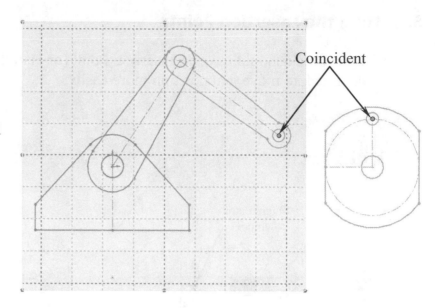

Coincident

- Add a **Coincident** relation between the centers of the 2 small circles as indicated.

7. Adding dimensions:

- Add a **6.000 in** dimension to define the spacing between the 2 parts.

Note: _Dimension to the centerline as noted to make a horizontal linear dimension._

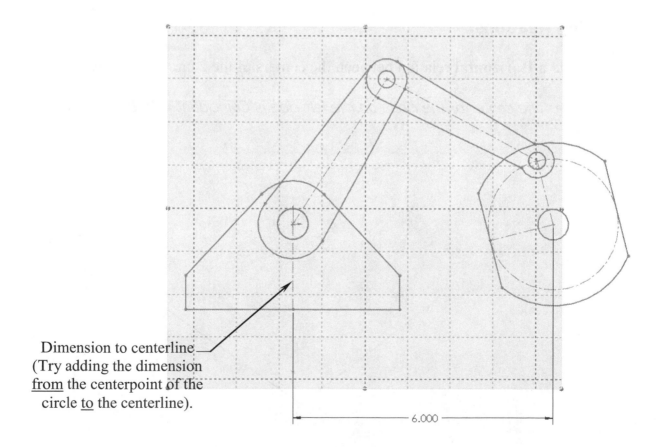

Dimension to centerline (Try adding the dimension from the centerpoint of the circle to the centerline).

6.000

8. Testing the relations between the blocks:

- Drag one of the vertices of the new part to see how the blocks respond.

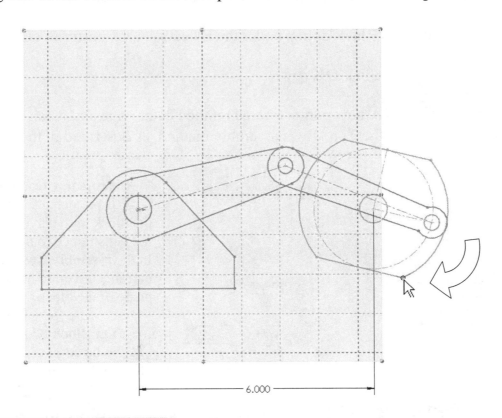

6.000

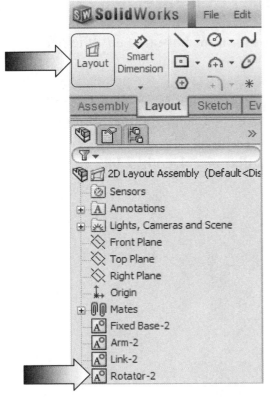

- **Click-off** the Layout command (arrow).

- Rename the new block to: **Rotator** (arrow).

- So far we have 4 different blocks, created as 2D-sketches in the assembly environment. The next step is to convert these blocks into 3D solid parts.

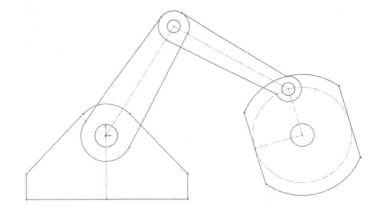

9. Converting a Block into a Component:

- Right click the name of the 1st block (Fixed Base) select **Make Part from Block**.

- Select the **On Block** option under the Block to Part Constraint dialog.

- Click **OK** .

- A new part is created on the Feature tree and it can be edited using the Top Down assembly method, as described in the next few steps.

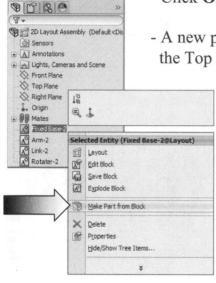

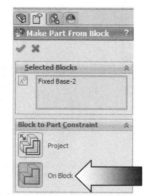

Project: Creates a part that is projected from the plane of the block in the layout sketch, but not constrained to be co-planar with. In the assembly, you can drag the part in a direction normal to the plane of the block.

On Block: Constrains the part to be co-planar with the plane of the block in the layout sketch.

10. Extruding the Fixed Base:

- Click the **Edit Component** button to edit the part Fixed Base.

- **Expand** the component Fixed Base, select the Sketch1, click **Extruded Boss/Base**, and set the following:

    * Type: **Mid Plane**   * Depth: **2.000 in**

- Click **OK** .

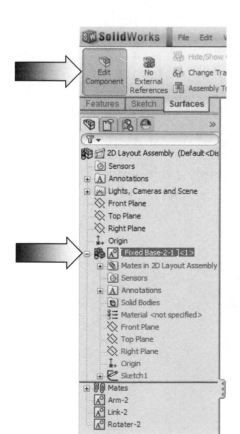

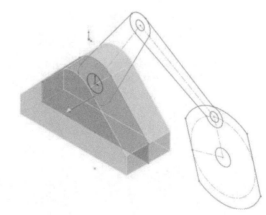

11. Adding fillets:

- Click the **Fillet/ Round** command.

- Enter **.500 in** for radius.

- Select the **2 edges** As indicated.

- Click **OK** ✔.

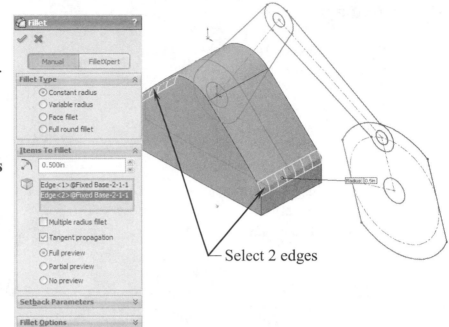

Select 2 edges

12. Shelling the part:

- Click the Shell command from the Features toolbar.

- Enter **.250 in** for wall thickness.

- Select the **7 faces** as noted.

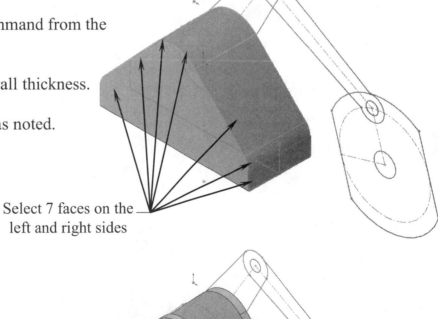

Select 7 faces on the left and right sides

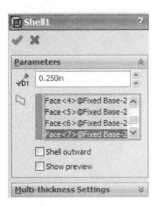

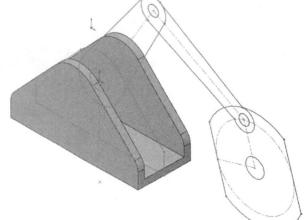

- Click **OK** ✔.

13. Adding a hole:

- Click the **Extruded Cut** command.

- Select **Though All** for both Direction1 and Direction2.

- Click in the **Selected-Contour** selection box and select the **circle** as shown.

- Click **OK** .

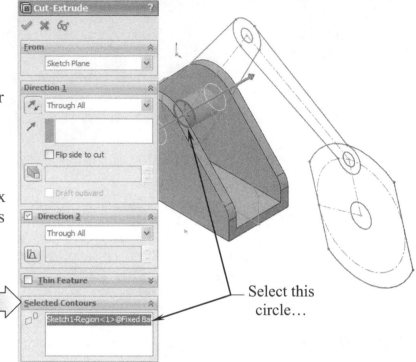

Select this circle...

- Click off the **Edit Component** command , the first part is completed.

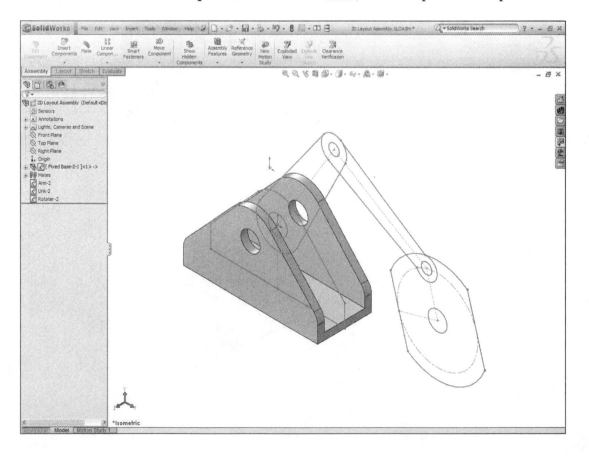

14. Converting the next block: (Repeating from step no. 8)

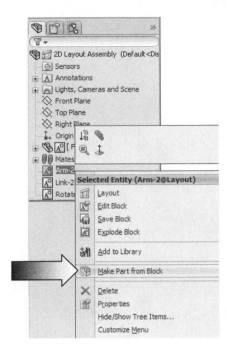

- Right click on the block named **Arm** and select **Make Part from Block**.

- Select the **On Block** option once again, from the **Block to Part Constraint** section.

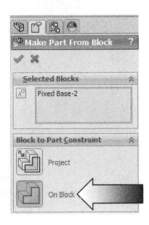

- A new part is created on the Feature Tree and it can be edited using the same method as the last one.

- Click **OK** .

15. Extruding the Arm:

- Select the part **Arm** from the Feature tree and click the **Edit Component** button.

- **Expand** the part **Arm**, select its sketch and click **Extruded Boss/Base**.

- Set the following:

    * Type: **Mid Plane**

    * Depth: **1.400 in**

- Click **OK** .

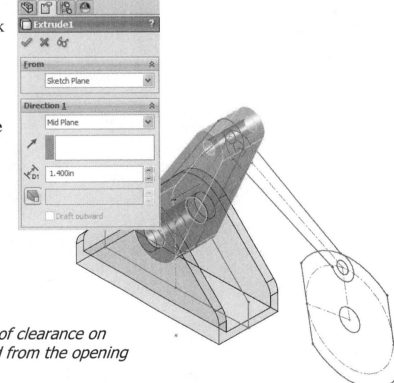

Note: _There should be a .050" of clearance on each side of this part, measured from the opening of the Fixed Base._

16. Adding a cut:

- Select the **Front** plane of the Part Arm and sketch the profile as shown.

- Use **Convert Entities** If needed and add the relations/dimensions to fully define the sketch.

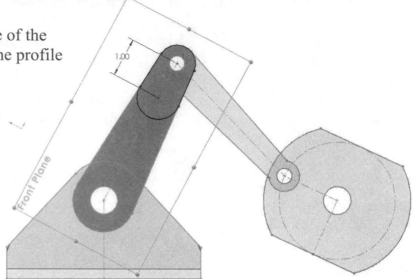

- Select the **Extruded Cut** command from the Features toolbar.

- Set the following:

* Type: **Mid Plane**

* Depth: **.900 in**

- Click **OK** ✓.

Note: _Make any adjustments if necessary to ensure proper fitsbetween the components so that they can move freely._

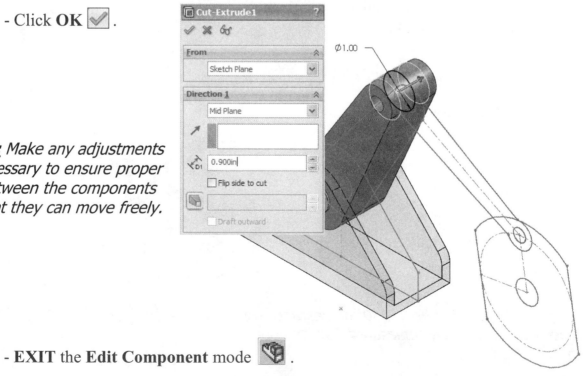

- **EXIT** the **Edit Component** mode.

17. Repeating:

- Repeat either the **step 8** or **step 13** and convert the next two blocks the same way.

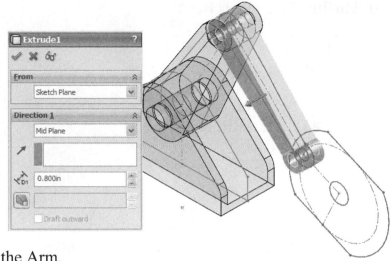

- Make the part **Link .800 in** thick as shown.

- Extrude with the **Mid Plane** type to keep the Link on the center of the Arm.

- **EXIT** the **Edit Component** mode  .

18. Using the Extrude-From option:

- The Extrude-From option allows a sketch to be extruded from a different location rather than from its own sketch plane. This new "location" can be either a plane, a surface of a part, or an offset distance which the user can control.

- Select the part **Rotator** and click **Edit Component** .

- Set the following:

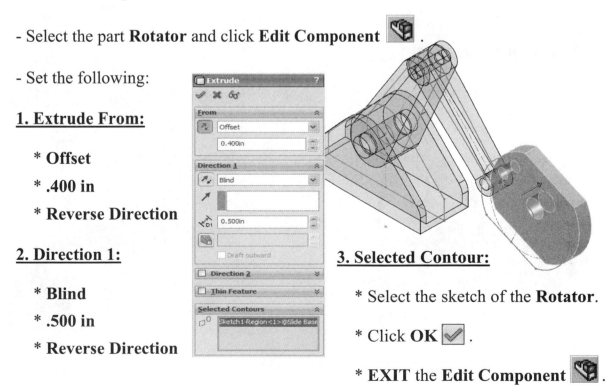

1. Extrude From:

   * **Offset**

   * **.400 in**

   * **Reverse Direction**

2. Direction 1:

   * **Blind**

   * **.500 in**

   * **Reverse Direction**

3. Selected Contour:

   * Select the sketch of the **Rotator**.

   * Click **OK** .

   * **EXIT** the **Edit Component** .

19. Hiding the sketches:

- For clarity, hide all sketches of the components.

- Right click on one of the sketch entities and select HIDE.

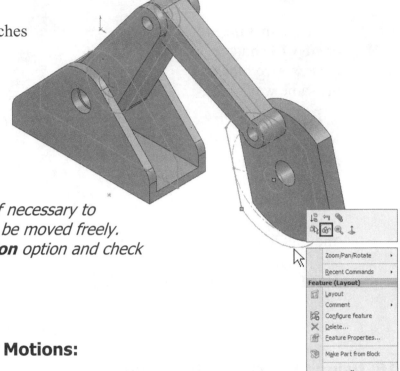

- *Note: Make any adjustments if necessary to make sure the components can be moved freely. Use the **Interference Detection** option and check for interferences, if any.*

20. Viewing the Assembly Motions:

- Drag the part **Rotator** back and forth to see how the components will move.

- Keep the part Fixed Base fixed and recreate any mates if necessary.

21. Saving your work:

- Save the assembly document as **Layout Assembly.sldasm**

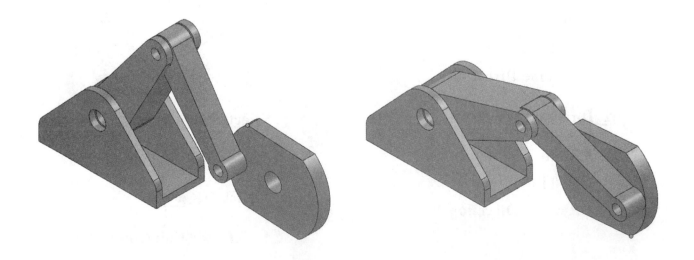

SolidWorks Animator – The Basics

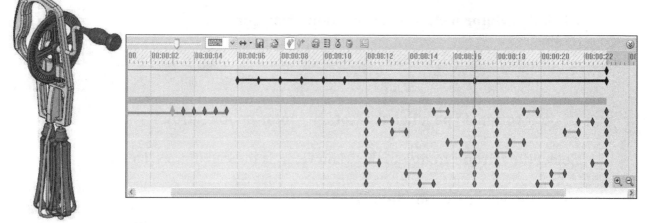

- You can use animation motion studies to simulate the motion of assemblies.

- The following techniques can be used to create animated motion studies:

* Create a basic animation by dragging the timeline and moving components.
* Use the Animation Wizard to create animations or to add rotation, explodes, or collapses to existing motion studies.
* Create camera-based animations and use motors or other simulation elements to drive the motion.

- This exercise discusses the use of all techniques mentioned above.

1. Opening an existing Assembly document:

- Open the file named: **Egg-Beater.sldasm** from the Training CD or from the web link.

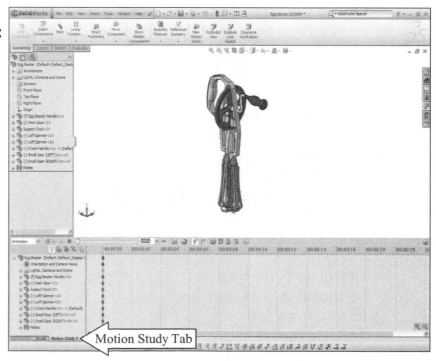

- Click the **Motion Study** tab to switch to the SolidWorks-Animation program (Motion Study1).

Motion Study Tab

2. Adding a Rotary Motor:

- Click the **Motor** icon from the **Motion Manager** toolbar.

- Under **Motion Type**, click the **Rotary Motor** option (arrow).

- Select the **Circular edge** of the Main Gear as indicated, for **Direction**.

- Click **Reverse direction** (arrow).

- Under **Motion**, select **Constant Speed**.

- Set the speed to: **30 RPM** (arrow).

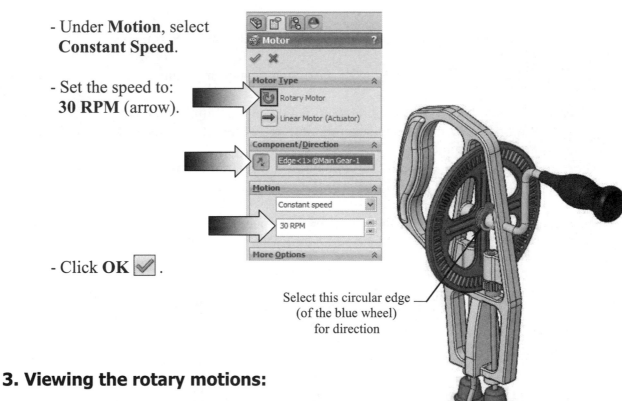

- Click **OK** ✔.

Select this circular edge (of the blue wheel) for direction

3. Viewing the rotary motions:

- Click the **Calculate** button on the **Motion Manager** (arrow).

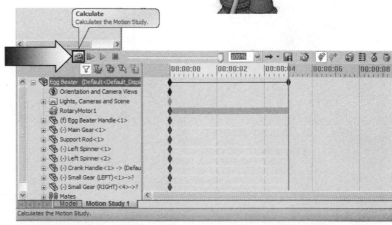

- The motor plays back the animation and by default, stops at the 5-second timeline.

4. Using the Animation Wizard:

- Click the **Animation Wizard** button on the **Motion Manager** toolbar.

- Select the **Rotate Model** Option from the **Animate Type** dialog.

- As noted in this dialog box, in order to animate the Explode or Collapse of an assembly, an exploded view must be created prior to making the animation.

- Click **Next** 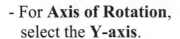.

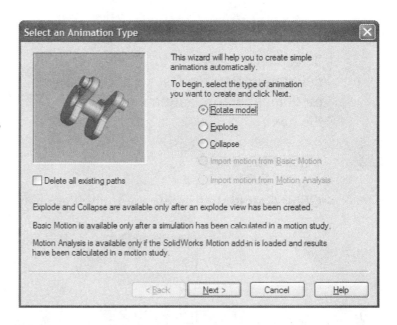

- For **Axis of Rotation**, select the **Y-axis**.

- For **Number of Rotation**, enter **1**.

- Select the **Clockwise** option.

- Click **Next** .

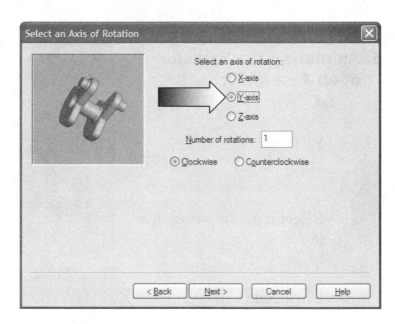

- To control the speed of the animation, the duration should be set (in seconds).

    * **Duration: 5** (arrow)

- To delay the movement at the beginning of the animation, set:

    * **Start time: 6** seconds

- This puts one-second of delay time after the last movement before animating the next.

- Click **Finish** Finish .

- Click **Calculate** to view the rotated animation.

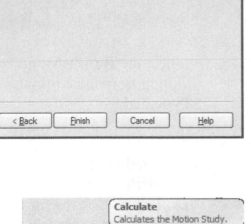

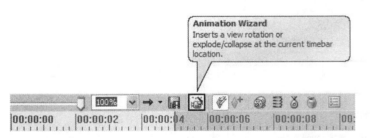

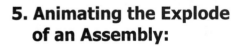

5. Animating the Explode of an Assembly:

- Click the **Animation-Wizard** button once again.

- Select the **Explode** option (arrow).

- Click **Next** Next > .

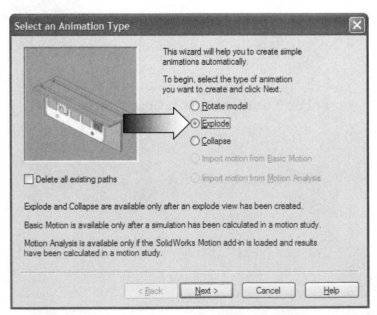

- Use the same speed as the last time

    * Duration: 5 seconds (arrow).

- Also put one-second of delay time at the end of the last movement.

    * Start Time: 12 seconds (arrow).

- Click **Finish** .

- Click **Calculate** to view the new animated movements.

- To view the entire animation, click:

Play from Start.

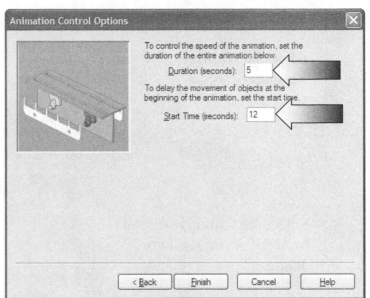

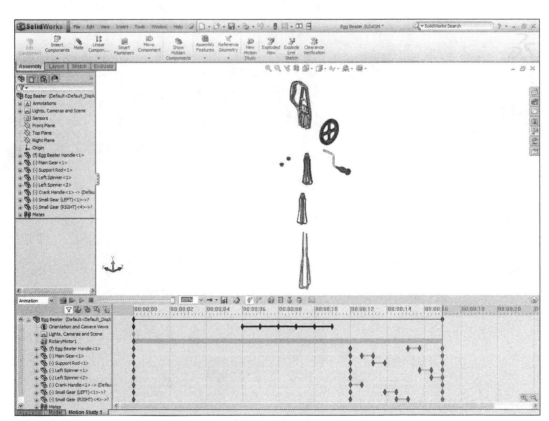

6. Animating the Collapse of the Assembly:

- Click the **Animation Wizard** button on the **Motion-Manager** toolbar.

- Select the **Collapse** option from the **Animate Type** dialog.

- Click **Next** Next > .

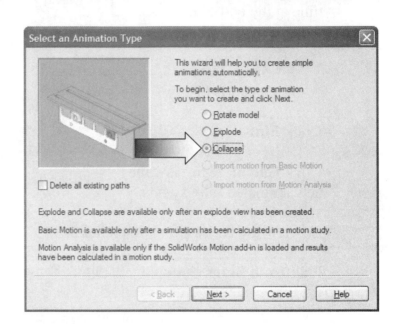

- Set the **Duration** to: **5 seconds**.

- Set the **Start Time** to: **18 seconds**.

- Click **Finish** Finish .

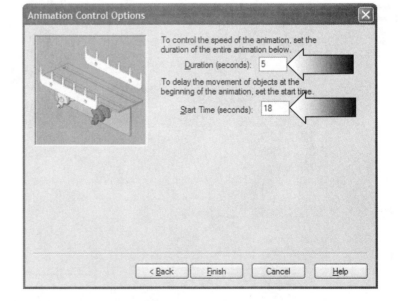

- Click **Calculate** to view the new animated movements.

- Click the **Play from Start** button  to view the entire animation.
Notice the change in the view? We now need to change the view orientation.

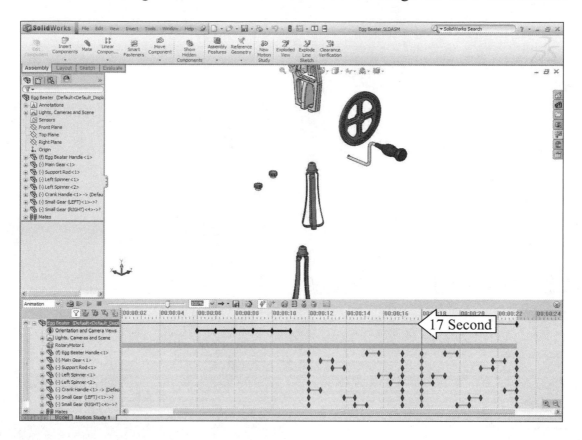

7. Changing the View Orientation of the assembly at 17-second:

- Drag the timeline to **17-second position**.

- From the MotionManager tree, right click on **Orientation and Camera Views** and un-select the **Disable View Key Creation** (arrow).

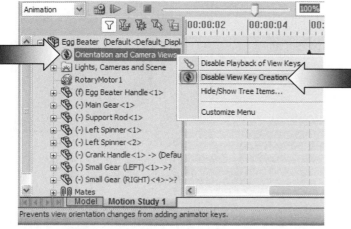

- Click the **Add/Update Key** (below).

- This key will allow modifications to the steps recorded earlier.

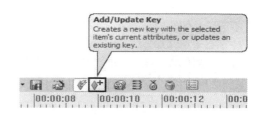

Add/Update Key
Creates a new key with the selected item's current attributes, or updates an existing key.

- Press the **F** key on the keyboard to change to the full screen – or – click Zoom to fit.

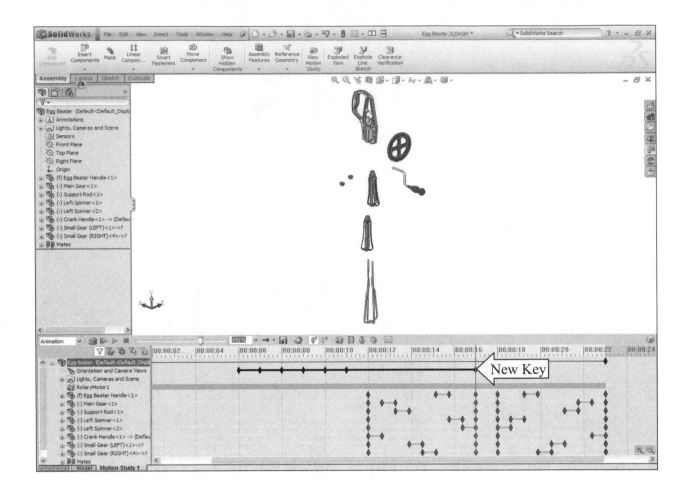

- The change in the view orientation from a zoomed-in position to a full-screen has just been recorded. To update the animation, press **Calculate.**

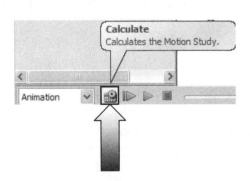

- The animation plays back showing the new Zoomed position.

Note: _This last step demonstrated that a key point(s) can be inserted at any time during the creation of the animation to modify when the view change should occur. Other attributes like colors, lights, cameras, shading, etc., can also be defined the same way._

- When the animation reaches the 23 second timeline, the assembly is shown as collapsed. We'll need to add another key and change the view orientation to full screen once again.

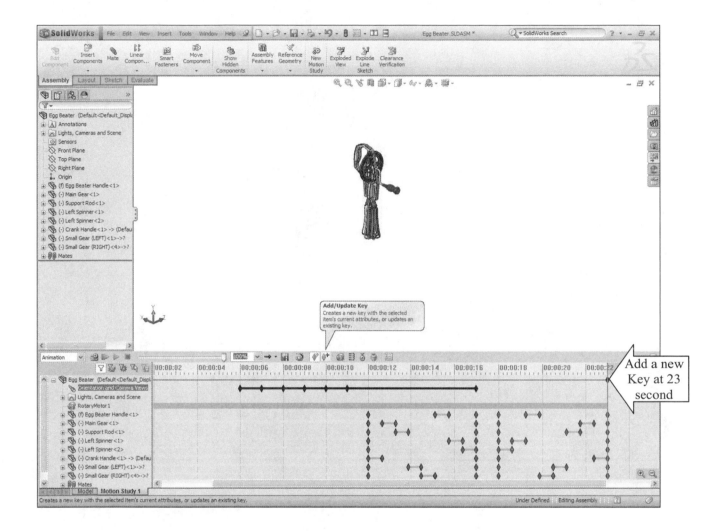

8. Changing the View Orientation of the Assembly at 23 second:

- Make sure the timeline is moved to **23 second position**.

- Click the **Add/Update Key** button on the MotionManager toolbar.

Note: *In order to capture the changes in different positions, a new key should be added each time. We will need to go back to the full screen so that more details can be viewed.*

- Press the **F** key on the keyboard to change to the full screen – or – click Zoom to fit.

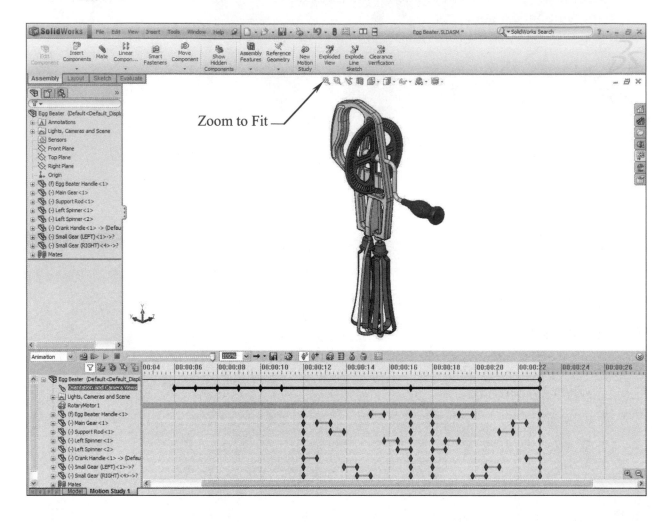

- Similar to the previous step, the change in the view orientation has just been captured.

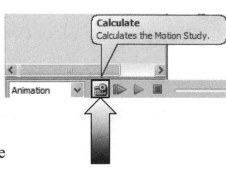

- To update the animation, press **Calculate.**

- The system plays back the animation showing the new zoom to fit position.

- Save your work before going to the next steps.

9. Creating the Flashing effects:

- Move the timeline to **3-second position**.

- Click the **Add/Update Key** button.

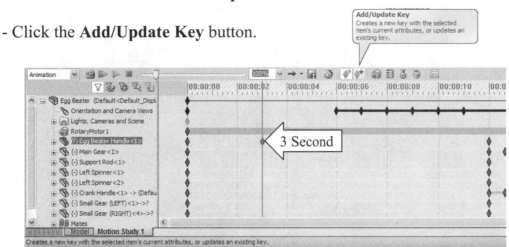

- We are going to make the Handle flash 3 times.

- Right click the part **Egg-Beater-Handle** from the Animation tree, go to **Component Display** and select **Wireframe**.

- Click **Calculate**.

- At this point, the Handle turns into Wireframe when the animation reaches the 3 second timeline and stays that way until the end.

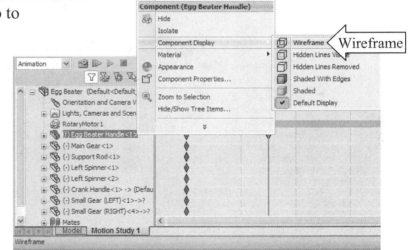

- Move the mouse cursor over the key point to display its key properties.

Place the mouse cursor over this key

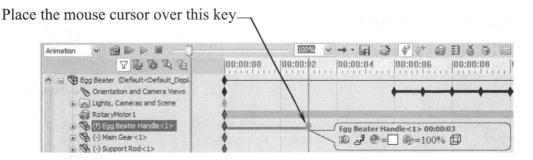

- Next, move the timeline to the **3.5 second position**.

- This time we are going to change the Handle back to shaded.

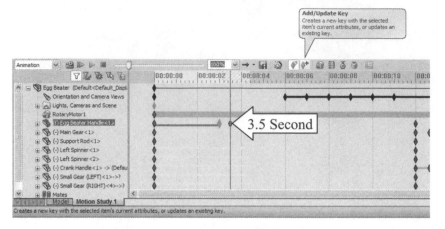

- Right click on the part **Egg Beater Handle**, go to **Component Display**, and select **Shaded with Edges**.

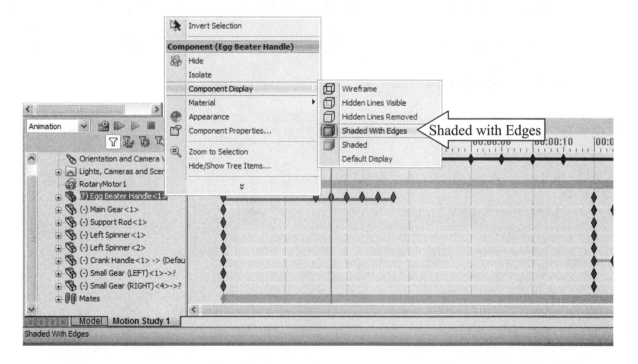

- Click **Calculate** 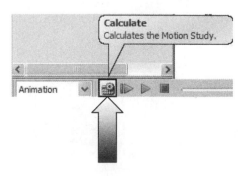.

- Since the change only happens within ½ of a second, the handle looks like it was flashing.

- Repeat the same step a few times, to make the flashing effect look more realistic.

4-second = Wireframe

3.5-second = Shaded with Edges

3-second = Wireframe

4.5-second = Wireframe

5-second = Shaded with Edges

5.5-second = Wireframe

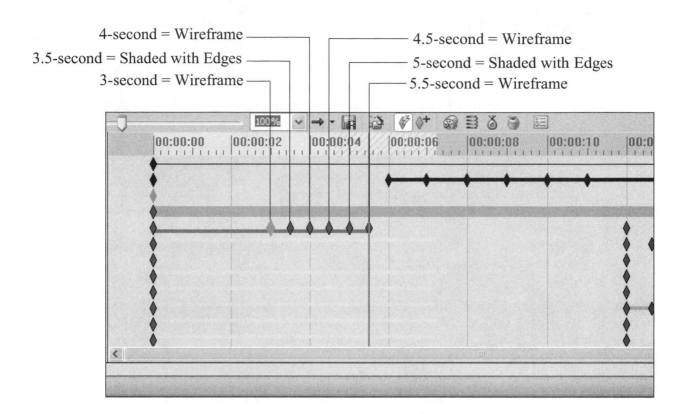

- Use the times chart listed above and repeat the step number 9 at least 3 more times.

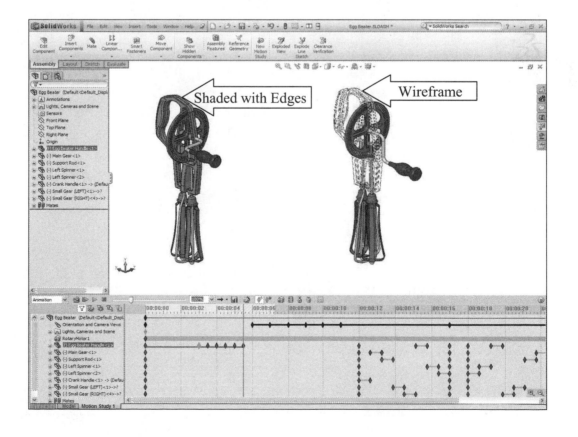

10. Looping the animation:

- Click the Playback Mode arrow and select **Playback Mode: Reciprocate** (arrow).

- Click **Play From Start** to view the entire animation again.

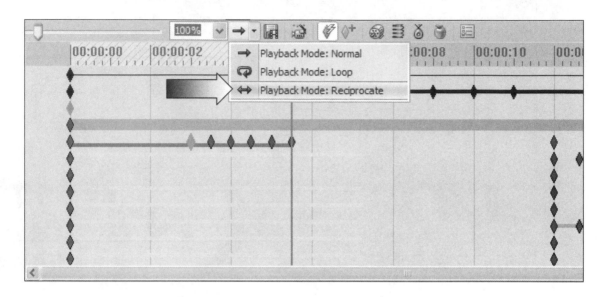

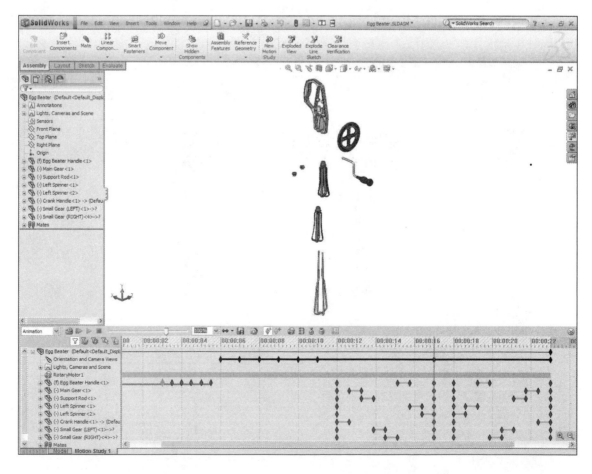

11. Saving the animation as AVI: (Audio Visual Interleaving):

- Click the **Save Animation** icon on the Motion Manager toolbar.

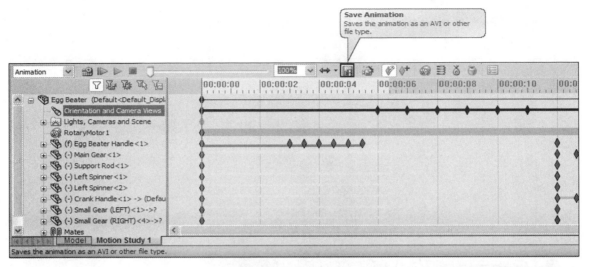

- Use the default name (Egg Beater) and other default settings.

- Click **Save**.

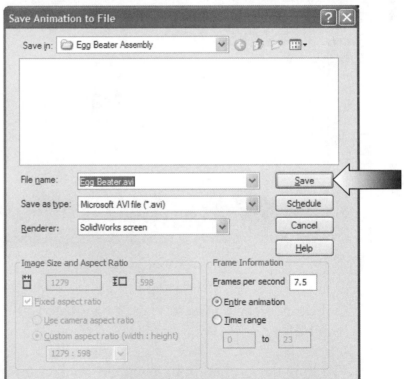

- The **Image Size** and **Aspect Ratio** (grayed-out) adjusts size and shape of the display. It becomes available when the renderer is PhotoWorks buffer.

- **Compression** ratios impact image quality. Use lower compression ratios to produce smaller file sizes of lesser image quality.

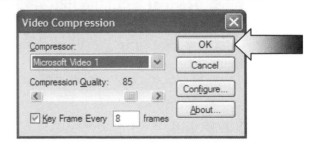

12. Viewing the Egg Beater AVI with Windows Media Player:

- **Exit** the SolidWorks program, locate and launch your **Windows Media Player**.

- **Open** the **Egg Beater.AVI** from Windows Media Player.

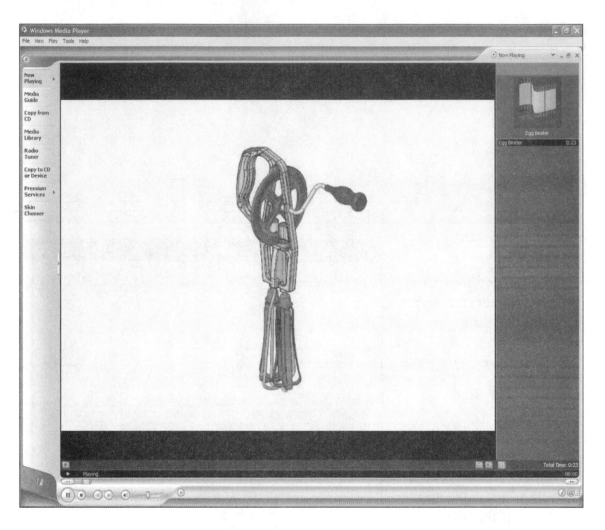

- Click the **Play** button to view the animated AVI file.

- To loop the animation in Windows Media Player, select **Repeat** from the Play dropdown menu.

- Also try changing the **Play Speed** from **Normal** to **Fast** and Play the animation again.

- **Close** and **exit** the Window Media Player.

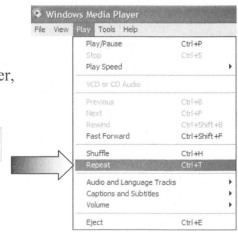

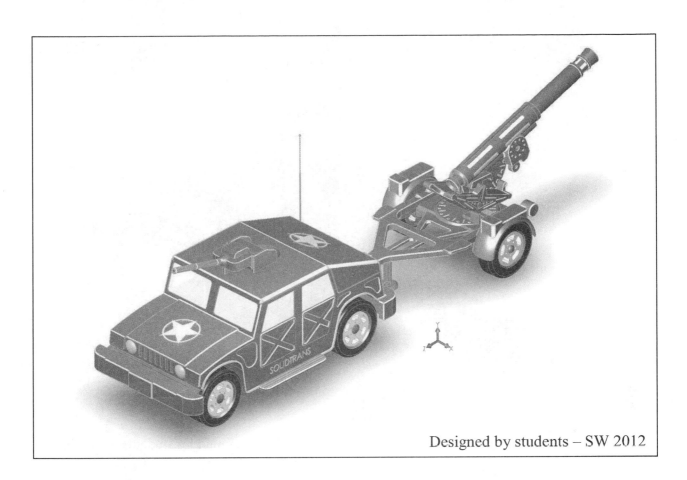

Designed by students – SW 2012

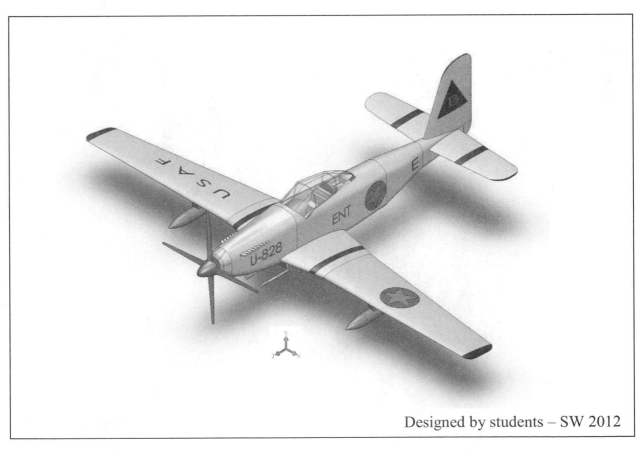

Designed by students – SW 2012

12-31

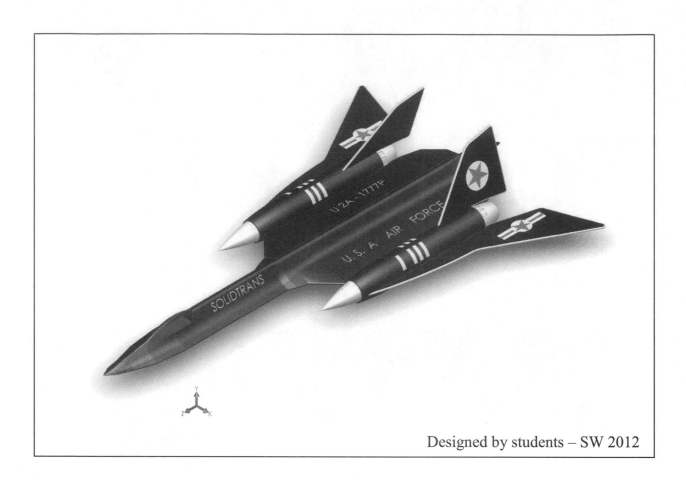

Designed by students – SW 2012

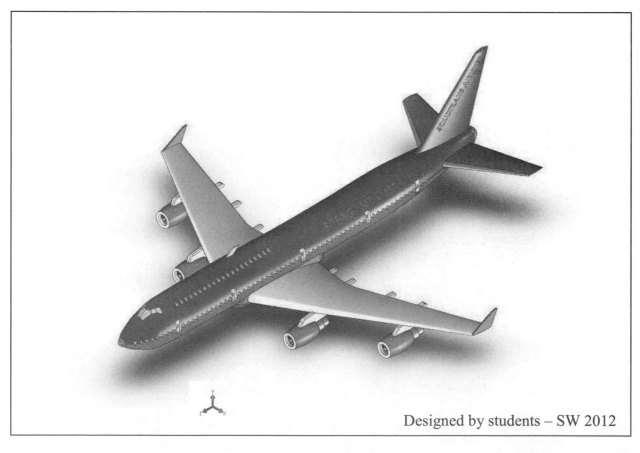

Designed by students – SW 2012

CHAPTER 13

Drawing Preparations

Customizing the Document Template

- Custom settings and parameters such as: ANSI standards, units, number of decimal places, dimensions and note fonts, arrow styles and sizes, line styles and line weights, image quality, etc., can be set and saved in the document template for current use or at any time in the future.

- All Document Templates are normally stored either in the templates folder or in the Tutorial folder:

    * (C:\Program Files\SolidWorks Corp\ SolidWorks\Data\Templates)
    * (C:\Program Files\SolidWorks Corp\ SolidWorks\Lang\English\Tutorial)

- By default, there are 2 "layers" in every new drawing. The "top layer" is called the **Sheet**, and the "bottom layer" is called the **Sheet Format**.

- The **Sheet** layer is used to create the drawing views and annotations. The **Sheet Format** layer contains the title block information, revision changes, BOM anchor, etc.

- The 2 layers can be toggled back and forth by using the FeatureManager tree, or by right clicking anywhere in the drawing and selecting: Edit Sheet Format / Edit Sheet.

- When the settings are done they will get saved in the Document Template with the extension: **.drwdot** (Drawing Document Template).

- This chapter will guide us through the preparations for a detailed drawing.

Drawing Preparations

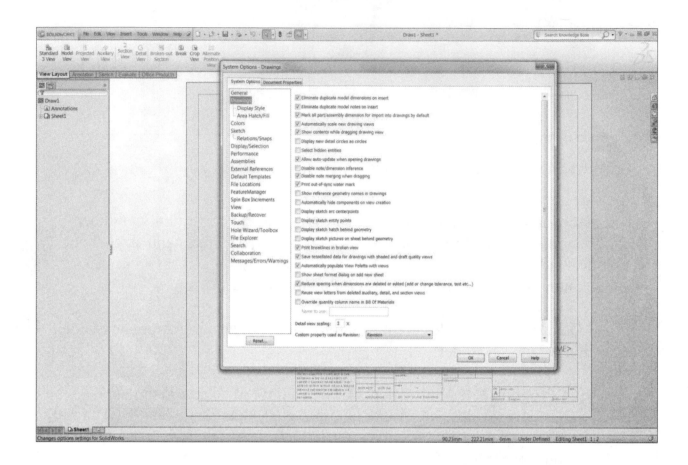

Dimensioning Standards: **ANSI**	Third Angle Projection
Units: **INCHES** – 3 Decimals	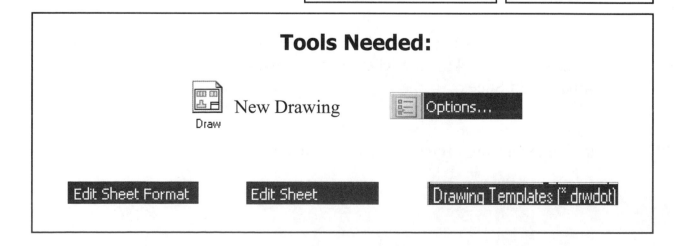

Tools Needed:

New Drawing

Draw

Options...

Edit Sheet Format

Edit Sheet

Drawing Templates (*.drwdot)

1. Setting up a new drawing:

- Select **File / New / Draw** (or Drawing) / **OK** 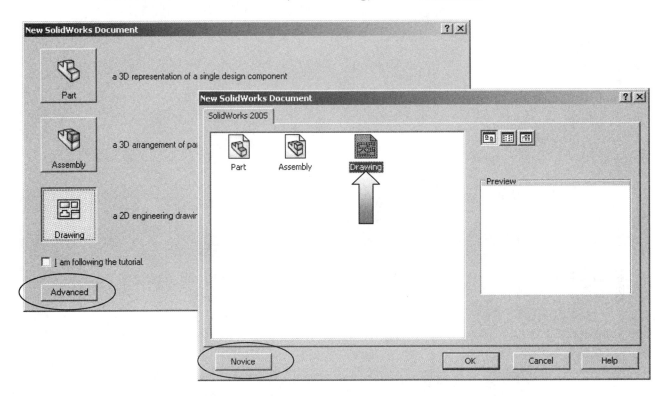 .

- By clicking on either **Advanced** or **Novice** (Circled), you can switch to the appropriate dialog box.

- Under Standard Sheet Size, choose **C-Landscape**.

- Uncheck the **Only Show Standard Format** check box (arrow).

- Click **OK** .

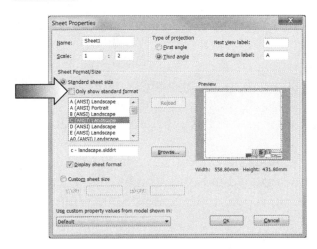

- The SolidWorks Drawing User Interface.

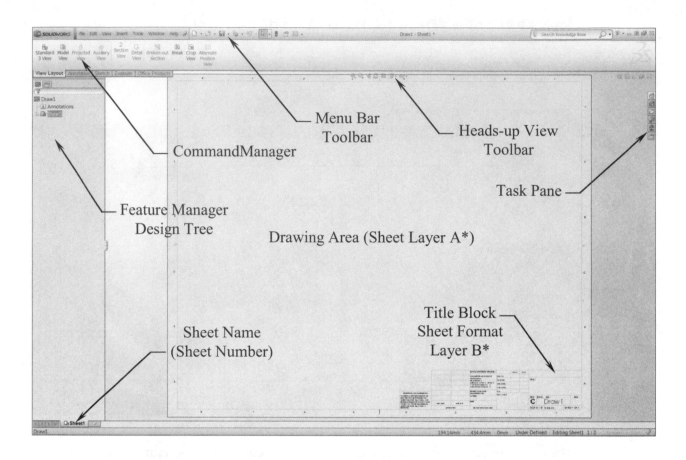

Menu Bar Toolbar

Heads-up View Toolbar

CommandManager

Task Pane

Feature Manager Design Tree

Drawing Area (Sheet Layer A*)

Title Block
Sheet Format
Layer B*

Sheet Name
(Sheet Number)

*A. By default, the **Sheet** layer is active and placed over the **Sheet Format** layer.

- The **Sheet** layer is used to create drawing views, dimensions, and annotations.

* B. The "bottom layer" is called the **Sheet Format** layer, which is where the revision block, the title block and its information are stored.

- The Sheet Format layer includes some links to the system properties and the custom properties.

- OLE objects (company's logo) such as .Bmp or .Tif can be embedded here.

- SolidWorks drawings can have different Sheet Formats or none at all.

- Formats or title blocks created from other CAD programs can be opened in SolidWorks using either DXF or DWG file types, and saved as SolidWorks' Sheet Format.

2. Switching to the Sheet Format layer:

- Right click in the drawing and select **Edit Sheet Format**.

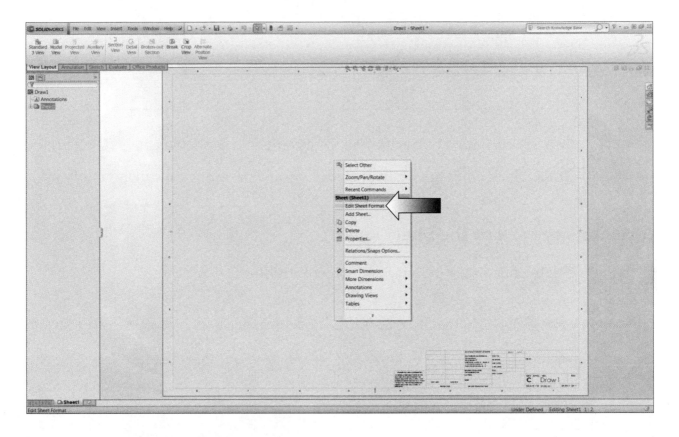

- Using the SolidWorks drawing templates, there will be "blank notes" already created for each field within the title block.

- Double click the blank note in the Company-Name field and enter: **SolidWorks.**

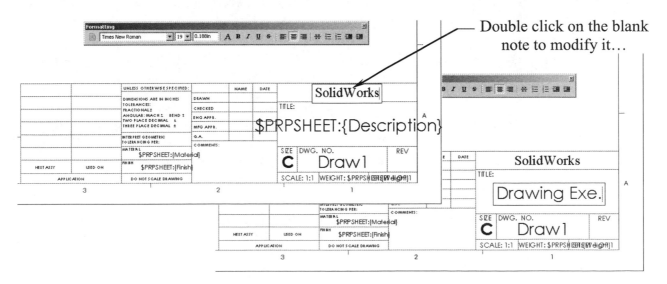

Double click on the blank note to modify it…

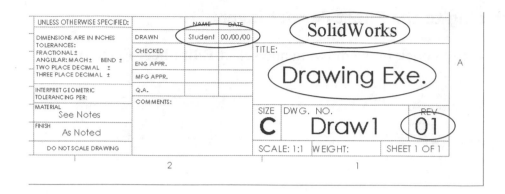

- Modify each note box and fill in the information as shown above (Circled).

- If the blank notes are not available, copy and paste any note then modify it.

3. Switching back to the Sheet layer:

- Right click in the drawing and select **Edit Sheet**.

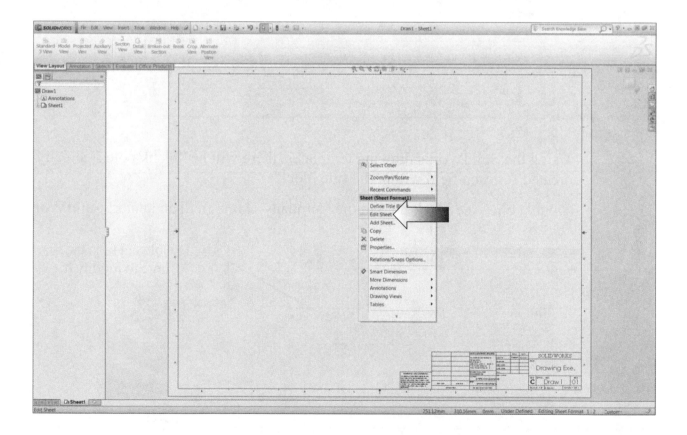

- The Sheet layer is brought to the top, all information within the Sheet Format layer is switched to the bottom layer.

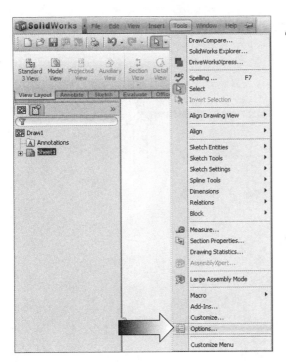

4. Setting up the Drawing Options:

- Go to **Tools / Options** .

- Select the **Drawings** options from the list.

- Enable and/or disable the drawing options by clicking on the check boxes as shown below.

NOTE:

For further information about these options, please refer to Chapter 2 in the: SolidWorks 2012 Part I - Basic Tools textbook (Essential Parts, Assemblies and Drawings).

- These parameters are examples for use with this text-book only; you may have to modify them to work with your application or company's standards

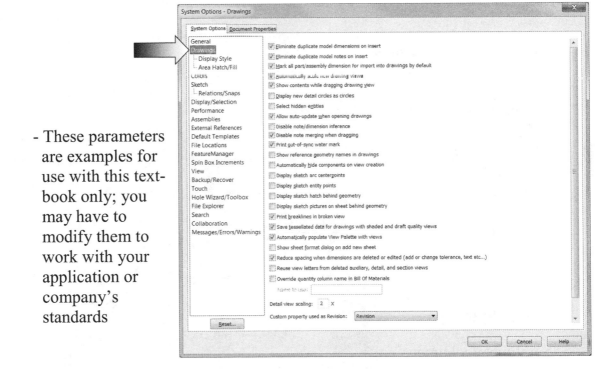

- The parameters that you are setting here will be save automatically as the default system options, and they will affect current and all future documents.

- Once again, enable only the check boxes as shown in the dialog above.

5. Setting up the Document Template options:

- Click the **Document Properties** tab.

- Select the **DRAFTING STANDARD** option.

- Change the default option to **ANSI**, which is an abbreviation of:

> **A**merican
> **N**ational
> **S**tandards
> **I**nstitute.

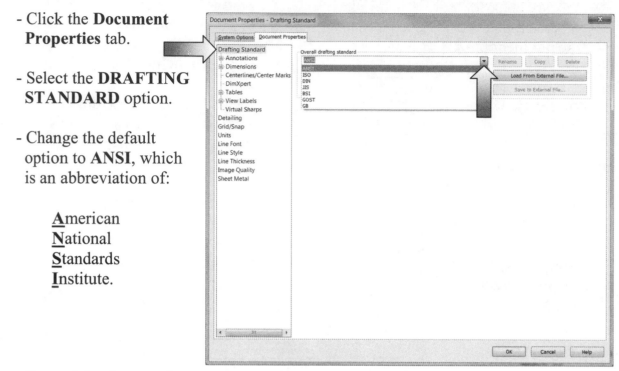

- Expand the **Annotations** options.

- Set the new parameters as shown.

- Click the **Font** button and select the following:

> **Century Gothic**
>
> **Regular**
>
> **13 points**

- Set the Note, Dimension, Surface Finish, Weld-Symbol, Tables, and Balloon to match the settings for Annotations.

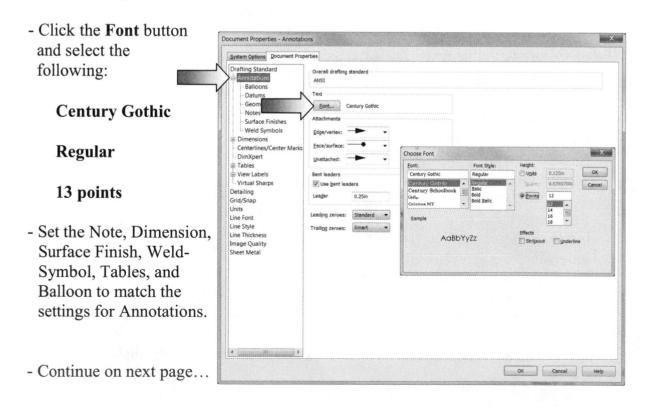

- Continue on next page…

- Refer to Chapter 2 in this textbook for other settings that are not mentioned here.

- Select the **Dimensions** option (arrow).

- Set the parameter in this section to match the settings in the dialog boxes.

- If the Dual Dimension Display is selected, be sure to set the number of decimal places for both of your Primary and Secondary dimensions.

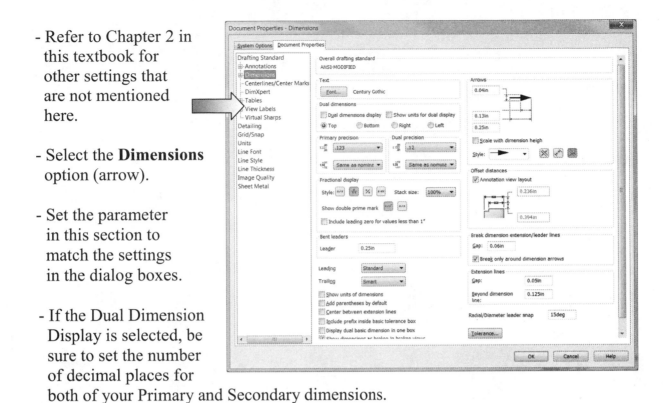

NOTE: Skip to the Units option below, if you need to change your Primary unit from Millimeter to Inches, or vice versa.

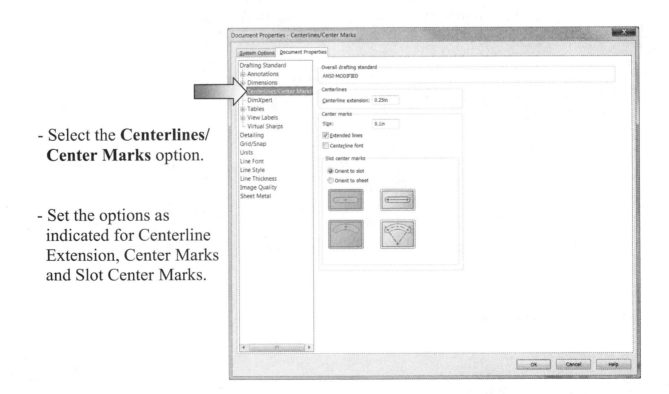

- Select the **Centerlines/ Center Marks** option.

- Set the options as indicated for Centerline Extension, Center Marks and Slot Center Marks.

- Select the **Tables / Bill of Materials** option.

- The B.O.M. is an Excel based template, set its parameters similar to the ones in Microsoft Excel such as: Border, Font, Zero Quantity Display Missing Component, Leading and Trailing Zeros, etc.

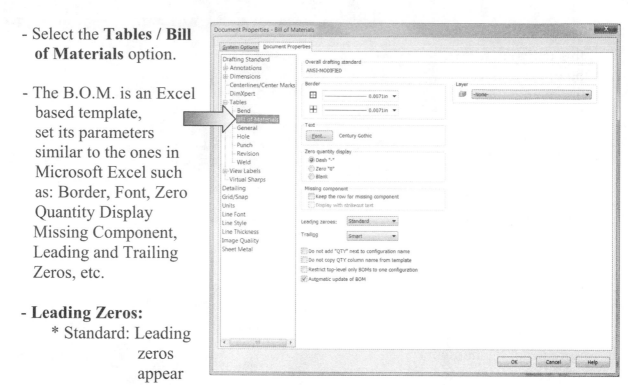

- Leading Zeros:

    * Standard: Leading zeros appear according to the overall drafting standard.

    * Show: Shows zeros before decimal point are shown.

    * Remove: Leading zeros do not appear.

- Trailing Zeros:

    * Smart: Trailing zeros are timed for whole metric values.

    * Standard: Trailing zeros appear according to ASME standard.

    * Show: Trailing zeros are displayed according to the decimal places specified in Units.

    * Remove: Trailing zeros do not appear.

- Select the **Tables / Revision** option.

- Set the document-level drafting settings for revision table like: Border, Font, Alphabet Numerical Control, Multiple Sheet Style and Layer.

- Select the **View Label / Detail** option.

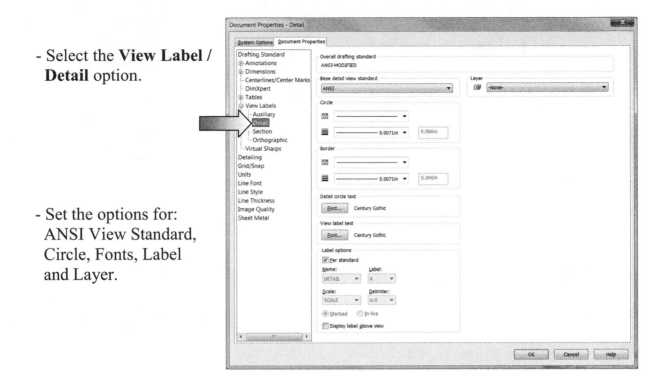

- Set the options for: ANSI View Standard, Circle, Fonts, Label and Layer.

- Select the **View Label / Section** option.

- Set the Line Style, Line Thickness, Fonts, Label, Scale, Layer, and Section Arrow Size.

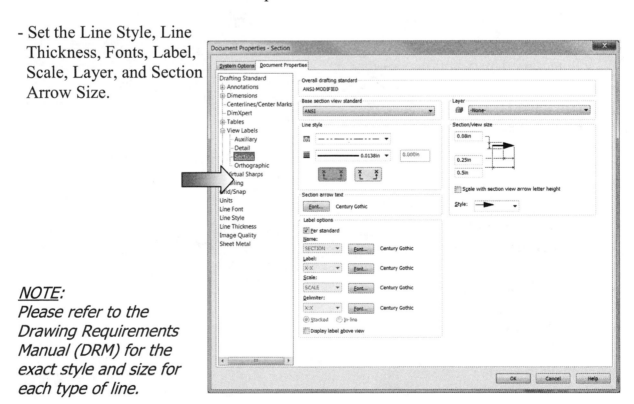

NOTE:
Please refer to the Drawing Requirements Manual (DRM) for the exact style and size for each type of line.

- Select the **Detailing** option.

- Set the Display Filters, Import Annotations, Auto Insert on View Creation, Area Hatch Display and View Break Lines.

- Select the **Units** option.

- Click the **IPS (Inch, Pound, Second)** system.

- Set the Length Units to: **3 Decimal Places (.123)**

- Other options can be set to meet your company's standards.

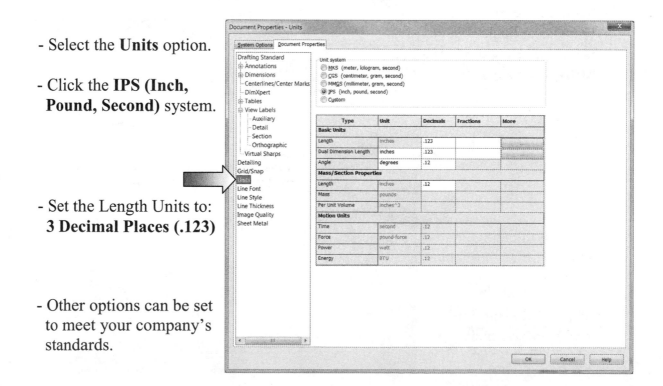

- Select the **Line Font** option.

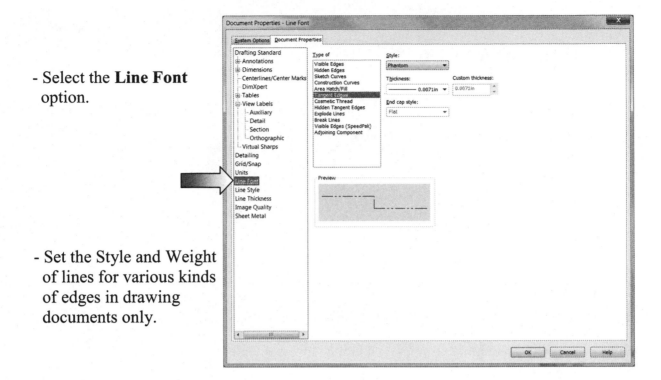

- Set the Style and Weight of lines for various kinds of edges in drawing documents only.

- Select the **Line Thickness** option.

- Set the **Line Thickness** to your own preferences.

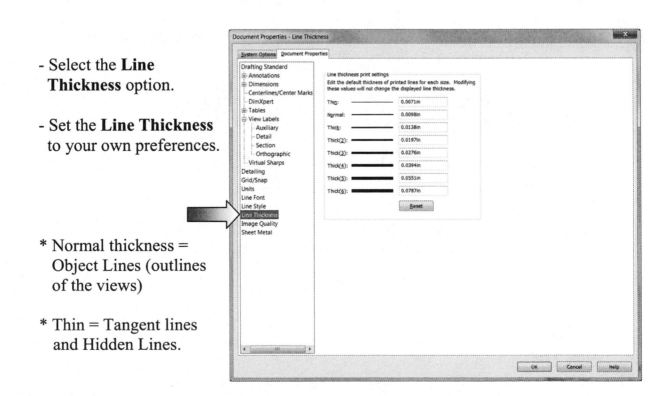

* Normal thickness = Object Lines (outlines of the views)

* Thin = Tangent lines and Hidden Lines.

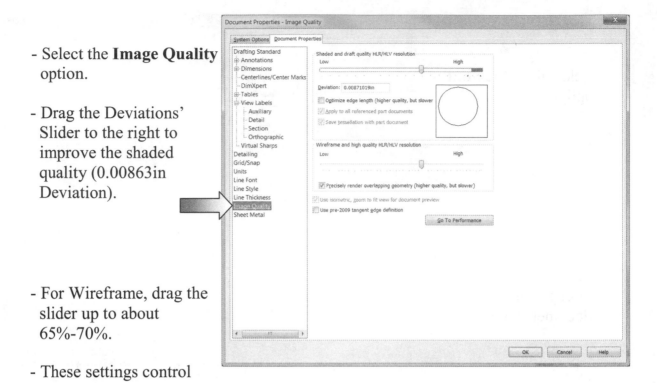

- Select the **Image Quality** option.

- Drag the Deviations' Slider to the right to improve the shaded quality (0.00863in Deviation).

- For Wireframe, drag the slider up to about 65%-70%.

- These settings control the tessellation of curved surfaces for shaded rendering output. A higher resolution setting results in slower model rebuilding but more accurate curves.

- Select the **Sheet Metal** option.

- Set the colors for Bend Lines, Form Features, Hems, Model Edges, Flat Pattern Sketch Color, and Bounding Box.

- Click **OK** [OK].

6. Saving the Document Template:

- Go to **File / Save As** and change the **Save As Type** to **Drawing Templates**.

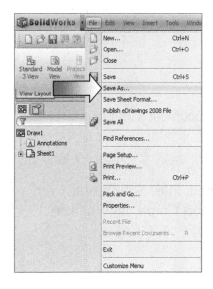
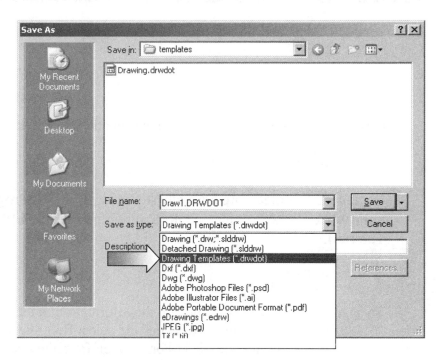

- SolidWorks automatically switches to the **Templates** folder (or **Tutorial** folder), where all SolidWorks templates are stored.

- Enter a name for your new template (i.e. C-Size Inch).

- Click **Save**.

- Close the document template.

Questions for Review

Drawing Preperations

1. Custom settings and parameters can be set and saved in the Document Template.
    a. True
    b. False

2. Document Templates are normally stored either in: (C:\Program Files\SolidWorks Corp\ SolidWorks\Data\Templates) OR (C:\Program Files\SolidWorks Corp\Lang\English\ Tutorial).
    a. True
    b. False

3. To access the sheet format and edit the information in the title block:
    a. Right click in the drawing and select Edit Sheet Format.
    b. Right click the Sheet Format icon from the Feature Tree and select Edit Sheet-Format.
    c. All of the above.

4. The **Sheet** layer is where the Title Block information and Revisions changes are stored.
    a. True
    b. False

5. The **Sheet Format** layer is used to create the drawing views, dimensions, and annotations.
    a. True
    b. False

6. Information in the Title Block and Revision Block are Fixed, they cannot be modified.
    a. True
    b. False

7. The Document Template is saved with the file Extension:
    a. DWG
    b. DXF
    c. SLDPRT
    d. DRWDOT
    e. SLDDRW

7. D
5. FALSE 6. FALSE
3. C 4. FALSE
1. TRUE 2. TRUE

CHAPTER 14

Assembly Drawings

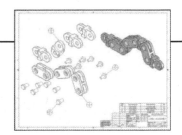

Assembly Drawings
Links Assembly

- Assembly drawings are created in the same way as part drawings, the same drawing tools and commands are used to create the drawing views and annotations. In an assembly drawing all components are shown together as assembled or as exploded.

- The standard drawing views like the Front, Top, Right, and Isometric views can be created with the same drawing tools, or they can be dragged and dropped from the View Pallet.

- When a cross section view is created, it will be cross hatched automatically and the hatch patterns that represents the part's material can be added and easily edited as well.

- A parts list or a Bill of Materials (B.O.M.) is created to report the details of the components such as:

* Materials.

* Vendors.

* Quantities.

* Part numbers, etc.

4	004-12345	Single Link	4
3	003-12345	Pin Head	6
2	002-12345	Alignment Pin	6
1	001-12345	Double Link	3
ITEM NO.	PART NUMBER	DESCRIPTION	QTY.

- The components will then be labeled with Balloons (or Dash Numbers) for verification against the Bill of Materials.

- This chapter discusses the basics of creating an assembly drawing using SolidWorks 2012.

Links Assembly
Assembly Drawings

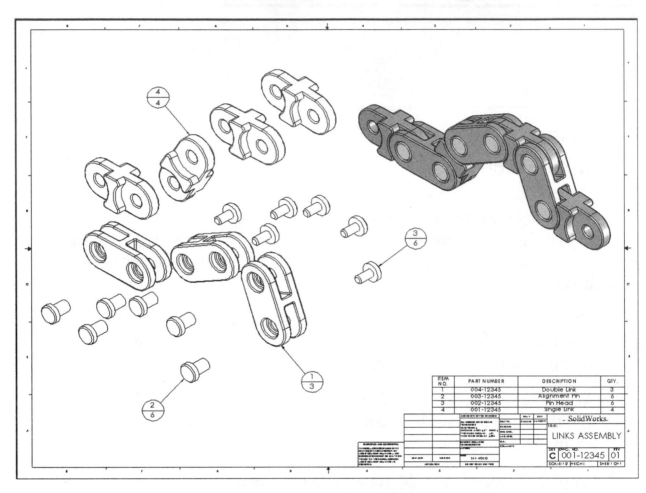

ITEM NO.	PART NUMBER	DESCRIPTION	QTY.
1	004-12345	Double Link	3
2	003-12345	Alignment Pin	6
3	002-12345	Pin Head	6
4	001-12345	Single Link	4

LINKS ASSEMBLY

C | 001-12345 | 01

Dimensioning Standards: **ANSI**	Third Angle Projection
Units: **INCHES** – 3 Decimals	

Tools Needed:

 New Drawing   Model View   Shaded View

Balloon   Bill of Materials    Properties...

1. Creating a new drawing:

- Select **File** / **New** / **Draw** (or Drawing) / **OK**.

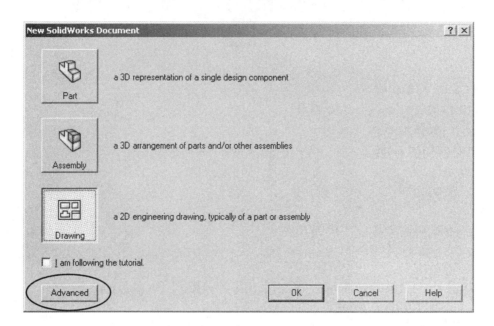

- Under Standard Sheet Size, select **C-Landscape** for paper size.

$$A = 8.5" \quad X \quad 11.00" \quad (Landscape)$$
$$B = 17.00" \quad X \quad 11.00" \quad (Landscape)$$
$$C = 22.00" \quad X \quad 17.00" \quad (Landscape)$$
$$D = 34.00" \quad X \quad 22.00" \quad (Landscape)$$
$$E = 44.00" \quad X \quad 34.00" \quad (Landscape)$$

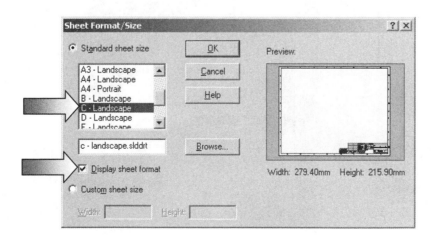

- Enable **Display Sheet Format** checkbox to display the revision and title blocks.

- Click **OK** [ΠK] .

- The Drawing template appears in the graphics area.

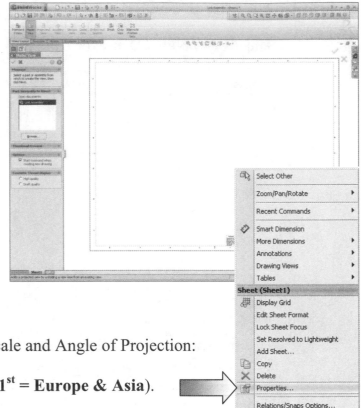

- Click **Cancel** (✖), the drawing views Scale and Projection type should be set up first.

- Right click in the drawing and select **Properties**.

- Set the Drawing Views Scale and Angle of Projection:

  (**3rd Angle = U.S. – OR – 1st = Europe & Asia**).

- Set **Scale** to **1 : 1** (full scale)

- Set **Type of Projection** to: **Third Angle** ⦿ Third angle

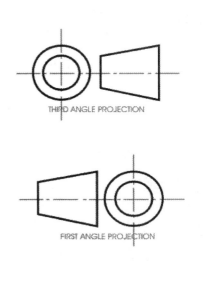

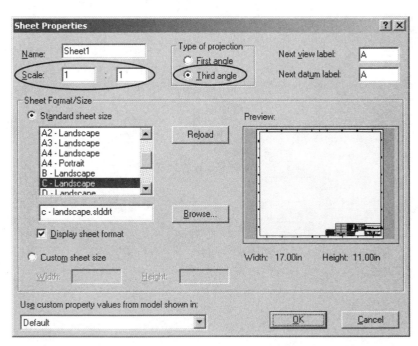

- Click **OK** [OK] .

2. Editing the Sheet Format:

- Right click inside the drawing and select **Edit-Sheet-Format**.

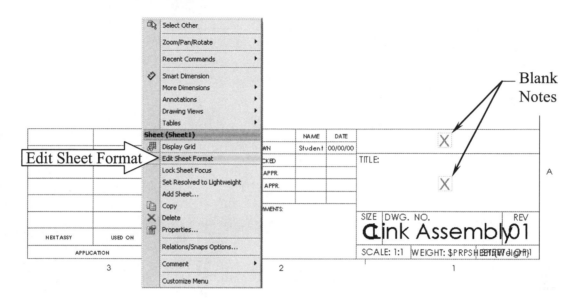

- The **Format** layer is brought up to the top.

3. Setting up the anchor point to attach the B.O.M.:

- Zoom in on the lower right side of the title block.

- Right click on the end point of the line (as shown) and
  select **Set-As-Anchor / Bill Of Materials**.

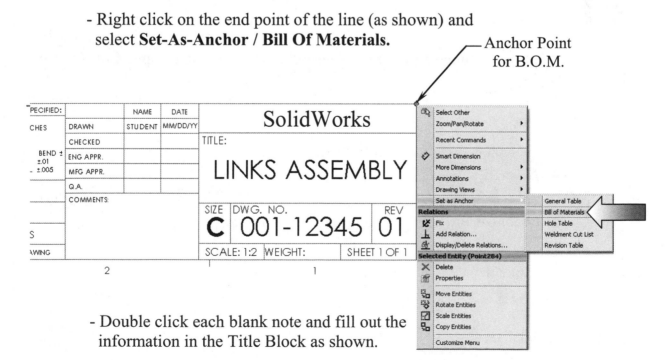

- Double click each blank note and fill out the
  information in the Title Block as shown.

4. Switching back to the Sheet layer:

- Right click inside the drawing and select **Edit-Sheet.**

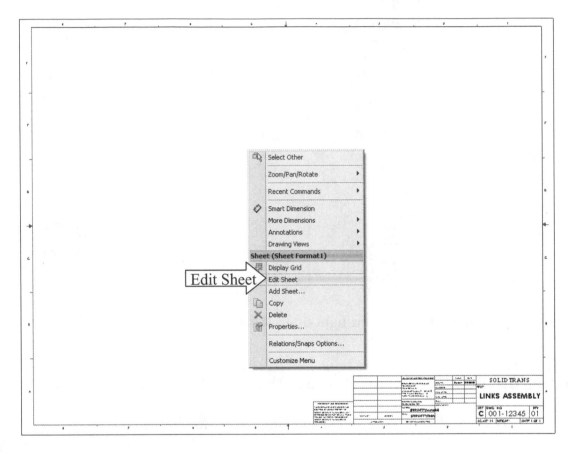

- **Change the Drawing Paper's color:**

- Select **Tools / Options / System Options / Colors / Drawing Paper Colors / Edit**.

- Select the **White** color and also enable: **Use Specified Color for Drawings Paper-Color** option.

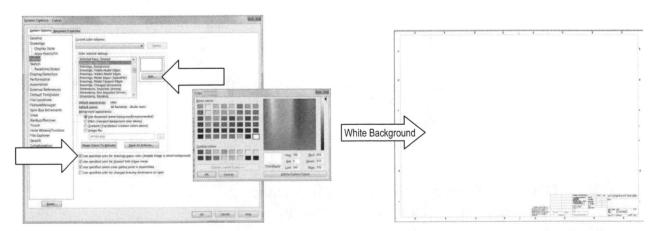

5. Opening an existing assembly document:

- Click the **Model View** command from the View Layout toolbar.

- Click the **Browse** button, locate and open your **Links Assembly** document.

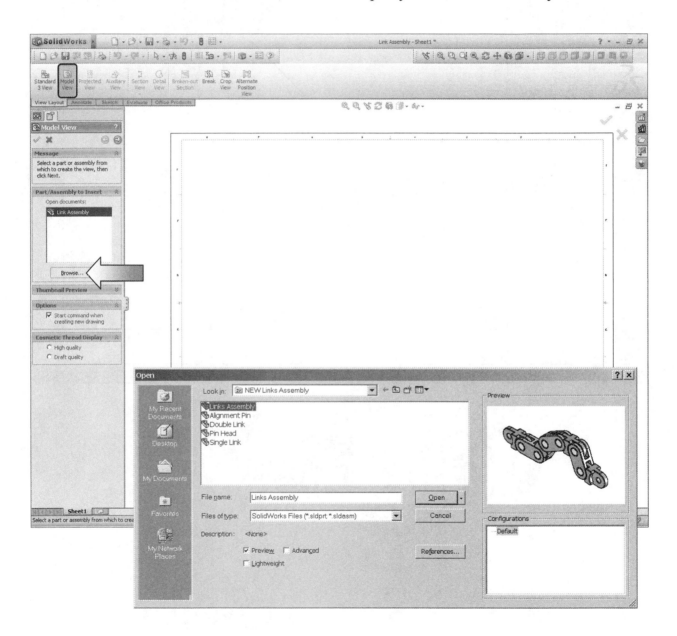

- There are several different methods to create the drawing views; in this lesson, we will discuss the use of the **Model-View** command first.

- Select the ISOMETRIC view button (Circled) and place the drawing view approximately as shown.

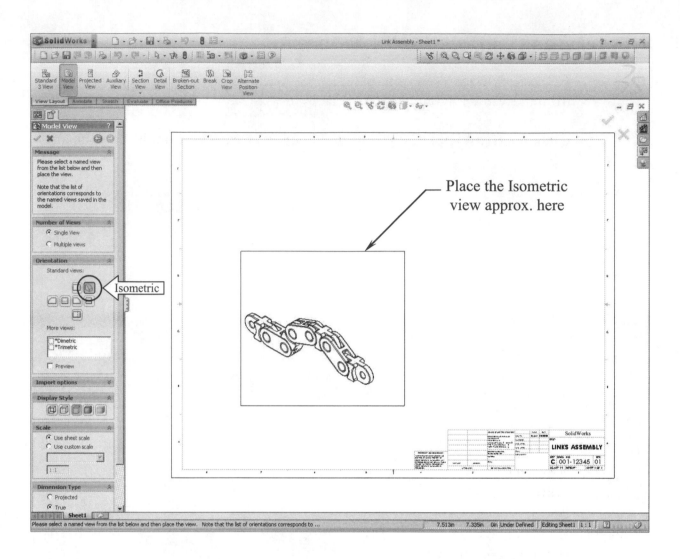

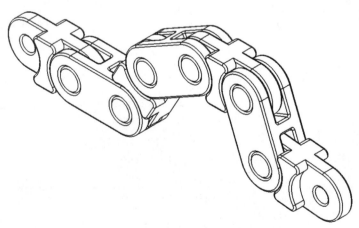

- The isometric view is created based on the default orientations of the last saved assembly document.

- Press **Ctrl + Tab** to toggle between the SolidWorks open documents.

6. Switching to the Exploded View state:

- Right click on the drawing view border and select **Properties**.

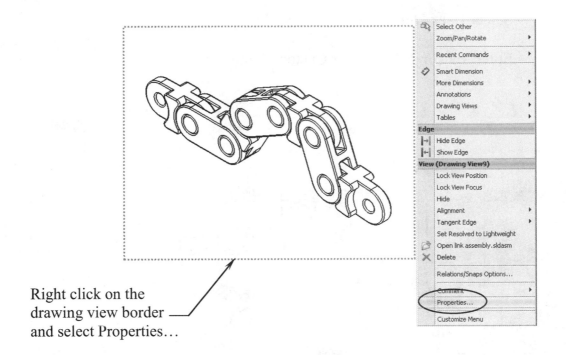

Right click on the
drawing view border
and select Properties...

- Enable the **Show In -
Exploded State** check box.

- The exploded checkbox is
only available if an exploded
view has been created earlier
in the assembly level.

- Click **OK** | OK |.

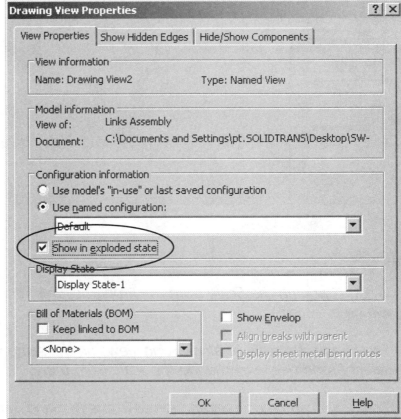

7. Changing the Scale of the Isometric Exploded view:

- Click the drawing view border to access the Properties tree.

- Select **User Defined** under the Scale section.

- Enter **3:2 (or 1.5 to 1)** for Custom Scale.

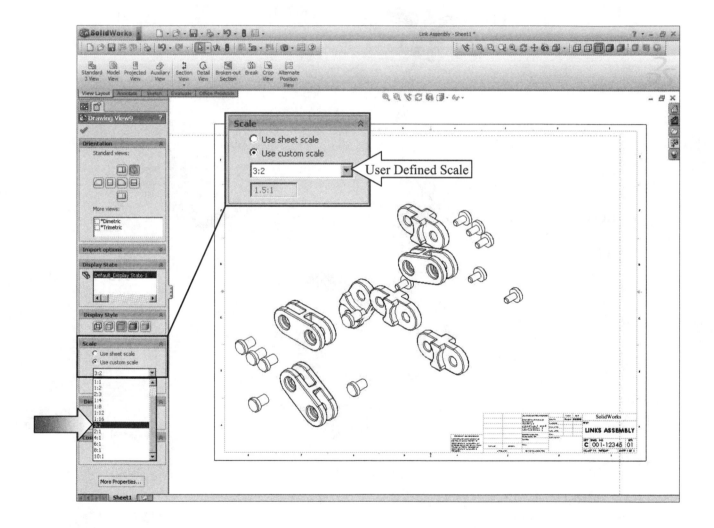

Notes:

- *When changing the Scale from the Properties tree, only the selected drawing view(s) will be affected.*

- *To change the scale of all drawing views on the same sheet, right click on the drawing, select Properties, and change the scale from there.*

- *The Scale can be pre-set and saved in the Drawing Template.*

8. Creating the 2nd Isometric View:

- Click the **Model View** command.

- Click **Next** and select the ISOMETRIC view under the Orientation Section.

- Place the drawing view approximately as shown.

- Click **OK** .

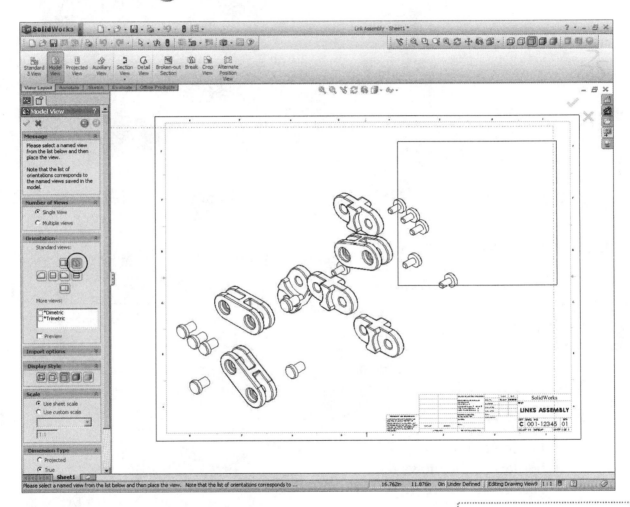

Note:

The drawing view borders appear on the screen but not on the printouts.

Drawing view border

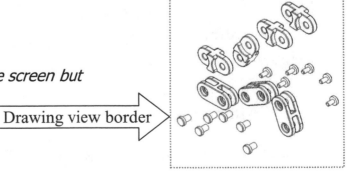

9. Changing Scale:

- Set the Scale option to: **Use Custom Scale**.

- Select from the list: **User Define**.

- Enter **3:2** for custom scale.

- Click **OK** .

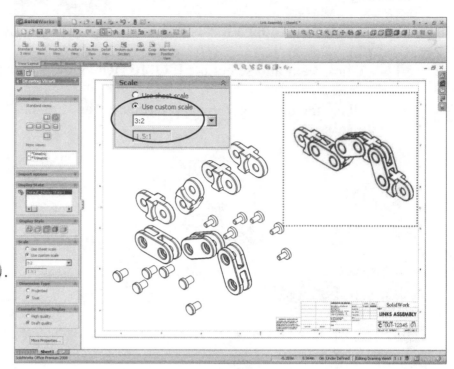

10. Switching to Shaded view:

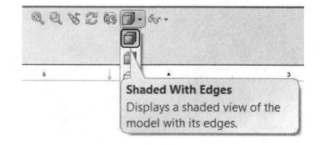

- Sometimes for clarity, a drawing view is changed to shaded instead of wireframe.

Shaded With Edges
Displays a shaded view of the model with its edges.

- The shaded view will be printed as shaded. To change the shading of more than one view at the same time, hold the control key, select the borders of the views then change the shading.

- Select the Isometric view border .

- Click **Shaded** or select **View / Display / Shaded with Edges**.

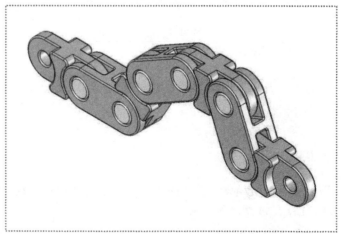

- The Isometric view is now shown as Shaded with Edges.

11. Creating a Bill Of Materials (B.O.M.):

- Click the Isometric view's border.

- Select **Insert / Tables / Bill Of Materials** – OR – Click the B.O.M. command from the **Tables** button.

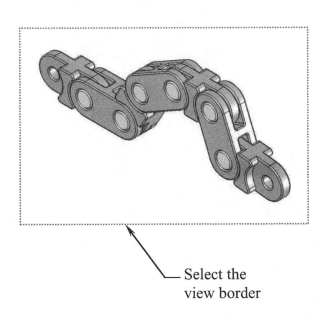

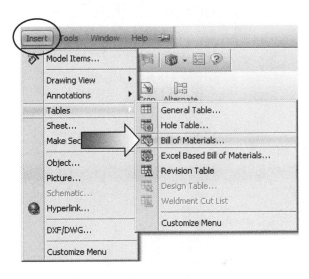

Select the
view border

- A BOM is created automatically and the information in the assembly document is populated with item numbers, description, quantities and part numbers.

- When the Bill Of Materials properties tree appears, select **Bom-Standard** (Circled) from the Table Template list (Circled) and Click **Open** [Open] .

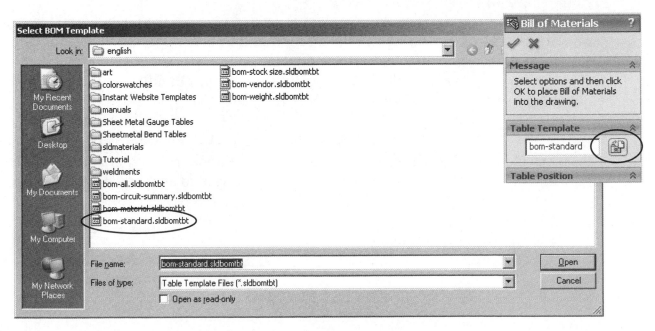

12. Selecting the B.O.M. options:

- Table Template: **BOM Standard.**

- Attach to Anchor Point*: **Cleared**.

- BOM Type: **Parts only**.

- Configuration: **Default**.

- Click **OK** [OK].

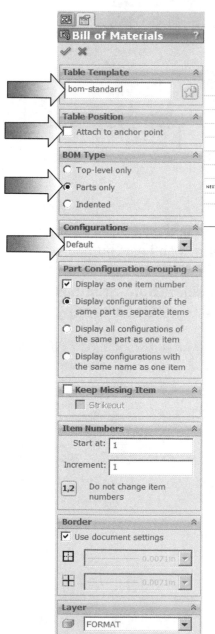

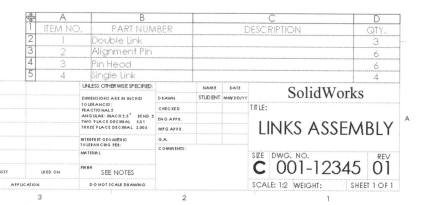

- The Bill Of Materials is created and anchored to the lower right corner of the title block, where the anchor point was set earlier.

* The Anchor point is set and saved in the Sheet Format layer. To change the location of the anchor point, first right click anywhere in the drawing and select Edit Sheet Format then right click on one of the end points of a line and select: Set-As-Anchor / Bill of Material.

- To change the anchor corner, click anywhere in the B.O.M, click the 4-way cursor on the upper left corner and select the stationary corner where you want to anchor the table (use the Bottom Right option for this lesson).

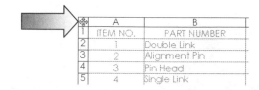

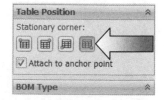

13. Modifying the B.O.M.:

- Double-click on the B.O.M. table to edit its content.

- Transfer the Part Number column over to the Description column.

- **To transfer Cell-By-Cell:**

In the Part Number column, double-click in a cell and select **Keep Link**.

Press **Cntrl + X** (Cut).

Enter a New Part Number.

Double-click a cell in the Description column and press **Control+V** (Paste) or simply re-enter the part name.

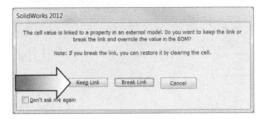

	A	B	C	D
1	ITEM NO.	PART NUMBER	DESCRIPTION	QTY.
2	1	Double Link	◁ Double Click	3
3	2	Alignment Pin		6
4	3	Pin Head		6
5	4	Single Link		4

- Click OK or click anywhere in the drawing when finished with editing. The BOM is updated accordingly.

ITEM NO.	PART NUMBER	DESCRIPTION	QTY.
1	001-12345	Double Link	3
2	002-12345	Alignment Pin	6
3	003-12345	Pin Head	6
4	004-12345	Single Link	4

SolidWorks

TITLE:

LINKS ASSEMBLY

SIZE	DWG. NO.	REV
C	001-12345	01

SCALE: 12   WEIGHT: SHEET 1 OF 1

UNLESS OTHERWISE SPECIFIED:
DIMENSIONS ARE IN INCHES
TOLERANCES:
FRACTIONAL±
ANGULAR: MACH±.5° BEND ±
TWO PLACE DECIMAL ±.01
THREE PLACE DECIMAL ±.005

INTERPRET GEOMETRIC
TOLERANCING PER:

MATERIAL

FINISH   SEE NOTES

USED ON   DO NOT SCALE DRAWING

NAME   DATE
DRAWN   STUDENT   MM/DD/YY
CHECKED
ENG APPR.
MFG APPR.
Q.A.
COMMENTS:

Note: *Refer to SolidWorks Online Help to learn more about customizing the B.O.M and how to create Custom Properties such as Part Numbers, Materials, etc.*

14. Reversing the column headers:

- Click anywhere in the B.O.M. table to access its **Properties**.

Click anywhere in the BOM to access its Properties…

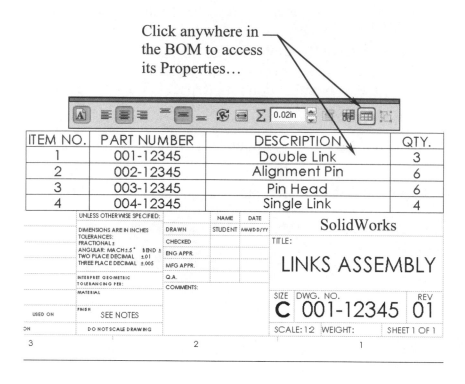

- An adjustment toolbar pops up on top of the BOM.

- Click the **Table Header** button.

- Click **OK** ✅.

Table Header Top/Bottom

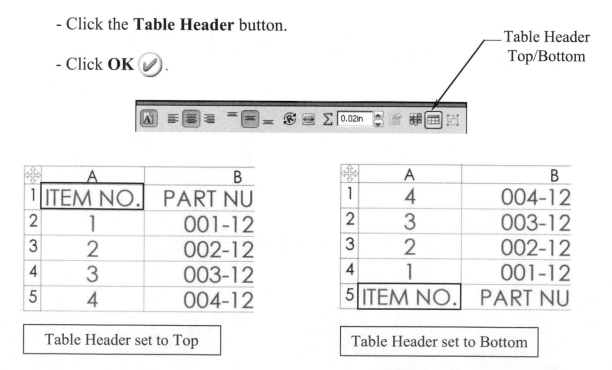

Table Header set to Top

Table Header set to Bottom

15. Adding Balloon callouts:

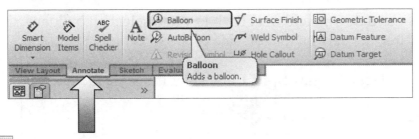

- Click  or select **Insert / Annotations / Balloon**.

- Click on the **edge** of the Single-Link. The system places a balloon on the part.

- The Item Number matches the one in the B.O.M. automatically.

- Click on the Double Link, the Alignment Pins, and Pin Heads to assign balloons to them.

Notes:
Balloons are similar to notes; they can have multiple leaders or attachment points.
To copy the leader line, hold down the CONTROL key, click and drag one of the arrows.

16. Changing the balloon style:

- Hold down the CONTROL key and select all balloons, the balloon Properties tree appears on the left side of the screen.

- Select **Circular Split Line** under the Style menu.

- Select **2 Character** size.

- Click **OK** ✓.

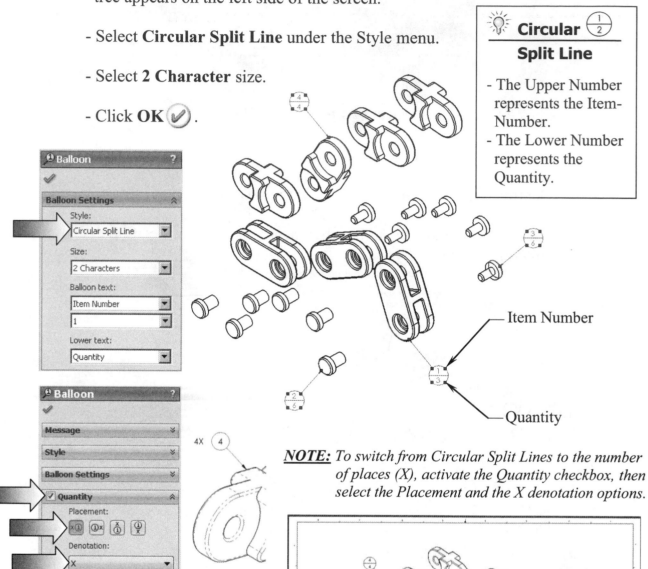

> 💡 **Circular** ①/②
>
> ──────────
>
> **Split Line**
>
> - The Upper Number represents the Item-Number.
> - The Lower Number represents the Quantity.

Item Number

Quantity

NOTE: *To switch from Circular Split Lines to the number of places (X), activate the Quantity checkbox, then select the Placement and the X denotation options.*

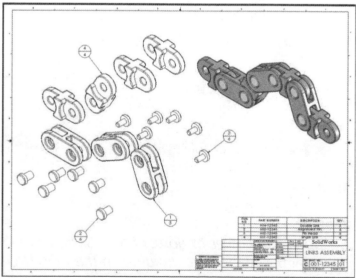

17. Saving your work:

- Select **File / Save As / Links-Assembly / Save**.

Questions for Review

Assembly Drawings

1. The drawing's paper size can be selected or changed at any time.
   - a. True
   - b. False

2. The First or Third angle projection can be selected in the sheet setup.
   - a. True
   - b. False

3. To access the sheet format and edit the information in the title block:
   - a. Right click in the drawing and select Edit Sheet Format
   - b. Right click the Sheet Format icon from the Feature Tree and select:
     Edit Sheet Format.
   - c. All of the above.

4. The BOM anchor point should be set on the Sheet Format not on the drawing sheet.
   - a. True
   - b. False

5. A Model View command is used to create Isometric views.
   - a. True
   - b. False

6. The Drawing views scale can be changed individually or all at the same time.
   - a. True
   - b. False

7. A Bill of Materials (BOM) can automatically be generated using Excel embedded features.
   - a. True
   - b. False

8. The Balloon callouts are linked to the Bill of Materials and driven by the order of the Feature Manager Tree.
   - a. True
   - b. b. False

8. TRUE
9. TRUE
5. TRUE
7. TRUE
3. C
4. TRUE
1. TRUE
2. TRUE

Exercise: Assembly Drawings

Go to: The Training CD.
Mini Vise folder.

1. Create an Assembly Drawing from the components provided.

2. Create a Bill Of Materials and modify the Part Number and the Description columns as shown.

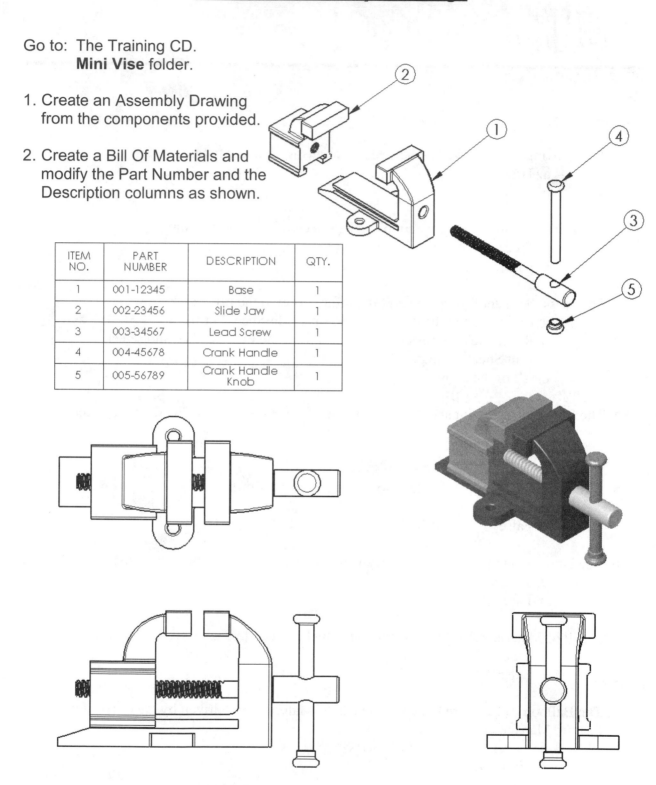

ITEM NO.	PART NUMBER	DESCRIPTION	QTY.
1	001-12345	Base	1
2	002-23456	Slide Jaw	1
3	003-34567	Lead Screw	1
4	004-45678	Crank Handle	1
5	005-56789	Crank Handle Knob	1

3. Save your work as: **Mini Vise Assembly.slddrw**

Exercise: Assembly Drawings

File Location:
Training CD
Egg Beater.sldasm

ITEM NO.	PART NUMBER	DESCRIPTION	QTY.
1	010-8980	Egg Beater Handle	1
2	010-8981	Main Gear	1
3	010-8982	Support Rod	1
4	010-8983	Right Spinner	1
5	010-8984	Left Spinner	1
6	010-8985	Crank Handle	1
7	010-8986	Small Gear (RIGHT)	1
8	010-8987	Small Gear (LEFT)	1

1. Create an Assembly Drawing with 5 views.

2. Add Balloons and a Bill Of Materials.

3. Save your work as: **Egg Beater Assembly**.

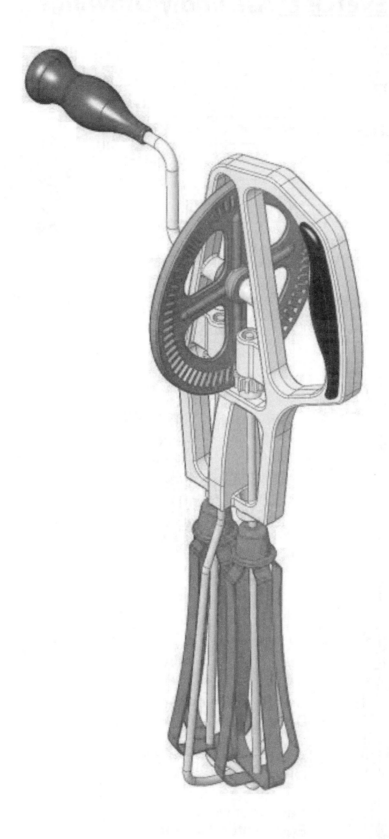

CHAPTER 13 (cont.)

Alternate Position Views

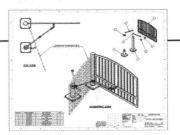

Assembly Drawings
Alternate Position Views

- Assembly drawings are created in the same way as part drawings, except for all components that are shown together as assembled or exploded.

- A Bill of Materials is created to specify the details of the components, such as: Part Number, Material, Weight, Vendor, etc.

- The BOM template can be modified to have more columns, rows, or different headers.

- Balloons are also created on the same drawing to help identify the parts from its list (B.O.M). These balloons are linked to the Bill of Materials parametrically, and the order of the balloon numbers is driven by the Assembly's Feature tree.

Alternate Position Views

- The Alternate Position View allows users to superimpose one drawing view precisely on another (open/close position as an example).

- The alternate position(s) is shown with phantom lines.

- Dimension between the primary view and the Alternate Position View can be added to the same drawing view.

- More than one Alternate Position View can be created in a drawing.

- Section, Detail, Broken, and Crop views are currently not supported.

Alternate Position Views
Assembly Drawings

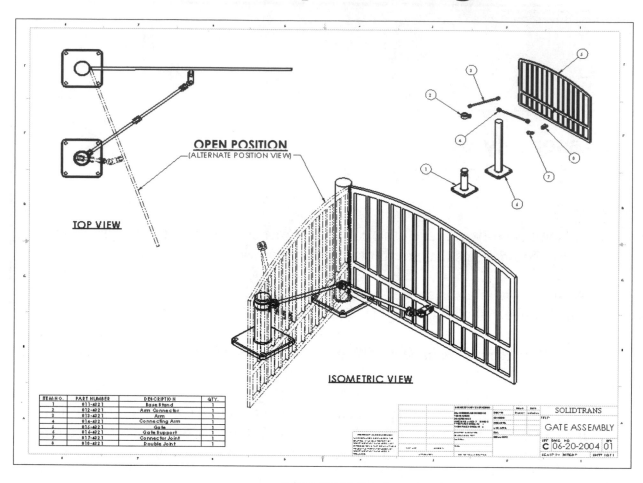

OPEN POSITION
(ALTERNATE POSITION VIEW)

TOP VIEW

ISOMETRIC VIEW

ITEM NO.	PART NUMBER	DESCRIPTION	QTY.
1	011-4221	Base Stand	1
2	012-4221	Arm Connector	1
3	013-4221	Arm	1
4	014-4221	Connecting Arm	1
5	015-4221	Gate	1
6	016-4221	Gate Support	1
7	017-4221	Connector Joint	1
8	018-4221	Double Joint	1

SOLIDTRANS

GATE ASSEMBLY

C 06-20-2004 01

Dimensioning Standards: **ANSI**
Units: **INCHES** – 3 Decimals

Third Angle Projection

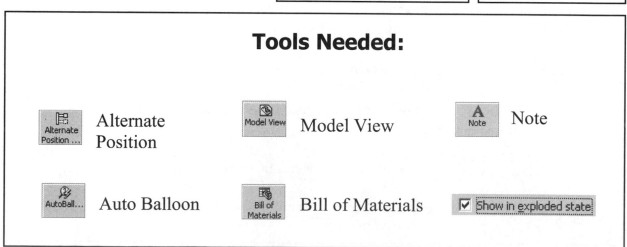

Tools Needed:

Alternate Position

Model View

Note

Auto Balloon

Bill of Materials

☑ Show in exploded state

1. Creating a new drawing:

- Select **File** / **New** / **Draw** (or Drawing) / **OK**.

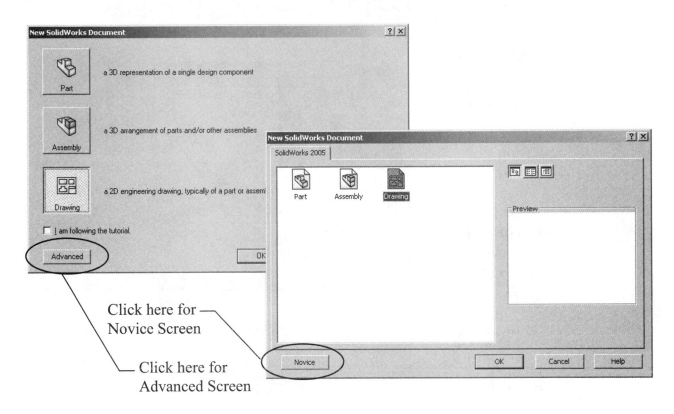

Click here for —
Novice Screen

— Click here for
Advanced Screen

- Under Standard Sheet Size, choose **C-Landscape**.

- Enable the **Display Sheet Format** check box.

- Click **OK** [OK] .

- Right click in the drawing
and select **Properties.**

- Set **Scale** to **1 : 1**
(full scale)

- Set **Type of Projection** to:
Third Angle [○ Third angle] .

- Click **OK** [OK] .

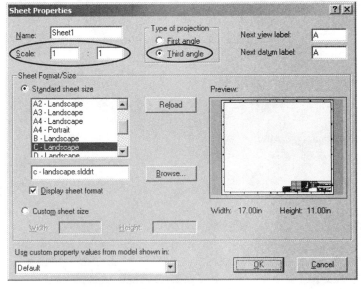

2. Creating the Isometric Drawing View:

- Click **Model View**, **Browse** to the **Gate Assembly** document, and click **Open**.

- Select the **Isometric** view from the Orientation section.

- Place the 1st drawing view (Isometric) approximately in the center of the sheet.

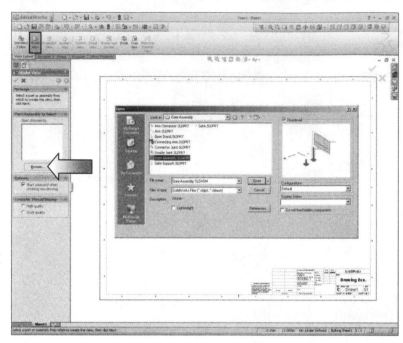

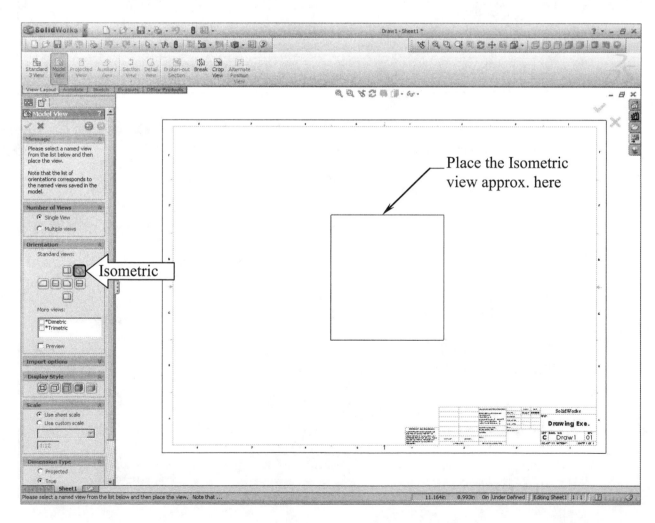

Place the Isometric view approx. here

Isometric

3. Changing the Drawing View Scale:

- Click on the Drawing View border and change the Scale to:

 * **Use Custom Scale.**

 * **User Defined.**

 * **Scale 1:3**

- Click **OK** ✅ .

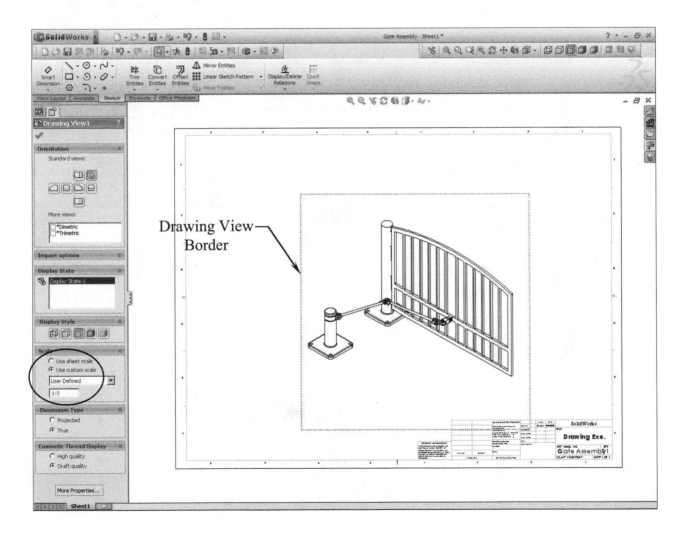

- The Isometric View is scaled to (1:3) or 1/3 time the actual size.

- When selecting the User Defined option you can enter your own scale, if the scale option that you want is not on the list.

4. Creating an Alternate Position drawing view:

Alternate Position View
Adds a view displaying a configuration of a model superimposed on another configuration of the model.

- From the Drawing Toolbar, click [Alternate Position ...] or select **Insert / Drawing View / Alternate Position View**.

- In the Configuration dialog, select the **Gate Open** configuration.

- Click **OK** ⊘.

- The new drawing view is shown with Phantom lines and it is superimposed over the original view.

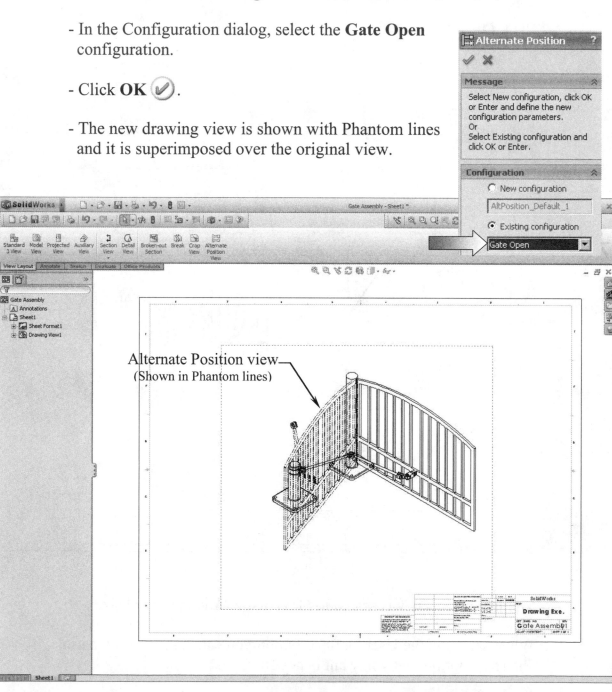

Alternate Position view
(Shown in Phantom lines)

5. Adding the Top Drawing view:

- From the Drawing Toolbar, click **Model View** or select:
Insert / Drawing View / Model.

- Click the **NEXT** arrow.

- Select the **TOP** view from the Orientation dialog.

- Place the Top drawing view approximately as shown.

- Click **OK** ✅.

- For clarity, change the view line style to Tangent Edges With Font. (Right click on the view's border, select Tangent Edge, and then click Tangent Edges with Font).

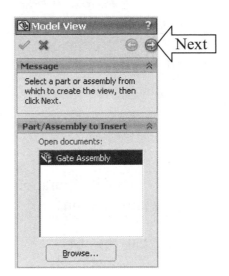

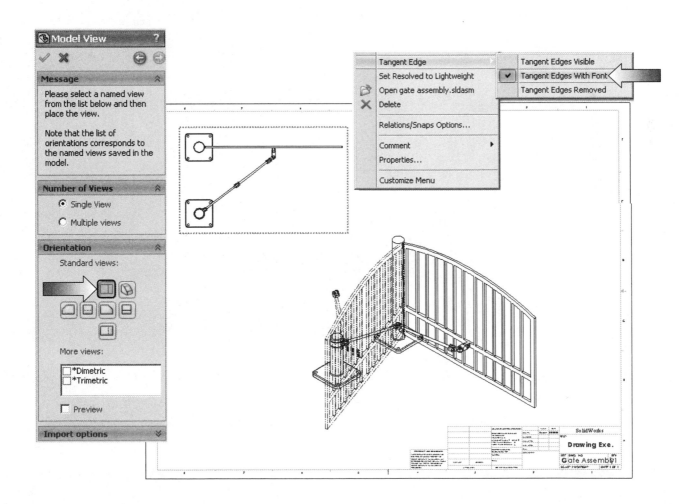

6. Creating an Alternate Position for the Top drawing view:

- Click the Top Drawing View's Border to activate.

- Click [Alternate Position ...] or select **Insert / Drawing View / Alternate Position**.

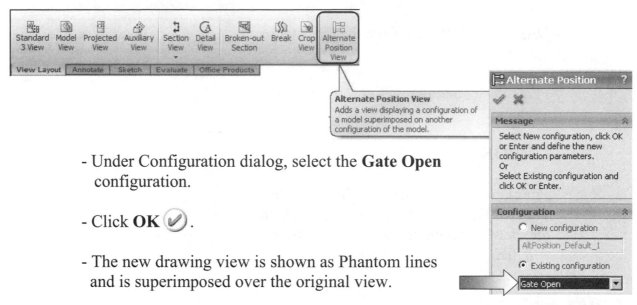

Alternate Position View
Adds a view displaying a configuration of a model superimposed on another configuration of the model.

- Under Configuration dialog, select the **Gate Open** configuration.

- Click **OK** ✓.

- The new drawing view is shown as Phantom lines and is superimposed over the original view.

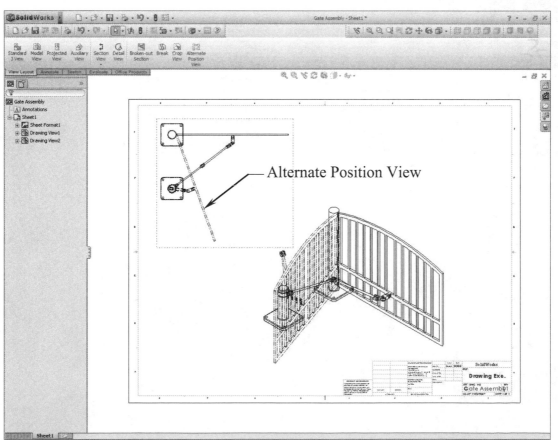

Alternate Position View

7. Adding Text / Annotations:

- Select the Top drawing view's Border to activate the view and click **Note** 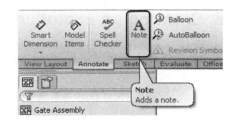 .

- Add the notes: **Top View** and **Isometric View** as shown.

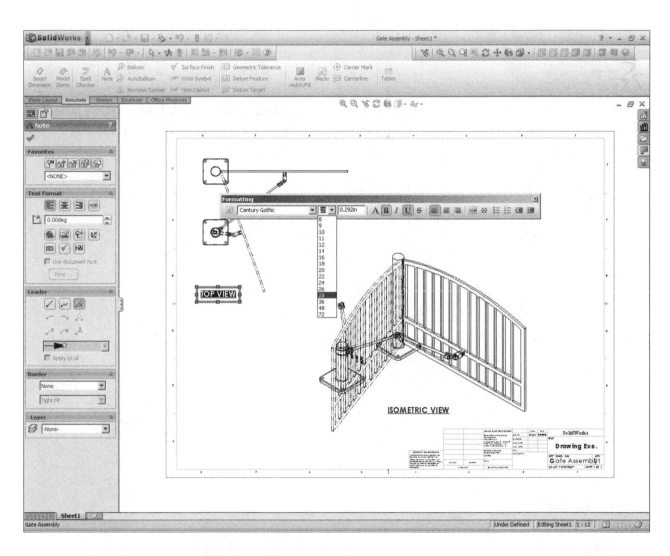

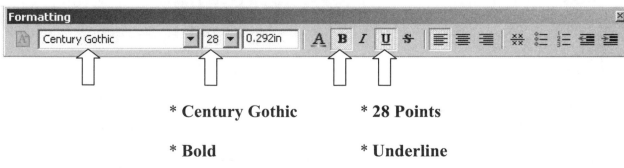

* **Century Gothic**   * **28 Points**

* **Bold**   * **Underline**

8. Creating an Exploded Isometric view:

- Click  or select **Insert / Drawing View / Model**.

- Click the **NEXT** arrow .

- Select the **Isometric** view from the Orientation dialog.

- Place the Isometric view on the upper right side of the sheet.

- Right click on the Isometric View's border and select Properties.

- Enable the **Show In Exploded State** check box (Arrow). The exploded view must be already created in the assembly for this option to be available in the drawing.

- Click **OK** .

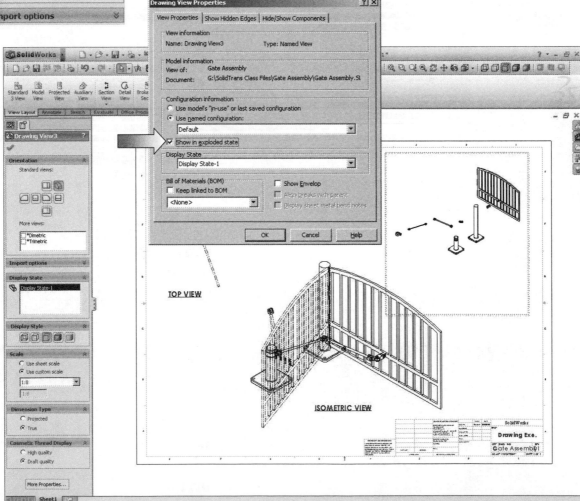

9. Adding Auto-Balloons to the Exploded view:

- Select the Isometric drawing view's border.

- Click AutoBall... or select **Insert / Annotations / AutoBalloon**.

- In the Auto Balloon properties tree, set the following:

* Balloon Layout: **Square**

* Ignore Multiple Instances: **Enable**

* Style: **Circular**

* Size: **1 Character**

* Balloon Text: **Item Number**

- Click **OK** OK .

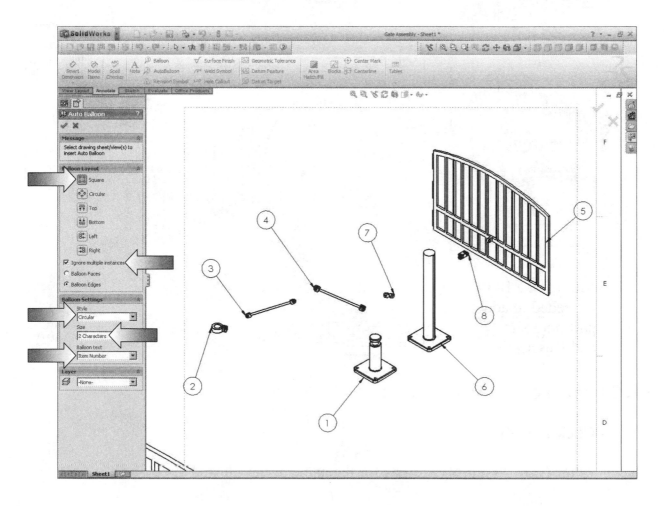

10. Adding a Bill of Materials to the Drawing:

- Click 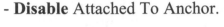 or select **Insert / Tables / Bill Of Materials**

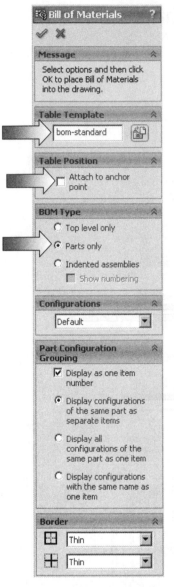

- Select **Bom-Standard** under Table Templates.

- **Disable** Attached To Anchor.

- Select **Parts Only** for BOM Type.

- Click **OK** OK .

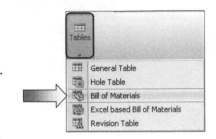

	A	B	C	D
1	ITEM NO.	PART NUMBER	DESCRIPTION	QTY.
2	1	011-4321	Base Stand	1
3	2	012-4321	Arm Connector	1
4	3	013-4321	Arm	1
5	4	014-4321	Connecting Arm	1
6	5	015-4321	Gate	1
7	6	016-4321	Gate Support	1
8	7	017-4321	Connector Joint	1
9	8	018-4321	Double Joint	1

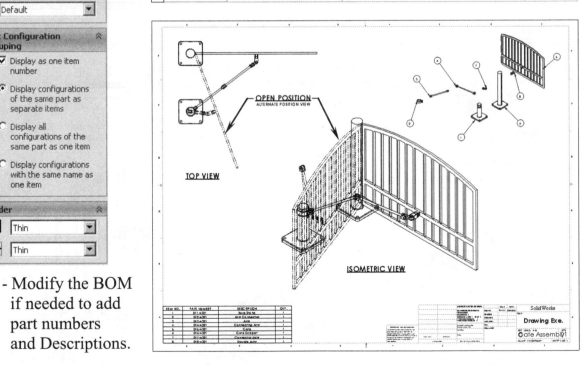

- Modify the BOM
  if needed to add
  part numbers
  and Descriptions.

11. Saving a copy of your work:

- Click **File / Save As.**

- Enter **Gate Assembly.slddrw** for the name of the file and click **Save.**

Questions for Review

Assembly Drawings

1. The Alternate Position command can also be selected from Insert / Drawing View / Alternate Position.
   a. True
   b. False

2. The Alternate Position command precisely places a drawing view on top of another view.
   a. True
   b. False

3. The types of views that are not currently supported to work with Alternate Position are:
   a. Broken and Crop Views
   b. Detail View
   c. Section View
   d. All of the above.

4. Dimensions or annotations cannot be added to the superimposed view.
   a. True
   b. False

5. The Line Style for use in the Alternate Position view is:
   a. Solid line
   b. Dashed line
   c. Phantom line
   d. Centerline

6. In order to show the assembly exploded view on a drawing, an exploded view configuration must be created first in the main assembly.
   a. True
   b. False

7. Balloons and Auto Balloons can also be selected from: Insert / Annotations / (Auto) Balloon.
   a. True
   b. False

8. The Bill of Materials contents can be modified to include the Material Column.
   a. True
   b. False

7. TRUE	8. TRUE
5. C	6. TRUE
3. D	4. FALSE
1. TRUE	2. TRUE

CHAPTER 15

Drawing Views

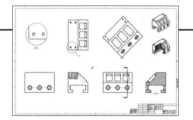

Drawing Views
Machined Block

- When creating an engineering drawing, one of the first things to do is layout the drawing views such as:

    * The standard Front, Top, Right, and Isometric views.

    * Other views like Detail, Cross section, Auxiliary views, etc., can be created or projected from the 4 standard views.

- Most of the drawing views in SolidWorks are automatically aligned with one another (default alignments); each one can only be moved along the direction that was defined for that particular view (vertical, horizontal, or at projected angle).

- Dimensions and annotations will then be added to the drawing views.

- The dimensions created in the part will be inserted into the drawing views, so that their association between the model and the drawing views can be maintained. Changes done to these dimensions will update all drawing views and the solid model as well;

- Configurations are also used in this lesson to create some specific views.

- This chapter will guide you through the creation of some of the most commonly used drawing views in an engineering drawing like: 3 Standard views, Section views, Detail views, Projected views, Auxiliary views, Broken Out Section views, and Cross Hatch patterns.

Machined Block
Drawing Views Creation

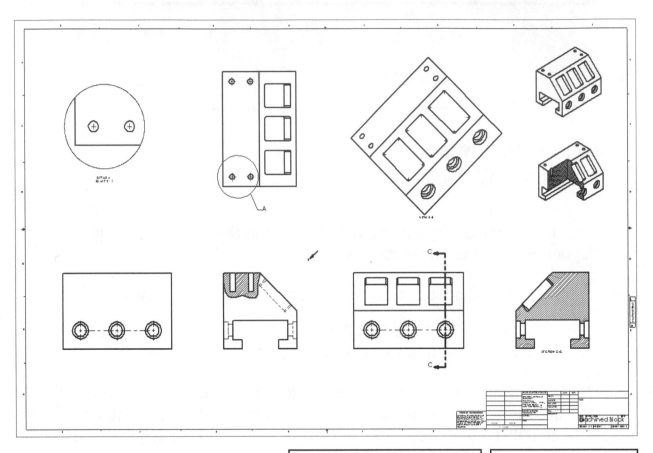

| Dimensioning Standards: **ANSI** | Third Angle Projection |
| Units: **INCHES** – 3 Decimals | |

Tools Needed:

 New Drawing   Model View   Projected View

 Auxiliary View   Detail View   Section View

 Broken Out Section   Area Hatch Fill   Note

1. Creating a new drawing:

- Select **File / New / Drawing** template.

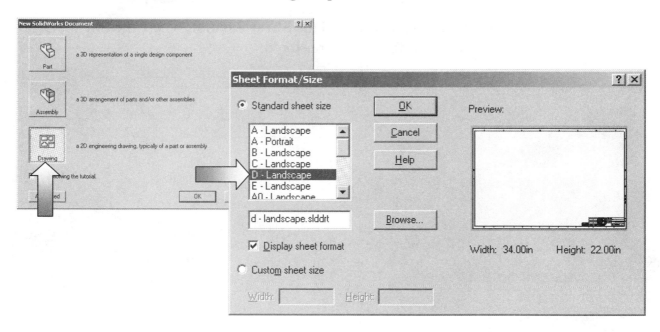

- Choose **D-Landscape** under Standard Sheet Size. (34.00 in. X 22.00 in.)

- Enable the **Display Sheet Format** check box to include the title block.

- Click **OK**.

- If the options
  above are not
  available, right
  click inside the
  drawing and select
  Properties.

- Click Third-
  Angle under
  Type of Projection.

- Select the D Land-
  scape paper size.

- Enable the Display
  Sheet Format box.

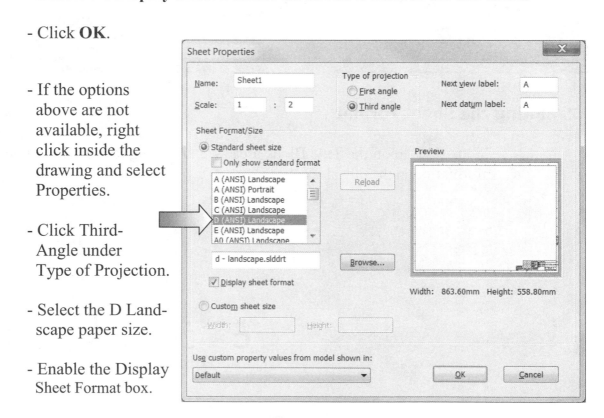

- The drawing templates come with 2 default "layers":

* The "Front layer" is called the **Sheet** layer, where drawings are created.

* The "Back layer" is called the **Sheet Format,** where the title block and the revision information are stored.

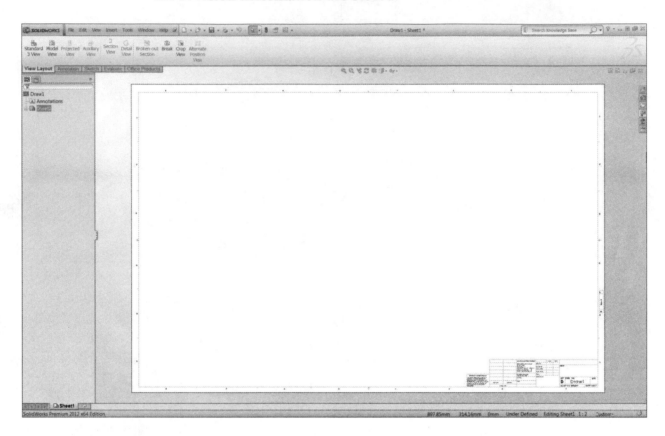

2. Editing the Sheet Format:

- Zoom 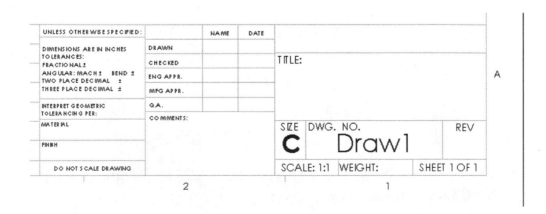 in on the Title Block area. We are going to first fill out the information in the title block.

UNLESS OTHERWISE SPECIFIED:		NAME	DATE		
DIMENSIONS ARE IN INCHES	DRAWN				
TOLERANCES: FRACTIONAL ± ANGULAR: MACH ± BEND ± TWO PLACE DECIMAL ± THREE PLACE DECIMAL ±	CHECKED			TITLE:	A
	ENG APPR.				
	MFG APPR.				
INTERPRET GEOMETRIC TOLERANCING PER:	Q.A.				
MATERIAL	COMMENTS:			SIZE DWG. NO. REV	
FINISH				**C** Draw1	
DO NOT SCALE DRAWING				SCALE: 1:1 WEIGHT: SHEET 1 OF 1	

- Right click in the drawing area and select **Edit Sheet Format.**

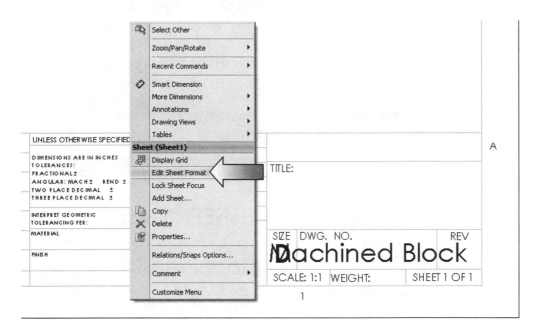

- The Sheet Format is brought up on top.

- New annotation and sketch lincs can now be added.

- Any existing text or lines can now be modified.

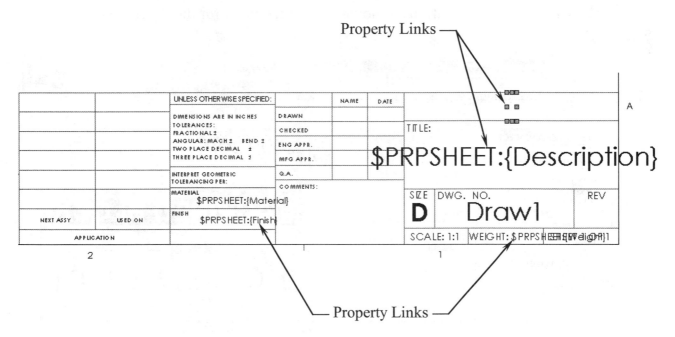

- Notice the link to properties text strings: "$PRPS". Some of the annotations have already been linked to the part's properties.

3. Modifying the existing text:

- Double click on the "Company Name" and enter the name of your company.

- Click 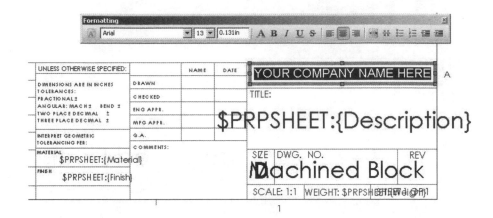 on the upper left of the Properties tree when done.

4. Adding the Title of the drawing:

- Double click on the PropertyLink in the Title area ($PRPSHEET:{Description})

- Type **Machined Block** for the title of the drawing.

- Enter the information as shown in the title block for the other areas.

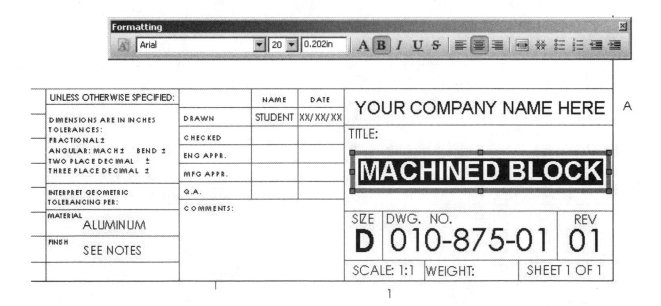

- Click **OK**.

5. Switching back to the drawing Sheet:

- Right click in the drawing and select **Edit Sheet**.

- The Drawing Sheet "layer" is brought back up on top.

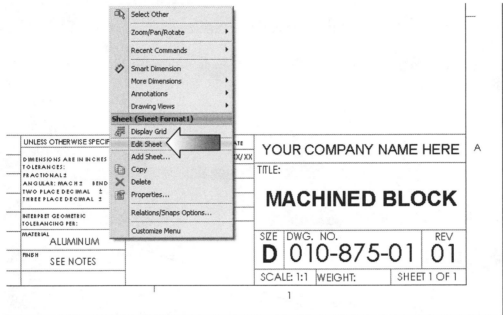

6. Accessing the View-Palette:

- The View Palette is located on the right side of the screen in the Task Pane area, click on its icon to access it.

Note: *If the drawing views are not visible on the View Palette window, click the Browse button ⬚ and open the part Machined block.*

- The standard drawing views like the Front, Right, Top, Back, Left, Bottom, Current, Isometric, and Sheet Metal Flat-Pattern views are contained within the View Palette window.

- These drawing views can be dragged into the drawing sheet to create the drawing views.

- The **Auto Start Projected View** checkbox should be selected by default.

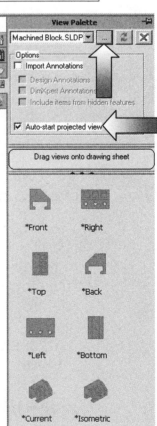

7. Using the View Palette:

- Click/Hold/Drag the Front view from the View-Palette and drop it in the drawing sheet, approximately as shown. Make sure the Auto-Start projected view checkbox is enabled (arrow).

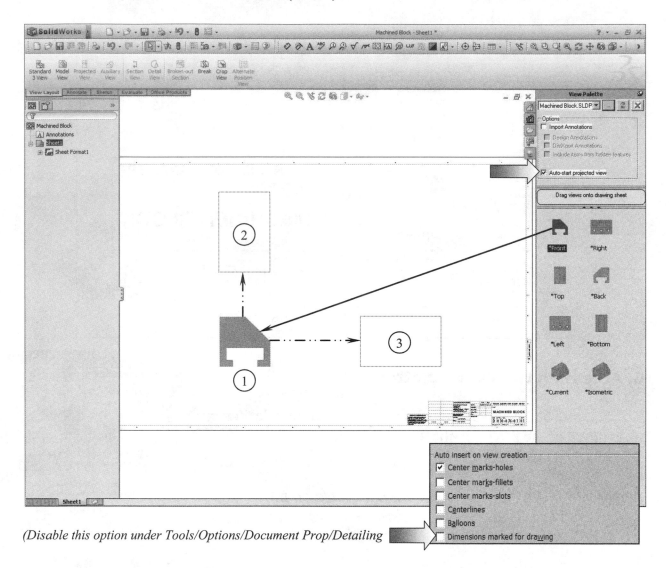

(Disable this option under Tools/Options/Document Prop/Detailing

- After the Front view is placed (position 1), move the mouse cursor upward, a preview image of the Top view appears, click in an approximate spot above the Front view to place the Top view (position number 2); repeat the same step for the Right view (position 3).

- All of the views from the View-Palette can be added to the drawing by using the same method.

- Click **OK** ✓ when you are finished with the first three views.

8. Adding an Isometric view:

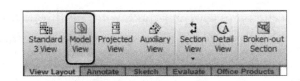

- Click [Model View] or select **Insert / Drawing View / Model View**.

- Click the NEXT arrow ➡.

- Select **Isometric** (Arrow) from the Model View properties tree and place it approximately as shown.

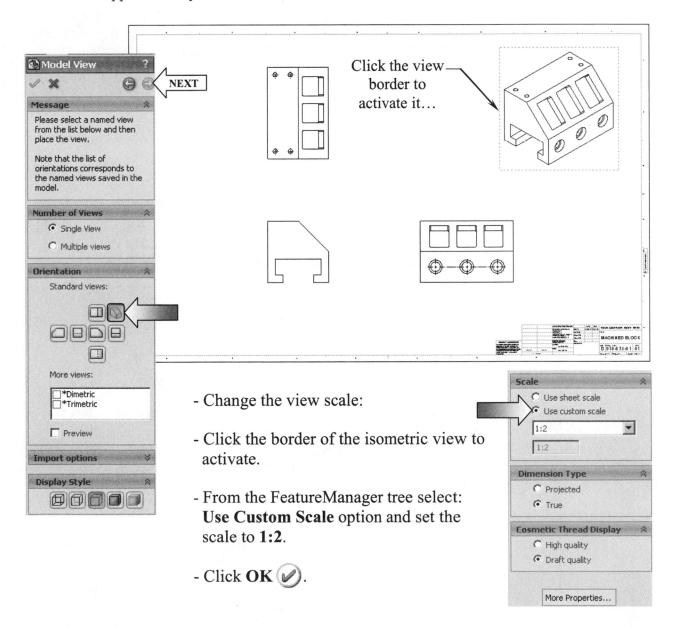

Click the view border to activate it...

- Change the view scale:

- Click the border of the isometric view to activate.

- From the FeatureManager tree select:
  Use Custom Scale option and set the scale to **1:2**.

- Click **OK** ✓.

9. Moving the drawing view(s):

- Position the mouse cursor over the border of the Front view and "Click/Hold/Drag" to move, all 3 views will move at the same time. By default, the Top and the Right views are automatically aligned with the Front view.

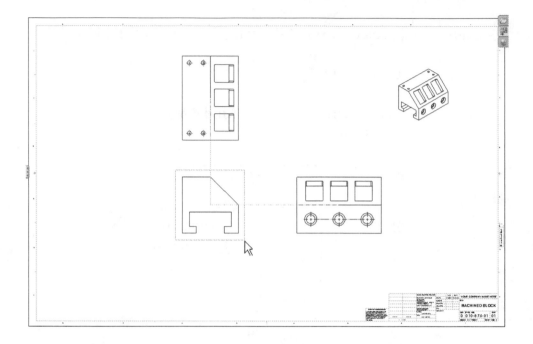

- When moving either the Right or the Top view, notice they will only move along the default vertical or horizontal directions. These are the default alignments when creating the standard drawing views.

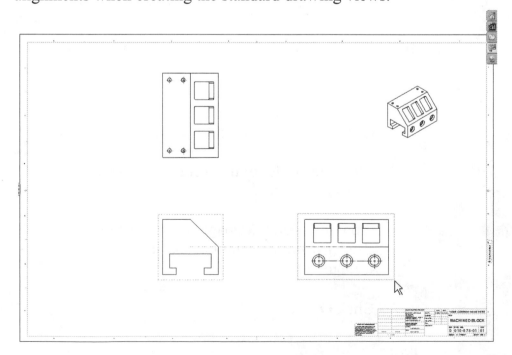

10. Breaking the alignments between the views:

- Right click inside the Top view or on its dotted border and select: **Alignment / Break-Alignment***.

- The Top view is no longer locked to the default direction, it can be moved freely.

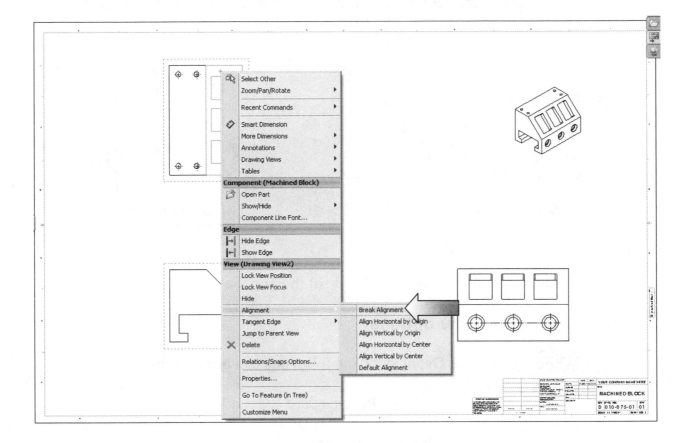

- Dependent views like Projected Views, Auxiliary Views, Section views, etc. will be aligned automatically with the views from where they were created. Their alignments can be broken or also reverted back to their default alignments.

- Independent views can also be aligned with other drawing views by using the same alignment options as shown above.

* To re-align a drawing view:

- Right click on the view's border and select **Alignment / Default-Alignment**.

11. Creating a Detail View:

- Click 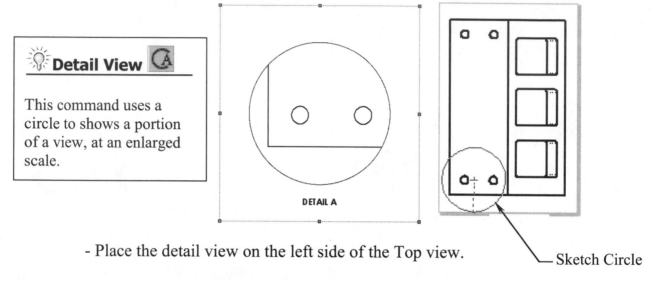 or select **Insert / Drawing View / Detail**.

- Sketch a circle approximately as shown on the Top drawing view.

- The system creates a Detail view automatically at the default 2 to1 scale.

> 💡 **Detail View**
>
> This command uses a circle to shows a portion of a view, at an enlarged scale.

DETAIL A

Sketch Circle

- Place the detail view on the left side of the Top view.

12. Using the Detail View options:

- While creating the Detail view, the following can be controlled:

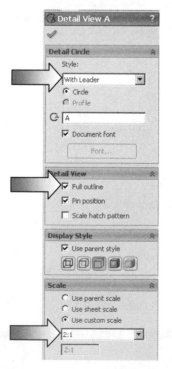

- Change Per-Standard style to **Width Leader**.

- Enable **Full Outline**.

- Use Custom scale of **2:1**.

- Click **OK** ✓.

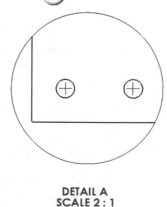

DETAIL A
SCALE 2 : 1

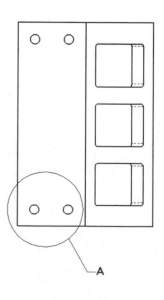

A

13. Creating a Projected View:

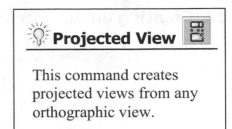

Projected View

This command creates projected views from any orthographic view.

- Click on the Front view's border to activate.

- Click 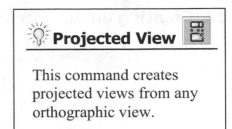 or select **Insert / Drawing View / Projected**.

- The preview of a projected view is attached to the mouse cursor, place it on the left side of the Front view.

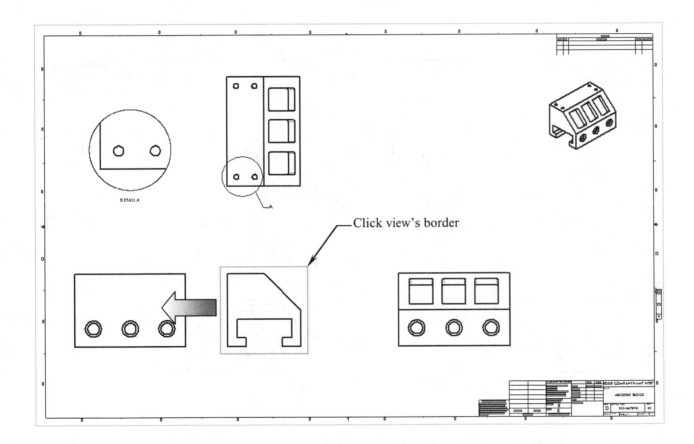

Click view's border

- Notice this view is also aligned automatically to the horizontal axis of the Front view. It can only be moved from left to right.

- For the purpose of this lesson, we will keep all of the default alignments the way SolidWorks creates them. (To break these default alignments at anytime, simply right click on their dotted borders and pick Break-Alignment).

14. Creating an Auxiliary View:

- Select the Angled-Edge as indicated.

- Click ⬨ or select **Insert / Drawing View / Auxiliary**.

- The system creates an Auxiliary view and attaches it onto your cursor.

- Place the Auxiliary view approximately as shown.

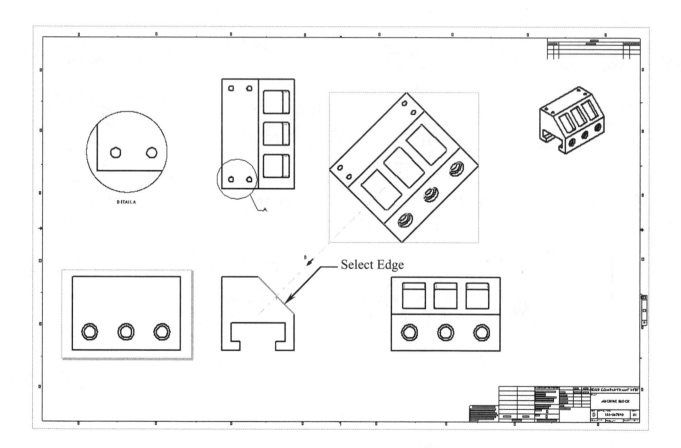

- The Auxiliary view is also aligned back to the edge from which it was originally projected.

- Use Break-Alignment option if needed to move the view to a different area.

15. Creating a Section View:

- Click 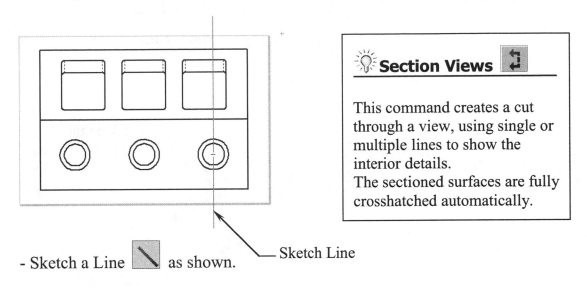 or select **Insert / Drawing View / Section**.

> ### 💡 Section Views
>
> This command creates a cut through a view, using single or multiple lines to show the interior details.
> The sectioned surfaces are fully crosshatched automatically.

- Sketch a Line ╲ as shown. ———— Sketch Line

- The preview of a section view appears, move the mouse cursor to the right-side and click to place the section view.

- The Section view is aligned horizontally with the view from which it was created and is cross-hatched automatically.

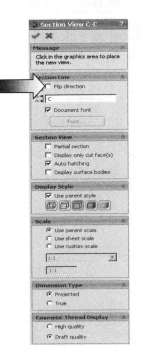

- To change the direction of the cut:

* Double Click on the section line and click Rebuild – OR –
* Enable Flip Direction checkbox in the FeatureManager tree.

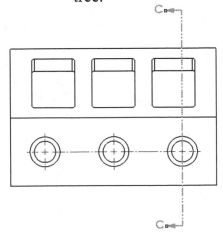

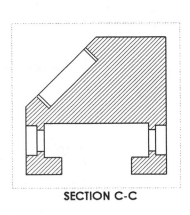

SECTION C-C

16. Showing the hidden lines in a drawing view:

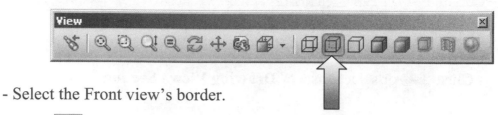

- Select the Front view's border.

- Click or select **View / Display / Hidden Lines Visible**.

- The hidden lines are now visible.

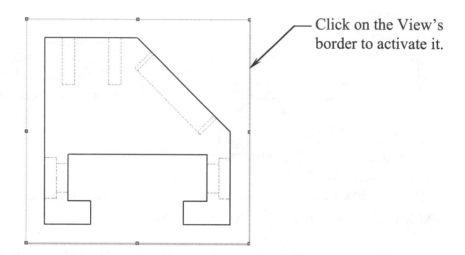

— Click on the View's border to activate it.

17. Creating a Broken-Out-Section:

> ### Broken Out Section View
>
> Creates a partial cut, using a closed profile, at a specified depth to display the inner details of a drawing view.

- Sketch a <u>closed</u> free-form shape on the Front view, around the area as shown (use either the Line or the Spline command to create the profile).

- Select the entire *Closed Profile.*

- Click  or select **Insert / Drawing View / Broken-Out-Section**.

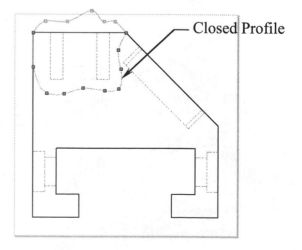

— Closed Profile

- Enable the **Preview** check box in the Properties tree ☑ Preview

- Enter **.500** in. for Depth 0.500in

- Click **OK** ✅.

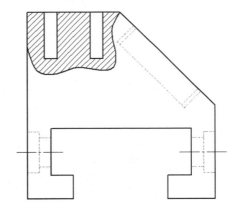

18. Adding a Cutaway view: (Previously created as a Configuration in the model).

- Click or select **Insert / Drawing View / Model**...

- Click on one of the view borders, the Model View Properties tree appears.

- Select **Isometric** (arrow) under Orientation window; use **Custom Scale** of **1:2**.

- Place the new Isometric view as shown.

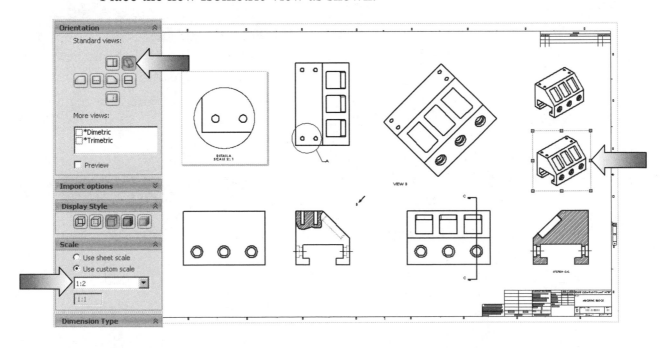

19. Changing Configurations: (From Default to Cutaway View).

- Right click on the new Isometric view's border and select **Properties.**

- Select the **Cutaway View** configuration under Default.

- Click **OK** [OK] .

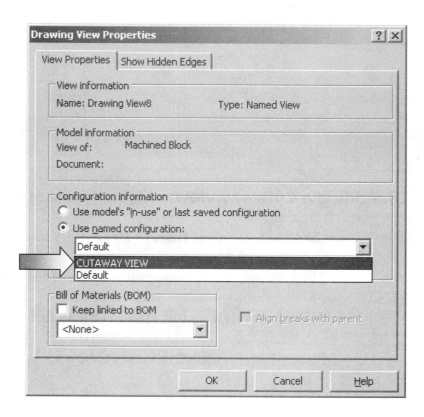

- The **Cutaway View** configuration is activated and the extruded-cut feature that was created earlier in the model, is now shown here.

- Since the cutout was created in the model, there is no crosshatch on any of the sectioned faces.

- Crosshatch is added at the drawing level and will not appeared in the model.

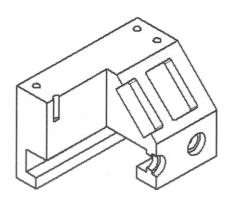

20. Adding crosshatch to the sectioned surfaces:

- Crosshatch is added automatically when section views are made in the drawing, since the cut was created in the model, we will have to add the hatch manually.

- Hold down the CONTROL key and select the 3 faces as indicated.

- Click 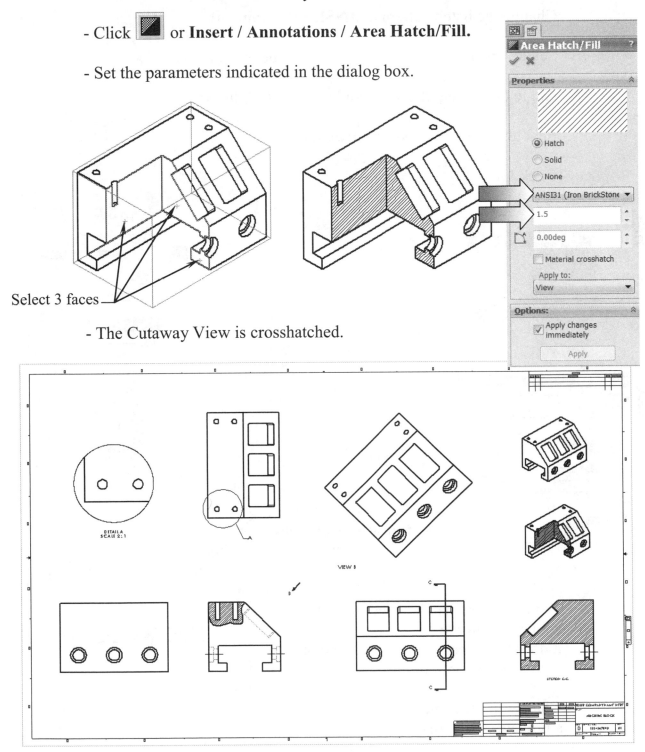 or **Insert / Annotations / Area Hatch/Fill.**

- Set the parameters indicated in the dialog box.

Select 3 faces

- The Cutaway View is crosshatched.

21. Modifying the crosshatch properties:

- Zoom in 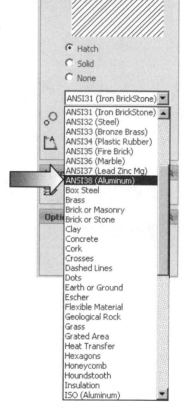 on the **Section C-C**.

- Click inside the hatch area, the **Area Hatch / Fill** properties tree appears.

- Change the hatch pattern to **ANSI38** (Aluminum).

- Scale: **1.500** (Sets the spacing between the hatch lines).

- Angle **00.00 deg**. (Sets the angle of the hatch lines).

- Enable: **Apply changes immediately**.

- Click **OK** OK .

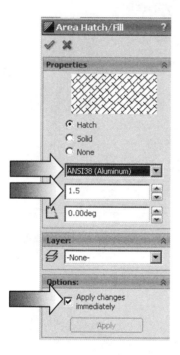

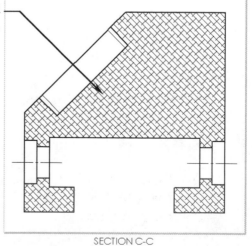

Change Hatch Pattern to match the previous settings.

- When the new hatch pattern is only applied locally to the selected view, it does not override the global settings in the system options.

- Change to the same hatch pattern for any views with crosshatch.

SECTION C-C

22. Saving your work:

- Select **File / Save As /**

- Enter **Machine Block-Drawing Views** for file name and click **Save**.

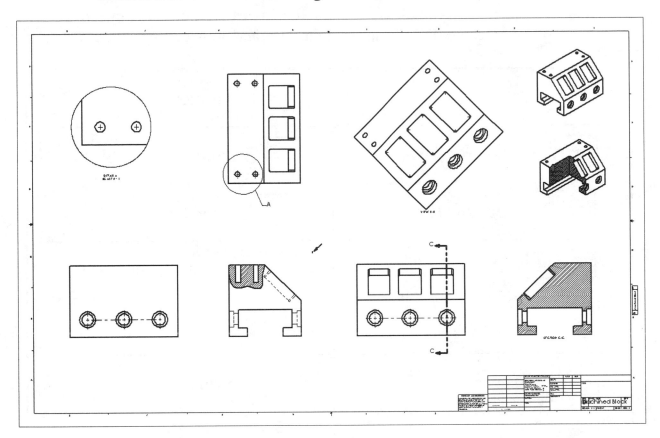

- The drawing views can also be changed from Wireframe to Shaded .

- The color of the drawing views is driven by the part's color. What you see here in the drawing is how it is going to look when printed (in color).

- Modifying the part's color will update the color of the drawing views automatically.

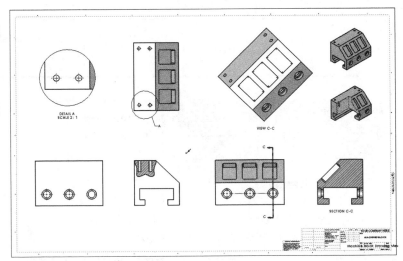

Geometric Tolerance & Flag Notes

Geometric Tolerance Symbols GCS are used in a Feature Control Frame to add Geometric Tolerances to the parts and drawings.

Symbol	Name	Symbol	Name
∠	Angularity	⊕	Position
↔	Between	⌓	Profile of Any Surface
○	Circularity (Roundness)	↗	Simple Runout
◎	Concentricity and Coaxially	↗	Simple Runout (open)
⌀	Cylindricity	—	Straightness
▱	Flatness	=	Symmetry
⌒	Profile of Any Line	↗↗	Total Runout
//	Parallelism	↗↗	Total Runout (open)
⊥	Perpendicularity	To access the symbol libraries, select: **Insert / Annotations / Note**

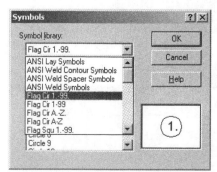

Circle 1-99	Square 1-99	Square/Circle 1-99	Triangle 1-99
①. ①	1. 1	1. 1	△. △
Circle A-Z	**Square A-Z**	**Square/Circle A-Z**	**Triangle A-Z**
Ⓐ. Ⓐ	A. A	A. A	△. △

Modifying & Hole Symbols

Modifying Symbols MC

Symbol	Name	Symbol	Name
℄	Centerline	Ⓣ	Tangent Plane
°	Degree	◸	Slope (Up)
⌀	Diameter	◿	Slope (Down)
S⌀	Spherical Diameter	◺	Slope (Inverted Up)
±	Plus/Minus	◹	Slope (Inverted Down)
Ⓢ	Regardless of Feature Size	□	Square
Ⓕ	Free State	⊠	Square (BS)
Ⓛ	Least Material Condition	ST	Statistical
Ⓜ	Maximum Material Condition	⌀	Flattened Length
Ⓟ	Projected Tolerance Zone	PL	Parting Line
Ⓔ	Encompassing	SolidWorks supports **ASME-ANSI Y14.5** Geometric & True Position Tolerancing

⊔ Counterbore (Spot face)   ⌄ Countersunk   ⊽ Depth/Deep   ⌀ Diameter

ASME (American Society for Mechanical Engineering)
ANSI Y14.5M (American National Standards Institute)
SYMBOLS DESCRIPTION

ANGULARITY:

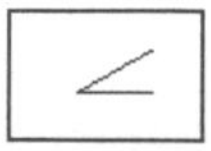

The condition of a surface or line, which is at a specified angle (other than 90°) from the datum plane or axis.

BASIC DIMENSION: | 1.00 |

A dimension specified on a drawing as BASIC is a theoretical value used to describe the exact size, shape, or location of a feature. It is used as a basis from which permissible variations are established by tolerance on other dimensions or in notes. A basic dimension can be identified by the abbreviation BSC or more readily by boxing in the dimension.

CIRCULARITY (ROUNDNESS):

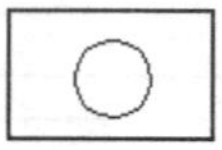

A tolerance zone bounded by two concentric circles within which each circular element of the surface must lie.

CONCENTRICITY:

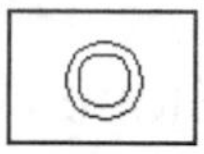

The condition in which the axis of all cross-sectional elements of a feature's surface of revolution are common.

CYLINDRICITY:

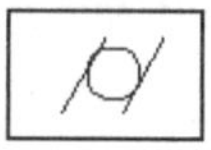

The condition of a surface of revolution in which all points of the surface are equidistant from a common axis or for a perfect cylinder.

DATUM:

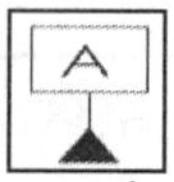

A point, line, plane, cylinder, etc., assumed to be exact for purposes of computation from which the location or geometric relationship of other features of a part may be established. A datum identification symbol contains a letter (except I, C, and Q) placed inside a rectangular box.

DATUM TARGET:

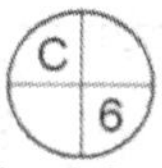

The datum target symbol is a circle divided into four quadrants. The letter placed in the upper left quadrant identifies it is associated datum feature. The numeral placed in the lower right quadrant identifies the target; the dashed leader line indicates the target on far side.

FLATNESS:

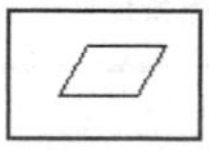

The condition of a surface having all elements in one plane. A flatness tolerance specifies a tolerance zone confined by two parallel planes within which the surface must lie.

MAXIMUM MATERIAL CONDITION: ⓂM
The condition of a part feature when it contains the maximum amount of material.

LEAST MATERIAL CONDITION: Ⓛ
The condition of a part feature when it contains the least amount of material. The term is opposite from maximum material condition.

PARALLELISM: //
The condition of a surface or axis which is equidistant at all points from a datum plane or axis.

PERPENDICULARITY: ⊥
The condition of a surface, line, or axis, which is at a right angle (90°) from a datum plane or datum axis.

PROFILE OF ANY LINE: ⌒
The condition limiting the amount of profile variation along a line element of a feature.

PROFILE OF ANY SURFACE: ⌓
Similar to profile of any line, but this condition relates to the entire surface.

PROJECTED TOLERANCE ZONE: Ⓟ
A zone applied to a hole in which a pin, stud, screw, etc. is to be inserted. It controls the perpendicularity of any hole, which controls the fastener's position; this will allow the adjoining parts to be assembled.

REGARDLESS OF FEATURE SIZE: Ⓢ
A condition in which the tolerance of form or condition must be met, regardless of where the feature is within its size tolerance.

RUNOUT: ↗
The maximum permissible surface variation during one complete revolution of the part about the datum axis. This is usually detected with a dial indicator.

STRAIGHTNESS: —
The condition in which a feature of a part must be a straight line.

SYMMETRY: =
A condition wherein a part or feature has the same contour and sides of a central plane.

TRUE POSITION: ⊕
This term denotes the theoretically exact position of a feature.

CHAPTER 15 (cont.)

Detailing

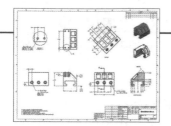

Detailing a drawing
Machined Block Details

- After the drawing views are all laid out, they will be detailed with dimensions, tolerances, datums, surface finishes, notes, etc.

- To fully maintain the associations between the model dimensions and the drawing dimensions, the Model Items options should be used. If a dimension is changed in either modes (from the solid model or in the drawing) they will both be updated automatically.

- When a dimension appears in gray color it means that the dimension is being added in the drawing and it does not exist in the model. This dimension is called a Reference dimension.

- SolidWorks uses different colors for different types of dimensions such as:
    * Black dimensions = Sketch dimensions (driving).
    * Gray dimensions = Reference dimensions (driven).
    * Blue dimensions = Feature dimensions (driving)
    * Magenta dimensions = Dimensions linked to Design Tables (driving).

- For certain types of holes, the Hole-Callout option should be used to accurately call out the hole type, depth, diameter, etc...

- The Geometric Tolerance option helps control the accuracy and the precision of the features. Both Tolerance and Precision options can be easily created and controlled from the FeatureManager tree.

- This chapter discusses most of the tools used in detailing an engineering drawing, including importing dimensions from the model, and adding the GD&T to the drawing (Geometric Dimensions and Tolerancing).

Machined Block
Detailing

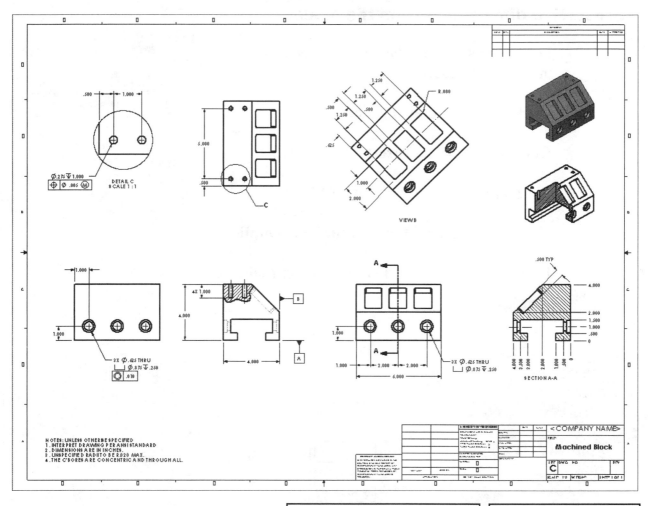

Dimensioning Standards: **ANSI**
Units: **INCHES** – 3 Decimals

Third Angle Projection

Tools Needed:

 Model Dimensions

 Geometric Tolerance

 Datum Feature Symbol

 Surface Finish

 Hole Callout

 Note

1. Opening the previous file:

- Click **File / Open** and open the document **Machined Block-Drawing View**.

2. Inserting dimensions from the model:

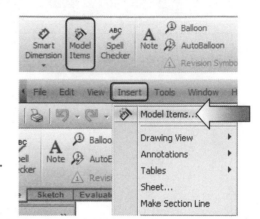

- Dimensions previously created in the model can be inserted into the drawing.

- Click the **Right** drawing view's border.

- Click 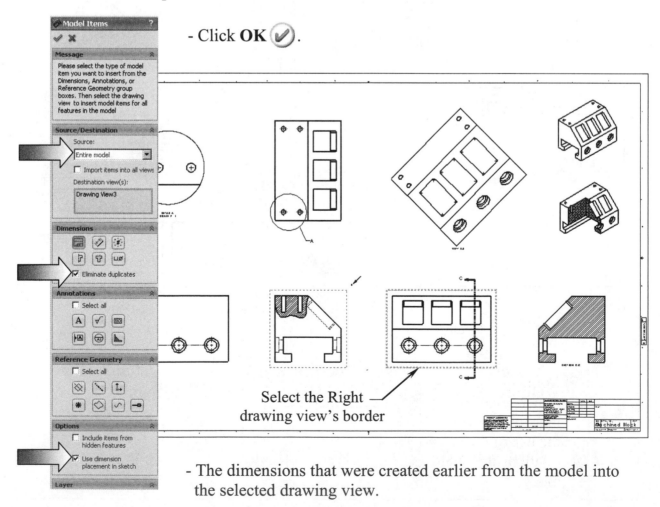 or select **Insert / Model Items**.

- For Source/Destination: **Entire Model**.

- Under Dimensions: Enable **Eliminate Duplicates**.

- Under Options: Select **Use Dimension Placement in Sketch**.

- Click **OK** ✅.

Select the Right drawing view's border

- The dimensions that were created earlier from the model into the selected drawing view.

3. Re-arranging the new dimensions: Zoom in 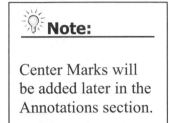 on the Right drawing view.

- Keep only the hole location dimensions and delete the others. The hole types and sizes will be added later.

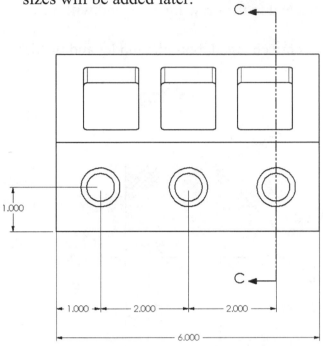

4. Inserting dimensions into the Section view:

- Select the Section view's border.

- Click 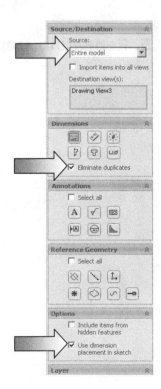 or select **Insert / Model Items**.

- The previous settings (arrow) should still be selected.

- Click **OK** ✔

- Some of the dimensions are missing due to the use of the relations in the model.

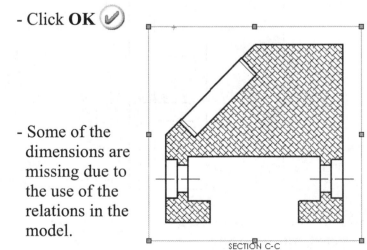

SECTION C-C

- The dimensions from the model are imported into the Section view.

- Use the Smart Dimension tool ⬦ to add any missing dimensions.

- These dimensions are attached to the drawing view and will move with the view.

- If any of these dimensions are changed, both the model and the drawing views will also change accordingly.

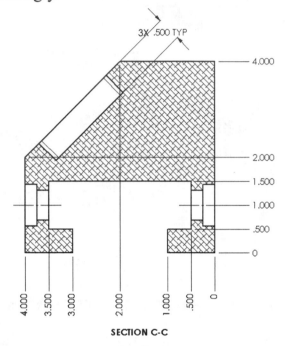

SECTION C-C

5. Repeating step 4: Insert the model's dimensions into the Top view.

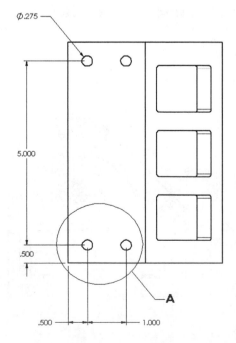

6. Adding dimensions to the Auxiliary view:

- Add any missing dimensions to the drawing view using the Smart Dimension command.

NOTE: _To add the Centerline symbol, select the Note command from the Annotation tab, click the Add Symbol button, then select the Centerline options from the list._

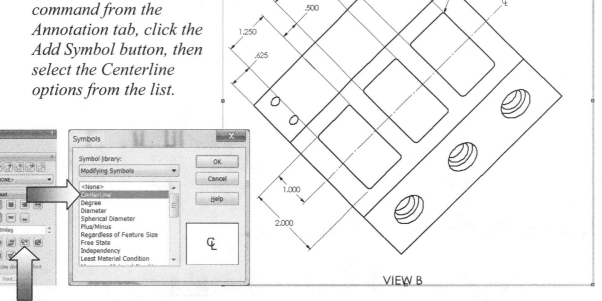

VIEW B

7. Adding the Center Marks:

- Zoom in on the Detail View.

- Click or select **Insert / Annotations / Center Mark**.

- Click on the edge of each hole to add Center Marks. The system places a Center Mark in the center of the hole.

Click on the circular edge to add Center Mark (skip this step if the center mark is already added).

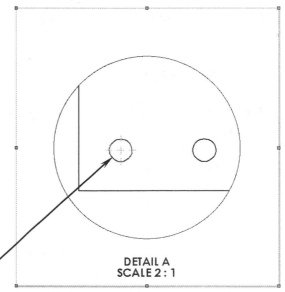

DETAIL A
SCALE 2 : 1

8. Adding center marks to the other holes:

- Click or select **Insert / Annotations / Center Mark**.

- Add a center mark to other holes by clicking on their circular edges.

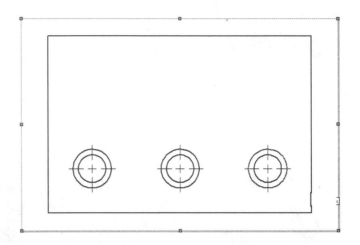

9. Adding the Datum Feature Symbols:

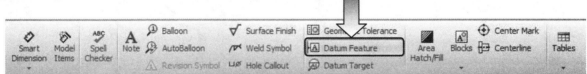

- Click or select **Insert / Annotations / Datum Feature Symbol**.

- Select edge 1 and place **Datum A** as shown.

- Select edge 2 and place **Datum B** as shown.

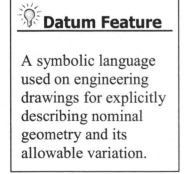

Datum Feature

A symbolic language used on engineering drawings for explicitly describing nominal geometry and its allowable variation.

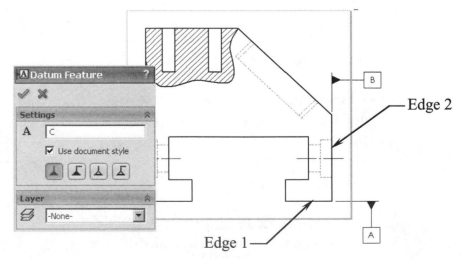

Edge 2

Edge 1

Datum Reference & Geometric Tolerance Examples

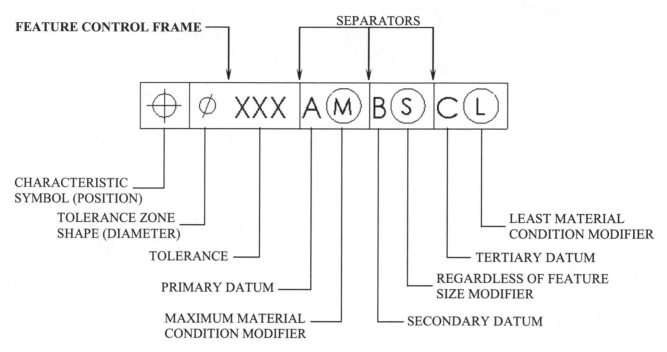

FEATURE CONTROL FRAME

SEPARATORS

CHARACTERISTIC
SYMBOL (POSITION)

TOLERANCE ZONE
SHAPE (DIAMETER)

TOLERANCE

PRIMARY DATUM

MAXIMUM MATERIAL
CONDITION MODIFIER

SECONDARY DATUM

REGARDLESS OF FEATURE
SIZE MODIFIER

TERTIARY DATUM

LEAST MATERIAL
CONDITION MODIFIER

💡 FEATURE CONTROL FRAMES

*A feature control frame symbolizes the
tolerance requirements for a feature of a
part. It can be added to a drawing note
for a feature tolerance, or can be specified
by running a leader line from the feature
control frame directly to the feature.
The box may be attached to an extension
line from the feature or it can be placed
on a dimension line. A feature can have
more than one feature control frame,
depending on its requirements.*

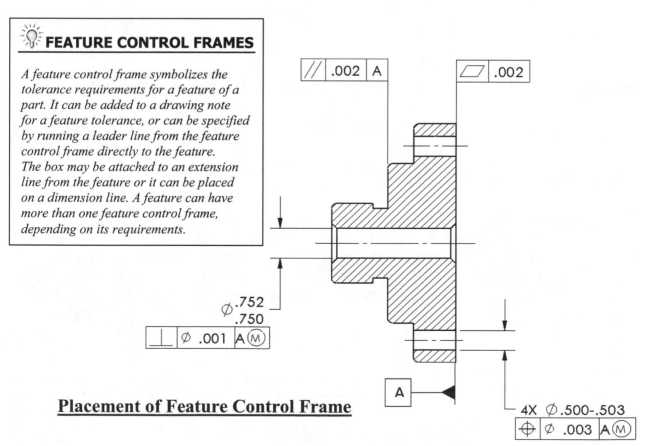

Placement of Feature Control Frame

10. Adding hole specifications using the Hole-Callout:

- Click or select **Insert / Annotations / Hole Callout**.

- Select the edge of the C'bore and place the callout below the hole.

- The system creates a callout that includes the diameter and the depth of the hole and the C'bore.

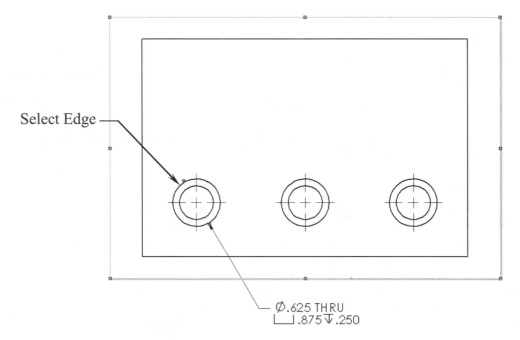

Select Edge

⌀.625 THRU
⊔.875 ▽.250

11. Adding Geometric Tolerances:

- Geometric dimensioning and tolerancing (GD&T) is used to define the nominal (theoretically perfect) geometry of parts and assemblies to define the allowable variation in form and possibly size of individual features and to define the allowable variation between features. Dimensioning and tolerancing and geometric dimensioning and tolerancing specifications are used as follows:

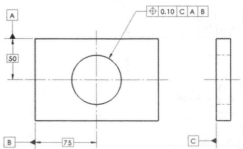

* Dimensioning specifications define the nominal, as-modeled or as-intended geometry. One example is a basic dimension.
* Tolerancing specifications define the allowable variation for the form and possibly the size of individual features and the allowable variation in orientation and location between features. Two examples are linear dimensions and feature control frames using a datum reference.

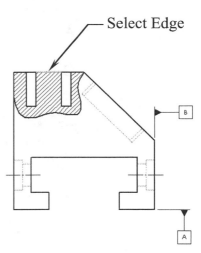

Select Edge

- Zoom in on the Front drawing view.

- Select the upper edge as shown.

- Click or select **Insert / Annotations / Geometric Tolerance**.

- The Geometric Tolerance Property appears.

- Click the **Symbol Library** dropdown list.

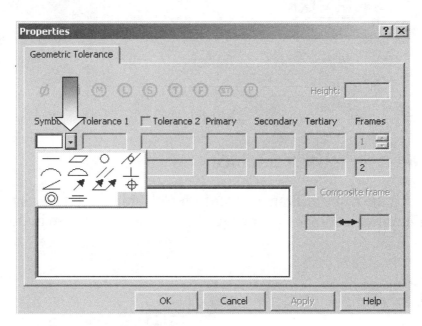

- Select **Parallelism** from the **Symbol** library list.

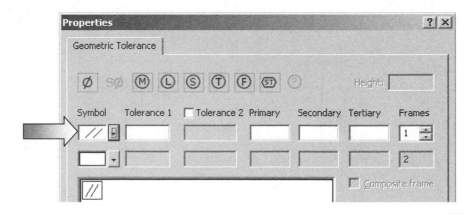

- Enter **.010** under Tolerance 1.

- Enter **A** under Primary reference datum (arrow).

- Click **OK** [OK] .

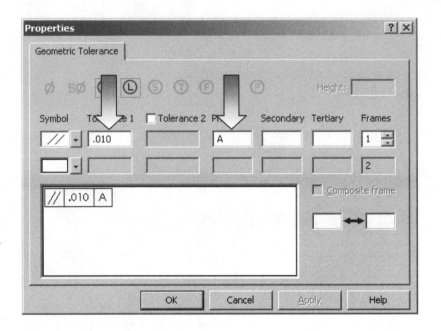

12. Align the Geometric Tolerance:

- Drag the Control Frame towards the left side until it snaps to the horizontal alignment with the upper edge, then release the mouse button.

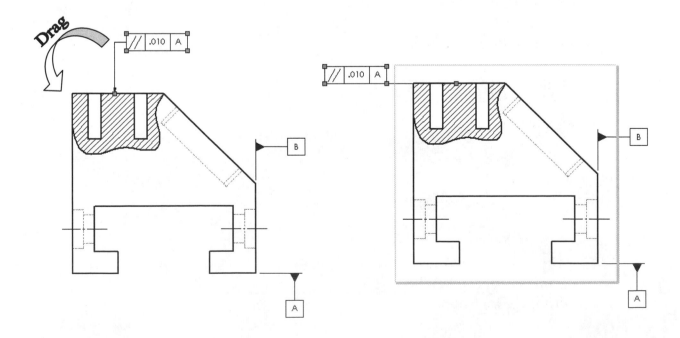

13. Attaching the Geometric Tolerance to the Driving dimension:

- Select the C'bore dimension. By pre-selecting a dimension, the geometric-tolerance will automatically be attached to this dimension.

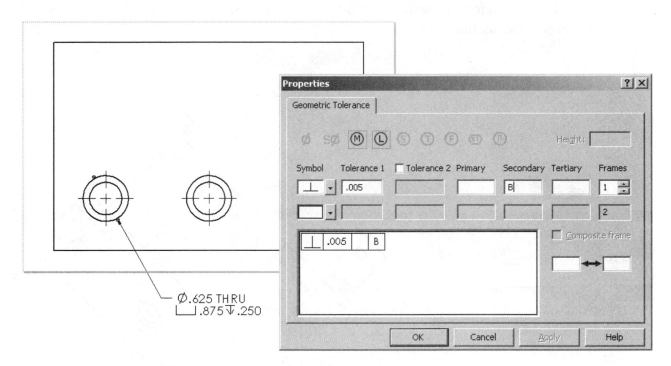

- Click 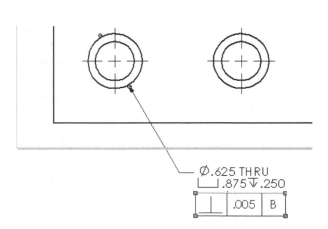 or select **Insert / Annotation / Geometric Tolerance**.

- Click the **Symbol Library** dropdown list ▼ .

- Select **Perpendicularity** ⟂ from the Symbol library list.

- Enter **.005** under Tolerance 1.

- Enter **B** under Secondary reference datum.

- Click **OK** ▢ OK ▢ .

- The Geometric Tolerance frame is attached to the driving dimension.

14. Adding Tolerance/Precision to dimensions:

- Select the dimension **.500** (circled).

- The dimension properties tree pops up, select **Bilateral** under the Tolerance/ Precision section.

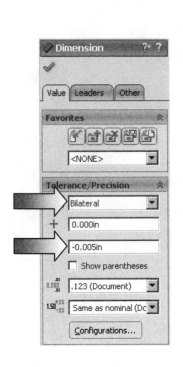

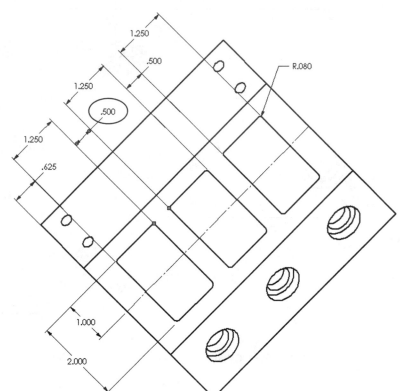

- Enter **.000 in**. for Max variation.

VIEW B

- Enter **.005 in**. for Min variation.

- Click **OK** ✓.

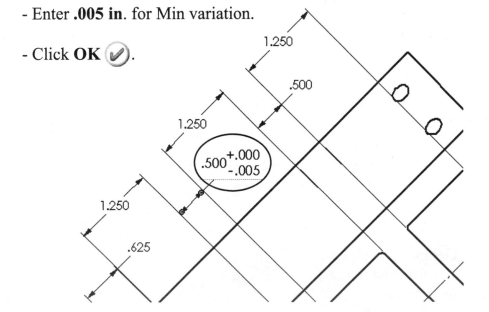

15. Adding Symmetric tolerance to a dimension:

- Select the width dimension **1.250** (circled) and the dimension properties tree appears .

- Choose **Symmetric** under Tolerance/Precision list (arrow).

- Enter **.003 in**. for Maximum Variation.

- Click **OK** ✅.

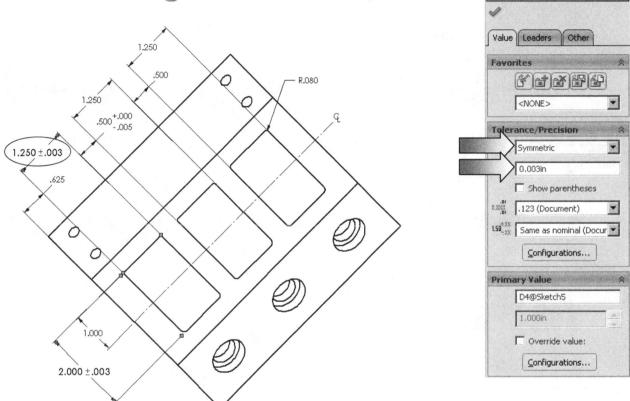

- Repeat step 15 and add a Symmetric tolerance to the height dimension: (**2.000 ±.003**).

- For practice purposes: Add other types of tolerance to some other dimensions such as Min – Max, Basic, Fit, etc..

16. Adding Surface Finish callouts:

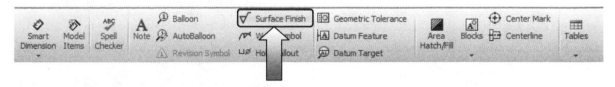

- Surface finish is an industrial process that alters the surface of a manufactured item to achieve a certain property. Finishing processes may be applied to: improve appearance and other surface flaws, and control the surface friction.

- Zoom in 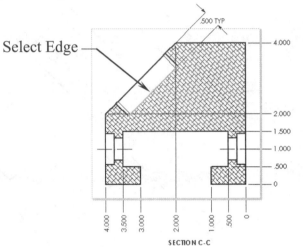 on the Section C-C.

- Select the edge as indicated.

- Click [✓] or select **Insert / Annotations / Surface Finish**.

- Choose **Machining-Required** [✓] under Symbol.

- Under **Maximum Roughness**, enter: **125**

- Under Leader, select: **Bent leader.**

- Click **OK** ✓.

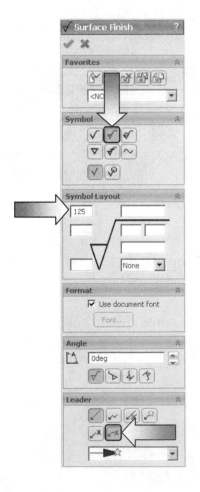

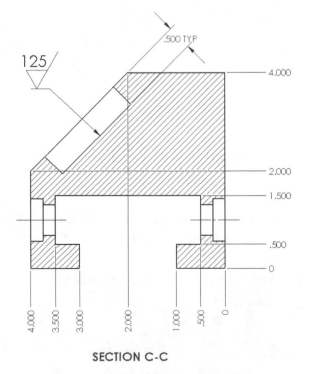

SECTION C-C

17. Adding non-parametric callouts:

- Click and add a diameter dimension to one circle.

- The dimension properties tree appears .

- Enter **4X** before <MOD-DIA>… or enter **4 PLCS** under callout.

- Click **OK** .

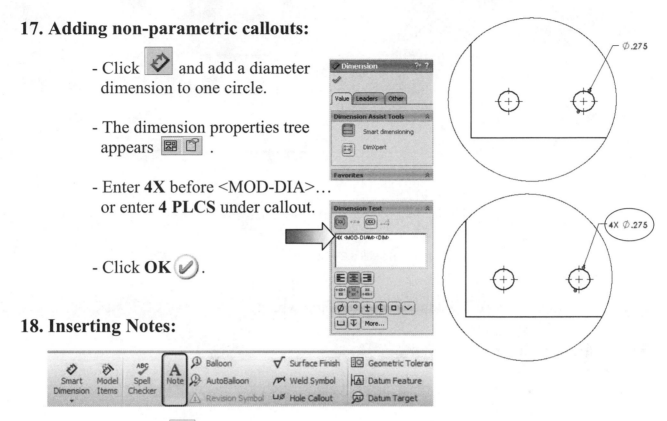

18. Inserting Notes:

- Zoom in on the upper left side of the drawing.

- Click **A** or select **Insert /Annotations / Note**.

- Click on an upper left area, approximately as shown, and a note box appears.

NOTE: *To prevent the note from moving, right click in the drawing and select:* **Lock-Sheet-Focus**.

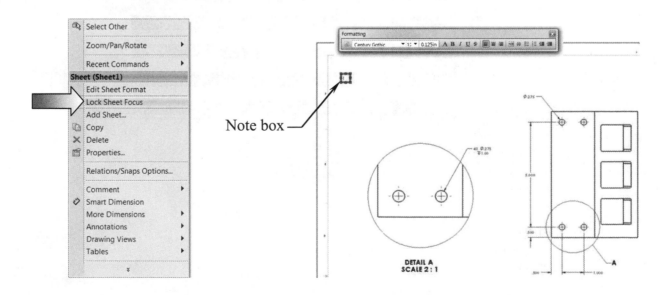

Note box

- Enter the notes below:

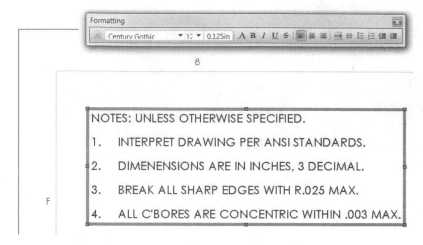

- Click **OK** when you are finished typing.

19. Changing document's font:

- Double click anywhere inside the note area to activate.

- Highlight the entire note and select the following:

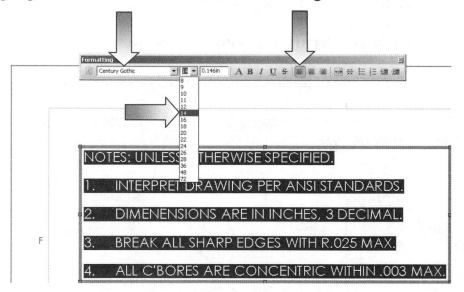

- Font: **Century Gothic**.

- Point size: **14**.

- Alignment: **Left**.

- Click **OK**.

20. Saving your work:

- Select **File / Save As**.

- Enter **Machined Block Detailing** for the name of the file.

- Click **Save**.

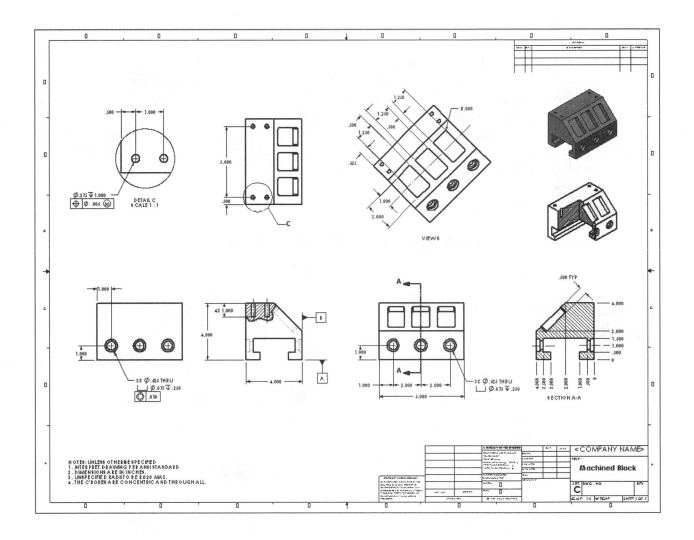

Questions for Review

Drawing & Detailing

1. Existing text in the title block can be edited when the Sheet-Format is active.
    a. True
    b. False

2. The standard drawing views can be created using the following method:
    a. Use Insert / Drawing views menu
    b. Use the Model-View command
    c. Drag and drop from an open window
    d. All of the above

3. View alignments can be broken or re-aligned.
    a. True
    b. False

4. The Detail-View scale cannot be changed or controlled locally.
    a. True
    b. False

5. The Projected view command projects and creates the Top, Bottom, Left, and Right views from another view.
    a. True
    b. False

6. To create an Auxiliary view, an edge has to be selected, not a face or a surface.
    a. True
    b. False

7. Only a single line can be used to create a Section view. The System doesn't support a multi-line section option.
    a. True
    b. False

8. Hidden lines in a drawing view can be turned ON / OFF locally and globally.
    a. True
    b. False

9. Configurations created in the model cannot be shown in the drawings.
    a. True
    b. False

9. FALSE
7. FALSE   8. TRUE
5. TRUE   6. TRUE
3. TRUE   4. FALSE
1. TRUE   2. D

Exercise: Detailing I

1. Create the **part** and **drawing** as shown.

2. The Counter-Bore dimensions are measured from the Top planar surface.

3. Dimensions are in inches, 3 decimal places.

4. The part is symmetrical about the Top reference plane.
   (To create the "Back-Isometric-View" from the model: hold the Shift key and push the Up arrow key twice.
   This should rotate the part 180°, then insert this view to the drawing using the Current View option).

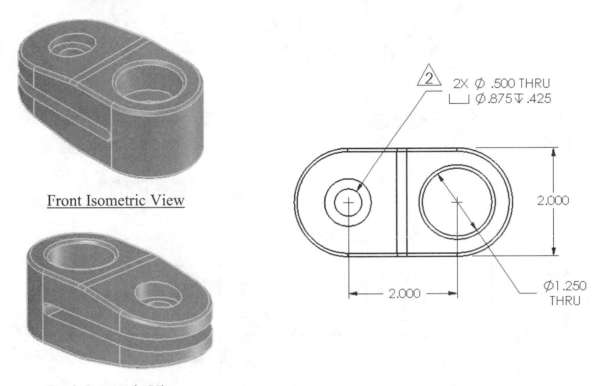

Front Isometric View

Back Isometric View

2X ⌀ .500 THRU
⌴ ⌀.875 ⤓ .425

2.000

2.000

⌀1.250
THRU

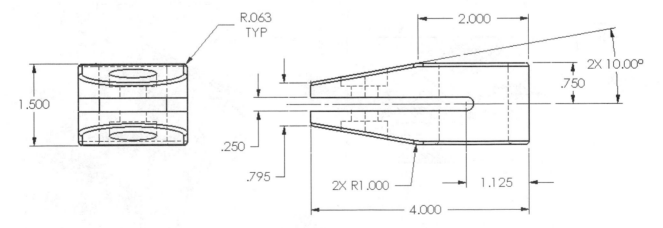

R.063
TYP

1.500

.250

.795

2X R1.000

2.000

2X 10.00°

.750

1.125

4.000

5. Save your work as: **Clamp Block**.

Exercise: Detailing II

1. <u>Open</u> the part named **Base Mount Block** from the training CD.
2. Create a drawing using the provided details.
3. Create the Virtual-Sharps where needed prior to adding the Ordinate Dimensions.
   (To add the Virtual Sharps: Hold the Control key, select the 2 lines, and click the Sketch-Point command).

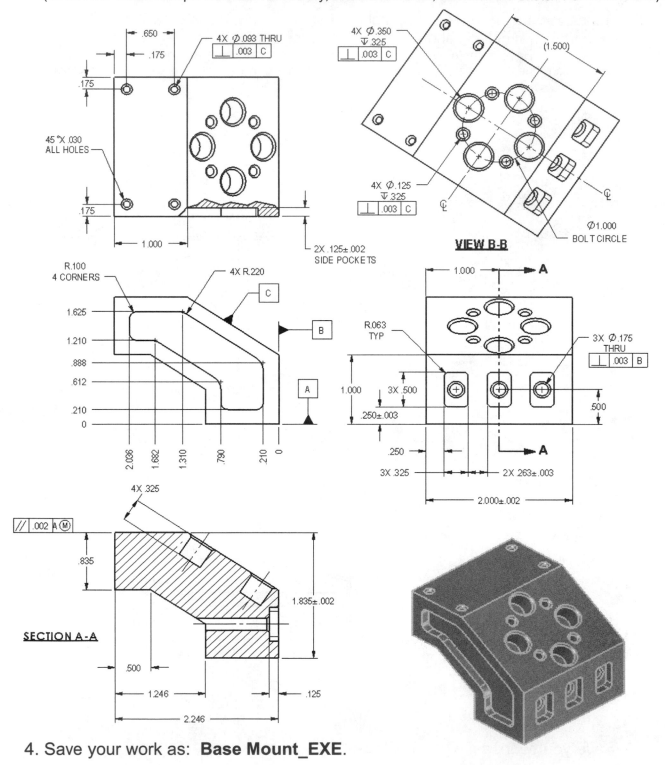

4. Save your work as: **Base Mount_EXE**.

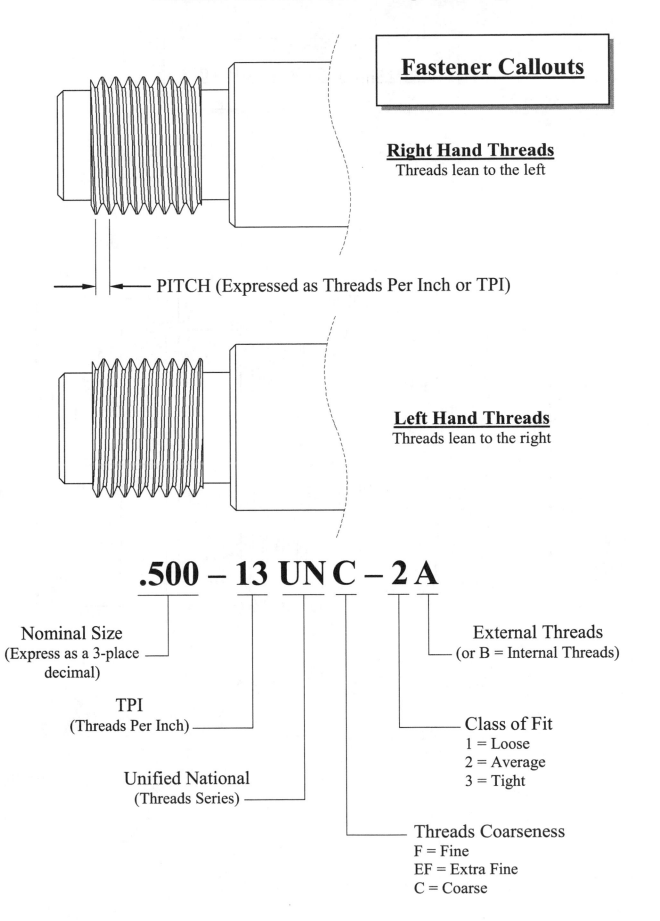

Fastener Callouts

Right Hand Threads
Threads lean to the left

PITCH (Expressed as Threads Per Inch or TPI)

Left Hand Threads
Threads lean to the right

.500 – 13 UN C – 2 A

Nominal Size
(Express as a 3-place decimal)

TPI
(Threads Per Inch)

Unified National
(Threads Series)

External Threads
(or B = Internal Threads)

Class of Fit
1 = Loose
2 = Average
3 = Tight

Threads Coarseness
F = Fine
EF = Extra Fine
C = Coarse

Thread Nomenclature

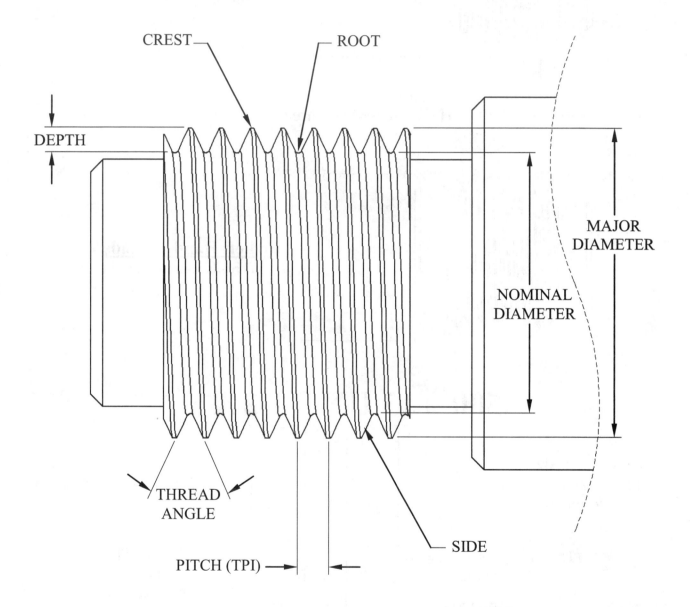

CREST

ROOT

DEPTH

MAJOR
DIAMETER

NOMINAL
DIAMETER

THREAD
ANGLE

SIDE

PITCH (TPI)

Geometric Dimensioning & Tolerancing

Reference Reading

Geometric Dimensioning & Tolerancing provide a vital link in the manufacturing field. It is used by engineers, designers, drafters, inspectors, machinists, and anyone involved in turning ideas into satisfactory products.

The engineer and designer can use geometric and position tolerances to communicate specifications clearly and accurately to the people who make the parts and to the inspector who will in turn, check the parts against the designer's drawings.

When properly applied the process of proper tolerancing will help eliminate or reduce problems which may occur later and products can be produced more accurately.

1. Opening an existing document: (optional)

- Open the document called **GD&T References.slddrw** from the Training folder.

- This drawing has a total of 4 sheets and for practice purposes we will add different geometric tolerances to the drawing views.

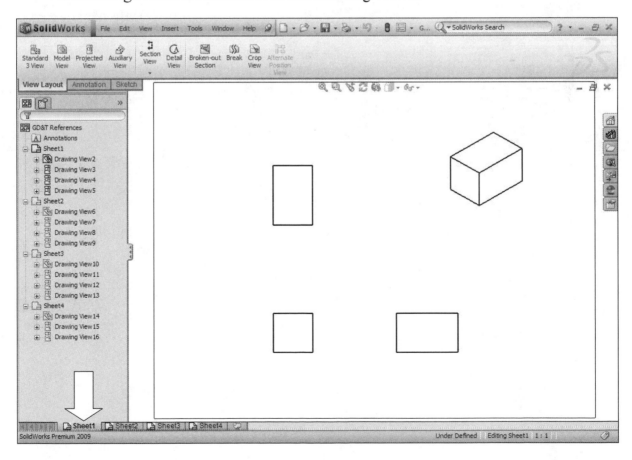

2. Adding the geometric tolerances:

- From the default sheet 1 use the Front drawing view, add a Flatness tolerance, and a Dimension with Symmetric tolerances as shown.

(For the Plus/Minus tolerance, add it from the Properties tree and switch back to the Annotation toolbar to add the Geometric Tolerance).

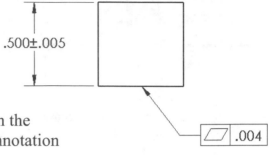

FORM Examples

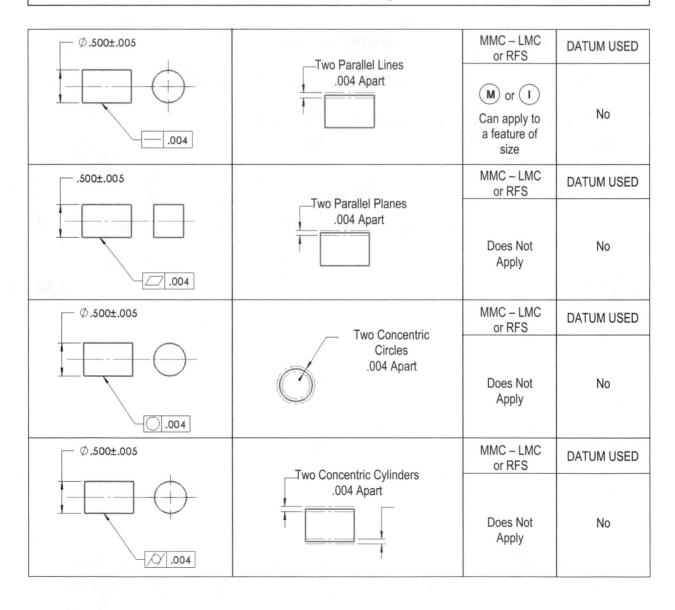

		MMC – LMC or RFS	DATUM USED
Ø.500±.005 ... .004	Two Parallel Lines .004 Apart	**M** or **I** Can apply to a feature of size	No
.500±.005 ... .004	Two Parallel Planes .004 Apart	Does Not Apply	No
Ø.500±.005 ... .004	Two Concentric Circles .004 Apart	Does Not Apply	No
Ø.500±.005 ... .004	Two Concentric Cylinders .004 Apart	Does Not Apply	No

ORIENTATION Examples

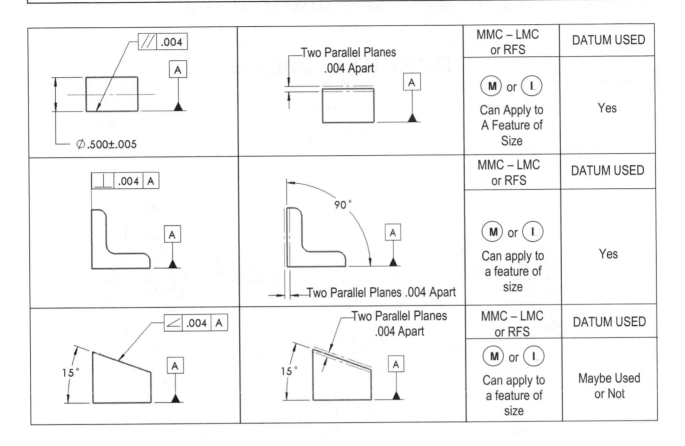

		MMC – LMC or RFS	DATUM USED
(//) .004 — A	Two Parallel Planes .004 Apart — A	(M) or (L) Can Apply to A Feature of Size	Yes
(⊥) .004 A — A	90° Two Parallel Planes .004 Apart — A	MMC – LMC or RFS	DATUM USED
		(M) or (L) Can apply to a feature of size	Yes
(∠) .004 A 15° — A	Two Parallel Planes .004 Apart 15° — A	MMC – LMC or RFS	DATUM USED
		(M) or (L) Can apply to a feature of size	Maybe Used or Not

PROFILE Examples

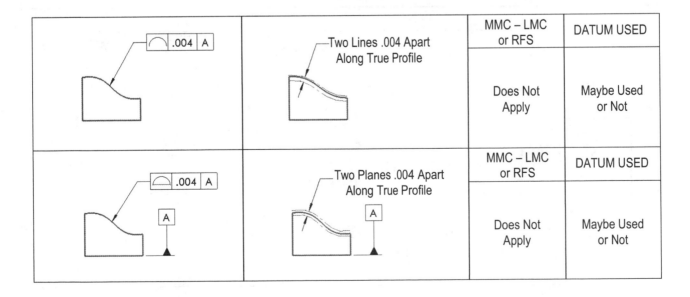

		MMC – LMC or RFS	DATUM USED
(⌒) .004 A	Two Lines .004 Apart Along True Profile		
		Does Not Apply	Maybe Used or Not
(⌒) .004 A — A	Two Planes .004 Apart Along True Profile — A	MMC – LMC or RFS	DATUM USED
		Does Not Apply	Maybe Used or Not

3. Adding more GD&T:

- Add the geometric tolerances for the RUNOUT and LOCATION as shown below.

RUNOUT Examples

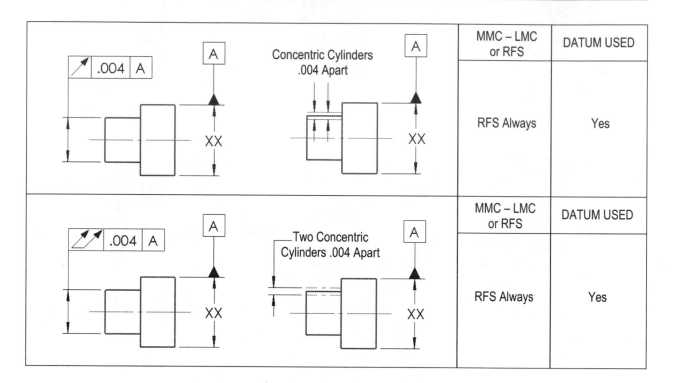

	MMC – LMC or RFS	DATUM USED
	RFS Always	Yes
	MMC – LMC or RFS	DATUM USED
	RFS Always	Yes

LOCATION Examples

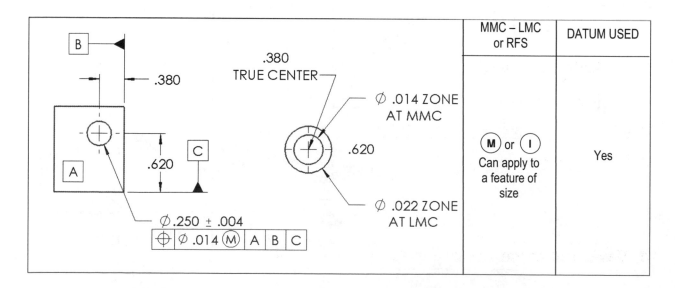

	MMC – LMC or RFS	DATUM USED
	Ⓜ or Ⓘ Can apply to a feature of size	Yes

LOCATION (cont.)

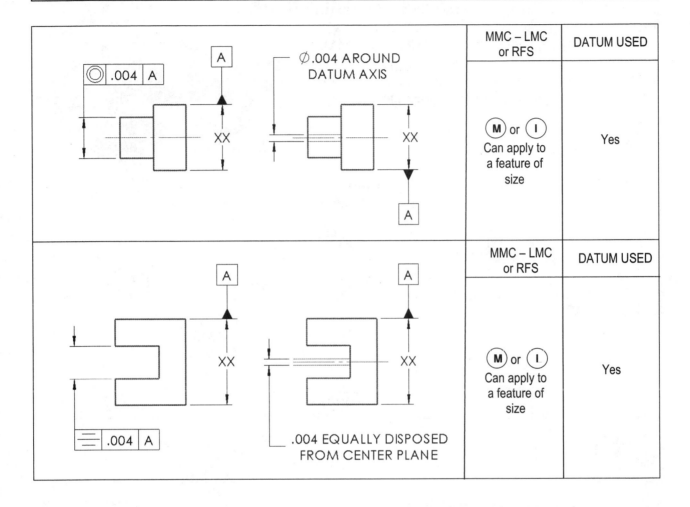

- Add the following tolerances to the other drawing views from sheet 1 through sheet 4.

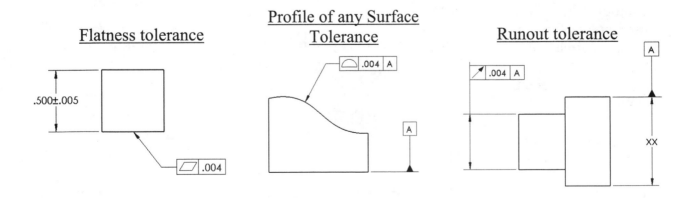

Flatness tolerance

Profile of any Surface Tolerance

Runout tolerance

4. Save and close the drawing.

Size at MMC – Maximum Material Condition

Part 1

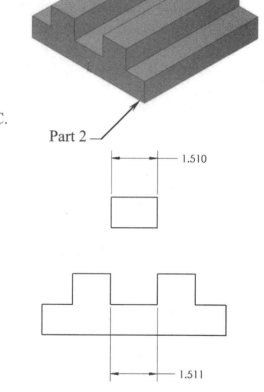

The 2 parts below are designed so that the Bar (part 1) will always fit into the slot of the Base (part 2), even when both are made at their most adverse condition of fit (MMC).

With the Bar (part 1) dimensioned at 1.500±.010, the MMC would be the largest within tolerance, or 1.510.

With the Slot (part 2) at MMC, it would be 1.511, the smallest within tolerance.

It can safely be predicted that the Bar will always be assembled in the Slot, even if both parts are at their MMC.

Part 2

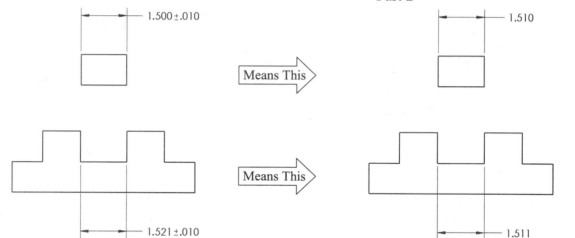

1.500±.010

Means This

1.510

1.521±.010

Means This

1.511

LMC – Least Material Condition

.500±.010

1.00±.03

Least Material Condition is a provision that is the opposite of Maximum Material Condition. The abbreviation is LMC. Its symbol in a tolerance frame is an L within a circle ⓛ.

Least Material Condition specifies that the tolerance applies when feature of size is made at its largest for an internal feature – or – at its smallest for an external feature.

Means This

Means This

Ø.510

Ø.97

Ø.490

Ø1.03

LMC ⓛ

MMC Ⓜ

5. Opening an Assembly Document:

- Open a drawing called **GD&T Assembly.sdldrw** (From the Training CD).

- This drawing has a total of 3 sheets. The **Sheet1** (arrow) is an assembly drawing, and **Sheet2** and **Sheet3** are the detail drawings.

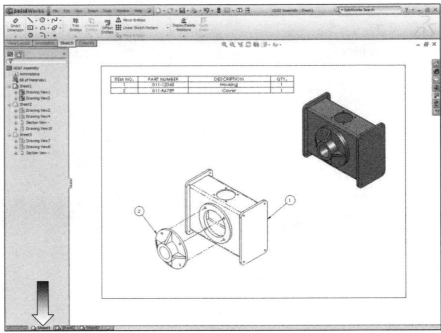

6. Switching the drawing sheet:

- Switch to **Sheet2** by clicking on its **Tab** at the bottom left of the drawing (arrow).

- We will create a new layer and move most of the dimensions into this layer, so that they can be toggled on or off quickly and easily.

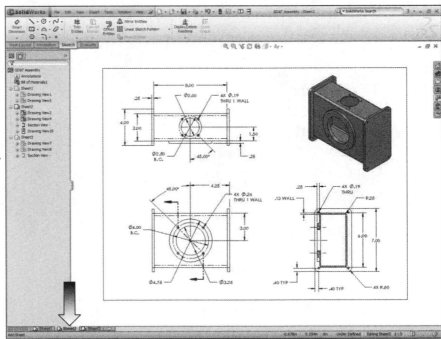

7. Creating a new Layer:

- Right click in an empty area as indicated and select the **Layer** toolbar (arrow) – OR – select **View / Toolbars / Layers**.

- Click the **layer button** on the Layer toolbar to access the layer properties.

Right click in this area and select the LAYER toolbar

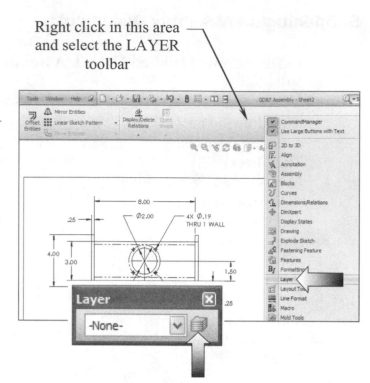

8. Grouping the Dimensions:

- Drag-Select to group all of the dimensions. Make sure only the dimensions are selected.

- To un-select entities like the Center-Mark, hold down the Control key and click on each mark to exclude them from the selection.

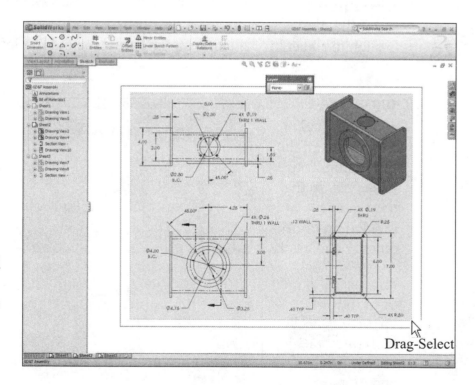

Drag-Select

9. Adding a Layer:

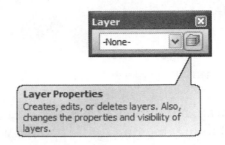

- While the dimensions are still highlighted, click the **New** button (arrow).

Layer Properties
Creates, edits, or deletes layers. Also, changes the properties and visibility of layers.

- A new layer is created and the default name is: **Layer0**.

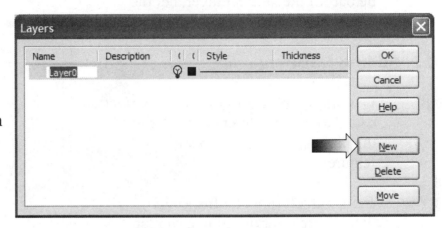

- The layer name can be changed to something more descriptive like: **Dimensions**.

10. Moving the dimensions into the Layer:

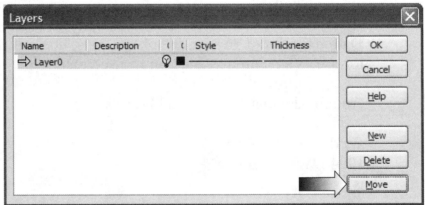

- Click the **Move** button (arrow) to move all of the selected dimensions onto the new layer.

- To verify that all dimensions have been moved, click the On/Off light bulb (arrow) a couple times, and then leave the layer **OFF**.

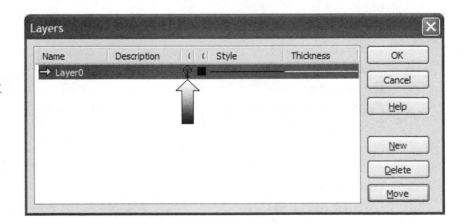

11. Switching Layer:

- Select the layer **None** from the Layer toolbar (arrow).

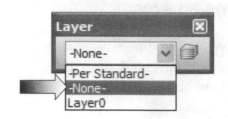

- This way, anything that we're going to add to the drawing (at this point) will be part of the Default layer, not the New layer.

12. Adding Datums:

- Datums are places of origin for perfect calculations or reference standards for the dimensions related to various features on parts.

- In manufacturing and Inspection, datums are established in a similar fashion with perfect surface tables or machine beds.

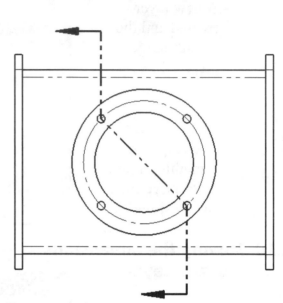

- Datums can also be invisible planes, axis, lines, or points for use as a theoretical basis of measurement.

- Add the datums **A**, **B**, **C**, and **D** as shown.

- By default, the new 1994 Datum symbol is used.

- If you need to switch back to the 1982 symbol, go to:

Tools / Options / Document-Properties, expand the **Annotation** option, click **Datums** and enable the check box for: **Display Datum per 1982**.

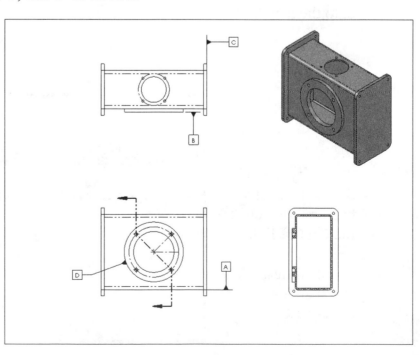

13. Adding Dimensions:

- Add the **Basic** dimensions as shown.

- Use the **Tolerance /Precision** on the Properties tree (arrow) to change to Basic dimensions.

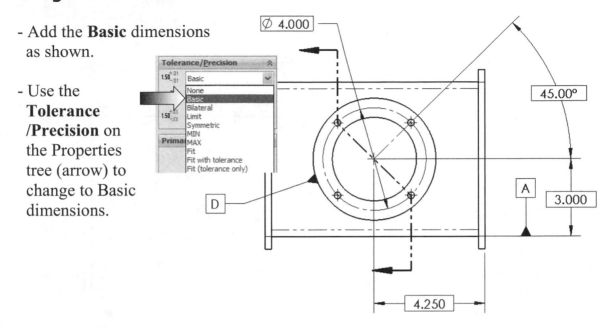

14. Adding the Tolerance/Precision:

- Add the hole diameter and location dimensions for use in this step.

- Add the **Symmetric** tolerances to the dimensions as noted (arrows).

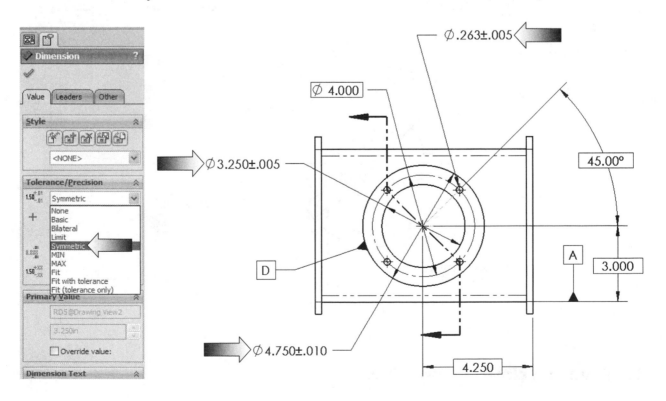

15. Adding the Geometric Tolerances:

- Add the **True Position** and the **Perpendicularity** tolerances to the dimensions as shown.

16. Repeating the process:

- Switch to the drawing **Sheet3** and add the dimensions and tolerances as indicated.

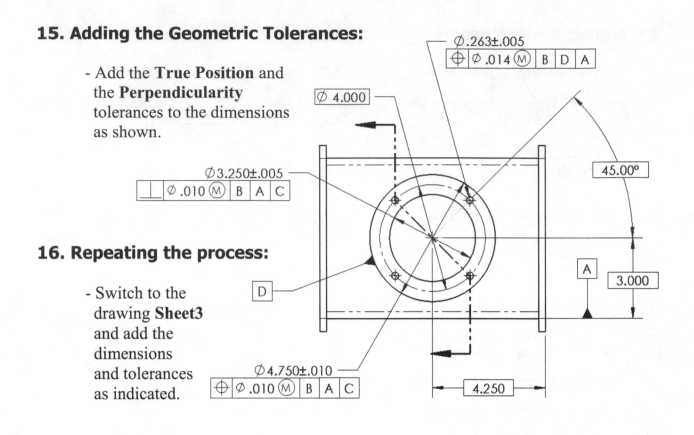

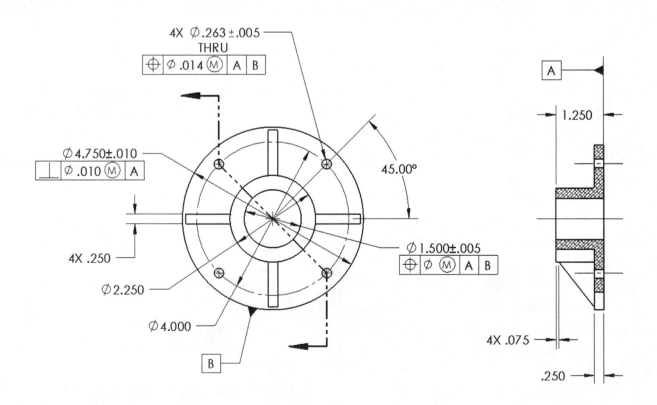

17. Save and close the drawing.

CHAPTER 16

Sheet Metal Drawings

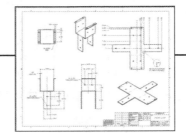

Sheet Metal Drawings
Post Cap

- When a *sheet metal Drawing* is made from a *sheet metal Part*, the SolidWorks software automatically creates a Flat Pattern view for use in conjunction with the Model View command.

- Any drawing views can be toggled to show the flattened stage, along with the bend lines. By accessing the Properties of the view, you can change from Default (Folded) to Flattened.

- By default, the Bend Lines are visible in the Flat Pattern but the Bend-Regions are not. To show the bend-regions, open the sheet metal part and right click the **Flat-Pattern** in the FeatureManager design tree, select **Edit Feature** and clear **Merge Faces**. You may have to rebuild the drawing to see the tangent edges.

- Both of the Folded and Flat Pattern drawing views can be shown on the same drawing sheet if needed. The dimensions and annotations can then be added to define the views.

- Changes done to the Sheet Metal part **will** reflect in the drawing views and the drawing itself can also be changed to update the sheet metal part as well. To prevent this from happening several options are available, refer to the Online Help from within the SolidWorks software for more details.

- This exercise will guide you through the basics of creating a sheet metal drawing and the use of the Default/Flat-Pattern configurations.

Post Cap
Sheet Metal Drawings

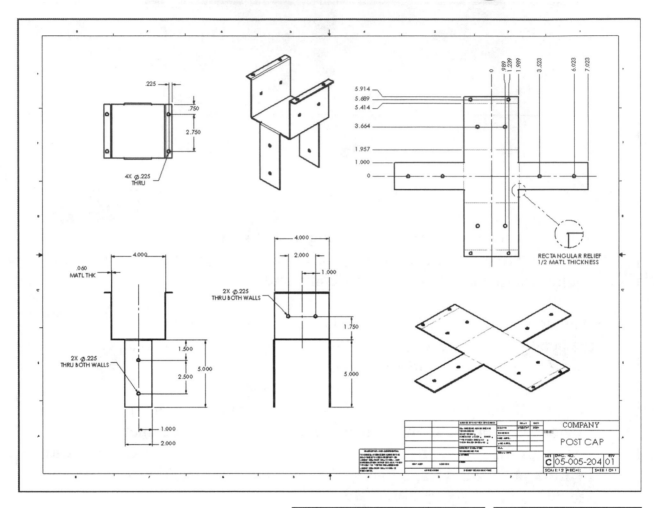

Tools Needed:

 New Drawing

Draw

 Model View

 Detail View

 Model Items

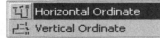 Horizontal Ordinate / Vertical Ordinate

 Properties...

1. Starting a new drawing:

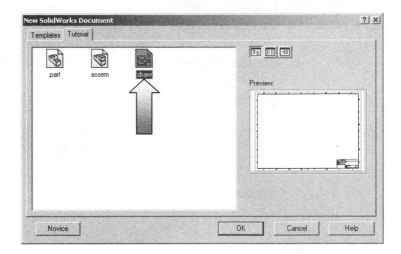

- Select **File / New / Draw** and click **OK**.

- _NOTE:_ _If you have already created and saved a template, you can browse and select the same template for this drawing._

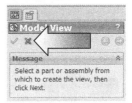

- Click the **Cancel** button (arrow). The drawing paper size, drawing view scale, and the projection angle must be set first.

- If the Sheet Properties dialog does not appear, right click in the default paper and select Properties.

- Set **Scale** to **1** to **1** and set **Type of Projection** to **Third Angle**.

- Select **C-Lanscape** sheet size.

- Enable **Display Sheet Format** and click **OK** .

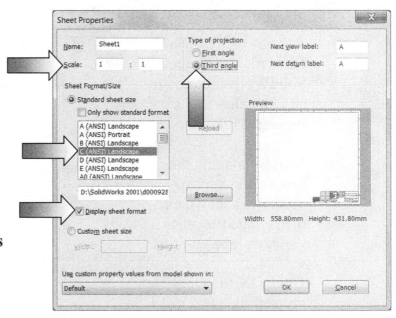

- Go to **Tools / Options** and change the **Units** to **IPS** (Inch / Pound / Second).

2. Creating the 3 Standard Views:

- Select **the Model View** command from the View Layout tab.

- Click the **Browse** Browse... button, from the CD open the part named **Post Cap**.

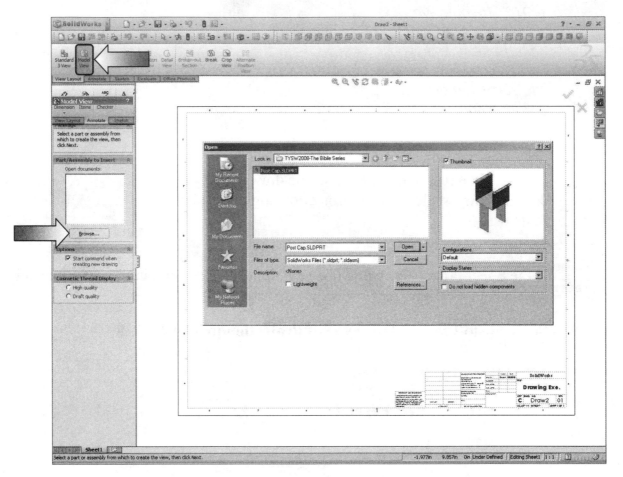

- Once a part is selected SolidWorks automatically switches to the ProjectedView mode.

- Start by placing the Front view approximately as shown and then create the other 3 views as labeled.

- Click OK to stop the projection.

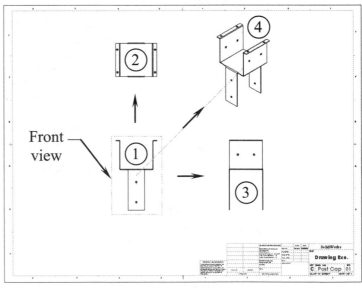

Front view

3. Re-arranging the drawing views:

- Re-arrange the drawing views to the approximate positions by dragging on their borders. A flat-pattern view will be placed on the right side of the drawing.

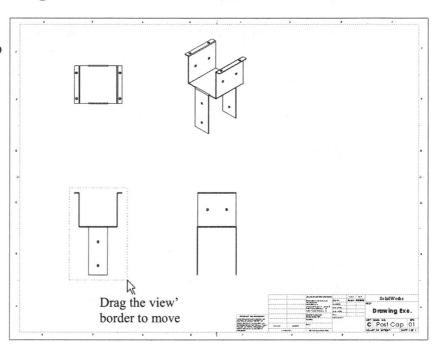

Drag the view' border to move

4. Creating the Flat Pattern drawing view:

- Select the **Model View** command 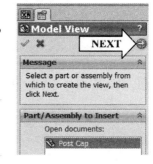, click Next , select the **Flat-Pattern** view (Arrow) from the list and place it approximately as shown.

- Bend notes must be turned off prior to creating the Flat Pattern view (Tools/Option/ Document Properties/Sheet Metal).

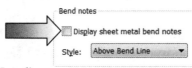

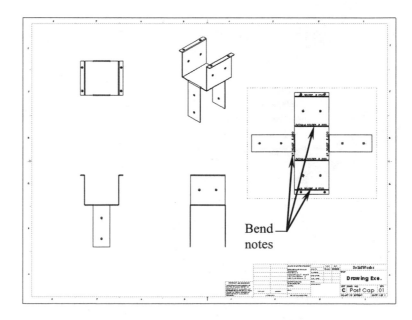

Bend notes

5. Creating a Detail view:

- Click the **Detail View** command 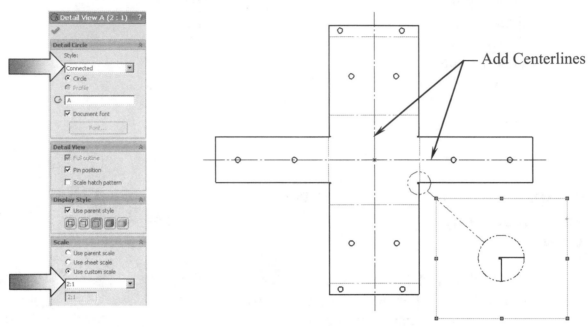 and sketch a Circle approximately as shown.

- Use the **Connected** option and **Custom Scale** of **2:1** (arrows).

Add Centerlines

6. Adding the Ordinate dimensions:

- Click the small arrow below **Smart Dimension** to access its options, and select: **Horizontal Ordinate Dimension** (arrow).

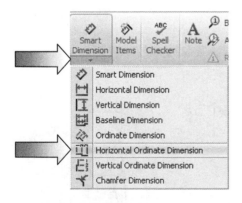

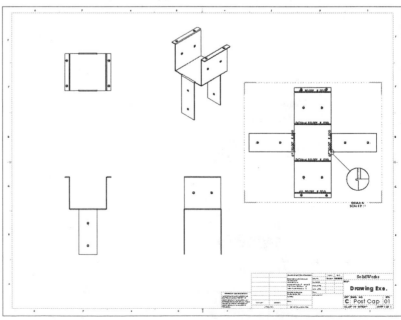

NOTE: Ordinate dimensions are a group of dimensions measured from a zero point. They are reference dimensions and their values cannot be used to change the model.

- Starting at the Vertical Centerline, add the Horizontal Ordinate dimensions as shown here.

- When you are done with adding the Horizontal Ordinate dimensions, right click anywhere in the drawing and select **More Dimensions / Vertical Ordinate**.

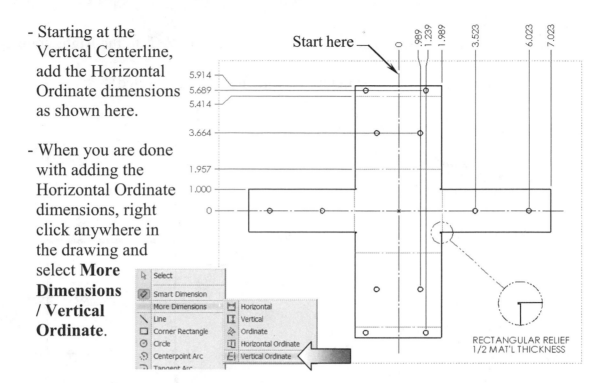

- Add the Vertical Ordinate dimensions as shown in the drawing view.

7. Adding the Model dimensions:

- Select the Front view's border to activate.

- On the **Annotation** tab, click the **Model Items** button, select: **Entire Model** and **Eliminate Duplicates**.

- Click **OK** ✅.

- Modify the dimensions and add the depth and the thickness callouts as shown.

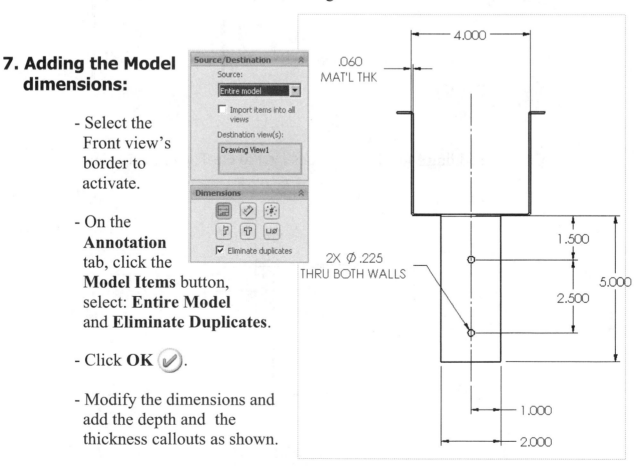

- Repeat step 6 and add the Model Dimensions 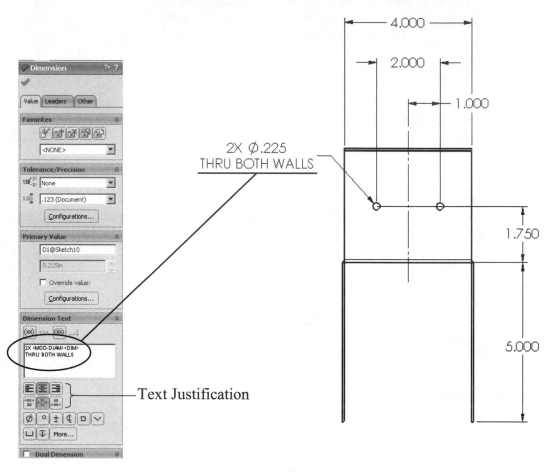 to the Right drawing view.

- Add the annotations below the dimension text (Circled).

- Continue adding Model Dimensions 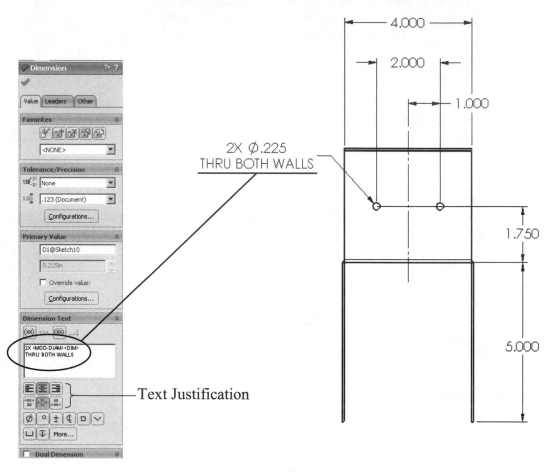 to the Top drawing view.

- Add annotations as needed.

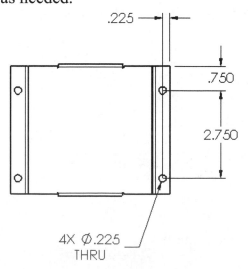

8. Creating the Isometric Flat Pattern view:

- Click the **Model View** command from the View Layout tab

- Click the **Next button** 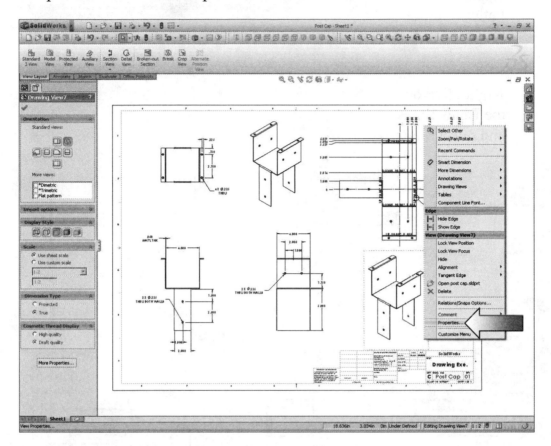 , select the Isometric View from the menu and place it below the flat-pattern view.

- Right-mouse click on the view's border and select **Properties** (Arrow).

- Change the **Default** to **Flat-Pattern** configuration and click **OK** OK .

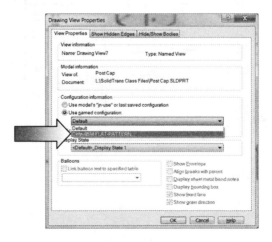

9. Showing the Bend Lines:

- Click the DrawingManager tab (arrow), go down the tree and expand the last Drawing view in the Feature Manager tree (click the + symbol).

- Expand the Flat Pattern option.

- Right click on the Bend-Lines and select **Show**.

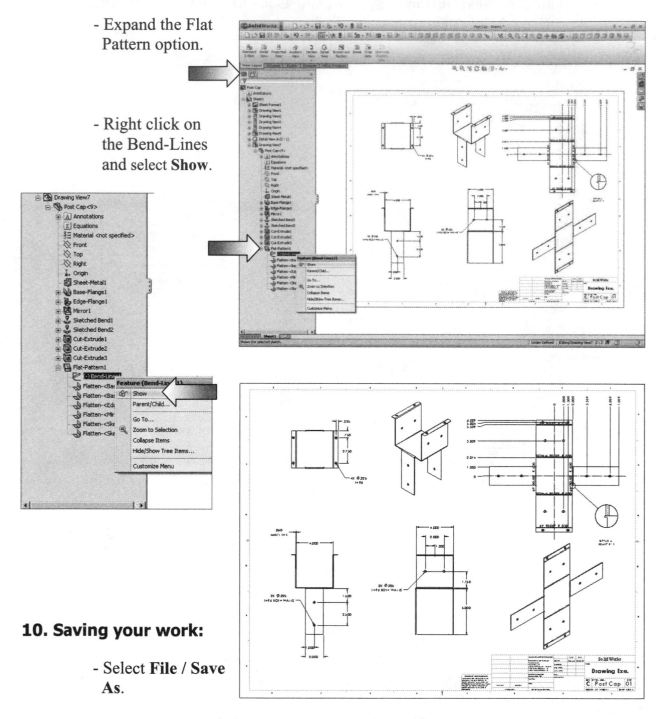

10. Saving your work:

- Select **File / Save As**.

- Enter **Post Cap.slddrw** for the name of the file.

- Click **Save**.

CHAPTER 16 (cont.)

AutoCAD To SolidWorks

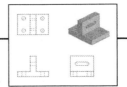

2D To 3D
Converting 2D AutoCAD files to 3D SolidWorks Parts

- The 2D to 3D options allow sketches and/or drawings created in SolidWorks or other CAD programs, like AutoCAD, to be converted into 3D solids.

- The sketches can be created in SolidWorks or imported as a DWG or DXF from other CAD sources. In either case, the sketch or the drawing should be a single sketch imported into a part template.

- The drawing can be Cut and Pasted into a sketch in a part template or can be imported into SolidWorks as a sketch in a part template, using the SolidWorks DXF/DWG import options.

- Once the drawing is imported or a sketch is created, follow the four easy steps to convert your sketch into a solid:

    * Edit the sketch.   * Extract the sketches (Front, Top, Right…)
    * Align the sketches.   * Extrude the sketch.

- This chapter and its exercises will guide you through some of the easiest techniques in converting an AutoCad 2D drawing into a SolidWorks 3D model, as well as using a built-in utility program called DXF/DWG Import by SolidWorks.

2D To 3D Conversions
Converting 2D AutoCAD DWG to 3D SolidWorks Model

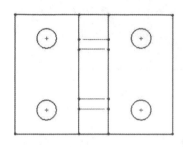

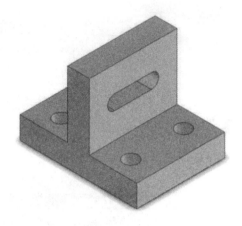

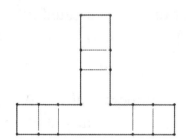

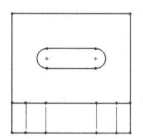

Dimensioning Standards: **ANSI**	Third Angle Projection
Units: **INCHES** – 3 Decimals	

Tools Needed:

Front	Top	Right	Left
Bottom	Back	Auxiliary	Create New Sketch
Repair Sketch	Align Sketch	Extrude	Cut

1. Creating the drawing in AutoCAD®:

- The orthographic views below have already been created in AutoCAD.

- The drawing has also been saved as **2Dto3D.dwg**.

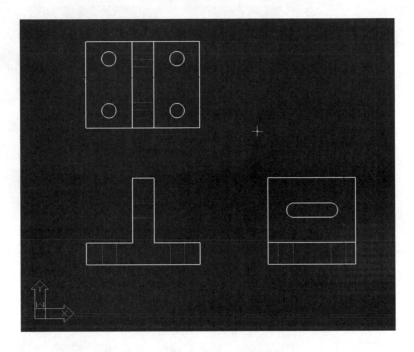

2. Opening the AutoCAD drawing from SolidWorks:

- In SolidWorks, click **File / Open**.

- Change the Files of Type to **Dwg** (*dwg), select the file **2Dto3D** and **open**.

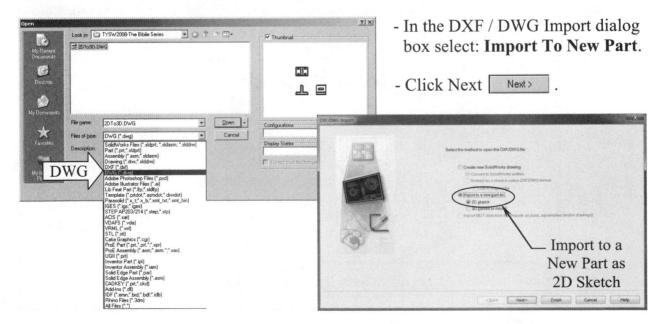

- In the DXF / DWG Import dialog box select: **Import To New Part**.

- Click Next Next > .

Import to a
New Part as
2D Sketch

- In the Document Settings dialog box, select **All Selected Layers** and **Add-Constraints** checkboxes.

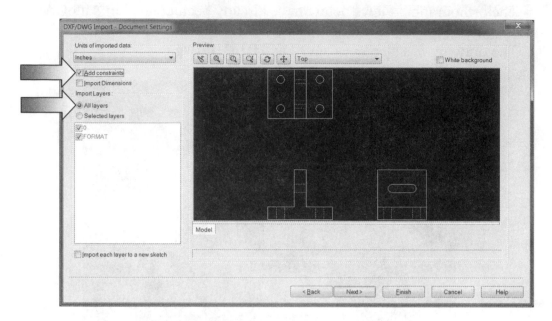

- Click **Next** [Next >].

- In the Drawing Layer Mapping dialog, select / set the following:

     * Merge points closer than **0.001**

     * White Background: **Enabled**.

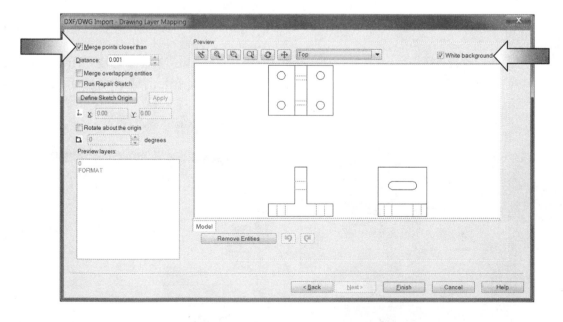

- Click Finish [Finish].

- The AutoCad drawing is placed onto the SolidWorks' Front plane, as a sketch.

- A 2D-To-3D toolbar pops up on the screen. (The 2D-To-3D toolbar can be toggled on/off under View / Toolbars / 2D-To-3D).

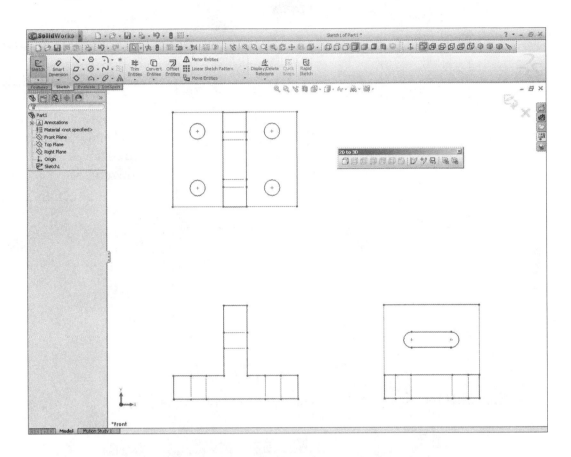

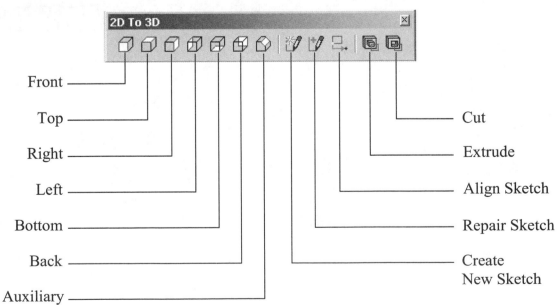

Front

Top

Right

Left

Bottom

Back

Auxiliary

Cut

Extrude

Align Sketch

Repair Sketch

Create New Sketch

3. Converting the sketches:

- Drag select (click-hold-drag) the Front view.

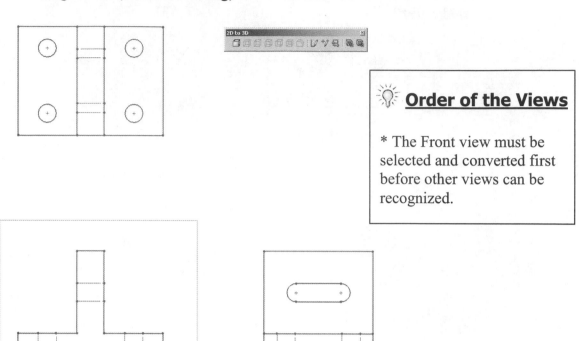

- Click FRONT in the 2D-To-3D toolbar.

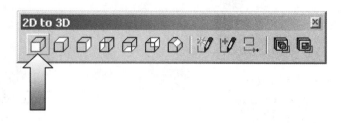

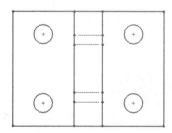

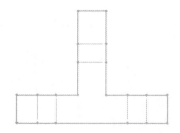

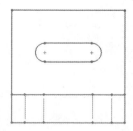

- The Front view is converted and turned into gray color.

- Drag select (click-hold-drag) the Top view.

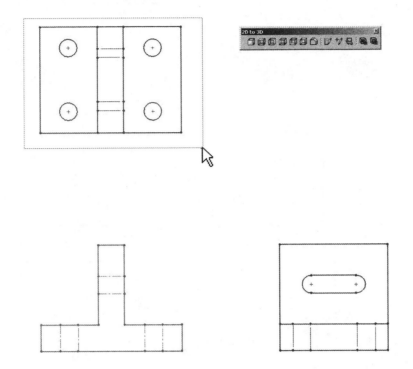

- Click TOP in the 2D-To-3D toolbar.

- The Top view is converted and rotated 90°.

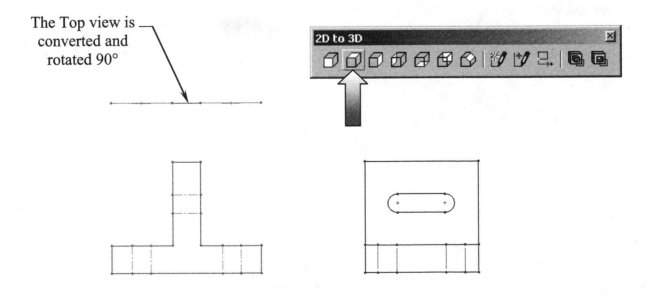

The Top view is converted and rotated 90°

- Drag select (click-hold-drag) the Right view.

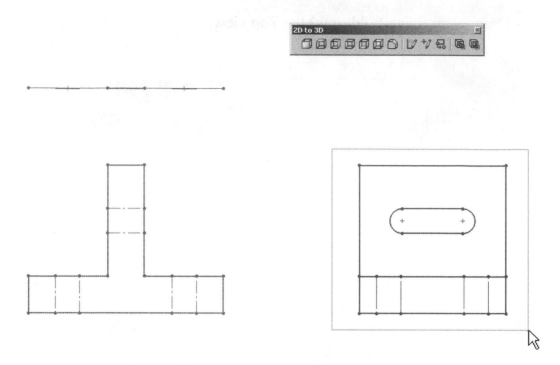

- Click RIGHT ⬚ in the 2D-To-3D toolbar.

- The Right view is converted and rotated 90°.

The Right view is converted and rotated 90°

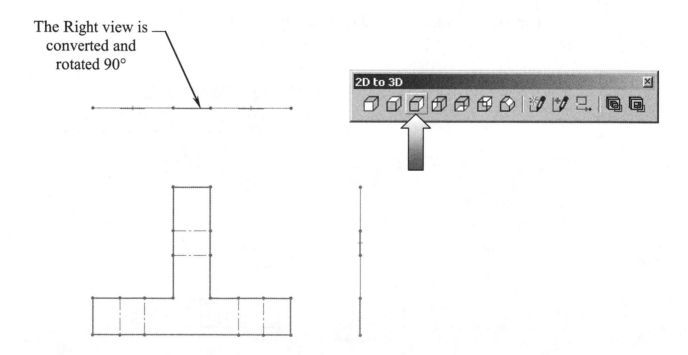

- Change to the Isometric view ⬢ (or press Cntrl + 8), the next step is to align the sketches before making the extrusions.

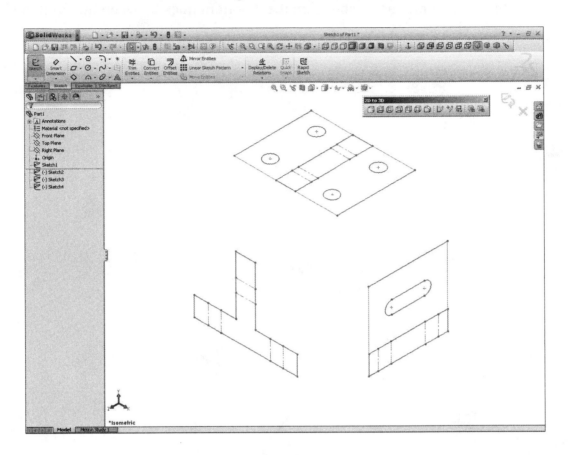

4. Aligning the three views:

- While holding the CONTROL key, select the **left-edge** of the Top view and the *left-edge* of the Right view as shown.

- Click ALIGN SKETCH ⬚ on the 2D-To-3D tool bar.

- The 2 selected views are aligned.

- Change to the Right view ⬢ to verify the result of the alignment.

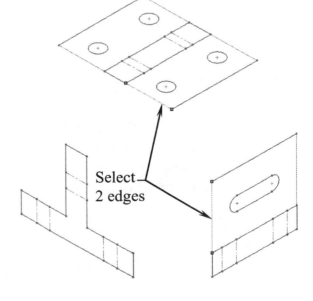

Select 2 edges

- Repeating the step 4:

- Repeat step number 4 and align the 2 bottom lines between the Front and the Right views.

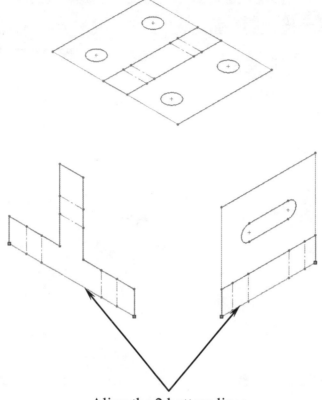

Align the 2 bottom lines.

5. Extruding the Base Feature:

- Select the profile of the Front view. (Right click on one of the lines and pick: **Select Chain**).

- The Select Chain option selects all connecting entities, regardless of their conditions.

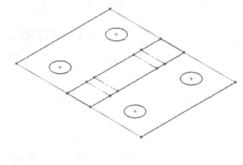

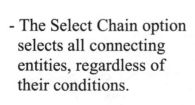

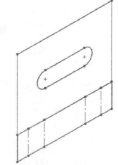

Right click and pick —— **Select Chain**.

- Click Extrude 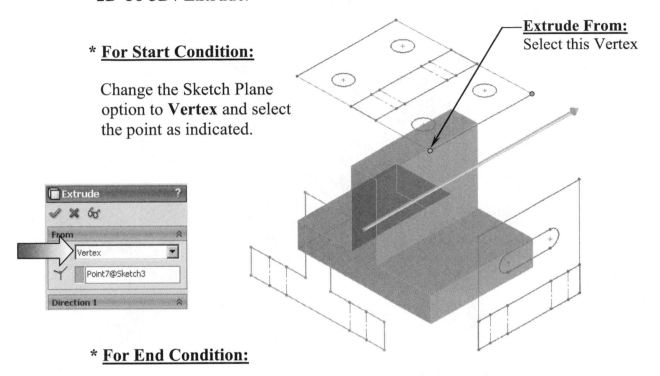 on the 2D-To-3D toolbar or select **Tools / Sketch Tools / 2D-To-3D / Extrude**.

Extrude From:
Select this Vertex

* For Start Condition:

Change the Sketch Plane option to **Vertex** and select the point as indicated.

* For End Condition:

Change the Direction 1 to **Up To Vertex** and select the point as indicated.

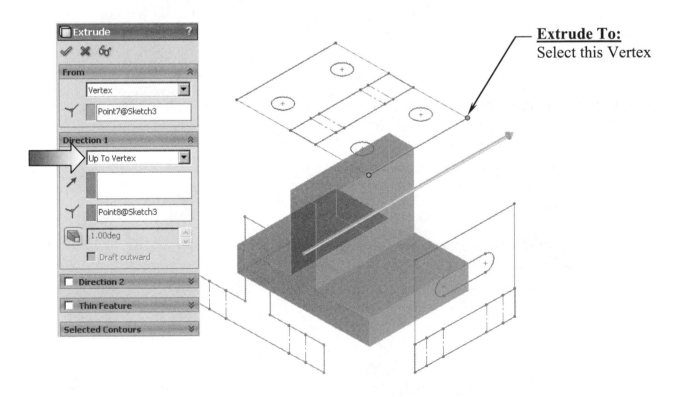

Extrude To:
Select this Vertex

- The solid feature is created from an imported drawing and is centered between the three views.

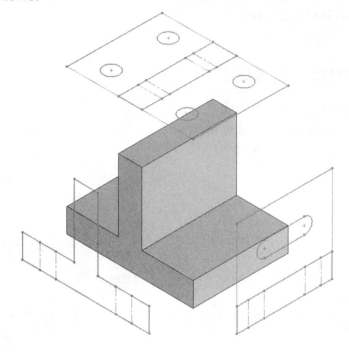

6. Creating the first Cut extrude, the 4 Holes:

- Select the **four circles** and press **Cut** on the 2D-To-3D toolbar.

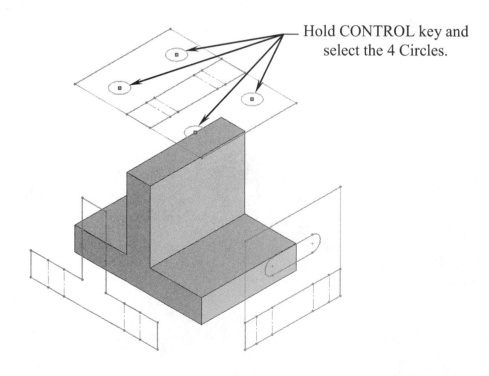

Hold CONTROL key and select the 4 Circles.

- Change the Direction 1 to **Through All**.

- Click **OK** 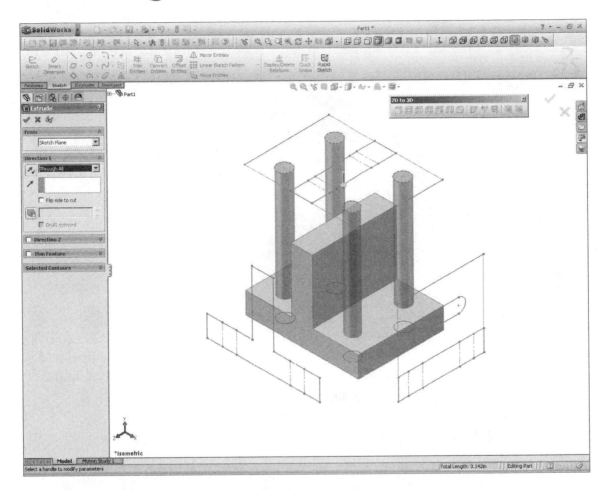.

- The Cut feature is created; rotate the part to verify the result.

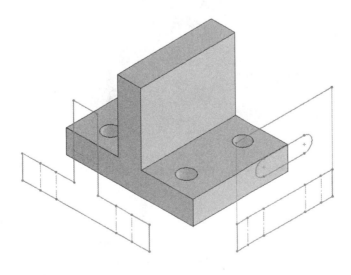

7. Create the second Cut extrude, the Center Slot:

- Right click on one of the lines of the slot and pick **Select-Chain**.

- Press **Cut** 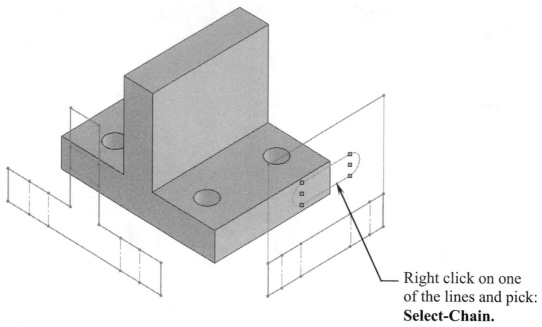 on the 2D-To-3D toolbar.

Right click on one
of the lines and pick:
Select-Chain.

- Change the Direction 1 to **Through All**.

- Click **OK** ✓.

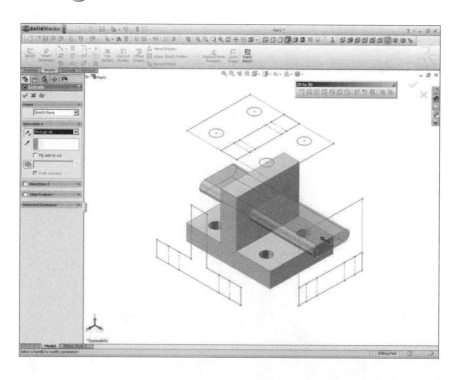

- The Slot feature is created; rotate the model to check out the cut.

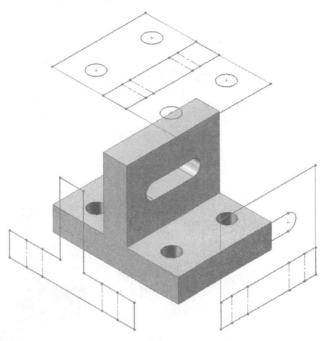

8. Hiding the Front sketch:

- Right click on one of the lines of the Front sketch and select **Hide.**

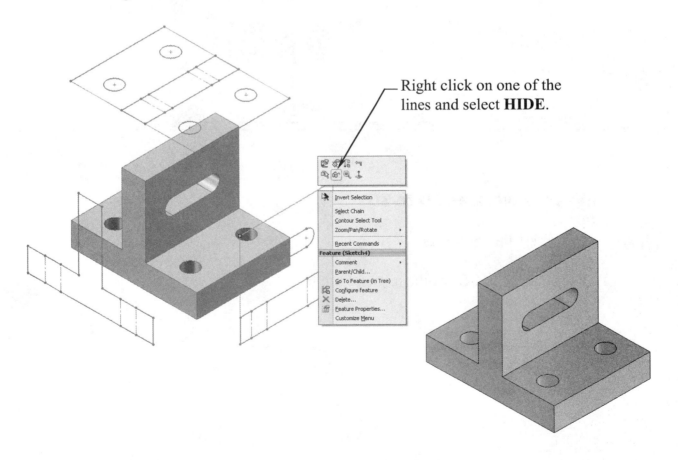

Right click on one of the
lines and select **HIDE.**

- The AutoCAD drawing has been converted into SolidWorks 3D solid model.

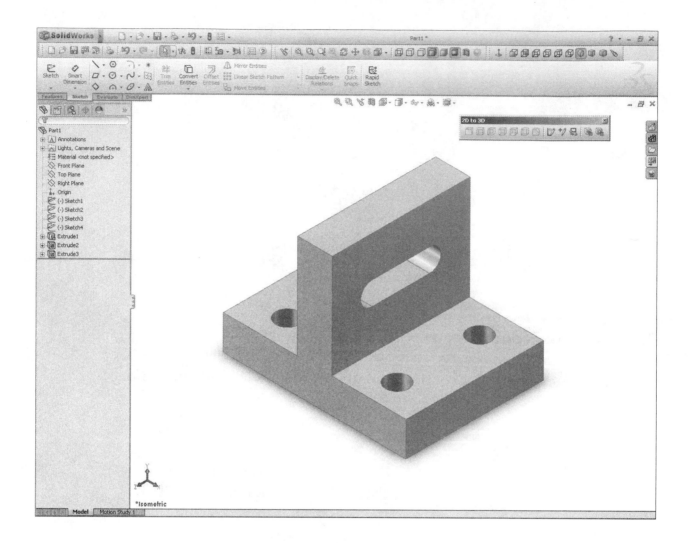

9. Saving your work as 2D to 3D:

- Click **File / Save As**.

- Enter **2D to 3D** for the name of the file.

- Click **Save**.

Questions for Review

2D To 3D

1. The 2D to 3D option allows sketches created in SolidWorks or other CAD software to be converted into 3D solid models.
   - a. True
   - b. False

2. Both .DXF and .DWG formats are supported for 2D to 3D conversion.
   - a. True
   - b. False

3. A .DWG document can be inserted into a new SolidWorks drawing or to a new part as a sketch.
   - a. True
   - b. False

4. The Front view does not have be selected and converted first, no sequence is required.
   - a. True
   - b. False

5. After the views are converted, they should be aligned with each other.
   - a. True
   - b. False

6. To select all sketch entities in a view press Control + A.
   - a. True
   - b. False

7. Before extruding, one view should be selected and a line or a dimension should be used to specify the depth.
   - a. True
   - b. False

8. A closed sketch profile can be used to make an Extruded-Cut only, not an Extruded-Boss.
   - a. True
   - b. False

7. True	8. False
5. True	6. False
3. True	4. False
1. True	2. True

<u>Exercise:</u> Modeling & Detailing III

1. Create the part and drawing as shown.
2. Dimensions are in inches, 3 decimal.
3. All connected edges are tangent.
4. Save the solid model and drawing as: **2D to 3D Part**.

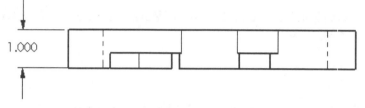

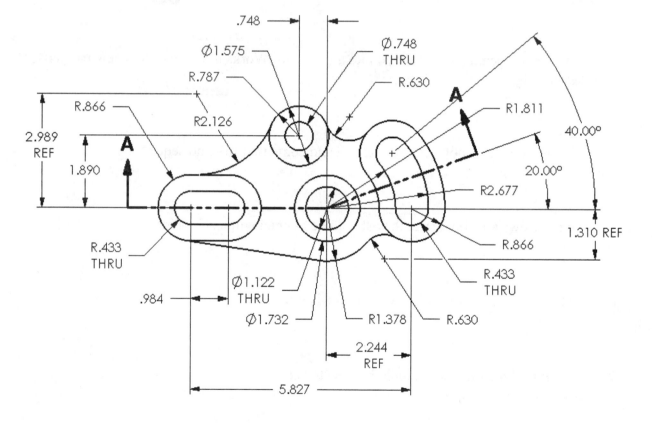

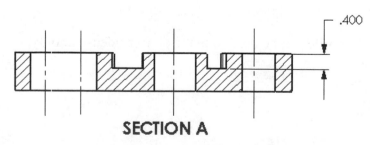

SECTION A

CHAPTER 16 cont.

SolidWorks e-Drawing & 3D Drawing View

eDrawing & 3D Drawing View

Soft-lock Assembly
eDrawing:

- eDrawing is one of the most convenient tools in SolidWorks to create, share, and view your 2D or 3D designs.

- The eDrawing Professional allows the user to create eDrawing markup files (***.markup**) that have markups, such as text comments and geometric elements.

- With eDrawing 2012 and SolidWorks® 2012, you can create an eDrawing from any CAD model or assembly from programs like AutoCAD®, Pro/E®, and others.

- The following types of eDrawing files are supported:
    * 3D part files (***.eprt**)
    * 3D assembly files (***.easm**)
    * 2D drawing files (***.edrw**)

3D Drawing View:

- The 3D drawing view mode lets you rotate a drawing view out of its plane so you can see components or edges obscured by other entities. When you rotate a drawing view in 3D drawing view mode, you can save the orientation as a new view orientation.

- 3D drawing view mode is particularly helpful when you want to select an obscured edge for the depth of a broken-out section view. Additionally, while in 3D drawing view mode, you can create a new orientation for another model view. 3D drawing view mode is not available for detail, broken, crop, empty, or detached views.

Soft-Lock Assembly
SolidWorks e-Drawing & 3D Drawing View

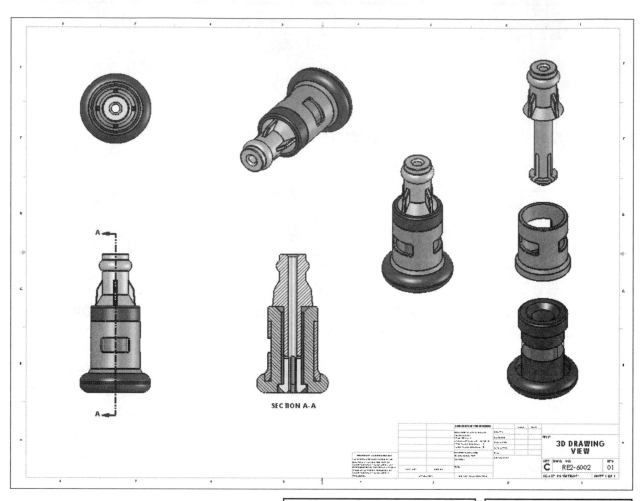

SECTION A-A

3D DRAWING VIEW

C   RE2-6002   01

Dimensioning Standards: **ANSI**	Third Angle Projection
Units: **INCHES** – 3 Decimals	

Tools Needed:

 SolidWorks e-drawing

 Play Animation

Stop Animation

 Rotate View

 3D Drawing View

1. Opening an existing drawing:

- Click **File / Open**.

- Select **3D Drawing View.slddrw** from the Training Files folder and open it.

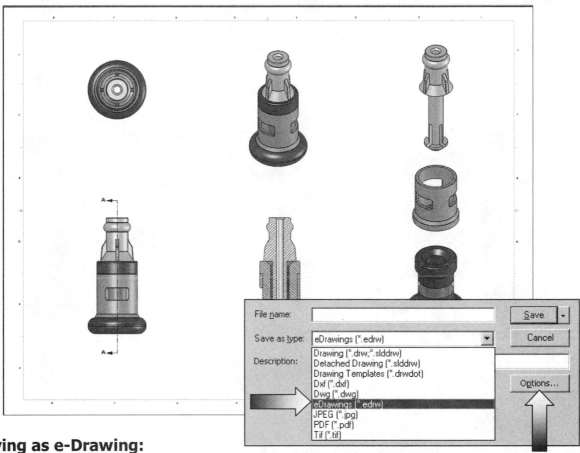

2. Saving as e-Drawing:

- Select **File / Save As.**

- Change the file format to **eDrawing** (*.edrw).

- Enter **3D Drawing View** as the file name.

- Click the Options button and enable **OK to Measure**.

- Click **Save**.

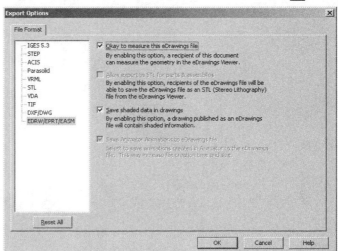

3. Working with eDrawing:

- Close out of SolidWorks and launch the **e-Drawing** program 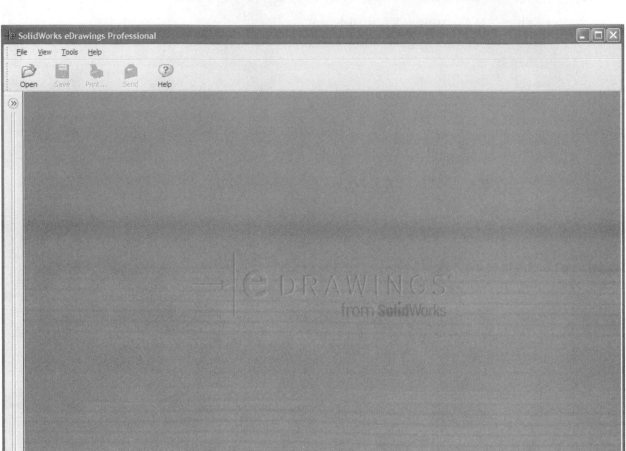 .

- Click **Open** .

- Select the document **3D-Drawing View .edrw** and click **Open**.

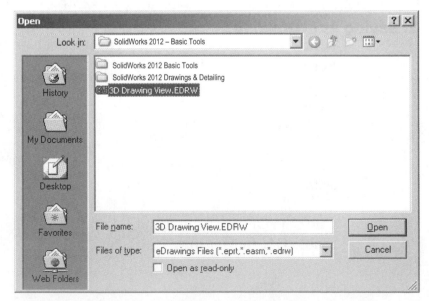

- The previously saved drawing is opened in the new User Interface .

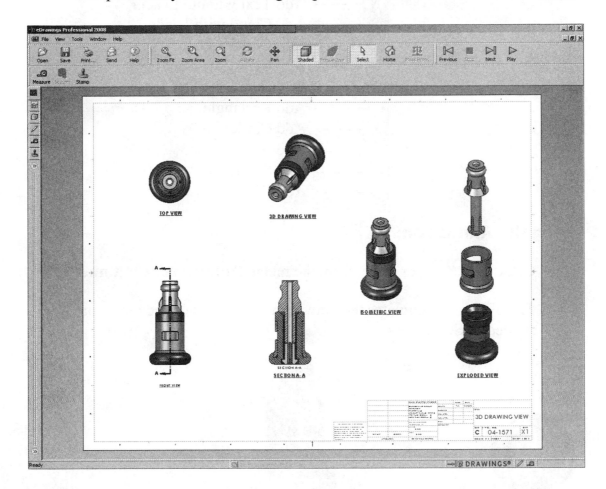

- The **eDrawing** toolbar:

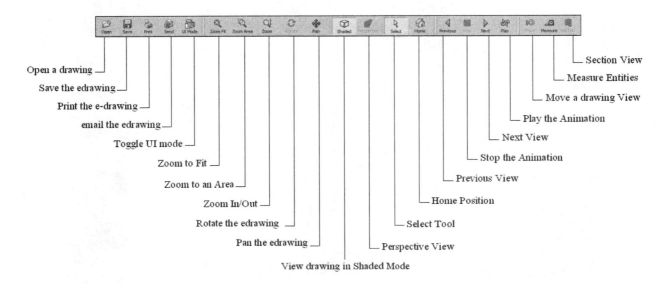

Open a drawing

Save the edrawing

Print the e-drawing

email the edrawing

Toggle UI mode

Zoom to Fit

Zoom to an Area

Zoom In/Out

Rotate the edrawing

Pan the edrawing

View drawing in Shaded Mode

Perspective View

Select Tool

Home Position

Previous View

Stop the Animation

Next View

Play the Animation

Move a drawing View

Measure Entities

Section View

- The **Markup** toolbar:

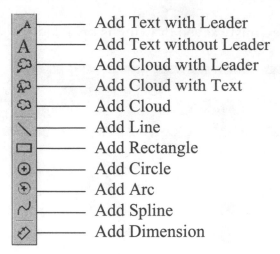

↗	Add Text with Leader
A	Add Text without Leader
☁	Add Cloud with Leader
☁	Add Cloud with Text
☁	Add Cloud
\	Add Line
☐	Add Rectangle
⊕	Add Circle
⊕	Add Arc
∿	Add Spline
⬦	Add Dimension

4. Playing the Animation:

- Click **Play** ▷ or select from the menu: **Animation / Continuous Play**.

- The eDrawing animates the drawing views based on the order that was created in SolidWorks.

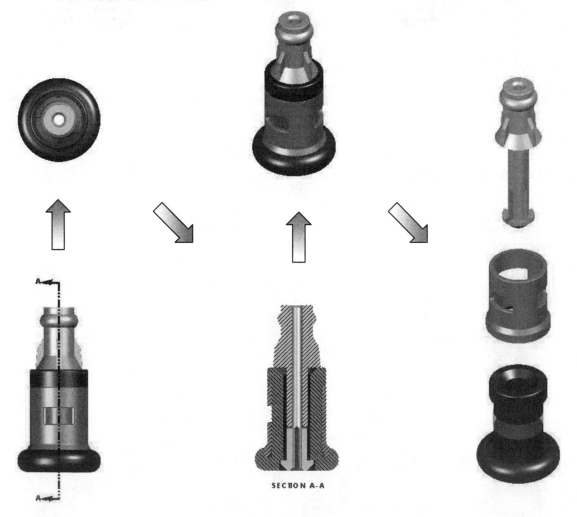

SECTION A-A

- Click **Stop** Stop or select from the menu: **Animation / Stop**.

- Click **Home** Home to return to the full drawing mode.

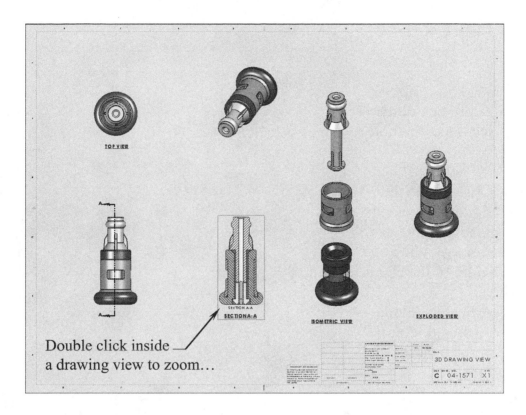

Double click inside a drawing view to zoom...

- Double click inside the Section view to zoom and fit it to the screen.

5. Adding the markup notes:

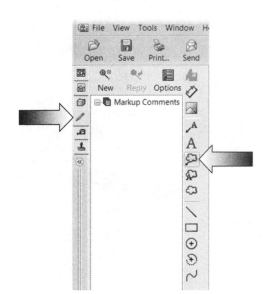

- Click the **Markup** button and select the **Cloud-With Leader** command (arrow).

- Click on the **Edge** of the bottom bore hole and place the blank note on the left side.

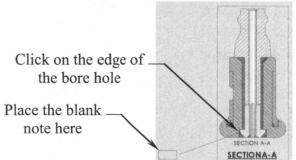

Click on the edge of the bore hole

Place the blank note here

- Enter the note: **Increase the Bore Diameter by .015"**.

- Click **OK** ✔.

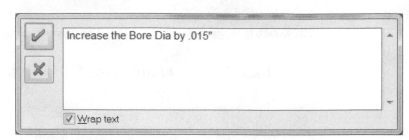

- Zoom out a little to see the entire note.

- Click inside the cloud; there are 4 handle points to move or adjust the width of the cloud.

- Adjust the cloud by dragging one of the handle points.

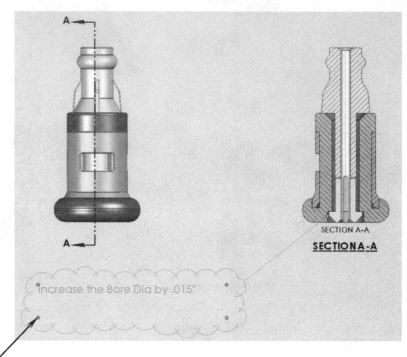

Drag handle point

6. Adding a "Stamp":

- Click the Stamp button.

- Locate the DRAFT stamp and drag/drop it on the upper corner of the drawing.

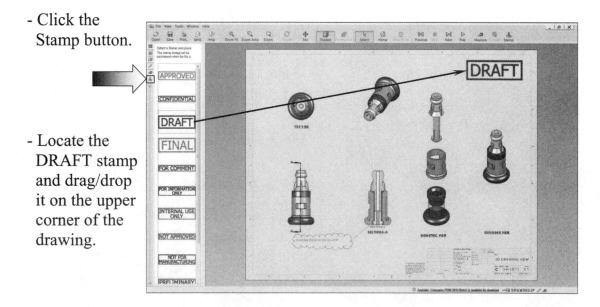

- Click THE **Home** button 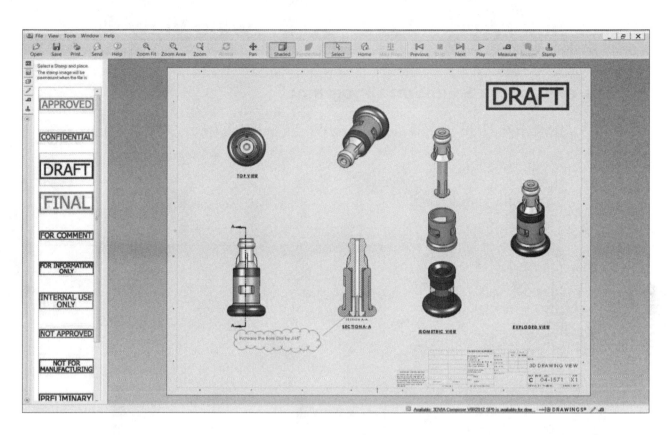 to return to the full drawing mode.

7. Saving as Executable file type:

- Click **File / Save As**.

- Select **eDrawing Executable Files (*.exe)** from the Save As Type menu & click **Save**.

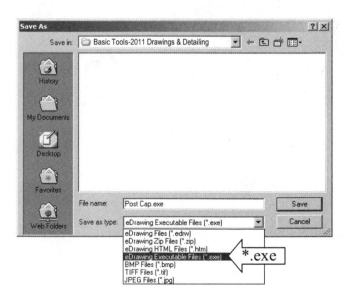

NOTES: *The .exe files are much larger in size than the Standard .edrw.*

The .edrw files require eDrawing Viewer or the eDrawing Program itself to view.

Continue...

SolidWorks 2012 - 3D Drawing View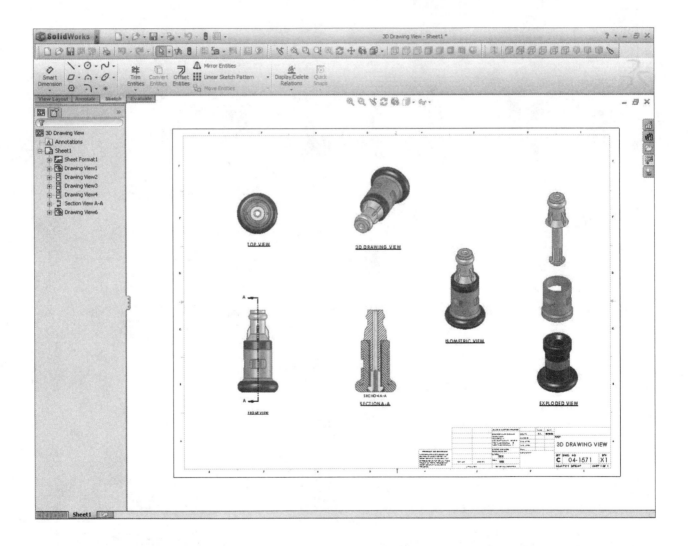

8. Returning to the SolidWorks Program:

- Switch back to the previous SolidWorks drawing (press Alt+ Tab).

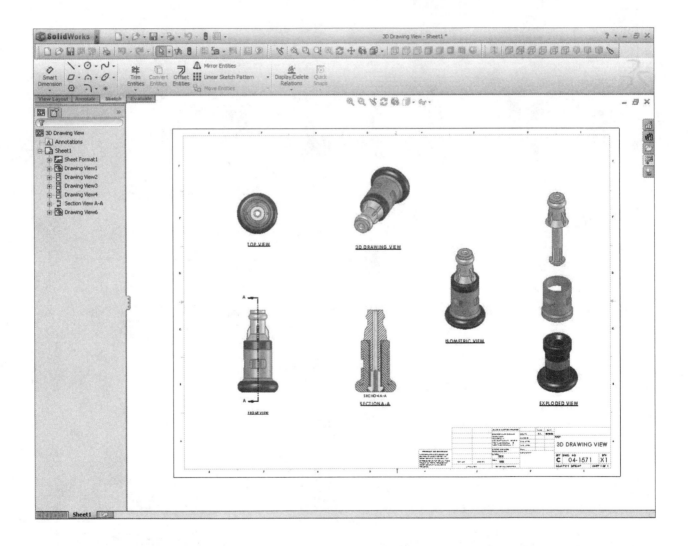

- 3D drawing view mode is particularly helpful when you want to select an obscured edge for the depth of a broken-out section view. Additionally, while in 3D drawing view mode, you can create a new orientation for another model view.

9. Using the 3D Drawing View command:

- Create another Top view and then click the drawing view's border to activate.

- Click 3D Drawing View icon  from the View toolbar (or under the **View /
Modify** menus).

- Select the Rotate tool and rotate the Top drawing to a different position
approximately as shown.

Original Drawing View

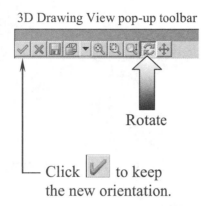

3D Drawing View pop-up toolbar

↑ Rotate

└─ Click ✓ to keep
the new orientation.

New 3D Drawing View

10. Saving the New-View orientation:

- Click Save on the 3D Drawing View pop-up toolbar.

- Enter: **3D Drawing View** in the Named View dialog. This view orientation will
be available under **More Views** in the **Model View PropertyManager** the next
time you insert a model view.

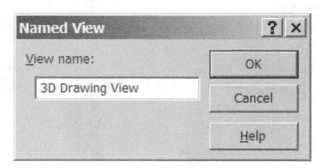

11. Testing out the new view:

- Delete the new view so that we can test out the one that we have just saved.

12. Inserting a Model View:

- Click **Model View**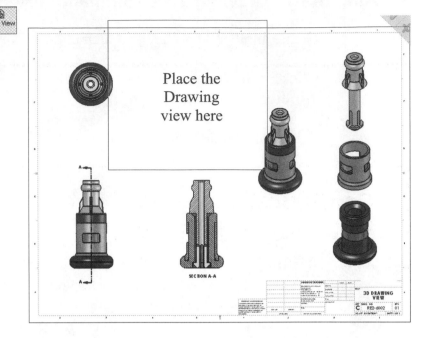

- Click the **NEXT** arrow.

- In the **Orientation** section, under **More Views**, select: **3D Drawing View**.

- Place the Custom Isometric View approximately as shown.

- Click **OK**.

- Access the properties of the view and click off Show-In-Exploded-State if needed.

13. Saving your work:

- Click **File / Save As**.

- Enter **3D Drawing View** as file name.

- Click **Save**.

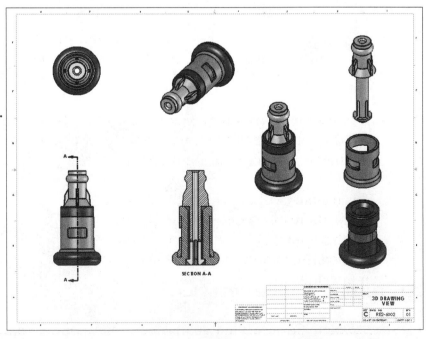

CHAPTER 17

Configurations – Part I

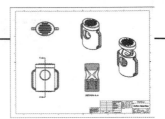

Configurations – Part I
Part, Assembly & Drawing

- Configurations allows SolidWorks users to create multiple variations of a part or assembly within the same document.

- Configurations provide a convenient way to develop and manage families of parts with different dimensions, components, or other parameters.

- In a **Part document**, configurations allow you to create families of parts with different dimensions, features, and custom properties.

- In an **Assembly document**, configurations allow you to create:

   * Simplified versions of the design by suppressing or hiding the components.

   * Families of assemblies with different configurations of the components, parameters, assembly features, dimensions, or configuration-specific custom properties.

- In a **Drawing document**, you can display different views of different configurations that you created earlier in the part or assembly documents by accessing the properties of the drawing view.

- This chapter will guide you through the basics of creating configurations in the part the assembly levels. Later on, these configurations will be called up in a drawing to display the changes that were captured earlier.

Configurations – Part 1
Part, Assembly & Drawing

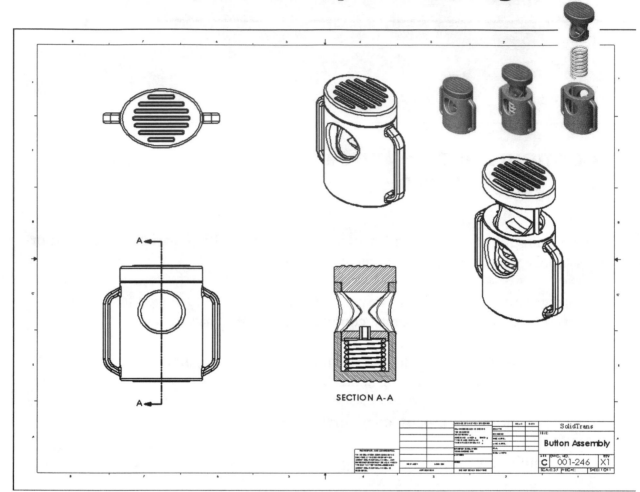

SECTION A-A

Button Assembly

SolidTrans

C | 001-246 | X1

Dimensioning Standards: **ANSI**	Third Angle Projection
Units: **INCHES** – 3 Decimals	

Tools Needed:

 Part document

 Assembly document

 Drawing document

Add Configuration

Default
Expanded

1. Opening the existing Assembly Document:

Go to: The Training CD
                  Button Assembly folder
                  Open **Button Assembly.sldasm**

2. Using Configurations in the Part mode:

- From the FeatureManager tree, right click on **Button Spring** and select **Open Part.**

- Change to the **ConfigurationManager** tree.

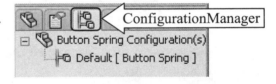

- Right click over the part named Button Spring and select **Add Configuration**.

- Enter **Compressed** under **Configuration Name.**

- Under Comment, enter: **Changed Pitch Dim. from .915 to .415**

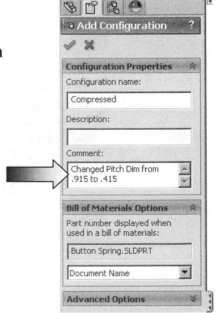

- Click **OK** .

3. Changing the Pitch:

- Switch back to the FeatureManager tree. (arrow).

- Expand the **Sweep1** feature (click the + symbol).

- Right click on the **Helix/Spiral1** feature and select **Edit Feature**.

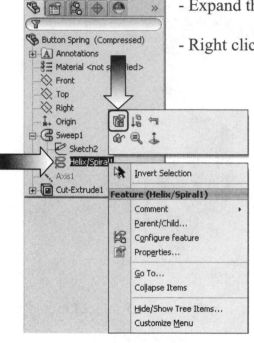

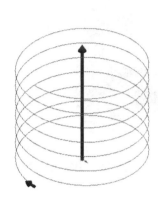

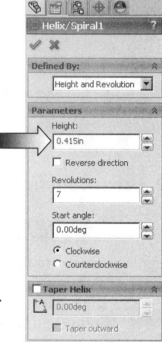

- Change the **Height** dimension to **.415** in.

- Click **OK** .

Default Configuration
(.915 Pitch)

Compressed Configuration
(.415 Pitch)

4. Using Configurations in the Assembly mode:

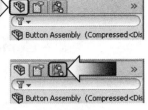

- Switch back to the Assembly document (**Cntrl + Tab**).

- Change to the **ConfigurationManager** tree.

- Right click over the name of the assembly and select: **Add Configuration**.

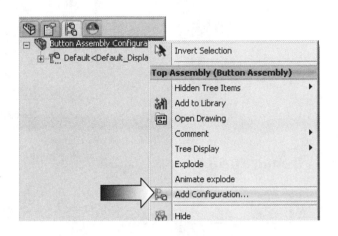

- Enter **Expanded** for Configuration Name.

- Click **OK** ✅.

5. Changing the Mate conditions:

- Switch back to the **FeatureManager** tree and expand the Mates group.

- Right click on the mate Coincident8 and select: **Suppress**.

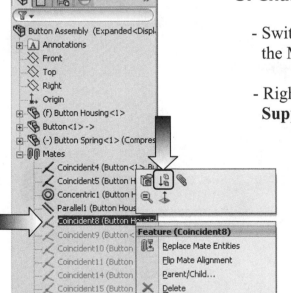

- By suppressing this mate, the Button (upper part) is no longer locked to the Housing and new Mates can be added to re-position it.

6. Adding new Mates:

- Add a **Coincident** Mate between the 2 faces of the two locking features.

Coincident Mate

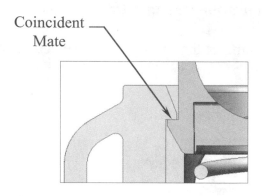

Default Assembly Configuration

7. Changing Configuration:

- Right click over the part named **Button Spring** and select **Component Properties**.

- From the Component Properties dialog box, select the **Default** Configuration.

- Click **OK** ✅.

Compressed Assembly Configuration

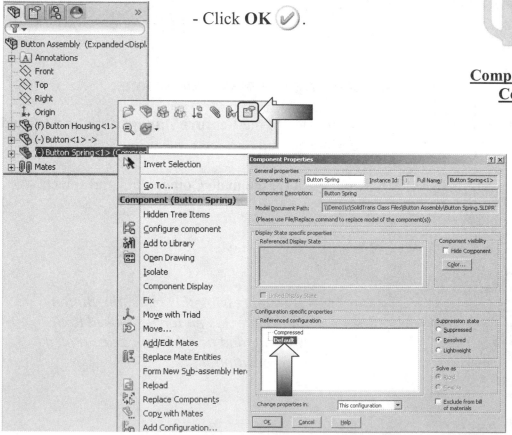

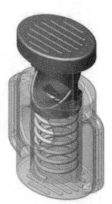

8. Using Configurations in the Drawing:

- Start a New drawing document; Go to **File / New / Draw** (or Drawing).

- Use **C-Landscape** paper size, **Scale: 3:1**

- Create the 4 standard views as shown below (using the **Default** Configuration).

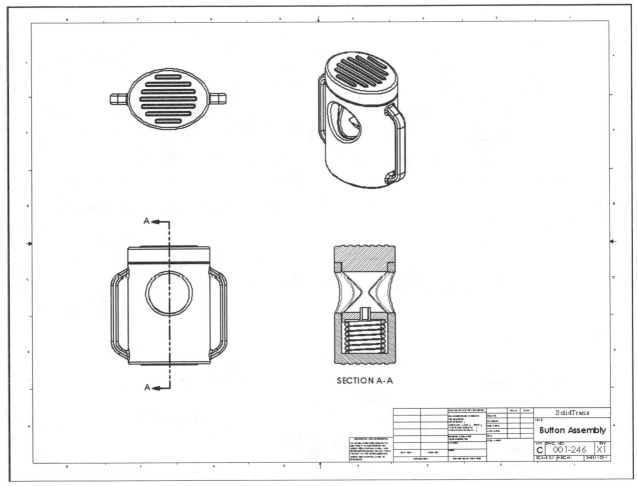

9. Creating a 2nd Isometric view:

- Create another Isometric view and place it approximately as shown.

Note: Copy and Paste also works; first select the Isometric view and press Cntrl+C, then click anywhere in the drawing and press Cntrl+V).

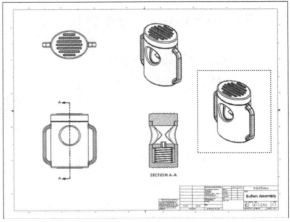

10. Changing the Configuration of a drawing view:

- Right click on the Isometric view's border and select **Properties**.

- Change from the **Default** configuration to **Expanded** configuration.

- Click **OK** 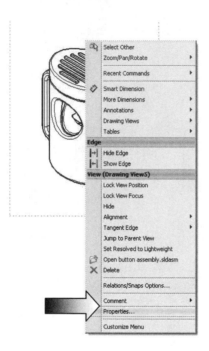.

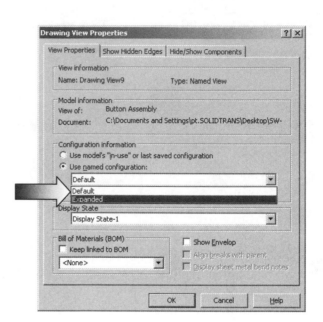

- The Expanded configuration is now the active configuration for this specific view.

11. Saving your work:

- Click **File / Save As**.

-Enter **Button Assembly** for the name of the file.

- Click **Save**.

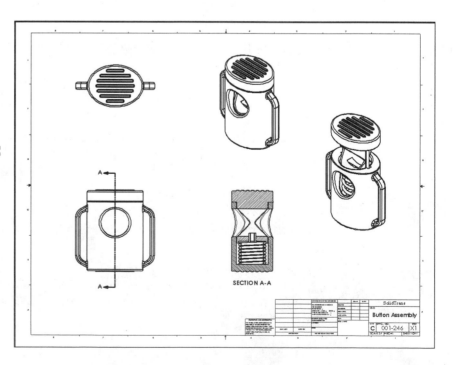

CHAPTER 17 (cont.)

Configurations – Part II

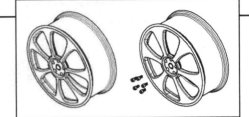

Configurations – Part II
Part / Assembly / Drawing

Configurable Items for Parts:

Part configurations can be used as follows:
* Modify feature dimensions and tolerances.
* Suppress features, equations, and end conditions.
* Assign mass and center of gravity.
* Use different sketch planes, sketch relations, and external sketch relations.
* Set individual face colors.
* Control the configuration of a base part.
* Control the configuration of a split part.
* Control the driving state of sketch dimensions.
* Create derived configurations.
* Define configuration-specific properties.

Configurable Items for Assemblies:

Assembly configurations can be used as follows:
* Change the suppression state (**Suppressed**, **Resolved**) or visibility (**Hide**, **Show**) of components.
* Change the referenced configuration of components.
* Change the dimensions of distance or angle mates, or suppression state of mates.
* Modify the dimensions, tolerances, or other parameters of features that belong to the assembly. This includes assembly feature cuts and holes, component patterns, reference geometry, and sketches that belong to the <u>assembly</u> (not to one of the assembly components).
* Assign mass and center of gravity.
* Suppress features that belong to the assembly.
* Define configuration-specific properties, such as end conditions and sketch relations.
* Create derived configurations.
* Change the suppression state of the Simulation folder in the Feature Manager design tree and its simulation elements (Suppressing the folder also suppresses its elements).

Configurations – Part II
Part, Assembly & Drawing

**6 Spokes
Configuration**

**7 Spokes
Configuration**

**7 Spokes with Bolts
Configuration**

Dimensioning Standards: **ANSI**	Third Angle Projection
Units: **INCHES** – 3 Decimals	

Tools Needed:

 Part document   Part

 Assembly document   Assembly

 Drawing document   Drawing

Feature Manager

 Configuration Manager

Part Configurations

This section discusses the use of Configurations in the part level, where the driving dimensions of the spokes-pattern will be altered to change the number of spokes in the part.

Opening the existing file:

     * Go to the Training CD.
     * Wheel Assembly folder.
     * **WHEEL.sldprt**

1. Part Configurations:

    - Change to the ConfigurationManager tree:

    - Click on the 3rd tab above the tree to change to the Configuration tree.

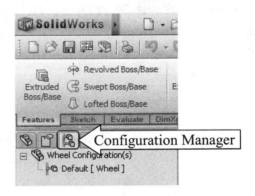

2. Creating a new configuration:

    - Right click over the name of the part and select **Add Configuration**.

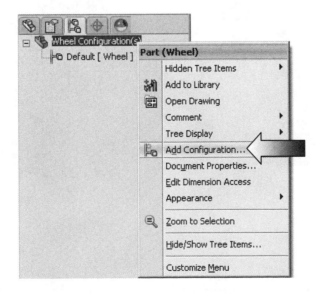

- For Configuration Name, enter:
  7 Spokes (arrows).

- Under Description, enter:
  Modified the No. of Spokes Pattern.

- Click **OK** 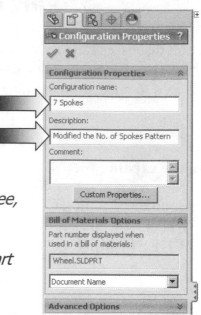.

NOTE:

To display the description in the FeatureManager tree, do the following:

From the FeatureManager tree, right click on the part name, go to Tree-Display, and select:
Show Feature Descriptions.

3. Changing the number of the Spokes:

- Switch back to the FeatureManager tree.

- Right click on the **Spokes Pattern** feature and select **Edit Feature** (Arrow).

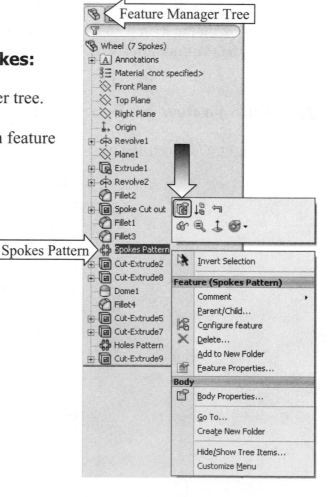

- Change the number of instances to **7** (Circled).

- Click **OK** .

NOTE:

Equations can be used to change the number of spokes and achieve the same result.

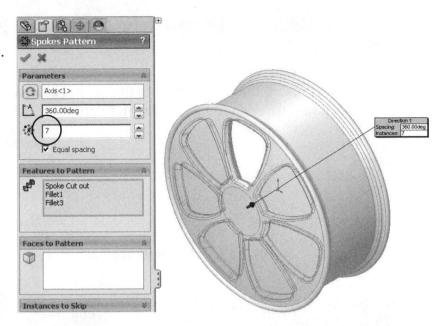

4. Viewing the configurations:

- Change to the ConfigurationManager tree.

- Double click on the **Default** configuration to see the 6-Spokes design.

- Double click on the **7 Spokes** configuration to view the new changes.

6 Spokes

7 Spokes

5. Saving the part:

- Save the part as a copy and name it: **WHEEL.sldprt**

Assembly Configurations

This section discusses the use of Configurations in the assembly level, where a Sub-Assembly is inserted and mated onto the Wheel as a new configuration, and any of the configurations created previously in the part level can be specified for use in the assembly level.

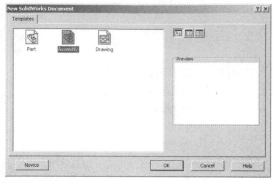

6. Starting a New assembly:

- Select **File / New / Assem**.

- Click the **Insert Component** command from the Assembly toolbar.

- In the **Insert Components** Dialog, enable the option **Graphics Preview** (arrow).

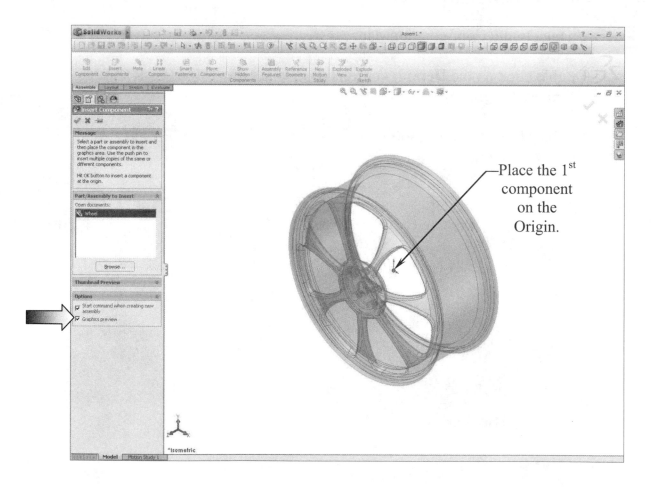

Place the 1st component on the Origin.

- Browse and open the part **Wheel** and place it on the Assembly's origin.

7. Assembly Configurations:

- Change to the ConfigurationManager tree.

- Right click on the Assembly's name and select **Add configuration** (Arrow).

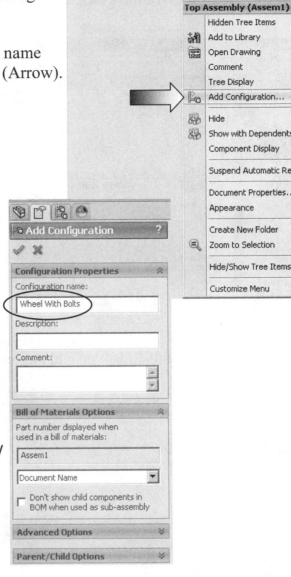

- For Configuration Name, enter: **Wheel With Bolts**.

- Click **OK** ⊘.

NOTE: A set of Bolts, which have been saved earlier as an assembly document, is going to be inserted into the Top Level Assembly and becomes a Sub-Assembly.

8. Inserting the Sub-Assembly:

- Click **Insert Components.**

- Click Browse... .

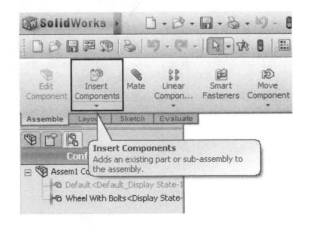

- Select the **Bolts Sub-Assembly** and click **Open**.
  (Go to the Training CD, Training Files, Part/Assembly Configs.).

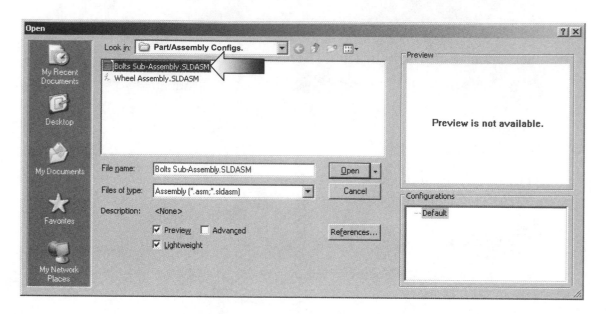

- Place the 6 Bolts Sub-Assembly approximately as shown.

Place the Bolt-Assembly approximately here.

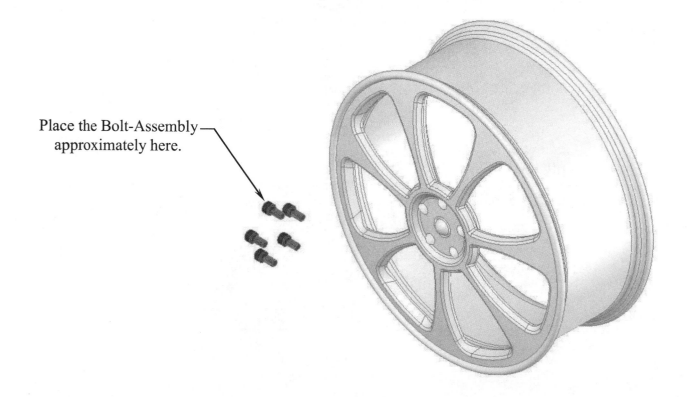

9. Mating the Sub-Assembly:

- Enable **Temporary Axis** from the **View** menu.

- Click **Mate** 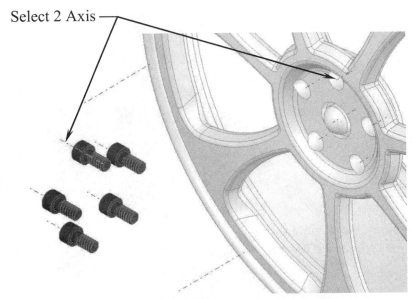 or select **Insert / Mate**.

- Select the center Axis of one of the Bolts and the mating Holes (pictured).

Select 2 Axis

- The system selects the Coincident mate automatically.

- Click either **Align** or **Anti-Align**, to flip the Bolts to the proper direction.

- Click **OK** ✓.

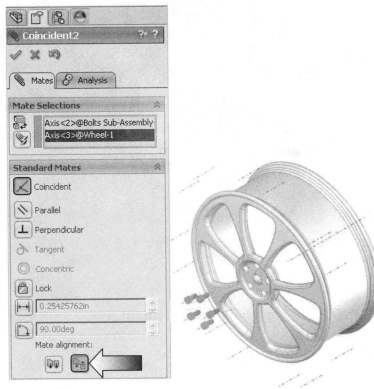

Coincident Mate the
Bolt and its mating face.

- Add a **Coincident** Mate
between the Bottom Face of
one of the Bolts and its mating
surface (pictured).

- Click **OK** 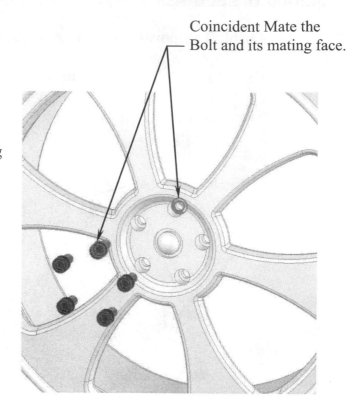.

Coincident Mate the
next 2 center Axis.

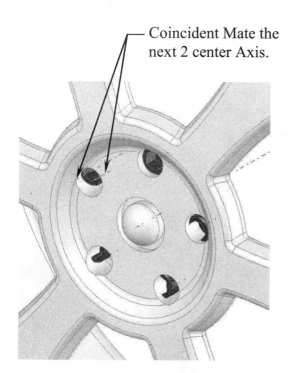

- Add another **Coincident**
Mate to the next 2 axis, to
fully center the 6 bolts.

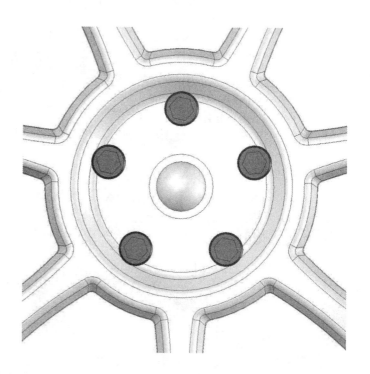

The Finished Assembly.

10. Viewing the Assembly Configurations:

- Change to the ConfigurationManager tree.

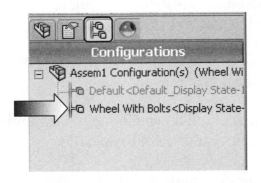

Wheel With Bolts Configuration

- Double click on the **Default** configuration.

- The Bolts Sub-Assembly is **Suppressed**.

- The **7 Spokes** pattern is displayed.

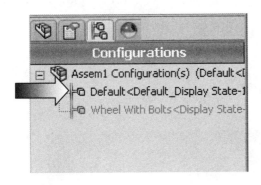

Default Configuration

- Make any necessary changes to the Number of Spokes pattern by accessing the Component's Properties and its Configurations.

- An assembly exploded view may need to be created for use in the drawing later.

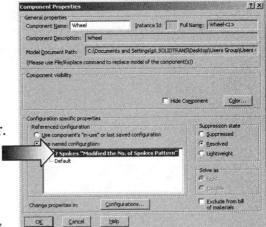

11. Saving your work:

- Save as **Part-Assembly Configurations**.

Drawing Configurations

Change Configurations in Drawing Views

- This section discusses the use of Configurations in the drawing level, where Configurations created previously in the part and assembly levels can be selected for use in the drawing views.

- To change the configuration of the model in a drawing view:

  * Right click a drawing view (or hold down **Ctrl** to select multiple drawing views, then right click) and select **Properties**.

- In the dialog box under **Configuration information**, select a different configuration for **Use- named configuration**.

1. Creating an assembly drawing:

- Go to **File / New / Drawing**.

- Use **C-Landscape** paper size.

- Set **Scale** to: **1 to 1**.

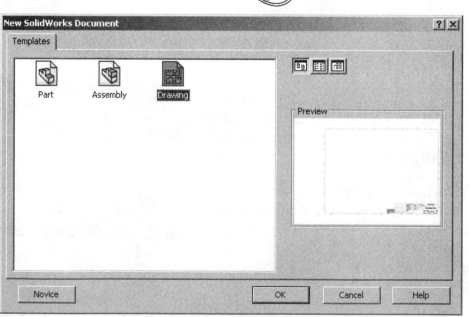

2. Creating the standard drawing views:

- Select **Model View** command .

- Click **Browse** .

- Select the **Wheel Assembly** and click **Open**.

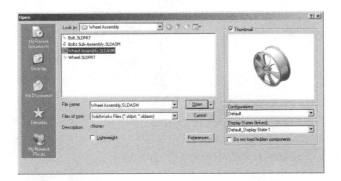

- Select the **FRONT** view from the Standard Views dialog and place it approximately as shown.

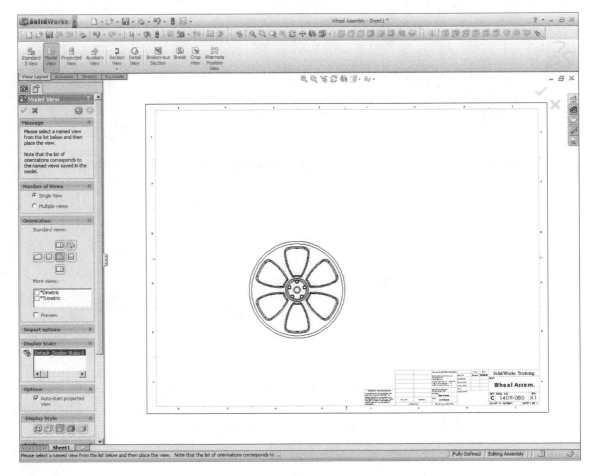

3. Auto-Start the Projected-View:

- If the option **Auto-Start Projected-View** is enabled, SolidWorks will automatically project the next views based on the position of the cursor.

- Place the Top view as pictured.

- Click **OK** ✅.

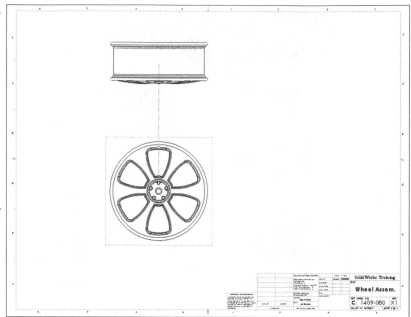

4. Creating the Aligned Section View:

- Select the Front drawing view's border to activate.

- Select the **Sketch** tab (Arrow), select the Line tool and sketch the 2 Lines as shown.

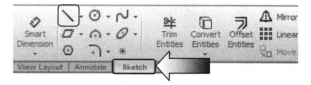

- Hold the **Control** key and select the Angled Line first, then the Vertical line after.

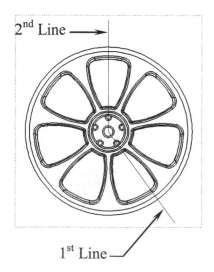

2nd Line ⟶

1st Line ⟍

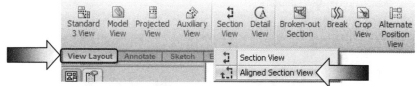

- Switch back to the View Layout tab (Arrow) and click the **Align Section View** command ⌐, (below the Section View command).

- <u>**Section Scope**</u>: is an option that allows components to be excluded from the section cut. In other words, when sectioning an assembly drawing view, you will have an option to select which component(s) is going to be effected by this section cut. This option is called Section Scope.

- In the Section Scope dialog box, enable **Auto Hatching** and if necessary, click **Flip Direction**.

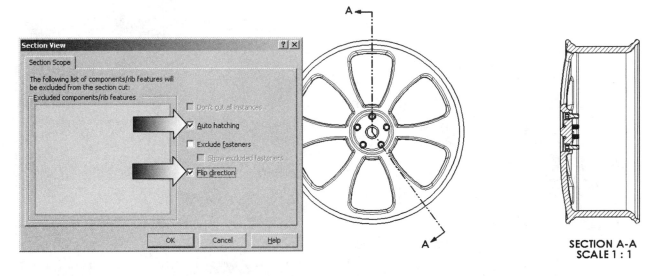

SECTION A-A
SCALE 1 : 1

5. Creating the Isometric view:

- Select the **Model View** command .

- Click **Next** .

- Select **Isometric** view from the Standard Views list.

- Place the Isometric view on the lower right side of the drawing.

- Click **OK** .

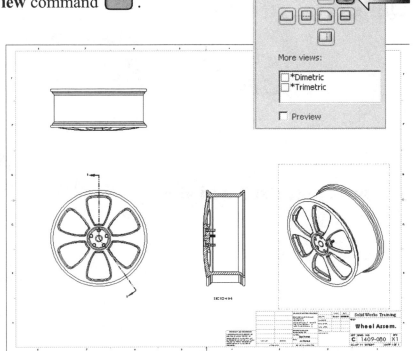

Displaying the Exploded View: (An exploded view must be created from the assembly level prior to showing it in the drawing).

- Right click on the Isometric drawing view's border and select **Properties**.

- Enable the **Show in Exploded State** check box.

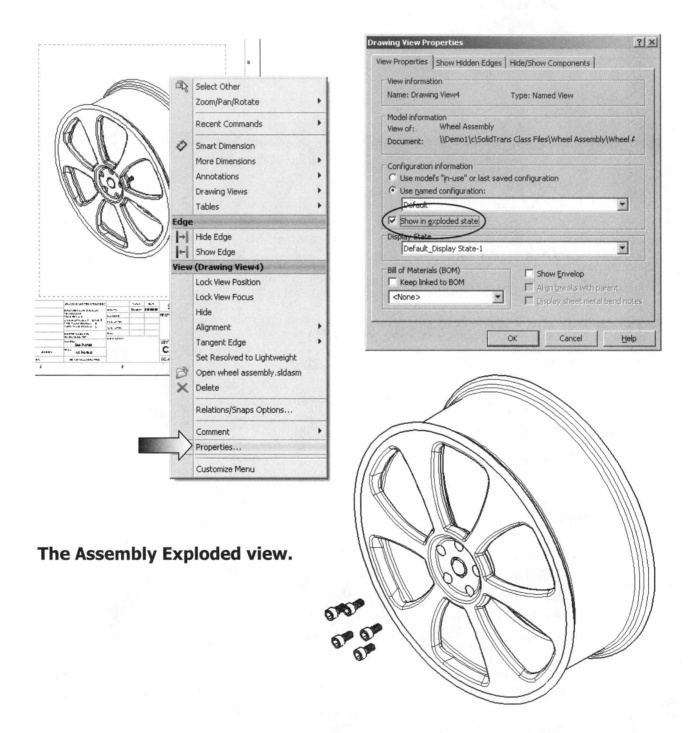

The Assembly Exploded view.

6. Changing Configurations:

- Use the **Model View** command and create 2 more Isometric views.

- Right click on the new Isometric drawing view's border and select **Properties**.

- Select the **Default** configuration.

- Set the 2ⁿᵈ Isometric view to the **6-Spokes** configuration (Switch to the Assembly document to modify the configurations).

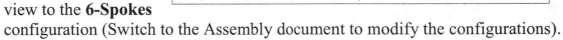

7. Adding Annotations:

- Click Note 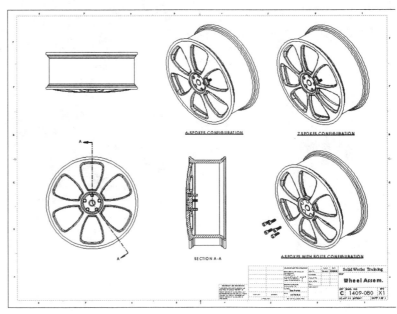 and add the call-outs under each drawing views as shown.

* 6 SPOKES CONFIGURATION.

* 7 SPOKES CONFIGURATION.

* 6 SPOKES WITH BOLTS CONFIGURATION.

8. Saving your work:

- Click **File / Save As**.

- Enter: **Drawing Configurations** for the name of the file.

- Click **Save**.

CHAPTER 18

Design Tables

Design Tables in Part, Assembly & Drawing

Design Table Parameters	Description (Legal values)
$PARTNUMBER@_____	- For use in a Bill of Materials.
$COMMENT@_____	- Any Description or text string.
$NEVER_EXPAND_IN_BOM@_____	- Yes/No to expand in B.O.M.
$STATE@_____	- Resolved = R, Suppressed = S
$CONFIGURATION@_____	- Configuration Name.
$SHOW@_____	- Has been Obsoleted.
$PRP@_____	- Enter any text string.
$USER_NOTES@_____	- Enter any text string.
$COLOR@_____	- Specifying 32-bit RGB color.
$PARENT@_____	- Parent configuration name.
$TOLERANCE@_____	- Enter tolerance keywords.
$SWMASS@_____	- Enter any decimal legal value.
$SWCOG@_____	- Enter any legal x,y,z value.
$DISPLAYSTATE@_____	- Display state name.

In a Design Table, you will need to define the names of the configurations, specify the parameters that you want to control, and assign values for each parameter. This chapter will guide you through the use of design tables in both the part and assembly levels.

Part, Assembly & Drawing
Design Tables

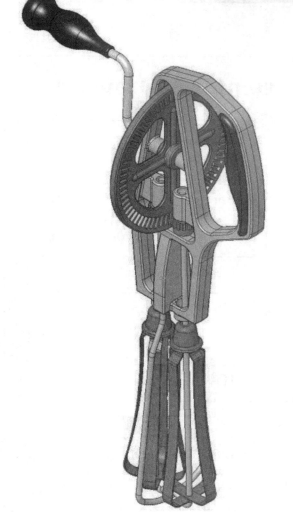

Design Table for: Egg Beater

	A	B	C	D	E	F	G	H	I	J
1	Design Table for: Egg Beater									
2		$state@Egg Beater Handle<1>	$state@Main Gear<1>	$state@Support Rod<1>	$state@Right Spinner<1>	$state@Left Spinner<1>	$state@Right Spinner<2>	$state@Left Spinner<2>	$configuration@Crank Handle<1>	
3	Default	R	R	R	R	R	R	R	Default	
4	Config1	R	S	S	S	S	S	S	Oval Handle	
5	Config2	R	R	S	S	S	S	S	Default	
6	Config3	R	R	R	S	S	S	S	Oval Handle	
7	Config4	R	R	R	R	S	S	S	Default	
8	Config5	R	R	R	R	R	S	S	Oval Handle	
9	Config6	R	R	R	R	R	R	R	Default	
10										

Sheet1

Dimensioning Standards: **ANSI** Units: **INCHES** – 3 Decimals	Third Angle Projection

Tools Needed:

 Design Tables / Microsoft Excel

 ConfigurationManager

Part - Design Tables

1. Copying the document:

- <u>Go to:</u> The Training CD
  Design Tables folder
  Part Design Table.sldprt

- **OPEN** a copy of the part
  document named:
  Part Design Table.sldprt

- This exercise discusses the
  use of Changing Feature
  Dimensions and Feature
  Suppression-States in a
  Design Table.

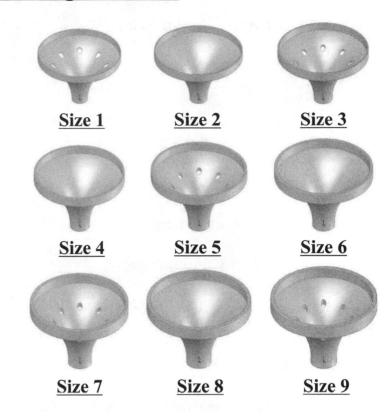

Size 1   Size 2   Size 3

Size 4   Size 5   Size 6

Size 7   Size 8   Size 9

- The names of the dimensions will be used as the column Headers in the design
  table.

- Go to the **View** menu and enable the option: **Dimension Names**.

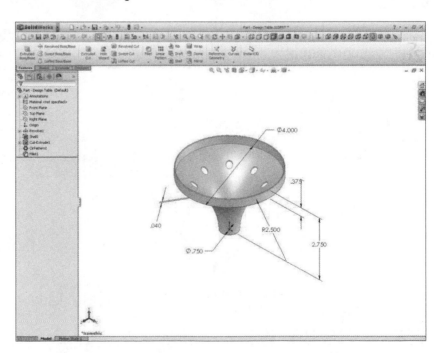

2. Creating a New Design Table:

- Click **Insert / Design Table**.

- Select the **BLANK** option from the Source section.

- Enable the option **Allow Model Edits to Update the Design Table**.

- Enable the options:

    * **New Parameters**

    * **New Configurations**

    * **Warn When Updating Design Table**

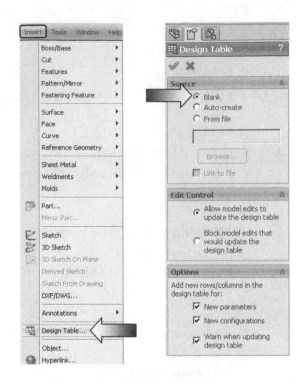

- Click **OK** .

- Click **OK** in the Add Rows and Columns Dialog box.

- The Microsoft Excel Work Sheet opens up.

- The cell A1 is filled in with the part's name.

- The cell B2 is automatically selected.

- The part's dimensions are going to be transferred over to the Excel Work Sheet in the next steps.

- Notice the names of the dimensions? They should be change to what they represented like: Wall Thk, Upper Dia, Height, Radius, Lower Dia., etc.

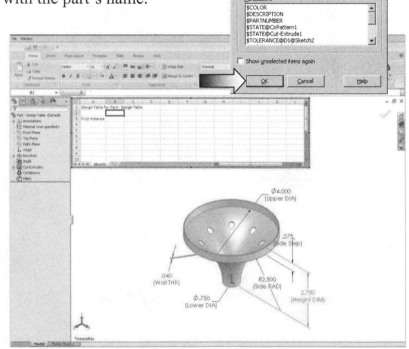

3. Transferring the Dimensions to the Design Table:

- Make sure the cell B2 is selected.

- Double click on the Height DIM 2.750

- The dimension is transferred over to cell B2.

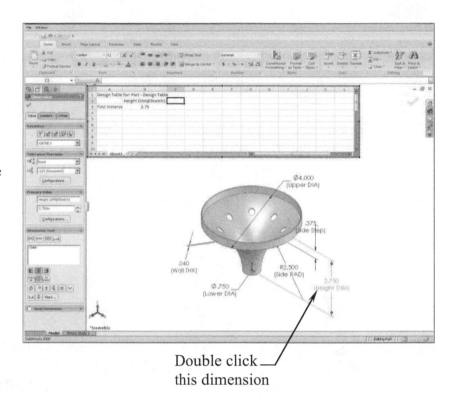

Double click this dimension

- Repeat the same step and transfer the other dimensions in the order as shown.

- Add configs. names: Size1 thru Size9.

	Height DIM@Sketch1	Upper DIA@Sketch1	Lower DIA@Sketch1	Side RAD@Sketch1	Side Step@Sketch1	Wall THK@Shell1
1 Design Table for: Part - Design Table						
2	Height DIM@Sketch1	Upper DIA@Sketch1	Lower DIA@Sketch1	Side RAD@Sketch1	Side Step@Sketch1	Wall THK@Shell1
3 Size1	2.75	4	0.75	2.5	0.375	0.04
4 Size2						
5 Size3						
6 Size4						
7 Size5						
8 Size6						
9 Size7						
10 Size8						
11 Size9						
12						

4. Using Excel's Addition Formula:

- Select the cell B3, type the equal sign (=), click the number **2.75** in cell B2, and then enter **+.125**

- Copy the formula to the cells below:

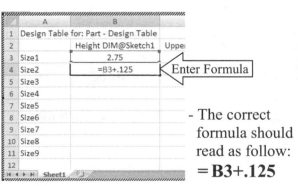

Enter Formula

- The correct formula should read as follow:
=B3+.125

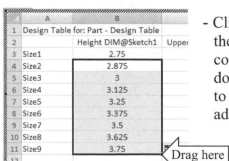

- Click and drag on the bottom right corner of cell B3, down to cell B11 to repeat the addition formula.

Drag here

	A	B	C	D
1	Design Table for: Part - Design Table			
2		Height DIM@Sketch1	Upper DIA@Sketch1	Lower DIA@
3	Size1	2.75	4	0.75
4	Size2	2.875	=C3+125	
5	Size3	3		
6	Size4	3.125		
7	Size5	3.25		
8	Size6	3.375		
9	Size7	3.5		
10	Size8	3.625		
11	Size9	3.75		
12				

	A	B	C	D
1	Design Table for: Part - Design Table			
2		Height DIM@Sketch1	Upper DIA@Sketch1	Lower DIA@
3	Size1	2.75	4	0.75
4	Size2	2.875	4.125	
5	Size3	3	4.25	
6	Size4	3.125	4.375	
7	Size5	3.25	4.5	
8	Size6	3.375	4.625	
9	Size7	3.5	4.75	
10	Size8	3.625	4.875	
11	Size9	3.75	5	
12				

- In cell C4 type:

= C3+.125

and copy the formula thru cell C11.

	A	B	C	D
1	Design Table for: Part - Design Table			
2		Height DIM@Sketch1	Upper DIA@Sketch1	Lower DIA@Sketch1
3	Size1	2.75	4	0.75
4	Size2	2.875	4.125	=D3+.0625
5	Size3	3	4.25	
6	Size4	3.125	4.375	
7	Size5	3.25	4.5	
8	Size6	3.375	4.625	
9	Size7	3.5	4.75	
10	Size8	3.625	4.875	
11	Size9	3.75	5	
12				

	A	B	C	D
1	Design Table for: Part - Design Table			
2		Height DIM@Sketch1	Upper DIA@Sketch1	Lower DIA@Sketch1
3	Size1	2.75	4	0.75
4	Size2	2.875	4.125	0.8125
5	Size3	3	4.25	0.875
6	Size4	3.125	4.375	0.9375
7	Size5	3.25	4.5	1
8	Size6	3.375	4.625	1.0625
9	Size7	3.5	4.75	1.125
10	Size8	3.625	4.875	1.1875
11	Size9	3.75	5	1.25
12				

- Cell D4 thru Cell C11, type:

= D3+.0625

and copy the formula.

	A	B	C	D	E
1	Design Table for: Part - Design Table				
2		Height DIM@Sketch1	Upper DIA@Sketch1	Lower DIA@Sketch1	Side RAD@Sketch1
3	Size1	2.75	4	0.75	2.5
4	Size2	2.875	4.125	0.8125	=E3+.0625
5	Size3	3	4.25	0.875	
6	Size4	3.125	4.375	0.9375	
7	Size5	3.25	4.5	1	
8	Size6	3.375	4.625	1.0625	
9	Size7	3.5	4.75	1.125	
10	Size8	3.625	4.875	1.1875	
11	Size9	3.75	5	1.25	
12					

	A	B	C	D	E
1	Design Table for: Part - Design Table				
2		Height DIM@Sketch1	Upper DIA@Sketch1	Lower DIA@Sketch1	Side RAD@Sketch1
3	Size1	2.75	4	0.75	2.5
4	Size2	2.875	4.125	0.8125	2.5625
5	Size3	3	4.25	0.875	2.625
6	Size4	3.125	4.375	0.9375	2.6875
7	Size5	3.25	4.5	1	2.75
8	Size6	3.375	4.625	1.0625	2.8125
9	Size7	3.5	4.75	1.125	2.875
10	Size8	3.625	4.875	1.1875	2.9375
11	Size9	3.75	5	1.25	3
12					

- Cell E4 thru Cell E11, type:

= E3+.0625

and copy the formula.

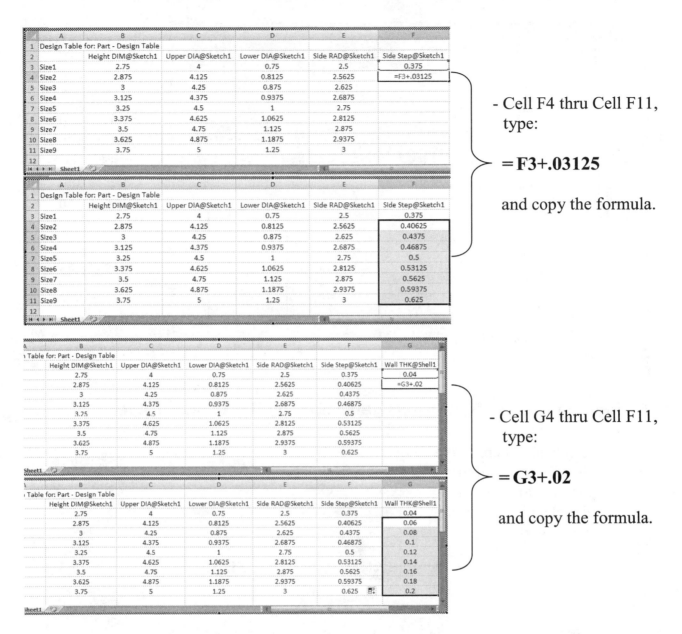

- Cell F4 thru Cell F11, type:

$$=F3+.03125$$

and copy the formula.

- Cell G4 thru Cell F11, type:

$$=G3+.02$$

and copy the formula.

5. Controlling the Suppression-States of the holes:

- Select the cell **H2** and double click on the **CutExtrude1** to transfer to cell H2.

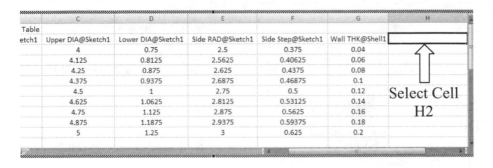

Select Cell H2

Double click

	B	C	D	E	F	G	H
1	for: Part - Design Table						
2	Height DIM@Sketch1	Upper DIA@Sketch1	Lower DIA@Sketch1	Side RAD@Sketch1	Side Step@Sketch1	Wall THK@Shell1	$STATE@Cut-Extrude1
3	2.75	4	0.75	2.5	0.375	0.04	UNSUPPRESSED
4	2.875	4.125	0.8125	2.5625	0.40625	0.06	
5	3	4.25	0.875	2.625	0.4375	0.08	
6	3.125	4.375	0.9375	2.6875	0.46875	0.1	
7	3.25	4.5	1	2.75	0.5	0.12	
8	3.375	4.625	1.0625	2.8125	0.53125	0.14	
9	3.5	4.75	1.125	2.875	0.5625	0.16	
10	3.625	4.875	1.1875	2.9375	0.59375	0.18	
11	3.75	5	1.25	3	0.625	0.2	
12							

Sheet1

- In Cell H3, replace the word **Unsuppressed** with the letter **U**.

	C	D	E	F	G	H	I
1							
2	Upper DIA@Sketch1	Lower DIA@Sketch1	Side RAD@Sketch1	Side Step@Sketch1	Wall THK@Shell1	$STATE@Cut-Extrude1	
3	4	0.75	2.5	0.375	0.04	U	
4	4.125	0.8125	2.5625	0.40625	0.06	S	
5	4.25	0.875	2.625	0.4375	0.08	U	
6	4.375	0.9375	2.6875	0.46875	0.1	S	
7	4.5	1	2.75	0.5	0.12	U	
8	4.625	1.0625	2.8125	0.53125	0.14	S	
9	4.75	1.125	2.875	0.5625	0.16	U	
10	4.875	1.1875	2.9375	0.59375	0.18	S	
11	5	1.25	3	0.625	0.2	U	
12							

Sheet1

- Enter **S** for: **Suppressed** in Cell H4.

- Enter **S** and **U** for all other cells as shown.

6. Viewing the Configurations generated by the Design Table:

- Click anywhere in the SolidWorks graphics area to close out of Excel and return to SolidWorks.

- Change to the ConfigurationManager tree.

- Double click on Size2 and then other sizes to see the parts that were created by the Design Table.

- Save your work as: **Part - Design Table**.

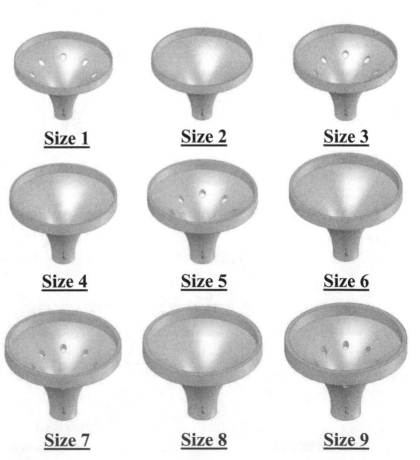

Size 1	Size 2	Size 3
Size 4	Size 5	Size 6
Size 7	Size 8	Size 9

Assembly - Design Tables

1. Copying the Egg Beater Assembly:

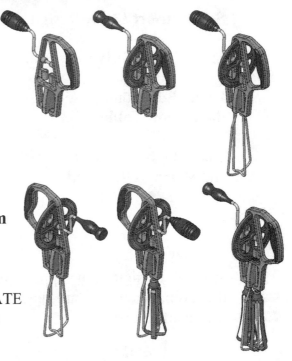

- <u>Go to:</u> The Training CD
          Design Tables folder
          Egg Beater Assembly Folder.

- Copy the entire content of the Egg-
  Beater-Assembly to your computer.

- **OPEN** the **Egg Beater Assembly.sldasm**

- This exercise discusses the use of the STATE
  and CONFIGURATION parameters in a
  Design Table.

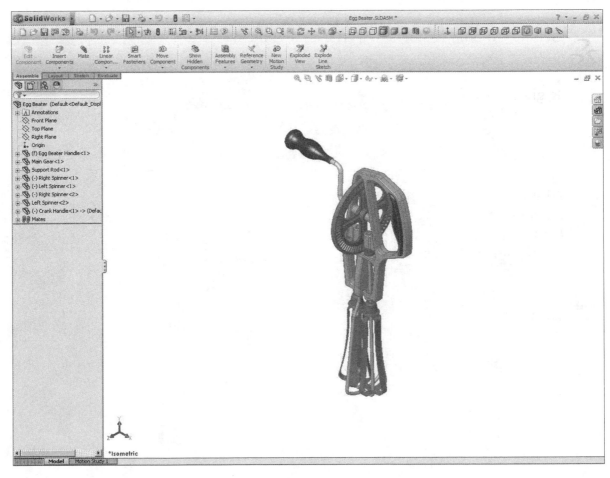

2. Creating a new Assembly Design Table:

- Select **Insert / New Design Table**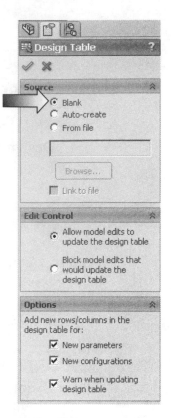

- From the property tree, under Source, select **Blank**.

- Under Edit Control, select **Allow Model Edits to Update the Design Table**.

- Under Options, enable **New Parameters**, **New Configs.**, and **Warn When Updating Design Table**.

- Click **OK** ✓.

- A blank Design Table appears on the SolidWorks' screen, the toolbars and the pull-down menus are now changed to Microsoft Excel.

- Set the Column Headers to Vertical Alignment.

- Right click on the row #2 (arrow), select Format Cells, click the Alignment tab and set the Orientation to 90 degrees.

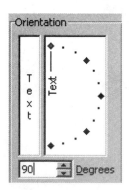

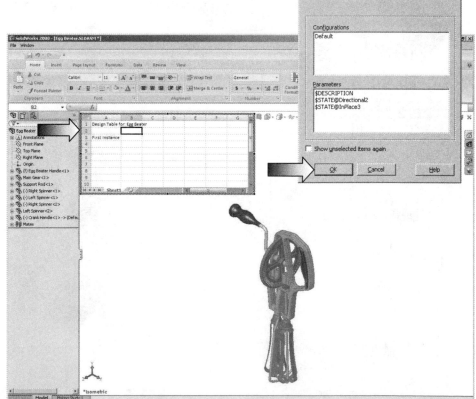

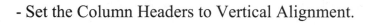

NOTE:

To create a design table, you must define the names of the configurations that you want to create, specify the parameters that you want to control, and assign values for each parameter.

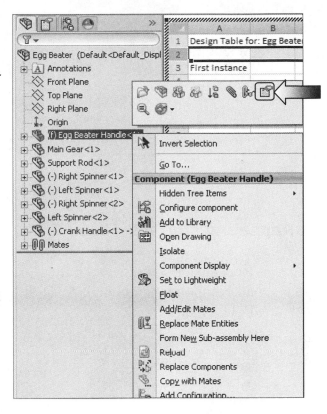

3. Defining the column headers:

- We are going to copy the name of of each component and paste it to the Design Table. They will be used as the Column Headers.

- Right click on the part named Egg Beater Handle and select: **Component Properties** (Arrow).

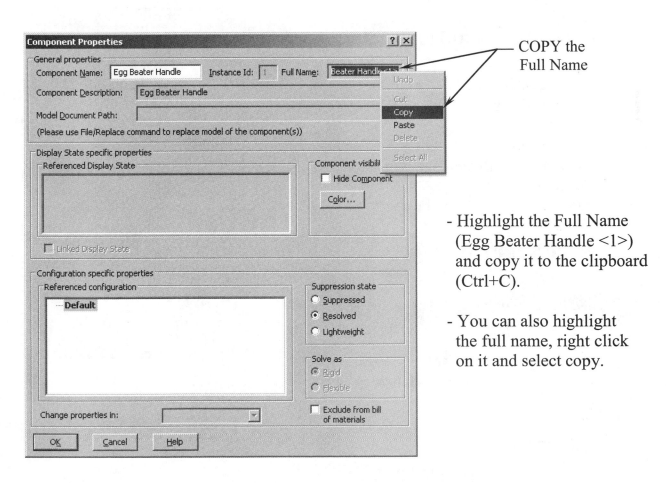

COPY the Full Name

- Highlight the Full Name (Egg Beater Handle <1>) and copy it to the clipboard (Ctrl+C).

- You can also highlight the full name, right click on it and select copy.

- Select the Cell C2 (arrow) and click **Edit / Paste** or press Ctrl+V.

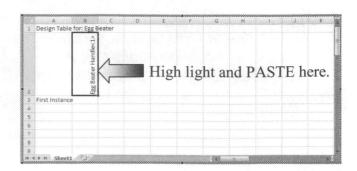

4. Repeating step #3: (Copy & Paste all components)

- Repeat step 3, copy and paste all components into cells C, D, E, F, G, H, and I.

5. Inserting the Control Parameters:

- For cells **B2** thru **H2**, insert the header: **$state@** before the name of each component.

Example:
$state@Egg Beater Handle<1>

- For cell **I2**, insert the header:

$configuration@

before the name of the component.

Example:
$configuration@Crank Handle<1>

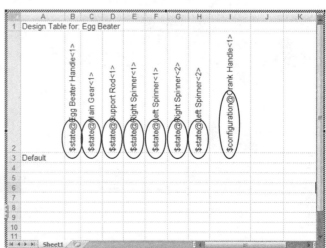

6. Adding the configuration names:

- The actual part numbers can be used here for the name of each configuration.

- Starting at **Cell A4**, (below Default), enter **Config1** thru **Config5** as shown.

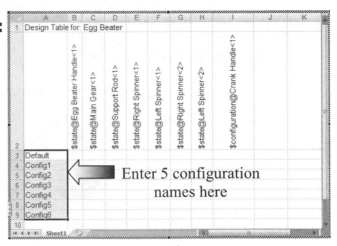

Enter 5 configuration names here

7. Assigning the control values:

- To prevent mistakes, type the letter R and letter S in each cell.

- Enter the values R (Resolved) and S (Suppressed) into their appropriate cells, from column B through column H.

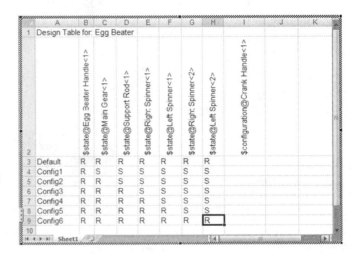

- For Column I, we will enter the names of the configurations instead.

- Select the cell **I3** and enter: **Default**.

- Select the cell **I4** and enter **Oval Handle**.

- Repeat the same step for all 6 configs.

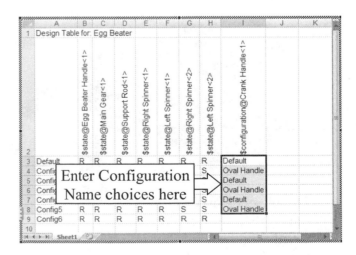

Enter Configuration Name choices here

8. Viewing the new configurations:

- Switch to the ConfigurationManager Tree.

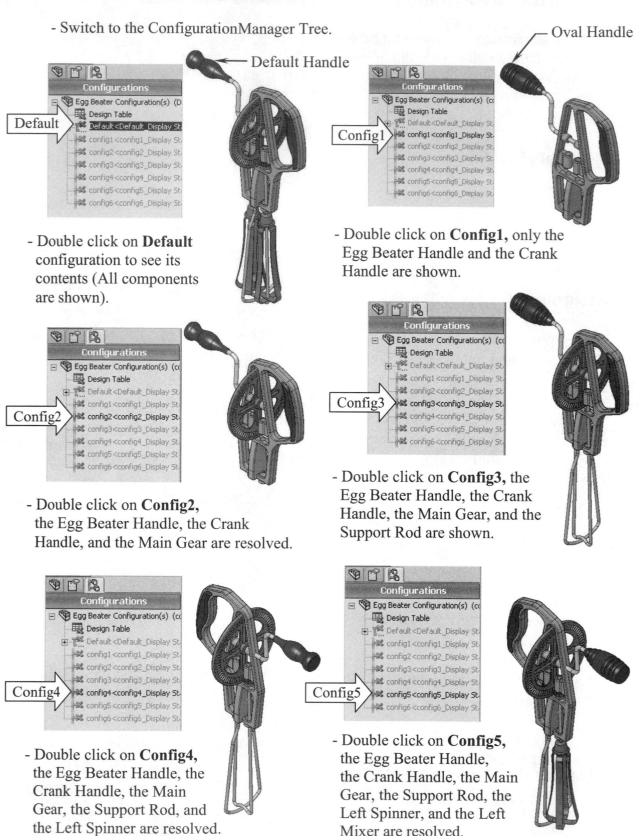

Default Handle

Oval Handle

Default

- Double click on **Default** configuration to see its contents (All components are shown).

Config1

- Double click on **Config1,** only the Egg Beater Handle and the Crank Handle are shown.

Config2

- Double click on **Config2,** the Egg Beater Handle, the Crank Handle, and the Main Gear are resolved.

Config3

- Double click on **Config3,** the Egg Beater Handle, the Crank Handle, the Main Gear, and the Support Rod are shown.

Config4

- Double click on **Config4,** the Egg Beater Handle, the Crank Handle, the Main Gear, the Support Rod, and the Left Spinner are resolved.

Config5

- Double click on **Config5,** the Egg Beater Handle, the Crank Handle, the Main Gear, the Support Rod, the Left Spinner, and the Left Mixer are resolved.

Exercise: Part Design Tables

1. Open the existing document named: **Part Design Tables_ EXE** from the Training CD.
2. Create a design table with 3 different sizes using the dimensions provided in the table.
3. Customize the table by merging the cells, adding colors, and borders.
4. Use the instructions on the following pages, if needed.

Design Table for: Part Design Tables_Exe									
	Lower Boss Thickness@Sketch	Upper Boss Thickness@Sketch	Center Hole@Sketch1	Upper Boss Dia@Sketch1	Lower Boss Dia@Sketch1	D1@Revolve1	Bolt Cicle@Sketch2	Hole on Flange@Sketch2	D3@CirPattern1	D1@CirPattern1
Size 1	0.25	0.25	0.5	1	2	360	1.5	0.25	360	4
Size 2	0.375	0.375	0.625	1.25	2.25	360	1.75	0.275	360	4
Size 3	0.5	0.5	0.75	1.5	2.5	360	2	0.3	360	4

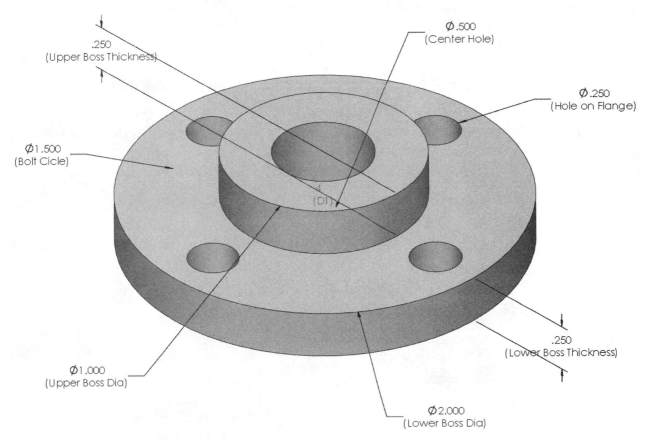

Ø.500
(Center Hole)

.250
(Upper Boss Thickness)

Ø.250
(Hole on Flange)

Ø1.500
(Bolt Cicle)

(D1)

.250
(Lower Boss Thickness)

Ø1.000
(Upper Boss Dia)

Ø2.000
(Lower Boss Dia)

1. Opening the Master part file:

- From the training CD, open the part named: **Part Design Tables_Exe**.
The dimensions in this part have been renamed for use in this ecercise.

2. Inserting a design table:

- From the **Insert** menu click **Tables / Design-Table**.

- Click the **Auto Create** button (default).

- Leave all other options at their default settings.

- Click **OK**.

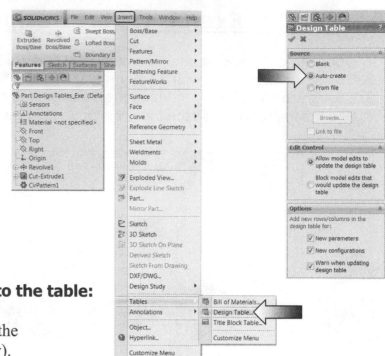

3. Adding model dimensions to the table:

- **Select all dimensions** in the Dimensions dialog (arrow).

- This option will export all dimensions from the part into the design table.

- Each dimension will be placed in its own column, in the order they were created.

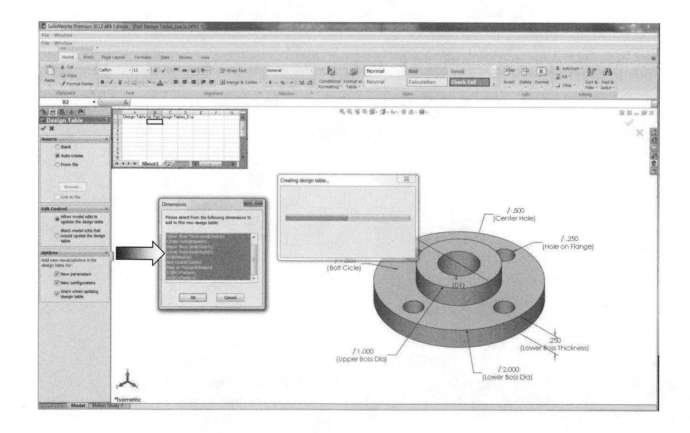

4. Changing the Configuration names:

- For clarity, change the name Default to **Size 1**.

- Create the next 2 configurations by adding the names **Size 2** and **Size 3**, on cell A4 and A5.

- Enter the **new dimensions** for the next 2 sizes.

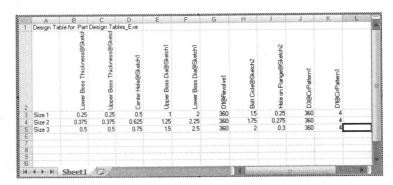

5. Viewing the new configurations:

- Click in the background anywhere. SolidWorks report dialog appears showing 3 new configurations have been generated by the design table.

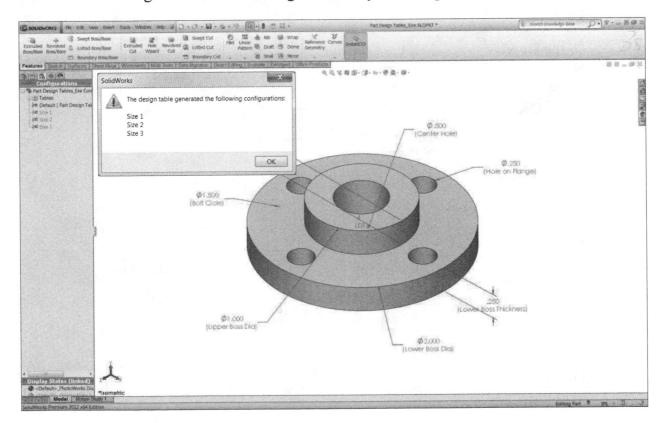

- Double click on the names of the configurations to see the changes for each size.

6. Customizing the table:

- Expand the **Tables** folder, right click on Design Tables and select **Edit Table**.

- Click OK to close the Rows and Columns dialog.

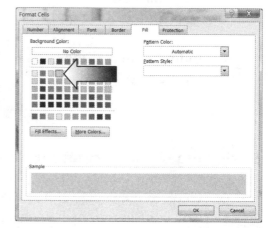

- Highlight the entire Row1 header, right click in the highlighted area and select: **Format Cell**.

- Click the **Fill** tab and select a color for the Row1.

- Change to the **Alignment** tab and enable the **Wrap Text** and **Merge Cells** check-boxes.

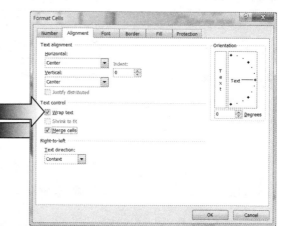

- In the **Border** tab, select the **Outline** button.

- Click OK.

- Repeat step 6 for other rows.

7. Saving your work:

- Click File / Save As.

- For file name, enter: **Part Design Table_Exe**.

- Click Save.

- Overwrite the file if required.

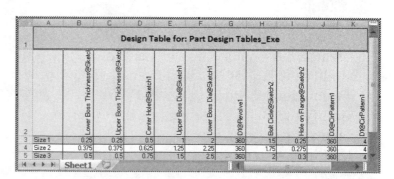

	A	B	C	D	E	F	G	H	I	J	K
1	Design Table for: Part Design Tables_Exe										
2		Lower Boss Thickness@Sketch1	Upper Boss Thickness@Sketch1	Center Hole@Sketch1	Upper Boss Dia@Sketch1	Lower Boss Dia@Sketch1	D1@Revolve1	Bolt Circle@Sketch2	Hole on Flange@Sketch2	D3@CirPattern1	D1@CirPattern1
3	Size 1	0.25	0.25	0.5	1	2	360	1.5	0.25	360	4
4	Size 2	0.375	0.375	0.625	1.25	2.25	360	1.75	0.275	360	4
5	Size 3	0.5	0.5	0.75	1.5	2.5	360	2	0.3	360	4

Level 2 Final Exam (1of2)

1. Open the existing assembly document named: **Bottom Up Assembly EXE** from the Bottom Up Assembly folder.

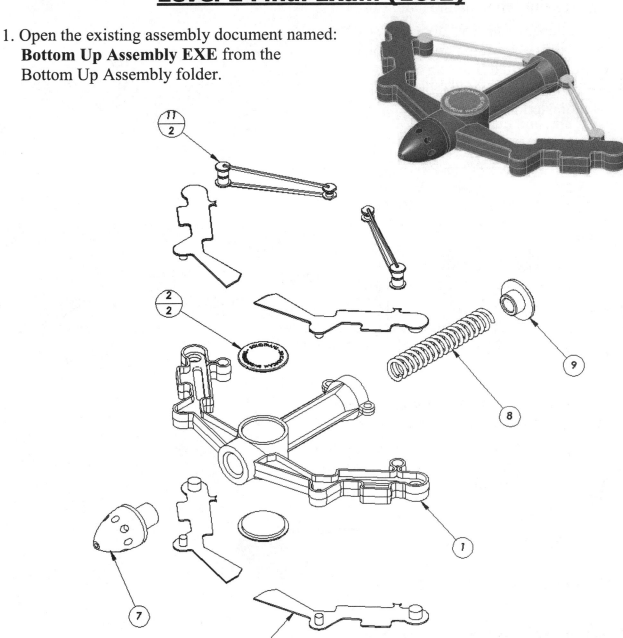

2. Create an Assembly drawing as shown.
3. Modify the Bill of Materials to match the information provided in the BOM.
4. Modify the Balloons to include the Quantity.
5. Save your drawing as: **L2 Final Assembly Drawing**.

ITEM NO.	PART NUMBER	DESCRIPTION	QTY.
1	010-123	Housing	1
2	020-123	Label	2
6	060-123	Cover Plate	4
7	070-123	Nose	1
8	080-123	Spring	1
9	090-123	End Cap	1
11	011-123	Support Arm	2

Level 2 Final Exam (2of2)

1. Open the existing Part document named:
   Nose.sldprt from the previous folder.
2. Create a detailed drawing as shown.
3. Add Dimensions and Geometric Tolerances
   as indicated in each view.

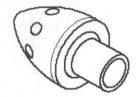

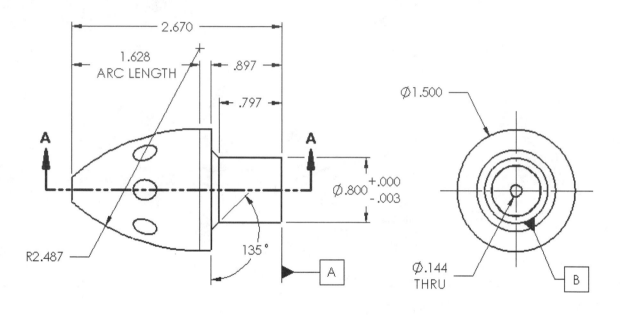

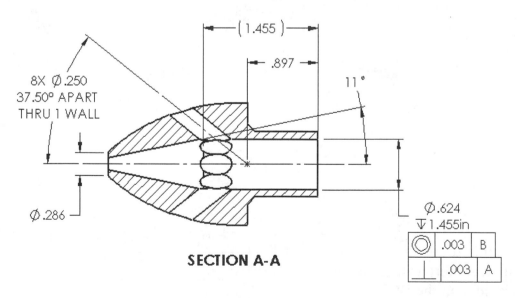

SECTION A-A

4. Add Datums and Annotations as specified.
5. Correct the Model's dimensions to match the drawing.
6. Save your drawing as: **L2 Final Drawing**.

TABLE OF U.S. MEASURES

LENGTH

12 inches	=	1 foot
36 inches	=	1 yard (or 3 feet)
5280 feet	=	1 mile (or 1760 yards)

AREA

144 square inches (in)	=	1 square foot (ft)
9 ft	=	1 square yard (yd)
43,560 ft	=	1 acre (A)
640 A	=	1 square mile (mi)

VOLUME

1728 cubic inches (in³)	=	1 cubic foot (ft)
27 ft	=	1 cubic yard (yd)

LIQUID CAPACITY

8 fluid ounces (fl oz)	=	1 cup (c)
2 c	=	1 pint (pt)
2 pt	=	1 quart (qt)
4 pt	=	1 gallon (gal)

WEIGHT

16 ounces (oz)	=	1 pound (lb)
2000 lb	=	1 ton (t)

TEMPERATURE Degrees Fahrenheit (°F)

32° F	=	freezing point of water
98.6° F	=	normal body temperature
212° F	=	boiling point of water

TABLE OF METRIC MEASURES

LENGTH

10 millimeters (mm)	=	1 centimeter (cm)
10 cm	=	1 decimeter (dm)
100 cm	=	1 meter (m)
1000 m	=	1 kilometer (km)

AREA

100 square millimeters (mm)	=	1 square centimeter (cm)
10,000 cm	=	1 square meter (m)
10,000 m	=	1 hectare (ha)
1,000,000 m	=	1 square kilometer (km)

VOLUME

1000 cubic millimeters (ml)	=	1 cubic centimeter (cm)
1 cm	=	1 milliliter (mL)
1,000 m	=	1 Liter (L)
1,000,000 cm	=	1 cubic meter (m)

LIQUID CAPACITY

10 deciliters (dL)	=	1 liter (L) - or 1000 mL
1000 L	=	1 kiloliter (kL)

MASS

1000 milligrams (mg)	=	1 gram (g)
1000 g	=	1 kilogram (kg)
1000 kg	=	1 metric ton (t)

TEMPERATURE Degrees Celsius (°C)

0° C	=	freezing point of water
37°C	=	normal body temperature
100° C	=	boiling point of water

SolidWorks 2012

Certified SolidWorks Professional (CSWP)

Certification Practice for the Core Examination

SolidWorks

**CERTIFIED
PROFESSIONAL**

Courtesy of Paul Tran, Sr. Certified SolidWorks Instructor

Certified-SolidWorks-Professional program (CSWP)
Certification Practice for the Core-Exam

Challenge I: Part Modeling & Modifications

Complete this challenge within 90 minutes

(The following examples are intended to assist you in familiarizing yourself with the structures of the exams and the method in which the questions are asked)

- Create this part in SolidWorks   - Unit: **Inches, 3 decimals**   - Origin: **Arbitrary**

- Drafting Standards: **ANSI**   - Material: **Cast Alloy Steel**   - Density: **0.264 lb/in^3**

1. Creating the 1st revolve body:

     - Sketch the profile as shown on the Front plane.

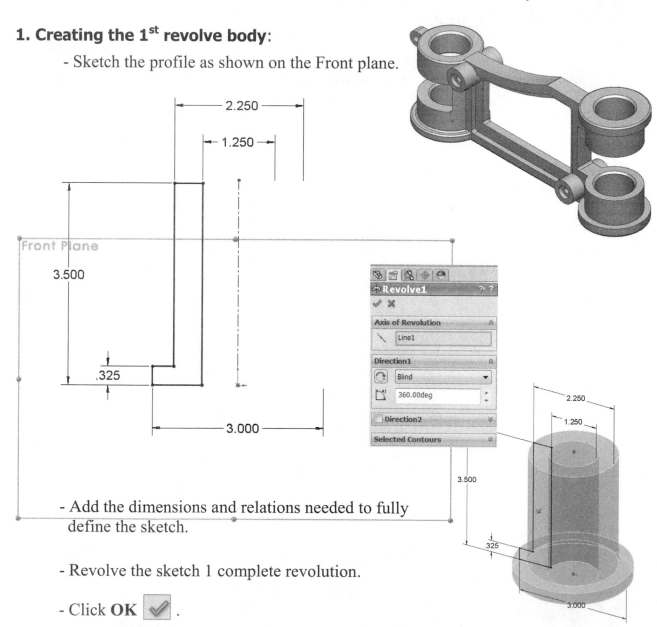

     - Add the dimensions and relations needed to fully define the sketch.

     - Revolve the sketch 1 complete revolution.

     - Click **OK** .

2. Creating the 2nd revolve body:

- Open a new sketch on the Front plane.

- Sketch a rectangle on the left side of a vertical centerline.

- Add the dimensions shown.

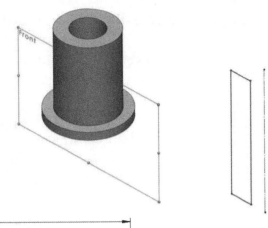

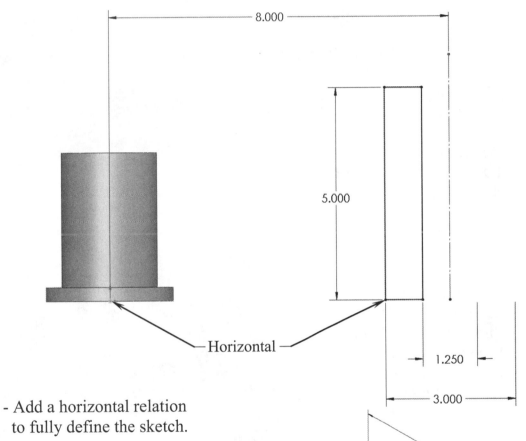

8.000

5.000

Horizontal

1.250

3.000

- Add a horizontal relation to fully define the sketch.

8.000

- Revolve the sketch 360 degrees.

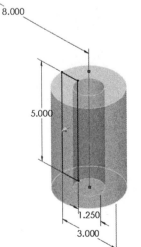

5.000

1.250

3.000

- Click **OK**.

3. Linking the dimension values:

- To save time on editing features later on, we will link some of the dimensions together.

- From the FeatureManager tree, right click on Annotations and enable both options:

  * **Display Annotations**

  * **Show Feature Dimensions**

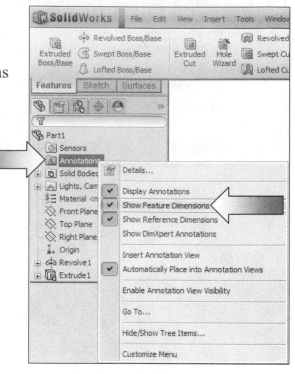

- At this moment, we will link the two ID dimensions (Ø1.250), by giving them the exact same name.

- Hold the Control key and select both ID dimensions (circled), right click on one of them and select: **Link Values** (arrow).

- Enter **ID Holes** for Name and click OK.

- The linked dimensions now have a red link symbol next to their values.

4. Creating the transition wall:

- Select the Front plane and open a new sketch.

- Sketch the profile as shown.

- Add the dimensions and the relations as indicated.

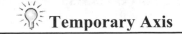

Temporary Axis

Enable the Temporary Axis from the View pull down menu.

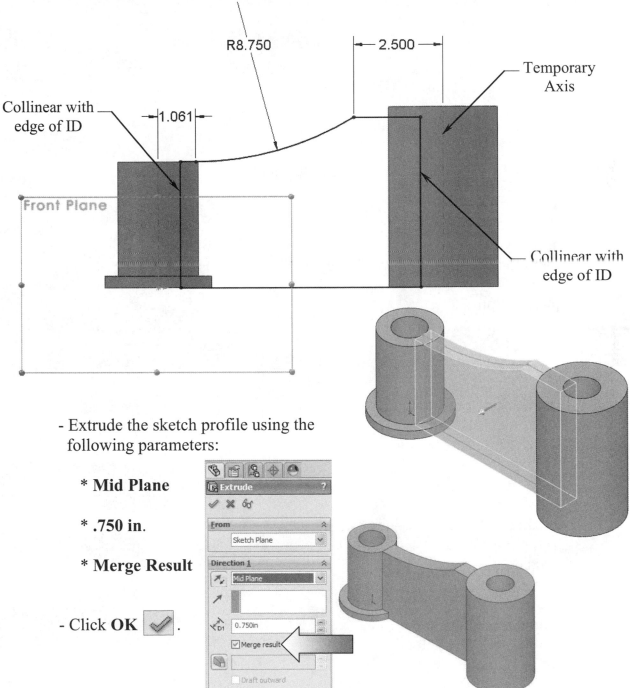

R8.750

2.500

Temporary Axis

Collinear with edge of ID

1.061

Front Plane

Collinear with edge of ID

- Extrude the sketch profile using the following parameters:

   * **Mid Plane**

   * **.750 in**.

   * **Merge Result**

- Click **OK** .

5. Creating a recess feature:

- Select the face as indicated and open a new sketch.

- Select the arc, the 2 lines, and click **Offset Entities**.

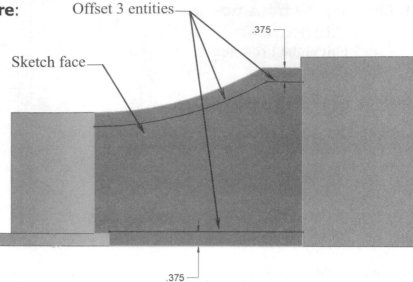

Offset 3 entities

Sketch face

.375

.375

- Enter **.375"** for offset distance and click OK.

- Add 2 more lines as shown and trim them to their nearest intersections.

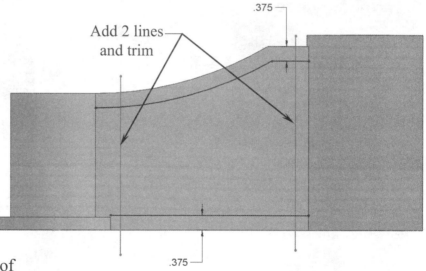

Add 2 lines and trim

.375

.375

- Add a sketch fillet of R.125 to 5 places.

- Enable the Temporary Axis and add the dimensions as shown to fully define this sketch.

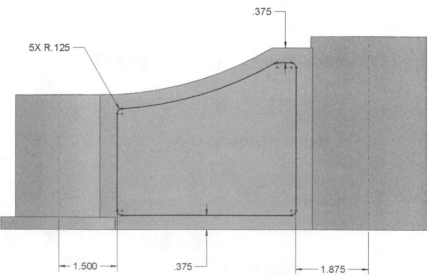

5X R.125

.375

1.500   .375   1.875

- Click **Extruded Cut** and use the following parameters:

   * **Blind**

   * **.215 in**.

- Click **OK** ✓ .

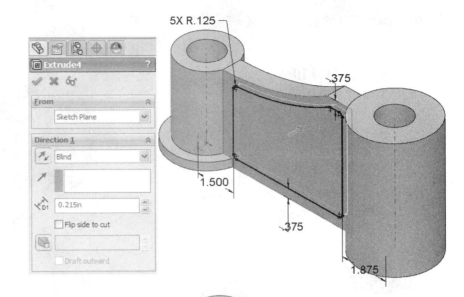

6. Mirroring the recess feature:

- Select the Front plane for use as the Mirror plane and click the **Mirror** Command from the Features toolbar.

- Click the recess feature either from the graphics area or from the FeatureManager tree.

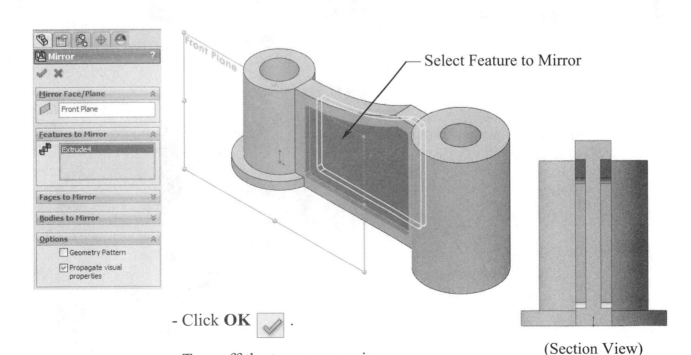

Select Feature to Mirror

(Section View)

- Click **OK** ✓ .

- Turn off the temporary axis.

7. Adding Fillets:

- Click the **Fillet** command and enter **.062** for radius value.

- Select the **6 edges** as shown.

- Click **OK**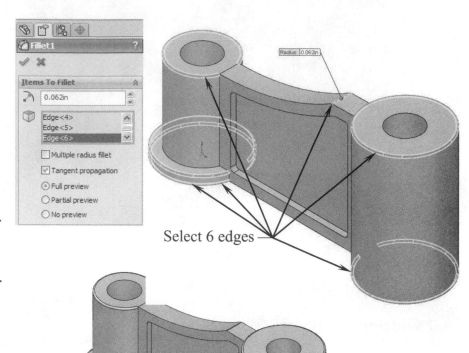

Select 6 edges

8. Changing dimension values:

- The grading scores are based on the mass of the part after certain changes. At this point, we will change several dimensions and see what the final mass may be.

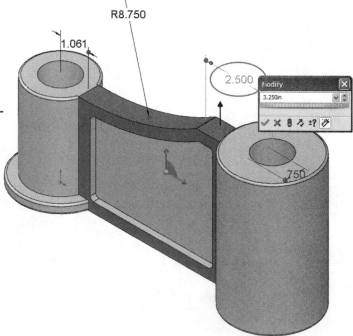

- Double click on the Transition-Wall to see its dimensions.

- Locate the **2.500"** dimension and change it to **3.250"**.

- Change the dimension
  8.000" to **8.750"**

- Click Rebuild
  or **Control + Q**.

8.000

Modify

8.750in

5.000

⌀3.000   ⌀1.250

9. Finding the mass of the part:

- Select **Tools / Mass Properties**.

- Enter the Mass here: _____ pounds.

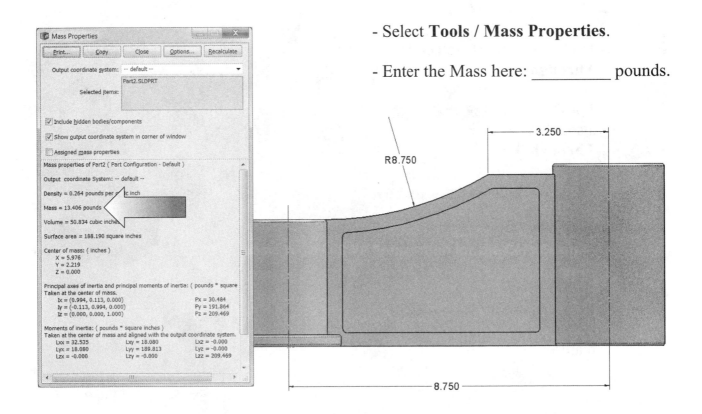

Mass Properties

Print...   Copy   Close   Options...   Recalculate

Output coordinate system: -- default --

Selected items: Part2.SLDPRT

☑ Include hidden bodies/components

☑ Show output coordinate system in corner of window

☐ Assigned mass properties

Mass properties of Part2 (Part Configuration - Default)

Output coordinate System: -- default --

Density = 0.264 pounds per cubic inch

Mass = 13.406 pounds

Volume = 50.834 cubic inches

Surface area = 188.190 square inches

Center of mass: (inches)
  X = 5.976
  Y = 2.219
  Z = 0.000

Principal axes of inertia and principal moments of inertia: (pounds * square)
Taken at the center of mass.
  Ix = (0.994, 0.113, 0.000)   Px = 30.484
  Iy = (-0.113, 0.994, 0.000)   Py = 191.864
  Iz = (0.000, 0.000, 1.000)   Pz = 209.469

Moments of inertia: (pounds * square inches)
Taken at the center of mass and aligned with the output coordinate system.
  Lxx = 32.535   Lxy = 18.080   Lxz = -0.000
  Lyx = 18.080   Lyy = 189.813   Lyz = -0.000
  Lzx = -0.000   Lzy = -0.000   Lzz = 209.469

R8.750

3.250

8.750

10. Adding the cut features:

- Select the Front plane and open a new sketch.

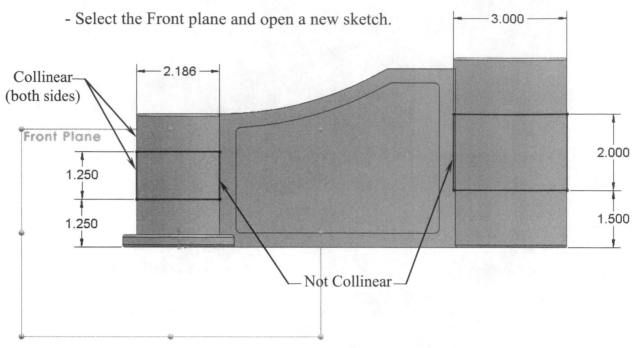

- Sketch the 2 rectangles as shown, and add dimensions/relations to fully define the sketch.

- Click **Extruded Cut**.

- Under Direction1, select: **Through All**.

- For Direction2 also select: **Through All**.

- Click **OK**.

- Rotate the part to verify the cut feature.

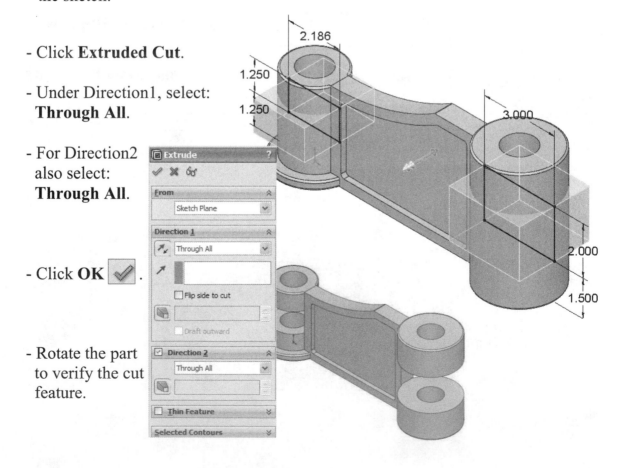

11. Adding fillets and chamfers:

- Click the Fillet command.

- Enter **.093"** for radius value.

- Select the **4 Edges** as noted.

- Click **OK**.

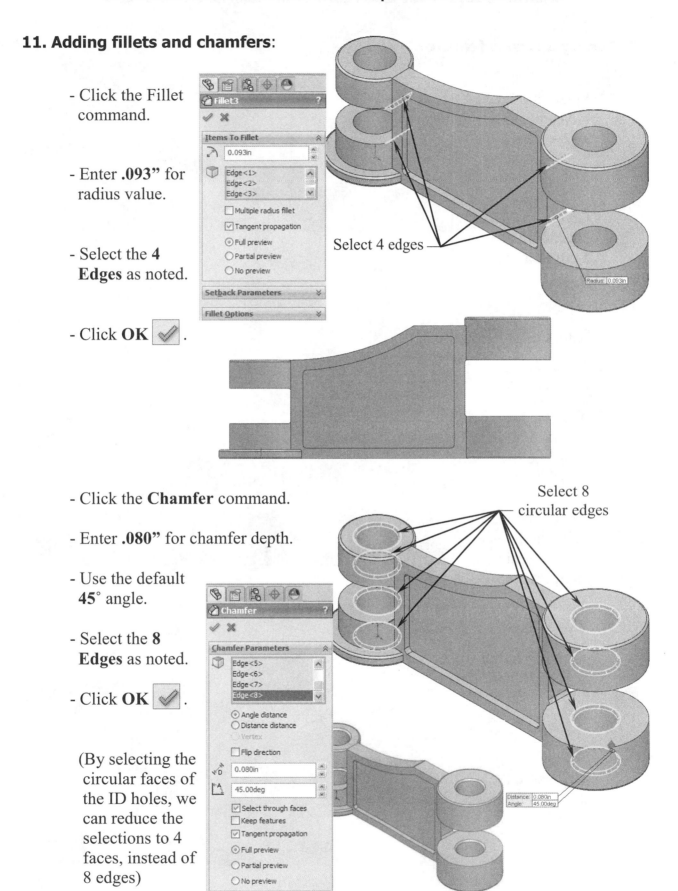

Select 4 edges

- Click the **Chamfer** command.

- Enter **.080"** for chamfer depth.

- Use the default **45°** angle.

- Select the **8 Edges** as noted.

- Click **OK**.

(By selecting the circular faces of the ID holes, we can reduce the selections to 4 faces, instead of 8 edges)

Select 8 circular edges

12. Adding a recess feature:

- Select the **face** as indicated and open a new sketch.

- Create an Offset of **.250"** from the **2 edges** as noted.

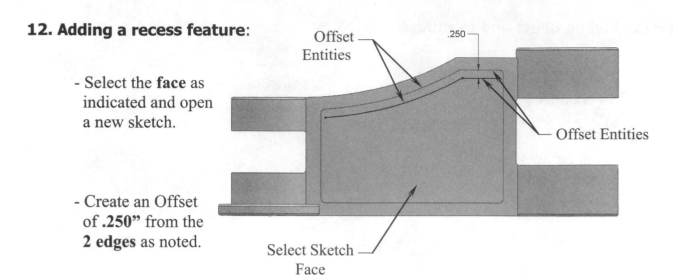

Offset Entities

.250

Offset Entities

Select Sketch Face

- Add **3 lines** approximately as shown.

- Add the dimensions as indicated in the image below.

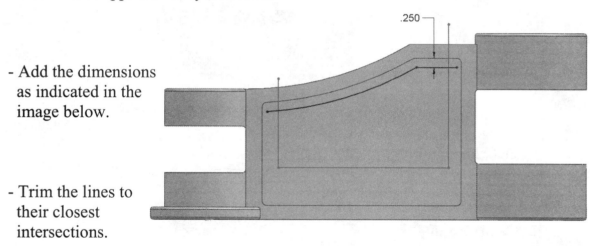

.250

- Trim the lines to their closest intersections.

- Add the **sketch fillets** of **R.093"** to **5 places**.

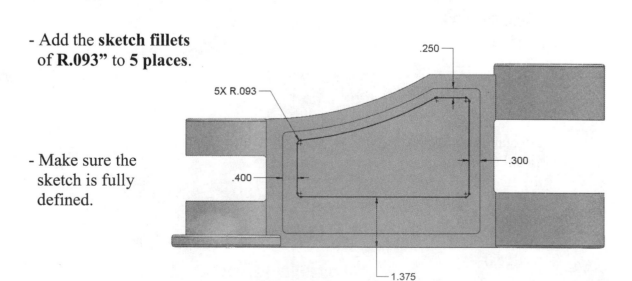

.250

5X R.093

.300

.400

- Make sure the sketch is fully defined.

1.375

- Click **Extruded Cut**.

- Under Direction1, select:
  Through All.

- For Direction2
  also select:
  Through All.

- Click **OK**.

- Rotate the part
  to verify the cut
  feature.

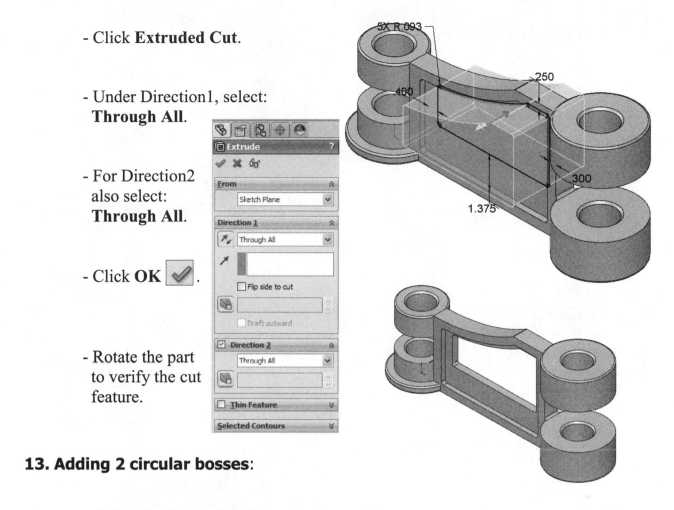

13. Adding 2 circular bosses:

- Select the Front plane from the FeatureManager tree and open a new sketch.

- Sketch 2 circles and add the dimensions as shown to fully define them.

- Link the diameter dimensions using the Link Values option. Rename them to:
  Cir_Bosses.

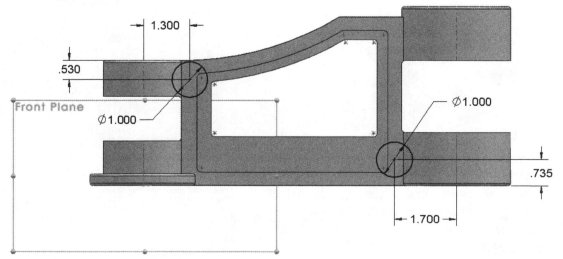

- Click **Extruded Boss/Base**.

- Under Direction1, select: **Mid Plane**.

- For extrude depth enter: **2.000in**.

- Click **OK** ✓.

- Change to the Top view (Control + 5) to verify the boss feature.

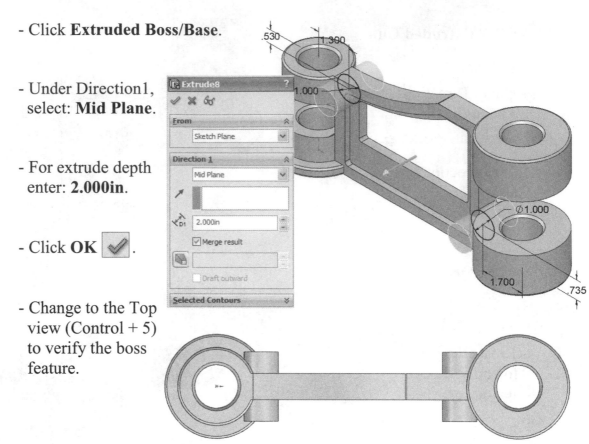

14. Finding the mass of the part*:

- Click **Tools / Mass Properties**.

- Locate the mass* (arrow) and enter

  it here _____ lbs.

* The mass of an object is the amount of material it contains.
A body with greater mass has more inertia; it needs a greater force to accelerate.
Weight depends on the force of gravity, but mass does not.

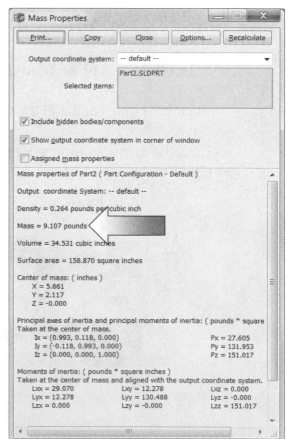

15. Modifying the feature dimensions:

- Locate the diameter
dimensions for the
2 ID holes (circled)
and change them
from: Ø1.250
to Ø **1.500"**.

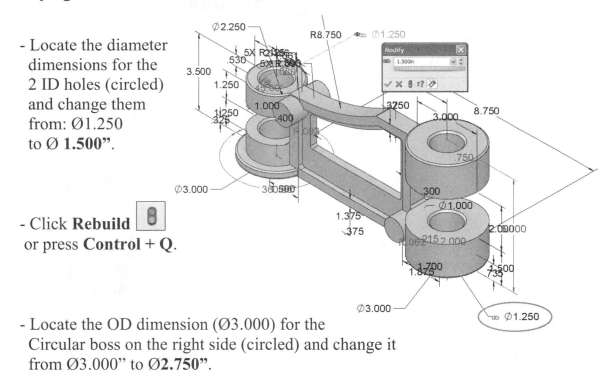

- Click **Rebuild**
or press **Control + Q**.

- Locate the OD dimension (Ø3.000) for the
Circular boss on the right side (circled) and change it
from Ø3.000" to Ø**2.750"**.

- Click **Rebuild**
or press **Control + Q.**

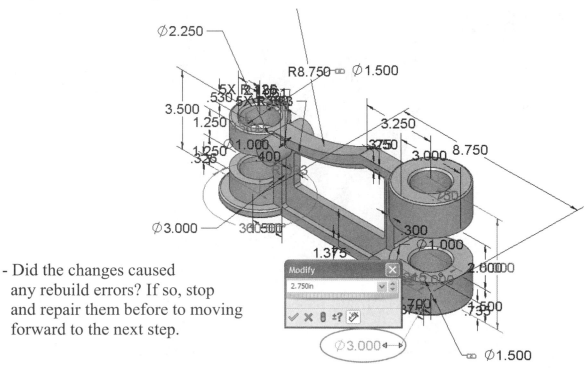

- Did the changes caused
any rebuild errors? If so, stop
and repair them before to moving
forward to the next step.

- Locate the OD dimension for the circular boss on the left (circled) and change it from Ø2.250 to **2.500"**.

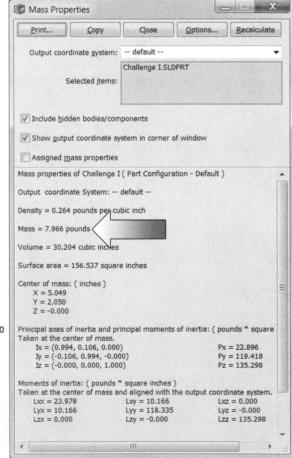

- Click **Rebuild** or press **Control + Q**.

16. Finding the mass of the part:

- Click **Tools / Mass Properties**.

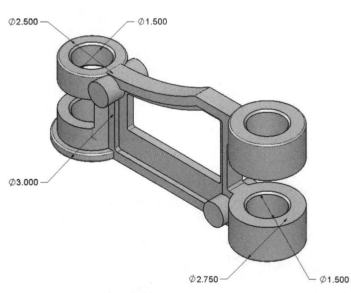

- Locate the mass (arrow) and enter it

here: _____ lbs.

17. Creating the Counter-Bores:

- Click the **Hole-Wizard** command from the Features toolbar.

- Select the following:

    * Hole Type: **Counterbore**

    * Standard: **Ansi Inch**

    * Type: **Binding Head Screw**

    * Size: **1/4**

    * Fit: **Normal**

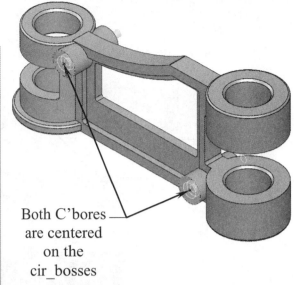

Both C'bores are centered on the cir_bosses

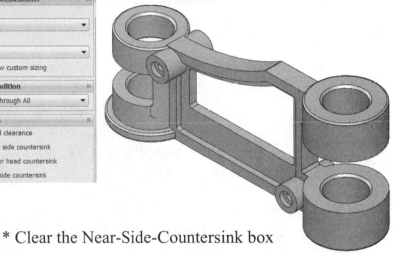

    * End Condition: **Through All**   * Clear the Near-Side-Countersink box

- Change to the **Positions** tab (circled) and place 2 Counter-bores on the same centers as the circular boss features, click OK when finished.

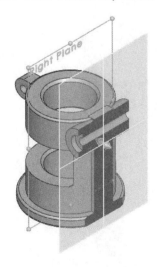

- Create a **Section View** similar to the one shown below to verify the 2 counter bores.

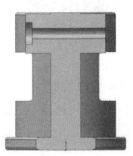

18. Adding a side tab:

- Open a new sketch on the Front plane.

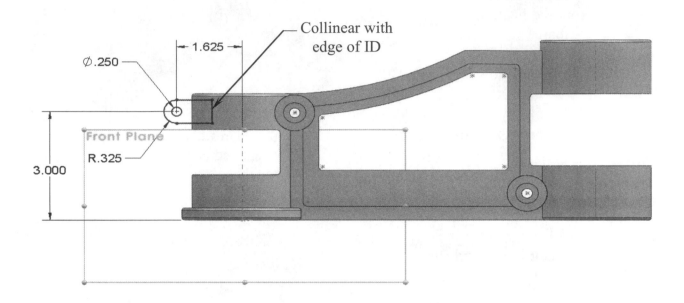

- Sketch the profile of the tab as show.

- Add the dimensions and relations needed to fully define the sketch.

- Click **Extruded Boss/Base**.

- Under Direction1, select: **Mid Plane**.

- For extrude depth enter: **.425 in**.

- Click **OK**.

- Rotate the part and Verify that the tab is centered on the Front plane.

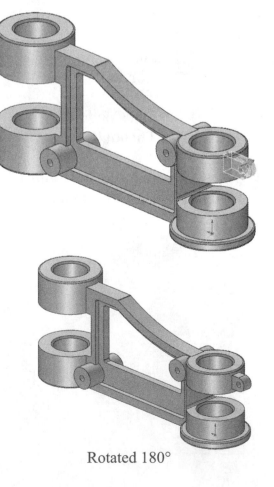

Rotated 180°

19. Modifying the recess feature:

- Locate the spacing dimension of the recess (1.375") and change to **.875"**.

- Click **Rebuild** [ ] .

- Find the final mass of the part and enter it here: _____ lbs.

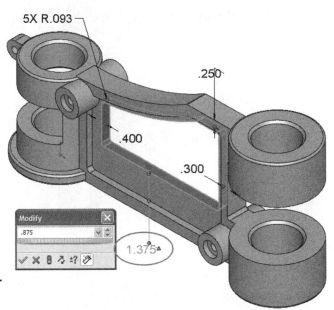

20. Modifying the Revolved feature:

- <u>Edit the sketch</u> of the **Revolved2** feature.

- Add 3 new lines as indicated.

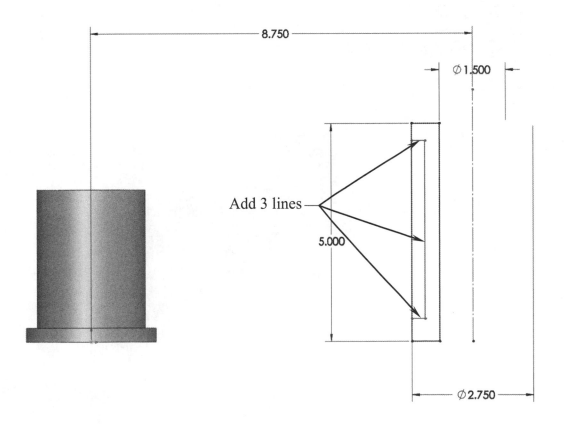

- Add the 3 dimensions (circled) to fully define this sketch.

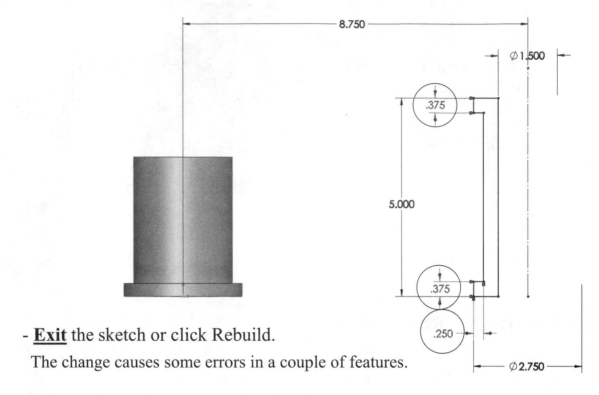

- **Exit** the sketch or click Rebuild.

  The change causes some errors in a couple of features.

- Edit the **Fillet1** feature and select the missing edge as noted.

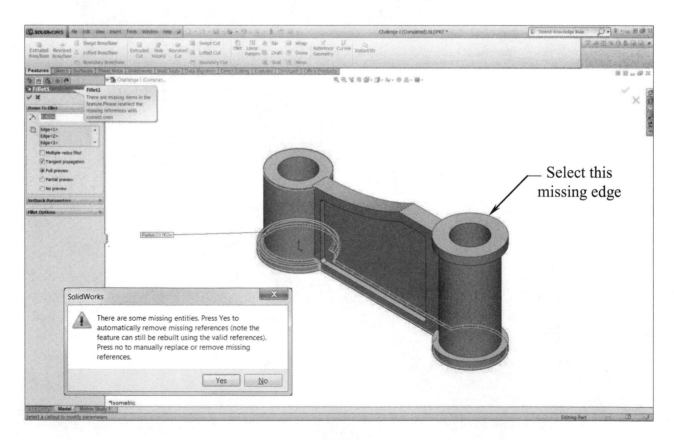

Select this missing edge

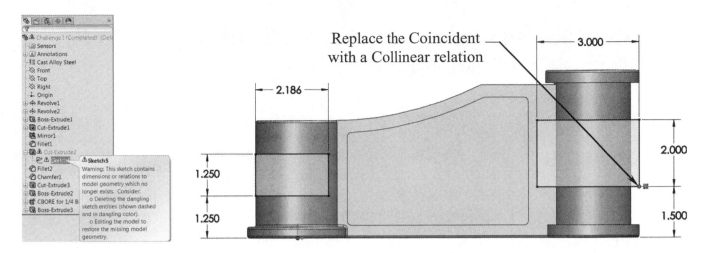

Replace the Coincident with a Collinear relation

- Edit the Sketch5 under the Cut-Extrude2. Replace the relation as noted. Click Rebuild.

- Find the final mass of the part and enter it here: _____ lbs.

21. **Saving your work**:

- Save your work as **Challenge1** and close the document when done.

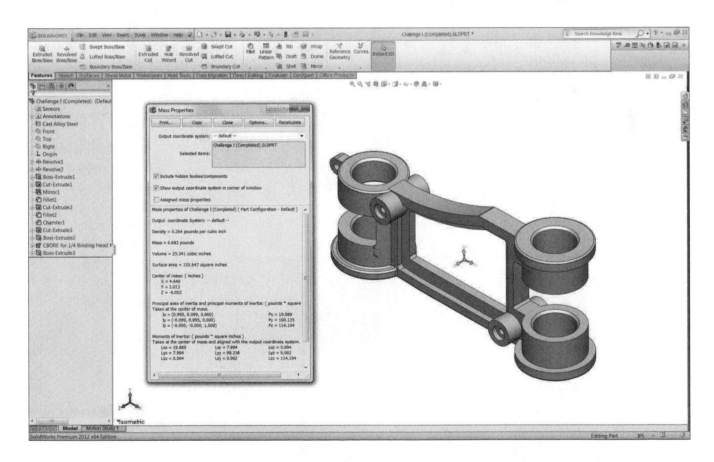

- Use the example file from the included CD to review the construction of the part, if needed.

Certified-SolidWorks-Professional program (CSWP)
Certification Practice for the Core-Exam

Challenge II-A: Part Configurations & Design Tables

Complete this challenge within 45 minutes

- Modify this part in SolidWorks   - Unit: **Millimeter, 2 decimals**   - Origin: **Arbitrary**

- Drafting Standards: **ANSI**   - Material: **Alloy Steel**   - Density: **0.008 /mm^3**

1. Opening the attached part named:

    Challenge II-A.

2. Setting the options:

    - Change the material to **Alloy Steel**.

    - Change the system options to match the settings above.

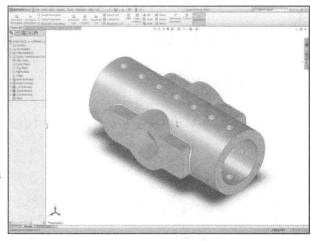

3. Switching Configuration:

    - Activate **Configuration A**.

4. Finding the current Mass:

    - Select **Tools/ Mass Properties**.

    - Enter the mass in grams:

    _____ grams.

NOTE: Material must be selected before calculating the mass of the part.

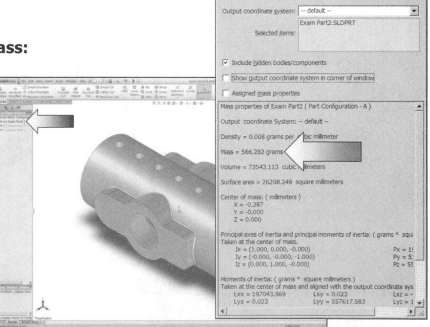

5. Adding a New Configuration:

- Create a <u>new configuration</u> named **D**, and enter the comment: **Added a 10mm hole**.

- Select the face as shown below and open a new sketch.

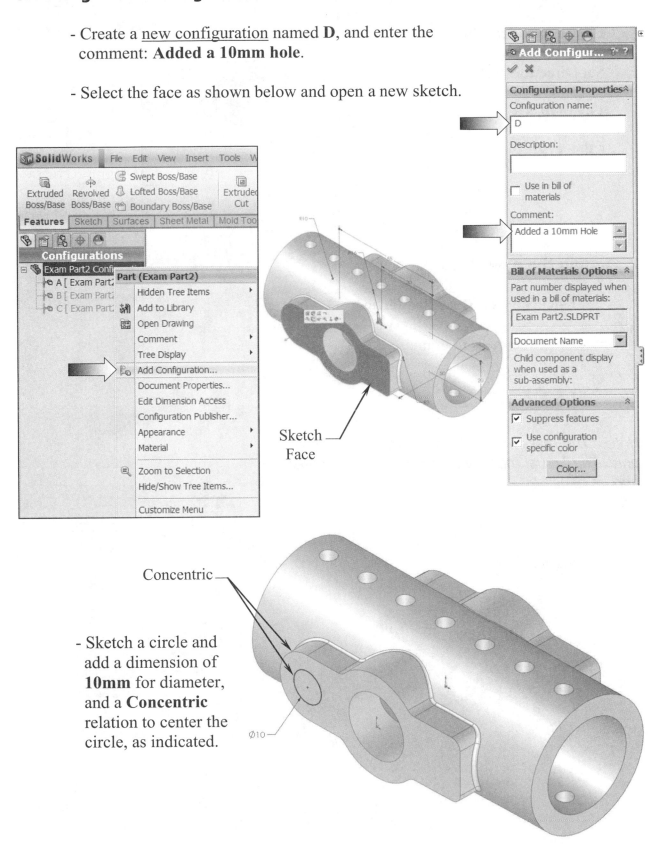

Sketch Face

Concentric

- Sketch a circle and add a dimension of **10mm** for diameter, and a **Concentric** relation to center the circle, as indicated.

6. Extruding a cut:

- Click **Extruded Cut**.

- Set Direction1 to:

  Through All.

- Click **OK** .

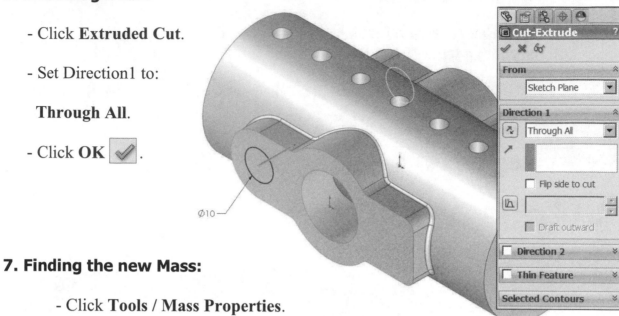

Ø10

7. Finding the new Mass:

- Click **Tools / Mass Properties**.

- Enter the mass in grams:

  _____ grams.

Note: The mass in the dialog boxes are examples only. The actual mass will be based on the material and its density.

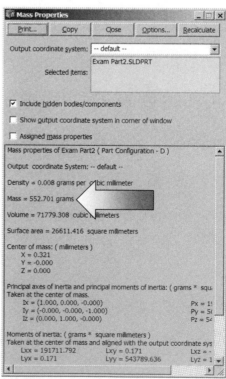

8. Switching configuration:

- Double click on **Configuration B** to make it active.

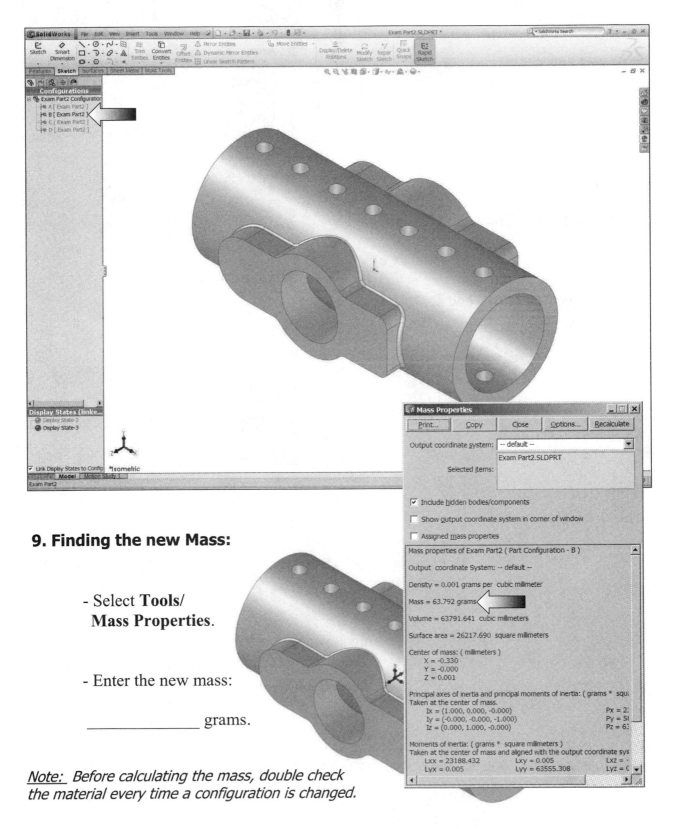

9. Finding the new Mass:

- Select **Tools/**
  Mass Properties.

- Enter the new mass:

_____ grams.

Note: _Before calculating the mass, double check_
the material every time a configuration is changed.

10. Creating a Design Table:

- Select **Insert/ Tables /Design Tables**.

- Click the **Auto-Create** option and leave all other option defaults.

11. Adding new Configurations:

- Right click on **Row4** and select **Copy**.

- Right click on **Row7** and select **Paste**.

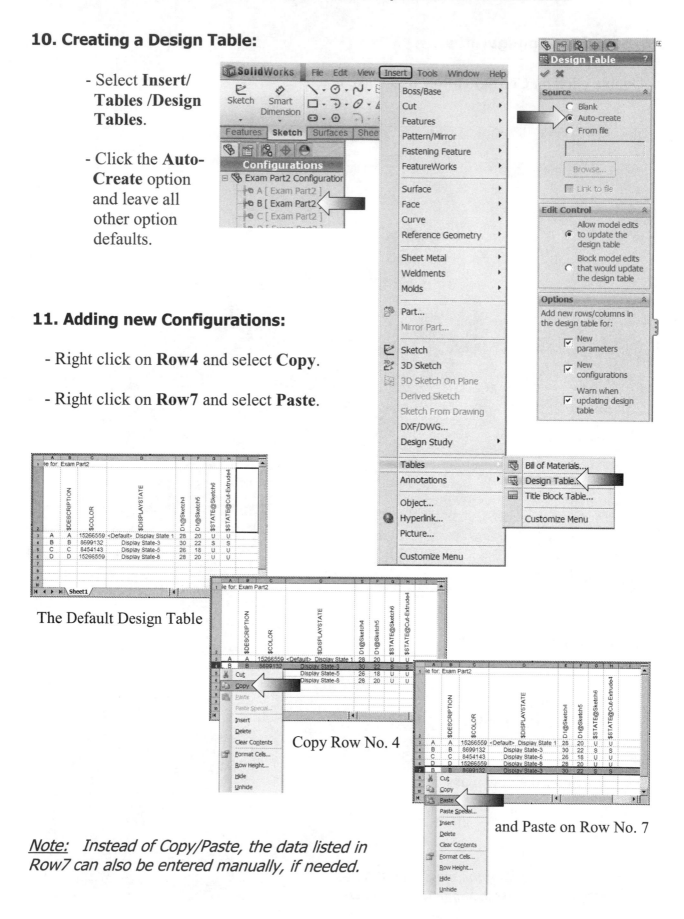

The Default Design Table

Copy Row No. 4

and Paste on Row No. 7

<u>Note:</u> Instead of Copy/Paste, the data listed in Row7 can also be entered manually, if needed.

12. Modifying the new configurations:

- Change the name of the new config. to **E**.

- Change the ID dimension on the body to **24**.

- Change the hole Diameter to **16**.

- Leave the Suppression States at Suppressed (S).

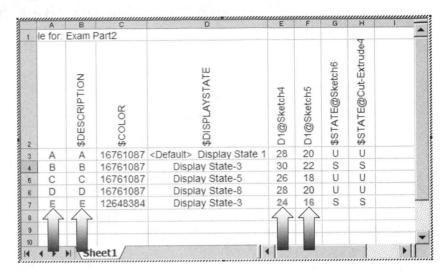

	A	B	C	D	E	F	G	H	I
1	le for: Exam Part2								
2		$DESCRIPTION	$COLOR	$DISPLAYSTATE	D1@Sketch4	D1@Sketch5	$STATE@Sketch6	$STATE@Cut-Extrude4	
3	A	A	16761087	<Default> Display State 1	28	20	U	U	
4	B	B	16761087	Display State-3	30	22	S	S	
5	C	C	16761087	Display State-5	26	18	U	U	
6	D	D	16761087	Display State-8	28	20	U	U	
7	E	E	12648384	Display State-3	24	16	S	S	
8									
9									
10									

Sheet1

- Click anywhere in the background to return to SolidWorks.

- Double click on **Configuration E** to activate.
(Click REBUILD to update the change of color).

13. Finding the final Mass:

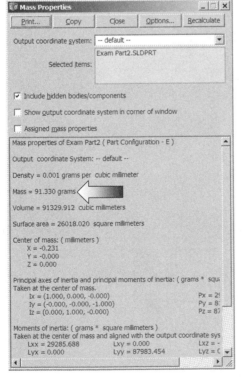

- Select **Tools/ Mass Properties**.

- Enter the final mass: _____ grams

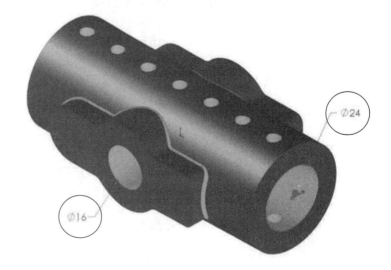

Configurations

- Exam Part2 Configuration
  - Tables
    - Design Table
  - A [Exam Part2]
  - B [Exam Part2]
  - C [Exam Part2]
  - D [Exam Part2]
  - E

14. Save your work as Challenge 2-A.

Certified-SolidWorks-Professional program (CSWP)
Certification Practice for the Core-Exam

Challenge II-B: Part Modifications

Complete this challenge within 30 minutes

- Modify this part in SolidWorks   - Unit: **Inches, 3 decimals**   - Origin: **Arbitrary**

- Drafting Standards: **ANSI**   - Material: **Alloy Steel**   - Density: **0.008 /mm^3**

1. **Opening the attached part named:**

   Challenge II-B.

2. **Setting the options:**

   - Change the material to **Alloy Steel**.

   - Change the system options to match the settings above.

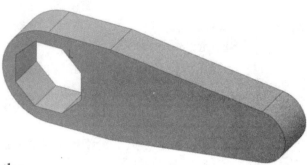

3. **Adding the 1st cut:**

   - Select the TOP plane and open a new sketch.

   - Sketch the profile shown below.

   - Add the dimensions and relations needed to fully define the sketch.

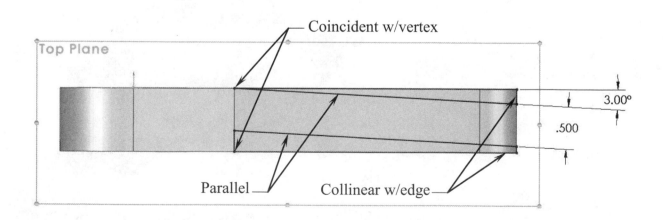

- Click **Extruded Cut**.

- Set Direction 1 to: **Through All**.

- Set Direction 2 also to: **Through All**.

- Click OK 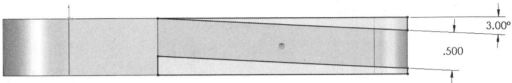.

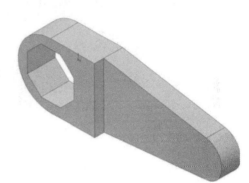

4. Finding the Mass:

- Select **Tools/ Mass Properties**.

- Enter the final mass: _____ pounds.

5. Adding the 2nd cut:

- Select the FACE as indicated and open a new sketch.

Sketch face

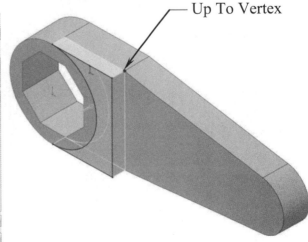

Up To Vertex

- Sketch the profile using the **Convert-Entities** option.

- Extrude Cut using the Vertex as noted.

- Click OK 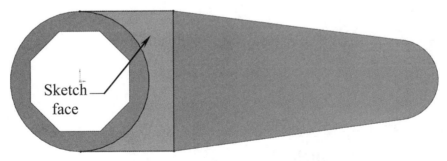.

6. Adding the 3rd cut:

- Select the FACE as indicated and open a new sketch.

- Create an offset of **.125"** from the **6 edges** as indicated.

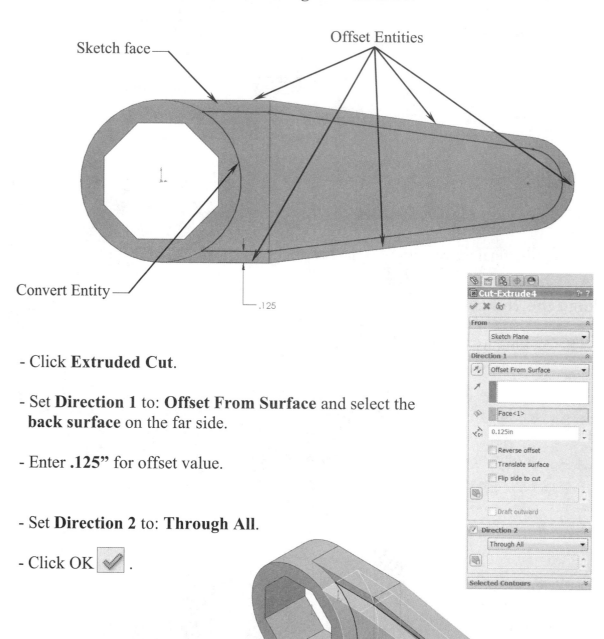

Sketch face

Offset Entities

Convert Entity

.125

- Click **Extruded Cut**.

- Set **Direction 1** to: **Offset From Surface** and select the **back surface** on the far side.

- Enter **.125"** for offset value.

- Set **Direction 2** to: **Through All**.

- Click OK.

7. Finding the Mass:

- Select **Tools/ Mass Properties**.

- Enter the final mass: _____ pounds.

8. Adding the 4th cut:

- Select the FACE as indicated and open a new sketch.

- Sketch a circle and a **.500"** diameter dimension.

- Add a Concentric relation as noted.

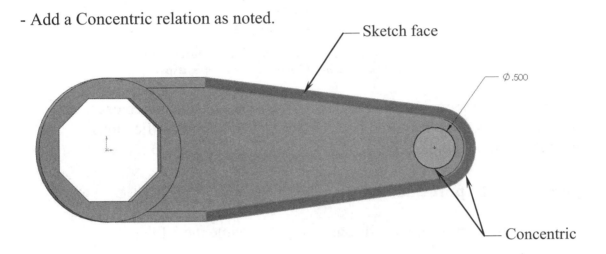

Sketch face

Ø .500

Concentric

- Click **Extruded Cut**.

- Set Direction 1 to: **Through All**.

- Click OK ✔ .

9. Finding the Mass:

- Select **Tools/ Mass Properties**.

- Enter the final mass: _____ pounds.

10. Saving your work:

- Click **File / Save As**.

- Enter **Challenge 2-B** for the name of the file.

- Click **Save**.

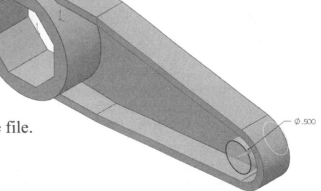

Ø .500

Certified SolidWorks Professional program (CSWP) Certification Practice for the Core-Exam

Challenge III: Bottom Up Assembly

Complete this challenge within 90 minutes

(The following examples are intended to assist you in familiarizing yourself with the structures of the exams and the method in which the questions are asked).

1. Assemble the components using mates.
2. Create a new coordinate system in the Assem.
3. Units: IPS (Inch/Pound/Second).

4. Detect and repair all interferences.
5. Mate modifications.
6. Decimal: 3 places.

1. Opening the 1st part document:

- Open the document named: **Base** from the Challenge 3 folder.

- This part will be used as the Parent component in the assembly.

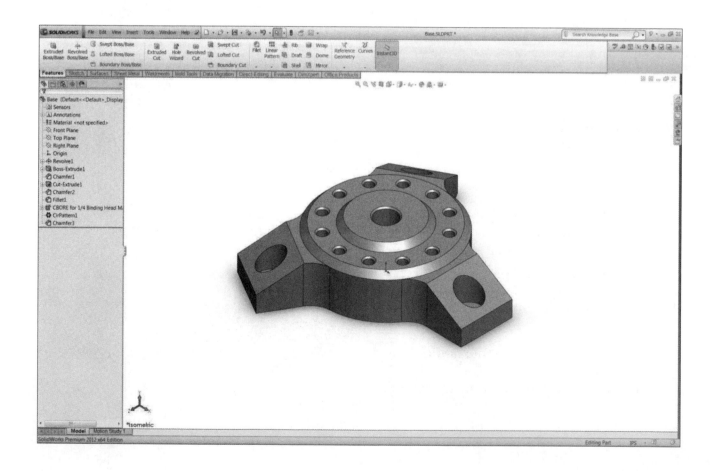

2. Transferring the part to Assembly:

- Select **Make Assembly From Part** from the **File** pull down menu (arrow).

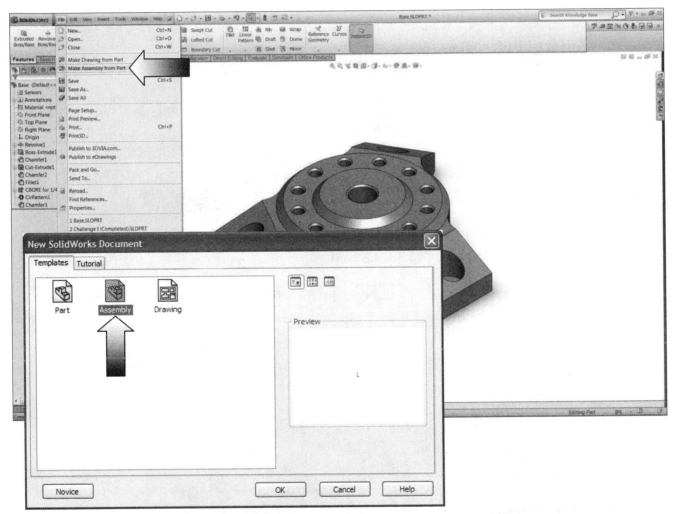

- Select the default **Assembly Template** and click **OK** [OK].

- Place the component on the assembly's origin as indicated.

- The 1st component should be fixed before other components can be mated.

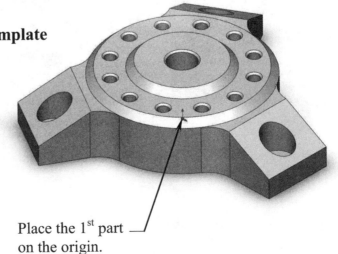

Place the 1st part on the origin.

3. Creating a Coordinate System:

- From the Assembly toolbar, click the Reference Geometry button and select the **Coordinate System** command – OR –

- From the pull down menu select: **Insert / Reference Geometry / Coordinate System**.

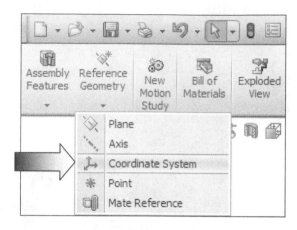

- Select the Corner-Vertex for **Origin**.

- Select the **X** and **Y** axis as indicated. Click Reverse Direction if needed.

- Leave the Z direction blank.

- Click **OK** [✓].

- This Coordinate System will be used to calculate the Center of Mass for all questions from here on.

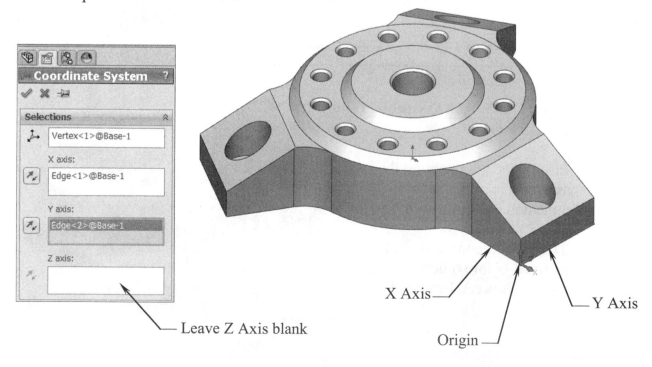

Leave Z Axis blank

X Axis

Y Axis

Origin

4. Inserting the 2nd component:

- From the Assembly toolbar, click the **Insert Component** command.

- Click Browse [Browse...] and open the component named: **Pivot**.

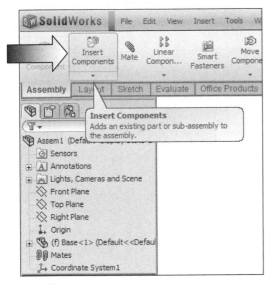
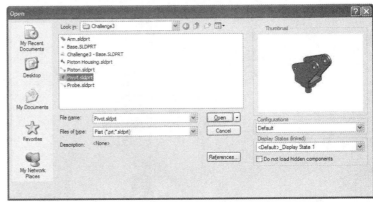

- Place the component approx. as shown below.

5. Adding the 1st mate:

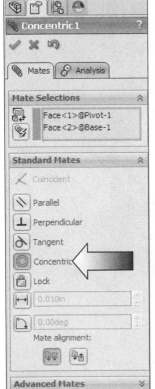

- From the Assembly toolbar, click **Mate**.

- Select the Circular Boss and the Hole as indicated.

- The **Concentric** mate is automatically created by default.

- Click **OK** [✓] .

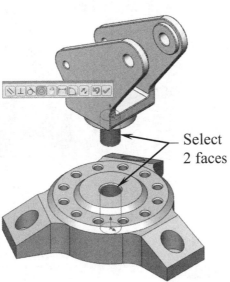

Select
2 faces

NOTE:

Most components will receive only 2 mates, since they were designed to move and rotate after everything is assembled.

Sometimes you may need to create the 3rd mate just to align the components. These mates should be suppressed prior to mating other components.

6. Adding the 2nd mate:

- Click **Mate** again if you are not already there.

- Select the <u>bottom face</u> of the Circular Boss and the <u>upper face</u> of the Base.

- The **Coincident** mate is added automatically.

- Click **OK** 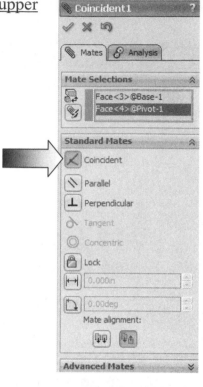.

Coincident

7. Adding the 3rd mate:

- Click **Mate** again.

- Select the FRONT of the Base and the FRONT plane of the Pivot.

- Click the **Parallel** mate option.

- Click **OK** ✓.

<u>NOTE:</u>
This parallel mate will align the 2 components for the time being, it will get changed to an Angle mate later on.

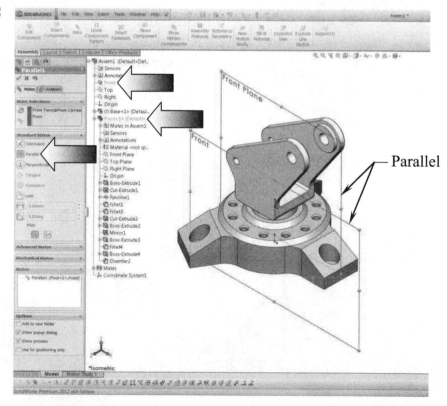

Parallel

8. Finding the Center Of Mass:

- Select **Tools** / **Mass Properties**.

- Change the default output coordinate to: **Coordinate System1**.

- Enter the Center Of Mass (in Inches).

X = _____

Y = _____

Z = _____

NOTE:
The center of mass shown in the dialog boxes are examples for use with this text only.

The actual mass properties of the components and the center of mass of the assembly depend upon the materials and the locations specified for each part in the assembly.

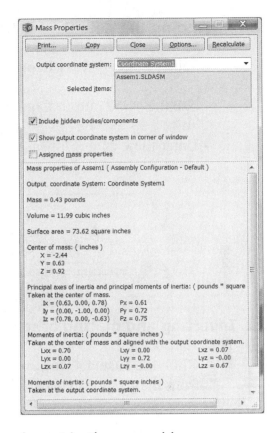

9. Creating an Angle mate:

- Expand the **Mate Group** from the bottom of the FeatureManager tree.

- Edit the **Parallel** mate, change it to **Angle** mate and enter **30.00deg**. Click **OK**.

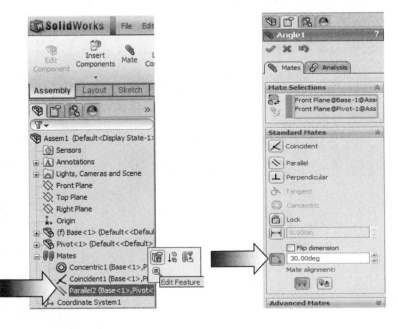

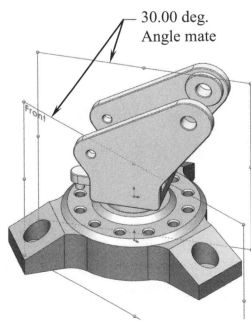

30.00 deg. Angle mate

10. Finding the new Center Of Mass:

- Select **Tools / Mass Properties**.

- Use the same output **Coordinate System1**.

- Enter the Center Of Mass (in Inches).

X = _____

Y = _____

Z = _____

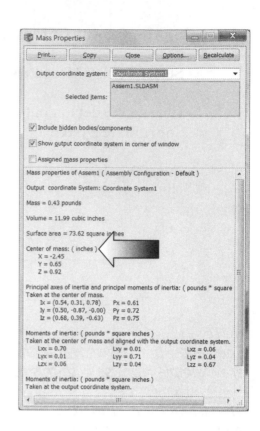

11. Inserting and mating other components:

- Click the **Insert Component** command from the Assembly toolbar.

- **Insert** and **Mate** the following components:

       * **Arm**   * **Probe**   * **Piston**   * **Piston Housing**

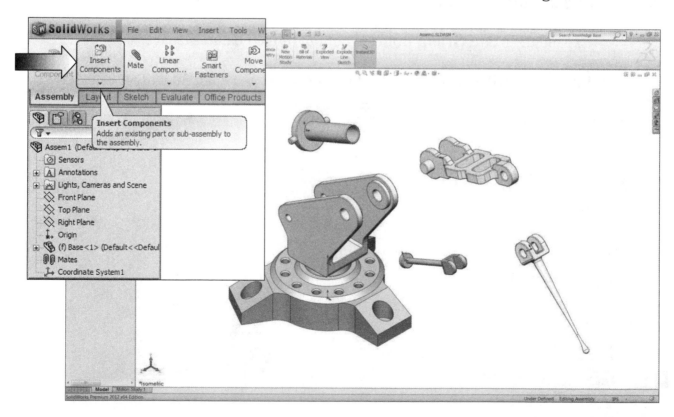

- Use the reference views below to mate the new components.

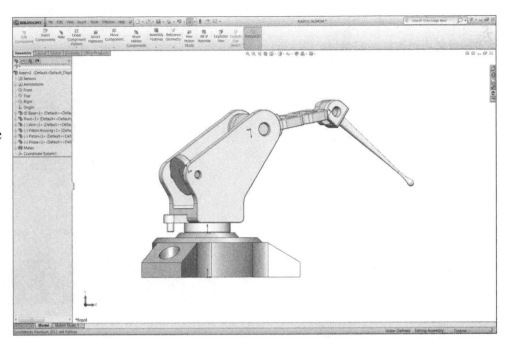

FRONT VIEW

- Use either of the Front planes on each component to center the components with Coincident mates

– OR –

use the **Width mate** option to achieve the same results.

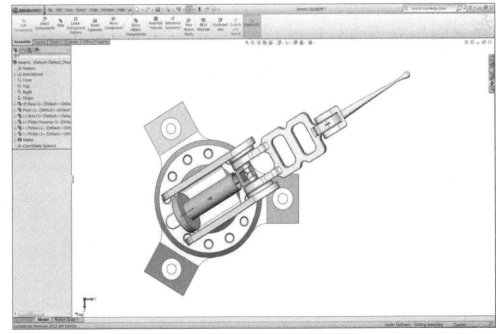

TOP VIEW

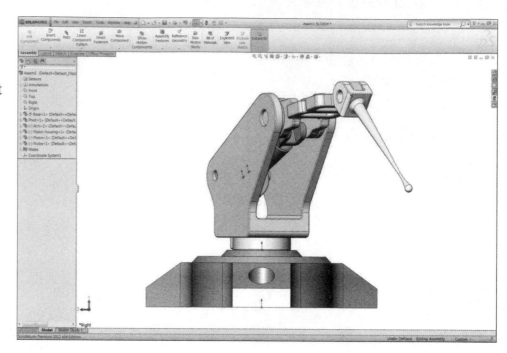

- Most component should have at least 1 degree of freedom left.

- You should be able to rotate the assembly back and forth, or up and down at this point.

RIGHT VIEW

12. Finding the new Center Of Mass:

- Select **Tools / Mass Properties**.

- Use the same output **Coordinate System1**.

- Enter the Center Of Mass (in Inches).

X = _____

Y = _____

Z = _____

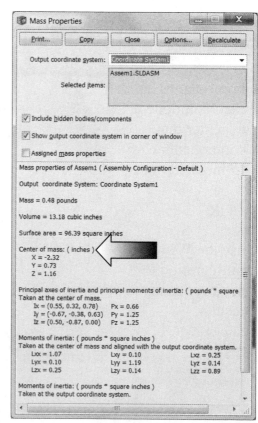

NOTE:
The current angle between the Base and the Pivot is still set at 30 degrees.

13. Changing the mate angle:

- Edit the **30deg** mate and change it to **180deg**.

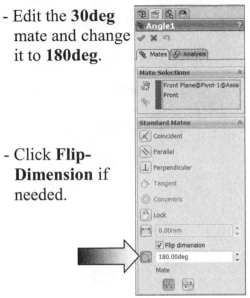

- Click **Flip-Dimension** if needed.

- Click **OK** ✓.

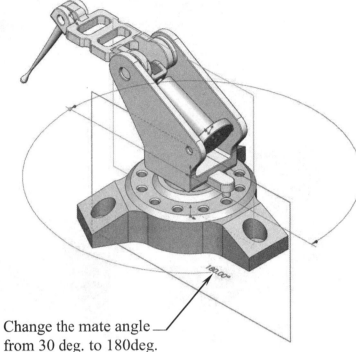

Change the mate angle from 30 deg. to 180deg.

14. Finding the final Center Of Mass:

- Select **Tools / Mass Properties**.

- Use the same output **Coordinate System1**.

- Enter the Center Of Mass (in Inches).

X = _____

Y = _____

Z = _____

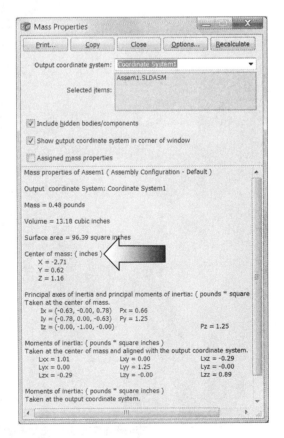

15. Save your work as Challenge 3.

NOTE: When you're ready to take the actual examination, log on to: **www.solidworks.com/sw/mcad-certification-programs.htm**, click on the CSWP option and select **purchase exam**. After the registration is completed, you will receive 2 emails from SolidWorks; one of them is the receipt for the purchase of the exam and the other have the instruction on how to download and take the exam.

If you passed, an email will be sent to you from the Grading server notifying you of the results and instructing you on how to print out your certificate. If you failed, there is a 30 day waiting period, you will need to register and pay for the exam and start the process over again.

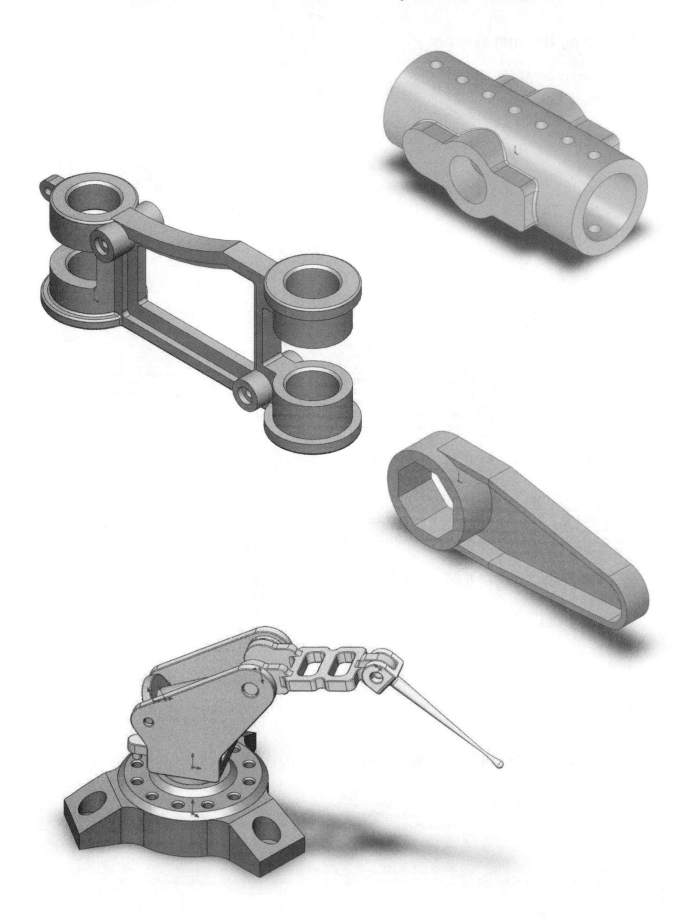

Glossary

Alloys:

An Alloy is a mixture of two or more metals (and sometimes a non-metal). The mixture is made by heating and melting the substances together.
Example of alloys are Bronze (Copper and Tin), Brass (Copper and Zinc), and Steel (Iron and Carbon).

Gravity and Mass:

Gravity is the force that pulls everything on earth toward the ground and makes things feel heavy. Gravity makes all falling bodies accelerates at a constant 32ft. per second (9.8 m/s). In the earth's atmosphere, air resistance slow acceleration. Only on airless Moon would a feather and a metal block fall to the ground together.
The mass of an object is the amount of material it contains.
A body with greater mass has more inertia; it needs a greater force to accelerate.
Weight depends on the force of gravity, but mass does not.

When an object spins around another (for example: a satellite orbiting the earth) it is pushed outward. Two forces are at work here: Centrifugal (pushing outward) and Centripetal (pulling inward). If you whirl a ball around you on a string, you pull it inward (Centripetal force). The ball seems to pull outward (Centrifugal force) and if released will fly off in a straight line.

Heat:

Heat is a form of energy and can move from one substance to another in one of three ways: by Convection, by Radiation, and by Conduction.

- Convection takes place only in liquids like water (for example: water in a kettle) and gases (for example: air warmed by a heat source such as a fire or radiator). When liquid or gas is heated, it expands and become less dense. Warm air above the radiator rises and cool air moves in to take its place, creating a convection current.
- Radiation is movement of heat through the air. Heat forms a match sets molecules of air moving and rays of heat spread out around the heat source.

- Conduction occurs in solids such as metals. The handle of a metal spoon left in boiling liquid warms up as molecules at the heated end moves faster and collide with their neighbors, setting them moving. The heat travels through the metal, which is a good conductor of heat.

Inertia:

A body with a large mass is harder to start and also to stop. A heavy truck traveling at 50mph needs more power breaks to stop its motion than a smaller car traveling at the same speed.
Inertia is the tendency of an object either to stay still or to move steadily in a straight line, unless another force (such as a brick wall stopping the vehicle) makes it behave differently.

Joules:

The Joules is the SI unit of work or energy.
One Joule of work is done when a force of one Newton moves through a distance of one meter. The Joule is named after the English scientist James Joule (1818-1889).

Materials:

- Stainless steel is an alloy of steel with chromium or nickel.

- Steel is made by the basic oxygen process. The raw material is about three parts melted iron and one part scrap steel. Blowing oxygen into the melted iron raises the temperature and gets rid of impurities.

- All plastic are chemical compounds called polymers.

- Glass is made by mixing and heating sand, limestone, and soda ash. When these ingredients melt they turn into glass, which is hardened when it cools. Glass is in fact not a solid but a "supercooled" liquid, it can be shaped by blowing, pressing, drawing, casting into molds, rolling, and floating across molten tin, to make large sheets.

- Ceramic objects, such as pottery and porcelain, electrical insulators, bricks, and roof tiles are all made from clay. The clay is shaped or molded when wet and soft, and heated in a kiln until it hardens.

Machine Tools:

Are powered tools used for shaping metal or other materials, by drilling holes, chiseling, grinding, pressing or cutting. Often the material (the workpiece) is moved while the tool stays still (lathe), or vice versa, the workpiece stayed while the tool moves (mill).
Most common machine tools are: Mill, Lathe, Saw, Broach, Punch press, Grind, Bore and Stamp break.

Newton's Law:

1. Every object remains stopped or goes on moving at a steady rate in a straight line unless acted upon by another force. This is the inertia principle.
2. The amount of force needed to make an object change its speed depends on the mass of the object and the amount of the acceleration or deceleration required.
3. To every action there is an equal and opposite reaction. When a body is pushed on way by a force, another force pushes back with equal strength.

Polymers:

A polymer is made of one or more large molecules formed from thousands of smaller molecules. Rubber and Wood are natural polymers. Plastics are synthetic (artificially made) polymers.

Speed and Velocity:

- Speed is the rate at which a moving object changes position (how far it moves in a fixed time).
- Velocity is speed in a particular direction.
- If either speed or direction is changed, velocity also changed.

Absorbed
A feature, sketch, or annotation that is contained in another item (usually a feature) in the FeatureManager design tree. Examples are the profile sketch and profile path in a base-sweep, or a cosmetic thread annotation in a hole.

Align
Tools that assist in lining up annotations and dimensions (left, right, top, bottom, and so on). For aligning parts in an assembly.

Alternate position view
A drawing view in which one or more views are superimposed in phantom lines on the original view. Alternate position views are often used to show range of motion of an assembly.

Anchor point
The end of a leader that attaches to the note, block, or other annotation. Sheet formats contain anchor points for a bill of materials, a hole table, a revision table, and a weldment cut list.

Annotation

A text note or a symbol that adds specific design intent to a part, assembly, or drawing. Specific types of annotations include note, hole callout, surface finish symbol, datum feature symbol, datum target, geometric tolerance symbol, weld symbol, balloon, and stacked balloon. Annotations that apply only to drawings include center mark, annotation centerline, area hatch, and block.

Appearance callouts

Callouts that display the colors and textures of the face, feature, body, and part under the entity selected and are a shortcut to editing colors and textures.

Area hatch

A crosshatch pattern or fill applied to a selected face or to a closed sketch in a drawing.

Assembly

A document in which parts, features, and other assemblies (sub-assemblies) are mated together. The parts and sub-assemblies exist in documents separate from the assembly. For example, in an assembly, a piston can be mated to other parts, such as a connecting rod or cylinder. This new assembly can then be used as a sub-assembly in an assembly of an engine. The extension for a SolidWorks assembly file name is .SLDASM.

Attachment point

The end of a leader that attaches to the model (to an edge, vertex, or face, for example) or to a drawing sheet.

Axis

A straight line that can be used to create model geometry, features, or patterns. An axis can be made in a number of different ways, including using the intersection of two planes.

Balloon

Labels parts in an assembly, typically including item numbers and quantity. In drawings, the item numbers are related to rows in a bill of materials.

Base

The first solid feature of a part.

Baseline dimensions

Sets of dimensions measured from the same edge or vertex in a drawing.

Bend

A feature in a sheet metal part. A bend generated from a filleted corner, cylindrical face, or conical face is a round bend; a bend generated from sketched straight lines is a sharp bend.

Bill of materials
A table inserted into a drawing to keep a record of the parts used in an assembly.

Block
A user-defined annotation that you can use in parts, assemblies, and drawings. A block can contain text, sketch entities (except points), and area hatch, and it can be saved in a file for later use as, for example, a custom callout or a company logo.

Bottom-up assembly
An assembly modeling technique where you create parts and then insert them into an assembly.

Broken-out section
A drawing view that exposes inner details of a drawing view by removing material from a closed profile, usually a spline.

Cavity
The mold half that holds the cavity feature of the design part.

Center mark
A cross that marks the center of a circle or arc.

Centerline
A centerline marks, in phantom font, an axis of symmetry in a sketch or drawing.

Chamfer
Bevels a selected edge or vertex. You can apply chamfers to both sketches and features.

Child
A dependent feature related to a previously-built feature. For example, a chamfer on the edge of a hole is a child of the parent hole.

Click-release
As you sketch, if you click and then release the pointer, you are in click-release mode. Move the pointer and click again to define the next point in the sketch sequence.

Click-drag
As you sketch, if you click and drag the pointer, you are in click-drag mode. When you release the pointer, the sketch entity is complete.

Closed profile
Also called a closed contour, it is a sketch or sketch entity with no exposed endpoints; for example, a circle or polygon.

Collapse

The opposite of explode. The collapse action returns an exploded assembly's parts to their normal positions.

Collision Detection

An assembly function that detects collisions between components when components move or rotate. A collision occurs when an entity on one component coincides with any entity on another component.

Component

Any part or sub-assembly within an assembly

Configuration

A variation of a part or assembly within a single document. Variations can include different dimensions, features, and properties. For example, a single part such as a bolt can contain different configurations that vary the diameter and length.

ConfigurationManager

Located on the left side of the SolidWorks window, it is a means to create, select, and view the configurations of parts and assemblies.

Constraint

The relations between sketch entities, or between sketch entities and planes, axes, edges, or vertices.

Construction geometry

The characteristic of a sketch entity that the entity is used in creating other geometry but is not itself used in creating features.

Coordinate system

A system of planes used to assign Cartesian coordinates to features, parts, and assemblies. Part and assembly documents contain default coordinate systems; other coordinate systems can be defined with reference geometry. Coordinate systems can be used with measurement tools and for exporting documents to other file formats.

Cosmetic thread

An annotation that represents threads.

Crosshatch

A pattern (or fill) applied to drawing views such as section views and broken-out sections.

Curvature

Curvature is equal to the inverse of the radius of the curve. The curvature can be displayed in different colors according to the local radius (usually of a surface).

Cut

A feature that removes material from a part by such actions as extrude, revolve, loft, sweep, thicken, cavity, and so on.

Dangling

A dimension, relation, or drawing section view that is unresolved. For example, if a piece of geometry is dimensioned, and that geometry is later deleted, the dimension becomes dangling.

Degrees of freedom

Geometry that is not defined by dimensions or relations is free to move. In 2D sketches, there are three degrees of freedom: movement along the X and Y axes, and rotation about the Z axis (the axis normal to the sketch plane). In 3D sketches and in assemblies, there are six degrees of freedom: movement along the X, Y, and Z axes, and rotation about the X, Y, and Z axes.

Derived part

A derived part is a new base, mirror, or component part created directly from an existing part and linked to the original part such that changes to the original part are reflected in the derived part.

Derived sketch

A copy of a sketch, in either the same part or the same assembly, that is connected to the original sketch. Changes in the original sketch are reflected in the derived sketch.

Design Library

Located in the Task Pane, the Design Library provides a central location for reusable elements such as parts, assemblies, and so on.

Design table

An Excel spreadsheet that is used to create multiple configurations in a part or assembly document.

Detached drawing

A drawing format that allows opening and working in a drawing without loading the corresponding models into memory. The models are loaded on an as-needed basis.

Detail view

A portion of a larger view, usually at a larger scale than the original view.

Dimension line

A linear dimension line references the dimension text to extension lines indicating the entity being measured. An angular dimension line references the dimension text directly to the measured object.

DimXpertManager

Located on the left side of the SolidWorks window, it is a means to manage dimensions and tolerances created using DimXpert for parts according to the requirements of the ASME Y.14.41-2003 standard.

DisplayManager

The DisplayManager lists the appearances, decals, lights, scene, and cameras applied to the current model. From the DisplayManager, you can view applied content, and add, edit, or delete items. When PhotoView 360 is added in, the DisplayManager also provides access to PhotoView options.

Document

A file containing a part, assembly, or drawing.

Draft

The degree of taper or angle of a face, usually applied to molds or castings.

Drawing

A 2D representation of a 3D part or assembly. The extension for a SolidWorks drawing file name is .SLDDRW.

Drawing sheet

A page in a drawing document.

Driven dimension

Measurements of the model, but they do not drive the model and their values cannot be changed.

Driving dimension

Also referred to as a model dimension, it sets the value for a sketch entity. It can also control distance, thickness, and feature parameters.

Edge

A single outside boundary of a feature.

Edge flange

A sheet metal feature that combines a bend and a tab in a single operation.

Equation
Creates a mathematical relation between sketch dimensions, using dimension names as variables, or between feature parameters, such as the depth of an extruded feature or the instance count in a pattern.

Exploded view
Shows an assembly with its components separated from one another, usually to show how to assemble the mechanism.

Export
Save a SolidWorks document in another format for use in other CAD/CAM, rapid prototyping, web, or graphics software applications.

Extension line
The line extending from the model indicating the point from which a dimension is measured.

Extrude
A feature that linearly projects a sketch to either add material to a part (in a base or boss) or remove material from a part (in a cut or hole).

Face
A selectable area (planar or otherwise) of a model or surface with boundaries that help define the shape of the model or surface. For example, a rectangular solid has six faces.

Fasteners
A SolidWorks Toolbox library that adds fasteners automatically to holes in an assembly.

Feature
An individual shape that, combined with other features, makes up a part or assembly. Some features, such as bosses and cuts, originate as sketches. Other features, such as shells and fillets, modify a feature's geometry. However, not all features have associated geometry. Features are always listed in the FeatureManager design tree.

FeatureManager design tree
Located on the left side of the SolidWorks window, it provides an outline view of the active part, assembly, or drawing.

Fill
A solid area hatch or crosshatch. Fill also applies to patches on surfaces.

Fillet
An internal rounding of a corner or edge in a sketch, or an edge on a surface or solid.

Forming tool

Dies that bend, stretch, or otherwise form sheet metal to create such form features as louvers, lances, flanges, and ribs.

Fully defined

A sketch where all lines and curves in the sketch, and their positions, are described by dimensions or relations, or both, and cannot be moved. Fully defined sketch entities are shown in black.

Geometric tolerance

A set of standard symbols that specify the geometric characteristics and dimensional requirements of a feature.

Graphics area

The area in the SolidWorks window where the part, assembly, or drawing appears.

Guide curve

A 2D or 3D curve used to guide a sweep or loft.

Handle

An arrow, square, or circle that you can drag to adjust the size or position of an entity (a feature, dimension, or sketch entity, for example).

Helix

A curve defined by pitch, revolutions, and height. A helix can be used, for example, as a path for a swept feature cutting threads in a bolt.

Hem

A sheet metal feature that folds back at the edge of a part. A hem can be open, closed, double, or tear-drop.

HLR

(Hidden lines removed) a view mode in which all edges of the model that are not visible from the current view angle are removed from the display.

HLV

(hidden lines visible) A view mode in which all edges of the model that are not visible from the current view angle are shown gray or dashed.

Import

Open files from other CAD software applications into a SolidWorks document.

In-context feature

A feature with an external reference to the geometry of another component; the in-context feature changes automatically if the geometry of the referenced model or feature changes.

Inference

The system automatically creates (infers) relations between dragged entities (sketched entities, annotations, and components) and other entities and geometry. This is useful when positioning entities relative to one another.

Instance

An item in a pattern or a component in an assembly that occurs more than once. Blocks are inserted into drawings as instances of block definitions.

Interference detection

A tool that displays any interference between selected components in an assembly.

Jog

A sheet metal feature that adds material to a part by creating two bends from a sketched line. (2)

Knit

A tool that combines two or more faces or surfaces into one. The edges of the surfaces must be adjacent and not overlapping, but they cannot ever be planar. There is no difference in the appearance of the face or the surface after knitting.

Layout sketch

A sketch that contains important sketch entities, dimensions, and relations. You reference the entities in the layout sketch when creating new sketches, building new geometry, or positioning components in an assembly. This allows for easier updating of your model because changes you make to the layout sketch propagate to the entire model.

Leader

A solid line from an annotation (note, dimension, and so on) to the referenced feature.

Library feature

A frequently used feature, or combination of features, that is created once and then saved for future use.

Lightweight

A part in an assembly or a drawing has only a subset of its model data loaded into memory. The remaining model data is loaded on an as-needed basis. This improves performance of large and complex assemblies.

Line

A straight sketch entity with two endpoints. A line can be created by projecting an external entity such as an edge, plane, axis, or sketch curve into the sketch.

Loft

A base, boss, cut, or surface feature created by transitions between profiles.

Lofted bend

A sheet metal feature that produces a roll form or a transitional shape from two open profile sketches. Lofted bends often create funnels and chutes.

Mass properties

A tool that evaluates the characteristics of a part or an assembly such as volume, surface area, centroid, and so on.

Mate

A geometric relationship, such as coincident, perpendicular, tangent, and so on, between parts in an assembly.

Mate reference

Specifies one or more entities of a component to use for automatic mating. When you drag a component with a mate reference into an assembly, the software tries to find other combinations of the same mate reference name and mate type.

Mates folder

A collection of mates that are solved together. The order in which the mates appear within the Mates folder does not matter.

Mirror

(a) A mirror feature is a copy of a selected feature, mirrored about a plane or planar face. (b) A mirror sketch entity is a copy of a selected sketch entity that is mirrored about a centerline.

Miter flange

A sheet metal feature that joins multiple edge flanges together and miters the corner.

Model

3D solid geometry in a part or assembly document. If a part or assembly document contains multiple configurations, each configuration is a separate model.

Model dimension

A dimension specified in a sketch or a feature in a part or assembly document that defines some entity in a 3D model.

Model item

A characteristic or dimension of feature geometry that can be used in detailing drawings.

Model view

A drawing view of a part or assembly.

Mold

A set of manufacturing tooling used to shape molten plastic or other material into a designed part. You design the mold using a sequence of integrated tools that result in cavity and core blocks that are derived parts of the part to be molded.

Motion Study

Motion Studies are graphical simulations of motion and visual properties with assembly models. Analogous to a configuration, they do not actually change the original assembly model or its properties. They display the model as it changes based on simulation elements you add.

Multibody part

A part with separate solid bodies within the same part document. Unlike the components in an assembly, multibody parts are not dynamic.

Native format

DXF and DWG files remain in their original format (are not converted into SolidWorks format) when viewed in SolidWorks drawing sheets (view only).

Open profile

Also called an open contour, it is a sketch or sketch entity with endpoints exposed. For example, a U-shaped profile is open.

Ordinate dimensions

A chain of dimensions measured from a zero ordinate in a drawing or sketch.

Origin

The model origin appears as three gray arrows and represents the (0,0,0) coordinate of the model. When a sketch is active, a sketch origin appears in red and represents the (0,0,0) coordinate of the sketch. Dimensions and relations can be added to the model origin, but not to
a sketch origin.

Out-of-context feature

A feature with an external reference to the geometry of another component that is not open.

Over defined

A sketch is over defined when dimensions or relations are either in conflict or redundant.

Parameter

A value used to define a sketch or feature (often a dimension).

Parent

An existing feature upon which other features depend. For example, in a block with a hole, the block is the parent to the child hole feature.

Part

A single 3D object made up of features. A part can become a component in an assembly, and it can be represented in 2D in a drawing. Examples of parts are bolt, pin, plate, and so on. The extension for a SolidWorks part file name is .SLDPRT.

Path

A sketch, edge, or curve used in creating a sweep or loft.

Pattern

A pattern repeats selected sketch entities, features, or components in an array, which can be linear, circular, or sketch-driven. If the seed entity is changed, the other instances in the pattern update.

Physical Dynamics

An assembly tool that displays the motion of assembly components in a realistic way. When you drag a component, the component applies a force to other components it touches. Components move only within their degrees of freedom.

Pierce relation

Makes a sketch point coincident to the location at which an axis, edge, line, or spline pierces the sketch plane.

Planar

Entities that can lie on one plane. For example, a circle is planar, but a helix is not.

Plane

Flat construction geometry. Planes can be used for a 2D sketch, section view of a model, a neutral plane in a draft feature, and others.

Point

A singular location in a sketch, or a projection into a sketch at a single location of an external entity (origin, vertex, axis, or point in an external sketch).

Predefined view
A drawing view in which the view position, orientation, and so on can be specified before a model is inserted. You can save drawing documents with predefined views as templates.

Profile
A sketch entity used to create a feature (such as a loft) or a drawing view (such as a detail view). A profile can be open (such as a U shape or open spline) or closed (such as a circle or closed spline).

Projected dimension
If you dimension entities in an isometric view, projected dimensions are the flat dimensions in 2D.

Projected view
A drawing view projected orthogonally from an existing view.

PropertyManager
Located on the left side of the SolidWorks window, it is used for dynamic editing of sketch entities and most features.

RealView graphics
A hardware (graphics card) support of advanced shading in real time; the rendering applies to the model and is retained as you move or rotate a part.

Rebuild
Tool that updates (or regenerates) the document with any changes made since the last time the model was rebuilt. Rebuild is typically used after changing a model dimension.

Reference dimension
A dimension in a drawing that shows the measurement of an item, but cannot drive the model and its value cannot be modified. When model dimensions change, reference dimensions update.

Reference geometry
Includes planes, axes, coordinate systems, and 3D curves. Reference geometry is used to assist in creating features such lofts, sweeps, drafts, chamfers, and patterns.

Relation
A geometric constraint between sketch entities or between a sketch entity and a plane, axis, edge, or vertex. Relations can be added automatically or manually.

Relative view
A relative (or relative to model) drawing view is created relative to planar surfaces in a

part or assembly.

Reload
Refreshes shared documents. For example, if you open a part file for read-only access while another user makes changes to the same part, you can reload the new version, including the changes.

Reorder
Reordering (changing the order of) items is possible in the FeatureManager design tree. In parts, you can change the order in which features are solved. In assemblies, you can control the order in which components appear in a bill of materials.

Replace
Substitutes one or more open instances of a component in an assembly with a different component.

Resolved
A state of an assembly component (in an assembly or drawing document) in which it is fully loaded in memory. All the component's model data is available, so its entities can be selected, referenced, edited, used in mates, and so on.

Revolve
A feature that creates a base or boss, a revolved cut, or revolved surface by revolving one or more sketched profiles around a centerline.

Rip
A sheet metal feature that removes material at an edge to allow a bend.

Rollback
Suppresses all items below the rollback bar.

Section
Another term for profile in sweeps.

Section line
A line or centerline sketched in a drawing view to create a section view.

Section scope
Specifies the components to be left uncut when you create an assembly drawing section view.

Section view
A section view (or section cut) is (1) a part or assembly view cut by a plane, or (2) a

drawing view created by cutting another drawing view with a section line.

Seed

A sketch or an entity (a feature, face, or body) that is the basis for a pattern. If you edit the seed, the other entities in the pattern are updated.

Shaded

Displays a model as a colored solid.

Shared values

Also called linked values, these are named variables that you assign to set the value of two or ore dimensions to be equal.

Sheet format

Includes page size and orientation, standard text, borders, title blocks, and so on. Sheet formats can be customized and saved for future use. Each sheet of a drawing document can have a different format.

Shell

A feature that hollows out a part, leaving open the selected faces and thin walls on the remaining faces. A hollow part is created when no faces are selected to be open.

Sketch

A collection of lines and other 2D objects on a plane or face that forms the basis for a feature such as a base or a boss. A 3D sketch is non-planar and can be used to guide a sweep or loft, for example.

Smart Fasteners

Automatically adds fasteners (bolts and screws) to an assembly using the SolidWorks Toolbox library of fasteners.

SmartMates

An assembly mating relation that is created automatically.

Solid sweep

A cut sweep created by moving a tool body along a path to cut out 3D material from a model.

Spiral

A flat or 2D helix, defined by a circle, pitch, and number of revolutions.

Spline

A sketched 2D or 3D curve defined by a set of control points.

Split line
Projects a sketched curve onto a selected model face, dividing the face into multiple faces so that each can be selected individually. A split line can be used to create draft features, to create face blend fillets, and to radiate surfaces to cut molds.

Stacked balloon
A set of balloons with only one leader. The balloons can be stacked vertically (up or down) or horizontally (left or right).

Standard 3 views
The three orthographic views (front, right, and top) that are often the basis of a drawing.

Stereolithography
The process of creating rapid prototype parts using a faceted mesh representation in STL files.

Sub-assembly
An assembly document that is part of a larger assembly. For example, the steering mechanism of a car is a sub-assembly of the car.

Suppress
Removes an entity from the display and from any calculations in which it is involved. You can suppress features, assembly components, and so on. Suppressing an entity does not delete the entity; you can un-suppress the entity to restore it.

Surface
A zero-thickness planar or 3D entity with edge boundaries. Surfaces are often used to create solid features. Reference surfaces can be used to modify solid features.

Sweep
Creates a base, boss, cut, or surface feature by moving a profile (section) along a path. For cut-sweeps, you can create solid sweeps by moving a tool body along a path.

Tangent arc
An arc that is tangent to another entity, such as a line.

Tangent edge
The transition edge between rounded or filleted faces in hidden lines visible or hidden lines removed modes in drawings.

Task Pane
Located on the right-side of the SolidWorks window, the Task Pane contains SolidWorks Resources, the Design Library, and the File Explorer.

Template

A document (part, assembly, or drawing) that forms the basis of a new document. It can include user-defined parameters, annotations, predefined views, geometry, and so on.

Temporary axis

An axis created implicitly for every conical or cylindrical face in a model.

Thin feature

An extruded or revolved feature with constant wall thickness. Sheet metal parts are typically created from thin features.

TolAnalyst

A tolerance analysis application that determines the effects that dimensions and tolerances have on parts and assemblies.

Top-down design

An assembly modeling technique where you create parts in the context of an assembly by referencing the geometry of other components. Changes to the referenced components propagate to the parts that you create in context.

Triad

Three axes with arrows defining the X, Y, and Z directions. A reference triad appears in part and assembly documents to assist in orienting the viewing of models. Triads also assist when moving or rotating components in assemblies.

Under defined

A sketch is under defined when there are not enough dimensions and relations to prevent entities from moving or changing size.

Vertex

A point at which two or more lines or edges intersect. Vertices can be selected for sketching, dimensioning, and many other operations.

Viewports

Windows that display views of models. You can specify one, two, or four viewports. Viewports with orthogonal views can be linked, which links orientation and rotation.

Virtual sharp

A sketch point at the intersection of two entities after the intersection itself has been removed by a feature such as a fillet or chamfer. Dimensions and relations to the virtual sharp are retained even though the actual intersection no longer exists.

Weldment

A multibody part with structural members.

Weldment cut list
A table that tabulates the bodies in a weldment along with descriptions and lengths.

Wireframe
A view mode in which all edges of the part or assembly are displayed.

Zebra stripes
Simulate the reflection of long strips of light on a very shiny surface. They allow you to see small changes in a surface that may be hard to see with a standard display.

Zoom
To simulate movement toward or away from a part or an assembly.

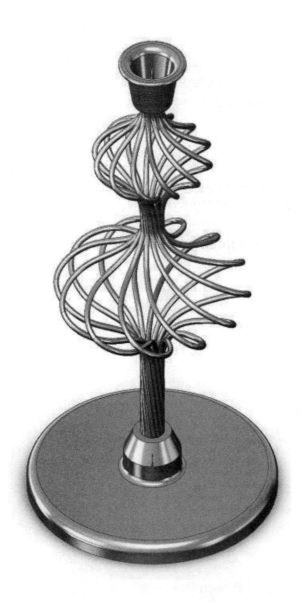

SolidWorks 2012

Student Testimonials

(Course Evaluations)

More than 6000 actual student testimonials to date.
Originals are filed at local SolidWorks Resellers and Academic Training Centers.

Student Testimonials

Joseph Hurlbut – NASA Ames Research Center
I cannot put into words sufficient praise for the product, program of instruction and the ability and approach of the Instructor. I've received a lot of training this year and I am happy to report that this course outshined all the others by far.

Carrie Keeney – Novera Optics
I had a great class with Paul. He is very knowledgeable and fun to work with. Thanks.

Kirk Sadler – Massie Research Labs.
The course objectives were clearly met and covered. My questions and concerns were answered and explained very clearly. I was very pleased with this course and the Instructor Paul Tran. This course has and will help me perform my job with more confidence and ease.

Joe Podhasky – Lynx Therapeutics
Paul was an excellent instructor, probably the best Technical Instructor I've ever had. He was very clear, knowledgeable and eager to help others.

Brent Rothert – Chahaya Optronics
A colleague of mine who completed this course earlier recommended it to me. He especially commented that Paul Tran was an excellent instructor and I agreed wholeheartedly. I am very fortunate to have taken this course from Paul.

Todd Rodericks – HealthTech
I have taken many PTC courses and none of them compare to the overall experience I had taking this course. Paul Tran did an exceptional job presenting the material in a clear concise fashion.

George Heropoulos – Leapfrog Toys
Most excellent instructor. Very clear, precise, professional and polite. Highly recommended.

Mike Donndelinger – Volex Inc.

Paul is a truly outstanding teacher. This was the best software training I have ever attended by far.

John Edwards – Marqun Corporation

Paul Tran is the best instructor of this kind that I have ever experience in twenty years of engineering practice. He has an exceptional talent for clearly and concisely presenting complicated materials.

Jill Cregan – Starion Instruments Inc.

I have no experience with any CAD programs. However, with the way Paul described and brought me through this course, I had no problems with keeping up. Excellent!

Paul Johnson – Impco Technology Inc.

Paul Tran was an excellent Instructor. He explained everything in a clear concise manner and was extremely helpful. I would recommend this course to anyone.

Rick Faeth – Cepheid

Although I am not a design engineer, I felt I learned a great deal about SolidWorks and how to create parts, assemblies and drawings. Paul Tran is extremely gifted and patient instructor.

Bob Lucero – Stryker Endoscopy

The instructor presented each topic very well. I was never lost during class, thanks.

Lich Tran – Sverdrup Technology

Very good instructor. He knows the materials in and out and explained it very well. He cares for the student's performance. I really like the one on one support by Paul. I would recommend the teacher and the course to all my friends.

Vincent King – Shur-Lok Corporation

This was my first exposure to this software. Paul was a very patient and competent instructor; I gained a lot of knowledge considering I had no experience before. Thanks

Hazen L. Hoyt – Aetas Corp.

Excellent course, excellent instructor. The best course I've ever experienced. Thanks Paul

Spencer Knock – Disneyland
I think Paul Tran is an excellent instructor. His years of experience in the field as well as with the software and his knowledge of how parts are actually manufactured are invaluable.

Michael Davison – Tsunami
Paul is such a good instructor that anytime he is offering a course in our area, we always send at least one company representative to receive his training.

David Gandocfo – Self Employed
I have been taking CAD training classes since 1985 but nothing compare to this course. Mr. Tran was the best instructor I have ever had. He was very informative and gave a lot of time to get everyone up to speed. Thanks.

Bob Pearce – TSK America
Paul Tran showed what a skilled and knowledgeable instructor should be like. He is very patient!! The software was easy to use but without Paul's shortcuts and tips and background experience, it may not have been as productive a class as it was for me.

Anthony Gonzalez – CD Alexander
The software is excellent, surpassed my expectations. The instructor was really outstanding, he took his time with students and he was very knowledgeable with all aspects of the software. Paul Tran made the course very productive and worthwhile.

Mark Tussey – Berkley Ind.
Paul was a fantastic instructor!!! He had such an interesting teaching method, easy to follow and understand the training sessions. Highly recommended.

Richard Loquet – Control Components Inc.
I enjoyed the course and appreciate the thoroughness of our instructor. He presented logical problems related to the work environments. My thanks to Paul Tran for a job well done.

Victor Ortiz – Verticom Inc.
Paul Tran was a very thorough instructor, very patient and went beyond the class content to answer our questions regarding problems in designs. Great job.

Tom Hansen – Paxton / Patterson

Paul was an excellent instructor. One of the best trainers I have seen in any setting. Very knowledgeable and patience. Amazing wealth of information. A true asset. He explained not only the concepts but took the time to explain the applications. I would highly recommend others to attend training with Paul.

Maithy Ngo – HCT Packaging

The instructor was clear, concise, knowledgeable, but more importantly patience, which I find is a valuable character in teaching. I would highly recommend his class to anyone.

Josh Leuenberger – CCI

Paul is a great instructor. I felt he provided additional tips not covered in the book. He also adjusted his pace to accommodate the slower students.

Arthur Wang – Self Employed

Paul Tran is an excellent instructor. He actually made the learning experience of Solidworks a pleasure. I look forward to taking more classes from him.

Angela Ji – Beckman Coulter

Paul Tran is an amazing instructor! He's thoroughly prepared, extremely knowledgeable, and endlessly patience in dealing with students, both advanced and novice. I wish all teachers were like him. :)

Katie Trinh – MicroVention

Being new to the CAD world, I learn so much about Solidworks, exceeding my expectation. Many thanks to the instructor. He's very professional, knowledgeable and always there to help.

Caesar Marmolejo – Moldex-Metric

Paul Tran is one of the most OUTSTANDING lecturers of Solidworks. I have tried the competitors' classes and lecturers do not compare to Paul Tran. I will take classes again with this reseller and Paul Tran. HE is the BEST.

Doug Nielsen – Hartwell Corp.

Paul was a fantastic instructor. He was very patience with those who've never touched SolidWorks, and equally helpful and informative to those with SW experience. Paul covered all book material as well as additional tips and tricks as time permitted.

SolidWorks 2012

Quick-Guide

Quick Reference Guide to SolidWorks 2012 command icons and toolbars.

SolidWorks® Quick-Guide

Quick Reference Guide To SolidWorks® 2012 Command Icons & Toolbars

The STANDARD Toolbar

- Creates a new document.
- Opens an existing document.
- Saves an active document.
- Make Drawing from Part/Assembly
- Make Assembly from Part/Assembly
- Prints the active document.
- Displays full pages as they are printed.
- Cuts the selection & puts it on the clipboard.
- Copies the selection & puts it on the clipboard.
- Inserts the clipboard contents.
- Deletes the selection.
- Reverses the last action.
- Redo the last action that was undone.
- Rebuilds the part / assembly / drawing.
- Saves all documents.
- Changes the color of the current selection(s).
- Edits material.
- Closes an existing document
- Shows or hides the Selection Filter toolbar.
- Shows or hides the Web toolbar.
- Displays Help topics for SolidWorks.
- Displays full pages as they will be printed.

The STANDARD Toolbar (Cont.)

- Loads or unloads the 3D instant website add-in
- Select tool.
- Reloads the current document from disk.
- Places an online order for a rapid prototype part.
- Checks read-only files for write access.
- Show/Edit the properties of the current selection.
- Changes options settings for SolidWorks.
- Tiles windows vertically, as non-overlapping.
- Tiles windows horizontally, as non-overlapping.
- Opens another window for the active document.

The SKETCH TOOLS Toolbar

- Sketches a rectangle from the center.
- Sketches a centerpoint arc slot.
- Sketches a 3-point arc slot.
- Sketches a straight slot.
- Sketches a centerpoint straight slot.
- Stretches sketch entities and annotations.
- Inserts an Equation Driven Curve.
- Sketches a 3-point arc.
- Inserts a picture into the sketch background.
- Creates sketched ellipses.

Quick Reference Guide To SolidWorks® 2012 Command Icons & Toolbars

The SKETCH TOOLS Toolbar

 Selects items for commands to act on.

 Sets up Grid parameters.

 Creates a sketch on a selected plane or face.

 Creates a 3D sketch.

 Scales/Translates/Rotates the current sketch.

 Moves or copies sketch entities and annotations.

 Scales sketch entities and annotations.

 Sketches an angle rectangle from the center.

 Sketches a parallelogram.

 Sketches a line.

 Creates a center point arc: center, start, end.

 Creates an arc tangent to a line.

 Sketches splines on a surface or face.

 Sketches a circle.

 Sketches a circle by its perimeter.

 Sketches a partial ellipse.

 Makes a path of sketch entities.

 Mirrors entities dynamically about a

 Insert a plane into the 3D sketch.

 Rotates sketch entities and

 Copies sketch entities and

 Sketches on a plane in a 3D sketch.

 Moves sketch entities without solving dimensions or relations.

The SKETCH TOOLS Toolbar (Cont.)

 Partial ellipses.

Adds a Parabola.

Creates sketched splines.

Sketches a polygon.

Sketches a rectangle.

Sketches a parallelogram.

Creates points.

Creates sketched centerlines.

Adds text to sketch.

Converts selected model edges or sketch entities to sketch segments.

Creates a sketch along the intersection of multiple bodies.

Converts face curves on the selected face into 3D sketch entities.

 Mirrors selected segments about a centerline.

 Fillets the corner of two lines.

Creates a chamfer between two sketch entities.

Creates a sketch curve by offsetting model edges or sketch entities at a specified distance.

Fits a spline to selected entities.

Trims a sketch segment.

Extends a sketch segment.

Splits a sketch segment.

Construction Geometry.

Creates linear steps and repeat of sketch entities.

Creates circular steps and repeat of sketch entities.

The SHEET METAL

Inserts a FlattenBends & a ProcessBends feature, A sheet metal feature will be added.

Shows flat pattern for this sheet metal part.

Shows part without inserting any bends.

Inserts a rip feature to a sheet metal part.

Inserts a Sheet Metal Base Flange or a Tab feature.

Inserts a Sheet Metal Miter Flange feature.

Folds selected bends.

Unfolds selected bends.

Inserts bends using a sketch line.

Inserts a flange by pulling an edge.

Inserts a sheet metal corner feature.

Inserts a Hem feature by selecting edges.

Breaks a corner by filleting/chamfering it.

Inserts a Jog feature using a sketch line.

Inserts a lofted bend feature using 2 sketches.

Creates inverse dent on a sheet metal part.

Trims out material from a corner, in a sheet metal

Inserts a fillet weld bead.

Converts a solid/surface into a sheet metal part.

Adds a Cross Break feature into a selected face.

The SURFACES Toolbar

Deletes a face or a set of faces.

Creates mid surfaces between offset face pairs.

Patches surface holes and external edges.

The SURFACES Toolbar (cont.)

Creates an extruded surface.

Creates a revolved surface.

Creates a swept surface.

Creates a lofted surface.

Creates an offset surface.

Radiates a surface originating from a curve, parallel to a plane.

Knits surfaces together.

Creates a planar surface from a sketch or A set of edges.

Creates a surface by importing data from a file.

Extends a surface.

Trims a surface.

Generating MidSurface(s).

Deletes Face(s).

Replaces Face with Surface.

Patches surface holes and external edges by extending the surfaces.

Creates parting surfaces between core & cavity surfaces.

Inserts ruled surfaces from edges.

The WELDMENTS Toolbar

Creates a weldment feature.

Creates a structure member feature.

Adds a gusset feature between 2 planar adjoining faces.

Creates an end cap feature.

Adds a fillet weld bead feature.

Trims or extends structure members.

The DIMENSIONS/RELATIONS Toolbar

 Inserts dimension between two lines.

 Creates a horizontal dimension between selected entities.

 Creates a vertical dimension between selected entities.

 Creates a reference dimension between selected entities.

 Creates a set of ordinate dimensions.

 Creates a set of Horizontal ordinate dimensions.

 Creates a set of Vertical ordinate dimensions.

 Creates a chamfer dimension.

 Adds a geometric relation.

 Automatically Adds Dimensions to the current sketch.

 Displays and deletes geometric relations.

 Fully defines a sketch.

 Scans a sketch for elements of equal length or radius.

 Automatically recognize tolerance features.

 Creates linked, unlinked, or collection pattern feature.

 Paints faces of toleranced features in different colors.

 Adds DimXpert location dimension.

 Adds DimXpert datum.

 Copies existing tolerance scheme to current configuration.

 Adds DimXpert size dimension.

 Adds DimXpert geometric tolerance.

 Deletes all tolerance data base.

 Adds new Tol Analyst.

The STANDARD VIEWS

 Front view.

 Back view.

 Left view.

 Right view.

 Top view.

 Bottom view.

 Isometric view.

 Trimetric view.

 Dimetric view.

 Normal to view.

 Links all views in the viewport together.

 Displays viewport with front & right views

 Displays a 4 view viewport with 1st or 3rd Angle of projection.

 Displays viewport with front & top

 Displays viewport with a single

The Block Toolbar

 Makes a new block.

 Edits the selected block.

 Inserts a new block to a sketch or drawing.

 Adds/Removes sketch entities to/from blocks.

 Updates parent sketches effected by this block.

 Saves the block to a file.

 Explodes the selected block.

 Inserts a belt.

Did you know??
* Ctrl+Q will force a rebuild on all features of a part.
* Ctrl+B will rebuild the feature being worked on and its dependants.

The FEATURES Toolbar

Creates a boss feature by extruding a sketched profile.

Creates a revolved feature based on profile and angle parameter.

Creates a cut feature by extruding a sketched profile.

Creates a cut feature by revolving a sketched profile.

Creates a sweep feature by sweeping a profile along a path curve.

Creates a cut by sweeping a closed profile along an open or closed path.

Creates a cut by removing material between two or more profiles

Creates a cut by thickening one or more adjacent surfaces.

Adds a deformed surface by push or pull on

Creates a lofted feature between two or more profiles.

Creates a solid feature by thickening one or more adjacent surfaces.

Creates a filled feature.

Chamfers an edge or a chain of tangent edges.

Inserts a rib feature.

Scales model by a specified factor.

Creates a shell feature.

Applies draft to a selected surface.

Creates a cylindrical hole.

Inserts a hole with a pre-defined cross section.

Puts a dome surface on a face.

Puts a shape feature on a face.

Applies global deformation to solid or surface bodies.

Wraps closed sketch contour(s) onto a face.

Moves / Sizes features.

Suppresses the selected feature or component.

Un-suppresses the selected feature or component.

Flexes solid and surface bodies

Creates a linear pattern using the selected feature(s).

Creates a circular pattern using the selected feature(s).

Mirrors a feature about a plane.

Creates a Curve Driven Pattern.

Creates a Sketch Driven pattern.

Creates a Table Driven Pattern.

Inserts a split Feature.

Combines two or more solid bodies.

Joins bodies from one or more parts into a single part in the context of an assembly.

Deletes a solid or a surface.

Inserts solid(s) or surface(s) into an existing open document.

Inserts a part from file into the active part document.

Moves/Copies solid and surface bodies or moves graphics bodies.

Merges short edges on faces

Pushes solid / surface model by another solid / surface model

Moves face(s) of a solid

Area fills faces or bodies into one or more contours.

Inserts holes into a series of parts.

Returns suppressed items with dependents to the model.

Cuts a solid model with a surface.

Adds material between profiles in two directions to create a solid feature.

Cuts a solid model by removing material between profiles in two directions.

Did you know??

* Right-mouse drag a component in an assembly rotates it.
* Left- mouse drag a component in an assembly moves it.

The **MOLD TOOLS** Toolbar

 Extracts core(s) from existing tooling split

 Constructs a surface patch

 Moves face(s) of a solid

 Finds & creates mold shut-off surfaces

 Inserts cavity into a base part.

 Scales a model by a specified factor.

 Applies draft to a selected surface.

 Inserts a split line feature.

 Creates an offset surface.

 Creates parting lines to separate core & cavity surfaces

 Creates a planar surface from a sketch or A set of edges.

 Knits surfaces together.

 Analyzes draft angles of faces, based on a mold pull direction.

 Inserts ruled surfaces from edges.

 Creates parting surfaces between core & cavity surfaces

 Creates multiple bodies from a single body.

 Inserts a tooling split feature.

 Identifies faces that form undercuts.

 Creates parting surfaces between the core & cavity.

 Inserts surface body folders for mold operation.

The **SELECTION** FILTERS

 Turns selection filters on and off.

 Clears all filters.

Selects all filters.

Inverts current selection.

The **SELECTION** FILTERS cont.

 Allows selection of edges only.

 Allows selection of faces only.

 Adds filter for Surface Bodies.

 Adds filter for Solid Bodies.

 Adds filter for Axes.

 Adds filter for Planes.

 Adds filter for Sketch Points.

 Adds filter for Sketch Segments.

 Adds filter for Midpoints.

 Adds filter for Center Marks.

 Adds filter for Centerline.

 Adds filter for Dimensions and Hole Callouts.

 Adds filter for Surface Finish Symbols.

 Adds filter for Geometric Tolerances.

 Adds filter for Notes / Balloons.

 Adds filter for Weld Symbols.

 Adds filter for Datum Targets.

 Adds filter for Cosmetic Threads.

 Adds filter for blocks.

 Adds filter for Dowel pin symbols.

 Adds filter for connection points.

 Allows selection filter for vertices only.

 Allows selection of weld symbols only.

 Allows selection of blocks only.

 Adds filter for routing points.

The FLYOUT Toolbar

2D to 3D.

Align.

Annotation.

Assemblies.

Curves.

Dimensions / Relation.

Drawings.

Features.

Fonts.

Line Formats.

Macros.

Molds.

Reference Geometry.

Quick snap filters.

Selection Filters.

Sheet Metal.

Simulation.

Sketch.

SolidWorks Office.

Splines.

Standard.

Standard Views.

Surfaces.

Tools.

View.

Web.

Weldments.

Block commands.

Explode sketch commands.

Table commands.

Fastening feature commands.

Creates a rounded internal or external fillet.

Linear Patterns Features, Faces and Bodies.

Creates various corner treatments.

Displays Deletes geometric relations.

Creates dimensions for one or more entities.

Adds an existing part or assembly.

Linear Patterns components in assembly.

Moves components in assembly.

Adds section view with a section line.

Creates various assembly features.

Toggles various view settings.

The SCREEN CAPTURE Toolbar

Copies the current graphics window to the clipboard.

Records the current graphics window to an AVI file.

Stops recording the current graphics window to an AVI file.

The Explode Line Sketch Toolbar

Adds a route line that connect entities.

Adds a jog to the route lines.

The LINE FORMAT Toolbar

Changes layer properties.

Changes line color.

Changes line thickness.

Changes line style.

Hides a visible edge.

Shows a hidden edge.

Changes line display mode.

The 2D-To-3D Toolbar

Makes a Front sketch from the selected entities.

Makes a Top sketch from the selected entities.

Makes a Right sketch from the selected entities.

Makes a Left sketch from the selected entities.

Makes a Bottom sketch from the selected entities.

Makes a Back sketch from the selected entities.

Makes an Auxiliary sketch from the selected entities.

Creates a new sketch from the selected entities.

Repairs the selected sketch.

Aligns a sketch to the selected point.

Creates an extrusion from the selected sketch segments, starting at the selected sketch point.

Creates a cut from the selected sketch segments, optionally starting at the selected sketch point.

The ALIGN Toolbar

Aligns the left side of the selected annotations with the leftmost annotation.

Aligns the right side of the selected annotations with the rightmost annotation.

Aligns the top side of the selected annotations with the topmost annotation.

Aligns the bottom side of the selected annotations with the lowermost annotation.

Evenly spaces the selected annotations horizontally.

Evenly spaces the selected annotations vertically.

Centrally aligns the selected annotations horizontally.

Centrally aligns the selected annotations vertically.

Compacts the selected annotations horizontally.

Compacts the selected annotations vertically.

Aligns the center of the selected annotations between

Creates a group from the selected items

Deletes the grouping between these items

Aligns & groups selected dimensions along a line or an arc

Aligns & groups dimensions at a uniform distances

The SIMULATION Toolbar

Stops Record or Playback.

Records Simulation.

Replays Simulation.

Resets Components.

Adds Linear Motor.

Adds Rotary Motor.

Adds Spring.

Adds Gravity.

The MACRO Toolbar

Runs a Macro.

Stops Macro recorder.

Records (or pauses recording of) actions to create a Macro.

Launches the Macro Editor and begins editing a new macro.

Opens a Macro file for editing.

Creates a custom macro.

The TABLE Toolbar

 Adds a hole table of selected holes from a specified origin datum.

 Adds a Bill of Materials.

 Adds a revision table.

 Displays a Design table in a drawing.

 Adds a weldments cuts list table.

 Adds a Excel based of Bill of Materials

 Adds a general table to a drawing sheet.

The REFERENCE GEOMETRY

 Adds a reference plane

 Creates an axis.

 Creates a coordinate system.

 Adds a reference point

 Specifies entities to use as references using SmartMates.

The SPLINE TOOLS Toolbar

 Adds a point to a spline.

 Displays points where the concavity of selected spline changes.

 Displays minimum radius of selected spline.

 Displays curvature combs of selected spline.

 Reduces numbers of points in a selected spline.

 Adds a tangency control.

 Adds a curvature control.

 Adds a spline based on selected sketch entities & edges.

 Displays all handles of selected splines.

 Displays the spline control polygon.

The ANNOTATIONS Toolbar

 Inserts a note.

 Inserts a surface finish symbol.

 Inserts a new geometric tolerancing symbol.

 Attaches a balloon to the selected edge or face.

 Adds balloons for all components in selected view.

 Inserts a stacked balloon.

 Attaches a datum feature symbol to a selected edge / detail.

 Inserts a weld symbol on the selected edge / face / vertex.

 Inserts a datum target symbol and / or point attached to a selected edge / line.

 Selects and inserts block.

 Inserts annotations & reference geometry from the part / assembly into the selected.

 Adds center marks to circles on model.

 Inserts a Centerline.

 Inserts a hole callout.

 Adds a cosmetic thread to the selected cylindrical feature.

 Inserts a Multi-Jog leader.

 Selects a circular edge or and arc for Dowel pin symbol insertion.

 Toggles the visibility of annotations & dimensions.

 Inserts latest version symbol.

 Adds a cross hatch patterns or solid fill.

 Adds a weld symbol on a selected entity.

 Adds a weld bead caterpillar on an edge.

The "Feathers"

 Lightweight component.

 Out-of-Date component.

 Hidden Lightweight component.

 Hidden, Out-of-Date and Lightweight.

The **DRAWINGS** Toolbar

Updates the selected view to the model's current stage.

Creates a detail view.

Creates a section view.

Inserts an aligned section using the selected line or section line.

Unfolds a new view from an existing view.

Generates a standard 3-view drawing (1st or 3rd angle).

Inserts an auxiliary view of an inclined surface.

Adds an Orthogonal or Named view based on an existing part or assembly.

Adds a Relative view by two orthogonal faces or planes.

Adds a Predefined orthogonal projected or Named view with a model.

Adds an empty view.

Adds vertical break lines to selected view.

Crops a view.

Creates a Broken-out section.

Inserts an Alternate Position view.

The **QUICK SNAP** Toolbar

Snap to points.

Snap to center points.

Snap to midpoints.

Snap to quadrant points.

Snap to intersection of 2 curves.

Snap to nearest curve.

Snap tangent to curve.

Snap perpendicular to curve.

Snap parallel to line.

Snap horizontally / vertically.

Snap horizontally / vertically to points.

Snap to discrete line lengths.

Snap to grid points.

Snap to angle.

The **LAYOUT** Toolbar

Creates the assembly layout sketch.

Sketches a line.

Sketches a rectangle.

Sketches a circle.

Sketches a 3 point arc.

Rounds a corner.

Trims or extends a sketch.

Adds sketch entities by offsetting faces, Edges curves.

Mirrors selected entities about a centerline.

Adds a relation.

Creates a dimension.

Displays / Deletes geometric relations.

Makes a new block.

Edits the selected block.

Inserts a new block to the sketch or drawing.

Adds / Removes sketch entities to / from a block.

Saves the block to a file.

Explodes the selected block.

Creates a new part from a layout sketch block.

Positions 2 components relative to one another.

Moves a component within the degrees of freedom defined by its mates.

The CURVES Toolbar

- Projects sketch onto selected surface.
- Inserts a split line feature.
- Creates a composite curve from selected edges, curves and sketches.
- Creates a curve through free points.
- Creates a 3D curve through reference points.
- Helical curve defined by a base sketch and shape parameters.

The VIEW Toolbar

- Displays a view in the selected orientation.
- Reverts to previous view.
- Zooms out to see entire model.
- Zooms in by dragging a bounding box.
- Zooms in or out by dragging up or down.
- Zooms to fit all selected entities.
- Dynamic view rotation.
- Scrolls view by dragging.
- Displays image in wireframe mode.
- Displays hidden edges in gray.
- Displays image with hidden lines removed.
- Controls the visibility of planes.
- Controls the visibility of axis.
- Controls the visibility of parting lines.
- Controls the visibility of temporary axis.
- Controls the visibility of origins.
- Controls the visibility of coordinate systems.

- Controls the visibility of reference curves.
- Controls the visibility of sketches.
- Controls the visibility of 3D sketch planes.
- Controls the visibility of 3D sketch
- Controls the visibility of all annotations.
- Controls the visibility of reference points.
- Controls the visibility of routing points.
- Controls the visibility of lights.
- Controls the visibility of cameras.
- Controls the visibility of sketch relations.
- Redraws the current window.
- Rolls the model view.
- Turns the orientation of the model view.
- Dynamically manipulate the model view in 3D to make selection.
- Changes the display style for the active view.
- Displays a shade view of the model with its edges.
- Displays a shade view of the model.
- Toggles between draft quality & high quality HLV.
- Cycles through or applies a specific scene.
- Views the models through one of the model's cameras.
- Displays a part or assembly w/different colors according to the local radius of curvature.
- Displays zebra stripes.
- Displays a model with hardware accelerated shades.
- Edits the real view appearance of entities in the model.
- Applies a texture to entities in a model.
- Changes the visibility of items in the graphics area.
- Controls visibility of the sketch grid.

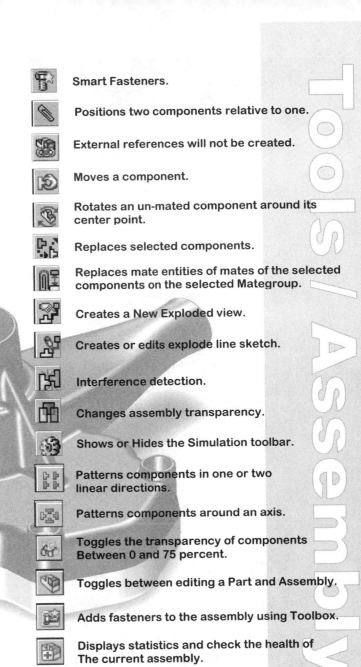

The **TOOLS** Toolbar

Calculates the distance between selected items.

Adds or edits equation.

Calculates the mass properties of the model.

Checks the model for geometry errors.

Inserts or edits a Design Table.

Evaluates section properties for faces and sketches that lie in parallel planes.

Reports Statistics for this Part/Assembly.

Deviation Analysis.

Runs the COSMOSXpress analysis wizard Powered by COSMOS.

Checks the spelling.

Import diagnostics.

Runs the DFMXpress analysis wizard.

Runs the DriveWorkXpress wizard.

Runs the COSMOSFloXpress analysis wizard.

The **ASSEMBLY** Toolbar

Creates a new part & inserts it into the assembly.

Adds an existing part or sub-assembly to the assembly.

Creates a new assembly & inserts it into the assembly.

Turns on/off large assembly mode for this document.

Hides / shows model(s) associated with the selected model(s).

Toggles the transparency of components.

Changes the selected components to suppressed or resolved.

Toggles between editing part and assembly.

Inserts a belt.

Inserts a new part into an

Smart Fasteners.

Positions two components relative to one.

External references will not be created.

Moves a component.

Rotates an un-mated component around its center point.

Replaces selected components.

Replaces mate entities of mates of the selected components on the selected Mategroup.

Creates a New Exploded view.

Creates or edits explode line sketch.

Interference detection.

Changes assembly transparency.

Shows or Hides the Simulation toolbar.

Patterns components in one or two linear directions.

Patterns components around an axis.

Toggles the transparency of components Between 0 and 75 percent.

Toggles between editing a Part and Assembly.

Adds fasteners to the assembly using **Toolbox**.

Displays statistics and check the health of The current assembly.

Patterns components relative to an existing Pattern in a part.

Shows hidden components.

Toggles large assembly mode for this document.

Checks assembly hole alignments.

Mirrors subassemblies and parts.

To add or remove an icon
to or from the toolbar, first select:

Tools/Customize/Commands
Next select a **Category**, click a button to see its description and then drag / drop the command icon into any toolbar.

Standard Keyboard Shortcuts

Rotate the model

* Horizontally or Vertically:	Arrow keys
* Horizontally or Vertically 90°:	Shift + Arrow keys
* Clockwise or Counterclockwise:	Alt + left or right Arrow
* Pan the model:	Ctrl + Arrow keys
* Zoom in:	Z (shift + Z or capital Z)
* Zoom out:	z (lower case z)
* Zoom to fit:	F
* Previous view:	Ctrl+Shift+Z

View Orientation

* View Orientation Menu:	Space bar
* Front:	Ctrl+1
* Back:	Ctrl+2
* Left:	Ctrl+3
* Right:	Ctrl+4
* Top:	Ctrl+5
* Bottom:	Ctrl+6
* Isometric:	Ctrl+7

Selection Filter & Misc.

* Filter Edges:	e
* Filter Vertices:	v
* Filter Faces:	x
* Toggle Selection filter toolbar:	F5
* Toggle Selection Filter toolbar (on/off):	F6
* New SolidWorks document:	F1
* Open Document:	Ctrl+O
* Open from Web folder:	Ctrl+W
* Save:	Ctrl+S
* Print:	Ctrl+P
* Magnifying Glass Zoom	g
* Switch between the SolidWorks documents	Ctrl + Tab

SW 2012 Sample Customized Hot Keys

Function Keys

F1	SW-Help
F2	2D Sketch
F3	3D Sketch
F4	Modify
F5	Selection Filters
F6	Move (2D Sketch)
F7	Rotate (2D Sketch)
F8	Measure
F9	Extrude
F10	Revolve
F11	Sweep
F12	Loft

Sketch

C	Circle
P	Polygon
E	Ellipse
O	Offset Entities
Alt + C	Convert Entities
M	Mirror
Alt + M	Dynamic Mirror
Alt + F	Sketch Fillet
T	Trim
Alt + X	Extend
D	Smart Dimension
Alt + R	Add Relation
Alt + P	Plane
Control + F	Fully Define Sketch
Control + Q	Exit Sketch

Part of SolidWorks 2012 – Basic Tools and Advanced Techniques

SolidWorks® Quick-Guide by Paul Tran – Sr. Certified SolidWorks Instructor
© Issue 9 / Jan-2012 - Printed in The United State of America – All Rights Reserved